I0131017

The Holocaust, Israel and 'the Jew'

The Holocaust, Israel and 'the Jew'

Histories of Antisemitism in Postwar Dutch Society

Edited by
Remco Ensel and Evelien Gans

Routledge
Taylor & Francis Group

LONDON AND NEW YORK

First published in 2017 by Amsterdam University Press Ltd.

Published 2025 by Routledge
4 Park Square, Milton Park, Abingdon, Oxon OX14 4RN
605 Third Avenue, New York, NY 10158

Routledge is an imprint of the Taylor & Francis Group, an informa business

© Remco Ensel & Evelien Gans / Taylor & Francis Group 2017

All rights reserved. No part of this book may be reprinted or reproduced or utilised in any form or by any electronic, mechanical, or other means, now known or hereafter invented, including photocopying and recording, or in any information storage or retrieval system, without permission in writing from the publishers.

Trademark notice: Product or corporate names may be trademarks or registered trademarks, and are used only for identification and explanation without intent to infringe.

ISBN: 9789089648488 (hbk)
ISBN: 9789462986084 (pbk)
ISBN: 9781003706526 (ebk)
NUR 689

Cover illustration: Graffiti on the poster of the musical 'Yours, Anne' in the Valkenburger-straat – incidentally the street which in the old Jewish Quarter of Amsterdam intersects the Anne Frank Straat (photo: Thomas Schlijper / Hollandse Hoogte, 2 January 2011)

Cover design: Coördesign, Leiden

DOI: 10.5117/9789462986084

Every effort has been made to obtain permission to use all copyrighted illustrations reproduced in this book. Nonetheless, whosoever believes to have rights to this material is advised to contact the publisher.

For Product Safety Concerns and Information please contact our EU representative:
GPSR@taylorandfrancis.com
Taylor & Francis Verlag GmbH, Kaufingerstraße 24, 80331 München, Germany

'A password to madness. Jew. One little word with no hiding place for reason in it. Say "Jew" and it was like throwing a bomb.'
— Howard Jacobson, *The Finkler Question* (2010)

Table of Contents

List of Illustrations

Preface

This book is about antisemitism and the stereotypical Jew in postwar Dutch society. When we embarked on this project we envisioned a series of interconnected chapters that follow the transfer of antisemitic tropes over time as manifested in everyday interactions, public debates, mass media, protests and commemorations. By investigating how old stories and vocabularies concerning 'the Jew' get recycled and adapted for new use, we sought to bridge early postwar antisemitism with current manifestations. While it is clear that Sartre's incisive view on 'the Jew' as a construct of the antisemite is still topical, we were not convinced that reflection on 'the [stereotypical] Jew' is a privilege of 'the [stereotypical] Antisemite'.[1] We therefore expressed a common ambition to cast our net wider and make an effort in exploring how 'real people', including Jews, have dealt with their stereotypical counterparts. By following a wide range of participants in the Dutch public debate – including Jewish and non-Jewish publicists, various solidarity movements and migrant interest groups – *The Holocaust, Israel and 'the Jew'. Histories of Antisemitism in Postwar Dutch Society* thus aims to demonstrate how in the Netherlands the Holocaust and the founding of Israel have come to act both as points of fixation for antisemitic expressions as well as building blocks for postwar Jewish identity.

The Netherlands may seem like an unlikely candidate for such an exploration of antisemitic stereotyping over time. The general feeling always has been that antisemitism in the Netherlands only exists in isolated incidents or in 'mild form'. When in the early 1880s the neologism *Antisemitismus* was coined, Dutch newspapers exclusively applied the term to incidents abroad. In several newspapers commentators wrote disapprovingly of the rise of the 'antisemitic movement' in Germany and the Habsburg Empire, but more than once they did so by simultaneously sneering about the assumed obtrusive presence of Jews. This was also the rhetorical strategy when finally a newspaper reported on a local incident. *'Anti-semitisme in Nederland'*, was the headline of *De Tijd* in 1890. The Catholic newspaper reported on the distribution of a periodical, *De Talmudjood*, in which Jews were literally portrayed as bloodsucking vampires.[2] Although the reporter expressed

1   Jean-Paul Sartre, *Réflexions sur la question juive* (Paris: Gallimard, 1946), Jean-Paul Sartre, *Anti-Semite and Jew* (s.l.: Schocken, 1948).
2   'There's only one way to get rid of those bloodsucking vampires ... deport them all, the whole bunch of Jews, to Russia where their friends will be so good as to send them to Siberia

his surprise, he nevertheless fully understood the rising tide in anti-Jewish sentiment: 'Even though we reject every attempt to root antisemitism in the Netherlands, we do feel obliged to point out the unhealthy and worrying developments, i.e. the way some Jews cash in on the economic downturn in agriculture .... The Jew is the natural enemy of agriculture .... What this means, history has shown.'

Despite these overt expressions of anti-Jewish sentiments in print, the early modern legacy of tolerance became part of national self-identification in the modern era. In this respect the Holocaust and the both relatively and absolutely high percentage of Jews murdered, when compared to other West-European countries, must have seemed like an enigma in the post-Liberation years. In any case, it didn't rhyme with the prevalent self-image of tolerance. Antisemitism turned out to have increased during the German occupation, burst into the open and even renewed itself during the post-Liberation years. Also, when it became taboo to express anti-Jewish feelings openly soon afterwards, it would never ever disappear.

At the beginning of the twenty-first century, the self-image of the tolerant nation came under pressure once again, under the influence of an escalating Israeli-Palestinian conflict, and a concomitant anti-multicultural and anti-Jewish mood. 'The stereotypical Jew' got deployed in a politics of national and ethnic identities, and real people bore the burden, as evidenced by the dissemination of anti-Jewish images and texts over the internet and a significant rise in so-called real life incidents. It is in light of these observations that we address in this volume the long-term unease with Jewish presence in Dutch society.

This book is one of the results of a research project, 'The Dynamics of Contemporary Antisemitism in a Globalising Context', that springs from an initiative by Evelien Gans and the NIOD Institute for War-, Holocaust- and Genocide Studies. The project was funded by NWO, the Netherlands Organisation for Scientific Research (NOW), and facilitated by the NIOD. The project aimed to investigate current anti-Jewish stereotypes in Dutch society focusing on some of its major ethnic groups. Earlier results of the project were both the publication, in 2014, of the monograph *Haatspraak. Antisemitisme – een 21ᵉ-eeuwse geschiedenis* by Remco Ensel, which was, just like this book, published by AUP (Amsterdam University Press), and,

with a free ticket.' In: 'Anti-semitisme in Nederland', *De Tijd, Godsdienstig-staatkundig dagblad*, 8 October 1890. *De Talmudjood* was then already published for three months, and due to its success upgraded to a bigger format.

with extra funding by the KNAW (Royal Netherlands Academy of Arts and Sciences), the website www.antisemitisme.nu (coordinated by Iwona Guść). In addition to publishing in academic media, we felt it was important to contribute to the public debate, in various media, about these crucial issues. With regard to this book, it is clear that it would have been incomplete without the valuable contributions of our co-authors Annemarike Stremmelaar (University Leiden), Katie Digan (University Ghent) and Willem Wagenaar (Anne Frank House).

Two notes about terminology are necessary. As the attentive reader probably noticed, we write antisemitism without hyphen, because, as Evelien Gans once put it, 'nothing like Semitism ever existed. The term anti(-)Semitism was an invention or construction of confirmed antisemites who, at the end of the nineteenth century, transplanted the designation of Semitic languages to a concept of social-political and racist Jew-hatred.' We wish to dissociate ourselves from this origin and take antisemitism to be the proper term for referring to hatred or antipathy of Jews. The unhyphenated spelling of antisemitism in this volume concurs with the recommendation by the International Holocaust Remembrance Alliance.[3]

We are furthermore aware of the public discussions about the use of 'Holocaust' to denote the systematic mass murder of Jews and other victim groups between 1939 and 1945. For a long time in the Netherlands the customary way to refer to the genocide and the German occupation alike was to speak of 'the war'. With respect to the Jewish victims, the term *Holocaust* (literally: burnt offering) has become both more conventional and controversial than *Shoah* (Hebrew for: destruction, calamity). While the title of this volume follows the series title, the NIOD Studies on War, Holocaust and Genocide, in our chapters we alternately use 'Holocaust' and the more appropriate term 'Shoah'.[4] Actually, the organised *persecution*

---

3   Evelien Gans, '"They have forgotten to gas you." Post-1945 Antisemitism in the Netherlands.', In: Philomena Essed and Isabele Hoving (eds.), *Dutch Racism* (Amsterdam/New York: Rodopi, 2014), 71-100: 95; David Hirsh, 'Anti-Zionism and Antisemitism: Cosmopolitan Reflections.' The Yale Hirsh Initiative for the Interdisciplinary Study of Antisemitism (YIISA) (Working Paper Series #1. New Haven, CT, 2007): 16; Memo on the spelling of antisemitism by the International Holocaust Remembrance Alliance (IHRA) (https://www.holocaustremembrance.com/).

4   *See, e.g.*, Dan Michman, 'Shoah, Holocaust, Churbn and More: On the Emergence of Names for the Lethal Nazi Anti-Jewish Campaign', Public Lecture At Wiener Library, 1 July 2015; Dan Michman, 'Waren die Juden Nordafrikas im Visier der Planungen zur Endlösung? Die "Schoah" und die Zahl 700.000 in Eichmanns Tabelle am 20. Januar 1942.' In: Norbert Kampe and Peter Klein (eds.) *Die Wannsee-Konferenz am 20. Januar 1942. Dokumente, Forschungsstand, Kontroversen* (Köln/Weimar/Wien: Böhlau, 2013), 379-397.

of the Jews started in 1933, when Hitler came into power in Germany, and went on wherever Nazism took over, as with the Anschluss in Austria, in March 1938.

We want to thank several institutions and individuals for their contributions and support with respect to the realisation of this book. In the first place NOW for recognising the academic and social relevance of our project. Secondly, we thank the NIOD for its confidence and its never-ending and generous support. These thanks most certainly also apply to the editors of the AUP-NIOD series for including our manuscript in an inspiring line of books. Both the Anne Frank House, the CIDI (Centre for Information and Documentation on Israel) and the Registration Centre for Discrimination on the Internet (MDI) helped us whenever we needed information and documentation. The same goes for the International Institute for Social History (IISH), the Netherlands Institute for Sound and Vision ('Beeld en Geluid') and the Dutch Institute in Morocco (NIMAR).

Subsequently we are grateful for the assistance of Rachid Aouled Abdallah, René Deelen, Gülsen Devre, Silke Eyt and Ralph Pluim who all did most important research in the context of this volume. We thank René Kok and Harco Gijsbers, both working in the audio-visual department of the NIOD, for their efforts to collect a large number of adequate photos and illustrations, and the National Archive (NA) for supplying us several photos for free. The Chair for Modern Jewish History at the University of Amsterdam (UvA) funded part of the illustrations.

Several translators have worked on our texts. We thank Jane Hedley-Prole and David McKay who translated the Introductory Essay, Beverley Jackson who translated the Epilogue, Luuk Arens and Han van der Vegt who translated or corrected the chapters in-between, and finally Asaf Lahat who edited the complete manuscript. All editorial decisions, including minor overlaps between different chapters, and any remaining errors are of course ours.

Valuable to us were all those – and we thank them collectively – who gave or sent us information during informal conversations or in e-mails about their experiences with antisemitism and other topics. Last but not least, we are grateful to those who spent time and energy with one or both of us during an interview. We name here: Mohammed Abdallah, Wim Bartels, Ronald van den Boogaard, Mellouki Brieuc-Cadat, Erwin Brugmans, Job Cohen, René Danen, Fatima Elatik, Joop Glimmerveen, Bertus Hendriks, Mohammed Jabri, Lody van de Kamp, Haci Karacaer, Sami Kaspi, Hans Knoop, Anneke Mouthaan, Ronny Naftaniel, Leo Nederstigt, Harry Polak,

Karen Polak, Mohamed Rabbae, Mehmet Sahin, Menachem Sebbag, Harry de Winter. Obviously we carry full responsibility for the translations of the interview excerpts, for the contexts in which these occur and for their interpretation.

Finally, while all our themes – the Holocaust, Israel, 'the Jew', and last but not least antisemitism – add up to a genuine minefield, we are happy we managed to finish the book in a spirit of excellent cooperation, mutual understanding and friendship.

Remco Ensel
Evelien Gans
Amsterdam, September 2016

1   Why Jews are more guilty than others ?[1]

An introductory essay, 1945-2016

Evelien Gans

Denkend aan Holland	Thinking of Holland
zie ik breede rivieren	I picture wide rivers
traag door oneindig	slowly meandering through
laagland gaan ...	unending lowland ...

The famous poet Hendrik Marsman (1899-1940) wrote these words in 1936, in a poem entitled 'Memory of Holland', later proclaimed Dutch poem of the century.[2] In that same year he published an article about the so-called 'Jewish Question', in which he postulated that Jews could not assimilate into Western society. The differences between 'them' and 'us' in terms of race, blood and origin, he wrote, were so unbridgeable that co-existence should 'if at all possible, be terminated and avoided'. In Marsman's view, the only solution was Zionism.[3] He did see Jews as possessing various positive qualities, including 'a distinctive kind of acuteness'. But he couldn't imagine them ever taking root in Holland.

Until fairly recently the Netherlands was internationally known as a tolerant country. Events such as the murders of the politician Pim Fortuyn (1948-2002) and the filmmaker and columnist Theo van Gogh (1957-2004), as well as the anti-Islam politics of both Fortuyn and Geert Wilders have upset this image.[4] This book focuses on the continuum of antisemitism, in various forms and gradations, before, during and particularly after 1945. The proverbial tolerance of the Dutch and their supposed tradition of non-violence have always been disputed, certainly in academic circles.

---

1   !: Irony mark, created by *Underware* and introduced in: 'Nieuw: een leesteken voor ironie', CPNB (foundation for the Collective Promotion for the Dutch Book), 13 March 2007.
2   This English version of the poem is a combination of a translation by the author (E.G.) and one by the Irish poet Michael Longley, who, in 1939, translated the first four lines as follows: 'Thinking of Holland / I picture broad rivers / meandering through / unending lowland'. For the whole poem, *see* http://4umi.com/marsman/herinnering (consulted 12 December 2015).
3   H. Marsman, 'Brief over de joodsche kwestie; antwoord aan Dr. G.D. Knoche', *Het Kouter* 1 (1936), 289-302, quoted in: Hans Anten, 'Bordewijk en de joden', *Nederlandse letterkunde* 7 (2002), 61-86: 8.
4   *See* chapters 12 and 18 (Epilogue).

Both tolerance and non-violence have had their limits. It is not as if there was never any hostility or violence towards, say, Catholics or, conversely, Protestants, political adversaries or outsiders.[5] The same applies to the Jews. In the fourteenth century, especially in the east of the country, entire Jewish communities were burnt at the stake. Just as elsewhere in Europe, they were held responsible for bringing the plague and other calamities.[6] But as of the sixteenth century, fleeing from the Inquisition in Spain and Portugal, and the pogroms in Eastern Europe, Jews found a relatively safe haven in the Dutch Republic – along with a great many religious, social and economic constraints. Here, too, certain cities and professions were out of bounds to Jews, and there were a great deal many more prohibitions, along with a host of anti-Jewish prejudices. But Jews were free to worship in their own communities and in a sense formed a little state within the state – the *'Joodsche Natie'* [Jewish Nation] – with its own jurisdiction and language. The government benefited from the international trade networks of these new citizens. No violent persecution took place. There were antisemitic incidents, disturbances, scandals – but no pogroms.

In the wake of the French Revolution came the Emancipation of 1796, when Jews in the Dutch Republic were granted the same rights and obligations as Gentiles. The Emancipation did not come about without a struggle. Jewish leaders and clergy feared the loss of the community's internal political influence, and a section of the Jewish population was afraid that the 'Jewish Nation' would lose its autonomy. Non-Jewish opponents stressed the danger of fraudulent business practices by Jews and, more generally, of growing competition for small and medium-size businesses. By the latter half of the eighteenth century, the number of Jews, and thus their share in trade, had increased considerably. The word 'Jew' came to be synonymous with shady trader and con man – *'smous'* the common term of abuse. Moreover, Jews were regarded as heathens and foreigners whose loyalty to the 'Dutch Nation' was questionable. The historian Rena Fuks-Mansfeld

5   See, e.g., Piet de Rooij, *Republiek van rivaliteiten: Nederland sinds* 1813 (Amsterdam: Mets & Schilt, 2002); Piet de Rooij, "'De reuk des doods." De fakkel van het antipapisme in Nederland 1848-1865.' In: Conny Kristel (ed.), *Met alle geweld. Botsingen en tegenstellingen in burgerlijk Nederland.* (Amsterdam: Balans, 2003), 60-77; Niek van Sas, 'Het beroerd Nederland. Revolutionair geweld en bezinning omstreeks 1800.' In: *ibid.*, 48-59.
6   For the position – and persecution – of the Jews in the Dutch Middle Ages *see*, B B.M.J. Speet, 'De Middeleeuwen.' In: J.C.H. Blom, R.G. Fuks-Mansfeld and I. Schöffer (eds.), *Geschiedenis van de Joden in Nederland* (Balans: Amsterdam, 1995), 21-49.

(1930-2012) summed it up as follows: 'an emancipation that was bestowed as reluctantly as it was accepted'.[7]

This led, by fits and starts, to a process of integration and assimilation, at different speeds and to varying degrees, of the various groups that made up the Jewish community. However, that certainly didn't put an end to social antisemitism in the form of exclusion and antisemitic stereotypes, or to religious or theologically motivated antisemitism, i.e. anti-Judaism. In 1878, Abraham Kuyper (1837-1920), the charismatic leader of the newly-formed Dutch Reformed Party, wrote a series of articles entitled *'Liberalisten en Joden'* [Liberals and Jews]. In his view, liberalism provided a cover under which Jews held absolute sway, not just in the Netherlands but throughout Europe, despite it being obvious that, as 'guests' of a Christian society, they should wield no political influence at all. Kuyper's views met with both outrage and approval.[8] In the 1930s and before, racist antisemitism had taken root in science and popular belief. Moreover, it became institutionalised and politically organised in National Socialist and Fascist organisations and movements like the Dutch National Socialist Movement (NSB).[9] In *Volk en Vaderland* [People and Fatherland], but also in several other papers and journals which were affiliated with the NSB such as *Het Nationale Dagblad* [National Newspaper] and *De Misthoorn* [The Foghorn] antisemitism was propagated already before the war, and even more so, during the occupation.[10] According to a senior NSB official in 1935 75% of the NSB members hold on to antisemitic beliefs.[11]

Inspired by nineteenth-century racial doctrines, a new racist form of antisemitism had emerged that, waving its pseudo-scientific publications, presented Jewishness as a biological issue: a dangerous, infectious virus transmitted from generation to generation. This racist antisemitism was new in that it ruled out any possibility of escape, even through conversion:

7   Rena Fuks-Mansfeld, 'Verlichting en Emancipatie omstreeks 1750-1814.' In: J.C.H. Blom, R.G. Fuks-Mansfeld and I. Schöffer (eds.), *Geschiedenis van de Joden in Nederland* (Balans: Amsterdam, 1995), 177-203: 203; Evelien Gans, *Jaap en Ischa Meijer. Een joodse geschiedenis 1912-1956* (Amsterdam: Bert Bakker, 2008), 32.
8   Evelien Gans, 'The Netherlands in the Twentieth Century.' In: Richard Levy (ed.), *Antisemitism. A Historical Encyclopedia of Prejudice and Persecution* (Santa Barbara/Denver/Oxford: ABC-CLIO, 2005), vol. 2, 498-500: 498.
9   J.C.H. Blom and J.J. Cahen, 'Joodse Nederlanders, Nederlandse joden en joden in Nederland.' J.C.H. Blom, R.G. Fuks-Mansfeld and I. Schöffer (eds.), *Geschiedenis van de Joden in Nederland* (Amsterdam: Balans, 1995), 245-310: 284-287.
10   Bas Kromhout, *Fout! Wat Hollandse nazi-kranten schreven over Nederland, verzet, Joden* (Amsterdam: Veen Media, 2016).
11   Bas Kromhout, 'Het ware gezicht van de NSB', *Historisch Nieuwsblad*, 24 November 2015.

Jewishness was in the Jews' blood.[12] A Dutch version was made of the German racist, antisemitic rhyme *'Ob Jud, ob Christ ist einerlei / in der Rasse liegt der Schweinerei':*

| *Wat de Jood gelooft, komt' d'r niet op an /* | Jewish or Christian it's all one / |
| *'t ras zelf is de zwijnepan* | It's their race that makes them scum[13] |

In 1940 Jewish integration was far from complete, and the degree of assimilation varied strongly within the community.[14] In his article, Marsman had explicitly placed Jews beyond the pale of Dutch society, but others did this more actively.

In March 1938, very probably on the instructions of NSB officials, around 10,000 cardboard 'railway tickets' were printed bearing the text: '1st CLASS / PASSENGER TRAIN TICKET / TO / JERUSALEM / ONE WAY / Never to RETURN / Valid from / Any station'.[15]

In 1934, the Dutch government had found it necessary to add two new articles to the Criminal Code concerning the defamation of a population group. It took this step largely because insults aimed at 'our Israelite fellow citizens' had taken on a kind of 'epidemic character'.[16] Before that time, only insults targeting individuals, primarily public officials, were grounds

---

12   Evelien Gans, '"They have forgotten to gas you." Post-1945 Antisemitism in the Netherlands.' In: Philomena Essed and Isabele Hoving (eds.), *Dutch Racism* (Amsterdam, New York: Rodopi, 2014), 71-100: 74.

13   Evelien Gans, 'Antisemitisme: evolutionair en multi-functioneel.' Paper presented at the *Anne Frank Stichting*, Amsterdam, 3 October 2007.

14   Evelien Gans, *De kleine verschillen. Een historische studie naar joodse sociaal-democraten en socialistisch-zionisten in Nederland* (Amsterdam: Vassallucci, 1999), 900-904 (English Summary); Gans, 'The Netherlands in the Twentieth Century', 498. Remco Ensel and Evelien Gans, 'The Bystander as a non-Jew.' Paper presented at the international conference *Probing the Limits of Categorization: The 'Bystander' in Holocaust History*, 24-26 September 2015, Amsterdam.

15   The misprint on the train tickets (Jerusalem instead of Jeruzalem) betrays the German origins; the tickets over there had been distributed in 1931, in Berlin: *De Telegraaf*, 31 March 1938; *Utrechts Nieuwsblad*, 30 March 1938; *Volksdagblad* and *Het Volk*, 29 March and 11 May 1938, NIOD, KA II 977 A.

16   Wetboek van Strafrecht [Criminal Code], 19th ed. [till 1968], ed. C. Fasseur (Zwolle: Tjeenk Willink, 1969), 69. Sections 137 a and b of the law turned against the abuse of public authorities. See, e.g., Esther H. Janssen, *Faith in Public Debate. An Inquiry into the Relationship between Freedom of Expression and Hate Speech Pertaining to Religion and Race in France, the Netherlands and European and International Law* (PhD thesis, Universiteit van Amsterdam, 9 September 2014) and Marloes van Noorloos, *Hate Speech Revisited. A Comparative and Historical Perspective on Hate speech Law in The Netherlands and England & Wales* (Cambridge: Intersentia, 2011).

Two examples of prewar antisemitic prints by the Dutch National-Socialist Movement (NSB)

Illustration 1 Cartoon by Maarten Meuldijk for the NSB newspaper, *Volk en Vaderland*, 25 June 1935

Illustration 2 Fake train ticket. German original, 1931

In gastvrij Nederland ... koekoek!

NIOD archive / Imagebase

4 - 38

1E KLAS
PERSONENTREIN NAAR
JERUSALEM
HEEN
en nooit meer
TERUG
0,00   1e
Geldig van uit
elk station

0838

NIOD archive / Imagebase

'In the hospitable Netherlands ... cuckoo!' In 1935 –, when the NSB had achieved a victory in the elections for the Dutch Provincial Councils – its journal *Volk en Vaderland*, published a cartoon that depicted 'the Jew' as a parasite: that is, like an alien cuckoo which devours all the food, while the native chicks are starving.

In March 1938, around 10,000 'railway tickets' were distributed in the Netherlands from the ranks of the NSB: 1st CLASS / PASSENGER TRAIN TICKET / TO / JERUSALEM / ONE WAY / Never to RETURN / Valid from / Any station'.

for criminal prosecution. The motive for adopting these new articles were concern not so much about Jews as about disturbances of the peace. Furthermore, an insult was defined by its form; supposed 'statements of fact' could still be made. It was a crime in 1940 to describe Jews as parasites, but not to express the underlying idea that Jews do well for themselves even in times of crisis.[17] In the Netherlands, 'the Jew' was also still very much seen as 'the Other', not just by National Socialist members and sympathisers, and in Christian circles, but also outside these groups.

During the Second World War, more Jews would be murdered in the Netherlands than in any other occupied country in Western Europe, both in relative and absolute terms: around 104,000 of the country's 140,000 Jewish citizens, that is to say 75%. The contrast between this fact and the Netherlands' above-mentioned reputation for tolerance would give rise to a concept that historians dubbed 'the Dutch paradox'.[18] During the German occupation, antisemitism in the Netherlands increased – as it did in other occupied countries in Europe – manifesting itself openly after the country's liberation in May 1945.[19] A case in point is the insult 'They have forgotten to gas you', a first, radical expression of how, after 1945, the Shoah or Holocaust was turned against the Jews. In June 1945, the re-established Jewish weekly *Nieuw Israëlietisch Weekblad* (NIW) called antisemitism 'Hitler's foremost legacy'.[20]

This study centres on the 'dark side' of the Dutch paradox, so to speak, and above all on its manifestations after 1945. It addresses processes of antisemitic stereotyping in the Netherlands by considering how the Shoah

17   Van Noorloos, *Hate Speech Revisited*, 199.

18   J.C.H. Blom, 'The persecution of the Jews in the Netherlands from a comparative international perspective.' In: Jozeph Michman (ed.), *Dutch Jewish History II* (Assen, Maastricht: Van Gorcum, 1989), 273-289: 289; Philo Bregstein, 'De Nederlandse paradox.' In: Philo Bregstein, *Het kromme kan toch niet recht zijn: Essays en interviews* (Baarn: de Prom, 1996), 45-72: 45-47; Wouter Ultee and Henk Flap, 'De Nederlandse paradox: waarom overleefden zoveel Nederlandse joden de Tweede Wereldoorlog niet?'. In: Harry Ganzeboom and Siegwart Lindenberg (eds.), *Verklarende sociologie. Opstellen voor Reinhard Wippler* (Amsterdam: Thela Thesis, 1996); Guus Meershoek, 'Een aangekondigde massamoord. Wat wisten Nederlanders van de jodenvervolging?', *De Groene Amsterdammer*, 31 January 2013.

19   *See* Dienke Hondius, *Terugkeer. Antisemitisme in Nederland rond de bevrijding.* With a story by Marga Minco (Den Haag: Sdu, 1998; revised version of 1990), translated version: Dienke Hondius, *Return: Holocaust Survivors and Dutch Anti-Semitism* (Westport, CO: Praeger, 2003); Evelien Gans, '"Vandaag hebben ze niets, maar morgen bezitten ze weer een tientje." Antisemitische stereotypen in bevrijd Nederland.' In: Conny Kristel (ed.), *Polderschouw. Terugkeer en opvang na de Tweede Wereldoorlog. Regionale verschillen* (Amsterdam: Bert Bakker, 2002), 313-353. *See*, e.g., chapters 2 and 3.

20   J.S. (Jacob) Soetendorp, 'Eerbied voor onze monumenten', *NIW*, 22 June 1945.

and Israel have come to function both as the most important new – that is, postwar – points of fixation for expressions of antisemitism, and at the same time, and not coincidentally, as the two most important building blocks of postwar Jewish identity.

Its contribution to the field of antisemitism studies is twofold. One original aspect is the effort to connect old stories and repertoires of stereotyping with new vocabularies and forms of deployment in a historical study that links early postwar everyday antisemitism with current manifestations. Secondly, by focusing on a wide range of participants in the public debate on the Shoah and Israel – including Jewish and non-Jewish public intellectuals, various solidarity movements and migrant interest groups – this volume presents the historical entanglements and global transfer of ideas about Jews on a national scale.

The Dutch case is of particular interest when tackling issues of stereotyping in the postwar era. As stated above, the relatively high percentage of Jews murdered during the war was difficult to reconcile with the tradition of tolerance that had become ingrained in the country's perception of its own identity. An increase of antisemitism was signalled, mainly by Jewish organisations, after the Yom Kippur War in 1973, and in response to several incidents thereafter. The details of these events did not generally come to the attention of the outside world, but several of them will be discussed in this book. At the beginning of this century, the self-image of the Netherlands as a tolerant nation came under pressure once again. Like other parts of the world, the country experienced outbursts of antisemitism, this time triggered by the clashes between Israelis and Palestinians after Ariel Sharon's visit to the Temple Mount, in September 2000, and in Jenin, in April 2002.[21] This was also the period of Fortuyn's rise to political prominence and subsequent assassination. Two years later, the Islamist assassination of Theo van Gogh led to a strong anti-multicultural and nationalist backlash. This event was felt to be the Dutch equivalent of the 9/11 attacks. What is hardly known beyond the Dutch borders, and increasingly forgotten or denied in the Netherlands itself, is that Theo van Gogh, resenting what he called the dominance of the Shoah, had been extremely provocative towards Jews in his pamphlets, columns and utterances – and later on, towards Muslims as well.

---

21   *See, e.g.,* Evelien Gans, "On Gas Chambers, Jewish Nazis and Noses." In: Peter R. Rodrigues and Jaap van Donselaar (eds.), *Racism and Extremism Monitor: Ninth Report.* Transl. Nancy Forest-Flier (Amsterdam: Anne Frank Stichting and Universiteit Leiden, 2010), 74-87: 75-76.

As mentioned before, Israel would become the second point of fixation for antisemitism after 1945. The initially hesitant support for Israel on the part of postwar Dutch governments developed into a strong sense of solidarity. The Six-Day War, or June War, of 1967 led to seemingly contradictory reactions in the Netherlands: an outburst of support in favour of Israel, along with more outspoken criticism of the occupation of the West Bank, Gaza and the Golan Heights. In 1969 the Dutch Palestine Committee was founded. At the same time, Moroccan and Turkish immigrants brought their mostly negative ideas about Israel and 'Zionism' with them, mingled with old, sometimes hostile images of 'the Jew' or nostalgic views on Jewish-Islamic coexistence in their respective home countries. This contributed to a broader aversion to Israel.

Against the background of the long-term debate on the Shoah and Israel, this study investigates the unease with the Jewish presence in Dutch society as manifested in commemorations of the Second World War, public debates, protests against Israel and everyday interactions. It shows the transfer of antisemitic tropes over time, between ethnic groups and across national borders. The emphasis is on qualitative historical research, with theory and analysis combined in a set of postwar narratives. All case studies are based on original research, drawing on a wide variety of sources, such as archival sources, newspapers and journals, websites, DVD's and music CD's, impromptu conversations and observations.

Operating in a minefield

A small book could be compiled of all the many different definitions of antisemitism drawn up and used as a yardstick by scholars, writers, institutes, monitors and bloggers. Two will be looked at here. According to the social historian Helen Fein (b. 1934), antisemitism is 'a persisting, latent structure of hostile beliefs toward *Jews as a collectivity*'. This wording forms, as it were, the body of her definition, which she continues by concluding that the 'hostile beliefs' she mentions manifest themselves,

> in *individuals* as attitudes, and in *culture* as myth, ideology, folklore, and imagery, and in *actions* – social or legal discrimination, political mobilization against the Jews, and collective or state violence – which results in and/or is designed to distance, displace or destroy Jews as Jews.[22]

---

22 Helen Fein, 'Dimensions of Antisemitism: Attitudes, Collective Accusations, and Actions.' In: Helen Fein (ed.), *The Persisting Question: Sociological Perspectives and Social Contexts of Modern*

Although Fein's definition is almost more of a miniature exposé, as a guideline it is certainly satisfactory in a number of respects. The description does justice to the complexity, the multi-layeredness and the persistence of the phenomenon, and makes clear that while hostile beliefs target the Jews as a group, they can manifest themselves at different levels: individual, cultural and political. Moreover, Fein postulates that antisemitic feelings need not necessarily lead to anti-Jewish behaviour.[23]

The Dutch social historian Dik van Arkel (1925-2010) defines antisemitism as 'Verbal or active manifestations of antagonism towards the Jewish group as such, 'irrespective of whether they are direct or indirect, intended or not'.[24] By speaking of 'active manifestations' and 'antagonism', his definition is more limited and less subtle than that of Fein. But like Fein, he posits that antisemitism can be purely verbal in nature, and he, too, adds an extra dimension: it is possible for antisemitism to be manifested indirectly and unintentionally.

Nevertheless, the usefulness of definitions is limited. Anyone speaking or writing about antisemitism will almost automatically find themselves embroiled in discussion. Just as 'the Jew' can represent the embodiment of the conflict with 'the Other', the concept of 'antisemitism' inevitably elicits opposition, polemics, denial and exaggeration. This ongoing debate and the different interpretations of antisemitism necessarily feature in this volume. A major obstacle for scholars and analysts of postwar antisemitism is that their findings tend to provoke disbelief and defensive reactions – often because people, consciously or unconsciously, use Nazi antisemitism and Jewish persecution as a yardstick. As long as the issue is not about politically organised antisemitism – about calls to exclude, discriminate against or persecute Jews, or programmes with that goal – the conclusion that certain verbal and written utterances are 'antisemitic' is very often seen as an

Antisemitism (Berlin: Walter de Gruyter, 1987), 67. Elsewhere Fein leaves out the characterisation 'persistent and latent', and speaks briefly of 'anti-Semitic beliefs and culture': *ibid.*, 85. Mark Cohen also offers an interesting definition: 'a religiously-based complex of irrational, mythical, and stereotypical beliefs about the diabolical, malevolent, and all-powerful Jew, infused, in its modern, secular form, with racism and the belief that there is a Jewish conspiracy against mankind': Mark R. Cohen, 'The "Convivencia" of Jews and Muslims in the High Middle Ages.' In: Moshe Maoz (ed.) *The Meeting of Civilizations. Muslims, Christians and Jewish* (Brighton, Portland: Sussex Academic Press, 2009), 54-65.

23 Fein, 'Dimensions of antisemitism', 85.

24 Dik van Arkel, *The Drawing of the Mark of Cain. A Socio-historical Analysis of the Growth of Anti-Jewish Stereotypes* (Amsterdam: Amsterdam University, Press 2009), 77.

exaggerated, moralistic, possibly even scandalous accusation – as casting unfair doubt on the integrity of the author or source in question.[25]

That attitude can lead to contemporary antisemitism being trivialised. People forget that antisemitism preceded Nazism, and that it did not disappear with the Nazis. They ignore the fact that antisemitism is not just a phenomenon, a term originally conceived by those who, because of their convictions, profiled themselves explicitly as antisemites, but has also entered common usage as 'an analytical or critical category'.[26] In other words, concluding that someone's words or deeds are antisemitic is not the same thing as claiming that someone is a 'Nazi' or even an 'antisemite'. The primary aim is to reach an analysis as such – an analysis founded on arguments. The charged debate about what may or may not be considered antisemitic is muddied yet further by those who, as soon as any criticism is expressed of Jews, Judaism or Israel, claim that it is 'antisemitic'. At the opposite end of the spectrum from those who trivialise antisemitism ('deniers') are those who exaggerate and exploit antisemitism to further their own (political) goals, or because of understandable, but not seldom unfounded fears ('alarmists').[27] In short, to make antisemitism an object of study is to enter an academic, political, social and emotional minefield.

A huge body of work exists on historical and contemporary manifestations of antisemitism, including after the Second World War. The Netherlands stands out for the paucity of its contribution to this corpus. Strikingly little Dutch research has been done on the history of antisemitism, either in previous centuries or after the war.[28] But then what could we add to

---

25 *See* chapter 13.

26 Robert Fine, 'Fighting with Phantoms: a Contribution to the Debate on Antisemitism in Europe', *Patterns of Prejudice* 43, 5 (2009), 459-479: 460, n. 2.

27 Fine, 'Fighting with Phantoms', 459*ff*; Evelien Gans, 'De strijd tegen het antisemitisme is verworden tot ideologie tegen moslims', *NRC Handelsblad*, 8 January 2011; *See* Ron van der Wieken, *Jodenhaat. Het verhaal van een uiterst explosief en destructief element in de westerse cultuur* (Amsterdam: Mastix Press, 2014), 14-16.

28 Before and after the Second World War, Dutch antisemitism was often dealt with in a very fragmented way in historical studies on Jewish history or quite different topics (like the Dutch labour movement): Evelien Gans, 'Gojse broodnijd. De strijd tussen joden en niet-joden rond de naoorlogse Winkelsluitingswet 1945-1951.' In: Conny Kristel (ed.), *Met alle geweld. Botsingen en tegenstellingen in burgerlijk Nederland* (Amsterdam: Balans, 2003), 195-213: 196-198. Since 1945, however, several studies have appeared that focus on antisemitism immediately after the Second World War (Hondius, *Terugkeer*, 1990/1998) and on the image of the Jew in Catholic and Protestant circles: Marcel Poorthuis and Theo Salemink, *Een donkere spiegel. Nederlandse katholieken over joden. Tussen antisemitisme en erkenning, 1870-2005* (Nijmegen: Valkhof Pers, 2006), and G.J. van Klinken, *Opvattingen in de gereformeerde kerken in Nederland over het Jodendom,1896-1970* (Kampen: Kok, 1996). Evelien Gans has published *Gojse nijd & joods narcisme. Over*

this prodigious international collection of books on antisemitism, both academic and non-academic? In the following sections we will expound the central questions of this book and the added value, the aims and the innovative aspects of our approach.

Stereotypes and points of fixation

In the first place this volume examines how, and by what dynamic processes, antisemitism, an age-old and global phenomenon, manifested itself in the Netherlands after 1945. As stated above, up to now, Dutch historians have not paid much attention to this subject, nor has it been much examined by historians outside the Netherlands.[29]

It is not for nothing that the term 'stereotype' appears frequently in this introduction. The second aim of this volume is to examine the historical and social development, function and relevance of antisemitic stereotypes. Stereotypes are manifestations of the view that people belonging to a certain group have specific characteristics – qualities that are predominantly, but not exclusively, negative. Stereotypes arise in a particular historical and social context and sometimes possess a grain of historical 'reality', albeit one which is exaggerated, distorted and removed from its historical context. For example, the Jews were forced by Christian society to specialise in money lending, and this led to the stereotype of the rich, materialistic Jew. But at least as often, stereotypes are completely irrational from the start (think of the Jewish child killer or the blood libel). These negative perceptions become fixed and take on a life of their own. The mechanism of 'collective liability' is directly linked to this. It suffices for one member of the group (or a few) to make a false step or commit a crime, for the whole group to be blamed.[30]

de verhouding tussen joden en niet-joden in Nederland (Amsterdam: Arena, 1994) and written several articles on the topic, which are occasionally mentioned in this book, particularly in the footnotes and bibliography; Remco Ensel (b. 1965) has published Haatspraak. Antisemitisme – een 21ᵉ-eeuwse geschiedenis (Amsterdam: Amsterdam University Press, 2014), which focuses on antisemitism, anti-Zionism and images of Jews in the Netherlands during the last decade, mainly, but not only, in the Moroccan-Dutch community.

29   An exception is Terugkeer by Dienke Hondius, mentioned above. In historical, chronological studies on Dutch and Dutch Jewish history, the theme 'antisemitism' is dealt with only briefly and in a fragmentary way: Gans, Gojse broodnijd, 196-197.

30   Gans, 'They have forgotten to gas you', 77; 'De grens van assimilatie verlegt zich keer op keer', (Interview with Evelien Gans) in: Bart Top, Religie en verdraagzaamheid. 10 gesprekken over tolerantie in een extreme tijd (Kampen: Ten Have, 2005), 47-60: 54-55.

Fein does not use the term 'stereotype', in contrast with the cultural historian George Mosse (1918-1999). 'Ideas can be weapons', Mosse said. It was 'the formation and diffusion of stereotypes and attitudes that paved the way to the rise of Nazism and favoured its success'.[31] Dik van Arkel even goes so far as to regard stereotypes as the backbone of antisemitism (and racism); their exclamatory power and functionality are of eminent importance to his work, as is clear from a whole series of articles and his magnum opus *The Drawing of the Mark of Cain: A Socio-historical Analysis of the Growth of Anti-Jewish Stereotypes* (2009).[32]

In a comparative analysis of various European countries, Van Arkel examines the conditions that allow antisemitism to grow into a political factor: stigmatisation of a minority by the elite or those in power, the creation of a social divide between majority and minority, whereby stereotypes and stigmas can no longer be corrected, and, finally, terrorisation of those who are unwilling to discriminate.[33] Anti-Jewish prejudices could never have become so deeply ingrained had not Christianity, as a young church, perceived Judaism as its greatest rival and seized upon ways of profiling itself as the only true heir of a common source. Dik van Arkel introduces the enlightening concept of 'secession friction'. A minority that distinguishes itself by a divergent interpretation of an element or elements of a shared ideology stands to gain by presenting itself as the only true heir of a once shared source. Accordingly, in the New Testament, the Jews serve as a 'marker of difference'. The Jew became the Christ killer in a predominantly Christian Europe.[34]

Van Arkel's focus was never systematically on contemporary history, nor did he devote much attention to the Netherlands. Nevertheless, his conceptual framework and also the kernel of his analysis – the emergence and function of stereotypes – transcend the time-specific, local nature of his research. Van Arkel coined the term 'genealogy of stereotypes', meaning that when stereotypes have a big enough social support base, they

---

31   Quoted in: Emilio Gentile, 'A provisional dwelling. The origin and development of the concept of fascism in Mosse's historiography.' In: Stanley G. Payne, David J. Sorkin and John S. Tortoise (eds.), *What History Tells. George L. Mosse and the Culture of Modern Europe* (Madison: The University of Wisconsin Press, 2004), 41-109: 50.

32   Van Arkel, *The Drawing of the Mark of Cain*, and Dik van Arkel, 'Genealogisch verband van antisemitische vooroordelen.' In: D. van Arkel et al. (eds.), *Wat is antisemitisme? Een benadering vanuit vier disciplines* (Kampen: Kok, 1991), 48-74.

33   Gans, 'Vandaag hebben ze niets', 325; Van Arkel, *The Drawing of the Mark of Cain*, 64-65, 119.

34   Nicholas de Lange, 'The origins of anti-Semitism: Ancient evidence and modern interpretations.' In: Sander L. Gilman and Steven T. Katz, *Anti-Semitism in times of crisis* (New York and London: New York University Press, 1991), 29-30; Van Arkel, *The Drawing of the Mark of Cain*, 114.

engender new ones, creating a network or system of linked stereotypes, stigmas and prejudices that connect different public domains. The first two are Christianity and the socio-economic sphere, which spawned the above-mentioned stereotypes of the Christ killer and the grasping, moneylending Jew, respectively.[35] Instead of a 'genealogy of stereotypes' one could also speak of a Pied Piper effect.[36]

Van Arkel's approach is also important because he is careful to avoid the post hoc fallacy. Although he occasionally makes the link with Nazi antisemitism and the Third Reich, he approaches antisemitism first and foremost as a phenomenon with an age-old, complex and dynamic history. This volume adopts the same perspective, in effect building on Van Arkel's work. The focus is on perceptions of Jews, anti-Jewish stereotypes, reasoning and actions after the Second World War. But it goes without saying that these did not appear out of the blue in 1945. They were grafted onto earlier perceptions and, moreover, did not stop developing in the years that followed. In this respect, the view of the historian Robert Chazan (b. 1936) is extremely enlightening: antisemitism develops by an evolutionary process and dialectical interplay. Blending a legacy from the past and new social circumstances, it results from constant interplay between old stereotypes and the reality of a changing historical context.[37] This work investigates which old stereotypes survived and played a role in a new historical context. Which ones were generated by changing circumstances, and which became dominant? It seeks to chart the interplay between old and new stereotypes.

Thirdly, unlike Van Arkel, the authors of this volume distinguish between stereotypes and their points of fixation. Old, familiar points of fixation were – and still are – the domains of religion ('the Christ killer'; Judas, 'the Jewish traitor'), the economy ('the grasping Jewish moneylender', 'the rich Jew') and sexuality ('the obscene Jew').[38]

From 1945 and 1948 onwards two new points of fixation appear, to which antisemitic stereotypes attach themselves. The first is the Shoah or Holo-caust ('they forgot to gas you'). A new question, certainly for a country such as the Netherlands that experienced Nazi occupation, is the extent to which

35   Van Arkel, 'Genealogisch verband van antisemitische vooroordelen', 15; Gans, *Gojse nijd & joods narcisme*, 15.

36   In Dutch: 'zwaan-kleef-aan-effect'; Gans, *Gojse nijd & joods narcisme*, 15.

37   Robert Chazan, *Medieval Stereotypes and Modern Antisemitism* (Berkeley: University of California Press, 1997),134-140.

38   Judas represents both the stereotype of the Jewish traitor and the Jew who will do anything for money ('a handful of pieces of silver'): an early form of the Pied Piper effect.

the Shoah itself influenced the development of postwar antisemitism and in that sense turned itself against the Jews.[39]

Israel became a second point of fixation. After a very complex previous history, its founding was politically legitimised by the United Nations in 1947, and morally legitimised by the Shoah and the fact that many nations had closed their borders to Jews before, during and after the Second World War. But before, and certainly after its establishment, the Jewish state was controversial – loved and hated, admired and vilified. Israel, too, or its politics, would increasingly work against not only itself but also, more generally, against 'the Jew'. Just as in the case of religion, the economy and sexuality, the two new points of fixation would regularly connect with one another – and with other points of fixation. How could Jews still invoke their victimhood, given the way in which they, or the Israelis (a distinction that is often not made) trampled upon the Palestinians? At the end of 2008, in response to constant rocket attacks from the Gaza Strip, Israel launched an offensive against Gaza, dubbed Operation Cast Lead, which attracted international criticism, being seen as a disproportionate reaction. The Dutch-based Centre for Information and Documentation on Israel (CIDI), which, although independent, cites solidarity with Israel as its key principle, was sent the following antisemitic hate mail: *'Hitler was een aardige man vergeleken bij de joden in Israel. Allemaal aan het gas die varkens en dan opvoeren aan de honden.'* [Hitler was a nice man compared to the Jews in Israel. Gas all those pigs and then feed them to the dogs].[40] This line of thinking results from looking through the prism of the Shoah at Jews in Israel. And the same principle operates in reverse. It is not for nothing that the Shoah and the preservation of the state of Israel are both crucial building blocks of postwar Jewish identity as well; we see a mirror image here.[41]

The Netherlands from a multicultural perspective

This book focuses on the postwar Netherlands as a multicultural society, and as the setting of a social phenomenon that provokes fierce debate in a global context.

---

39   In this book the authors alternately use the terms Shoah and Holocaust.
40   Elise Friedmann, *Monitor antisemitische incidenten in Nederland: 2008. Met een verslag van de Gazaperiode: 27-12-2008 – 23-1-2009* (Den Haag: CIDI, 2009), 25.
41   See Gans, *Jaap en Ischa Meijer*, 11.

These two photos mirror a main theme of this book: both the Holocaust and Israel as points of fixation for postwar reflections on 'the Jew'. At different moments in time very diverse groups of people, for most divergent goals, nonetheless gather at the same *lieu de mémoire*: the National Monument at Dam Square in Amsterdam.

Illustration 3   Photo of a protest against the expiration of war crimes on Dam Square, 28 February 1965

Photo: Arthur Bastiaanse / ANP

Former camp prisoners, some of whom have a yellow badge in the form of the Star of David pinned on their coat, protest against the premature expiration of German war crimes, 28 February 1965. The protest signs read: 'Former prisoners of Auschwitz protest against premature expiration', 'Our millions of dead demand justice' and 'Monday protest meeting at Krasnapolsky' (which refers to the hotel behind the Monument).

**Illustration 4   Photo of a demonstration against the military operation in Jenin on
Dam Square, 13 April 2002**

Photo: Bram Buddel / De Beeldunie

'Palestine is one big concentration camp,' 'Zionism is Racism'. Demonstration
on Dam Square against the Israeli military operation in the Jenin refugee
camp, 13 April 2002. The Star of David – also the symbol on the Israeli flag – is
equated with a Swastika.

Certain manifestations, patterns and turning points will become visible – several of which have a more or less typically Dutch flavour, and quite a few of which parallel Western European or global developments. Unlike in some other countries in Western and especially Eastern Europe, there has hardly been any physical violence against Jews in the Netherlands since the Second World War. Verbal and social antisemitism, however, have remained serious issues. The so-called swastika epidemic (the chalking of swastikas on synagogues and other Jewish institutions), which originated in West Germany in 1959-1960 and spread throughout the world from there, was copied in the Netherlands only sporadically. But because it took place right across the border, in a country that had recently occupied the Netherlands, it was the subject of intense debate and made an impact on the Dutch Jewish community. After the Eichmann trial in 1961, and partly in connection with the worldwide publicity that the trial generated, the 1960s saw several anti-Jewish incidents, which will be dealt with in the following chapters. Apparently, figuring out how to cope with the legacy of the Shoah was an ongoing process. One relevant factor, for Jews and Gentiles alike, is which generation was dominant in the political and cultural establishment and in public debate.

This factor may be most relevant to the Dutch debate on Israel. As mentioned above, the Six-Day War or June War of 1967, was a turning point in the Netherlands and throughout Europe, after which sympathy for Israel declined, although it certainly did not disappear. This decline in sympathy took place more slowly in the Netherlands than elsewhere. In the Arab world, Zionism and the founding of Israel had been fiercely rejected from the start; in 1967 the aversion increased enormously. Moroccan immigrants to the Netherlands brought this political baggage with them, including their memories and perceptions of the place of 'the Jew' in their mother country and in the world. Much the same can be said of Turkish immigrants – even though Turkey had a much more ambivalent relationship to Israel than Morocco and other Arab countries. Precisely because of its solidarity with Israel, the Netherlands was hard hit by the Arab oil embargo of 1973, in the wake of the Yom Kippur War. The political and economic harm done to Dutch trade and commercial relations by this measure, as well as the responses to it, will be examined in this book. The country's political stance towards Israel changed, as did the degree of organisation among Jews in the Netherlands, which monitored not only antisemitism but also what they took to be political manifestations of anti-Israel sentiment, and took action when they saw the need for it. Anti-Israeli tendencies were reinforced by the Lebanon War of 1982 – after which the Netherlands contributed to the international peacekeeping force – and the Intifadas of 1987 and 2000,

Israel's military actions and reactions, and the military operation in Gaza, Cast Lead, in 2008/9. These events had a particular impact on opinion in Moroccan-Dutch and Turkish-Dutch communities. In Dutch government circles, however, which were usually dominated by Christian Democrats and Liberals, a benevolent stance continued to prevail. Yet in all strata of Dutch society, to differing degrees, a fateful triangle of antisemitism, anti-Zionism and criticism of Israel was at work.[42]

The fourth aim of this volume is, while keeping in mind the patterns described above, to adopt an innovative approach by putting the spotlight on different population groups and their perceptions of Jews – on their interactions with 'the Jew'. An important question in our research is the extent to which the ideas and stereotypes about Jews held by Moroccan and Turkish newcomers changed and became connected – in whatever direction – with perceptions that were current in their new home country.[43]

The very first group to be considered is the dominant majority among the Dutch population – the so-called native Dutch. The members of this group are Christian, or they or their forefathers were raised in the Christian tradition – by now they are often completely or largely secular. In any event, they identify with, see themselves as and are perceived as being both the heirs and representatives of dominant, mainstream ('Dutch') history and culture – however volatile and mutable these concepts might be. Naturally, this approach has its limitations. The native Dutch community is by no means a homogenous group. Its members come in all shapes and sizes, in terms of age, gender, generation, social background, religion, ideology and political affiliation. Moreover, they think and act in a specific historical and social context. Several groups fall into grey areas, like those who are partly of Indonesian descent, known as Indos, and the Moluccan-Dutch community. So this category is intended merely as an initial, rough demarcation.

The (Dutch) Jews – also far from being a uniform population group – occupy an intriguing middle ground here. In late December 1945 the Jewish population of the Netherlands stood at 21,674; by 1947 that number had risen to an estimated 28,000 – only a quarter of what it had been before the war.[44] These survivors would fan out into numerous, very diverse groups – or

42   Gans, 'They have forgotten to gas you', 90-94.
43   In the mid-1960s, Morocco and Turkey replaced Spain and Italy as the main countries supplying migrant labour: Rob Witte, 'Al eeuwenlang een gastvrij volk'. Racistisch geweld en overheidsreacties in Nederland 1950-2009 (Amsterdam: Aksant, 2010), 63.
44   Chaya Brasz, 'Na de Tweede Wereldoorlog: van kerkgenootschap naar culturele minderheid.' In: J.C.H. Blom, R.G. Fuks-Manfeld and I. Schöffer (eds.), Geschiedenis van de joden in Nederland (Amsterdam: Balans, 1995), 351-403: 351-352.

remain lone wolves – in terms of their religious and political leanings, social position and involvement in Jewish causes such as Zionism.[45] Interestingly, the Dutch Marxist and Zionist Sam de Wolff (1878-1960) primarily saw Jews as 'a community with a common destiny' [*Schicksalgemeinschaft* in German; *lotsgemeenschap* in Dutch]. According to De Wolff, even before the war they had come to belong to two such communities: the Jewish and the Dutch, along with a double nationality and loyalties, having lived for centuries in the Low Countries.[46]

How Jews in the Netherlands have perceived antisemitism since 1945 is strongly bound up with their experiences prior to and especially during the German occupation, as well as the place they have assigned the Shoah in their lives and world view. Other contributory factors are the extent to which they see themselves as Dutch or as Jews, or both – or as one more than the other; whether they were born before, during or after the war – a factor which in fact applies, in varying degrees, to every population group examined here; and their views on Israel and degree of solidarity with the Jewish state. In this volume, Jews are not only seen as being 'acted upon' – as the passive target of antisemitism. They are also active players, who can opt to be silent, to shrug off what they have seen or experienced, to make themselves heard or to take action. In the fifth place, this is, in fact, an innovative approach in itself. Most literature on antisemitism focuses on antisemitism, its manifestations and on those who practice and/or preach it. Moreover, much literature separates the analysis of antisemitism completely from that of Israeli politics.

In the first decade of the twenty-first century, when this research project was conceived, the perpetrators of antisemitic utterances or aggression who were taken to court still came primarily from extreme right-wing and neo-Nazi circles. They too are discussed in this book.[47] But media attention was devoted primarily to the acts of Dutch citizens of Moroccan origin. An

---

45   *See* Gans, *De kleine verschillen*, 556*ff*; Chaya Brasz, 'Onontbeerlijk maar eigengereid. De zionistische inmenging in de naoorlogse joodse gemeenschap.' In: Conny Kristel (ed.), *Binnenskamers. Terugkeer en opvang na de Tweede Wereldoorlog. Besluitvorming* (Amsterdam: Bert Bakker, 2002), 235-260; Conny Kristel, 'Leiderschap na de ondergang. De strijd om de macht in joods naoorlogs Nederland.' In: *ibid.,* 209-234.

46   Gans, *De kleine verschillen*, 279*ff*, 391*ff*; Evelien Gans, 'Sam de Wolff (1878-1960): een typisch geval van én-én.' In: Francine Püttmann et al. (ed.), *Markante Nederlandse Zionisten* (Amsterdam: De Bataafsche Leeuw, 1996), 50-63: 53, 56-58.

47   Remco Ensel and Annemarike Stremmelaar, 'Speech acts: Observing antisemitism and Holocaust education in the Netherlands.' In: Gunther Jikeli and Allouche-Benayoun (eds.), *Perceptions of the Holocaust in Europe and Muslim Communities: Sources, Comparisons and Educational Challenges* (Dordrecht: Springer, 2013), 153-171. *See* chapter 4.

incident when Moroccan youths shouted antisemitic slogans and played
football with wreaths laid on Dutch Remembrance Day on 4 May 2003
caused a public outcry. 'Hamas, Hamas, all Jews to the gas' was, originally,
a slogan that native Dutch football fans would and still do chant at matches
where their team was playing against Ajax, Amsterdam's football club, traditionally labelled as 'Jewish'. Later this slogan was shouted by Moroccans on
the street, and during anti-Israel demonstrations.[48] That fact prompted the
authors of this work to look back in time to see how Moroccan migrants in
the Netherlands related to Dutch perceptions of Jews, Israel and the Shoah.

Just as we find when looking at the make-up of the Dutch or Dutch
Jewish population, there is no such thing as 'the' Dutch Moroccan. People
of Moroccan origin fall into different groups, in their own perception and
in how they are looked upon. Just like Jews, they can emphasise their Dutch
and Moroccan identities in differing combinations and gradations. In this
respect they have a hyphenated identity – like many other population
groups, such as Dutch Jews.[49]

The first generation of migrant workers cherish a nostalgic picture of
Jews and non-Jews living harmoniously side by side in their mother country,
back in the old days. In their view, Zionism and Israel disrupted what was
originally a peaceful relationship. In the Arab world as a whole, especially
since 1967, anti-Zionism, often involving antisemitic stereotypes, has become rampant. Commentators across the international scene argue that a
'new antisemitism' has arisen – 'new' in that 'Israel' has been substituted
for 'the Jew'. This is a controversial idea. As Robert Chazan has pointed
out, antisemitism has 'renewed' itself time and again, in a dialectical and
evolutionary process. From 1967 onwards 'Israel' did indeed constitute a
crucial point of fixation, but is the issue not primarily about 'new' environ-
ments and regions in which antisemitism has become reinforced, often to a
very extreme degree? Right from the outset, Israel was the object of sharp
debate, a debate that would sometimes – and nowadays with increasing
frequency – cross over into antisemitism. But alongside this phenomenon,
old forms of antisemitism continued to exist, while new ones came into
being.[50]

48 *See also* Ensel, *Haatspraak*; Gans, 'On Gas Chambers, Jewish Nazis and Noses', 84.
49 Heba M. Sharobeem, 'The hyphenated identity and the question of belonging. A study of
Samia Serageldin's *The Cairo House*', *Studies in the Humanities* 30, 1 & 2 (2003), 60-84. Remco
Ensel applies this concept in the Dutch context and translated it as 'koppelteken-identiteit':
Ensel, *Haatspraak*, 216, 222, 237, 242, 275, 331, 336. *See, e.g.*, chapter 14.
50 For the debate on 'new antisemitism', *see* Helga Embacher, 'Neuer Antisemitismus in Europa – ein historischer Vergleich.' In: Moshe Zuckerman (ed.), *Antisemitismus – Antizionismus*

Mohammed Bouyeri, born in the Netherlands in 1978, is not typical of his generation in one respect – he murdered Theo van Gogh – but in many other ways he is. Second-generation Moroccan migrants like him have at most heard family stories about Moroccan Jews, but have no personal experience or memories of such co-existence. They grew up in the Netherlands where, as they saw it, Jews were perceived as victims, while actually belonging to the establishment and, in Israel, pursuing ruthless anti-Palestinian policies. The seeds for identification and a sense of solidarity with Palestinians had already been sown in Morocco, and these feelings became gradually stronger in the Netherlands, not just among the younger generations.

Again, more generally, the self-image of Moroccans changed in that the religious component became increasingly dominant, relegating the national component more to the background. In the course of the 1990s, adherence to Islam became a trend in the Moroccan – and Turkish – communities. Among young people, in particular, living as a conscious, active Muslim provided a counterbalance to cultural and social rootlessness, and the experience or perception of belonging to a discriminated population group. In the case of a small minority, including Bouyeri, this led to political Islamisation and fiercely anti-Western views, including antisemitism and hatred of Israel.[51] Anti-Israel, anti-Judaism and anti-Jewish feelings, most certainly, also exist more widely in Muslim circles, albeit, often in a less extreme form.

In today's largely secularised Western Europe, conservative segments of the Muslim population have ideas and traditions that depart from the mainstream on issues such as the position of women, homosexuality and apostasy. These views tend to provoke surprise and, in extreme cases, aversion, fear and hatred. Actually, discriminatory views of this kind are also present within – admittedly smaller – Christian fundamentalist and Jewish ultra-orthodox circles. Muslims too are targets of fear and hatred, because of their religious or cultural identity: anti-Muslim racism, anti-Muslim xenophobia, and most common by now, though not unchallenged, generally

– *Israelkritik. Tel Aviver Jahrbuch für deutsche Geschichte* XXXIII (Göttingen: Wallstein Verlag, 2005), 50-69; Jonathan Judaken, 'So, what's new? Rethinking the "new" anti-Semitism' in a global age', *Patterns of Prejudice*, 42, 5/5 (2008), 531-560; Esther Webman, 'The challenge of Assessing Arab/Islamic Anti-Semitism', *Middle Eastern Studies*, 46, 5 (September 2010), 677-697; Ensel, *Haatspraak*, 330-331; Véronique Altglas, 'Anti-Semitism in France: past and present', *European Societies* 14, 2 (2012), 259-274; Alejandro Baer and Paula López, 'The blind spots of secularization. A qualitative approach to the study of antisemitism in Spain', *European Societies* 14, 2 (2012), 203-221; Robert Fine and Glynn Cousin, 'A common cause. Reconnecting the study of racism and anti-Semitism', *European Societies* 14, 2 (2012),166-185.

51   Helga Embacher and Margit Reiter (eds.), *Europa und der 11. September 2001* (Wien, Köln, Weimar: Böhlau Verlag, 2011); Ensel, *Haatspraak*, 271-291.

referred to as Islamophobia, all of which generalise, and therefore stereo-type, by definition. Geert Wilders, the leader of the right-wing populist Freedom Party (PVV), is an undisguised example of this phenomenon in the Netherlands. Signals of Muslim emancipation and integration – such as the Muslim boat in Amsterdam's Gay Pride festival, as well as the particularly good educational performance of Muslim girls – are often overlooked. Obviously, the long series of attacks by Al-Qaida, Islamic State (IS) and other Islamic terrorist organisations, some of which have had Jewish targets, have roused anxiety and anger. These feelings are quite understandable, but Wilders does capitalize on them and reinforces them, in every possible way.[52]

The question arose as to why relatively little antisemitism was reported among the Turkish community. Were they perhaps not averse to Jews for historical reasons – because of the Jews' relatively favourable status in the Byzantine and Ottoman Empires and, as of 1923, Turkey, as compared to Christian Europe? And did the reasonably cordial – or at least not hostile – though increasingly delicate relations between the Turkish and Israeli governments play a role here? Just like the Moroccans, most Turks were Muslims – so did that prove there wasn't a connection between Islam and antisemitism? Or was the Turkish community so closed that very few controversial reports reached the outside world? According to informal sources, antisemitism did exist among Turks – also in the Netherlands. An incident arose concerning an Iranian television series *Zahra's Blue Eyes* (2004), copies of which were covertly sold in Turkish mosques in 2004 and 2005. Besides anti-Israeli and anti-Zionist elements, the series also portrayed outright antisemitic stereotypes. Gradually, more reports were heard of antisemitic incidents within the Turkish community.[53] That raised plenty of questions and provided grounds for also turning the spotlights on the Turkish community in the Netherlands, which, like the Moroccan community, forms a large and heterogeneous group.

52   *See, e.g.*, chapters 10, 17 and 18. There is quite some literature – and polemic – on the parallels and differences between antisemitism and Islamophobia. One of the most well-known but also controversial books is by Matti Bunzl, *Anti-Semitism and Islamophobia: Hatreds Old and New in Europe* (Chicago: Chicago University Press, 2007). *See also* Jaël Elkerbout, 'Fear and Hatred of "the Other": Comparing Stereotypes of Anti-Semitism and Islamophobia' (Master thesis, Conflict Resolution and Governance, Universiteit van Amsterdam) (unpublished).
53   Inspraak Orgaan Turken (IOT), 'Quickscan antisemitisme in de Turkse gemeenschap in Nederland': www.republiekallochtonie.nl/userfiles/files/Quickscan%20iot%20antisemitisme. pdf. The Dutch current affairs TV programme *NOVA* devoted an item to the illegal sale of *Zahra's Blue Eyes* on 18 June 2005 with the cooperation of Evelien Gans. Esther Brommersma, '*Filmvertoning Zahra's Blue Eyes*', 9 June 2006 (unpublished) (Personal Archive Evelien Gans).

In the sixth place, this volume will examine both the differences and similarities in images and stereotypes among the three above-mentioned population groups and, where possible, their resultant interaction. Reference has already been made to the leader of the Dutch Anti-Revolutionary Party, Abraham Kuyper, and his agitation against the pernicious Jewish influence in politics and elsewhere; he saw Judaism and godless liberalism as being hand in glove.[54] The fact that in conservative, and Christian circles, especially, 'the Jew' embodied the dangerous, perverse aspects of modernity was mentioned earlier. Christian groups – and they were not alone – seized on the Talmud as a source of accusations against the Jews. Mohammed Bouyeri, mentioned above, did exactly the same. He, too, used Talmud texts to claim, among other things, that the Jews were responsible for the pernicious democratic system. In doing so, he drew on a publication by two American Christian antisemites, Michael A. Hoffman and Alan R. Critchley: *The Truth about the Talmud*, which was posted, in a poor translation, on the site islamawakening.com.[55] In conservative Catholic circles, especially before but even after the war, Jews were the embodiment of communism, 'Jewish Bolshevism' or 'Judeo-Bolshevism'. In its most extreme form, this attitude was manifested in the refusal of the Dutch Catholic Church to condemn the 1946 pogrom in Kielce, Poland.[56] The Catholic periodical *De Linie* [The Line] approvingly quoted the Polish cardinal August Hlond, who condemned the pogrom but explained it by reference to the large number of Jews in the Polish Communist governing cadres.[57]

Similar views were held by the Islamic-Turkish movement Milli Görüş which, inspired by religious and nationalist principles, sought a third way between capitalism and communism, and which had branches outside Turkey, including in Germany and the Netherlands. A pamphlet published in 1982 by a Turkish cultural centre in Amsterdam largely visited by right-wing Turkish migrants, warned against the dangers of Zionism and

54 Abraham Kuyper, *Liberalisten en Joden* (Amsterdam: Kruyt, 1878); Gans, 'Netherlands in the Twentieth Century', 498.
55 Ensel, *Haatspraak*, 289, 400 and chapter 14. *See, e.g.*, the English version: Michael A. Hoffman and Alan R. Critchley, *The Truth about the Talmud. Judaism's Holiest Book* (Coeur d'Alene, Idaho: Independent History and Research, 1998) (consulted 9 February 2014). On this bluntly antisemitic Dutch-language site (consulted 9 February 2014) the Talmud is one of the goals of anti-Jewish hatred, Holocaust denial included.
56 Poorthuis and Salemink, *Een donkere spiegel*, 217, 359, 358-361, 375; *De Linie*, 26 juli 1946, 2 August & 6 September 1946.
57 *De Linie*, 26 July 1946, 2 August 1946, 6 September 1946. *See, e.g.*, Lowe, *Savage Continent*, 206.

communism as the antitheses of Islam. 'The Jew' formed the link between the two ideologies.[58]

Meanwhile, people associated with Christian churches continued to make anti-Jewish religious statements. The Goerees, an 'evangelist couple', were a Protestant *cause célèbre* in the 1980s; they claimed that the Holocaust was God's punishment for the rejection of Christ and regarded Israel as the ideal location for a Christian eschatology.[59] The same phenomenon could be observed among Catholics. In the 1980s, two editors of the Catholic periodical *Bazuin* [Trumpet] were convicted in court (and acquitted on appeal). Their activities had included publishing an open letter that described the new wave of theological interest in Israel as naive and 'born of belated guilt feelings about the Shoah'. They had also urged theologians to come to the aid of the true victims of their day, arguing that 'the name of Israel' had come to refer more truly to 'the forcibly scattered and displaced Palestinian people' than to their Jewish counterparts.[60]

Mention is made above of the emergence of two new points of fixation for postwar antisemitism: the Shoah and Israel. Both feature in the views of all the examined population groups. The only difference is in where emphasis is placed. In the perceptions of Moroccans and Turks, the Palestinian-Israeli conflict ranks very high, though Israel's popularity has also progressively diminished among the native Dutch population. In the case of all three of the above-mentioned population groups, 'competing victimhood' emerges as a factor. The fact that the Jews were the pre-eminent victims of Nazi genocides would, even though partially and at times wholly recognised, be denied all over again, trivialised and contradicted – often

---

58   *See* chapter 10.

59   The Goerees were associated with the *Jezus Beweging Nederland* ['Dutch Jesus Movement'] and the *Stichting Evangelieprediking* ['Gospel Preaching Association'] See: E.G. Hoekstra and M.H. Ipenburg, *Wegwijs in religieus en levensbeschouwelijk Nederland: handboek religies, kerken, stromingen en organisaties* (Kampen: Kok, 2000). Jenny Goeree-Manschot has a website: www. jennygoeree.com. One of the statements that led to a court case was that 'one can conclude from the Bible that everything done to Jews, including the Holocaust, is their own fault'. A civil suit and criminal prosecution followed: Bas van Stokkom, Henny Sackers and Jean-Pierre Wils, *Godslastering, discriminerende uitingen wegens godsdienst en haatuitingen. Een inventariserende studie* (Ministerie van Justitie, 2006), 79. *See, e.g.,* chapter 8.

60   Poorthuis and Salemink, *Een donkere spiegel*, 70-71. Another source of inspiration was the Israeli chemist Israel Shahak, an anti-Zionist, who had written about the supposed age-old hatred towards Christians in orthodox Judaism, argued for the abolition of the religion on these grounds, and criticised Zionism for using a combination of the aforementioned hatred and the entire history of anti-Jewish persecution to legitimise the Zionist persecution of the Palestinians: *ibid. See, e.g.,* chapter 8.

provoking a furious defence by Jews. It has gradually become standard practice to invoke Israel to support the argument that it is time to stop putting all the emphasis on 'Jewish suffering'. The circle is then complete – Jews are not just there to be gassed, they are the Nazis of today, with the Palestinians as the new Jews: 'Hitler was a nice man compared to the Jews in Israel. Gas them all …' The comparison with Hitler and the 'Jews in Israel', to the detriment of the latter, illustrates the phenomenon of *nivellering* [levelling] – reducing existing differences in position, circumstances, motives, dilemmas and emotions between victim, perpetrator, bystander and accomplice.

Antisemitism as a multifunctional projection screen: Why the Jews?

'Why the Jews?' is a question which time and again has puzzled scholars, students, adults, children, and all kinds of people in the academic, public and private spheres, whether Jews or Gentiles. This section introduces a number of concepts developed by other scholars of antisemitism who tried to answer this question, and shows their interrelationships. We hope that by applying and combining these concepts, and by introducing and using concepts of our own, we can deepen both academic and public understanding of and insight into contemporary antisemitism, including the Dutch version. We attach great importance to a multidisciplinary approach. To succeed in their aims, antisemitism studies must, at a minimum, draw on history, sociology and psychology.

The planned title of this book was 'Why Jews are more guilty than others?', but we abandoned this idea because of the risk that readers would miss the irony, and therefore the concealed analytical meaning of the phrase. If those words are taken literally – 'Why Jews are more guilty than others' – they seem to have roughly the same implications as those of the notorious German Nazi Julius Streicher: *'Die Juden sind unser Unglück'* ('The Jews are our misfortune'). The real point of our original title, however, was to express why it has been so tempting, and remains tempting even today, to assign disproportionate guilt to the Jews for all sorts of catastrophes and unwanted developments. What has made 'the Jew' such a good scapegoat, to this day? This tendency is not limited to Christians or Muslims, the *petit bourgeoisie* or the establishment, the left or the right. Jews are seen as 'guilty' by a wide array of nations, groups and individuals, who may have very different or entirely contradictory objectives, opinions, interests, and ideals. 'The Jew' is evidently a multifunctional projection screen.[61] That has remained true after the Shoah, or Holocaust – in other words, since 1945 – and after the foundation of Israel three years later, right up to the present.

The phrase 'Why Jews are more guilty than others!' was inspired by George Orwell's famous maxim, 'All animals are equal, but some animals are more equal than others.' Orwell expresses something timeless: there is an ideology, a theory – but actual practice deviates from it. Jesus preached love and tolerance. According to John 8:7, he said, 'He that is without sin among you, let him first cast a stone ...' But the same Christian tradition taught that, although all people are 'sinful', Jews are more so than others. After all, they had refused to acknowledge the true Messiah, and then they had nailed him to the cross.

The Enlightenment and the French Revolution proclaimed the ideals of Liberty, Equality and Fraternity in a new, modern world to be designed from the ground up. Yet this did not prevent their exponents from excluding Jews in many ways – both Jews who openly wanted to maintain their Jewish identity, whether in a religious or non-religious sense, and those who showed a high degree of assimilation, but not enough to satisfy the non-Jews. In psychoanalytic terms, this phenomenon has been called a *double bind*, a term coined, in the context of Jewish studies and of antisemitism, by the historian Sander Gilman (b. 1944).[62] Actually, this *double bind* doesn't apply solely to Jews. Other minorities, such as Dutch people of Moroccan and Turkish descent, are confronted with the same mechanism.[63]

The firm foundation for hatred of Jews laid by the Christian tradition has already been mentioned as a causal factor behind the almost inexhaustible repertoire of antisemitism, alongside the impact of socio-economic envy, rivalry and resentment – exacerbated by the Pied Piper effect. But there are still other possible responses to the ever-fascinating question, why the Jews in particular? And therefore to the provocative, fictional challenge, 'Why Jews are more guilty than others'. The tenacity and diversity of antisemitism,

61   Evelien Gans organised an international symposium (under the auspices of the Menasseh ben Israel Institute, Amsterdam), titled *'The Jew' as a multifunctional projection screen. The dynamics of contemporary anti-Semitism in a globalizing context*, 12 May 2010, Amsterdam; amongst the speakers were Prof. Dr Werner Bergmann (Zentrum für Antisemitismusforschung, Berlin), Prof. Dr Moishe Postone (University of Chicago) and Dr Esther Webman (University of Tel Aviv).

62   Sander Gilman, *Jewish Self-Hatred. Anti-Semitism and the Hidden Language of the Jews* (Baltimore, Maryland: The Johns Hopkins University Press, 1986), 3; Gans, *De kleine verschillen*, 207; and for the double bind in a study of 'established and outsiders' in Moroccan society: Remco Ensel, *Saints and Servants in Southern Morocco* (Leiden, Köln: Brill, 1999), 9-12.

63   'De grens van assimilatie verlegt zich keer op keer', 58.

as well as the many questions about the reasons behind it, have inspired psychoanalysts to try to shed light on the phenomenon. In *Der Mann Mozes und die monotheïstische Religion* [*Moses and Monotheism*] (1939), Freud drew a connection between the Jewish tradition of circumcision and the fear of castration that he felt this must arouse among non-Jews. As a second major factor, he suggested that Christians feel envious of the Jews as the first-born, chosen children of God. Freud's thinking was revolutionary in exposing the role of unconscious drives in human life. Aggressive tendencies play an especially central role: 'It is always possible to unite considerable numbers of men in love towards one another, so long as there are still some remaining as objects for aggressive manifestations' (*Civilization and Its Discontents*, 1929).[64] Furthermore, he accorded at least as much weight to the irrational as he did to the rational.[65]

Five years after Freud's death, in June 1944, a number of psychoanalysts and sociologists in exile, including such prominent intellectuals as Theodor Adorno, Max Horkheimer, Ernst Simmel and Otto Fenichel, held a symposium in San Francisco on the subject of antisemitism – motivated not only by the genocide of European Jews that was then taking place, but also by mounting anti-Jewish sentiment in the United States. In 1946 their essays were published in the collection *Anti-Semitism: A Social Disease*. Simmel (1882-1947) opened his introduction with a concise, crystal-clear statement that prefigures Saul Friedländer's concept of 'redemptive antisemitism' with respect to the Nazis[66]: 'The anti-Semite hates the Jew because of his belief that the Jew is responsible for his unhappiness. He persecutes the Jew because he feels persecuted by him.'[67] The most useful instruments or

64 Sigmund Freud, *Civilization and Its Discontents* (London: Penguin, 2002); first Austrian edition: Sigmund Freud, *Das Unbehagen in der Kultur* (Wien: Internationaler psychoanalytischer Verlag, 1930).
65 Gans, *Gojse nijd & joods narcisme*, 24-25.
66 Saul Friedländer (b. 1932) described redemptive antisemitism as coupling murderous anger to an 'idealistic' target. It was not enough for the Jews to dominate the world: they wanted to destroy it. The parasite that was consuming the healthy Aryan body from within – or the mighty Jew that would sweep away the foundations of Germany, and then the world – had to be made visible and then eradicated before it was too late: it was 'them' or 'us'. Indeed, the aim was to destroy not just Jews of flesh and blood, but everything that had become contaminated with the Jewish 'spirit' – in other words, with 'The Jew': Saul Friedländer, *Nazi-Duitsland en de joden I: De jaren van vervolging 1933*-1939 (Utrecht: Het Spectrum, 1998), 16, 121-123, and idem, *Nazi-Duitsland en de joden II: De jaren van vernietiging* (Amsterdam: Nieuw Amsterdam, 2007), 17. *See, e.g.*, chapter 15.
67 In German: 'Der Antisemit hasst den Juden, weil er glaubt, dass der Jude an seinem Unglück schuld ist. Er verfolgt den Juden, weil er sich von ihm verfolgt fühlt': Ernst Simmel, 'Einleitung.' In: Ernst Simmel (ed.), *Antisemitismus* (Frankfurt am Main: Fischer Taschenbuch Verlag, 1993), 12-19:

concepts that psychoanalysis provides for gaining a better understanding of antisemitism are, without a doubt, 'projection' and 'repression' – two 'defence mechanisms', in the jargon of the field.[68]

The psychoanalytic approach does not come close to exhausting the explanatory factors. Another important feature of the antisemitic stereotype is the image of the Jew as both parasitic and all-powerful – Janus-faced.[69] 'The Jew' was feared and despised, admired and envied. He was – and is – both inferior and superior, powerful and dangerous but also weak and unmanly. There are no limits to the possibilities that 'the Jew' presents. The diverse historical manifestations of antisemitism – the broad range of prejudices and stereotypes, which both complement and contradict each other – are what makes it so persistent, flexible, and multifunctional. They allow it to serve as a frame, an explanatory model for all sorts of social and political problems that are experienced as threatening to some degree.[70] Similarly, Dik van Arkel has argued that one remarkable characteristic of antisemitism is its ability to develop new beliefs, time after time, about the 'degeneracy' of 'the Jew'; crucially, the 'Christ killers', after an initial period of tolerance, were massacred during the Crusades. This introduced a dimension of violence, which later became associated with the social question, and the stereotype of the 'Jewish usurer'. That paved the way for the transition to a secular ideology. Van Arkel describes this development as 'accusatory innovation' and argues that it has played a decisive role in the spread of antisemitism, setting it apart from other forms of racism.[71]

15 (Original edition: *Antisemitism. A social disease* (New York/Boston: International University Press, 1946).

68   For definitions of psychological and psychoanalytical concepts like projection and repression, we use: Harry Stroeken, *Nieuw psycho-analytisch woordenboek – begrippen, termen, personen* (Amsterdam: Boom, 2000). Projection: activity with the help of which one wrongfully describes wishes or thoughts one denies or rejects for oneself, to another person or matter. So, it is a defence mechanism: *ibid.*, 180-181. Repression: 'Push away thoughts, images, memories or wishes into the unconscious or trying to keep it there': *ibid.*, 209. For a more extensive elucidation: *ibid.*

69   *See, e.g.*, Friedländer, *Nazi-Duitsland en de joden I*, 121; Gans, 'They have forgotten to gas you', 74. For how the stereotype of the Jew as a parasite became current, *see, e.g.*, Sven Oliver Müller, *Deutsche Soldaten und ihre Feinde. Nationalismus an Front und Heimatfront im Zweiten Weltkrieg* (Frankfurt am Main: S. Fischer, 2007), 65.

70   *See, e.g.*, Gans, 'They have forgotten to gas you', 94.

71   Van Arkel, *The Drawing of the Mark of Cain*, 391ff, 394-395, 417. In his recent Dutch-language book *Anti-Joodse beeldvorming en Jodenhaat* [Anti-Jewish Image and Jew-hatred] (Hilversum: Verloren, 2016), on the history of Western European antisemitism, Chris Quispel builds on the work of Van Arkel. For instance by means of the concept of 'labelled interaction', explaining how (forced) Jewish economic specialisation confirms already fixed anti-Jewish stereotypes.

Contradictions between stereotypes do not diminish their impact. The function of stereotypes is to create order in chaos, to gain control of events and clarify conflict situations by making causal connections. The people who use them seek, find and contrive evidence to support their stereotypical views in any way they can. You might ask, how can 'the Jew' be a Bolshevist one moment and a capitalist the next? This is because behind the scenes, these two stereotypes work hand in hand. Furthermore, both capitalism and Bolshevism fall outside of national frameworks – just like 'the Jew' – and they are both the degenerate projects of a modernity run amok.[72] Stereotypes are self-justifying.[73] Still other explanations have been offered of the multifunctionality of 'the Jew', some of which are closely linked to the ones already discussed. The frequent social role of the Jews as intermediaries is another answer to the question of why they, in particular, formed such an obvious target of exclusion and hostility. 'The Jew' occupies a whole series of intermediary roles, which stem from his status as outsider, such as the medieval Jew in Western Europe, seen as a creditor moving between the local population and the ruler and, in the magical scenes in bestiaries, as half-animal, half-human;[74] or the Jew as an effeminate

Contrary to Van Arkel, however, Quispel has written a chronological, more general and at the same time well-wrought history of antisemitism in Western Europe – including the Netherlands – until the first decade of the twenty-first century. One might say that our book begins where his last chapter on postwar Europe, titled 'Nobody is an antisemite anymore', ends: *ibid., e.g.*, 12, 90, 120, 267-279.

72   See Blom and Cahen, 'Joodse Nederlanders, Nederlandse joden en joden in Nederland', 283. Steven Beller states that both capitalism and socialism were felt as two sides of a modernisation which would be harmful to the more traditional economic branches. Jews were attracted to both, various other population groups felt threatened by them: Steven Beller, '"Pride and Prejudice" or Sense and Sensibility"?' In: Daniel Chirot and Anthony Reid (eds.), *Essential Outsiders. Chinese and Jews in the Modern Transformation of Southeast Asia and Central Europe* (Seattle and London: University of Washington Press, 1997), 99-124.

73   Yaacov Schul and Henri Zukier, 'Why do stereotypes stick?' In: Robert Wistrich (ed.), *Demonizing the Other. Antisemitism, Racism, and Xenophobia* (London and New York: Routledge, 1999), 31-43; Chris Quispel, 'Introduction.' In: Van Arkel, *The Drawing of the Mark of Cain*, 11-19: 17-18. Images of Jews and non-Jewish 'Slavs' in the Soviet Union, emaciated and reduced by wartime conditions to dressing in rags, confirmed the belief on the part of the Wehrmacht and SS that both groups were *Untermenschen* [subhumans]: Sönke Neitzel and Harald Welzer, *Soldaten. Protokolle vom Kämpfen, Töten und Sterben* (Frankfurt am Main: S. Fischer, 2011). And when, despite the stereotype of Jews as lazy and averse to manual labour, a Jew proved to be a hard worker, one could always fall back on the stereotype of the sly, untrustworthy Jew who is merely pretending.

74   See the 'bestiaries', moralising animal stories about 'the Jew' as the owl or the ass: Van Arkel, *The Drawing of the Mark of Cain*, 415. There was also the image of the menstruating male Jew, see Henri Zukier, 'The transformation of hatred: Antisemitism as a struggle for group identity.'

man (and a homosexual); as positioned between white Europeans and colonised peoples; or as an artisan and shopkeeper, between the elite and the industrial proletariat. According to the social psychologist Henri Zukier, it is the hybrid Jew, the Jew as a 'transitional figure', who exposes a society's weak points and the mutability of its boundaries and dividing lines, thus disturbing the peace and embodying fear and insecurity.

> The imaginary Jew obsesses society as one who crosses boundaries, combines contradictory features, breaches the barriers of the natural species and otherwise violates the order of nature.[75]

Zukier contends that the historical role of the Jew as an outsider and intermediary created the psychological distance that made demonisation possible.[76]

Jews' intermediary role offered advantages both to them and to non-Jews, for instance by permitting the money markets that society required. The American sociologists R.E. Park (1864-1944) and E.V. Stonequist (1901-1979) introduced the concept of the 'marginal man', which they claimed was applicable to Jews in the diaspora. Jews were among those who identified with two or more social groups. That made the modern Jew a 'cultural hybrid', as they put it, unfettered by provincialism and endowed with a creative potential that enabled him or her to 'see the life of the environing nation from the outside as well from the inside'. Yet Park and Stonequist were not at all blind to the fact that this role made Jews not only productive, but also vulnerable, as targets of opposition from both spheres of influence.[77]

The German historian Klaus Holz (b. 1960) introduced the concept of 'the Jew' as *der Dritte* [the third party].[78] The whole world can be organised according to the fundamental pattern of 'us' and 'them', except for 'the Jew', who disrupts this unambiguous two-way distinction. Jews fall outside the

---

In: Robert Wistrich (ed.), *Demonizing the Other*, 118-130: 126; *See, e.g.*, '... the Jew is the feminised Other ...'; Gilman, *The Jew's Body*, 76. The virulent antisemitic leader of the Dutch SS, Henk Feldmeijer, referred to Jews and Bolshevists as '*beestmenschen*' [beast people]: Bas Kromhout, *De voorman. Henk Feldmeijer en de Nederlandse SS* (Amsterdam: Atlas Contact, 2012).

75   Zukier, 'The transformation of hatred', 126. *See also*: Amir Vodka, *The Human Chameleon. Hybrid Jews in Cinema* (PhD thesis, University of Amsterdam, 5 July 2016). Vodka looks, on the contrary, at the Hybrid Jew emphatically in positive terms (PhD thesis, Universiteit van Amsterdam, 9 September 2014)

76   *Ibid.*, 126-127.

77   Gans, *De kleine verschillen*, 17-18.

78   Klaus Holz, *Die Gegenwart des Antisemitismus. Islamistische, demokratische und antizionistische Judenfeindschaft* (Hamburg: Hamburger Edition, 2005) 30.

framework of 'one people, one state, one nation'. This leads to their image as possessors of a secret, supranational power, who are plotting not only to rule the world but also to undermine the 'natural' differences between all its peoples, races and religions. Which reminds us of the never-ending impact of the infamous *Protocols of the Elders of Zion* – a fabricated document which purports to be the minutes of a secret meeting of Jewish leaders. The Protocols were published in 1903 and have been reprinted in all major languages ever since, notwithstanding the fact that it was exposed as a forgery as early as 1921.[79]

From this perspective, Jews embody universalism and cosmopolitanism. Holz writes, *"'Der Jude' als Dritter transzendiert, bedroht und zersetzt die binäre Unterscheidung zwischen uns und den anderen, dank deren die partikulare Gruppenidentität konstruiert wird'* ([The Jew as third party transcends, threatens and breaks down the binary distinction between us and the others, on which the group bases its particular identity]. The Jews can neither become a 'normal people' nor come to feel at home [*heimisch werden*] among one of the 'normal peoples'.[80] The Dutch poet Marsman, in 1936, had pinned his hopes on the former of these two possibilities – a Jewish state – and given up on the achievement of the latter.

As Holz sees it, 'the Jew' is the antagonist of all *Wir-Gruppen* [Us Groups], at both the national and transnational levels. Antisemitism therefore occurs at both of these levels: not only one's own group, but a range of groups, can collectively feel threatened by 'the Jew', seen as the *Weltfeind* [World Enemy].[81] The World Wide Web embodies this development. The internet is both a symbol and an instrument of a world in which the mutual dependence between people and countries around the globe is increasing daily, in economic, political and cultural terms. 'The Jew' can be found there in countless manifestations, and usually in a negative light. Building on Shulamit Volkov's concept of antisemitism as a 'cultural code',[82] one might well ask whether contemporary antisemitism has not become an integral part of a global, digital culture.

As noted above, Jews are seen as 'guilty' by a wide variety of nations, groups and individuals, who may have very different or entirely contradictory objectives, opinions, interests and ideals. In that sense, it is reasonable

79 The tenacity might be located in the seeming truthfulness of the genre of conference proceedings: Richard Levy, *Antisemitism in the modern world. An anthology of texts* (Lexington, MA, Toronto: D.C. Heath and Company, 1991), 147. *See, e.g.,* chapter 7.

80 Holz, *Die Gegenwart des Antisemitismus*, 33-34.

81 *Ibid.*, 36.

82 Shulamit Volkov, *Antisemitismus als kultureller Code. Zehn Essays* (München: Beck, 2000).

to assert that 'the Jew' can serve as a negative source of social cohesion. Holz's concept of 'the Jew' as a third party can be connected to one of the English historian Steven Beller's conclusions about the role of Jews in Vienna from the late nineteenth century onwards. In the city of Vienna, which was expanding enormously because of an influx of immigrants with a remarkably wide range of nationalities, antisemitism facilitated what Beller (b. 1958) calls 'negative integration'. Hostility toward Jews enabled newcomers to win a place for themselves by defining and approaching each other in terms of what they were *not*: namely, Jewish.[83]

In our own day, antisemitism can still serve as a negative – although often not a lasting – source of social cohesion or solidarity between individuals, national organisations or international groups. For instance, temporary alliances – sometimes unwitting, unintended or half-hearted – occasionally arise between right-wing extremists and Muslim and Islamist groups, or between the far right and the far left. Holocaust denial can be observed in various forms and gradations both among right-wing extremists and in Muslim circles. The extreme or radical left and the extreme right are sometimes strange bedfellows in matters regarding Israel, as will be made clear in several chapters of this book.[84]

'The Jew' can also be a source of solidarity between fundamentalist Christians and Palestinians. The highly controversial film *The Passion of the Christ* (2004), made by the Catholic fundamentalist Mel Gibson (b. 1956), which was a huge success at the box office, continued the old tradition of holding the Jews responsible for Christ's death, and used the techniques of modern cinematography to create a highly visceral, almost pornographic presentation of its violent story: the lashing, the journey to the cross, and the crucifixion. Around the world, the film provoked heated debate about whether it was antisemitic. Enlightened Christians, in the Netherlands and elsewhere, opposed the film, but others saw it as an excellent instrument for missionary work.[85] In the Arab world, the film drew full houses, even though Christ is a minor religious figure in Islam. Despite this different cultural

83   Steven Beller, '"Pride and Prejudice" or "Sense and Sensibility"?'
84   *See, e.g.*, chapter 4.
85   Rianne Wijmenga, 'De passie van de toeschouwer. Receptieonderzoek naar de reacties van het publiek op Mel Gibsons *The Passion of the Christ*' (MA thesis, Universiteit van Amsterdam, 29 April 2011, www.slideshare.net/RianneWijmenga/ma-thesis-film-studies-rcw) (consulted 15 June 2015); *See, e.g.*, Sergio I. Minerbi, 'The Passion by Mel Gibson: Enthusiastic Response in the Catholic World, Restrained Criticism by the Jews', *Jewish Political Studies Review* 17:1-2 (Spring 2005): www.jcpa.org/phas/phas-minerbi-s05.htm; Frank Rich, '2004: The Year of "The Passion"', *The New York Times*, 19 December 2004.

heritage, the film offered Muslims plenty of opportunities for identification, equating the despicable role of the Jews in the crucifixion with Israel's role in the Middle East and, in particular, the Israelis' treatment of the Palestinians. Yasser Arafat, the leader of the PLO, called Gibson's *Passion* a 'moving and historical' film, and his aide said that the Palestinians still endured the same kind of pain as Jesus on a daily basis.[86] The 'hybrid Jew' with a Janus face, *der Dritte* – these concepts are as relevant as ever.

'The Jew' as both victim and victimiser: a continuing postwar theme

This section revolves around the argument that Jewish victimhood has turned against 'the Jew'. Paradoxically, the stereotype of 'the powerful Jew' has been reinforced by his role as victim.

That brings us back to the image of the 'Janus-faced' Jew – powerful and powerless, prosperous and impoverished, cowardly and cruel, inferior and superior – along with the notion of 'the Jew' as 'the guilty victim'. In the postwar period, one such stereotypical duality, one Janus face in particular, has gradually become the most prominent: the dual role of victim and perpetrator, victim of the Nazis and their collaborators during the Shoah, and perpetrator of injustices against the Palestinians in Israel and in Gaza and the West Bank. This Janus face is not a Dutch invention; it is perceived around the world. It is also directly connected to the above-mentioned phenomena of *nivellering* [levelling] and of the reversal of perpetrator and victim. 'Victim' and 'perpetrator' form an explosive combination. Victims arouse not only compassion, but also revulsion. Compassion is the twin brother of revulsion, wrote the Dutch Jewish lawyer and author Abel Herzberg (1893-1989), a survivor of the Bergen-Belsen concentration camp, as early as 1950. He saw this as an explanation for the increase in antisemitism in the Netherlands after the war.[87]

Jewish survivors also aroused feelings of rivalry and envy: envy of 'the Jew', who presents himself as the ultimate victim. We regard this as a crucial component of antisemitism and ambivalence toward Jews: goyish envy, Gentiles' envy of talents, qualities and privileges supposedly possessed by

86   *See* (website) Palestinian National Authority State Information Service, International Press Centre, 10 March 2004; (website) RKK, Katholiek Nederland, 21 March 2004.

87   Abel J. Herzberg, *Kroniek der Jodenvervolging 1940-1945* (Amsterdam: Meulenhoff, 1978), 25 (reprint of: *Onderdrukking en verzet*, 1950). *See, e.g.*, chapters 2, 3 and 5.

Jews.[88] These feelings underlay arguments that, after all, the Jews weren't the only ones who had suffered in the war, were they? And there were plenty of mass murders before the Holocaust, weren't there – not to mention the many 'Holocausts' that took place after 1945. Where there were feelings of guilt and shame – perhaps a sense of not having done enough, a sense that one could or should have done more to help Jews – those could also lead to irritation and aggression. The Dutch Jewish historian Jacques Presser (1899-1970), who had gone into hiding and survived the war, wrote – three years after Herzberg and again in reference to postwar antisemitism – that guilt among non-Jews must have played a major role. Was it any wonder that so many people who had fallen short 'took vengeance on those who so painfully reminded them of their failures: the surviving Jews?' It was inherent to the human spirit, he wrote, to hate the people you have hurt.[89]

Changing power relations through history have an undeniable influence on the prominence of particular stereotypes. Israel – with its series of military victories over Arab countries, its repressive policies and forceful domination of the Palestinians, and, more generally, its outspokenly assertive if not offensive stance – has unmistakably shifted the stereotype of the craven, powerless Jew to the background and brought that of the powerful Jew to the fore.[90] In contrast, for many Jews outside its borders, Israel has become not only a living *lieu de mémoire* [site of memory], anchoring the recollection of a horrific past, but also a form of compensation for that past and a source of pride in the ability to forge a new Jewish future.[91] They have no intention of letting that be taken away from them, despite growing criticism from outsiders. Since the Six-Day War in June 1967, more and more Jewish committees, task forces and lobbying groups have emerged in the Netherlands and elsewhere – not only stepping forward as defenders of the Jewish state, but also making a clean break with the reticence of earlier generations regarding expressions of antisemitism.[92] This assertiveness can even lead to the rejection of all criticism of Israel, Jews or Judaism. That could be described as Jewish narcissism: a self-image organised entirely around the two poles of suffering and pride. Whatever does not fit is denied or ignored.[93]

88   Gans, *Gojse nijd & joods narcisme;* Gans, 'They have forgotten to gas you', 78.
89   Jacques Presser, *Ondergang. De vervolging en verdelging van het Nederlandse jodendom,* II (The Hague: Staatsuitgeverij, 1965), 518-519.
90   Evelien Gans, 'De Joodse almacht. Hedendaags antisemitisme', *Vrij Nederland,* 29 november 2003.
91   Idem, De kleine verschillen, 898.
92   *See* chapters 5, 6 and 8.
93   Gans, *Gojse nijd & joods narcisme,* 46-48; idem, 'They have forgotten to gas you', 81-84.

After 1945, there was a counterweight to antisemitic statements: support
and solidarity from non-Jews, which was accepted with both gratitude and
scepticism. The term philosemitism was heard with some frequency. The most
flattering interpretation of this phenomenon is as the idealisation of Jews;
the least flattering is as the other side of the antisemitic coin, the love of Jews
simply because they are Jews – just as much of a stereotype as antisemitism.[94]

The power of 'the Jew' gradually seems to have become the central
theme of antisemitism today. In his analysis of modern antisemitism,
the Jewish-American sociologist Moishe Postone (b. 1942) emphasises
its supposedly anti-hegemonic nature. It was for this very reason that
traditional socialism made use of it, portraying the Jews as the capitalist
enemy. The nineteenth-century socialist August Bebel (1840-1913) called
this short-sighted strategy the 'socialism of fools'.[95] Social democrats in
the Netherlands, though certainly less radical than their predecessors,
were not immune to antisemitism either. Henri Polak (1868-1943), the well-
known Jewish Diamond Union leader, wrote a pamphlet, at the request of
several of his Jewish party members, in which he refuted a large number of
antisemitic remarks and prejudices they had been confronted with. It is also
noteworthy that, after years of unsuccessful attempts, the Dutch branch of
the internationally active socialist-Zionist organisation *Poale Zion* [Workers
of Zion] was founded in 1933. Socialism alone was no longer enough for its
members.[96] The Dutch socialist anarchist Domela Nieuwenhuis (1846-1919),
a former Lutheran minister, was triply prejudiced; he not only carried the
anti-Jewish baggage of Martin Luther (1483-1546), but also, following in
the footsteps of the widely read utopian socialist and anarchist thinker
Pierre Joseph Proudhon (1809-1865), stigmatised the Jews both as inveterate
hucksters and as the mainstays and profiteers of the capitalist system. As
late as 1912 he wrote in racist terms, in the *Vrije Socialist* [Free Socialist] that
if the Jews 'wanted to live on the basis of equal rights with other races', they
should stop 'forming a clique in their ghetto, always favouring their own
nation in trade, and carefully preventing every mixing of race.'[97]

94   *See, e.g.*, chapters 5, 6, 8 and 18.

95   For August Bebel, *see* Van Arkel, *The Drawing of the Mark of Cain*, 24-25.

96   Gans, *De kleine verschillen*, 42, 492, and for Poale Zion: *ibid., passim.* Henri Polak, *Het 'wetenschappelijk' antisemitisme. Weerlegging en betoog* (Amsterdam: Blitz, 1933). Because of his fierce
attacks against (also Dutch) antisemitism in his journalistic columns, the mainly non-Jewish
party leadership would reproach him for his allegedly over-emotional, even 'hysterical' stance:
ibid., 86-90. *See, e.g.*, Ensel and Gans, 'The bystander as a non-Jew'.

97   Jan Willem Stutje, *Ferdinand Domela Nieuwenhuis. Een romantisch revolutionair* (Amsterdam: Atlas/Contact, 2012), 193-98; *See, e.g.*, Gans, *De kleine verschillen*, 48.

Postwar groups within the leftist, anti-capitalist and anti-colonialist movement have also taken an antisemitic line, precisely because of a perceived Jewish – and Israeli – hegemony. All forms of racism use essentialist biological and cultural categories to explain complicated social and historical categories, according to Moishe Postone. But what is specific to antisemitism is its populist and apparently anti-hegemonic and anti-globalist nature.

> Whereas most forms of race thinking commonly impute concrete bodily and sexual power to the Other, modern anti-Semitism attributes enormous power to Jews, which is abstract, universal, global, and intangible.[98]

The importance that Postone attaches to the 'all-powerful, elusive Jew', and to antisemitism's appeal as an anti-hegemonic interpretive framework, is very persuasive, as is his emphasis on the political and economic domains. But alongside this approach, we also want to emphasise the envy of 'the Jew' as 'the ultimate victim', or as an object of sexual revulsion, fascination and resentment. This erotic dimension, it should be added, involves not only the attribution of 'concrete bodily and sexual power to the Other', as in the case of racism against blacks. Suspicions of perversion play an equal, if not greater, role. Moreover, some recent Dutch and international historiography on the Second World War is riddled with stereotypes of the Jews as passive, obedient victims.[99]

There is one final, crucial aspect of the supposition of Jewish power in postwar antisemitism. As observed above, 'the Jew' as victim arouses both compassion and revulsion. Paradoxically, the stereotype of 'the powerful Jew' has actually been reinforced in the postwar period by his role as victim. First of all, 'the Jew' is resented for claiming to be the 'ultimate victim' and accused of maintaining a monopoly on suffering at the expense of non-Jewish victims. Secondly, Jewish victims are accused of using their professed status as victim as an instrument of power – of cashing in on it, in political, material, moral and emotional ways.

Three pieces make up the suit of this stereotypical Jew. In France, the French comedian Dieudonné M'bala M'bala (b. 1966), who is of Cameroonian and Breton origin, illustrates the third piece – the 'jacket'. He has drawn a

---

98   Moishe Postone, 'History and Helplessness: Mass Mobilization and Contemporary Forms of Anticapitalism', *Public Culture* 18, 1 [special issue on *Anticapitalism, Xenophobia, Imperialism*], 93-110: 99.
99   *See* chapters 12 and 13.

direct link between the roles of victim and perpetrator with his antisemitic jokes about the Shoah or about leading Jews and gas chambers, his rants against 'the system' in France, and his accusation that the Jews were the driving force behind the transatlantic slave trade. 'He hits France where it hurts – in the memory of the Holocaust,' the Moroccan-Dutch writer Hassan Bahara wrote in *De Groene Amsterdammer*, a progressive and independent weekly magazine of current affairs.[100] When a victim becomes a perpetrator in someone else's eyes, that not only neutralises and even annihilates earlier claims of victimhood (acknowledged or otherwise), but also provides an opportunity to free oneself of any feelings of guilt and shame: we are even, at the very least. Dieudonné appeals not only to young people in immigrant communities in the French *banlieues*, but also to young ethnically French people and to those who feel drawn to 'far-left radical chic'.[101] Again, 'the Jew' serves as a negative source of social cohesion.[102]

The same tendencies are visible in the Netherlands. Just as in France, the Shoah is the Achilles heel of Dutch society. And here too, Israel's actions – and sometimes its very existence – have excited growing controversy. The stereotype of the Jew forms the link between the Shoah and Israel. To sum up, the third piece of the puzzle is 'the Jew's' complex role, not only as Janus-faced victim and perpetrator, but also as *Dritte*; 'the Jew' falls outside the apparent dichotomy of victim and perpetrator, and arouses all the more animosity and hatred because he is felt to *pose* as a victim while *actually* being a victimiser. The tangled combination of these two roles, victim and victimiser, has given postwar antisemitism a powerful new dimension.

Organisation of the book

Apart from this introductory chapter and the epilogue, this collection has four parts, ordered in a systemic, cohesive way. The first part, *Post-Liberation Antisemitism*, focuses on antisemitic, dubious and ambivalent statements, opinions and feelings about 'the Jew' from 1945 to the 1960s. In chapter 2, 'The Jew as a Dubious Victim', Evelien Gans both investigates the importance of

---

100 Hassan Bahara, 'Een antisemitische ananas. De ongemakkelijke populariteit van Dieudonné', *De Groene Amsterdammer*, 16 January 2014; zie ook: Pascal Bruckner, 'Racisme tegen blanke bestaat heus, Dieudonné', *NRC Handelsblad*, 11 /12 January 2014. For parallels and differences between Dieudonné and Theo van Gogh: Jaap Cohen, 'Provoceren: over de top kwetsend of heel erg lomp', *NRC Next*, 5 February 2014.
101 Bahara, 'Een antisemitische ananas'.
102 In the Netherlands, the same goes for Theo van Gogh, *see* chapter 12.

the psychological factor in postwar antisemitism – building on the German concepts of secondary antisemitism and *Schuldabwehrantisemitismus* – and identifies a gap in Dutch historical writing about both the phenomenon of antisemitism and its psychological dimension. She relates this to the widespread antisemitic curse, 'They have forgotten to gas you'.

Chapter 3, 'The Meek Jew – and Beyond', opens with a discussion of a suit against a former member of the Dutch wartime resistance who accused the Jews of meekness. Again, Gans shows how the Shoah, or Holocaust, came to be used against the Jews, in this case through accusations by former resistance members and others that the Jews had not put up any, or not enough, resistance to the Nazis – the old stereotype of the 'cowardly Jew'. She describes turning points such as the Eichmann trial (1961) as well as the dissenters who argued that relatively many Jews were involved in the resistance. In this chapter, the vague outlines also become visible of a parallel world in Israel: 'the Jew' was regarded both as a brave fighter and as a perpetrator of injustices against 'the Arabs' – the first, still sporadic expressions of anti-Zionist dissent, which very occasionally crossed the line into antisemitism.

Chapter 4, *'Alte Kameraden'*, is a joint 'project' of Remco Ensel, Evelien Gans and Willem Wagenaar. Until now, there has been very little research into antisemitism in Dutch neo-Nazi and far-right circles, partly because even though there was antisemitism in those circles, there was also a taboo, at first, on revealing it to outsiders. This essay unveils some of the first covert signals. It addresses Holocaust denial in the Dutch context in connection with efforts to cast former ss and NSB (Dutch Nazi party) members in the role of victim, also examining overtly antisemitic acts and statements. In the 1970s, the direct influence of the 'veterans' began to wane. A new political party, the *Nederlandse Volks-Unie* [Dutch People's Union] aimed its poison arrows at the new group of immigrants from the Mediterranean region, but was also unique in that its own writings expressed antisemitic attitudes.

In chapter 5, 'Jewish Reactions', Gans describes how Jews responded to expressions of anti-Jewish feeling, examining antisemitic incidents that varied from verbal abuse to the desecration of Jewish cemeteries and a scandal among university students. The responses were highly diverse: swearing back, starting a fistfight, emigrating to Israel, keeping silent, withdrawing and ignoring the problem, and taking the stance, dominant in leading circles of Zionists and politically conscious Jews, that antisemitism was the problem of non-Jews. This point of view emerges clearly from the culminating section of chapter 5, a lengthy debate on this issue published in the Dutch Jewish magazine NIW. In less than twenty years' time, beliefs about what 'Jewish dignity' required would undergo a complete reversal.

After this discussion of the Shoah as a point of fixation for postwar antisemitism, part II, *Israel and 'The Jew'*, turns to Israel. In chapter 6, 'Philosemitism? Ambivalences regarding Israel', Gans explores the complex phenomenon of philosemitism in general, and particularly in relation to the attitude of the Netherlands toward Israel. Although guilt feelings clearly play a role, the Dutch government was late to recognise Israel, mainly for political and strategic reasons. But during the Suez crisis in 1956, the Netherlands became an outspoken friend of Israel, and in 1967, during the Six-Day War, this 'special relationship' reached its height. A turning point came in 1967 as well, however – a year of paradoxes that ushered in a period of divided loyalties, among both Jews and non-Jews.

In chapter 7, 'Transnational Left-wing Protest and The Powerful Zionist', Remco Ensel describes the evolution of protest in Dutch left-wing circles against Israel's policies on the Palestinians, with the *Nederlands Palestina Komitee* [Dutch Palestine Committee] as the fulcrum. The stereotype of the 'Powerful Zionist' arrived on the scene – and was here to stay. Furthermore, Moroccan immigrants – mainly intellectuals, as individuals and in small groups – began making common cause with already existing anti-Israeli activism, although their emphases were sometimes distinctly different.

Gans goes into 'divided loyalties' more deeply in chapter 8, 'Israel: Source of Divergence', in which the contrasts come into sharper focus. While in 1973, the Netherlands was the target of an Arab boycott because it was 'friendly to Israel', it later became clear that many Dutch companies had escaped this boycott by signing what was known as a *'niet-Jood verklaring'* ['non-Jew declaration'], more or less with the knowledge of the Dutch government. This scandal, as well as a more general tendency toward greater criticism of Israel and the fear that antisemitism was on the rise, led to the formation of several powerful, pro-active Jewish organisations, such as STIBA and CIDI, which came out in support of Israel and took on antisemitism.

In chapter 9, '"The Activist Jew" Responds to Changing Dutch Perceptions of Israel', Katie Digan continues the examination both of the growing criticism of Israel in various, mainly left-wing, circles, and of activism among Jews, concentrating on the small radical Jewish group that called itself the *Joodse Defensie Liga* [Jewish Defence League]. The central topic is an incident in which the League barged into the radio studio of the progressive left-wing broadcasting company VPRO, which was then airing a number of programmes on the Palestinians, including one on torture by Israel. Progressive intellectuals and different groups of Gentiles and Jews – both fiery left- and right-wingers and moderates – debated the thorny question of the line between criticism of Israel and antisemitism.

In Chapter 10, 'Turkish Anti-Zionism in the Netherlands', Annemarike Stremmelaar describes experiences in the Netherlands in the 1980s with expressions of antisemitic sentiment by representatives of Dutch Muslim organisations. With political Islam on the rise internationally, Muslims in the Netherlands became familiar with the language and concepts of Islamic ideology, which involved negative stereotypes of Jews and Zionism. During demonstrations against Israel in the Netherlands, ethnically Turkish supporters of a radical Turkish imam in Germany characterised Jews as bloodthirsty occupiers of Palestine and enemies of Islam. The groups in question were regarded as radical and extreme by the large majority of Muslim organisations in the Netherlands.

This brings us to part III of the book: *The Holocaust-ed Jew' in Native Dutch Domains since the 1980s.* In Chapter 11, 'The Jew' in Football: To Kick around or to Embrace', Gans addresses the issue of football-related antisemitism up to the present day. This phenomenon, targeting Jewish football clubs and players, had its origins in the pre-war Netherlands and continued after the war. The Amsterdam club Ajax was still seen, largely mistakenly, as a Jewish club. What changed, in the 1980s, was that supporters of rival clubs began to insult Ajax with slogans and songs that linked traditional antisemitic put-downs to the Holocaust in various ways. Football, or soccer, antisemitism is a global phenomenon. The main questions explored in this chapter are why the Shoah entered the domain of football in the 1980s and why Ajax supporters (*Ajacieden*) have so stubbornly clung to their nickname of 'Jews' or 'Super Jews'.

The Holocaust also became a subject of satire and pornography in the 1980s. Gans opens chapter 12, 'Pornographic Antisemitism, Shoah Fatigue and Freedom of Speech', by looking at the historical origins of the image of the 'perverse Jew', showing that it dates back many centuries. As mentioned above, the film director and columnist Theo van Gogh was the master of linking the perverse Jew to the Holocaust. Van Gogh, who had many admirers and even some followers, took a similarly pornographic approach to Muslims, systematically calling them 'goat fuckers', all in the name of defending absolute – that is, unrestricted – freedom of speech and, later, of combating the threat of the 'multicultural society' (read: 'Islam'/'Muslims'). The overarching themes of this chapter are the right to free speech and political incorrectness, projected onto the image of 'the Jew'.

This is followed, in chapter 13, '*Historikerstreit*: The Stereotypical Jew in recent Dutch Holocaust Studies', by an exploration of the theme of 'historical incorrectness' with regard to the Shoah and the role of the Jews themselves with respect to their persecution. Ensel and Gans describe an influential tendency in Dutch historiography that involves depicting 'the

Jew' as passive, resigned and obedient. This stereotype evidently appeals to a broad public, considering the popularity of the two historians. The phenomenon of levelling, briefly mentioned above, plays a key role in this tendency. Themes such as rehabilitation and the absolution of guilt (or alleged guilt) also resurface.

Part IV, *Generations. Migrant Identities and Antisemitism in the Twenty-first Century*, focuses on the Moroccan-Dutch and Turkish-Dutch populations. In the twenty-first century, antisemitism became part of a politics of ethnic identity. Chapter 14, '"The Jew" vs. "The Young Male Moroccan": Stereotypical Confrontations in the City', looks at the new manifestations of anti-Israeli protest and everyday antisemitism. In particular, Ensel investigates the ways in which members of the second generation in immigrant communities are actively opposing the Dutch system of power relations as they perceive it, with the Moroccan-Dutch and other Muslim groups in the Netherlands and elsewhere at the bottom of the heap. In demonstrations against Israel, in songs, on the internet and in day-to-day confrontations in the streets, we see that 'the Jew' symbolises the power against which they are fighting.

The focus of chapter 15, '*Conspiracism*: Islamic Redemptive Antisemitism and the Murder of Theo van Gogh', is the Islamisation of the image of 'the Jew' as a symbol of the powerful, secular West. Specifically, Ensel scrutinises the writings of Mohammed Bouyeri, Theo van Gogh's assassin. Bouyeri and those who share his opinions have emphasised the corrupt and conspiratorial nature of the Jews and used this as the basis for an ideology which Ensel links to Saul Friedländer's concept of redemptive antisemitism.

In chapter 16, 'Reading Anne Frank. Confronting Antisemitism in Turkish communities', Annemarike Stremmelaar describes how Turkish-Dutch organisations and individuals have handled antisemitism since 2000. The organisation Milli Görüş, which has its roots in Turkish political Islam and controls many European mosques, has been criticised by the Dutch authorities and media as a source of antisemitic and anti-Western views. Among the Milli Görüş rank and file, expressions of antisemitism have been observed, such as anti-Jewish conspiracy theories and descriptions of Israel as an evil force. The issue has exposed serious disagreements within and between mosque boards, whose positions have ranged from taking a stand against antisemitism to ignoring or even practicing it. Stremmelaar goes into detail about a case in 2013 in which a group of young Dutch people of Turkish descent said on television that they hated Jews.

In chapter 17, 'Holocaust Commemorations in Postcolonial Dutch Society', Ensel describes how the first and the second/third generations in immigrant communities in the Netherlands are involved in Holocaust commemoration.

This chapter was prompted by a series of incidents in 2003-2004 in which children, adolescents and adults disrupted commemorative events. The interrelationships between different and sometimes antagonistic perspectives on the past – specifically, on the Shoah, transatlantic slavery and Palestine – are analysed in terms of two concepts: secondary antisemitism and Michael Rothberg's 'multidirectional memory'.

In 'Instrumentalising and Blaming "the Jew"', this book's epilogue, Evelien Gans argues that the Second World War, the Shoah, 'the Jew', Israel and antisemitism will remain subjects of 'a never-ending debate'[103] in the Netherlands and elsewhere. This final chapter ties together strands from some of the preceding ones and touches on a few recent developments. New topics include the rise of the politician Geert Wilders, his Islamophobic *Partij van de Vrijheid* (Freedom Party; PVV) and his instrumentalisation of 'the Jew', the debate on the ban on ritual slaughter as well as the impact of the bloody attacks by Muslim extremists on Charlie Hebdo in Paris and Jewish targets in Toulouse, Brussels, Paris and Copenhagen on debates in the Netherlands about free speech and antisemitism.

---

103 History as *'een discussie zonder einde'* [literally: A discussion without ending] was a famous statement of the equally famous Dutch historian Pieter Geyl (1887-1966) in Pieter Geyl, *Napoleon for and against* (New Haven: Yale University Press, 1949; first Dutch edition 1946) and idem, *Die Diskussion ohne Ende. Auseinandersetzungen mit Historikern* (Darmstadt: Gertner, 1958).

Part I
Post-Liberation Antisemitism

Illustration 5   A photo of the Jewish Quarter in the postwar years

Boris Kowadlo / Jewish Historical Museum / Dutch Photo Museum / Heirs Kowadlo

The Weesperstraat (Amsterdam) in the heart of the barren Jewish Quarter in the postwar years, as captured by Boris Kowadlo (1911-1959). During the German occupation, Kowadlo had been active in the resistance group of photographers 'The Underground Camera'.

2   'The Jew' as Dubious Victim

Evelien Gans

In October 1948, the Amsterdam City Council discussed inappropriate police behaviour, including an incident involving an officer who had received disciplinary punishment for making 'harmful antisemitic remarks to two Jewish girls'. These incidents were not isolated, the spokesman of the Communist Party said. During the German occupation, the police force had been eager to act against Jews, and it had not been able to rid itself of this tendency since.[1] The incident had been raised by the former resistance newspaper *Het Parool*. The officer concerned had stopped the two cycling Jewish girls, and the following dialogue ensued:

> Does your father make so much money that you can afford to get yourself fined?
> My father is dead, officer.
> Did you bring a towel and a bar of soap?
> No, officer.
> More's the pity. Otherwise, I could have sent you to the gas chamber.[2]

Het Parool asked the police about the matter. Initially, the commissioner spoke of an 'inappropriate joke', but eventually, he promised disciplinary punishment. The two Jewish girls did not file a complaint. The remark was clearly antisemitic: the Jews were verbally sent to the gas chamber in retroaction. This was a new, post-Holocaust stereotype. The identification of Jews with gas and the gas chamber – 'the Jew' is there to be gassed – would remain an important item in the antisemitic repertoire.[3] This chapter

---

1   *De Waarheid*, 27 January 1949. For the Dutch police during the German occupation: Guus Meershoek, *Dienaren van het gezag. De Amsterdamse politie tijdens de bezetting* (Amsterdam: Van Gennep, 1999).

2   *Het Parool*, 1 October 1948, NIOD, KB II, 307.

3   Evelien Gans, '"Hamas, Hamas, all Jews to the gas". The history and significance of an antisemitic slogan in the Netherlands, 1945-2010.' In: Günther Jikeli and Joëlle Allouche Benayoun (eds.), *Perceptions of the Holocaust in Europe and Muslim Communities. Sources, Comparisons and Educational Challenges* (Dordrecht: Springer, 2013), 85-103; Evelien Gans, '"They have forgotten to gas you": Post-1945 Antisemitism in the Netherlands.' In: Philomena Essed and Isabel Hoving (eds.), *Dutch Racism* (Amsterdam, New York: Rodopi, 2014), 71-100.

describes how the Shoah or Holocaust became something that could be held against the Jews in the postwar Netherlands.

Antisemitism had not disappeared from the Netherlands; it acquired a number of new dimensions. We will here elucidate the genesis and development of the curse 'They have forgotten to gas you'. The next chapter will show how the historically developed stereotype of the 'cowardly Jew' acquired a new content and function. Important here are the concepts, developed in Germany, of secondary antisemitism and *Schuld- und Erinnerungsabwehrantisemitismus* [antisemitism as defence against guilt and unwanted memory]. By demonstrating that these concepts are also relevant for the Netherlands, psychology is granted its rightful place in the analysis of Dutch postwar antisemitism and the changing or unchanging image of 'the Jew'. The victimhood of the Jews not only gave rise to astonishment and empathy, but also to aversion, aggression and competitive victimhood.

Antisemitism as Defence against Guilt and Unwanted Memory: the Psychological Aspect

Of the 140,000 Jews living in the Netherlands, approximately 104,000 were killed during the Second World War, that is to say 75%. That percentage is considerably higher than in the other Western European countries occupied by Germany. International comparative research has established that by far the most important reason for this was the nearly unrestricted control of the German police over organisation and execution of the deportations, and the ideologically very motivated and extremely antisemitic ss regime. Other important aspects were the failed rise of organised national resistance because the Dutch economy, and therefore the food situation, remained relatively prosperous during the first few years, the fact that there were comparatively few escape opportunities from the (relatively densely populated) Netherlands, and the fact that the Netherlands distinguished itself by its legalistic and comparatively cooperative attitude. The vulnerable position of the Jews was enhanced – and in part symbolised – by the legalistic approach of the Jewish Council, which was directly supervised by the ss and had extremely little room to manoeuvre.[4] It wasn't until April

4   Pim Griffioen and Ron Zeller, *Jodenvervolging, in Nederland, Frankrijk en België. Overeenkomsten, verschillen, oorzaken* (Amsterdam: Boom, 2011), 17, 1025. In this short summary, not all relevant aspects, let alone the clarifying details, can be treated. *See* for a survey and analysis of the historiography of the persecution of the Jews in France, the Netherlands and Belgium:

1943, when the *Arbeitseinsatz* of Dutch men was extended, that hiding places became available on a large scale. But by then, most Jews had already been deported.[5] The pillarisation of Dutch society, i.e. the segmentation of society into various denominational and ideological 'pillars', restricted the availability of hiding places. As historian Bob Moore said, when the Jews needed help 'there were still social and cultural barriers which had to be broken down'.[6] The historical sociologist Helen Fein introduced the concept of 'the universe of obligation': 'that circle of persons toward whom obligations are owed, to whom the rules apply and whose injuries call for expiation of the community'.[7] For most non-Jews, Jews were not a natural part of their 'universe of obligation'. Nonetheless, 28,000 Jews, a fifth of all Jews in the Netherlands, would go into hiding and around 8,000 of them would be betrayed or traced.[8]

Griffioen and Zeller, *Jodenvervolging*, 17-65, and Pim Griffioen and Ron Zeller, 'Comparing the persecution of the Jews in the Netherlands, France and Belgium, 1940-1945: Similarities, differences, causes.' In: Peter Romijn et al. (eds.), *The Persecution of the Jews in the Netherlands, 1940-1945: New Perspectives* (Amsterdam: Vossiuspers, 2012), 55-91; see Bob Moore, *Victims and Survivors: the Nazi Persecution of the Jews in the Netherlands, 1940-1945* (London: Arnold, 1997); J.C.H. Blom, 'De vervolging van de joden in internationaal vergelijkend perspectief', *De Gids* 150, 6/7 (June/July 1987), 494-507. This article has been reprinted several times, for instance in: J.C.H. Blom, *Crisis, bezetting en herstel. Tien studies over Nederland 1930-1950* (The Hague: Nijgh & Van Ditmar Universitair, 1989), 134-150 and J.C.H. Blom, 'The persecution of the Jews in the Netherlands in a comparative international perspective,' *European Jewish Quarterly* 19 (1989), 331-251.

5   In May 1943, approximately 39,000 Jews were living legally in Amsterdam (of these, a relatively large number went into hiding): J.T.M. Houwink ten Cate, 'Het jongere deel. Demografische en sociale kenmerken van het jodendom in Nederland tijdens de vervolging.' In: *Oorlogsdocumentatie 1940-1945. Jaarboek van het Rijksinstituut voor Oorlogsdocumentatie* (Amsterdam: Walburgpers, 1989), 9-66, specifically 51, note 162.

6   Moore, *Victims and Survivors*, 162. Hans Blom also devotes a lot of attention to the effect of pillarisation (in Dutch: *verzuiling*), the process in which 'integrated subcultures[*zuilen*] emerged which cut across class lines uniting disparate economic and social groups on the basis of their religious affiliation', producing four central 'pillars': Roman Catholic, Calvinist, Social Democrat and Liberal (Moore, *Victims and Survivors*, 23).

7   Helen Fein, *Accounting for Genocide: National Responses and Jewish Victimization During the Holocaust* (repr. 1984; Chicago/London: University of Chicago Press, 1979), 4; Dienke Hondius, *Gemengde huwelijken, gemengde gevoelens. Hoe Nederland omgaat met etnisch en religieus verschil* (The Hague: Sdu Uitgevers, 2001; rev. ed. of 1999), 104. I Thank Dienke Hondius.

8   Marnix Croes and Peter Tammes, *'Gif laten wij niet voortbestaan.' Een onderzoek naar de overlevingskansen van Joden in de Nederlandse gemeenten 1940-1945* (Amsterdam: Aksant, 2004) 174*ff*, 471. Croes and Tammes talk of at least 27,995 Jews in hiding. Griffioen and Zeller give a number of 28,000: *Jodenvervolging in Nederland*, 572. Chaya Brasz mentions the number of betrayed Jews of 8,000, a few thousand who escaped abroad and ca. 8,000 survivors who were (relatively) sheltered by their marriage to a non-Jewish partner in: Chaya Brasz, 'Na de

In Dutch historiography, the role and development of antisemitism in respect of the high number of Dutch deportations has received scant attention, despite the fact that during the German occupation antisemitism did not decrease but grew, as reported on in the clandestine press from 1942 onwards. This lack of attention undoubtedly ensues from the absence of both virulent, political antisemitism in the Dutch past and of a tradition in the research of antisemitism in general. In international comparative perspective, Dutch antisemitism during the Second World War is obscured by antisemitism in Belgium, France and other countries.[9] In the Netherlands, however, political and racist antisemitism did indeed exist, primarily, but not solely, among the small minority group of National Socialists.[10]

Passive, or latent, antisemitism, based on deep-rooted Christian, socio-economic and cultural prejudices and anti-Jewish stereotypes, was much more widespread. Dutch Jewish circles call this phenomenon *risjes*: a deeply ingrained anti-Jewish mentality consisting of explicit or implicit prejudice and malice against Jews, without culminating in public or political statements or actions.[11] With reference to Germany, Helen Fein has pointed out that to carry out the Shoah it was extremely relevant that the Nazis' political and ideological antisemitism could connect with milder forms of antisemitism. Anti-Jewish prejudices and resentment among the population would prevent resistance against the persecution of the Jews.[12] Moore has remarked

Tweede Wereldoorlog: van kerkgenootschap naar culturele minderheid.' In: J.C.H. Blom, Rena Fuks-Mansfeld and I. Schöffer (eds.), *Geschiedenis van de joden in Nederland* (Amsterdam: Balans, 1995), 351-352.

9   See Guus Meershoek, 'Een aangekondigde massamoord. Wat wisten de Nederlanders van de Holocaust?', *De Groene Amsterdammer*, 30 January 2013, 30-33.

10   There is a plethora of literature on the National Socialist Movement (NSB) in the Netherlands; most recent are: J.M. Damsma, *Nazis in the Netherlands: a social history of National Socialist collaborators, 1940-1945* (PhD thesis, Universiteit van Amsterdam, 2013): http://dare.uva.nl/record/448535; Tessel Pollmann, *Mussert & Co. De NSB-Leider en zijn vertrouwelingen* (Amsterdam: Boom, 2012); Robin te Slaa and Edwin Klijn, *De NSB. Ontstaan en opkomst van de Nationaal-Socialistische Beweging, 1931-1935* (Amsterdam: Boom, 2009). For racist-antisemitic utterances in diaries of non-NSB Dutch people, see Remco Ensel and Evelien Gans, 'De inzet van joden als 'controlegroep'. Bart van der Boom en de Holocaust', *Tijdschrift voor Geschiedenis* 126, 3 (2013), 388-396: 395; English extended version: Remco Ensel and Evelien Gans, 'We know something of their fate. Bart van der Boom's history of the Holocaust in the Netherlands': https://independent.academia.edu/Remco Ensel and https://independent.academia.edu/EvelienGans.

11   The Jewish author Siegfried van Praag (1899-2002) defined 'risjes' as 'mini-antisemitism': Justus van de Kamp and Jacob van der Wijk, *Koosjer Nederlands. Joodse woorden in de Nederlandse taal* (Amsterdam, Antwerp: Contact, 2006), 510.

12   Helen Fein, 'The Impact of Antisemitism on the Enactment and Success of "the Final Solution of the Jewish Question."' In: Helen Fein, *The Persisting Question: Sociological Perspectives and Social Contexts of Modern Antisemitism* (Berlin: Walter de Gruyter, 1987), 283-284. About

that many people in the Netherlands still considered the Jews 'strangers who had brought their misfortune upon themselves or had deserved it'.[13] Like Fein, the Dutch historian Dienke Hondius has stressed the importance of passive forms of antisemitism during the German occupation. According to Hondius, an 'everyday image of a common difference and some social distance between Jew and non-Jew' could be enough to obstruct effective solidarity with and help to the persecuted Jews during the war.[14] Up to now, the question of whether this passive antisemitism influenced the process that resulted in the dismissal of Jews by the Dutch administration and the unwillingness of a majority of the Dutch people to take more risks to help them, is still subject to debate, both in Dutch historiography and in Dutch society.[15]

With regard to the position of the Dutch administration which did not escape to England, but remained behind, the Dutch historian Peter Romijn concluded in his book *Burgemeesters in oorlogstijd* [Mayors in wartime] (2006), among other things, that, in practice, the Dutch mayors sacrificed the Jewish population to the general interest and the maintenance of the infrastructure: 'The incapability of the Dutch authorities to develop a collective strategy against the anti-Jewish politics was an important factor in the success of these politics.'[16] The political scientist Guus Meershoek characterised the stance of the Dutch authorities, when compared to the

Germany, Fein writes that only a minority were virulent antisemites; many more were 'passive antisemites, accepting the need to exclude the Jews'. On this point, Fein concurs with the historian Ian Kershaw who strongly stresses the aspect of 'indifference'. Saul Friedländer (*Nazi Germany and the Jews. Volume I: The Years of Persecution, 1933-1939* (New York: Harper Collins, 2007) discusses the importance of what he calls 'ordinary antisemitism'. He perceives its existence as one of the reasons why in Germany, resistance against the antisemitic politics of a relatively small group did not occur, in: Frank Diamand, *When Memory Comes. A Film about Saul Friedländer* (2012).

13 Moore, *Victims and Survivors*, 250, 258.
14 Dienke Hondius, *Oorlogslessen. Onderwijs over de oorlog sinds 1945* (Amsterdam: Bert Bakker, 2010), 38; *see* Hondius, 'De holocaust als hype. Goldhagen onderscheidt maar twee groepen Duitsers: daders en slachtoffers. Daartussenin zit niets', *De Groene Amsterdammer*, 23 April 1997. Gans and Ensel, 'Wij weten iets van hun lot. Nivellering in de geschiedschrijving' ; Evelien Gans, 'They have forgotten to gas you', 80.
15 *See* chapter 13.
16 Peter Romijn, 'Ambitions and Dilemmas of Local Authorities in the German Occupied Netherlands, 1940-1945.' In: Bruno De Wever, Herman van Goethem and Nico Wouters (eds.) *Local Government in Occupied Europe (1939-1945)* (Gent: Academia Press, 2006), 33-66; Peter Romijn, *Burgemeesters in oorlogstijd. Besturen onder Duitse bezetting* (Amsterdam: Balans, 2006), 464, 671.

authorities in other parts of occupied Europe, as 'blind subservience'.[17] In
2012, the lawyers Corjo Jansen and Derk Venema analysed how the Supreme
Court, the highest Dutch court of law, let the dismissal of their Jewish
President pass without any protest. This attitude marked the beginning
of their attitude of compliance towards the German occupier, including
signing the so-called *Ariërverklaring* [Aryan declaration] which separated
Gentiles from Jews.[18] However, on the point of identifying (social and latent)
antisemitism and analysing its role in the stance of administration and
authorities these and other historians and scholars are remarkably reserved.

On the basis of divergent sources and literature, it is certain that it was
a lot harder to provide hiding for Jewish people than for other people in
need: 'Often, they found the doors closed'.[19] Fear of severe punishment on
discovery and feelings of impotence played an important, possibly even
decisive role. But the aversion to Jews enhanced the passiveness of the
Dutch population, in the opinion of Loe de Jong (1914-2005) in one of the
volumes of his life's work, *Het Koninkrijk der Nederlanden in de Tweede
Wereldoorlog* [The Kingdom of the Netherlands during the Second World
War] (1969-1988). 'When the persecution of the Jews became more severe,
antisemitism increased'.[20] For instance, a number of rumours circulated
about untrustworthy and miserly Jews in hiding who had betrayed their
hosts and pretended not to have money to avoid having to contribute to the

17   Meershoek, *Dienaren van het gezag,* 214.
18   Corjo Jansen and Derk Venema, *De Hoge Raad en de Tweede Wereldoorlog. Recht en rechts-beoefening in de jaren 1930-1959* (Amsterdam: Boom, 2012).
19   *See* Ben Sijes, 'Enkele opmerkingen over de positie van de Joden in de Tweede Wereldoorlog in Nederland', *Jaarboek van de Maatschappij der Nederlandsche Letterkunde te Leiden,* 1973-1974 (Leiden, 1975), 14-38: 35; *see* Jacques Presser, *Ondergang. De vervolging en verdelging van het Nederlandse Jodendom* (The Hague: Staatsdrukkerij, 1965), II: 255; Loe de Jong, *Het Koninkrijk der Nederlanden in de Tweede Wereldoorlog* (The Hague: Martinus Nijhoff, 1976), VII: 463; Moore, *Victims and Survivors,* 178-179; G.J. van Klinken, *Opvattingen in de gereformeerde kerken in Nederland over het Jodendom, 1896-1970* (Kampen: Kok, 1996), 431. Loes Gompes. *Fatsoenlijk land. Porgel en Porulan in het verzet* (Amsterdam: Rozenberg Publishers, 2013) 58; Ensel and Gans, 'De inzet van joden als: "controlegroep"', 393.
20   For instance, Loe de Jong, *Koninkrijk,* VII: 462-463, 440-441. Sijes, 'Enkele opmerkingen', 129-130. Evelien Gans, '"Vandaag hebben ze niets, maar morgen bezitten ze weer een tientje." Antisemitische stereotypen in bevrijd Nederland.' In: Conny Kristel (ed.), *Polderschouw. Terugkeer en opvang na de Tweede Wereldoorlog. Regionale verschillen* (Amsterdam: Bert Bakker, 2002), 313-353: 317. For postwar antisemitism in the Netherlands, *see* Dienke Hondius, *Terugkeer. Antisemitisme in Nederland rond de bevrijding.* With a story by Marga Minco (1990; rev. ed. The Hague: Sdu, 1998), translated as *Return. Holocaust Survivors and Dutch Anti-Semitism* (Westport: Praeger, 2003).

expenses of their stay. Here, the ancient stereotypes of Judas and Shylock shook hands.[21]

Loe de Jong also addressed the reason behind the growing array of negative feelings towards Jews in the Netherlands during the German occupation. First, there was the gradually implemented isolation which allowed non-Jews to get used to the idea that Jews belonged to a different kind of humanity. This isolation alone made the anti-Jewish measures, accompanied with antisemitic propaganda, very effective.[22] Secondly, the propaganda appealed especially to those who already had reservations or prejudices against Jews: they could now easily mould their worries and problems into a Dutch version of the sentiment: *'Die Juden sind unser Unglück!'* Thirdly, De Jong writes, people's secret shame about their lack of courage could 'easily be reasoned away by assuming that the Jews were not worth the risks one could take on their behalf'. For that reason, people became susceptible to any argument that could put Jews, in the present or past, in a bad light: their disproportionally large influence in the pre-war Netherlands, their betrayal of the people who offered them hiding places, etc.[23] The phenomenon of *blaming the victim* – De Jong had not picked up the expression when it was coined in 1971 – thus fed on antisemitic prejudices.[24]

The historian Jacques Presser (1899-1970), a colleague of De Jong, and featuring already in the introductory essay, listed many antisemitic state-ments from after the liberation (e.g. 'There are actually still too many Jews in the Netherlands'), and remarked on how peculiar it was that these 'might also be considered from the perspective of many similar statements made during the occupation'.[25] There was, in other words, a line of continuity between antisemitism before, during and after the war, within an always changing historical context. Dutch opinion polls of July 1945 indicate that nearly 60 percent of those polled thought that the Dutch people had acted

---

21 Gans, 'Vandaag hebben ze niets', 316.

22 As the premise for antisemitism and racism, the social historian Dik van Arkel saw, apart from stigmatisation and terrorisation, the establishment of social distance, which made it impossible to correct stigmas and stereotypes: Gans, 'Vandaag hebben ze niets', 325; Chris Quispel, 'Introduction.' In: Dik van Arkel, *The Drawing of the Mark of Cain. A Socio-historical Analysis of the Growth of Anti-Jewish Stereotypes* (Amsterdam: Amsterdam University Press, 2009), 11-19.

23 De Jong, *Koninkrijk*, VII, 435. In 2014 a voluminous biography of Loe de Jong was published: Boudewijn Smits, *Loe de Jong 1914-2005. Historicus met een missie* (Amsterdam: Boom, 2014).

24 'Blaming the victim' was coined by the psychologist William Ryan in his study *Blaming the victim* (New York: Pantheon Books, 1971).

25 Presser, *Ondergang*, II: 515-516.

'indifferently' or 'badly'.[26] These polls are only a snapshot of a period, directly after the liberation. Soon afterwards, a dominant image took root, which put national suffering and unity at the forefront, framed the Second World War between the opposites of resistance and collaboration, and showed little interest in either the attitude of the non-Jewish majority during the occupation or in the persecution of the Jews. These images only started to shift in the 1960s.[27] The dominant image before the 1960s of 'resistance versus collaboration', however, would probably, as the July 1945 polls show, always have a more hidden counterpart: that of 'indifference' and 'bad behaviour'.

When, over the course of 1945, the fate of the deported Jews was established with certainty, it became increasingly necessary for the Dutch people to exonerate themselves. Shortly after the war, the historian Richter Roegholt (1925-2005) wrote that there was a vague collective sense of guilt that was obscured through collective repression.[28] The lawyer and writer Abel Herzberg, the historians Jacques Presser, Loe de Jong and Roegholt – the latter by far the youngest of the three and the only non-Jew – considered it only natural to use psychological and psychoanalytical concepts such as shame and repression in their analyses.[29] This attitude can also be seen in the relative ease with which they included the phenomenon of antisemitism, albeit to a limited extent, in their analyses. In 1945, the sociologist and social democrat Hilda Verwey-Jonker (1908-2004) bluntly wrote that the majority of the Dutch people were well aware that they had behaved 'utterly miserably' towards their Jewish fellow-countrymen. Now they sought to justify

26 Ismee Tames, *Besmette jeugd. Kinderen van NSB'ers na de oorlog* (Amsterdam: Balans, 2009), 77. Tames remarks that this negative judgment especially concerned the 'weak' attitude; sympathy for the Germans or National Socialism came within the 'heavier' category.
27 *See* Frank van Vree, *In de schaduw van Auschwitz. Herinneringen, beelden, geschiedenis* (Groningen: Historische uitgeverij, 1995); Frank van Vree, 'De dynamiek van de herinnering. Nederland in een internationale context.' In: Frank van Vree and Rob Laarse (eds.), *De dynamiek van de herinnering. Nederland en de Tweede Wereldoorlog in een internationale context* (Amsterdam: Bert Bakker, 2009), 17-40.
28 Richter Roegholt, *Amsterdam in de 20ᵉ eeuw – deel II (1945-1970)* (Utrecht, Antwerp: Het Spectrum, 1979), 109-111.
29 In his work, the Dutch psychoanalyst Louis Tas (1920-2011), himself a Bergen-Belsen survivor, elaborated on the importance of 'shame', among other things in dealing with the war past (also or especially for Jews). *See* Willem Heuves and Ad Boerwinkel (eds.), *Een wijze van kijken: psychoanalyse en schaamte. Liber Amicorum voor Louis Tas* (Amsterdam: Het Spinhuis, 1996). For definitions of psychological or psychoanalytical concepts such as shame, repression and projection, *see* Harry Stroeken et al., *Nieuw psycho-analytisch woordenboek; begrippen, termen, personen* (Amsterdam: Boom, 2000), 180-181. Shame develops when one wants to deflect imminent rejection, but cannot find an explanation, an excuse or a correction.

themselves by criticising the Jews. Antisemitism was compensation for a lack of national pride.[30] People did indeed feel guilty – especially in social democratic and liberal circles, which were the strongest protesters against antisemitism.[31] The historian A.E. (Dolf) Cohen (1913-2004), former deputy director of the National Institute for War Documentation (RvO, now NIOD), founded in 1945, and a close colleague of De Jong, wrote ten years after the liberation in a (posthumously published) essay how antisemitism had grown during the German occupation. Explanatory factors were the Jewish exceptional and humiliating position, the inevitable tensions between Jews and Gentiles at hiding places, the alleged ingratitude of Jews after the war and the conflicts between Jews and Gentiles who had guarded Jewish possessions. His statements were confirmed by several members of the scholarly board of the institute. Moreover, Cohen wrote in his article that in 1955 there was still 'an undercurrent' of antisemitism.[32]

On close consideration it is remarkable that the younger generation of historians and other researchers never or hardly ever looked at the role of psychological and antisemitic aspects – and the connection between the two during the occupation.[33] For the older generation, it was apparently more acceptable, or indeed even 'normal' not to make a distinction between emotions and psychology on the one hand and their own specific discipline, on the other. For them, 'Freud' was still very much alive. As for the mention of Dutch antisemitism before, during and after the war, apart from their expertise concerned, Herzberg, De Jong and Presser will have been less reluctant because, as Jews, they were simply 'experts by experience'. They knew all too well that antisemitism was not a Nazi invention, but an ingredient that simply had its place in the lives of Jews and non-Jews. Or, as another Jewish historian, Jaap Meijer (1912-1993), would put it: 'Actually, I always

30   Hilde Verwey-Jonker in *Vrij Nederland*, 24 November 1945, quoted in Martin Bossenbroek, *De Meelstreep. Terugkeer en opvang na de Tweede Wereldoorlog* (Amsterdam: Bert Bakker, 2001), 266; *see* Gans, 'Nu hebben ze niets', 313, 326-329, 331.

31   In 1948, the 'meek, amenable, even assisting Dutch people' brought a blush to the cheeks of a reporter of *Elseviers Weekblad*: Klaas Alkema and Ger van der Drift, 'Mist tussen de dijken. De stemming in de weekbladpers en de opvang van oorlogsslachtoffers', in: Kristel, *Polderschouw*, 263-292: 289.

32   A.E. Cohen, 'Tien jaar na de bevrijding van nationaal-socialisme en jodenvervolging in Nederland' (1955) and 'Verslag van bespreking, 8 October 1956.' In: J.C.H. Blom et al. (eds.), *A.E. Cohen als geschiedschrijver van zijn tijd* (Amsterdam: Boom, 2005), 317-328: 321-322, 328. *See also* Epilogue.

33   For instance in the publications by J.C.H. Blom: note 4 and 8, and Blom, 'The persecution of the Jews in the Netherlands and Griffioen and Zeller, *Jodenvervolging*. The same goes for Romijn, *Burgemeesters in oorlogstijd*.

consider antisemitism as something very normal.'[34] In this regard, these Jewish historians implicitly or explicitly integrated a Jewish perspective in their approach.

Generally speaking, it is not possible to give a profound explanation of both the phenomenon and the function of antisemitism only based on religious, economic and political factors. Inevitably, the epithets 'assumed' and 'supposed' are linked to the image of 'Jewish treason', 'Jewish prosperousness' or 'Jewish power': this is about generalisation, the mechanism of 'collective liability', about a projection of one's own feelings of impotence and frustration, and about more or less conscious and hidden desires – about internalised stereotypes and so-called goyish envy – the envy of supposed Jewish qualities, talents and privileges.[35] An explanation of antisemitism has to include a psychological dimension.

In 2013, Guus Meershoek wrote that, due to the results of international comparative research by the Dutch historian J.C.H. (Hans) Blom (b. 1943) in the 1980s, which proved the number of Jews deported from the Netherlands was exceptionally high, the emphasis shifted even more to the Dutch circumstances under which the Holocaust could have taken place. This was first experienced as shocking, then as shameful and then resulted in a defensive reaction. Meershoek, author of a study on the Dutch police in wartime, critically observed that those reactions resulted in considering it obvious that the Dutch were not to blame for the miserable fate of the Jews living in the Netherlands. Hence, Meershoek questioned the ingrained notion of 'Dutch tolerance' and, with that, the concept of the 'Dutch paradox'.[36] It is striking that he used the terms 'shameful', 'guilt' and 'defensive reaction'. In this respect, he also used – albeit not very elaborately – the psychological approach of the first generation of postwar historians, and, more explicitly, that of *Gojse nijd & joods narcisme* [Goyish envy & Jewish narcissism] by Evelien Gans (b. 1951).[37]

---

34 Evelien Gans, *Jaap en Ischa Meijer. Een joodse geschiedenis 1912-1956* (Amsterdam: Bert Bakker, 2008), 217.

35 Evelien Gans, *Gojse nijd & joods narcisme. Over de verhouding tussen joden en niet-joden in Nederland* (Amsterdam: Arena, 1994).

36 *See* for the concept of the Dutch paradox, chapter 1. Meershoek, 'Een aangekondigde massamoord'. Ido de Haan, 'The paradoxes of Dutch history. Historiography of the Holocaust in the Netherlands'. In: David Bankier and Dan Michman (eds.), *Holocaust Historiography in Context: Emergence, Challenges, Polemics and Achievements* (Jerusalem: Yad Vashem, Berghahn Books, 2008), 355-376.

37 Gans, *Gojse nijd*. Martin Bossenbroek argues the phenomenon of *blaming the victim* is one of the explanations of postwar misunderstanding and lack of consideration for 'Jewish grief'. He also mentions the possible connection which Hilda Verwey Jonker (*see* note 30) made

Secondary Antisemitism

In Germany, academics have used psychology and psychoanalysis to analyse postwar antisemitism from the very start. In the 1950s, the German
philosopher and sociologist Theodor Adorno (1903-1969) coined the term
Schuld- und Erinnerungsabwehrantisemitismus, which means, according
to Werner Bergmann, one of the pioneers in the research of postwar antisemitism in Germany and Europe, that

> *Juden als ein Kollektiv gesehen werden, das durch Seine blosse Existenz die*
> *Erinnerung an Verbrechen wach halt – näherhin die Erinnerung an den*
> *Antisemitismus und der Schuld der Deutschen vor 1945.* [Jews are seen as
> a collective that, solely through its existence, keeps a crime alive – the
> memory of antisemitism and the guilt of the Germans before 1945.][38]

In the early 1960s, Peter Schönbach, a fellow researcher and kindred mind
of Adorno's at the Frankfurter Schule, introduced the concept of 'secondary
antisemitism'.[39] 'Secondary' because it did not refer to the antisemitism
which had led to the Shoah, but to the ways in which people tried to deal
with its character and results, with the charged past and the horrors inflicted upon the Jews. A new branch grew on the antisemitism 'tree': a more

between 'sense of guilt' and postwar antisemitism, but does not confirm this: Bossenbroek,
De Meelstreep, 265-266, 297, 503-504, 516, 573, 576. For criticism of aspects of Bossenbroek's
approach: Evelien Gans, 'Gojse broodnijd: de strijd tussen joden en niet-joden rond de naoorlogse
Winkelsluitingswet 1945-1951.' In: Conny Kristel (ed.), *Met alle geweld: botsingen en tegenstellingen in burgerlijk Nederland* (Amsterdam: Balans, 2003),195-213: 200; and Evelien Gans, *De
weg terug. Het kantelend zelfbeeld van de joodse historicus Jaap Meijer (1912-1993)* (Amsterdam:
Vossiuspers, Amsterdam University Press, 2003), 16. In their book on the Dutch Supreme Court,
Jansen and Venema refer, when describing the Nazi strategy of 'setting traps' in order to reach
their goals to socio-psychological literature: *Hoge Raad*, 327.
38 Werner Bergmann, '"Störenfriede der Erinnerung." Zum Schuldabwehr-Antisemitismus
in Deutschland.' In: Klaus-Michael Bogdal, Klaus Holz and Matthias N. Lorenz (eds.), *Literarischer Antisemitismus nach Auschwitz* (Stuttgart, Weimar: J.B. Metzler, 2007), 13-35: 13. Defence
(*Abwehr*): 'Banning or triggers connected to unwelcome images from one's consciousness, as
well as the situations summoning those triggers.' In: Harry Stroeken, *Nieuw psycho-analytisch
woordenboek: begrippen, termen, personen* (Amsterdam: Boom, 2000), 18.
39 Theodor W. Adorno, 'Zur Bekämpfung des Antisemitismus heute.' In: Rolf Tiedeman (ed.),
Theodor W. Adorno. Kritik. Kleine Schriften zur Gesellschaft (Frankfurt am Main: Suhrkamp Ver-
lag, 1971), 105-133: 107-108, 107, 109. Werner Bergmann, 'Sekundärer Antisemitismus.' In Wolfgang
Benz et al. (eds.), *Handbuch des Antisemitismus. Judenfeindschaft in Geschichte und Gegenwart*,
Bd. 3: *Begriffe, Theorien, Ideologien. Im Auftrag des Zentrums für Antisemitismusforschung*
(Berlin, New York: De Gruyter, K.G. Saur Verlag, 2010), 300-302.

subtle, indirect form that manifested itself not in spite of, but precisely as aftermath and result of the Shoah. Again, 'defence' and 'projection' play a central role here. The painful memory of 'Auschwitz' and the associated feelings of guilt and shame, sometimes experienced as enforced, were shifted onto the Jews and used against them. To put it provocatively: 'The Germans will never forgive the Jews for Auschwitz.'[40]

People want to draw a *'Schlussstrich'* [end line] and consider the Holocaust *'wenigstens geringer dimensioniert und vergleichbarer mit den Untaten anderer Nationen'* [at least not as pronounced and more comparable to crimes of other nations].[41] This is 'sabotaged' by the Jews who act as an obstacle on the road to 'normalisation' of the past.[42] Furthermore, their very victimhood seems to make the Jews invulnerable: *'Man darf ja gegen Juden heute nichts sagen'* [These days, one may not say anything against Jews], according to Adorno, who in this way tried to show that the public taboo on antisemitism spawned a new antisemitic argument.[43] In secondary antisemitism, new stereotypes such as the 'ultimate Jewish victim' inflating itself with 'moral authority', attach themselves to old images of the resentful, money- and power-hungry Jew.[44] The typically German terms *Schuld-und Erinnerungsabwehr* [defence against guilt and memory] and *Schlussstrichbedürfnis* [need for closure], however, refer to universal concepts. The concept of secondary antisemitism is not only applicable to Germany or Austria, but also to formerly occupied Europe, where the Jews are equally the embodiment of the *'Verbrechensgeschichte'* [Crime history] inflicted upon them.[45] One of the characteristics of secondary antisemitism Bergmann mentions is: *'Juden wird eine Mitschuld an Hass und Verfolgung gegeben'* [The Jews partly have themselves to blame for the hatred and

40   According to the Israeli psychoanalist Zvi Rex, quoted in: Henryk Broder, *Der Ewige Antisemit. Über Sinn und Funktion eines beständigen Gefühls* (Frankfurt am Main: Fischer, 1986), 125.
41   Wolfgang Benz, 'Zwischen Antisemitismus und Philosemitismus: Juden in Deutschland nach 1945.' In: Katja Behrens (ed.), *Ich bin geblieben – warum? Juden in Deutschland – heute* (Gerlingen: Psychosozial-Verlag, 2002), 7-33: 9.
42   *Ibid.*
43   Adorno,'Zur Bekämpfung', 115.
44   Lars Rensmann and Julius H. Schoeps (eds.), *Feindbild Judentum. Antisemitismus in Europa* (Berlin: Verlag für Berlin-Brandenburg, 2008), 16.
45   Werner Bergmann and Rainer Erb, *Antisemitismus in der Bundesrepublik Deutschland. Ergebnisse der empirischen Forschung von 1946-1989* (Opladen: Verlag Leske und Budrichs 1991), 231. The Jews are assumed to use the 'Moralkeule Auschwitz' ('the moral bludgeon of Auschwitz') against non-Jews: Lars Rensmann, *Democratie und Judenbild. Antisemitismus in der politischen Kultur der Bundesrepublik Deutschland* (Wiesbaden: Verlag für Sozialwissenschaften, 2004), 162.

persecution].[46] Indeed, within the context of the persecution of the Jews, the boundaries between 'blaming the victim' and (secondary) antisemitism are extremely porous.[47]

In the Netherlands, researchers have not or hardly applied these originally German concepts. But here too, the return of the Jews from the camps and out of hiding was confronting. Why would secondary antisemitism and 'Schuld- und Erinnerungsabwehrantisemitismus' not be applicable to an occupied country such as the Netherlands, where the vast majority of the Jewish population had been deported and killed, and where the non-Jewish population needed to find a way to relate to this fact? As early as 1944, Dutch resistance fighter Gerrit van der Veen (1902-1944) said that 'a large part of the Dutch population had abandoned their Jewish fellow-countrymen, and had even, to make life easier, taken refuge in antisemitism'. This was understandable, because when someone is in misery, you want this to be his own fault: '... If you are bad, you are punished. The persecution of the Jews is punishment indeed, therefore the Jews are bad.[48]

In 1946, Jews and non-Jews united in the Hollandsche Schouwburg Committee (referring to the theatre that served as the assembly point from where most Jews in Amsterdam were deported to transit camp Westerbork), to prevent this building from ever being used again as a cinema or theatre. They proposed a worthier function for the theatre.[49] A reporter, and sympathiser of the initiative, was reproached for belonging to those Jews who 'in word and writing discredit the behaviour of their fellow Jews and create an atmosphere that enables antisemitism'. The reporter concerned typified this statement as an expression of 'the vilest form of antisemitism, namely that which makes the Jews themselves responsible for the suffering that others inflict upon them'.[50] These antisemitic reactions were clearly linked to an aversion against a lasting reminder of the mass deportations.

46 Bergmann, 'Sekundärer Antisemitismus', 301.
47 Recent empirical research has confirmed secondary antisemitism as a reaction to the image of the ever continuing suffering of the Jews on the basis of the crimes committed against them in the past: R. Imhof and R. Banse, 'Ongoing victim suffering increases prejudice: the case of secondary antisemitism', Psychological Science 20 (2009),1443-1447. I thank Werner Bergmann.
48 Gerrit Jan van der Veen, De Vrije Kunstenaar, 15 March 1944; see Gans, Gojse nijd, 30-34. I thank Guus Meershoek.
49 For the history of the Hollandsche Schouwburg: Frank van Vree, Hetty Berg and David Duindam (eds.), De Hollandsche Schouwburg. Theater, deportatieplaats, plek van herinnering (Amsterdam: Amsterdam University Press, 2013).
50 Alkema and Van der Drift, 'Mist tussen de dijken', 290-291. The sympathiser was a reporter and – to be precise – not a Jew.

'They Have Forgotten to Gas You'

The superlatively aggressive way of treating Jewish people was expressed in the abusive remark, 'They have forgotten to gas you'. This new stereotype – the Jews are there to be gassed – was inspired by the persecution of the Jews itself. It was the worst thing you could say to a Jew, and that is how it was felt. During the introductory conversation to a training analysis, a Jewish psychoanalyst told her (non-Jewish) analyst in training that he should feel free and, indeed, obliged to say anything that came to his mind: 'Even if it is something along the lines of, "They have forgotten to gas you"'.[51] Precisely this curse has the effect of the 'ultimate offence'. According to the American philosopher Judith Butler (b. 1956), a certain expression, or language, only becomes insulting because of the history it contains. The Holocaust is inevitably part of the penalisation of antisemitic utterances.[52]

As mentioned before, the more traditional stereotypes that put 'the Jew' down as a traitor (Judas) and a miserly, cunning materialist (Shylock) had circulated during the German occupation and were generally countered by critical comments in the clandestine press.[53] After the liberation, these and other stereotypes were adapted to the new context of the liberated, but still unsettled, Dutch society. People suspected repatriating Jews of first digging up their bank notes, then taking the best jobs to drive off with the biggest cars. They were supposed to play the first fiddle, sometimes literally, instead of acting modestly and showing gratitude for the help people had offered them at the risk of their own lives.[54]

---

51   Email by Hans Wiersema to Evelien Gans, 26 March 2012.

52   Judith Butler, *Excitable Speech: A Politics of the Performative* (New York: Routledge, 1997). In 2007, a Dutch translation of *Excitable Speech* appeared [*Opgefokte taal: een politiek van de performatief*] with a preface in which Butler refers to the murder of Theo van Gogh, among other things. *See* Padu Boerstra, 'Woorden zijn soms ook daden,' *Filosofie magazine* 3 (2007), 16-17, 19-20. The anthropologist Tzvetan Todorov wrote in *Les Morales de l'histoire* (Paris: B. Grasset, 1991): 'Speaking is acting: the racist treatise is not only an incitement to action, but it is an act itself', quoted in: Dick van Galen Last, 'Wetenschapsbeoefening en revisionisme.' In: Jaap van Donselaar, Teresien de Silva and W. Sorgdrager (eds.), *Weerzinwekkende wetenschap. Holocaustontkenning en andere uitingen van historisch revisionisme* (Amsterdam: Anne Frank Stichting, 1998), 16-33: 31.

53   *See, e.g.*, Gans, 'Vandaag hebben ze niets', 317.

54   *Ibid.*, and Gans, 'Gojse broodnijd'. Evelien Gans, 'Over gaskamers, Joodse Nazi's en neuzen.' In: Peter Rodrigues and Jaap van Donselaar (eds.), *Monitor Racisme & Extremisme. Negende Rapportage* (Amsterdam: Anne Frank Stichting, Amsterdam University Press, 2010), 129-152. English version: Evelien Gans, 'On gas chambers, Jewish Nazis and noses.' In: Peter Rodrigues and Jaap van Donselaar, (eds.), *Racism and Extremism Monitor. Ninth Report* (Amsterdam: Anne Frank Stichting, Universiteit Leiden, 2010), 74-87.

Many of these accusations had a materialistic connotation. The antisemitism in the postwar Netherlands can partly be explained from socio-economic factors. In many cases, people wanted to keep what they had received in keeping: objects such as a Persian carpet, a fur coat or precious tableware, to which they had become attached or which had replaced their own worn-out possessions. Immediately after the war, with dearth everywhere, Jewish survivors returned to reclaim their houses, jobs, companies, clients, money and other possessions. Some non-Jewish Dutch people saw them as competitors. They had become used to the absence of Jews. Here, one's own material interest directly connects to psychological factors and emotions such as greed and envy. These were projected onto the stereotype of the materialistic, greedy, rich Jew.[55] The Dutch authorities also played their part. For instance, recent research has shown that the City of Amsterdam 'deliberately' charged Jewish survivors ground rent arrears and fines for the period during which they were unable to live in their houses, because they had been deported or had gone into hiding. This is only the most recent example of a long series of abuses. Directly after 1945 – also outside of Amsterdam – all sorts of other taxes were levied without justification. Rehabilitation was hard-fought, both legally and politically.[56]

These kinds of measures were not confined to the Netherlands. In several other formerly occupied countries the same happened, and in a more violent way, for instance in France.[57] In his book on the aftermath of the Second World War, *Savage Continent* (2012), the British historian Keith Lowe states that properties of deported Jews (or of those who had managed to go into hiding or escape to neutral territory) were considered 'a resource that could

55   *Ibid.* See Gans, 'They have forgotten to gas you', 77-81.
56   Hinke Piersma and Jeroen Kemperman, *Openstaande rekeningen: de gemeente Amsterdam en de gevolgen van roof en rechtsherstel, 1940-1950* (Amsterdam: Boom, 2015). For Dutch restitution, *see also* A.J. van Schie, 'Restitution of economic rights after 1945.' In: Jozeph Michman and Tirtsah Levie (eds.), *Dutch Jewish History. Proceedings of the Symposium on the History of the Jews in the Netherlands* (Jerusalem, Tel Aviv: Tel Aviv University, Hebrew University of Jerusalem, 1984), 401-420; Gerard Aalders, *Berooid. De beroofde joden en het Nederlands restitutiebeleid sinds 1945* (Amsterdam: Boom, 2001); A.J. van Schie, 'A Disgrace? Postwar Restitution of Looted Jewish Property in the Netherlands.' In: Chaya Brasz and Yosef Kaplan (eds.), *Dutch Jews as perceived by themselves and by others. Proceedings of the Eighth International Symposium on the History of the Jews in the Netherlands* (Leiden: Brill, 2001), 393-404; Wouter Veraart and Laurens Winkel (eds.), *The Post-War Restitution of Property Rights in Europe: Comparative Perspectives* (Amsterdam: Scientia Verlag, 2011). *See also*: Epilogue.
57   When, for example, Jewish survivors claimed back their properties in France, this led (especially in Paris and Toulouse) to anti-Jewish demonstrations and attacks: Pieter Lagrou, 'Victims of genocide and national memory', *Past & Present* 154 (February 1997), 181-222: 184-185; *see* Hondius, *Terugkeer*, 204.

be shared by everyone'.[58] In Central and Eastern Europe, where non-Jewish people were considerably poorer and had suffered more than those in Western Europe, anti-Jewish violence occurred on a daily basis after the end of the war. This included excesses like pogroms such as the infamous one in the Polish city of Kielce and in other Polish villages.[59] Less known, but not less gruesome, is the pogrom in postwar Hungary – in the village of Kunmadaras where, just like in Kielce, the violence started with the rumour of the ritual murder of a Christian child, but where socio-economic motives and goyish envy were the decisive factors.[60] Lowe mentions a *witz* [Jewish joke] circulating in Hungary. A Jewish camp survivor meets a Christian friend in Budapest who asks him how he is doing. Don't ask, says the Jew. I came back from the camp and now I have nothing but the clothes on your back. Lowe writes that the joke would work in any Eastern European city, adding 'plus a good many in the West'.[61]

Lowe does not only pay attention to the material drive behind post-liberation antisemitism. He also traces the key to the general and comforting myth that one had survived the war as a people, even as nations of Europe, and that many had resisted the Nazis with truly heroic courage. The tale the Jews told did not correspond to this story.

> They were a reminder of former failings at every level of society. Their very presence was enough to create discomfort, as though they might at any moment reveal an embarrassing secret.[62]

Lowe does not name this phenomenon and does not elaborate further on it. But, as a matter of fact, he describes the mechanisms that led to *Schuld- und Erinnerungsabwehrantisemitismus.*

The same applies to the Netherlands. The Jews were assumed to have cashed in on the war, both materially and morally. They supposedly claimed the right to being more pampered and favoured 'because they had suffered

---

58   Keith Lowe, *Savage Continent. Europe in the Aftermath of World War II* (London: Viking, 2012), 200.

59   Jan T. Gross, *Fear: Anti-Semitism in Poland after Auschwitz: An Essay in Historical Interpretation* (Princeton: Princeton University Press 2003).

60   Lowe, *Savage Continent*, 202. A remarkable documentary was made about the pogrom in Kunmadaras: András Surányi, Sándor Simó and Edit Kőszegi, *Midön a vér* [Bloodplot. Bloodlibels after the Holocaust] (1992). I thank András Kovács.

61   Lowe, *Savage Continent*, 197. Chris Quispel, *Anti-Joodse beeldvorming en Jodenhaat* (Hilversum: Verloren, 2016), 267-271.

62   *Ibid.*

so much'. And, if it were true that they had suffered so much, why had they not become better persons? They, who had lost all their relatives, 'still feel the urge to hunt down furniture that was once theirs'.[63] These kinds of reproaches reveal the goyish envy towards 'the Jew' as 'the ultimate victim'. Through it all, you can see the Christian idea that 'suffering purifies'. The sufferings of the Jews should have made them more spiritual and less materialistic. Whether made consciously or subconsciously, all these remarks turned the Shoah against the Jews. Had the Jews really deserved the help people gave them? An explicitly religious form of this sentiment was the complaint among both conservative Protestant and Catholic circles that the Jews had brought the persecution upon themselves: by crucifying Christ and subsequently maintaining that he was not the long-awaited Messiah.[64]

As always, it would be wrong to generalise. Many non-Jews helped 28,000 Jews to go into hiding and there were plenty examples of 'guardaryans' (in Dutch: *bewariërs* which is a wordplay on the guarding of Jewish property by 'Aryans'), who painstakingly guarded the possessions given in keeping. Many Jews and non-Jews, journalists, Zionists, opinion makers and politicians, zealously fought against anti-Jewish prejudices. But they did so as individuals. For the Dutch government never took a clear stance against what it considered 'latent antisemitism'. It did use anti-Jewish sentiments as an argument in its decision not to take certain measures which benefited Jews, such as the admission of Jewish refugees. It was assumed this would only have strengthened 'latent antisemitism' among the population, for instance in view of the housing problem. This behaviour implicitly confirmed the prejudice among the population, and the existence of an element of 'goyish envy'.[65]

While most (secondary) antisemitic stereotypes elaborated on existing prejudice, this did not apply to the abusive remark: 'They have forgotten to gas you'. The police officer who had asked two girls whether they had a piece of soap and a towel with them to be able to 'put them in the gas chamber', did not base his comment on an old extermination method. Reports and rumours about gassing already circulated during the German occupation, but they weren't fully confirmed until after the liberation,

---

63   Letter, 21 July 1945, NIOD, VN, inv.nr. 576; Letter,17 July 1945, NIOD, VN inv.nr. 575; *see* Gans, 'Vandaag hebben ze niets', 342.

64   *See* for these sentiments: Van Klinken, *Opvattingen in de gereformeerde Kerken*, 414-417; Alkema and Van der Drift, 'Mist tussen de dijken', 288-289; Marcel Poorthuis and Theo Salemink, *Een donkere spiegel. Nederlandse katholieken over joden. Tussen antisemitisme en erkenning, 1870-2005* (Nijmegen: Valkhof Pers, 2006), 527-529.

65   Gans, 'Vandaag hebben ze niets', 324-325; Gans, 'Hamas, Hamas, all Jews to the gas', 89.

when the press reported on it and Jewish survivors returned. Between mid-September and mid-November 1945, the so-called (Bergen-)Belsen trial took place in Germany, and many SS commanders, guards and *kapos* were tried – including some who had worked at Auschwitz. Therefore, several Jewish survivors gave detailed testimonies about the setup and the execution of the murders. In Dutch newspapers, journalists described the obscuring procedures surrounding the gas chamber, by highlighting the 'towel' and 'soap', as cynical destruction requisites.[66]

This information instilled astonishment and empathy, but also a defensive reaction, and it served as an instrument to voice aversion and aggression towards Jews. It wasn't until 1948 that the antisemitic gassing remark reached the press – following the incident with the Amsterdam police officer. But from many individual testimonies, it appears to have entered the language shortly after the liberation to never disappear again: for example, on the tram or train, in shops, in queues before shops and distribution offices, after traffic accidents, in rows between neighbours and at work.[67] There were children who returned from hiding, only to have this insult thrown at them. Diego Rodrigues Lopes (b. 1936) witnessed how, on the tram, three men shouted 'they have forgotten to gas you' at his grandfather, an impeccably dressed gentleman ('with a Jewish nose, a goy would say').[68] Ron van der Wieken (b. 1946) returned to the Netherlands with his parents, where the family moved into the house of an aunt who had been murdered.

> I think I was about four years old. When the bell rang, I opened the door of our house in Scheveningen with my mother. The knife grinder asked whether we had any work for him. My mother thanked him politely, whereupon he walked off crossly and shouted at us: "They have forgotten to gas you". My mother shut the door and started to cry (probably the

---

66   See for instance: *Het Limburgsch Dagblad*, 22 September 1945; *Veritas: katholiek 14-daagsch blad voor Maastricht*, 22 September 1945, *De Heerenveensche Courier*, 24 September 1945; *De Waarheid*, 22 September 1945.

67   Email by Ernst Verduin to Evelien Gans, 30 January 2013; Emails by Joke Sterringa to Evelien Gans, 30 January and 6 February 2013; Johan Jongejan to Evelien Gans, 27 and 31 January 2013, 6 and 14 February 2013 and several emails from other respondents.

68   Telephone interview with Diego Rodrigues Lopes, 6 June 2012. See Almar Tjepkema and Jaap Walvis, *'Ondergedoken.' Het ondergrondse leven tijdens de Tweede Wereldoorlog* (Weesp: De Haan, 1985), 159-160.

reason why I still remember it); to my question of why, she answered:
"That was a very stupid man."[69]

In many cases, adults, like Diego's grandfather, just shrugged, but in some
instances Jewish boys and men picked a fight. It appears that antisemitic insults were less tolerated than before the war and that fists were used earlier.
These individual cases could lead to a conviction in court, for instance in the
case of Emanuel Aalsvel, for whom this was the final straw: he emigrated to
Israel.[70] In mid-1947, the KNVB (Royal Dutch Football Association) organised
a course for referees on how to deal with antisemitism on the field.[71]

Antisemitism did not induce all Jews to move to Israel, opt for 'innere
Emigration' or fight it out. Some thought this contested insult was so insup-
portable and inacceptable that they went to court. This can be deducted
from newspaper articles, court reports and files from the 1950s and 1960s.
The courts also employed a hierarchy of standards. A form of jurisprudence
developed in which one of the two main antisemitic insults, 'They have
forgotten to gas you', was punished more severely than Rotjood [Rotten
Jew].[72] Convictions depended on whether the judge thought it was a deliberate insult of a population group, as described in the introductory chapter.
And the severity of the sentence varied depending on the circumstances in
which the insult was made, the character of the 'perpetrator' and that of the
'victim' – and the personal considerations and legal interpretation of the
judge. In 1955, a construction worker in Hilversum became incensed when,
during sales at the local clothes shop, his wife had to stand back in line in
order to buy the blouse she had chosen earlier on, in his opinion contrary
to what had been agreed. He had scolded the son of the owner: 'You are all
swindlers. It is a good thing they have gassed you all in the war. It's just a
pity they forgot you.' In appeal, the judge changed his original sentence,
a forty-guilder fine, to an unsuspended one-week jail sentence, probably
because the suspect showed no remorse.[73] That was not the case for the
deckhand of the ferry across the Amsterdam IJ. In 1957, he shouted at a
driver, who he thought 'looked Jewish' and had squeezed his car onto the
ferry at the very last moment, that 'Hitler had not picked the right moment

69 Emails by Ron van der Wieken to Evelien Gans, 20 and 27 June 2012.
70 Gans, 'They have forgotten to gas you', 71.
71 Evert de Vos, '"Verliest den moed toch niet." Joodse voetbalclubs in Amsterdam 1908-1948'
(Doctoral thesis, Social History, Universiteit Leiden, October 2000), 60. I thank Evert de Vos.
72 Vrij Nederland, 27 January 1962, NIOD, KB II 307A. Within the short scope of this chapter, I
can refer to only some of the court cases.
73 Het Parool, 28 April 1955.

to stop gassing people'. During the trial he hung his head in shame and
pleaded guilty: he did not at all wish those people what had been inflicted
upon them. The judge reduced the 150-guilder fine, demanded by the district
attorney, to a third of the sum and

> reminded the deckhand who, on the evidence of his accent, did not
> originate from the capital, what the hundred thousand Jews deported
> from Amsterdam had meant for the city ....[74]

In February 1964 and May 1968, the insults 'They gassed the good people,
but they should have gassed you' and 'Rotten Jews, they have forgotten to
gas you' led to fines of forty and twenty guilders, respectively.[75] The insult
'They have forgotten to gas you' could be heard on the street, in the pub,
in shops and in workplaces; it was vulgar and mainly used by people who
were not high up on the social ladder. It could be about a contested seat, at
a bus stop or on the train – a matter of territorial rage.[76]

The 'well-educated' with anti-Jewish prejudices had a better training
in when and what to say. They kept their anti-Jewish ideas to themselves,
or, as the Spanish expression says, *solapado* – under their revers. Or they
wrote them down in documents which were never meant to be revealed,
but nevertheless would be brought into the open. Like the public prosecutor
who, in 1949, had characterised a Jewish applicant for naturalisation as
'the type of a rich Jew'.[77] And the highly esteemed professor of law Adriaan
Pitlo (1901-1987) who appeared to have written in his diaries that 'many of
us' had had bad experiences with Jews in hiding. Those Jews had kept their
jewellery for themselves: 'What Hitler left us, is a piece of antisemitism. Not
Hitler is to blame, but the Jews themselves. Lots of Jews have abused the
help that was given to them by non-Jews.'[78]

The insult 'They have forgotten to gas you' was an expression of resentment and acute anger against Jews who were assumed to call the shots
again, or to be able to do so in the near future. In that sense, it tied in with
old stereotypes of the rich, materialistic, powerful Jew. But the conflict

---

74 *Het Vrije Volk*, 16 December 1957, NIOD, KB II, 307.

75 *Nieuwsblad van het Noorden*, 11 February 1964 and *Friese Koerier, onafhankelijk dagblad voor
Friesland en aangrenzende gebieden*, 2 May 1968.

76 *Paraat*, 22 December 1945.

77 *Nieuwe Rotterdamse Courant*, 4 April 1952; The case became public, by accident, because of
an official investigation.

78 Joggli Meihuizen, *Sans égards. Prof. mr. A. Pitlo en zijn conflicten met joodse juristen* (Amsterdam: Boom, 2007), 65.

of interest also escalated because of the rancour regarding the 'ultimate victim': 'the Jew' who was traditionally pushy and rude, and now thought he was entitled to extra consideration and mollycoddling. As if the Jews were the only ones who had suffered. Victim competition and protest against a supposed hierarchy of suffering played an important role here. And from whatever annoyance or resentment the insult was born, it was directly inspired by the persecution of the Jews itself. Similarly, the weekly and former resistance journal *Vrij Nederland* published a survey of antisemitic incidents with the caveat that it was only a selection from many more available examples. And not everything reached the newspapers. From time to time, they would receive clippings from local newspapers and news leaflets, which reported many dubious incidents. But they were not always considered national news.[79] In other words, the journal emphasised that what was in the paper was only the tip of the iceberg. This must have been even truer for the anti-Jewish insults that reached the courts. The insulted parties will not always have had the energy to sue. The aggressive verbal identification between Jews and 'gas' was there to stay.[80] It would relocate to other social domains, such as football stadiums, demonstrations and the internet, and in connection to the politics of Israel.

79   *Vrij Nederland*, 27 January 1962.
80   A fairly recent example is that, in the summer of 2015, a judge sentenced a person who had hurled at someone, 'They should have gassed you', to forty hours of community service: Anne Vegterlo, 'Hitlergroet is geen discriminatie', *NRC Handelsblad*, 26 August 2015.

3 The Meek Jew – and Beyond

Evelien Gans

Court cases constitute a formal platform where all manner of conflicts between individual citizens and social groups are settled – within the framework of the law.[1] This makes them the yardstick by which we can determine what was deemed legally tolerated within a specific historical context. In February 1949, the court of Amsterdam held a remarkable session. A Jewish lawyer, one of the founders of the former resistance newspaper *Het Parool*, had filed a complaint against a – non-Jewish – Dutch Reformed resistance fighter.[2] During the war, the Jewish lawyer Hans Warendorf (1902-1987) had managed to escape to England in time, but several of his *Parool* friends and resistance comrades had been arrested and killed. Among them were a number of Jews: Maurits Kann (1894-1942), Jaap Nunes Vaz (1906-1943) and Sieg Vaz Dias (1904-1943).[3] The accused, Klaas Norel (1899-1971), for that matter, had an excellent reputation as a resistance fighter, committed to working for the illegal National Organisation for Assistance to People in Hiding (LO) and to publishing the Reformed former resistance newspaper *Trouw*. He was also the author of a very popular Second World War novel for young adults: *Engelandvaarders* [England paddlers] (1945).

Already during the occupation, rumours circulated about Jewish people in hiding betraying their protectors. Moreover, soon after the liberation, people were saying that the Jews had not put up any resistance to the Nazis. The latter view was also disseminated by Norel in a number of passages he had written in the eighth volume of the series 'History of the Occupation Years': *De Tyrannie verdrijven* [Dispelling the Tyranny].

> The Jews did not offer resistance to the pogroms. On the occasion of the closure of the Leiden University and the February 1941 strike in Amsterdam, others entered the lists for them ....[4]

---

1   For a small part, this chapter is an adaptation of: Evelien Gans, 'Disparaging responsibility. The stereotype of the Passive Jew as a legitimizing factor in Dutch remembrance of the Shoah'. In David Wertheim (ed.), *The Jew as Legitimation* (forthcoming).

2   *NIW,* 30 January 1948; *Het Parool*, 6 February 1948; *Trouw,* 18 February 1949, NIOD, KB I 5145.

3   For the history of the illegal *Het Parool*: Madelon de Keizer, *Het Parool 1940-1945. Verzetsblad in Oorlogstijd* (Amsterdam: Otto Cramwinckel, 1991).

4   Quoted in: *Het Parool*, 6 February 1948 NIOD, KB I 5145. *See also Algemeen Handelsblad*, 18 February 1949. Intended is, among other things, the famous lecture on 26 November 1940 by

In short, the Jews had left it to others to fend for them; they themselves had not been able to. As early as July 1945, the Jewish psychiatrist Coen van Emde Boas (1904-1981) wrote that people had started to consider Jews once more as Jews, among other things, due to the necessity to help them in that capacity against the Germans. Their elimination and isolation had led to estrangement, aversion and a sense of superiority. These sentiments had then been enhanced by pity and by the position of non-Jews as 'helpers' and of Jews as 'helped'.[5]

Norel did not stop at the above-mentioned quote. He also wrote that Jews were simply not willing to make an effort when there was no chance of success, as there had not been when it came to fighting. What surprised him was that, initially, they had made so little effort to evade the grasp of the Germans, 'For the Jews may not be heroes, they are most certainly cunning'. The only thing that could motivate Jews was their property. They had meekly collaborated with their registration, but when it came to handing in their radios and bicycles, 'they had run like hares'. Even those with 'a slightly Jewish appearance' still submitted to wearing the Star of David.

> They only awoke when the Nazis extended their greedy fingers towards their property and household effects. And then, with a vengeance, with great cunning, they hid untold millions from the enemy. But this could not be accomplished with cunning alone. They needed help. And help was generously offered, by the Dutch.[6]

Here, the Jew is characterised as un-Dutch and thoroughly materialistic, but above all as passive. Just like the other stereotypes, the cowardly Jew who fails to become a hero goes back a long way. The same goes for the myth of Jewish passivity. In biblical times, the Jewish people were considered an experienced military opponent. In the Diaspora, the Jews nurtured a different image: as a non-Christian minority, they were not allowed to carry weapons; only much later would they be able to serve in national armies. This fact, combined with the inability of the Jews to defend themselves with weapons against pogroms and other acts of violence, fed the stereotype of the passive, cowardly Jew as regards physical defence, use of weapons and

Professor Cleveringa, in which he protested against the dismissal of his Jewish colleagues, upon which the Germans (temporarily) closed the university. *See also* NIW, 30 January 1948.

5   Evelien Gans, *Gojse nijd & joods narcisme. Over de verhouding tussen joden en niet-joden in Nederland* (Amsterdam: Arena, 1994), 31-32.

6   *Het Parool*, 6 February 1948.

(lack of) masculinity.[7] Phenomena such as the seventeenth- and especially eighteenth-century Jewish bands of robbers[8] and self-defence groups of Russian Jews against pogroms[9] could not change this. Strengthening Jewish self-awareness was an important secondary goal for both (Jewish) social-ism and Zionism. In 1929, after Palestinian Arabs had massacred Jews in Hebron, the Dutch Jewish union leader Henri Polak (1869-1943) said: 'We are no longer the people whose bent figures move among the shadows of the houses .... We do not resign, we do not bow. The times have changed and we have changed.'[10]

After the war, the stereotype of the cowardly, obedient Jew acquired a new function. In general, it enabled people to argue that, if the Jews had not resisted the Nazis, why should non-Jews have put their lives, families and belongings at stake to save them? In Norel's opinion, the resistance was blameless anyway. Had he and his comrades not fought to the last ditch to defend the nation and its people? Had they not made an effort for the Jews? Certainly – but the question was how much priority they had given to helping the Jews?[11] The stereotype of the passive Jew can be seen in this postwar context as an expression of secondary antisemitism,

7   Ben Braber, *Zelfs als wij zullen verliezen. Joden in verzet en illegaliteit, 1940-1945* (Amsterdam: Balans, 1990), 11-12; Evelien Gans, '"Vandaag hebben ze niets, maar morgen bezitten ze weer een tientje." Antisemitische stereotypen in bevrijd Nederland.' In: Conny Kristel (ed.), *Polderschouw. Terugkeer en opvang na de Tweede Wereldoorlog. Regionale verschillen* (Amsterdam: Bert Bakker, 2002), 313-353: 321.
8   Rena Fuks-Mansfeld, 'Verlichting en emancipatie omstreeks 1750-1814.' In: J.C.H. Blom, R.G. Fuks-Manfeld and I. Schöffer (eds.), *Geschiedenis van de joden in Nederland* (Amsterdam: Balans, 1995), 177-203: 181; Evelien Gans, *Jaap en Ischa Meijer. Een joodse geschiedenis 1912-1956* (Amsterdam: Bert Bakker, 2008), 31.
9   Evelien Gans, *De kleine verschillen die het leven uitmaken: een historische studie naar joodse sociaal-democraten en socialistisch-zionisten in Nederland* (Amsterdam: Vassalucci, 1999), 24.
10   Gans, *De kleine verschillen*, 79. Polak was not a member of organised Zionism, but did sympathise with Zionism.
11   It has now been established that between the summer of 1942 and the summer of 1943, when most deportations took place, there was no National Organisation for Assistance to People in Hiding (LO) in Amsterdam, where most of the Jews lived. The four non-Jewish resistance organisations that would later merge with the LO only made a small contribution to supplying hiding places for Jews. The LO itself would later admit to having been directed more to supplying massive help to other, larger (i.e. non-Jewish) groups. Most of the Jews were helped by 'small Jewish organisations, in which students did magnificent work': Loes Gompes, *Fatsoenlijk land. Porgel en Porulan in het verzet* (Amsterdam: Rozenberg Publishers, 2013), 128-129. Other small resistance groups were indeed active in supplying hiding places for Jews. Moreover, the so-called Free Groups Amsterdam (VGA) were active in this field. 20% of their members had a Jewish background: H van Riessen and Rogier van Aerde (eds.), *Het grote Gebod; Gedenkboek van het verzet van LO en LKP* (first ed. 1951; Kampen: Kok, 1989), 12.

especially when accompanied with the suggestion that 'the Jew' had a hand in his own elimination because of an accumulation of typically 'Jewish characteristics': cunning but subservient, protective of property but not combative. This position – as taken up by Norel – could be used to avoid a sense of responsibility, guilt and shame. The Jew and the Dutch were functioning as communicating vessels: the more cowardly the Jew, the braver the help-offering Dutch.

The 'heroic resistance fighter' versus the 'passive Jew'

During the trial against resistance fighter Klaas Norel, Warendorf declared that he had lodged his complaint on behalf of his Jewish friends who had died in the resistance. He argued that many Jewish Dutch people had participated in the resistance, despite their extremely difficult position. Compared to that of non-Jewish Dutch people, their participation percentage had been remarkably high. Therefore, Warendorf stated, Norel had falsified history and posterity should not be given a wrong representation of the position of the Jews.[12] Warendorf's statements were not solely based on his own experience, but also on the first research results of the historian Loe de Jong, director of the National Institute for War Documentation (RvO). The Jews had indeed offered resistance 'to the pogroms', for instance in 1941, in fights with the NSB and with a gang of thugs in Amsterdam's Jewish quarter; they had also contributed to the resistance at universities and to the February Strike. 'Dutch people of Jewish descent' (De Jong mentioned several names) had been active in all segments of the resistance. If desired, the RvO would be able to supply more data. In a letter, put at the disposal of Warendorf, De Jong concluded that the percentage of Jews participating in resistance activities 'was certainly not lower than that of other Dutch people, only a small minority of whom, as we know, participated in the resistance against the occupier'.[13] What was remarkable about this case

12   The letter dates from 17 February 1949, and from this and other remarks by Warendorf, it appears that, during the first trial, he also explicitly used data originating from Loe de Jong and the RvO, though not extensively: *see Het Parool*, 18 February 1949. *See also* Noord-Hollands Archief, Haarlem, Archief Gerechtshof Amsterdam, inv.nr. 489-177/197/345, record of the session 5th chamber court Amsterdam 17 February 1949. In later years the RvO would become the RIOD (State Institute for War Documentation) and then NIOD.

13   Loe de Jong to J.C.S. Warendorf, 17 February 1949, NIOD, Corresp. Archive Loe de Jong, 1948-1949, ser adv. Lies Keja, resistance fighter, fiercely turned against Norel's stereotypes and referred to the five Jewish founders of *Het Parool*, among whom Warendorf, adding that she

was the emphasis put by the district attorney on the fact that the Jews had demonstrated their combative spirit in Palestine.[14] So at this very moment, in the postwar Netherlands, one is confronted with 'the fighting Jew' in Palestine as the counterpart of 'the cowardly Jew'.

Norel was acquitted. The magistrate ruled that the challenged passages showed a 'lack of tact and had been wrongfully formulated in a generalising manner', but he did not think that they were proof of deliberate insult.[15] The sentence hinged on whether or not the insult had been deliberate. In April 1951, the case was heard on appeal. Once again, the case was surrounded with a lot of publicity, but his acquittal, sometime later, went largely unnoticed.[16]

Norel was certainly not the only resistance fighter to make dismissive statements about Jews, but there were also counter-voices in these circles.[17] In 1948, a member of the Dutch Organisation of Former Political Prisoners (Expogé) proposed to open the ranks to those persecuted because of their 'race'. 'Fascism' had tried to exterminate the Jews because of their being Jewish. Most members voted against the proposal. Jews could only join if they had been active in the resistance. 'Jews who were imprisoned only for being Jewish do not belong with us.'[18]

At best, going into hiding was rated as 'passive' resistance. The Dutch government also decided not to put Jewish people in hiding in the category

could name dozens of other Jews with whom she had worked during the occupation: *Het Vrije Volk*, 12 February 1948, NIOD, KB I 5145 (Klaas Norel); *see* De Keizer, *Het Parool 1940-1945*.

14   *Het Parool*, 18 February 1949, NIOD, KB I 5145.

15   *Ibid.*, 15 March 1949, NIOD, KB I 5145, *Trouw*, 3 March 1949. During the trial at the Amsterdam court, Van Lier was president, Kist was district attorney: *De Waarheid*, 18 February 1949; defence lawyer was W. de Vries: *Trouw*, 18 February 1949.

16   The final verdict was only reported by *De Waarheid*, 27 April 1951. *See also* Noord-Hollands Archief, Haarlem, Archief Gerechtshof Amsterdam, Archiefstuk 561-201, Arr. No. 468, Rolnr. 545/49. I thank Willem Wagenaar.

17   The Frisian former resistance fighter Abe Brouwer wrote in the same key as Norel in *Tusken Dea en Libben* [Between death and life] (Bolsward: Osinga, 1946). Already during the war resistance organisations made a distinction between those who were forced to hide for 'reasons of principle' and (in the negative sense) Jews: Ewoud Kieft, *Oorlogsmythen. Willem Frederik Hermans en de Tweede Wereldoorlog* (Amsterdam: De Bezige Bij, 2012), 256-257. The former resistance fighter (and Frisian) Anne de Vries sr. criticised the antisemitic attitude among his former comrades, himself included: Anne de Vries, 'Het opgejaagde volk.' In: K. Norel et al., *Den vijand wederstaan: Historische schetsen van de Landelijke Organisatie voor hulp aan onderduikers, landelijke knokploegen en centrale inlichtingendienst* (Wageningen: Zomer & Keuning, 1946), 23; *see* G.J. van Klinken, *Opvattingen in de Gereformeerde Kerken in Nederland over het Jodendom, 1896-1970* (Kok: Kampen, 1997), 440-442.

18   For this and other arguments: Gans, 'Vandaag hebben ze niets', 338.

of the 'persecuted'. This meant that Jews were not eligible for the 1947 Special Pension Law.[19] As from the Treaty of Luxemburg, in September 1952, the West German government started the *Wiedergutmachung,* a financial compensation scheme for those who had been persecuted by the Nazis because of their race, belief or world view. The scheme was primarily aimed at Jewish survivors – and also for *'14.000 Juden, die in der Illegalität haben leben müssen'* [14,000 Jews who were forced to live illegally].[20] But Expogé felt passed over and managed to put pressure on the Dutch government by exerting its moral authority. The former resistance fighters were converted into 'resistance victims' making them eligible for compensation. The total sum of money available, however, remained the same, so in order to keep the individual payments equally high the government decided to replace, surreptitiously, Jewish people in hiding for resistance people: a shameless exchange, according to the historian Hinke Piersma, who states that all 'solutions' worked out badly for the Jewish war victims.[21] It may seem remarkable that the resistance changed its image from 'fighter' to 'victim', but it also fits in with the phenomenon of victim competition. There were, of course, protests from the Jewish side. But, as often happened when Jews protested against the maintenance of rules perceived as disadvantageous or against the lack of compensation, they were reminded of their duty to be grateful for the assistance offered during the occupation.[22]

In most resistance novels, Jews play the part of helpless victims whose main role is to highlight the resistance's heroism.[23] In 1945, the Catholic novelist Antoon Coolen (1897-1961), who had been active in the literary resistance movement, described how he watched, with trepidation, a nightly round-up.[24] He was filled with disgust towards the Germans and with pity towards the Jews. But there was also another sentiment.

19   Hinke Piersma, *Bevochten recht. Politieke besluitvorming rond de wetten voor oorlogsslachtoffers* (Amsterdam: Boom, 2010), 29.
20   *Ibid.*, 93-94.
21   *Ibid.*, 93-94; 96; *Contactblad Stichting 1940-1945,* Fall 2010, 10-12.
22   Piersma, *Bevochten recht,* 97-98; Gans, 'Vandaag hebben ze niets', 332*ff*; Gans, 'Gojse broodnijd', 199.
23   Until 1947, Willy Corsari (1897-1998), Maurits Dekker (1896-1962) and Bert Voeten (1918-1992), among others, were representatives of this approach: Douwe Hettema, 'Nederlandse verzetshelden en joodse onderduikers. De Duitse bezetting in de romanliteratuur.' In: Conny Kristel (ed.), *Polderschouw. Terugkeer en opvang na de Tweede Wereldoorlog. Regionale verschillen* (Amsterdam: Bert Bakker, 2002), 355-377.
24   J. van Oudheusden et al. (eds.), *Brabantse biografieën. Levensbeschrijvingen van bekende en onbekende Noordbrabanders.* Vol. 2 (Amsterdam, Meppel: Uitgeverij Boom and Stichting

I am one of those who are no friends to the Jews. We have something against the bad manners of the race. But look at this, why does that group of Jews, so meekly gathered, stay on that nightly piece of pavement? They are guarded. And even if they were not guarded, they would probably still not dare to run.[25]

The conservative and idiosyncratic mayor of Gorinchem, L.R.J. Ridder van Rappard (1906-1994), had been fired by the Nazis for being one of the instigators of the protest against the large-scale *Arbeitseinsatz* of students and municipal staff in Germany. He had not taken a similar stand as regards the Jews. In his postwar memoir he wrote that he bitterly reproached himself for his failure to take preparatory measures to safeguard and rescue 'these threatened fellow-countrymen', let alone to actually save them. This lament however, was followed by the remark that 'far too many Jews, with astonishing acquiescence' had let themselves be taken to the slaughter.[26]

In 1950, the lawyer Abel Herzberg published the historical study *Kroniek der Jodenvervolging* [Chronicle of the Persecution of the Jews]. A year later, he published *Tweestromenland* [Between the Streams] the diary he had kept at the Bergen-Belsen concentration camp. In *Kroniek*, Herzberg voiced his opinion that the persecution of the Jews was not part of Dutch, but of Jewish and German history. According to the historian Conny Kristel, Herzberg thus declared the Dutch people collectively innocent of the persecution of the Jews.[27] And although several reviews did indeed think that the persecution of the Jews was a blot on the conscience of Dutch society, there were also reviews that agreed with Herzberg and completely ignored the responsibility of Dutch society.[28] These focused on the perpetrators – and on the victims. In reference to the high number of Jews killed, the newspaper *Heerenveense Koerier,* for instance, pointed out the Jewish disinclination to

Brabantse Regionale Geschiedbeoefening, 1994), quoted at: www.thuisinbrabant.nl/personen/c/ coolen,-antoon

25   Anton Coolen, *Bevrijd vaderland* (Rotterdam: Nijgh & Van Ditmar, 1945), 107. Photo round-up D Willinkplein: Gans, *Jaap en Ischa Meijer,* 205. Image library NIOD.

26   Peter Romijn, *Burgemeesters in oorlogstijd. Besturen tijdens de Duitse Bezetting* (Amsterdam: Balans, 2006), 468-472: 464. This concerns: L.J.R. Ridder van Rappard, *Hoe was het ook weer. Burgemeester voor, tijdens en direct na de bezetting van het Koninkrijk der Nederlanden in de Tweede Wereldoorlog* (Meppel: Boom, 1979).

27   Conny Kristel, *Geschiedschrijving als opdracht. Abel Herzberg, Jacques Presser en Loe de Jong over de jodenvervolging* (Amsterdam: Meulenhoff, 1998), 177, 241.

28   *Ibid.,* 241-242.

go into hiding: 'Many Jews who could have gone into hiding did not want to: out of fear, out of solidarity, out of inertia'.[29]

The reviews of *Tweestroomenland* also focused on the attitude of the Jews. *Het Volksweekblad* (edited by the Catholic Capuchins) praised Herzberg's factual description of 'that fighting, complaining, stealing community of concentration camp inhabitants'.[30] When the Catholic Teachers' Society St Bonaventura's weekly wrote that the book showed 'how the Jews there [in Bergen-Belsen] had made their camp life hell through their selfish fear', the left-wing weekly *De Groene Amsterdammer* accused the author of antisemitism.[31] In this case too, there were voices contradicting the image of the Jews as weak-willed, cowardly victims, and the camp inhabitants as devoid of solidarity and ethics.

The Jewish victim at the Eichmann Trial (1961)

The kidnapping of former ss *Obersturmbannführer* Adolf Eichmann in 1960 and his subsequent trial in Israel, in 1961, put the Jewish victims in the spotlight again, from various angles. Their attitude and position during the war and the occupation would be defended, bemoaned, denied and contemplated.

In the diverse literature on the dynamics of historiography and the memory of the war in and outside of the Netherlands, the Eichmann trial has been called a breakthrough: never before had the world been so explicitly confronted with the exceptional nature of the Nazi extermination politics and testimonial descriptions of it.[32] The horrific details about the annihilation of the Jews in Europe concentrated on the question of how it had been possible that this murder, preceded by systematic deprivation of rights and by deportation, had taken place. Although the trial first and foremost revolved around Eichmann's role in the organisation, the attention to the position of other people, directly or indirectly involved, spread out like an ink blot. 'Eichmann was not alone', was the significant motto of a meeting in Amsterdam on 12 April 1961.[33]

29   *Ibid.*, 241.
30   *Ibid.*, 240.
31   *Ibid.*
32   Frank van Vree, *In de schaduw van Auschwitz. Herinnering, beelden, geschiedenis* (Groningen: Historische Uitgeverij, 1995), 113.
33   *Het Vrije Volk*, 13 April 1961, NIOD, KB 1972 B.

The issue of whether or not non-Jewish Dutch people had acted weakly, indifferently or self-sacrificially first surfaced in 1961 and led to an infinite discussion, both in historiography and in the public debate.[34] It is equally important to note that the attention focused on the Jews, partly in the same way as it had, following Abel Herzberg's publications. In the process, the statement by former resistance fighter Klaas Norel – 'The Jews did not offer resistance to the pogroms' – was granted a new lease of life. This time the stereotype recurred in Israel as symbolised by the refrain of the question asked by the Israeli district attorney Gideon Hausner to the witnesses during the Eichmann trial: 'Why didn't you resist?'

It is relevant to take an interest in the extent and the manner of Jewish resistance during the Shoah as long as there is room for differentiation, reflection and analysis. A debate on 'Jewish resistance' does not necessarily have to result in blaming the victim – and with that, in many cases, in antisemitism. But if the fundamental question is whether the victims had 'sufficiently' resisted, we should be on our guard for the suggestion of the 'guilty victim', in part responsible for or guilty of his downfall.

A fierce international academic debate arose, in which the most famous Jewish participants, the Americans Raul Hilberg (1926-2007) and Hannah Arendt (1906-1975), opposed the Eastern Europeans Philip Friedmann (1901-1960) and Ben-Zion Dinur (1884-1973), on the issue of the existence and relevance of Jewish resistance and of the distinction between 'passive' and 'active' Jewish resistance.[35] Against this background – and partly preceding

34 Most recently, on the occasion of the publication of Bart van der Boom's book *Wij weten niets van hun lot. Gewone Nederlanders en de Holocaust* (Amsterdam: Boom 2012); Bart van der Boom, 'Ordinary Dutchmen and the Holocaust: a summary of findings.' In: Peter Romijn et al. (eds.), *The Persecution of the Jews in the Netherlands 1940-1945. New Perspectives* (Amsterdam: Vossiuspers UvA, 2012), 29-52; Evelien Gans and Remco Ensel, 'Wij weten iets van hun lot. Nivellering in de geschiedenis', *De Groene Amsterdammer*, 13 December 2012, 32-35; Remco Ensel and Evelien Gans, 'Wij weten iets van hun lot ii', *De Groene Amsterdammer*, 6 February 2013 (www.groene. nl/commentaar/2013-01-30/nederlanders-en-de-jodenvervolging); and Remco Ensel and Evelien Gans, 'De inzet van joden als "controlegroep". Bart van der Boom en de Holocaust', *Tijdschrift voor Geschiedenis* 126, 3 (2013), 388-396. *See* Christina Morina, 'The "Bystander" in recent Dutch historiography', *German History* 32, 1 (2013), 101-111. *See* chapter 13.

35 In his *The Destruction of the European Jews* (Chicago: Quadrangle Books, 1961), Hilberg made short shrift of the concept of 'passive' resistance, which, in his opinion, was a 'fatal and completely inadequate strategy against the National Socialist annihilation machine'. He even went as far as to speak of the 'role of the Jews in their own destruction'. Hence, he opposed Friedman and Ben-Zion Dinur who had interpreted a passive attitude during the Second World War as a form of spiritual resistance. In *Eichmann in Jerusalem* (New York: Viking Press, 1963), Hannah Arendt based her argument strongly on Hilberg, but did not concur with his opinions on 'Jewish acquiescence'. She put the blame – as far as the Jews were concerned – primarily on

it – Herzberg, Presser and De Jong also testified. All three – De Jong as the last one[36] – recognised the value of passive resistance, for instance fleeing and going into hiding, and the impossibility of armed resistance. 'How can you fight without weapons and surrounded by children and old and ill people?', Herzberg wrote as early as 1951.[37] In 1961, in an article in *Het Vaderland*, Presser made two statements about Jewish resistance in the Netherlands during the German occupation. The Germans overestimated their resistance as much as the Dutch underestimated it. Jewish resistance was proportionally larger than non-Jewish resistance.[38] In less cautious sentences, Presser formulated what Loe de Jong had written in the letter used as evidence in the trial against Norel. Later, historians would take Presser's statements as the point of departure for further research and would confirm them to a large extent. Moreover, the distinction between 'active' and 'passive' resistance is mostly surpassed and replaced by a considerably larger, more nuanced array of categories, as identified, for the Dutch context, by the historian Ben Braber in his study *This cannot happen here* (2013). Braber remarks that the lack of interest in Jewish resistance in Dutch historiography could be explained by the stubborn postwar image of the Jews as 'passive victims'.[39] In *Jewish Resistance against the Nazis* (2014), many facts, myths – like the one of the Jews led like sheep to the slaughter –, prejudices, omissions and distortions with regard to Jewish resistance are dealt with academically and on an international scale. One of many conclusions why the myth of Jewish passivity is so tough, despite being ahistorical, is that it

---

the Jewish leadership and the Jewish Councils. Hilberg and Arendt were subsequently attacked by a younger generation which sided with Friedman and Dinur; for instance the originally Polish historian Nathan Eck and the originally Lithuanian lawyer Jacob Robinson, who refused only to consider *armed* resistance as 'resistance': Kristel, *Geschiedschrijving als opdracht*, 122*ff*; see Ben Braber, *This cannot happen here. Integration and Jewish Resistance in the Netherlands, 1940-1945* (Amsterdam: Amsterdam University Press, 2013), 2-3.

36   In his evidence against Norel, De Jong had emphasised the relatively large contribution from the Jews to the resistance, but in *Koninkrijk*, he initially stressed the (historically developed) passive attitude of the Jews: Kristel, *Geschiedschrijving als opdracht*, 114.

37   *Ibid.*, 103.

38   *Het Vaderland*, 4 May 1961. *See* J. Presser, 'Het verzet van joden in Nederland 1940-1945.' In: Jacques Presser, *Schrijfsels en Schrifturen* (Amsterdam: Moussault, 1961), 138, 146; Presser, *Ondergang*, II: 5.

39   Braber, *This cannot happen here*, 8; see Gompes, *Fatsoenlijk land*, 11, 130. Internationally groundbreaking in the further elaboration, analysis and nuancing of the Jewish resistance were the historians Yehuda Bauer, Dan Michman and Michael Marrus: Braber, *This cannot happen here*, 3-5; see R. Rozett, 'Jewish Resistance.' In: D. Stone (ed.), *The Historiography of the Holocaust* (Basingstoke: Palgrave Macmillan, 2004), 341-363.

is 'more comfortable to blame the victim'.[40] The book tackles the question of what actions should *count* as resistance, emphasising all sort of 'passive' forms of resistance in dangerous and dead-end situations.[41] One article on Jewish resistance in the Netherlands mainly focuses on many various forms of 'active' Jewish resistance, varying from armed raids and killings of Nazis to providing hiding addresses.[42]

Although Presser paid ample attention to the solidarity demonstrated by the non-Jewish resistance, he also pointed out the ambivalent attitude of many fiercely anti-German resistance fighters. Not uncommonly, they had given their lives for their fatherland and for their Jewish fellow citizens, but were 'nonetheless openly Jew haters'.[43] Here, Presser publicly discussed antisemitism among resistance circles. In 1965, he would publish *Ondergang* [The destruction of the Dutch Jews] (1965). The book made a huge impact and would be more influential than the Eichmann trial because of its focus on the Netherlands – especially on the attitude of the non-Jewish Dutch population. In *Ondergang*, Presser wrote that it was easier to assume that the Jews meekly went to the slaughter, quietly accepting their fate, than to indicate 'the historical negligence of the Dutch people, so many of whom have left these Jews to their fate'.[44] Hence, the image of 'Jewish resignation' alleviated the sense of one's own shortcomings, according to Presser. Here, Presser exposed the phenomenon of blaming the victim and retorted the question of who was to blame to the Dutch non-Jews, who had taken a passive stance.

Moreover, just like Hannah Arendt[45] – and in opposition to Herzberg – Presser and De Jong were extremely negative about the role of the Jewish Council which had been established by the Nazis. In De Jong's opinion, by carrying out the most evil orders from the Germans, it had strengthened 'the image of the subservient, servile, cowardly Jew'. But any tendency contrary to this had remained hidden. 'The fact that Jews had contributed a very

---

40 Richard Middleton-Kaplan, 'The Myth of Jewish passivity.' In: Patrick Henry (ed.), *Jewish Resistance Against the Nazis* (Washington D.C.: The Catholic University of American Press, 2014), 3-26: 21-22. For this aspect of 'comfort' *see* Patrick Henry, 'Introduction. Jewish Resistance Against the Nazis.' In: *ibid.*, XIII-XXXVIII, and: Yehudi Lindeman and Hans de Vries, '"Therefore Be Courageous, Too." Jewish Resistance and Rescue in the Netherlands.' In: *ibid.*, 185-219: 218.

41 Berel Lang, 'Why Didn't They Resist More?' In: *ibid.*, 27-39: 30.

42 Lindeman and De Vries, '"Therefore Be Courageous, Too"', 187.

43 *Het Vaderland*, 4 May 1961.

44 Quoted in: Kristel, *Geschiedschrijving als opdracht*, 110.

45 Hannah Arendt, *Eichmann in Jerusalem. A Report on the Banality of Evil* (New York: Viking Press, 1963).

workable share to the illegality was only known to their fellow-resistance fighters.[46]

Here, three different historians *and* Jewish survivors struggled with the question: 'did they (the Jews, so at the same time: we, ourselves) resist, and if so, how?' The physician, psychiatrist, writer and Auschwitz survivor Elie Cohen (1909-1993) also testified to this struggle, when he reported on the Eichmann trial for the Dutch press. Cohen did not discuss the resistance in terms of 'active' or 'armed' versus 'passive', but of 'massive' versus 'individual' resistance. There had been a lot of individual resistance: some Jews had to be dragged from their homes, caught in hiding or gone on the run. Among the many factors that made massive resistance impossible, Cohen also included the question of whether the Jews could have expected 'sufficient support from the outside world'.[47] The Jews had no alternative to thinking 'things would turn out all right', for where should they expect deliverance? It is striking that Cohen took a stance against what he considered the short-sighted amazement in Israel during the Eichmann trial about the huge number of Jews who 'had been led to the slaughter without any resistance'. The Israelis should not forget that with their own government, president and army they formed a unity, especially after 1948, which had been completely out of reach for the Jews during the occupation.[48]

Under the influence of the extensive reporting on the Eichmann trial in the Dutch press, the broader public began to join the debate. In a letter to the editor of the liberal newspaper *Algemeen Handelsblad*, which had initially been fiercely anti-German during the occupation, an anonymous K.B. voiced his opinion that Jewish resistance would have been possible only in Amsterdam, where the largest number of Jews had been living. Instead of playing a leading part in that, the Jewish Council had assisted the Nazis in the execution of the anti-Jewish measures. The Council, and particularly its two Presidents (David Cohen [1882-1967] and Abraham Asscher [1880-1950]) had known that the 'emigration', as presented in the propaganda, would never materialise, but that the Jews were deported to camps to be killed.

---

46   De Jong, *Koninkrijk*, 7, 435-436. Later historiographers could judge more nuanced, characterising the Jewish Council as 'instrument and victim': Kristel, *Geschiedschrijving als opdracht*,
135*ff*; see Gompes, *Fatsoenlijk land*, 130.

47   *NIW*, 9 June 1961 NIOD, KB I 1976. Cohen mentioned further factors that made large-scale
resistance, hiding and flight impossible: the systematic misinformation by the Nazis, the lack
of capable Jewish leaders, the lack of weapons and of knowledge of the gas chambers, and the
responsibility towards their own relatives. *See also Het Parool*, 19 May 1961.

48   *NIW*, 9 June 1961.

They had facilitated this massacre in order to save their own lives.[49] There was a flood of criticism of the position and the role of the Jewish Council, but this was a very extreme expression of it. More important was that here, a normative criterion was born, that it so say whether one knew – or did not know – what fate lay in store for the Jews.[50]

The writer responded to an article on the Eichmann trial in the *Algemeen Handelsblad*, in which the newspaper had protested against the one-sided emphasis put by both Israeli judges and Dutch commentators on the question of whether the Jews had not offered resistance. According to the newspaper, this was a 'painful' – later it called it 'hurtful' – question that inflicted yet more feelings of guilt upon Jewish fellow-countrymen than they already had to deal with. Moreover, they had indeed joined the 'initially inexperienced resistance', and going into hiding had also been a form of resistance. The *Algemeen Handelsblad* also spoke out against naming the Jewish Council as the prime source of evil. Dutch civil servants had also stamped a 'J' on the identity cards, and tram and railway personnel had arranged transports.

> How often – out of fear – did the neighbours keep their doors shut, or did shopkeepers ensure that especially marked Jews did not enter their shops after curfew? Who was behaving like a lamb? That is the question that many should ask.[51]

Just as Presser had done, the *Algemeen Handelsblad* reversed the question: why had so few non-Jews offered assistance?[52] But as late as 2012, Professor of Criminology Alette Smeulders said, in her inaugural lecture at the University of Tilburg, that Hannah Arendt had been 'one of the first to point at the *fact* that the Jews had played a part in their own destruction'.[53]

---

49 *Algemeen Handelsblad*, 26 May 1961.

50 *See* note 35 and chapter 13.

51 *Algemeen Handelsblad*, 9 May 1961. In its reaction afterwards, the board of editors wrote that the order which the occupying powers had given the presidents of the Jewish Council was just as 'inhuman' as the whole situation in which the Jews found themselves: *Algemeen Handelsblad*, 26 May 1961.

52 In its reaction to K.B., the *Algemeen Handelsblad* board of editors wrote, among other things, that the Jews had been forced to make choices that could not be made by 'logical reasoning, a considered weighting': *Algemeen Handelsblad*, 26 May 1961.

53 Alette Smeulers, 'In opdracht van de staat: gezagsgetrouwe criminelen en internationale misdrijven.' Inaugural speech, Tilburg University, 27 April 2012, 7 (italics added). I thank Abram de Swaan. *See also* chapter 13.

In this debate there were readers who reacted, from different ends of the spectrum, to the, in their opinion, unbalanced reporting. Some thought that during the Eichmann trial, the Dutch resistance and the help offered to the Jews were underestimated. Others, to the tune of 'Eichmann was not alone', uttered scepticism about the size of the help and referred to a 'German-like: *Wir haben es nicht gewusst*'.[54] The latter statement was partly a reaction to another letter to the editor, in which the author wondered why, if so many Jews could not imagine what their fate would be, the non-Jews would not argue along similar lines? At the time, he himself had known nothing about a 'ruthless extermination' of the Jews. But he also admitted that, if the news had reached him, he would not have been willing to give credence to it. 'Possibly, there lies my guilt – our guilt.'[55] This caused a furious reaction that affirmed that everyone could have known the truth about the fate of the Jews.

> ... In heaven's name what else could one think, with these bestial transports taking place under everyone's eyes, of complete Jewish families, young and old, even from hospitals and institutions. Only the manner of the destruction was initially unknown.[56]

This writer, Dr F.J. Krop, followed Eli Cohen's argument about the attitude of many deported Jews: how could they '... contemplate an inevitable end without clutching at a straw: "It will not be as bad as all that"?' Possibly, 'We, their non-Jewish fellow-countrymen' could not face the truth either, because this would amount to the recognition that, individually and collectively, we have failed, for instance because of the risks to our own families. Here, Krop rebelled against both the absolute evaluation of 'knowing' ('Only the manner of the destruction was initially unknown') and the extenuating effect of comparing the possibilities, considerations and dilemmas of Jewish and non-Jewish Dutch people. The Jews had no other options than hoping

---

54   L. Boas in *Algemeen Handelsblad*, 17 May 1961, and J.M. de Cassières in *Vrij Nederland*, 25 June 1961. For an early Dutch usage (March, 1944) of the expression '*Wir haben es nicht gewusst*' (attributed to the Germans): Remco Ensel, *Haatspraak. Antisemitisme – een 21ᵉ-eeuwse geschiedenis* (Amsterdam: Amsterdam University Press, 2014), 118-119.

55   This was formulated in a way to suggest that the writer had indeed heard about the extermination, but had thought or tried to think that this was incorrect. 'We were inundated with propaganda. What was the truth?' *Algemeen Dagblad*, 20 April 1961. The letter was signed 'Oculus'.

56   *Algemeen Dagblad*, 22 April 1961.

for the best – while the non-Jews were first and foremost driven by fear for their own risks.

Making light of the Jewish resistance and the 'absence of knowledge' as forms of guilt alleviation and extenuation: these factors played a part in the debate – but the line of antisemitism was not crossed. This did happen in a column of a Belgian illustrated journal that could also be found in the Netherlands 'on many reading tables in cafes' – and caused fierce commentary.[57] The columnist in question posed the 'existential' question of how the human mind of the ss, but also of their victims, the Jews, could become so deformed. See, for instance, the Jew in the corpse-burning squad, who had to burn the bodies of the gassed Jews, including those of his own two daughters: 'I am convinced that I would have refused to do that .... You can hang me, my friend. Rather that, than wasting the last shimmer of human dignity.' That also applied to the orchestra of sixty Jewish musicians who played while the 'death squad' went to work, not to mention what one knew from the earlier trials: Jewish kapos were 'often more ruthless than the ss themselves'.[58]

As victims, Jews could fill people with aversion in two ways: as passive and cowardly, or conversely as at least as bad as their persecutors. The article in *De Post* did not meet with sympathy, though, at least openly. The Eichmann trial engendered a stronger awareness of involvement in the Dutch population with regard to the persecution of the Jews, but one could ask oneself whether this also yielded more insight into the position and mental world of the witnesses – and with them, of the Jews as persecuted people. The political scientist Ido de Haan (b. 1963) states that this is not the case: the testimony was predominantly experienced as painful.[59]

And there, or perhaps therefore, manifested itself also the phenomenon of underplaying the role of Eichmann and levelling out (in Dutch: *nivelleren*) the attitude of victim, bystander and perpetrator, as had happened in *De Post* – albeit more subtly. In the progressive, sophisticated weekly *Hollands*

57 According to the writer Simon Carmiggelt in a column in which he pointed to an antisemitic approach in the same period, also in *De Post*, but in another issue: *Het Parool*, 4 May 1961.

58 *De Post*, 14 May 1961.

59 Ido de Haan, *Na de ondergang. De herinnering aan de jodenvervolging in Nederland, 1945-1995* (The Hague: Sdu, 1999), 180-181. In reference to the bystanders, De Haan refers to what the historian Bart van der Boom would later call the 'myth of the guilty bystander', *see* Remco Ensel and Evelien Gans, 'We know something of their fate. Bart van der Boom's history of the Holocaust in the Netherlands.' By now, two biographies of Adolf Eichmann have definitively established that he was a convinced and fanatic antisemite: David Cesarini, *Eichmann. His Life and Crimes* (London: Heinemann, 2004) and Bettina Stangneth, *Eichmann Before Jerusalem: The Unexamined Life of a Mass Murderer* (New York: Alfred A. Knopf, 2014).

Weekblad a barbed polemic ensued about the person of Eichmann. True to the view of Eichmann being just a cog in the Shoah machinery, one author stated that he himself could also have been an Eichmann. Many 'loves' could induce a man to sit behind a desk and become a murderer. One could even feel guilty when one wasn't. The suspect was exchangeable.[60] He gained support, but was also harshly criticised by well-known publicists like Aad Nuis (1933-2007) and Renate Rubinstein (1929-1990). Nuis sneered that Roukens (the author) had discovered that 'there lurked a beast in everyone'.[61] When Roukens defended himself against the reproach of not identifying with the Jews, arguing that he hadn't gone through what they had, Rubinstein threw him this one-sided identification in his face. According to her, most people had such an 'instinctive aversion to the victims of horrible deeds' that they preferred to forget them, adding that applying your ability to identify only to those of your own kind was a form of antisemitism.[62]

From cowardly to courageous to cruel

In 1949, during the court case against Klaas Norel, the district attorney had pointed out that, in Palestine, the Jews had shown their combative spirit.[63] The Protestant newspaper *Trouw* had even reported that on the question of whether the Jews were 'heroes', the events in Palestine had given a clear answer.[64] As stated earlier, one could interpret those sayings as counter-images of the stereotype of the meek Jew presented by Norel and others.

Beyond that, however, directly after the liberation, albeit sporadically, a more extreme counter-image of the cowardly Jew, the cruel Jew, turned up, mainly in more or less fundamentalist Catholic, and in pro-Arab, mostly academic, circles. These two circles seem to have been interconnected and mainly targeted the Jews fighting in Palestine – the so-called Zionists –,

---

60 *Hollands Weekblad* 3, 163 (20 December 1961). In this context Roukens, probably the Catholic folklore scholar Winand Roukens (1896-1974), mentioned a whole list of 'loves': 'love for science, technology, the nation, freedom, the system, a father, a religion, even for a distant relative who will become a victim of our work; because he does the same work as we do, but happens to be born in a different region'.

61 *Hollands Weekblad* 37, 29 December 1961.

62 *Vrij Nederland*, 3 February 1962; quoted in: *Hollands Weekblad* 141, 14 February 1962.

63 *Het Parool*, 18 February 1949, NIOD, KB I 5145.

64 *Trouw*, 18 February 1949.

the nascent Jewish state, and afterwards the state of Israel, founded in May 1948. An example of this pattern was a report by the Christian (Protestant) weekly *De Spiegel* on the journey of the *Exodus*, the ship that openly, and against the British Mandate authorities' rules, tried to (illegally) transport Jewish immigrants to Palestine. The *Exodus* initiative was meant both as a serious attempt to bring motivated Jewish survivors to the place they wanted to but were not yet allowed to go, as well as a pro-Zionist strategy to force a breakthrough in the restrictive British immigration policy. With regard to the latter *De Spiegel* didn't shrink from calling the '*Exodus* stunt' in 1947 '*Goebbeliaans*' (after the Third Reich Minister of Propaganda, Joseph Goebbels). The same article also accused the Jews of 'Eastern cruelty', having killed two British soldiers.[65] Actually, the Dutch Government had been late in recognising Israel, de facto in January 1949 and de jure a year later. The main reason was that they tried (in vain) to prevent the independence of their colony, the Dutch Indies, through military means while, at the same time, they didn't want to insult the mainly Islamic Indonesian independence movement and population by recognising a Jewish ('Zionist') state.[66]

The real giant in the background, however, was the Vatican. On the basis of the replacement theology (i.e. Christianity is the only legitimate successor and substitute of and for Judaism) the Jews no longer held any right to the Holy Land, the Church itself being the 'new Israel'. The Vatican also worried about the position of the Palestinian refugees, among those of Christian belief. All this was accompanied by explicitly antisemitic language and stereotypes, broadcasted by Radio Vaticana. Revengeful Jews would be able to use their 'economic preponderance, their nearly mystic expansionism and the almost total denial of the wishes of others, which characterises the Zionists as a group'. These and similar utterances culminated in a statement by the Vatican, issued on 9 November 1949, calling Zionism a 'sort of Nazism'.[67]

---

65   *De Spiegel*, 4 October 1947.
66   For the developments in the relationship between the Netherlands and Israel, R.B. Soeten-dorp, *Het Nederlandse beleid ten aanzien van het Arabisch-Israëlisch conflict 1947-1977* (Meppel: Krips Repro, 1982); R.B. Soetendorp, 'The Netherlands and Israel: from a special to a normal relationship', *Internationale Spectator* 43 (November 1989), 697-700; Fred Grünfeld, *Nederland en het Nabije Oosten. De Nederlandse rol in de internationale politiek ten aanzien van het Arabisch-Israëlisch conflict 1973-1982* (Deventer: Kluwer, 1991); Frans Peeters, *Gezworen vrienden. Het geheime bondgenootschap tussen Nederland en Israël* (Amsterdam, Antwerp: L.J. Veen, 1997).
67   Marcel Poorthuis and Theo Salemink, *Een donkere spiegel. Nederlandse katholieken over joden. Tussen antisemitisme en erkenning 1870-2005* (Nijmegen: Valkhof, 2006), 533-534.

In the Netherlands, Catholic institutions and media generally followed their Mother Church. In his 'Prayer for Palestine', Archbishop Jan de Jong (1885-1955) advocated a 'spiritual crusade' in favour of the preservation of Palestine. In 1949, the Dutch Catholic Church founded the Pro Palestine Committee.[68] The pivot of this Committee was the Dominican J.P.M. van der Ploeg (1909-2004) who later became Professor of Biblical Studies at the Catholic University of Nijmegen. His anti-Zionism already originated from before the war when he wrote a pamphlet called *Het Joodsche Vraagstuk. Een maatschappelijk probleem* [The Jewish Question. A Social Problem] (February 1940), in which he not only condemned Zionism, but also typified Jews as representatives of a dangerous modernity, making use of several antisemitic stereotypes. Jews were atheists, perverts (with only a small number of children) and possessed traits like noisiness and lack of modesty.[69] He was the one who shortly after the creation of Israel, in 1949, in a letter to a priest had condemned Zionism as 'a new sort of Nazism' as well as an ideology of 'colonisation connected to theft and murder'. The priest, Toon Ramselaar (1899-1981), one of the later founders of the Catholic Council for Israel, rejected Van der Ploeg's statements – demonstrating that there were other opinions within more enlightened Catholic circles.[70] But in general, for quite some time the Catholic milieu remained more reluctant than others to embrace Israel.

The change came at the Second Vatican Council, or Vatican II (1962-1965). This unique assembly of representatives of the Church was established to address a number of urgent issues in the postwar modern world. One of these pressing matters certainly was the relationship of the Catholic Church and of Catholics towards Judaism and Jews. After long deliberations the assembly agreed on a document, *Nostre Aetate* (1965), in which it was established that Jews could not be held responsible for the crucifixion of Christ. The Jewish roots of Christianity were furthermore recognised and the Covenant between God and the people of Israel was no longer denied. The age-old designation of Jews as 'perfidious' was removed. The Pope declared himself against antisemitism directed 'against Jews at any time and by anyone'. The text, however, reveals a certain disunity. The 'principle' of Jewish deicide was not abjured or renounced. *Nostre Aetate* still said that, at the time, the Jewish authorities and their

---

68 *Ibid.*, 355, 535. It was, for that matter, also De Jong, who, in 1942, had openly protested against the persecution of the Jews: *ibid.*, 497.
69 *Ibid.*, 477-479.
70 *Ibid.*, 541. This 'Katholieke Raad voor Israël' was founded in 1951: *ibid.*, 538.

followers had insisted on the death of Christ, but that what had been done to Him 'cannot be charged against all the Jews, without distinction, then alive, nor against the Jews of today'.[71] So Vatican II did not solve all dilemmas or rub off all sensibilities. The Holocaust and the foundation of Israel remained delicate questions. An interesting detail is that quite some converted Jews would be closely associated with the materialisation of *Nostre Aetate*.[72]

A striking controversy took place in the, in itself polemic, student journal *Propria Cures* (*PC*) in 1958. This happened two years after the Suez Crisis when, following the Egyptian nationalisation of the Suez Canal, France, England and Israel attacked Egypt, but had been blown the whistle on by the United States. By then, the Dutch government stood solidly behind Israel.[73] Openly critical stances against the Jewish state were rare. In *PC*, the medical student A. Verhagen stated that, as far as he was concerned, Israel didn't have to disappear into the sea, but that the arrogant Zionism should disappear. Verhagen openly declared to be an anti-Zionist, belonging to the *'Arabo-phielen'* – and a Catholic. He had connections with the *Nederlands-Arabische Kring* [Dutch Arab Circle] and appeared to be well-informed on several issues. He debunked a number of Zionist myths like the one that the around 750,000 Arabs who had left Palestine had done so voluntarily after being called to do so by Radio Cairo and against the wish of the Jewish population. Contrary to what was told, Israel had had, at least from June 1948 onwards, a military dominance thanks to arms supplied by the Soviet bloc. He mentioned the bloodbath in the Palestinian village Deir Yassin, brought about by the Israeli army. According to Verhagen, the Palestinians had fallen victim to feelings of guilt, which were actually legitimate, by the 'civilised world'.[74]

---

71   Declaration on the relation of the Church to non-Christian Religions proclaimed by His Holiness Pope Paul VI on October 28, 1965, www.vatican.va/archive/hist_councils/ii-vatican_council/documents/vat-ii_decl_19651028_nostra-aetate_en.html (consulted on 23 July 2012). For the debunking of the Jews as the initiators of the crucifixion of Christ in Biblical times: Marvin Perry and Frederick Schweitzer, *Antisemitism. Myth and Hate from Antiquity to the Present* (New York: Palgrave Macmillan 2002), 17.

72   John Connelly, 'From enemy to brother.' A lecture on the international conference *The Jew as legitimation*, Menasseh Ben Israël Instituut, Amsterdam, 29 August 2013 (to be published); John Connelly, *From enemy to brother. The revolution in Catholic teaching on the Jews, 1933-1965* (Cambridge, MA: Harvard University Press, 2012); Remco Ensel, *Haatspraak*, 53; Remco Ensel, 'Katholieke kabouters en pro-Palestijns protest in Nederland', 1 March 2015 (unpublished).

73   *See* chapter 6.

74   A.R.H.B. Verhagen, 'Israël de zee in?', *Propria Cures*, 3 May 1958. Verhagen was right, according to the Israeli historian Avi Shlaim. In the very first phase of the war the Israeli army

Several of his views have been confirmed, later, since the 1980s, by New Historians in Israel such as Bennie Morris and Tom Segev.[75] Verhagen's Jewish opponents, however, trusted the information which reached them via Israeli media and the BBC, which had, for example, mentioned the Arab League's message to cause a 'momentous massacre' in Israel and the fact that in Haifa the Jewish population had urged the Arabs to stay. They called Deir Yassin a shameful case of Jewish terrorism, condemned by the well-thinking part of Israel's Jewish population, but also (unlike Verhagen) mentioned the bloodbath in Kfar Etzion, where 120 Jews had been murdered, about as many Palestinian victims as in Deir Yassin. Against Verhagen's denial of the Jews' historical right on Israel they claimed the decision of the United Nations in 1947 which formed the basis of Israel's right to exist. It was Israel's most ardent wish to have peace with its neighbours, on the condition and understanding that 'a historical process could be interpreted according to one's own wishes, but was not reversible'.[76] This was, for them, the crux that Verhagen, however, did not accept.

Some of Verhagen's opponents wrote that after the Second World War there no longer existed an anti-Zionist grouping worth mentioning among the Jewish people: thus, differentiating between anti-Zionism and anti-Jewish had become impossible – a statement which is, still, highly controversial. Verhagen, in a retort, voiced the complaint that there were Zionists who, by calling their opponents 'antisemites', practised terror in favour of Israel.[77] Did Verhagen express himself in an antisemitic way? In some cases he did. Strikingly, he emphasised the money that Jews used to get hold of, in the past, but now in Israel too. The Jews were actually *'steppenzwervers'* [steppe tramps] who, after the Babylon Exile, stuffed grasshoppers and made 'money and proselytes'. Most conspicuously was that Verhagen could not resist the urge to refer, on several occasions, to the Nazi ideology and practices. He wrote that the false 'Jewish propaganda'

was under-armed, but this changed after the arrival of Czech arms. From the start, Israel had more armed men (and women) than the mutually divided and badly coordinated Arab armies: Avi Shlaim, 'Israel and the Arab Coalition in 1948.' In: Eugene Rogan and Avi Shlaim (eds.), *The War for Palestine: Rewriting the United States and the Israeli-Palestinian Conflict History of 1948* (Cambridge: Cambridge University Press, 2001), 79-103.

75   An important study on (the debate about) the changing historical image and narratives with regard to Israel and Zionism: Laurence Silberstein, *Postzionism debates. Knowledge and power in Israeli culture* (London: Routledge, 1999). For Morris and Segev: *ibid.*, 96-102.

76   H.R. Eyl, 'De oliebronnen van Verhagen', *Propria Cures*, 10 May 1958; A.S. Reiner and H.J. Kisch, 'Verhagen de pekel in?', *Propria Cures*, 10 May 1958.

77   A.R.H.B. Verhagen, 'Terreur', *Propria Cures*, 17 May 1958.

caused a kind of irritation of which one had been sick and tired during the (German) occupation. Military successes were not pragmatically analysed, but attributed to Jewish superiority towards the Arabs, to an *'Übermensch-idylle'* – he spoke of a 'Blitzkrieg'. In fact, the Israeli successes were based on 'the same foundation as those of the Nazis'. Deir Yassin and similar massacres showed a similarity with *'Nazi-atrociteiten'* [Nazi atrocities].[78]

Verhagen's most fierce antagonist was the American-born Michael Chayes – also a medical student and one of the editors of PC. Chayes made some sharp observations, blaming Verhagen of using the 'well-known stereotype of the rich Jews', attacking him hard about his comparison between the Israelis and the Nazis and referring to literature and documentaries on the Holocaust. Moreover, he wasn't afraid to admit that there 'are bad things done in Israel', but what did Verhagen expect? 'You may have started out expecting the Jews to be "Übermenschen" ... but ... I don't think they're better or worse than most people in the world'.[79] According to Chayes, Jews were no saints, but wanted their own land, self-respect and respect from others. He himself, however, showed no respect for his opponent, calling him the prototype of the 'little antisemite', the *'ingekankerde'* [inveterate] antisemite '... without whose support the leaders could never execute their hideous plans', but especially by exposing him as a frustrated Catholic. 'I'm going to CRUCIFY you'. He wished Verhagen's blood would wash away the sins of 'All Race Haters'.[80] It was mainly because of this anti-Catholic outburst that the other PC editors felt compelled to distance themselves from Chayes, with whom they actually sympathised.[81]

Chayes' final explosion can be typified as an example of extreme anti-antisemitism – even of anti-goyism.[82] At the same time, he and other

78 Verhagen, 'Israël de zee in?'.
79 Michael Chayes, 'Just a Jew-hater', *Propria Cures*, 17 May 1958. Capitals in the text by Chayes himself.
80 *Ibid.*
81 T. Sontrop, H. Brandt Corstius, H.U. Jesserun d'Oliveira and H. Leupen, 'Tegen een over-slaande stem', *Propria Cures*, 24 May 1958. For other reactions, *see ibid.*, 17, 24 and 31 May 1958, and: 'Het slot erop' (De Redactie), *Propria Cures*, 14 June 1985.
82 The term anti-antisemitism is mostly used to express the struggle and actions against (supposed) antisemitism. Anti-goyism is a much more complicated concept. It is used by Jews and non-Jews to criticise Jews who are convinced of their own Jewish (for example) moral and intellectual superiority and harbour contempt against non-Jews *as* non-Jews (Gentiles). But the term is also used as an antisemitic or dubious 'trick': disposing legitimate Jewish criticism as 'anti-goyism'.

critics of Verhagen can be considered as the forerunners of a new Jewish
generation in the early 1970s, which, unlike Abel Herzberg's generation,
would put up a fight, openly and decidedly, against anything and anybody
they considered antisemitic.[83] And with respect to Israel, the polemic in
PC, which went on for weeks, can serve in many ways as an early model
for a dialogue of the deaf which would, in many variations, recur in the
Netherlands (and elsewhere) countless times – often with fixed political,
historical, emotional and, in the long run, sometimes nearly ritualised
arguments.

Finally, it could happen that in 1969, nine years after the opening of
the Anne Frank House, Anne Frank, by then the icon of Jewish suffering,
was not only ridiculed, but even turned into a perpetrator in the, again,
very polemical magazine for the progressive, unruly youth, *Aloha.* Alive
and kicking, hiding in a convent, living on the profits of her diary, she
told her readers – in a fictitious interview – that it was exactly the Jewish
spinelessness that had caused 'us, Jews' so much misery. No more of that
anymore. She had realised it was her duty to actively support Israel's cause,
mobilising Dutch Jews for the war against the 'Arab danger' and establishing
military training camps for the Jewish youth. Anne was thinking of setting
up her headquarters in the Anne Frank House in Amsterdam. 'The tourists
could keep coming quietly', but all proceeds would from now on be put 'in
our arms fund'.[84]

Now *Aloha* was a satirical magazine and explicitly wanted to push the
boundaries. But putting words in Anne Frank's mouth in such a manner
can be seen as crossing those boundaries: 'Immediately marching on to
Cairo, blow up the pyramids, filling up the whole Nile valley and putting
all those hashish smokers in their tent dresses to the sword.'[85] In one,
albeit satirical, article Jews were, again, pictured as cowards, responsible
for their own misery, then financially profiting from this misery, and
finally as racists who wanted to get rid of the Arab 'tent dressers' most
violently.

83   *See* chapters 4, 6, and 9.

84   Quoted in: *Het Parool,* 19 December 1969. *Aloha* was the successor, in 1969, of the alternative
music journal *Hitweek.* The form of a fictitious interview proved to be popular: in January 1993
it returned in the Groninger student journal *Nait Soez'n.* In this case Anne Frank lived on in
Argentina as a transsexual. The author's motive was to denounce the 'prostitution' of the Jewish
genocide in order to legitimate the violation of human rights: Gans, *Gojse nijd,* 78-79. The author,
Peter Middendorp, still defended his article in 2014: *de Volkskrant,* 1 November 2014.

85   *Ibid.*

Note that this happed in 1969, two years after the Six-Day (or June) War which had turned Israel into an occupying force. The year 1967 would prove to be a turning point after which the Israeli military and administrative policies towards the Palestinians would be weighted more and more against Jewish victimhood in general and during the Second World War specifically. This could culminate in the reversal of victim and perpetrator. On the one hand, the stereotype of the cowardly Jew would pale in comparison with the stereotype of the belligerent, blood-thirsty Jew in Israel. On the other, the stereotype of the passive, resigned Jew, especially during the Nazi occupation, would never wholly disappear and even revive in recent Dutch historiography about the Second World War and the Shoah[86] – this is the Janus face of 'the Jew'.

86 *See* chapter 13.

4   *Alte Kameraden*

Right-wing Antisemitism and Holocaust Denial

Remco Ensel, Evelien Gans and Willem Wagenaar

After 1945, more than 100,000 Dutch were imprisoned on suspicion of treason, aiding the enemy, joining a foreign army, personal enrichment or acts of violence.[1] Many were detained in camps without a clear notion of the legal consequences. In this legal no man's land guards could act independently and take violent and humiliating sanctions against prisoners.[2] An alleged target of this (partly) private justice was Meinoud Rost van Tonningen, virulent antisemite, prominent member of the National Socialist Movement (NSB), MP and chairman of the Dutch National Bank during the occupation. After the war, his wife, F.S. (Florrie) Rost van Tonningen-Heubel (1914-2007), embarked on a personal campaign to prove that her husband had been terrorised and either killed in imprisonment or driven to commit suicide. There is no evidence for this allegation, says Van Tonningen's biographer David Barnouw, but the widow's campaign does reflect a broad-based, deeply-felt sense of injustice among 'war veterans' and political delinquents. 'Black Widow Rost van Tonningen' became a key figure in one of these small groups of 'war veterans' as well as an icon of the persistent yet marginal presence of National Socialism in postwar Dutch society.[3] In 1969, the Dutch public was first introduced to this stately lady and her posh accent in a documentary on Anton Mussert, leader of the NSB, by the starting director Paul Verhoeven (b. 1938).[4] More media appearances ensued. Rost van Tonningen consistently played down the Holocaust, praising Adolf Hitler, expressing resentment about the handling of her husband and complaining about the incessant misreading of the honest intentions of her ideological

---

1   J. S. Hoek, *Politieke geschiedenis van Nederland. Oorlog en herstel* (Leiden: A.W. Sijthoff, 1970), 195-226.

2   Heleen Grevers, *Van landverraders tot goede vaderlanders: de opsluiting van collaborateurs in Nederland en België, 1944-1950* (Amsterdam: Balans, 2013): 'These camps circumvented the controlling power of justice and subsequently developed into closed institutions where at some locations inmates were treated violently.'

3   David Barnouw, *Rost van Tonningen. Fout tot het bittere eind* (Amsterdam: Walburg Pers, 1994).

4   *Portret van Anton Adriaan Mussert* (direction Paul Verhoeven, 1968).

**Illustration 6   Photo of a protest against the pension for the neo-nazi widow of a
nazi in The Hague, 27 November 1986**

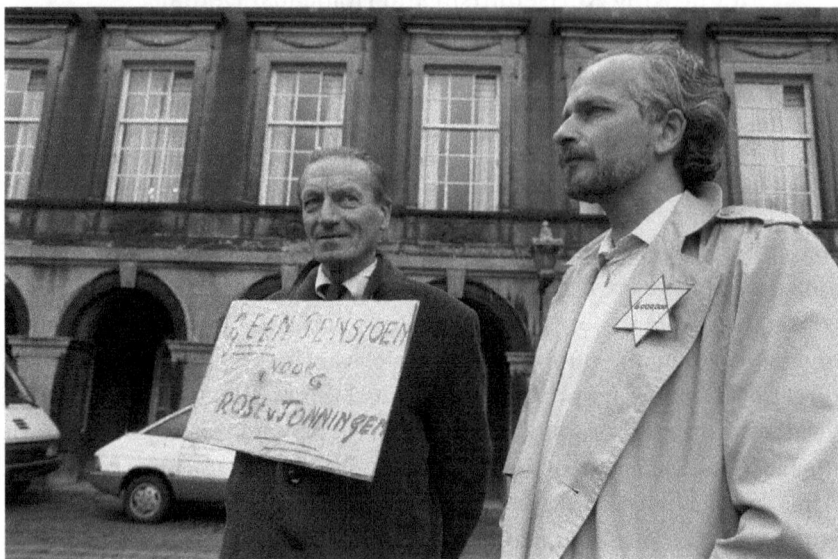

C. Croes / Anefo / Nationaal Archief, 27 November 1986

In 1986, debate and protest arose when it became known that F.S. (Florrie)
Rost van Tonningen-Heubel (1914-2007), the widow of a major Dutch Nazi and
a prominent neo-Nazi and distributor of neo-Nazi publications in her own
right, received a widow's pension because of her husband's parliamentary
seat before the war.

kin. Her villa *Ben Trovato* in the small town of Velp became a meeting place
for neo-Nazis and Flemish nationalists. Under the name *'Consortium De
Levensboom'* ('The Tree of Life Consortium'), the villa doubled up as the
distribution centre of publications about neo-Nazism and Holocaust denial,
including *Die Auschwitz-Lüge* by Thies Christophersen, published in 1973.
Rost van Tonningen was handed several convictions for distributing these
publications as well as for the publication of her autobiography.

    Thanks to her extravagance and elitist diction, the 'black widow' seemed
able to neutralise the weight of postwar neo-Nazism. As if by celebrating
the summer solstice – big news in 1983 – Nazism became German folklore
celebrated by naive people. Her behaviour, however, in actual fact revealed
the relationship between first-generation Nazi sympathisers, many of whom

had been tried after the war, and a new generation of neo-Nazis. Her closest opponents have always taken her seriously and persisted in obstructing her propaganda activities.

This chapter addresses the effects of wartime National Socialism and antisemitism. It focuses on the first postwar decades and briefly touches upon the post-1970 period.

Political delinquents

In the late 1940s and early 1950s, after their release, those who had been imprisoned because of their National Socialist sympathies and aiding the enemy started to look each other up again. The activists among them saw themselves as the losers of the war, but also as victims of their political opponents. There was a strong sense of injustice. Those who were ideologically engaged had, in their view, genuinely tried to create a better society and had, hence, been unfairly punished after the war as traitors, profiteers or accomplices to genocidal violence. The delinquents were rather nostalgic about the occupation period.[5] In a way the sense of community and the drive to reorganize among certain sympathizers of the NSB, former collaborators and delinquents was mirrored in the spirit of solidarity among resistance fighters in postwar society (even though very soon differences of opinion became manifest). Equally postwar justice, i.e. debates about requests for pardon for convicted war criminals or resentment about class justice – 'the bigwigs are not addressed', led to a lot of emotions throughout the whole of society.[6]

After a difficult time in prison, most political delinquents withdrew in shame or for fear of their past being revealed. Others organised themselves in newly founded organisations to let off steam and enable others to fight for a revival of National Socialism.[7] Initially the *Alte Kameraden* collided with

5   These feelings are extensively addressed in the widow's autobiography: F.S. Rost van Tonningen-Heubel, *Op zoek naar mijn huwelijksring* (Erembodegem: De Krijger, 1993).
6   Ido de Haan, *Na de ondergang. De herinnering aan de jodenvervolging in Nederland, 1945-1995* (The Hague: Sdu, 1999). Especially the imprisonment and partly release of the so-called Four, later Three of Breda (among whom were German chief of the SD, Willy Lages, and the officer responsible for the deportations, Ferdinand aus der Fünten) yielded much public debate: Hinke Piersma, *De drie van Breda. Duitse oorlogsmisdadigers in Nederlandse gevangenschap, 1945-1989* (Amsterdam: Balans, 2005).
7   Ismee Tames, *Doorn in het vlees. Foute Nederlanders in de jaren vijftig en zestig* (Amsterdam: Balans, 2013), 102.

the widespread aversion against NSB members as traitors and so-called '*foute Nederlanders*' [Dutch who had been on the 'wrong' side during the war]. Subsequently revulsion about the Holocaust became an obstacle to their ambition of reviving their political objectives, as the historian Ismee Tames notes in her study about 'Wrong Dutchmen in the 1950s and 1960s'. Tames describes the different strategies adopted by former political delinquents to 'neutralise' the Holocaust.[8] Former delinquents referred, for example, to the miserable conditions in which 'wrong Dutchmen' had lived in the internment camps. In an attempt to taint the moral purity of those who had, allegedly, chosen the 'good side', they also pointed to the Allied bombings. The number of victims and the suffering caused by these bombings almost equalled the 'abuses' on the German side. Another strategy was to deny their role in the destruction of the Jews. Finally, some played down or flatly denied the Holocaust.

The first viable organisation was the *Stichting Oud Politieke Delinquenten* (SOPD), founded in 1951 to provide individual and collective support to its members, for example former prisoners who had lost their pension entitlements. The anthropologist Jaap van Donselaar (b. 1953) characterised the SOPD as a 'precursor of a political party with a National Socialist foundation'.[9] The authorities kept a close and suspicious eye on the organisation, as they did on all initiatives and organisations founded by former 'wrong' Dutch. In 1958, for example, the police in Amsterdam kept an eye out for two former political delinquents released from prison. The first one was former radio propagandist G.P. Smis (1898-1969), the author of, among other works, the populist novel *De smederij bij den Westertoren* [The Smithy at the Western Tower] (1942), which contained anti-Jewish elements. The other was Sam Oly, a policeman who had reported many Jews to the Germans. Allegedly, the two were planning to publish a book about the idealism of Dutch National Socialists, including strong criticism of postwar justice.[10]

1953 saw the founding of the *Nationaal Europese Sociale Beweging* (NESB) with Jan Aksel Wolthuis (1933-1983) and Paul van Tienen (1921- ca. 1994) as its flag bearers. During the war, Wolthuis had been a supporter of Rost van Tonningen's radical antisemitic and so-called *Völkisch* National Socialist wing within the NSB. As a member of the Waffen-SS, Van Tienen had fought

8   Tames, *Doorn in het vlees*, 58.

9   Jaap van Donselaar, *Fout na de oorlog. Fascistische en racistische organisaties in Nederland, 1950-1990* (Amsterdam: Bert Bakker, 1991), 50. The SPODs precursor was Comité 1945-1950.

10   *Het Vrije Volk*, 18 September 1958. The book has indeed been written, in various versions, but it was never published. The manuscript, titled *Peccavi, arm vaderland*, is held by the Letterkundig Archief in The Hague.

on the Eastern Front. One sympathiser claimed that, as a young member of the Waffen-SS, Van Tienen had witnessed the conquest of the Ukrainian town Lviv.[11] If this is correct, it is very well possible that Van Tienen took part in the *razzias* (Nazi raids) and massacres of Jews in that city in June 1941.[12] Or at the least that he must have known about it. While Van Tienen and Wolthuis presented themselves as outright neo-Nazis, the NESB only implicitly referred to the Nazi ideology. Their texts contained words like *landverhuizing* [emigration] and 'emigration policy' (instead of *Lebensraum*), 'family and population policy' (and not race policy), 'social peace', *'indamming van de vakbonden'* [containment of the trade unions] and the creation of *'beroepsgemeenschappen'* [professional communities], thus avoiding the word 'corporatism' and openly declaring war to the parliamentary democracy; and finally a 'national' and 'social' Europe (a veiled reference to the Third Reich) as a third power between the 'East' (communism) and 'West' (capitalism). This veiled language served the movement's goal to run in the parliamentary elections. The party's principles did not mention anti-semitism – but they did mention the aim of removing the Ambonese (from the former Dutch East Indies) from Dutch society. This explicit xenophobia was a precursor of the radical right-wing focus on Mediterranean migrant workers in the 1970s. Within the NESB there was a silent agreement not to mention 'the Jewish question' during meetings and in public. But it was on the agenda: 'Why would you stress something that is blatantly obvious?', said one former member of the NESB.[13] The members knew where they stood. It was not necessary to express anti-Jewish feelings.

The authorities responded with a swift legal reaction, house searches, arrests and a court case. Eventually, the Supreme Court banned the organisation in 1956, after a long and erratic legal procedure, on the ground of the *Besluit Ontbinding Landverraderlijke Organisaties* [Resolution concerning the Dissolution of Treasonable Organisations]. The course of justice revolved around the question whether the new NESB was a continuation of the old NSB, in line with their similar names. NESB's works lacked any mention of antisemitism. Was this political opportunism, as Van Donselaar suggested

11   E. Peijster, Paul van Tienen, en...., *Mededelingen van Actie De Vrije Richting* – The Hague (Extra Edition) (probably published late August 1966; this on the basis of a letter and report by the BVD (national security service) to the Ministry of Internal Affairs, 23 September 1966), 10-11: 10.

12   *See* Saul Friedländer, *The Years of Extermination. Nazi Germany and the Jews, 1939-1945* (New York: Harper & Collins, 2007); Karel C. Berkhoff, *Motherland in Danger. Soviet Propaganda during World War II* (Cambridge MA, London: Harvard University Press, 2012), 152, 224.

13   Van Donselaar, *Fout na de oorlog*, 68; Tames, *Doorn in het vlees*, 112.

in his study?[14] If so, those involved had well calculated that the war, the oppression and the Shoah were still too fresh in the collective memory to publicly ventilate antisemitic feelings.

The outlawing sent out a signal to postwar right-wing extremists in the Netherlands: it was, at that stage, not possible for National Socialists to organise themselves for political purposes.[15] Things were different when they limited themselves to organising social activities, meetings and mutual support and assistance. The consequence of the sentences for NESB's board was that, in the following years, these right-wing extremists would only organise themselves in various more socially-oriented groups offering support and acting as a network for 'former political delinquents'. One such group was HINAG, a lobby and support organisation for disabled ex-soldiers who had served on the Eastern Front, relatives of victims and political prisoners. In 1955, there was a short-lived attempt to start a new political organisation, the National Opposition Union (NOU).

So the 1956 ban in itself was not an obstacle to forming an organisation; it was more due to their social focus that, until the 1970s, these organisations stayed under the public radar. They could be organisations with social objectives, which, more privately, as we will see, engaged in publishing material that played down or denied the Holocaust.

Another strategy of 'former political delinquents' was to seek refuge at existing political parties, such as the rural protest party *Boerenpartij* (BP), founded in 1958. Its anti-parliamentary discourse, which praised the 'ordinary Dutch', gradually attracted more and more supporters. The *Boerenpartij* provided shelter for (former) National Socialists such as Wolthuis, but in public the party's top brass distanced themselves from 'fascism'. Members with a National Socialist past managed to become a force within the party, but this did not involve the transfer of a National Socialist ideology.[16] It was, at the most, the party's idealisation of rural life and strong nationalism which differed from the ideologies of other existing parties. As for its populism and support for small entrepreneurs, we can draw a certain parallel with the contemporary Poujadism in postwar France.[17]

14   Van Donselaar, *Fout na de oorlog*, 63.

15   P.R.A. van Iddekinge and A.H. Paape, *Ze zijn er nog. Een documentatie over fascistische, nazistische en andere rechtsradicale denkbeelden en activiteiten na 1945* (Amsterdam: De Bezige Bij, 1970), 281.

16   Van Donselaar, *Fout na de oorlog*, 132. Paul Lucardie, *Nederland stromenland: een geschiedenis van de politieke stromingen* (Assen: Van Gorcum, 2002), 52.

17   Sean Fitzgerald, 'The Anti-Modern Rhetoric of Le Mouvement Poujade', *The Review of Politics* 32, 2 (1970), 167-190 and about the antisemitic connotation of Poujade: Richard C. Vinen, 'The

The *Boerenpartij* joined the 1960 elections and got only 0.05% of the votes. Three years later they won 2.3% of the votes and 3 of the 150 available seats in parliament. In 1966, there was a row when it emerged that one of the party's members of the Senate had been a member of the National Socialist Dutch Workers Party, which had an even more radical agenda than the NSB and had used strong antisemitic language, particularly in a war journal. The senator in question eventually resigned on his own accord. In the 1970s, BP sympathisers emerged in the newly founded *Nederlandse Volks-Unie* (NVU).

Antisemitism and revisionism

The aforementioned NESB, founded in 1953 and outlawed in 1955, had one member, also mentioned above, who presented himself as an outspoken antisemite. In 1951, former Waffen-SS man, book trader and NESB party leader Paul van Tienen attended a meeting of the fascist European Social Movement in Malmö. After the war, Sweden was a cradle of neo-Nazism, antisemitism and fascism. From here, many brochures and pamphlets were distributed. Sweden was suitable for these activities because it was possible to build on a pre-war Nazi movement, but also because, towards the end of the war, National Socialists abroad transferred large sums of money to the country. Wealthy Swedish industrialists were also involved in the movement.[18] In 1950, *Het Vrije Volk* reported about the transit, from Sweden, of anti-Jewish pamphlets written in Dutch.[19] Five years later, there were concerns about the Swede Einar Aberg who distributed antisemitic pamphlets in Western Europe and South America.[20] In the Netherlands, Paul van Tienen acted as the distributor of such neo-Nazi materials. The important role of Holocaust denial and 'revisionism' in these materials was unique for the Dutch postwar period. Van Tienen fought his 'battle against the false interpretation of the history' of the Second World War in *Sociaal Weekblad*, the journal of which he was the editor since 1953 and which was renamed two years later as the *Nederlands Archief der Conservatieve Revolutie* (NACR).[21] It was the first time that revisionist historiography openly

End of an Ideology? Right-Wing Antisemitism in France, 1944-1970', *The Historical Journal* 37, 2 (1994), 365-388: 383.

18   Van Donselaar, *Fout na de oorlog*, 53.

19   *Het Vrije Volk*, 10 January 1950.

20   *De Volkskrant*, 3 June 1955; see Iddekinge and Paape, *Ze zijn er nog*, 348-349.

21   Although 'people [in the Netherlands] would rather be accused of arson or theft than of conservatism ...', politicians rarely use the term: Hermann von der Dunk, 'Conservatism in the

appeared in the Netherlands, a long time before Florrie Rost van Tonningen-Heubel became a distributor and shortly after the French *négationniste* Paul Rassinier published, in 1950, his *Le Mensonge d'Ulysse* and Gerald Reitlinger radically downsized the number of Jewish victims in his *The Final Solution,* which was published in Great Britain in 1953.[22]

In brief, Van Tienen's revisionism reduced all evil, including the bad intentions on the German side, to virtually zero and blamed the Allies for the Second World War. Van Tienen aimed for a rehabilitation of National Socialism – mainly as *the* counterforce against 'international bolshevism'.[23] Initially, he did this in a concealed way, by taking a stand against Eisenhower, the US President, in November 1955. Eisenhower was a man who 'did not rule, but was being ruled'. By his advisers and, most of all, by Bernard Baruch, according to Van Tienen. Although he did not use the word 'Jewish', he did talk about 'dark forces behind the scenes'.[24] Van Tienen's argumentation bore all the hallmarks of Judeo-Bolshevism which saw Jews and communists as an equally big threat to world peace.[25]

In 1960, Van Tienen went one step further when the kidnapping of Adolf Eichmann in Argentina by the Israeli secret services hit the headlines of the world. This year, in fact, marks the start of active Holocaust denial and downplaying in the Netherlands. It came down to the paradox that more knowledge of the Holocaust led to the phenomenon of trying to debunk this information. Despite Eichmann's relatively low rank as ss *Obersturmbannführer,* his role as head of the notorious *Referat* IV B 4 department (for 'Jewish affairs'), which resorted under the Gestapo, had played a crucial role in the organisation of the deportations and destruction of European Jewry. Van Tienen disagreed with that.

In three brochures about the 'Eichmann affaire', Van Tienen did mainly two things. First, he tried to demonstrate that Eichmann's efforts had always been aimed at organising, at the first opportunity, the emigration of Jews. Initially from Germany itself, and, after the outbreak of the war,

Netherlands', *Journal of Contemporary History* 13, 4 (1978), 741-763.

22   Paul Rassinier, *Le Mensonge d'Ulysse: regard sur la littérature concentrationnaire* (Bourg-en-Bresse: Editions Bressanes, 1950); Gerhard Reitlinger, *The Final Solution* (London: Sphere Books, 1953).

23   *NIW,* 21 April 1961, NIOD, KB II 2290.

24   Iddekinge and Paape, *Ze zijn er nog,* 48 (n. 1).

25   *See* for the conflation of Jews and communists, and the belief in a worldwide conspiratorial Judeo-Bolshevism, Johannes Rogalla von Bieberstein, 'Judeo-Bolshevism.' In: Richard S. Levy (ed.) *Antisemitism. A Historical Encyclopedia of Prejudice and Persecution.* Vol. 1 (Santa Barbara: ABC-CLIO, 2005), 389-391; André Gerrits, *The Myth of Jewish Communism: A Historical Interpretation* (New York: Peter Lang, 2009).

from occupied Europe. In that sense, Van Tienen took the name of the *Zentralstelle für Jüdische Auswanderung,* set up by Eichmann, very literally.[26] There was no indication whatsoever that Eichmann had played a role in the *Endlösung* of the Jewish question, Van Tienen claimed. On the contrary, the Allies had sabotaged Eichmann's plans by closing their borders to Jewish immigrants – particularly the French who had rejected Eichmann's proposal to allocate Madagascar as Jewish territory, and the English who had blocked Jewish immigration in Palestine.[27]

In addition, and directly related to his attempt to rehabilitate Eichmann, Van Tienen questioned the facts and figures with regard to 'the killing of six million Jews', which he deliberately put between inverted commas.[28] That was mainly the case in his third brochure, *Het lot van de Joden: waan en werkelijkheid* [The Fate of the Jews. Illusion and Reality]. One of the few sources quoted by Van Tienen in his brochures was Reitlinger's *The Final Solution.* In his brochures, Van Tienen endorsed Reitlinger's obsessive 'recount' and even went one step further by also putting 'Auschwitz' and 'gas chamber' between inverted commas. 'The gas chamber' was, after all, used as a *deus ex machina*, a final means of rescue, against anybody who realised that 'history cannot be written in black and white with impunity'. This made it even more important to unearth the truth. According to Van Tienen it was about time to put an end to the profound indignation at every attempt to check the correctness of the 'astonishing number of Jews' who have allegedly been murdered. All those who, even to a very modest extent, supported the National Socialist movement, were being blamed for what was today considered 'the biggest crime of all times'. And even if it were true that Hitler needed the Jews, at the time, as a scapegoat, today's scapegoats were the National Socialists.[29] This was a remarkable example of perpetrator-victim reversal.

According to Van Tienen, there was no convincing evidence for the systematic extermination of the Jews. The correct figure would probably be 'in the order of three hundred thousand' victims.[30] The most reliable calculation

---

26 *NIW,* 21 April 1961, NIOD, KB II 2290. (Paul van Tienen), *De mislukking van Eichmanns emigratie-politiek*, NACR brochure 109, NIOD, Br 7076, 22.
27 (Paul van Tienen), *De kwestie Eichmann in een nieuw licht*, NACR brochure 108, NIOD, Br 707512-13; (Paul van Tienen), *De mislukking van Eichmanns emigratie-politiek*, NACR brochure 109, NIOD, Br 7076, 17-20, 26-31.
28 See *De mislukking van Eichmanns emigratie-politiek*, 33.
29 (Paul van Tienen), *Het lot van de Joden: waan en werkelijkheid*, NACR brochure 110, NIOD, Br 7077, 51.
30 *Ibid.*, 52.

put the number at 'at least 200,000 and at the most 300,000 Jewish victims of criminal actions'. In addition, not all Jewish victims had been killed by the Germans. Nevertheless, the fate of the Jews, even if instead of 6 million around 250,000 of them were killed, remained a tragedy.

> ... but their fate is no longer an 'unequalled low point in the history of humanity', as today is being claimed, if we consider that an estimated same number of people – 250,000 – were killed within 24 hours by the criminal phosphor bombings on Dresden in February 1945.[31]

In other words: one crime could be crossed out against the other. The figure of 250,000 for Dresden tends to falsification. After the war, Germany put the number of civilian victims at 25,000; recently, this figure has been downsized to 18,000.[32]

Van Tienen distributed neo-Nazi materials from a bookstore in Utrecht. In the 1960s, he became well-known after the daily newspaper *Het Parool* reported about him selling the antisemitic book *Adolf Hitler – Sein Kampf gegen die Minusseele.* This led to a criminal case and a six-month prison sentence. Van Tienen was caught when two reporters presented themselves as clients pretending to be interested in the above-mentioned notorious antisemitic book which claims Jews have extremely dangerous 'sub-souls', identifies them with Satan and typifies them as 'vampires living off other populations': a strong brew of modern and medieval stereotypes. Van Tienen was accused of breaching article 137d, for possessing and distributing *Minusseele,* containing passages which 'insult the Jewish community in Dutch society'.[33] The police in Utrecht established that Van Tienen had quite a large group of regular customers for whom he collected his materials, mainly from abroad.[34] While waiting for his appeal to be heard in court, Van Tienen fled to Spain where he lived until his death in about 1994.[35] After his escape to Spain, Van Tienen was convicted in absentia. In appeal, Van Tienen was convicted to a prison sentence and a five-year ban on exercising the

31   (Paul van Tienen), *Het lot van de Joden en het Derde Rijk*, quoted in: Van Donselaar, *Fout na de oorlog*, 102.

32   We thank Joost Rosendaal for the references. *Erklärung der Dresdner Historikerkommission zur Ermittlung der Opferzahlen der Luftangriffe auf die Stadt Dresden am 13./14. Februar 1945,* Dresden, 1 October 2008.

33   *Utrechts Nieuwsblad,* 3 November 1964, *Trouw,* 12 November 1965.

34   *Het Parool,* 23 October 1964.

35   Van Donselaar, *Fout na de oorlog*, 105-109; author of *Adolf Hitler etc* is W. van Asenbach; *see Algemeen Handelsblad*, 2 March 1967.

**Illustration 7   A news clipping on the distribution of neo-Nazi material in
newspaper *Het Parool*, 23 October 1964**

NIOD, KB I 6742

In the early postwar years former Waffen-ss member Paul van Tienen acted as
the distributor of neo-Nazi materials and publications on Holocaust denial. In
the 1960s two reporters had presented themselves as clients in his bookstore
after which he was brought to trial and convicted (in absentia).

profession of book trader. That makes him the only right-wing extremist until the 1970s to have been convicted for antisemitic group insult.

So, until the 1970s, when the political party *Nederlandse Volks-Unie* launched itself as the heir of the extremist right-wing body of thought, there are no known legal cases in which an extreme right-wing motive or extreme right-wing perpetratorship has been legally demonstrated. But there have been incidents of antisemitic vandalism in which extreme right-wing motivations may have played a role. Between 1964 and 1966, for instance, there was a series of vandalism incidents at Jewish cemeteries and a synagogue in the eastern region of the Achterhoek. In this context, the political scientist Rob Witte points to the large number of NSB supporters in this eastern border region during the war.[36] Hence, this may have been a case of personal continuity of Nazi sympathisers during and after the war.

Was Van Tienen a loner? In 1964, there was a demonstration against Van Tienen in The Hague, but he also received support. He was praised by the journal of a small group called *Actie De Vrije Richting*. This journal was entirely filled by *Einzelgänger* E. Peijster, an anti-communist with fascist and National Socialist sympathies. Like a growing number of other publicists, Van Tienen allegedly 'honestly' challenged a lot of deliberately false war propaganda. The image of Van Tienen marching in front of legions of black shirts was concocted by 'drunken teetotallers suffering from hallucinations and crooked noses'.[37]

In July 1960, another former National Socialist had anticipated the trial against Eichmann by, on the one hand, denying or playing down the Holocaust and, on the other, questioning Eichmann's guilt. In a letter to the editor of the weekly *Haagse Post* R.N. de Ruyter van Steveninck (1894-1963), former NSB member, German SS member and mayor of Leiden during the war, wrote that 'the number of Jews who were really *"greifbar"* for Hitler, had been one and a half million at the most'.[38] He doubted whether there had been gas chambers. De Ruyter probably partly borrowed his figures from Van Tienen's journal.[39] The *Haagse Post* published eight outraged reactions, including one by publicist H. Wielek (the pen name of Wilhelm

---

36   Rob Witte, *'Al eeuwenlang een gastvrij volk'. Racistisch geweld en overheidsreacties in Neder-land 1950-2009* (Amsterdam: Aksant, 2010). In the same period a wave of incidents with swastika graffiti on synagogues and cemeteries (known as the *Schmierwelle* or Swastika Epidemic) swept across Germany and, to a lesser extent, the Netherlands.

37   Henri Knap in *Het Parool*, 27 June 1964.

38   Quoted in: De Haan, *Na de ondergang*, 170.

39   *Haagse Post*, 23 July 1960. Jan Vrijman also mentioned that in December 1947, De Ruyter van Steveninck had been sentenced to ten years in prison, in 1948 to four and a half years, and was

Kweksilber, 1912-1988), author of the first publication on the Shoah in the Netherlands, *De oorlog die Hitler won* [The war that Hitler won] (1947), who showed how De Ruyter falsified his sources, and one by journalist and film-maker Jan Vrijman (1929-1997) who lifted the lid on the war background of the challenged author.[40] De Ruyter was allowed to challenge the reactions and stuck with the central message of his argumentation: that he considered the design of such a murder factory by developed people less likely than that the gas chambers were a product of anti-German propaganda. Considering the doubts about their existence, he followed a well-known strategy used by revisionists, calling for an independent investigation, 'unlike for example Nuremberg, where the victors tried the losers'.[41] The *Haagse Post* said it had published De Ruyter's piece to show that those who, here and in Germany, wanted to prove *'dass es nicht wahr ist'* were more dangerous than Eichmann. Because 'Eichmann is not a threat to the future – those others are'.[42]

The extreme right after 1970

From the early 1970s, the character of the extreme right in the Netherlands changed. Personal Second World War experiences became less leading within extreme right formations. A new generation was entering the scene, one that was less marked by the war. There was less reminiscing about the past and the agenda increasingly also included issues related to current political and social situations. The search for a social and political role for 'former political delinquents', an important activity of the extreme right in the 1950s and 1960s, slowly moved into the background. This had two visible consequences. First, the emergence of political movements which profiled themselves on new 'racial issues'. These movements focused on new minority groups such as migrant workers and Surinamese (who had migrated to the Netherlands after the colony's independence in 1975). Second, the rise of a new generation of right-wing extremists with no war background and often born after the war. In the 1970s and 1980s, this generation started

---

released in November 1949. *Vrij Nederland* expressed its surprise at his release: *Vrij Nederland*, 30 July 1960.

40   *Haagse Post*, 23 July 1960.

41   *Ibid.*, 30 July 1960.

42   *Ibid.*, 23 July 1960. The magazine used De Ruyter Steveninck's German expression.

Illustration 8   Photo of a demonstration against airtime for an extreme right party, 18 May 1981

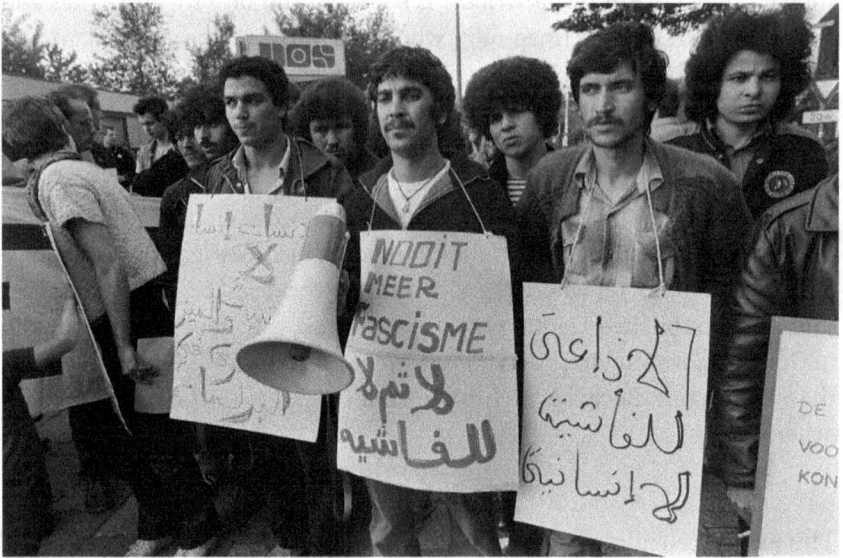

Hans van Dijk / Nationaal Archief

Protest in front of the office of the Netherlands Broadcasting Service (NOS) against airtime for the extreme right party *Nederlandse Volks-Unie* (NVU).The party, home to both old and neo-Nazis, targeted foreign migrants and Jews alike. See also Illustration 29.

to look for ways to make National Socialism acceptable again. The most important organisation was the *Nederlandse Volks-Unie*.[43]

When the NVU was founded, in 1971, it was not much different from the other extreme right-wing groups that had been active in the preceding period: populated by former members of the SS and NSB, struggling to find a balance between transparency and the threat of being banned, and focused on the Second World War. Yet a new voice was emerging within the NVU. One that demanded attention for a new and current problem: the growing presence of new groups of immigrants. The new sound came from Joop Glimmerveen, a newcomer on the extreme right-wing scene.

43 Carolien Bouw, Jaap van Donselaar and Carien Nelissen, *De Nederlandse Volks-Unie: portret van een racistische splinterpartij* (Amsterdam: Wereldvenster, 1981).

The accountant Glimmerveen, born in 1928, did not have an active war background. And although – in the midst of the Cold War – he had a strong anti-communist world view he had only very recently got involved with the extreme right. So Glimmerveen did not carry the weight of a war past and the subsequent repression of an older generation of right-wing extremists. Commenting on his initial period at the NVU, he said in 2012: 'It was all about the rehabilitation of former NSB members. I did not disapprove of that, but I found contemporary politics more interesting. There were other problems .... Yes, those people had been members of the NSB. I hadn't.'[44]

In addition to the arrival of migrants from Surinam and the Mediterranean, the rise of so-called 'youth styles', which started in the 1960s, also played a role. Youths were starting to adopt approaches to life and to each other based on specific lifestyles. Particularly 'skinheads' and football hooligans tended to get involved with extreme right-wing formations like the NVU (see Illustration 28). And that created a two-faced party. On the one hand, this was a new and modern extreme right-wing party with young supporters, provocative and – adapted to the 1970s – mainly focused on new migrants and, in the middle of the Cold War, communism. On the other hand, it had a lasting, sometimes more or less explicit, focus on the Third Reich and traditional National Socialism with a fascination for paraphernalia, clothes and display of symbols. Neo-Nazism developed into a subculture with its own dress code, forms of sociability and music. The green bomber jackets and the jackets of the 'Lonsdale youngsters' (referring to a clothing brand that became popular among right-wing sympathizers because of the letters 'nsda', i.e. one letter short of the acronym of the German Nazi party) became a familiar sight in the 1980s and 90s. It led to a political debate about a ban on the use of clothing symbolism. In some instances white supremacist, xenophobic and antisemitic sympathies coincided. This was for example the case with a small youth group in the new town of Almere that set fire to a synagogue and an Islamic primary school. More generally, it was found that some Lonsdale youngsters moved towards even more radical persuasions.[45]

The NVU had to deal with strong opposition from the legal authorities and the party was even officially outlawed, albeit not disbanded, in the late 1970s. Things went quickly downhill when, in 1980, it also had to compete

44 Interview Willem Wagenaar and Katie Digan with Joop Glimmerveen, The Hague, 3 October 2012.

45 J. van der Krogt, *Rechtsextremisme op het internet*. Meldpunt discriminatie internet, 2009 (www.magenta.nl).

with the newcomer *Centrumpartij* which had an anti-foreigner agenda without a National Socialist connotation.[46] In 1982 the *Centrumpartij* won one seat in Dutch Parliament, something the NVU had never achieved and would never achieve. Glimmerveen was relieved of duty. In 1996 he returned when Eite Homan and Constant Kusters, two neo-Nazis, i.e. of the second and third generation, successfully appealed to him to revive the NVU. In the following years, the party mainly profiled itself through public demonstrations. Initially, these were unannounced small-scale gatherings, to avoid bans and counter-actions. As of 2001, however, the party won the right to demonstrate in an administrative court case. Demonstrations then became the party's main activity.

What was the role of antisemitism within the NVU? On the basis of the party magazine, '*Wij Nederland*',[47] and on the basis of an interview with party leader Glimmerveen it appears that there was a lot of sympathy for Third Reich heroism. Initially, this did not lead to a focus on Jews or the Holocaust. Glimmerveen did however reveal in an interview that he 'didn't find the racial laws of Nuremberg horrendous'.

Mein Kampf contains a lot of good things. I personally find that thing with the Jews exaggerated. Those pages that go on and on about Jews preying on white boys, I find them exaggerated. But don't forget that the racial laws in Israel go much further than those of Nuremberg. I don't find racial laws horrendous, the *Endlösung*, that was of course horrible. Maybe not six million Jews have been murdered, perhaps four million, Jewish scholars say, two and a half million. But it did happen of course, without a doubt. And for us that is the biggest handicap, the Second World War is for us the biggest handicap.[48]

Glimmerveen's remark that the Holocaust and the Second World War are 'the biggest handicap' for the current dissemination of his political ideas fits into the well-established sense that the Holocaust was in the way of a healthy view on Nazism. Without that mass murder National Socialism would 'become a world view like any other'. In the interview Glimmerveen played down the Holocaust, appealing to, of all people, 'Jewish scholars'.[49]

46   Kees Brants and Willem Hogendoorn, *Van vreemde smetten vrij. Opkomst van de Centrumpartij* (Bussum: De Haan, 1983).
47   The first issue of *Wij Nederland* was published in March 1971.
48   *Vrij Nederland*, 2 August 1975.
49   Jaap van Donselaar, *De staat paraat? De bestrijding van extreem-rechts in West-Europa* (Amsterdam: Babylon De Geus, 1995).

The ideological behaviour of the early NVU can be characterised as the realisation that the party carried the weight of the history of the Holocaust and the Second World War with it. That weight posed great limitations to the possibility of successfully grabbing public attention for its National Socialist ideas. At the same time, the party did not distance itself from antisemitism.

Towards the late 1970s, the party's tone changed and, for the first time, it denied the Holocaust. The direct cause for that was the American TV series 'Holocaust', broadcast in the Netherlands in 1979. The series triggered a lot of media attention and a big public debate.[50] A pamphlet appeared which passed the series off as 'heinous propaganda of lies' to 'push the Germans in the corner again and obtain subsidies'. Moral blackmail resulting in financial gain (through state support) acted as the underlying antisemitic stereotypes, which were actually very typical, also more in general, for postwar antisemitism. The pamphleteer was tried, fined and handed a conditional prison sentence.[51] As far as we know, he was not associated with the NVU. This was the first conviction for insulting Jews because of their race on the ground of article 137c ('group insult') since Paul van Tienen's conviction (on the ground of article 137d which focused on distribution) in the 1960s.

About the role of the TV series Glimmerveen said: 'It was very much in the picture at the time and of course we took our position.' In the first issue of *Wij Nederland*, in 1979, the Holocaust was, for the first time, explicitly denied and typified as 'THE LIE of the twentieth century'.[52] All that was, so it appears, a consequence of 'taking a position', as mentioned by Glimmerveen. That issue of *'Wij Nederland'* also contained a positive review of the standard work and 'milestone in US Holocaust denial' for Holocaust deniers, *The Hoax of the 20ᵗʰ century* by Arthur Butz (1976).[53] It set a trend. Later issues reviewed books by other Holocaust deniers.[54] Glimmerveen explained this sudden change, whereby the Holocaust was not just strongly played down, but simply denied, as follows:

50   The series also caused a big outcry among extreme right-wing groups in other countries. In Germany, TV stations and transmission masts were guarded during broadcast after threats by neo-Nazis (*Leeuwarder Courant* 23 January 1979).

51   Court of Arnhem, 4 June 1982: LBR, *Rechtspraak Rassen discriminatie,* ed. 1995, 32*ff.*

52   *Wij Nederland,* January 1979.

53   Roni Stauber, 'Holocaust Denial, Negationism, and Revisionism.' In: Richard S. Levy (ed.), *Antisemitism. A Historical Encyclopedia of Prejudice and Persecution.* Vol. 1 (Santa Barbara: ABC-CLIO, 2005), 319-322.

54   For example the books by Richard E. Harwood, Udo Walendy, Arthur Butz and Thies Christophersen in *Wij Europa,* January 1981.

Yes, at first I was convinced that it had happened. But well, then I received books by Rassinier. Rassinier was a Communist. So why would that man ... and I also read about a German socialist from Vienna, who had been there for years, in Auschwitz, but he was not aware of anything! Well, that makes you think.[55]

Although the biographical details are not entirely correct, Glimmerveen probably referred to the above-mentioned Thies Christophersen who was stationed in a camp near Auschwitz. The publication of his *Die Auschwitz-Lüge* in 1973 had a big impact in Germany and the Netherlands. After wandering through Germany and Denmark Christophersen eventually ended up in Belgium where he died in 1997.[56]

For most NVU sympathizers the war had become a *postmemory* passed on by those who had actually experienced it.[57] An exception is Et Wolsink who became actively involved in the NVU from 1978 onwards. Wolsink's joining the NVU played an important role in the suddenly harsher antisemitic tone. During the Second World War Wolsink had voluntarily joined the German army. Most of the signed antisemitic articles in *Wij Nederland* during this period were written by him. In 1984, Et Wolsink published the article *'Bent U Antisemiet?'* [Are you an antisemite?]. In it, he called the Holocaust a fairy tale and stated that the Jews had started the Second World War. He also wrote about 'Jewish parasites':

In those ghettos they were waiting, profiting from weak spots in German society, manipulating with capital and quickly got the white community in a stranglehold.[58]

The persecution of Jews in the Third Reich was, according to Wolsink, a response to this behaviour. The 'internment camps' were only intended for Germany's enemies. It wasn't until 1985 that Wolsink used the present tense in one of his contributions, stating that the Jews should go 'back' to Israel. In a following issue he named international Zionism as the main enemy. The Zionists were, after all, out for world hegemony.[59] That was the first time the NVU targeted Israel shortly after the period in which, due to

55   Interview Joop Glimmerveen, by Katie Digan and Willem Wagenaar, 3 October 2012.
56   Roni Stauber, 'Auschwitz lie'. In: Richard S. Levy (ed.), *Antisemitism*, 45.
57   For the concept of Postmemory *see* Marianne Hirsch, *The Generation of Postmemory: Writing and Visual Culture After the Holocaust* (Columbia University Press, 2012).
58   *Wij Nederland,* June 1984.
59   *Ibid.,* January 1985.

the war in Lebanon and the massacre in Sabra and Shatila, Israel was also being more criticised in the Netherlands.[60]

Party leader Joop Glimmerveen managed to surround himself with a number of youths. With this group he increasingly looked for provocation and confrontation through demonstrations and other street actions. Those actions led to several antisemitic incidents. For example, on a number of occasions the demonstrators shouted slogans like: *'Juden vergasen'*, *'NSB okee, Joden weg ermee'*. In 1983, there was an unusual incident. The grave of Nehemia de Lieme, a prominent pre-war Zionist, was destroyed and his skull was stolen. NVU slogans were found in the area around the cemetery.[61]

In conclusion, we see how at the start of the 1970s there was more or less a split in the public character of extreme right-wing political formations, due to the rise of the *Nederlandse Volks-Unie* (NVU) as the most important exponent. Before that, there were loners and organisations with a sociable character. These networks, including the group around Florrie Rost van Tonningen, however, continued to exist after 1970. The NVU gradually emerged as a party with an antisemitic voice and a prominent place for Holocaust denial. In the 1980s antisemitism within the NVU becomes rougher. The younger generation seemed freer with regard to profiling Nazism than the generation which had personally experienced a more controlled and suspicious climate. Nevertheless, a veteran such as Wolsink managed to make his mark on the party's ideology.

Around the turn of the century, in the Netherlands as elsewhere, the internet gave a new boost to the distribution and exchange of neo-Nazi and antisemitic texts, imageries and paraphernalia. Magenta, a Dutch anti-racism monitor dedicated to internet hate speech, began to document the proliferation of websites with a neo-Nazi or antisemitic signature: the Dutch branch of the international Stormfront, known for its Holocaust denial, is the largest; other sites are Blood & Honour, New National Unity, Youth Storm, etc. Magenta furthermore observed a 'symbiotic relationship' between online contact and offline gatherings. This accounts for example for music events and war-related commemorations. Recently protests connected to the refugee crisis in 2015-2016 were joined, and in some instances hijacked, by members of the NVU and other right-wing organisations.[62]

In 2007, 'black widow' Florrie Rost van Tonningen died. Her grave quickly became a pilgrimage destination for a younger generation of Nazis. The

60 *See* part II.
61 *Afdruk*, May 1984.
62 *See* Epilogue.

Volks-Unie organized a service at the cemetery which was filmed and posted on YouTube. Constant Kusters (b. 1970), the local party leader of the *Nederlandse Volks-Unie*, told his 'comrades' about the exemplary role of Rost van Tonningen. Kusters 'praised Germany's role in the Second World War' and described the members of the Dutch Waffen-ss as heroes, exactly like Rost van Tonningen had done for years. In the forest near her grave he predicted that he and his supporters would seize power of 'those 150 idiots in the parliament'.[63]

---

63   'Treurmars rond Rost verloopt in alle rust,' *De Gelderlander* 2 June 2007.

5   Jewish Responses to Post-Liberation Antisemitism

Evelien Gans

In the early 1960s, the Netherlands was confronted with the so-called *Schmierwelle*. This Swastika Epidemic which had started in Germany in December 1959, when neo-Nazis painted swastikas on a newly opened synagogue in Cologne, swept like a tidal wave across Germany and many other countries in Europe, even reaching South Africa, Australia and the United States. In the Netherlands, a Jewish cemetery had been vandalised, on several locations swastikas had been painted and various prominent Jews in Amsterdam had received anonymous threatening letters: 'Jews not welcome'.[1] There weren't that many incidents during the Dutch *'hakenkruis-rage'* [swastika craze][2], but there was a lot of consternation, particularly due to the huge scale of this antisemitic wave in the country of the former occupier.[3]

In 1962, the tombstones of the Jewish cemetery in Enschede were dam-aged and the windows of the *shul* in Amersfoort were smashed.[4] Most of all, an incident at the elitist student association *Amsterdamsch Studenten Corps* (ASC) raised a public outcry. Despite (or because of?) the extensive coverage of the Eichmann trial, during ASC's initiation ceremonies, its *feuten* (freshmen who join the ceremonies as aspiring members), with their heads shaved and nude torsos, were put together in a narrow space, were yelled at: *'We gaan Dachautje spelen'* [We're going to play the Dachau game]. A Jewish freshman who complained because he had lost relatives in Dachau was called a *'vuile rotjood'* [filthy Jew].[5] The incident turned into a

---

1   See *Trouw*, 4 January 1960, NIOD, KB II 307; see Witte, *'Al eeuwenlang een gastvrij volk.'*, 59-61. See for an early analysis of the incidents in the United States: Howard J. Ehrlich, 'The Swastika epidemic of 1959-1960: Anti-Semitism and community characteristics', *Social Problems* 9, 3 (1962), 264-272.

2   The term *'hakenkruisrage'* was used by the *Algemeen Handelsblad*, 5 January 1960, NIOD, KB II 454; see *Algemeen Handelsblad*, 4 January 1960, *de Volkskrant*, 4 and 5 January 1960, VVN, 16 January 1960; see Jaap van Donselaar, *De staat paraat? De bestrijding van extreem-rechts in West-Europa* (Amsterdam: Babylon De Geus, 1995); Witte, *'Al eeuwenlang een gastvrij volk'*, 59-60.

3   See Van Donselaar, *De staat paraat.*

4   *NIW*, 19 October 1962, NIOD, KB II 307 A. For vandalism at the Jewish cemetery in Enschede, see *Deventer Courant*, 5 October 1962, NIOD, KB II 307 A.

5   Literally in Dutch: 'vuile rotjood'; see *Algemeen Dagblad*, 9 and 10 October.

national scandal. Because of the agitation among Dutch Jews caused by this and other recent antisemitic incidents, the *Nieuw Israëlietisch Weekblad* (*NIW*) decided to organise a debate in October 1962 with Abel Herzberg and four other prominent Jews, in order to address issues such as how seriously Jews were to take these antisemitic incidents. In September 1961, with the Eichmann trial still in full swing, Herzberg had already lectured the Dutch Jews and their mouthpiece, the NIW, because of their defensive attitude. He accused them of ignoring the trial's historical significance and worse, of hardly writing anything about this event of world proportions. If at least, Herzberg said, they had sided with opponents of the trial, but no, they chose not to take sides at all. They just walked away, did not want to be confronted with the past, open old wounds, have their peace disturbed. Someone had even dared to describe the trial as a form of 'Jewish masochism'.[6] Was Herzberg right? Were Jews ignoring the growing international public debate about the Shoah? And, more importantly within the context of this book: how did they act when confronted with current antisemitic abuse? On the one hand, Herzberg was too generalising; Jewish circles did report about the Eichmann trial. Furthermore, Herzberg specifically addressed the *organised* Jewish community and not Jews who did not fit into this category, but were still engaged.[7] On the other hand, after the liberation, many Jews had indeed been inclined to turn their backs (as much as possible) to the wartime period and the misery it had caused. Typically, when after the war the Hollandsche Schouwburg Committee started looking for a suitable use of this former deportation location, the Jewish community sent out a strong message calling for the demolition of the despised building.[8] Only later there was gradually more attention for the history of the persecution of the Jews and for their experiences and memories – also in Dutch society as a whole.

6   *Levend Joods geloof,* September 1961.

7   *See, e.g., NIW* of 21 April 1961 with an article in which the author says he is pleased that Israel had given the trial a solid legal foundation. And *see, e.g.,* the involvement of the journalist and writer Renate Rubinstein and the participation of the author Marga Minco (b. 1920) at the meeting in Krasnapolsky on 12 April 1961. Rubinstein's father was Jewish and Minco was Jewish; neither of them was member of a Jewish organisation, *Het Vrije Volk,* 13 April 1961, NIOD, KB 1972 B.

8   *See* Evelien Gans, 'Sam de Wolff, 1878-1960' and Bart Wallet, '"Een levend gedenkteken." Israël, joods Nederland en de herinnering aan de Shoa.' In: Frank van Vree, Hetty Berg and David Duindam (eds.), *De Hollandsche Schouwburg. Theater, deportatieplaats, plek van herinnering* (Amsterdam: Amsterdam University Press, 2013), 200-209, 190-199.

Jewish reactions: lashing out

The responses of Jews to antisemitic abuse varied enormously. This had
been the case right from the liberation. What did Jews do when someone
made an antisemitic remark? Some sued their assailant, as described in
chapter two. Others lashed out – in complete defiance of the image of
the cowardly, passive Jew who willingly endures the abuse. With respect
to postwar violence, Keith Lowe's *Savage Continent* paints a picture of a
postwar Europe that has grown into a continent where violence, at both
individual and collective level, has become commonplace among a range
of ethnic and national groups. Violence against women and rape became
a mass phenomenon, particularly, but definitely not exclusively, among
Russian troops. One of the ways in which British, American and Russian
troops initially responded to the terrible situations they stumbled into in the
concentration and extermination camps they were liberating, was: to take
revenge on the Germans who were still there, starting with the ss troops.
The confrontation with the violence and degeneration in the camps 'had a
way of implicating everybody, even the liberators'.[9]

The United Nations Relief and Rehabilitation Administration (UNRRA),
which was mainly involved in supporting and repatriating so-called *Displaced Persons*, was also concerned about possible acts of violence by former
Jewish concentration camp prisoners. After all, they had been exposed to all
kinds of human cruelty, 'and they place no value on human life whatsoever'.[10]
On several occasions, during the first stage of the liberation of a camp, Allied
troops would hand over or leave captured ss troops and other camp guards
to the former Jewish prisoners to do with them as they pleased. Apart from
these handovers, they initially let prisoners who wanted to take revenge on
their former henchmen have a go. The same thing also happened outside
the camps where ss troops, kapos, pro-Nazi Germans, suspected pro-Nazi
Germans or not even that, were badly beaten and killed.[11]

9   Keith Lowe, *Savage Continent. Europe in the Aftermath of World War II* (London: Viking,
2012), 88. The quote is taken from Robert Abzug, *Inside the Vicious Heart. Americans and the
Liberation of Nazi Concentration Camps* (Oxford: Oxford University Press, 1985), 93; *see* Lowe,
Savage Continent,78-88.

10   *Ibid.*, 49.

11   *Ibid.*, 88-93. The American military governor Lucius Clay noticed in 1947 that Jewish
Displaced Persons (DPs) 'in spite of their natural hatred of the German people ... have been
remarkably restrained in avoiding incidents of a serious nature with the German population ....';
ibid., 89. In Bergen-Belsen, British soldiers put the SS soldiers in a circle and told a group of
women: 'Go ahead and throw stones': Evelien Gans, *Jaap en Ischa Meijer. Een joodse geschiedenis
1912-1956* (Amsterdam: Bert Bakker, 2008), 396.

This was, of course, not an exclusively 'Jewish phenomenon'. On the contrary, the revenge of other nationalities and groups, like the millions of forced labourers and *Displaced Persons* on, first of all, Germans, but also on Italians, Hungarians and others who had been part of the Axis powers, was many times larger and more extreme. Among the Russians, and those within their sphere of influence, the violence was, in general, much more extreme than in the West. Revenge was, as Lowe shows, a cropped-up desire that was passionately satisfied by many people, after their long-desired liberation or conquest, and sometimes even served as a guiding principle.[12] In the Netherlands, members of the NSB and other 'wrong' Dutchmen were also abused and, in a number of instances, killed in the roundup locations and camps where they were held, for a short or longer period, after their arrest.[13] On a more general level, the government and authorities were very concerned about what they perceived as a strongly increased blurring of moral standards and degradation among the population as a result of the occupation.[14]

The psychiatrist Elie Cohen, figuring in chapter 2, has tried to describe the scars left behind by living and surviving in a ruthless setting, among Jewish camp survivors – whom Cohen called *'wij concentrationnaires'* [we concentrationaires]. For a long time, their only goal had been to get enough food and clothes and be in the best possible work commando, almost without any room for empathy. Detached from conventions and common moral judgments, their behaviour had become a lot rougher. In postwar society they went straight for their target, spoke their minds and certainly did not treat their fellow citizens with kid gloves. This gave their behaviour, Cohen wrote in *Beelden uit de nacht. Kampherinneringen* [Images from the Night. Camp Memories], 'a certain raw edge, which, of course, must have often had a repulsive and very unpleasant effect on others'.[15] Their faith in humanity had not exactly improved. They had, so they thought, learned to understand man like he really was and could see right through everybody. That had given Cohen and others a sense of 'standing above everybody you engaged with'. It was a distorted sense of superiority, according to Cohen, but

12   *See* Lowe, *Savage Continent,* part III, 'Vengeance', 75-184. There is also a taboo on 'Jewish revenge', see the indignation following the publication of John Sack's *An Eye for an Eye: The Untold Story of Jewish Revenge Against Germans in 1945* (New York: Basic Books, 1993): *ibid.,* 182.
13   *See* Ismee Tames, *Besmette jeugd. Kinderen van NSB'ers na de oorlog* (Amsterdam: Balans, 2009), 121-124.
14   *See* Herman de Liagre Böhl and Guus Meershoek, *De Bevrijding van Amsterdam: een strijd om macht en moraal* (Zwolle: Waanders, 1989).
15   Elie Cohen, *Beelden uit de nacht. Kampherinneringen* (Baarn: de Prom, 1992), 175.

understandable, because the experiences of others often seemed futile in comparison to their own experiences – which, from an objective viewpoint, they often were. It took time for the *concentrationnaires* to adapt themselves and allow their interlocutors to tell their story, without laughing in their faces.[16]

There was indeed a brutalisation of behaviour and language among Jewish survivors in the initial postwar period – especially among camp survivors. They had to get out of the habit of swearing and cursing at the slightest, and of quickly and sneakily snatching things to eat or stealing handy items.[17] It is unknown if some Jews already had a short fuse before the war, or if they had become so stressed out and hardened due to their war experiences that it wasn't until after 1945 that the slightest suspicion of aversion made them go berserk. It may well have been a sum of pre- and postwar factors; it certainly wasn't as if every Jewish survivor started picking fights after the liberation. However, it was highly likely that among many of them, the natural rejection of physical violence had been, to some extent, sometimes strongly, eroded.[18] After 1945, Jewish football players were, again, confronted with, often very violent, antisemitism on the pitch. In October 1947, *Onze Revue*, the magazine of the predominantly Jewish football club *Wilhelmina Vooruit*, noted a rise in antisemitism. Jewish football players were also less tolerant than in the 1930s and were more likely to pick a fight after antisemitic abuse, write about it in club magazines or file a complaint with the national football association KNVB.[19]

At the Jewish nursery and primary school Rosj Pina, which opened its doors in Amsterdam in 1947, there were a few Jewish teachers who beat up pupils they considered disobedient and difficult. It was, of course, also a

---

16 *Ibid.*, 176; see Gans, *Jaap en Ischa Meijer*, 381-382.

17 See Jaap Meijer, in: Gans, *Jaap en Ischa Meijer,* 368, 382, and Hannie Liebman-Wolff and Abraham Linda, in: *ibid.*, 384.

18 There exists a great deal of literature on the field of Jewish survivor's trauma and also concerning the question as to what psychological harm was done before, during and after the war. We only name here: Martin S. Bergmann and Milton E. Jucovy (eds.), *Generations of the Holocaust* (New York: Columbia University Press, 1990, with new pref. and postscripts; orig. 1982: Basic Books); Hans Keilson, *Sequential traumatization in children: a clinical and statistical follow-up study on the fate of the Jewish war orphans in the Netherlands* (Jerusalem: The Magnes Press / The Hebrew University, 1992). And from a European and political perspective: Jolande Withuis and Annet Mooij (eds.), *The Politics of War Trauma. The Aftermath of World War II in Eleven European Countries* (Amsterdam: Aksant, 2010).

19 Evert de Vos, "'Verliest den moed toch niet". Joodse voetbalclubs in Amsterdam 1908-1948' (Doctoral thesis, Social History, Universiteit Leiden, October 2000), 54-55, 70-71. *See also* chapter 11.

time in which it was more accepted to hit children in school and at home, but the surviving stories also point to disproportionate anger, even in the context of that period. The pupils themselves were, like their teachers, badly mangled by the war and some were unruly and wild. Some pursued children from the nearby public primary schools, calling them *goyim*. Such aggressive – or assertive – behaviour was all the easier because these Jewish children were all in a Jewish school and, hence, acted as a collective.[20]

Both children and adults avoided antisemitic abuse, sought confrontation, withdrew, shrugged their shoulders, lodged complaints or used their fists. It is impossible to find out how many Jews literally went on the attack after being abused for being a Jew. That same Diego who witnessed how his grandfather ignored the men in the tram telling him 'they forgot to gas you', on his second day in school beat up a classmate who called him a 'bloody Jew'.[21] They also called Frank Diamand (b. 1939) who, together with his parents had survived Bergen-Belsen, a 'bloody Jew'. He handed his jacket to a friend and then beat his assailant to pulp.[22]

The market salesman and metal worker Barend de Hond (1907-?) was a special case. He was the only person to have escaped from a group of four hundred Jewish men arrested during the first big razzia in Amsterdam in February 1941. The others had been humiliated, beaten and chased along for hours to Waterlooplein before being deported, via a detour, to Mauthausen where they all died shortly afterwards. This razzia led to the February Strike of 25 and 26 February, but also created, in conjunction with the death reports which arrived from Mauthausen in a very quick succession, a climate of permanent fear among the Jewish population. De Hond survived the war. When a man in a café on Rembrandtplein started provoking him and finally said: 'I hate all Jews', he did not know he was dealing with an amateur wrestler. De Hond threw him together with his chair, across the terrace and onto the tram tracks and then knocked the man unconscious when he returned. Looking back, De Hond said:

---

20   Gans, *Jaap en Ischa Meijer*, 470-474. Before the war, fighting between Jewish and Christian children in Amsterdam (and also between Catholic and Protestant children) was fairly frequent. For these and other forms of pre-war antisemitism in Amsterdam, *see* Philo Bregstein and Salvador Bloemgarten (eds.), *Herinnering aan Joods Amsterdam* (Amsterdam: De Bezige Bij, 1978), 189-203.

21   Telephone interview with Diego Rodrigues Lopes, 6 June 2012; *see* chapters 2 and 3,

22   Conversation with Frank Diamand, 21 April 2007.

After the war, antisemitism was there again. I am not a fighter, but after the war I had to appear in court six or seven times ... for fighting with antisemites.[23]

The NIW reported on two trials, in January and February 1949, where the accused were, respectively, a non-Jew and a Jew. The first suspect, biscuit producer J.M., was accused of verbally abusing the second suspect, and his company of cherry eating Jews, with antisemitic insults such as 'they should have gassed you all' and of making 'nose movements'. Merchant H.W. had reacted by giving him 'a terrible beating'.[24] The biscuit producer was found not guilty because of non-concurring witness statements and, hence, a lack of evidence. His lawyer argued that J.M. had actually done a lot for Jews during the war, but had received little recognition for that. A few days later, the Jewish suspect was given a fifty-guilder fine. The court did not hand out the one-month prison sentence that was demanded, in view of the positive report on the suspect and his wartime experiences and those of his wife, an Auschwitz survivor. A one-month prison sentence would, however, have been fitting, according to the judge, if the suspect shared the views of his lawyer, M. Knap. This lawyer, also a Jew, had made a remarkable plea. He admitted that it was not allowed by law to hit someone. But the ruling against the other suspect (acquittal) proved how unsatisfactory the sense of justice remained when Jews followed the course of justice. His client was deeply grieved and he was not an isolated case.

Every day across the world Jews are taunted and scorned. I would like to let you know that I was pleased when the suspect told me how he had reacted. I would have done exactly the same. Antisemitism has risen enormously after the war ....[25]

The lawyer talked about a 'natural right to defence in case of offended pride'. 'The victim' only had himself to blame for the beating. Knap also told the court that postwar Jews had changed. 'We are less inclined to tolerate things, both individually and nationally.'[26]

---

23   Quoted in: Bregstein and Bloemgarten, *Herinnering aan Joods Amsterdam*, 323. For Barend de Hond, *see also*: *ibid.*, 31-32, 128-129, 313.

24   *NIW*, 11 February 1949. It was not uncommon for the insulting (non-Jewish) party and the, in response to that, abusive (Jewish) party to be tried separately: Evelien Gans, *Antisemitisme? Het beeld van 'de Jood' in Naoorlogs Nederland* (unpublished typoscript).

25   *NIW*, 11 February 1949.

26   *Ibid.*

Jewish responses: collective protest as the exception

Nevertheless, most Jews probably reacted like the parents of Ron van der
Wieken and their friends who, after the liberation, discussed their lives on
long summer nights in Scheveningen. One of the topics were the antisemitic
expressions after the war. Usually, the atmosphere was subdued, along the
lines of 'That's how it is, there is not much you can do about it' and 'What do
they know, those *goyim,* they all have *risjes*', according to Van der Wieken.
His father and a few friends, who had served as soldiers in the Princess Irene
Brigade or elsewhere, took a more militant stance. They believed that the
right thing to do was to lash out. But, as far as Van der Wieken knows, that
had never actually happened.[27]

The first public war monument founded by Jews was one that expressed
gratitude to the non-Jews who had come to their help. But that, of course, did
not mean that gratitude was the most dominant feeling among Jews. This
can also be deducted from the fights and confrontations described above.
Gratitude certainly did not prevail among the radical current within the
Zionist movement, a faction within the Dutch Zionist Union which was,
already before the war, an ideological activist advance guard, traversing
various Zionist strands and openly and strongly condemning assimilation, and not afraid to raise the issue of home-grown antisemitism. Jewish
culture and active emigration to (what was then still) Palestine (*aliya*)
were also high on the agenda.[28] In February 1947 the *Leeuwarder Courant*
concluded that a gap had grown between Jews and non-Jews that had not
existed before the war. Jews threw themselves with 'fanatic passion' at
the question of how to move on from here and simplified the answer to a
choice between Palestine and assimilation. Non-Jews looked at them with
'a certain strangeness and, sometimes, a certain unwillingness'.

> Unlike before it is not possible to discuss the path and fate of the Jews in
> a peaceful atmosphere; every word that is being said about it, no matter
> how well-intended, triggers a sharp irritability. It is as if the unheard
> cries of fear of the gassed are still floating in the air in despair, asking
> for accountability ....[29]

27 Email by Ron van der Wieken to Evelien Gans, 20 June 2012. For the term 'risjes': *see* chapter 1.
28 *See* note 32 on radical Zionism.
29 *Leeuwarder Courant*, 26 February 1947.

As an important illustration of what he meant, the journalist described
how at the recent general assembly of the Dutch Zionist Union (NZB), the
chairman of the NZB had declared that almost everywhere in the world
antisemitism was on the rise, that England waged a reign of terror in
Palestine and that a Jewish community outside Palestine was no longer
viable. The assembly took a radical stance against the Dutch missionary
work among the Jews and an equally radical position against the UN plan
to divide Palestine between Jews and Arabs. The NZB would ask the Dutch
government to support the aim of one undivided Jewish Palestine. At the
same time, it noted that on this issue the Jews' wishes fell on deaf ears
within the government and that goodwill among the Dutch population
was on the wane. These Zionists were prepared to put up with the fact that
such views would lead to a growing distance from the population in their
'guest countries', the *Leeuwarder Courant* said. 'They saw it as inevitable
....' The reporter was shocked about what he apparently experienced as a
one-sided opposition against the Netherlands. He had felt torn between
'intense and sometimes breathtaking compassion and indignation about
the ... unheard-of presumptuousness of these people', whom he suddenly
experienced as complete strangers.[30] The *Leeuwarder Courant* probably did
not know that after the war the radical Zionists were initially controlling
the NZB, as mentioned above. Salomon Kleerekoper (1893-1970), socialist,
Zionist and Professor of Economics, was also part of this engaged and self-
conscious company. He made the provocative statement that there was only
one choice for Jews: Zionist or assimilation.[31] During the first years after the
war, the radical Zionists also had a strong representation within re-founded
Jewish organisations and postwar reconstruction institutions. One of them
was NZB chairman Jaap van Amerongen (1913-1995), whom the *Leeuwarder
Courant* described as the personification of 'blind self-righteousness' and
'outrageous arrogance'.[32] When Van Amerongen and his family went on an

30 *Ibid.*

31 Gans, *De kleine verschillen*, 391.

32 For Jaap van Amerongen's role in the Dutch Zionist movement and, after 1948, in Israel (as
Ja'akov Arnon), *see ibid., passim.* See for the role of the radical Zionists and the power struggle
between the various Jewish groups in the Netherlands, *ibid.*, 577-631. *See also* Conny Kristel,
'Leiderschap na de ondergang. De strijd om de macht in joods naoorlogs Nederland.' In: Conny
Kristel (ed.), *Binnenskamers. Terugkeer en opvang na de Tweede Wereldoorlog. Besluitvorming*
(Amsterdam: Bert Bakker, 2002), 209-234, and: Chaya Brasz, 'Onontbeerlijk maar eigengereid.
De zionistische inmenging in de naoorlogse joodse gemeenschap' In: Kristel, *Binnenskamers*,
235-260.

aliya shortly before the foundation of Israel, Kleerekoper succeeded him as NZB's chairman.

Several radical Zionists had only one foot in the Netherlands, ready to leave for Palestine. But until that time they were, unlike most other Jewish survivors, looking for a confrontation with non-Jewish society and, if needed, with other Jews. They were the engine behind the foundation of the Joodse Ereraad [Jewish Council of Honour] which was to manage the purging process within the Jewish community – first of all of both chairmen of the Jewish Council, the classicist David Cohen (1882-1967) and the diamond trader and politician Abraham Asscher (1880-1950), and of the other board members. Kleerekoper, Van Amerongen, Jozeph Michman (at the time still Melkman; classicist and historian, long-standing editor in chief of NIW) (1914-2009) and their sympathisers denounced the slow restitution of equal rights to the Jews in the Netherlands, the myth of the February Strike (was that not also the last time that the people in Amsterdam had stood up for their Jewish population?), postwar Dutch antisemitism and the passive attitude of the Dutch authorities and the majority of the population with regard to the persecution of the Jews. If most of these radical Zionists had stayed in their country of birth, they might have been able to raise more attention for Dutch antisemitism. But because mentally they had already partly said farewell to their country of birth, it was easier for them, less painful, to openly denounce anti-Jewish tendencies in the Netherlands during and after the occupation.[33] All those who were not planning to emigrate, to Israel or elsewhere – or who had serious doubts about it, including Zionists – stood to benefit more, for the time being, from a qualified and distanced view on the attitude of non-Jewish Dutch. They were focusing on a fresh start or a relatively harmonious life in the Netherlands.

That made it difficult to take a stand, especially at a political level. As mentioned above, in 1960 the Dutch authorities, in breach of the German guidelines, excluded Jews who had gone into hiding from the *Wiedergutmachung* funds in favour of former resistance fighters who, basically, were not eligible for these funds. Protests from the Jewish side were suppressed with the warning that it would not be in the Jews' interests if they opposed benefit payments to former members of the resistance. The advisory committee for the benefit payments of war victims, known as the *Drees Committee* (1961),

---

33 For the actions of the Jewish Council of Honour and the course of the Jewish purging, *see* Gans, *De kleine verschillen*, 603-631. For the position of the radical Zionists, *ibid.*, 741-767. Salomon Kleerekoper would stay in the Netherlands and remained a criticaster, also with regard to Israel: *ibid.*, 774-782, 791-799.

had even considered whether it should pay families of Jewish victims less than those of non-Jews, because 'the current Jewish generation is better off than the average non-Jew in the Netherlands'.[34] This was not only a call on the duty of Jews to be grateful, but also a snide reference to the stereotype of the Rich Jew who had to make sure not to cause any envy. It was a subtle way to warn about the risk of an antisemitic backlash. The Jewish (religious) organisations got the message. They did not follow up their initial protests with further action, as this '[would] not make a good impression'.[35]

It looks as if, at this stage, Jewish protests' only chance of success was to act collectively and openly and with full support from non-Jews. There was certainly protest – albeit not very coordinated – against the slow and whimsical restitution of legal rights, lost or stolen houses, possessions and money to Jews, and against the temporary continuation of the (Nazi) ban on the Jewish ritual of slaughter without pre-stunning.[36] There was also a long-lasting unsuccessful resistance from the Jewish side against the continuation of the anti-Jewish restrictions in the shop closure law imposed by the German occupier. In this specific case, the tide only started to turn when the Jewish community joined forces and openly voiced their opinion by sending requests to the city council of Amsterdam and the Parliament. They were now supported by, among others, prominent non-Jewish sympathisers such as Arnold d'Ailly, mayor of Amsterdam. In various phases the law was gradually adjusted with regard to the crucial point for Jews: the permission to keep a shop open on Sundays instead of Saturdays (i.e. the Sabbath). In 1959, the regulation was restored to its 1935 level; Jewish shopkeepers were allowed to keep their shops open until 6 pm on Sundays. So it took almost fifteen years to 'bring a satisfactory end to this long battle', noted

34   Officially, '*Commissie van Advies inzake uitkeringen ten gunste van Nederlandse slachtoffers van de Nationaal-Socialistische vervolging*'; Hinke Piersma, *Bevochten recht. Politieke besluitvorming rond de wetten voor oorlogsslachtoffers* (Amsterdam: Boom, 2010), 95. *See also* chapter 2.

35   Piersma, *Bevochten recht*, 97. The reasoning that those who had been persecuted as a result of active acts of resistance would be more entitled to social benefits than those merely persecuted for being Jewish, also contained despise for an alleged Jewish passivity: *ibid.*, 101.

36   There is quite a lot of documentation about the postwar struggle by Jews to restore their right to ritually slaughter animals, p.p. J. Tal (Chief Rabbi), A. Salomons (secretary) to Mr Snuyff, 5 December 1946, Archive NIHS, 46-48, M-Z; *NIW*, 10 February 1950. *See also* Jaap Cohen, 'De slachtstrijd is weer opgelaaid', *NRC Next*, 28 June 2011; Bas Kromhout, 'Kritiek op ritueel slachten is soms antisemitisch. Dierenbeschermers wilden in 1945 Duits verbod handhaven' (Interview with Evelien Gans) *Historisch Nieuwsblad* (April 2011), 28; Bart Wallet, 'Rituele slacht en godsdienstvrijheid in een seculiere samenleving,' *Religie & Samenleving*, 7, 2 (September 2012), 166-183. This subject is also addressed in the Epilogue.

the Permanent Committee of the Dutch-Israeli Congregation [*Nederlands Israëlietisch Kerkgenootschap*; NIK].[37]

The Schokking affair

It wasn't until the so-called Schokking affair that attention for anti-Jewish sentiments led to a national debate. In 1956, the *Haagsch Dagblad* revealed that, during the German occupation, in his previous position as mayor of the village of Hazerswoude, the mayor of The Hague, F.M.A. Schokking, had turned over a Jewish family in hiding to the German Security Service (SD). Almost the entire political, constitutional and religious establishment intervened in his defence. The case was already known, but put aside. At the time, the Jewish man in question, Jacob Pino, had allegedly behaved strangely and irresponsibly; as a result he was suspected of being a collaborator. Now, fourteen years later, impure (left-wing) motives had led to the *Haagsch Dagblad's* initiative, according to those who came to Schokking's defence.[38] A number of professors, including the historian P.J. Bouman, professors of law R.P Cleveringa, C.H.F. Polak and B.V.A. Röling, and the poet M. Vasalis called for an end to the postwar purge.[39] Minister Beel of Internal Affairs, of the Catholic party KVP, who knew Schokking's dossier because of his appointment, but who had ignored Pino's case as not relevant, set up an investigative committee headed by the President of the Supreme Court, J. Donner. In its final report the committee warned of 'wisdom in hindsight' and fully cleared Schokking.

But, entirely unexpectedly, that was not the end of the story. When Schokking felt strong enough to sue the *Haagsch Dagblad* at the Disciplinary Board of the Federation of Dutch Journalists (FJN), it backfired on him. Thorough investigative journalism revealed that Pino had not at all been guilty of collaboration. This undermined the foundation of Schokking's defence and the Donner committee's report concerning a number of other issues. The fact that Schokking's behaviour was a flagrant breach of what should have been expected from him, was underlined by an alliance between

37   Gans, 'Gojse broodnijd', 212.
38   For an extensive treatment of this case, *see* De Haan, *Na de ondergang*, 106-118.
39   The stance of the poet M. Vasalis, pseudonym of Margaretha Drooglever Fortuyn-Leenmans (1909-1998), who engaged in acts of resistance during the war, is remarkable. Her opinion might have been partly formed through her friendship with Professor Bert Röling, *see* Maaike Meijer, *M. Vasalis. Een biografie* (Amsterdam: G.A. van Oorschot, 2011). The Schokking affair is not mentioned in the biography.

progressive groups within the (former) resistance, politics and journalism. A climate was emerging in which the situation of the Pino family was also put in the broader context of the persecution of the Jews. Eventually, so many murky things emerged that Schokking's position became untenable. He was given an honourable resignation and, within a year, appointed as dike warden (chair of a water board).[40]

In his history of the Shoah's postwar memory, the political scientist Ido de Haan rightly argued that in the Schokking affair – and in the 1950s and 1960s in general – the Jewish voice was unable to make its mark on the public perception of the persecution of the Jews. On the contrary, it was the non-Jews who stood up for them. And when Jews *did* speak for themselves, this generally generated hostile reactions and antisemitic prejudices. For example, by the right-leaning resistance publication *Voormalig Verzet Nederland* (VVN), which said that the stereotype of the 'typically nervous, scared Jew' applied to Pino. And by the spokesperson of the Liberal Party VVD, W. Ritmeester, who argued that he had come across many Jews of all sorts, 'in addition to brave also cowardly', and that the Pino family had fitted into the category 'difficult' and had deserved an extremely powerful reprimand.[41] Similar to the trial against Klaas Norel (as described in chapter 2), it was another projection of the image of the nervous, cowardly, unreliable and collaborating Jew. Supportive voices about the 'agony' of the Jews who had gone into hiding, about how their nervousness made sense, fell on deaf ears because of the tough mass of stereotypes.[42]

The Dachau game

The fact that there wasn't a lot of coordinated protest didn't mean that the phenomenon of postwar antisemitism did not interest Jews in the Netherlands. The NIW quite frequently wrote about incidents which the magazine perceived as antisemitic – sometimes in a bitter tone, but often in a distanced or sarcastic way. That was one of the traditional ways in which Jews had protected and shielded themselves, among their own, against the *goyim*. Sometimes also provocatively, like the song that was sung in

40 De Haan, *Na de ondergang*, 115-116.
41 *Ibid.*, 112-116. Actually, the same VVN also denounced antisemitism on several occasions. In 1958, for instance, it concluded, on the basis of a number of examples, that the statement that after World War Two antisemitism in the Netherlands had further increased, was probably correct: Gans, *Antisemitisme?*.
42 *Ibid.*, 110-111.

the old Jewish quarter of Amsterdam before the war, and which captured the stereotype of the Christ killer under the motto 'The best defence is a good offense':

Zeven spijkers, zeven krammen	Seven nails and clamps from us
Daar hebben we Jezus aan opgehangen[43]	It took to put Jesus on the cross

But in line with the Zionist inspired conviction that arguments against antisemitism were not very effective, and that it was, basically, a problem of the non-Jews, it definitely wasn't a favourite topic in the NIW. Furthermore, the NIW was not a player in the national field, usually adopted an aloof or cautious attitude, and focused on its own circle.

The most important incident in the early 1960s was the above-mentioned 'Dachau game', by the student association *Amsterdamsch Studenten Corps* (ASC). The term 'Dachau game' was used by the president of NIA (*Nos Iungit Amicitia*), ASC's student society committee charged with the initiation. He had shouted 'We are going to play the Dachau game' to the *feuten* [freshmen] with their heads shaved and naked torsos, in a narrow space. That one Jewish student who complained about this was hurled at, 'Shut up, filthy Jew', as mentioned above, made aspiring member Wim Noordhoek, who wasn't Jewish himself, decide to leave, which triggered the scandal.[44] When an internal complaint fell on deaf ears, the press was alerted and the 'Dachau game' became a national scandal. The university said it was shocked, and the issue was addressed by the city council and in Parliament.[45] The debate in the press was mainly about whether this was a case of antisemitism.

---

43   Bregstein and Bloemgarten, *Herinnering aan Joods Amsterdam*, 191. Translation: Luuk Arens. For such a distanced and sarcastic approach, *see, e.g.*: 'Vraag op redactiebespreking: Wat doen wij aan die antisemietische pastoor uit Leende? Besluit: Niets', *NIW*, 29 October 1965, NIOD, KB II, 307 B.

44   The contested 'Dachau game' returned in different contexts, for example: '*Foeten*, shut up or we will go and play the Dachau game down in the basement': *Algemeen Dagblad*, 9 October 1962; according to the newspaper the term was used several times. Most newspapers only reported 'Filthy Jew'. Some mentioned that the father or both parents or relatives of the protesting *feut* had been killed in Dachau.

45   *See Algemeen Dagblad*, 9, 10 and 17 October 1962; *Haagse Post*, 27 October 1962, *Het Parool*, 9 October 1962 and many other newspapers and magazines: NIOD, KB II 307 A; *see* Piebe Theeboom, '150 jaar Corps in Amsterdam: een geschiedenis van het ASC/AVSV.' In: J.W. Ebbinge et al. (ed.), *Wij Amsterdamsche Studiosi. 150 jaar ASC/AVSV* (Amsterdam: ASC/AVSV, 2002), 12-206. The concentration camp Dachau was originally set up for political prisoners, but they were gradually joined by various other groups of prisoners, mainly Jews. *NIW*, 19 October 1962, NIOD, KB II 307 A. For a more thorough report, *see also Algemeen Handelsblad*, 22 and 23 October 1962.

Illustration 9   A news clipping on an incident with a student initiation ceremony from the *Haagse Post*, 27 October 1962

Afsluitingsritueel (met varken) van de groentijd van het Amsterdams Studenten Corps
„O, was ik maar bij moeder thuis gebleven…" (groentijdlied) pag. 7

NIOD KB II 307a

In 1962, it became publically known how the most 'established' Amsterdam student association threatened a group of freshmen with going to 'play the Dachau game' during its annual initiation ceremony. The incident turned into a national scandal, triggered by a photo which actually dated from the year before.

In the student journal *Propria Cures* (PC), its editor defined the antisemitic component as follows.

Whether the members in question of the students' union are really anti-semites, or irresponsible youths, hardly matters. This sort of behaviour makes antisemitism *bon ton* among hundreds of future students ….[46]

46   Referred to in *Het Parool*, 9 October 1962. This reasoning could also be applied to the anti-Jewish chants of the supporters of clubs playing against Ajax, *see* chapter 11.

It was not the first and certainly not the last time that the question was asked to what extent they were dealing with 'real' antisemites. But *PC* made it clear that the question was basically not relevant: it was about what was being said, and what effect this could have. The former Reformed resistance newspaper *Trouw* also appeared not to take an interest in the concept of the 'real' antisemite. The newspaper wrote that people talked about antisemitism – and in general – as if it were a strange disease, because that made it easy to blame it on lunatics and criminals.[47] *Het Parool* quoted the student Michiel Cohen de Lara who confirmed that during the initiation in question he was ordered to sing an antisemitic song, which he had refused.[48] The left-leaning former resistance weekly *Vrij Nederland* reported that the 'Dachau game' had, in some instances, led to exaggerated reactions, like the demand for a 'new Nuremberg' and the remark that it would be better to put an end to the 5 May liberation celebrations. At the same time, the magazine condemned *de Volkskrant* which had supported the rector of ASC's senate in his firm denial that this was a case of antisemitism. The weekly, significantly, referred to the Catholic roots of both *de Volkskrant* itself and of the contested president and his NIA student union committee member. But *De Telegraaf,* which had collaborated with the Nazis during the German occupation and was now right-leaning, had stood up for the two members of the association who were 'unquestionably not antisemitic'.[49] The original motivation of whistle-blower Max Arian (b. 1940), political science student and ASC member, was to tackle the initiation practice, or even abolish it, rather than denounce antisemitism. But as he learned more details, the latter motive became increasingly important to him.[50] He had initially tried to accept the ASC senate's argument that within the student union it was equally possible to say dirty Frisian or dirty Catholic instead of filthy Jew, but subsequently rejected that as a fallacy. The senate had not understood 'how much I was emotionally involved in this case as a Jew'.[51] While the 'Dachau game' in itself may have served as a fitting description of the 'initiation ritual', in 2012 Arian stated that in addition there were also clearly antisemitic expressions.[52]

47   *Trouw*, 20 October 1962.
48   Earlier, *Het Parool* had erroneously reported that the student in question was ordered to sing 'Und wir fahren gegen Engeland': *Het Parool*, 22 October 1962.
49   *Vrij Nederland*, 20 October 1962.
50   Emails by Max Arian to Evelien Gans, 1 February 2012. *See also* emails sent by Fred Borensztajn, Pitt Treuman and Philip van Tijn to Evelien Gans on 2 and 3 February 2012.
51   *Het Parool*, 20 October 1962, NIOD, KB II 307 A.
52   Email by Max Arian to Evelien Gans, 1 February 2012.

But the antisemitism factor soon disappeared off the radar. The ASC implemented a number of reforms. The initiation period was still based on the principle of inequality, but almost all elements of physical violence were banned, like the notorious *'indikken'* (literally, 'thicken', squeezing many people together in a confined space), which had led to the expression 'Dachau game' to begin with, *'kikkeren'* (frog jumping), ripping up clothes, etc. The head shaving practice remained in place, though.[53] On the basis of the committee's report, set up by the Rector of the University, J. Kok, fourteen leading students of the ASC were suspended for a few months. This was a case of collective guilt as 'a result of an old-fashioned and wrong system'. It had nothing to do with antisemitism, according to Kok. The denounced expressions were more based 'on ignorance and lack of insight and originality, than on something that smelled of antisemitism'.[54] But the Dutch Zionist Student Organisation (NZSO) saw antisemitism during the initiation period as something inevitable. In a letter sent to the student journal *Propria Cures* it stated that Jews would always be confronted with antisemitism. The time that Jews kept quiet 'for fear of a conflict with their non-Jewish environment is, however, gone', according to the Zionistic organisation. Only after effective punishment and reform of the initiation would Jews again be able to join one of the student associations without loss of self-respect. In its response, a second *PC* editor – with a diametrically different approach than that of his fellow editor – accused the NZSO of making an unfair division between Jews and non-Jews. He said the evil was implicated in the initiation as such. The NZSO was, hence, guilty of an 'easy use of the word antisemitism'.[55]

The fact that tempers had flared so much, had a lot to do with the political and cultural climate of the period in question. The first seeds of a rebellious democratisation had germinated – at universities more and more students joined alternative, mostly progressive student associations, and

---

53 *Vrij Nederland*, 3 November 1962. 'Playing Dachau' became winged words for excesses occurring during the initiation periods of Dutch students' unions (corpora), *see* e.g. Rob van Eeden's blog at www.robvaneeden.nl/html/archief_januari_2007.html (consulted 5 March 2013); *Limburgsch Dagblad*, 31 August 1991. In 2012, there was an outcry about an 'initiation' at a party organised by the actors of the TV series 'Feuten', inspired by elitist student unions, including their initiations, because some visitors had allegedly been insulted and humiliated, for example by being forced to make the Hitler salute: *de Volkskrant*, 12 April 2012. Philip Huff's novel *Niemand in de stad* (Amsterdam: De Bezige Bij, 2012) about members of the ASC also mentions homophobia and antisemitism as fixed ingredients of this culture: *NRC Handelsblad*, 3 February 2012.

54 De Haan, *Na de ondergang*, 119.

55 *Ibid.*, 120. Voor *PC* editor Verstegen, *see* earlier in this chapter.

in 1963 the Student Union (SVB) was founded.[56] Furthermore, the war and the persecution of the Jews had become more familiar issues. Only a few months earlier, in May 1962, Eichmann had been hanged. The entire country was hooked to Dr Loe de Jong's TV series *De Bezetting* [The Occupation] about the Netherlands in 1940-1945. One person wrote a letter wondering if members of the student association in question had ever heard about the annual Remembrance Day and the fallen resistance fighters. 'Have they never watched any films about the concentration camps, never read anything about the Eichmann trial, never watched the extraordinary TV programmes of Dr L. de Jong ...?'[57]

On the evening of 1 February 1963, the Dutch Dachau commemoration committee came to Leiden University, upon an invitation by the Leiden student contact commission, to put an end to the ignorance among students about 'Dachau'. Formers prisoners, including author Nico Rost (1896-1967) and poet Ed Hoornik (1910-1960), talked about their experiences. The evening's theme was the resistance, as was the case for the organising Dachau committee associated with the Organisation of Former Political Prisoners, Expogé. The information evening was attended by only thirty students.[58] But a few months earlier, in Amsterdam, hundreds of students had come to Kriterion, a student cinema, for the screening of *Nuit et Brouillard* [Night and Fog] (1955) by film director Alain Resnais, 'the famous documentary about the horrors of German concentration camps'. Later that week two more screenings would follow. Here too, the event was triggered by the 'recent excesses during initiation' and 'Dachautje spelen' in particular. Around fifteen members of the student association were among the attendees; no members of the senate, which had approved the initiative, were present.[59] Resnais' documentary had premiered in the Netherlands in 1957; the year after the Anne Frank House had been saved from demolition – and the year before, finally, it was decided to convert the Hollandsche Schouwburg into a remembrance site. These were all small steps in an awareness process

56 Theeboom, '150 jaar Corps in Amsterdam', 107.
57 *Het Parool*, 15 October 1962, NIOD, KB II 307 A. Frank van Vree, *In de schaduw van Auschwitz. Herinneringen, beelden, geschiedenis* (Groningen: Historische Uitgeverij, 1995), 57-88.
58 *Algemeen Handelsblad*, 1 February 1963, NIOD, KB II 307 A. Expogé published two articles about the incident: Aalders, 'Dachau-spel' and 'De groentijd-incidenten en de concentratiekampen', *Aantreden. Orgaan van de Nederlandse Vereniging van Ex-politieke Gevangenen uit de Bezettingstijd*, 17, 11 (November 1962), 401-405.
59 *Het Vrije Volk*, 29 October 1962.

that brought the war closer, especially the persecution of the Jews, with the Eichmann trial as an important accelerator.[60]

A typical indication of how erratic this development was – not only in the Netherlands – was the absence of the word 'Jews' in *Nuit et Brouillard,* even though the film was actually about the persecution of the Jews.[61] The fact that there was gradually and explicitly more attention for the persecution of the Jews does not mean that there was a lot of reflection on antisemitism in Dutch society. While former resistance fighters like cartoonist and social democrat Jan Rot (1892-1982) clearly denounced *'Dachautje spelen'* as a 'disgusting antisemitic expression',[62] *Propria Cures* had silenced the Zionist students on that issue. The magazine was, however, right when it noted that the NZSO, 'considering its specific views [was] hardly representative of Dutch students of Jewish descent in general'.[63] Antisemitism in the Netherlands was only experienced as a relevant theme or problem by a few. A number of students who had left the ASC in protest, such as Max Arian, also drew a line under their experience with antisemitism to dedicate themselves to the ideals of student unions and a more democratic society or explicitly organised on the basis of socialism.[64]

Jewish debate

Despite its overall reluctant attitude towards the topic of antisemitism, in October 1962 the NIW offered a platform for a thorough and historical debate on precisely that issue between a number of prominent Dutch Jews, or 'wise men': the lawyer and professor Isaac Kisch (1905-1980), the economist Salomon Kleerekoper (1893-1970), the lawyer and author Abel Herzberg (1893-1989), Salco Hertzberger, MD (1913-1979) and two – at the time much less prominent – Jews from a younger generation: the chemist Manfred Gerstenfeld (b. 1937) and the political scientist Isaac Lipschits

60 The commentator in the Dutch version of this French documentary was the author Victor van Vriesland: *Het Vrije Volk,* 19 May 1957. *See also* Van Vree, *In de schaduw van Auschwitz,* 98-99.
61 In Israel, this universalistic approach led to a heated political debate which, initially, led to a limited number of screenings: Nitzan Lebovic, 'An Absence with Traces: The reception of Nuit et Brouillard in Israel.' In: Ewout van der Knaap (ed.), *Uncovering the Holocaust: The international reception of Night and Fog* (London: Wallflower Press, 2006), 86-105.
62 *VVN,* 25 oktober 1962, NIOD, Kb II 307.
63 De Haan, *Na de ondergang,* 120
64 That was true for Max Arian and several of his fellow members: Emails by Max Arian to Evelien Gans, 1 February 2012.

(1930-2008), who chaired the debate. The NIW assured its readers that it would not abandon its principled stance: the incidents which leading up to the debate had in fact not deserved all the pages devoted to them. With the Simchat Torah (Rejoicing of the Law) holiday around the corner, people in Israel and here had more important and more joyful preoccupations. But because, according to chairman Lipschits, 'a certain anxiety' was growing in the Jewish community about a series of events in recent weeks, they had decided, after all, that it was important to ask a few authoritative figures to discuss their opinion about these 'aspects of the Jewish issue'.[65]

All five participants were Zionists and more or less shared the opinion put forward by Herzberg and cherished by Zionism that antisemitism was not a Jewish problem. It was 'a problem of civilisation of the non-Jew'.[66] Hence, they all agreed – with the exception of one – that it was up to non-Jews to do something about it or not. Kleerekoper said he had only noted a very small increase in antisemitism. He believed that basically little had changed since the liberation: in the first period after the war a more or less virulent anti-semitism had been noticeable in the Netherlands.[67] Kleerekoper was very much inclined to play down the level of antisemitism in the Netherlands. He pointed to the politically and culturally 'strong philosemitic overcurrent' in the Netherlands which, he suspected, was caused by a sense of guilt.[68] He did, however, refer to the 'swastika vandalism' of a few years ago and, of course, to neo-Nazi Paul van Tienen's outrageous activities.[69]

So the 'Dachautje spelen' incident did not make any impression on Kleere-koper; he considered it a 'completely irrelevant question'. Herzberg did not agree with that. He did agree on other matters. On this point Herzberg uttered the timeless and oft-quoted words: '... and if the gentlemen want to be antisemites, then let them do as they please.' But he made an excep-tion when it came to the 'Dachau game'. Apparently, those student society members identified with the persecutors – and there may have been an antisemitic element to that. Herzberg himself had become convinced that 'cruelty is an infectious disease, but also something that is longed for'. He

65 'Geen joods probleem, maar een beschavingsprobleem', NIW, 19 October 1962, NIOD, KB II 307 A.
66 Ibid.
67 NIW, 19 October 1962.
68 At the same time, radical and critical Jews like Kleerekoper had a sceptical approach to philosemitism: at some point it could backfire, Kleerekoper admitted. For Kleerekoper's approach to antisemitism, see Gans, De kleine verschillen, 285ff, 358ff, 797. Kleerekoper's Het antisemitisme en zijn randverschijnselen was published posthumously (Deventer: Van Loghum Slaterus, 1970). For philosemitism, see chapter 6.
69 NIW, 19 October 1962. See chapter 4.

wondered, for example, if all the publicity about 'Poland' in the context of the Eichmann trial had not only a deterring effect, but also triggered a certain 'desire' – a craving for violence or sadism.[70]

Unlike (the younger) Gerstenfeld, Kisch and Hertzberger were not in favour of Jewish protests denouncing antisemitism, however tempting it may have been. According to Kisch, Dutch society lived with those Jews who had returned as if they were ghosts. Non-Jewish patients of Hertzberger, who was a GP, told him that there was still a lot of antisemitism: 'Behind the Jews' backs, at dinner parties, at birthday parties, during ordinary meetings, in pubs ....' Kisch talked about antisemitism as an 'infectious disease', Hertzberger as an 'endemic disease', which however was not 'virulent'. And if you couldn't stand it, you should go to Israel.[71]

Unlike Herzberg, Kleerekoper did not talk in psychological terms about a desire for cruelty as a general human trait. He did, however, see all the attention for the Eichmann trial as *gefundenes fressen* for former sympathisers of the meanwhile executed war criminal, i.e. for former ss soldiers. Furthermore, it was remarkable that Kleerekoper believed that too much publicity, whether for the Eichmann trial, Anne Frank and the *Achterhuis* or other 'Jewish misery', contained 'an element of self-pity'. Not that the Jewish people had no reason to complain about what had been done to them. But one should rather keep one's complaints to oneself. As the old Yiddish saying goes: *'De kinnes behoren thuis gezongen te worden'* [sing your sorrows at home]. That was sometimes lacking nowadays.[72] Kleerekoper, who never shied away from unconventional opinions, seems to point here to the danger of (Jewish) narcissism – referred to in the introductory essay – a psychoanalytical term to describe a person whose disproportionate sense of self-esteem hides the opposite: a deep sense of insecurity. Here, Jewish narcissism is freely interpreted as the tendency among Jews to reduce their own self-image to two extremes: suffering and pride; pride also as compensation for the suffering.[73] But Kleerekoper also noted the possibility

---

70 *Ibid.*

71 *Ibid.*

72 *Ibid.* Interestingly enough, just like Herzberg and Kleerekoper, albeit from an completely different perspective, the challenged journalist himself had also expressed his doubt in *De Post* (*see* chapter 3) about whether the Eichmann trial would lead to renewed sympathy for the Jews and renewed indignation about the Germans: *De Post*, 14 May 1961.

73 Gans, *Gojse nijd & joods narcisme*, 47-48; Evelien Gans, '"They have forgotten to gas you." Post-1945 Antisemitism in the Netherlands', in: Philomena Essed and Isable Hoving (eds.) *Dutch Racism* (Amsterdam, New York: Rodopi, 2014), 71-100: 84.

that when Jews got or demanded a lot of attention for their victimisation, this would, eventually, backfire at them.[74]

In fact, that is what happened right from the start. By verbally, retroactively sending 'the Jew' to the gas chamber, by accusing him of intolerance, by reducing him to an aggressive, complaining and stealing camp prisoner, by downplaying or denying his victimisation, and by playfully pushing him into a camp setting.

Less than two months after NIW's debate by authoritative Jews, the Amsterdam branch of the NZB hosted its first lecture in a 'Jewish problem' series about the 'psychological aspects of antisemitism'. The lecturer was Dr Hans Keilson, introduced as psychiatrist and author of the novel *In de ban van de tegenstander* (1959) [The Death of the Adversary].[75] Hans Keilson (1909-2011) was a German Jew who had fled to the Netherlands in 1936, and had been taking part in resistance activities while in hiding during the German occupation. After the liberation he became very closely involved, as a psychiatrist, in the treatment of Jewish war orphans. In his lecture in Amsterdam, Keilson, like Hertzberger, talked about antisemitism as an 'endemic disease' unrelated to time and place. Like his predecessors he said that antisemitism should be considered 'a problem of non-Jewish civilisation'. Also like them, he assumed that discussions with antisemites were pointless because this was a 'specific irrational prejudice'. Keilson added that it was actually just as impossible to discuss antisemitism with Jews, 'because we are all completely emotionally charged'. Keilson pointed out that people from a wide range of backgrounds were getting together and mobilising themselves under the joint banner of antisemitism – a function of antisemitism which the historian Steve Beller called 'negative integration'.[76]

Keilson mainly differed from Kleerekoper and his followers by emphatically using both a sociological and psychoanalytical set of tools. The fact that it was fashionable to talk about being 'in' and 'out' did not, according to Keilson, make these concepts less relevant when applied to antisemitism. It is the 'in' group which turns the minority group, in this case the Jews, into an 'out' group and exaggerates its alleged inferior characteristics. Keilson also introduced the concept of ethnocentrism: putting one's own people at

74 For the emergence of an (alleged) culture of complaining: Gans, *Gojse nijd & joods narcisme*, 121-122; Jolande Withuis, *Erkenning. Van oorlogstrauma naar klaagcultuur* (Amsterdam: De Bezige Bij, 2005).

75 *NIW*, 14 December 1962.

76 For Steve Beller and the concept of 'negative integration', *see* chapter 1.

the centre – but without actually saying that this was applicable to Zionism. As a psychoanalyst he explicitly used the concept of projection and the example of the dictator who, in times of crisis, was able to put the blame for everything that went wrong 'on the easy projection screen that are the Jews'. Even though their names are not mentioned in NIW's report, Keilson undoubtedly tapped into the ideas of the sociologists and philosophers Adorno and Horkheimer of the *Frankfurter Schule*. During their exile in the United States the latter two had developed, in collaboration with psychoanalysts such as Ernst Simmel and Otto Fenichel, an analysis of antisemitism in which psychoanalytical categories played a crucial role.[77] Keilson also talked in relation to the psychological phenomenon of 'projection' of the 'authoritarian personality' with its non-channelled urges, for whom it is particularly tempting to take their own failings out on others, and who is, as such, more susceptible than others to antisemitism.[78]

In 1965, after the publication of *Ondergang*, Presser's much talked about *j'accuse* as well as his obituary,[79] many more heated debates about antisemitism and the attitude of the Dutch population during and after the German occupation would follow in the NIW among a younger generation. And later again, during the 1970s, the idea among Jews that it was 'beneath Jewish dignity' to protest against antisemitism, would acquire another, almost opposite meaning, if not make a complete turnabout. 'Jewish dignity' would express itself in a state of permanent alertness and militancy, and in judicial and other kinds of protests – all from a predominantly Jewish side.[80]

77 *See* chapter 1. Introductory essay.

78 *NIW*, 14 December 1962; *see* Ernst Simmel, Theodor W. Adorno and Elisabeth Dahmer-Kloss (eds.), *Antisemitismus* (Frankfurt a. M: Fischer Verlag, 1993). For the psychological and psychoanalytical dimension, *see also* chapter 2.

79 Van Vree, *In de schaduw van Auschwitz*, 104.

80 *See* chapters 6 and 8.

Part II
Israel and 'the Jew'

6 Philosemitism?

Ambivalences regarding Israel

Evelien Gans

Research into the relations between the Netherlands and Israel provides a dominant image of a 'special relationship' – a relationship between two 'sworn friends'.[1] The question is to what extent that image is correct. And if it is, what the explanatory factors are for this relation. Could it be reduced to a sense of guilt because of the deportation and murder of so many Jews from the Netherlands, even emphasised by the fact that their number was high in proportion to other Western European occupied countries? In the discussion between prominent Jewish intellectuals as mentioned in chapter 5, the economist Salomon Kleerekoper came up with the term philosemitism to depict the dominant attitude among the Dutch Gentile population towards the Jews. At the same time, however, he reminded his discussion partners of the acute antisemitism in the first years after the liberation. Moreover, he and his partners in dialogue had come together on the request of the Jewish weekly *Nieuw Israëlietisch Weekblad* (NIW) to reflect on several antisemitic incidents that took place in the beginning of the 1960s.

So, how should we conceive the concept of philosemitism – a fascinating but also highly complex and multi-interpretable phenomenon? This chapter opens exactly with this question, trying to provide some answers. Subsequently we shall turn to the attitude of the Dutch population and government towards Israel, and will examine and address a similar coincidence of philosemitic and antisemitic tendencies. Taking into account doubts, countervoices, ambivalent or critical attitudes, this chapter looks, more in general, at how the approach of the Netherlands towards Israel has shifted. Which interests have guided the Dutch government? And how did Dutch Jews relate to Israel and to what they regard, within this context, as antisemitism? There was a wide range of opinions among Jews. This

---

1   R.B. Soetendorp, 'The Netherlands and Israel: from a special to a normal relationship', *Internationale Spectator* 43 (November 1989), 697-700; F. Grünfeld, *Nederland en het Nabije Oosten: de Nederlandse rol in de internationale politiek ten aanzien van het Arabisch-Israëlisch conflict 1973-1982* (Deventer: Kluwer, 1991), 31; Frans Peeters, *Gezworen vrienden. Het geheime bondgenootschap tussen Nederland en Israël* (Amsterdam/Antwerp: L.J. Veen, 1997).

chapter looks at the shifting approaches towards Israel among both Jews and non-Jews until the 'watershed' of 1967.

Philosemitism and sense of guilt

The term philosemitism, described by Van Dale, the leading dictionary of the Dutch language, as *'Joodsgezindheid'* [Jewish disposition], can be interpreted in various ways. It literally means 'love for Jews', i.e. the opposite of antisemitism in its most embryonic form: aversion or hatred of Jews. Philosemitism can be interpreted as a genuine sympathy for Jews. But like antisemitism, philosemitism is often based on generalisations; both phenomena need the addition 'love or hate for Jews *as Jews*', i.e. *because* they are Jews. In the case of philosemitism this leads to a false bottom, because it, again, puts Jews at the risk of being turned into a stereotype of 'the Jew' just as antisemitism does. In which case, the 'love' (for Jews) is automatically triggered at the push of a button, ignoring who those complex human beings of flesh and blood, to whom we have to relate, *really* are. By strictly pursuing this line of reasoning philosemitism is the flip side of the same coin.[2] In Jewish circles people therefore tend to take a negative, or at least sceptical or suspicious, view of philosemitism. The Jewish poet Saul van Messel (the pseudonym of the historian Jaap Meijer) wrote the following short poem, entitled *'filosemiet'* (1967):

erger dan / haat die / beledigen / kan:	worse than / hate which / can / offend:
vriendschap / waartegen /	friendship / against which /
ik mij niet / verdedigen kan	I cannot / defend.[3]

Soon after the liberation feelings of guilt about people's own shortcomings regarding the Jews during the German occupation emerged – although it

---

2   Evelien Gans, 'Over gaskamers, Joodse nazi's en neuzen.' In: Peter Rodrigues and Jaap van Donselaar (eds.), *Monitor Racisme en Extremisme. Negende rapportage* (Anne Frank Stichting, Amsterdam University Press: Amsterdam, 2010), 141.

3   (Translation by E.G.) Saul van Messel, *Zeer zeker en zeker zeer. Joodse gedichten.* Haagse Cahiers 10 (Rijswijk Z.H.: De Oude Degel, 1967). Meijer systematically refused to use capital letters in his poetry. For Jaap Meijer, see the first part of the double biography of father Jaap and son Ischa Meijer: Evelien Gans, *Jaap en Ischa Meijer. Een joodse geschiedenis* (Amsterdam: Bert Bakker, 1994). In his novel *De laatste oorlog* [The last war] (2016), the Dutch author Daan Heerma van Voss (b. 1986) called the philosemite 'the nice neighbour of the antisemite', quoted in: Arjen Fortuin, 'Wat haalt de filosemiet nu weer in zijn hoofd?', *NRC Handelsblad*, 15 January 2015.

is difficult to establish to what extent. On the opposite side, people suppressed, denied or pushed aside those potential feelings of responsiblility or
guilt, for which they, subsequently, were rebuked by others. On 11 January
1947, F.R.A. Henkels wrote that during the war years 'we' had done *'iets'*
[something] for the Jews. To him, that word captured 'a lot of impotence,
helplessness, fear, unwillingness and all other things, which, combined,
define our shame and mourning'.[4] August Henkels was a Reformed clergy-
man who co-founded, during the war, *De Blauwe Schuit*, a publishing house
which illegally published, among other things, the *Chassidische Legenden*
[Chassidic Legends] (1941) by the artist and printer Hendrik Werkman (1882-
1945), who was executed in the final year of the war.[5] In his article, Henkels
commented on an antisemitic remark made by a friend, who had told him
that Jews were sending him letters about houses that were theirs, but had
ended up being managed by his company as a result of an NSB *Verwalter*
[custodian]. 'Real Jewish letters', Henkels' friend had said: *'zo springerig
en brutaal'* [jumpy and cheeky]. He added that he would usually let them
sweat for a while, before sending back a 'teasing letter'.[6]

Henkels referred to the incident in the context of his question whether
people sometimes believed that they had done all they could for the Jews,
'and that this unpleasant chapter had been closed with the liberation ....' He
had told his friend to tick off, trying to make clear in what kind of situation
returning Jews found themselves. It was a matter of doing something for
the Jews now, in the present: 'It is not over, it has only just started.' Henkels
decided to learn more about all things Jewish, for example by reading *Het
Joodse vraagstuk* [The Jewish Question] (1946) by his Reformed colleague
Dr M.C. Slotemaker de Bruine. He also called for an active and conscious
engagement with the Jewish fate, 'because *our* fate is at stake. Fate and
salvation – it's about those two things.'[7] So Henkels was referring to shame,
mourning and feelings of guilt. He challenged what the Germans would

---

4   *Tijd en Taak*, 11 January 1947.
5   Henkels was co-author; Werkman was arrested and executed shortly before the liberation:
B.H. Spaanstra-Polak, 'Werkman, Hendrik Nicolaas (1882-1945).' In: *Biografisch Woordenboek
van Nederland.* http://resources.huygens.knaw.nl/bwn1880-2000/lemmata/bwn2/werkman
[12-11-2013]. The collection was republished in 1967: *Chassidische Legenden van Martin Buber, ed.
J. Martinet, m.m.v. F.R.A. Henkels en prenten van H.N. Werkman* (Haarlem: Grafische Bedrijven,
1967).
6   Apparently a case of *Schuldwehrantisemitismus*. Henkels wrote that this friend had also
had a hard time himself during the war, without further explaining this, *Tijd en Taak*, 11 January
1947.
7   *Ibid.*; M.C. Slotemaker de Bruine, *Het Joodse vraagstuk* (Nijkerk: Callenbach, 1946).

coin *Schlussstrichbedürfnis* and encouraged a thought-out solidarity with
the Jews. Did that make him a philosemite?

As mentioned, philosemitism, just like antisemitism, is a flexible concept,
and distrust can quickly lead to an overly negative interpretation. In the
volume *Philosemitism in History* (2011), the historians Jonathan Karp and
Adam Sutcliffe question the widespread interpretation of philosemitism
as, basically, a disguised form of antisemitism.[8] As expressed in the above-
quoted short poem by Van Messel, a poetical variation of the oft-quoted
taunting Jewish joke:

Q: Which is preferable – the antisemite or the philosemite?
A: The antisemite. At least he isn't lying.[9]

Karp and Sutcliffe, on the other hand, say that it is too simple to merely view
philosemitism as a mirror image of antisemitism, characterised by twisted
and exaggerated views on Jews and Jewry. In fact, they warn for what the
historian Salo Baron (1895-1985) has been calling, critically, the 'lachrymose
conception' of Jewish history.[10] They illustrate this with a long list of examples of how Jews figured as God's chosen people, not only in Christianity,
and how, since Greek and Roman times, they have been admired because
of presumed positive characteristics, such as superior intelligence, vitality
and intensity, business acumen, ethnic loyalty, cultural cohesion, family
engagement, moral refinement and will to survive. Examples abound of

8   Adam Sutcliffe and Jonathan Karp, 'Introduction. A Brief History of Philosemitism.' In: Adam
Sutcliffe and Jonathan Karp (eds.), *Philosemitism in History* (New York: Cambridge University
Press, 2011), 1-26: 4-5.
9   Adam Sutcliffe and Jonathan Karp, 'Introduction', In: Jonathan Karp and Adam Sutcliffe
(eds.), *Philosemitism in history* (New York: Cambridge University Press, 2011), 1-26: 1. The saying
also circulates in Dutch Jewish circles: *Wie is minder erg – de antisemiet of de filosemiet?/ De
antisemiet, die liegt tenminste niet.*
10   *Ibid.*, 4. Salo Baron, *Social and Religious History of the Jews* (Philadelphia: Jewish Publication
Society of America, 1937); Salo Baron, 'Newer Emphases in Jewish History.' In: Salo Baron, *History
and Jewish Historians: Essays and Addresses* (Philadelphia: Jewish Publication Society of America,
1964), 90-108. In their approach, Karp and Sutcliffe oppose other researchers and scholars, who,
in their view, followed an overly simplistic approach, like Frank Stern, in: *The Whitewashing of the
Yellow Badge: Antisemitism and Philosemitism in Postwar Germany* (London: Heinemann, 1992)
and Phyllis Lassner and Lara Trubowitz (eds.), *Antisemitism and Philosemitism in the Twentieth
and Twenty-first Centuries* (Newark: University of Delaware Press, 2008), 4-5. This approach
to philosemitism has also become current in the Netherlands, *see, e.g.*, Grünfeld, *Nederland
en het Nabije Oosten*, 38: 'After all, philosemitism is also essentially a form of antisemitism,
as paradoxically as it may sound'. In a note Grünfeld refers to C.P. van Andel, *Jodenhaat en
jodenangst. Over meer dan twintig eeuwen antisemitisme* (Amersfoort: De Horstink, 1984), 187.

how Jews and Jewry, exactly as a counterpoint, as the ultimate 'Other', have been a source of inspiration.[11]

Hence, they have analysed the complex interaction between admiration and rancour, between positive and negative views Jews have always been generating, and simply define philosemitism as 'the idealisation of Jews and Jewry'. They want to expose where this idealisation becomes problematic, but also investigate the meaning and role of positive perceptions of Jews.[12] Karp and Sutcliffe thus leave the option of genuine sympathy for Jews open.[13]

Nevertheless, idealisation implies that those idealised can take a deep tumble once they no longer meet the ideal image. Furthermore, there is only a gradual difference between idealisation and zealotry, with stereotyping engrained in both phenomena. The glorification of Jews always has an inherent ambivalence; a 'double agenda' is never far away. From Tacitus to Nietzsche, from Milton to Lenin: apart from admiration there was also rejection and aversion. Ambivalence lies in how, in Western political imagination, Jews are role models of both particularism and cosmopolitanism. So, in one draw of breath, you can be a shining example for one and a scapegoat for the other; and for all parties, in a positive, but certainly more often in a negative sense, as a projection screen and legitimation.

This almost structural ambivalence also manifests itself in the genesis of the term philosemitism. As would be the case with the term 'political correctness', in another time period, the term philosemitism was coined as a derisive label by opponents, in this case mostly politically organised German antisemites around 1880. Those labelled 'philosemites' initially experienced this label as anything but complimentary. Although they did not see themselves as antisemites – a label reserved for those explicitly describing themselves as such – that did not mean that they did not share many of the same stereotypical ideas about Jews with 'real' antisemites. The solution of the Jewish question as championed by antisemites, however – curtailing the newly acquired rights of the Jews or even removing them entirely from society – went much too far for them. In that sense, they were anti-antisemites. It is very well possible, according to the historian Lars Fischer, that someone who would today be considered an antisemite, would have been seen as an anti-antisemite in the German Empire.[14]

---

11 Sutcliffe and Karp, 'Introduction', 6-21.
12 *Ibid.*, 5-6, 10. *See* chapter 18.
13 *Ibid.*, 2.
14 Lars Fischer, 'Anti-"Philosemitism" and Anti-Antisemitism in imperial Germany.' In: Karp and Sutcliffe, *Philosemitism in History*, 170-189: 170-171.

The Shoah has not made the interaction between Jews and non-Jews easier. Where had all those philosemites been during the persecution of the Jews? Jews were inclined to wonder.[15] That did not make it easier for non-Jews to ventilate their criticism or, conversely, admiration regarding Jews without being branded either an antisemite or philosemite. The path to a 'normalisation'of the relations between Jews and non-Jews has many obstacles and, after 1945, next to the Shoah, Israel would become the most important obstacle. The question remains, however, whether normalisation should be the objective or if it's even realistic. Using the elusive concept of 'normalisation' as a yardstick is also, Karp and Sutcliffe rightly argue, a-historical and counterproductive.[16] Furthermore, the question is whether a majority of Jews, when it comes down to it, would actually appreciate what is commonly considered normalisation. There is also a lot of ambivalence on the Jewish side, because, for example, consciously or unconsciously, Jews can be attached to the 'specialness' of their own status.[17]

So philosemitism, like antisemitism, is an extremely complex phenomenon, and often has a hidden meaning. Sometimes it's mainly *le ton qui fait la musique*. Pastor Henkels, who urged his readers to dedicate themselves, in the present, to the Jewish cause, seems genuinely angry, worried and engaged, without the overcompensation or zealotry characterising the suspicious form of philosemitism. At the same time, his reference to Slotemaker de Bruine and his *Het Joodse vraagstuk* (1946), largely written from a Christian perspective, and to the common destiny of Jewry and Christianity, also emanates a religiously inspired philosemitism. This was both based on a modern, constructive interpretation of the relationship between Christianity and Jewry and, indeed, on a sense of guilt. In 1962, the psychiatrist Hans Keilson (1909-2011), who is also briefly quoted in chapter 5, spoke, without any restraint, about the 'current philosemitic position of the churches', which could be traced back to repentance about what happened during the war. Keilson implicitly expressed his distrust

15   See Wulf Kansteiner, 'What is the Opposite of Genocide? Philosemitic Television in Germany, 1963-1995.' In: Karp and Sutcliffe, *Philosemitism in History*, 289-313: 289. In a fascinating way, Wulfsteiner shows how TV producers in West Germany slip on the 'slippery terrain between anti- and philosemitism' with an uneasy, artificial and blundering form of philosemitism, thus (partly) paradoxically laying the foundation for the future 'surprisingly self-critical historical culture' in German culture and society: *ibid.*, 313.

16   Karp and Sutcliffe propose normalisation as an abstract sort of compromise which still remains the goal of the Jewish and non-Jewish liberal spectrum, 'A Brief History of Philosemitism', 1-2.

17   *See* Evelien Gans, *Gojse nijd & joods narcisme. Over de verhouding tussen joden en niet-joden in Nederland* (Amsterdam: Arena, 1994), 128-129.

when he explained this philosemitism by referring to the discovery that an attack on Christianity had been hidden behind antisemitism.[18]

The Reformed pastor Dr M.C. Slotemaker de Bruine, who was well-known in the Netherlands, had been active for some time as liaison between the Council for Church and Israel, founded by the Reformed Synod, and the so-called Christian Jews in Westerbork.[19] He had no guilty conscience, at least not in 1946. That year he actually praised 'the spontaneous solidarity with the Jews, displayed by the churches, during their persecution of these last years'. In his introduction of *Het Joodse vraagstuk*, the book recommended by his colleague Henkels, Slotemaker explicitly wrote that his wasn't 'a typical philosemitic writing'.[20] That was correct. Although he did mention, among other things, philosemitic characteristics of the Jewish people, such as 'historical depth', 'great cultural talent' and 'extraordinary intensity', those went hand in hand with characterisations such as a 'hardly concealed sense of superiority' and 'egocentric attitude' of, among others, – but definitely not exclusively – 'many Jews in hiding'. On the one hand, Slotemaker adopted a very nuanced stance in the fierce ongoing battle about the future of the Jewish war foster children and war orphans whose parents had been killed, i.e. whether they should stay with their non-Jewish foster families or be placed into a Jewish family or setting. On the other hand, however, Slotemaker strongly opposed special or preferential treatment of Jewish survivors. 'The fact that they have been discriminated against by the occupying administration as "Jews" is no reason to now favour them as "Jews".'[21] This meant he supported the initial fallacy of the Dutch government to make no distinction between Jews and non-Jews, as opposed to the Nazis, thereby hardly or not at all accommodating Jews as genocide victims.[22]

Kees Stip (1913-2001), a poet of epigrams, produced a mocking example of philosemitic zealotry. Stip was one of those who, late 1967, wrote about their

18   *NIW*, 14 December 1962.
19   J.F.L. Bastiaanse, *De Jodenzending en de eerste decennia van de Hervormde Raad voor Kerk en Israël 1925-1965: een generatie in dienst van de Joods-Christelijke toenadering* (Zoetermeer: Boekencentrum, 1995), I: 265-280, II. Note 4.8, 777.
20   Slotemaker de Bruine, *Het Joodse vraagstuk*, 5, 195.
21   *Ibid.*, 130, 149, 152, 182, 191-194. For the complex postwar case of the Jewish war orphans in the Netherlands, *see* Elma Verhey, *Om het joodse kind* (Amsterdam: Nijgh & Van Ditmar, 1991).
22   Evelien Gans, *De kleine verschillen die het leven uitmaken: een historische studie naar joodse sociaal-democraten en socialistisch-zionisten in Nederland* (Amsterdam: Vassalucci, 1999), 567-568; Evelien Gans, 'Gojse broodnijd: de strijd tussen joden en niet-joden rond de naoorlogse Winkelsluitingswet 1945-1951.' In: Conny Kristel (ed.), *Met alle geweld: botsingen en tegenstellingen in burgerlijk Nederland* (Amsterdam: Balans, 2003), 195-213: 200.

indignation about an antisemitic incident at a school in the southern town of Venlo. A teacher had accused a Jewish pupil of committing a *'Jodenstreek'* [Jew trick], because he hadn't handed in his jotter. Stip sarcastically postulated that, at first sight, it seemed as if the antisemites too had not survived the war. The remaining Jews – friends, even competitors – 'come back to life in an angelic form'. Their positive characteristics were praised – the negative ones not mentioned. But that meant they were supposed to behave accordingly. The Jewish pupil in Venlo had not and therefore had, so his teacher claimed, done his people an ill service.[23] In this case idealisation turned into the opposite, to put it very mildly. What Stip meant was that non-Jews were always quick off their mark to spot the devil behind a Jew in his angelic guise. And without specifically mentioning the word philosemites, he did ridicule them. It was about non-Jews who were slightly infected by a *'Heiniaanse Weltschmerzbacil'*. You could recognise them 'because they preferred Mendelssohn to Beethoven and Mahler to Bruckner'.[24]

Stip's newspaper column was published in December 1967, the year in which a short, fierce and decisive war had raged in the Middle East – triumphantly dubbed the Six-Day War by the winner Israel, its sympathisers and allies; the Arab losers and their supporters preferred the more neutral term June War. 1967 turned out to be a crucial year for the developments in the Middle East. After a period of a threat of war and bloodthirsty rhetoric by Arab countries, which had immersed the Jewish state in an atmosphere of tension and fear, Israel had gone on the attack. It had conquered the Sinai, including the Gaza strip, from Egypt, the West Bank, including East Jerusalem, from Jordan, and the Golan Heights from Syria. In 1947 and 1948, during Israel's Independence War, some 700,000 Palestinians had fled the war violence or been driven away by Israeli troops – a disastrous event for this people, known as (Al) Nakba. Now, another 200,000 to 300,000 Palestinians left the Western Jordan Bank and Gaza – mainly from existing refugee camps – and a further 50,000 to 100,000 Arabs left the Golan.[25] Israel then held absolute sway in what has since been known – in different forms – as the 'occupied territories'.

Just before the war the very existence of the Jewish state seemed to be hanging by a thread. After the war, which according to many Israel had

23   *Haarlems Dagblad,* 6 December 1967; *see also Trouw,* 30 November and 11 December 1967; *Haarlems Dagblad,* 19 March 1968, and *Algemeen Handelsblad,* 25 March 1968.
24   Kees Stip, in: *Haarlems Dagblad,* 6 december 1967, hereby referring to the German-Jewish writer and poet Heinrich Heine (1797-1856).
25   Gans, *De kleine verschillen,* 822.

managed to win amazingly swiftly, the Netherlands was hit by a wave of solidarity with the small brave 'David' and his fight against the Arabian 'Goliath'.[26] People put stickers with 'We are behind Israel' on their cars and a national collection for Israel raised a staggering twelve million guilders within two weeks.[27] Initially, critical voices towards the Jewish state were very rare, but they were heard and closely followed by the Jewish community. Looking back in 1971, the chairman of the Dutch Zionist Union (NZB) said that after the Six-Day War the time of philosemitism – which was always going to be subject to wear and tear – was over. By that, he did not mean to say that the Netherlands had become an antisemitic country.[28] In practice, it often turned out that philosemitism and antisemitism were, after all, not simply interchangeable. A journal reported that even though psychologists would claim that anti- and philosemitism had the same origin, for Jews who had long suffered 'the hot hate of antisemitism, the cooling affection of philosemitism was definitely preferable'.[29] In fact, antisemitism – see the previous chapters – had never disappeared. In this context referring to philosemitism, actually seems detached from 'the Jew' or Jewry. This time seems to imply an almost unconditional embrace of Israel. That is in itself a relevant change in concept and approach, though 'the Jew' and Israel would remain intertwined. The handle that the Netherlands offered Israel did indeed gradually become more loose after 1967: a paradoxical year in terms of the relations between Jews and non-Jews – in the Netherlands and also elsewhere in the world.

Not immediately friends with Israel

Had sense of guilt or idealisation led to a positive, 'philosemitic' approach to Israel immediately after the war? In 1948, the sympathy of a large part of the population – led by the pro-social democratic segment – went out to

26 *Ibid.*, 896.
27 Website Anne Frank Stichting, Education; 'Wij staan achter Israël': www.annefrank.org/nl/Educatie/Discriminatie-in-Nederland/Kronieken/Kroniek-antisemitisme/Omslag-in-publieke-opinie/Wij-staan-achter-Israel/ (consulted 24 June 2015) *See also* R.B. Soetendorp, *Het Nederlandse beleid ten aanzien van het Arabisch-Israëlisch Conflict 1947-1977* (Meppel: Krips Repro, 1982) 98-100; Jan Dirk Snel, 'Nederland en de band met Israël. Sympathie voor een jonge staat", *Historisch Nieuwsblad* 5 (2008): www.historischnieuwsblad.nl/nl/artikel/10671/nederland-en-de-band-met-israel.html
28 *Leeuwarder Courant*, 3 March 1971.
29 *Algemeen Dagblad*, 3 August 1967, NIOD, KB II 454.

Israel; 54% believed that the Netherlands should recognise the new state.[30] The government, however, was remarkably late with both its *de facto* and *de jure* recognition of Israel. The main reason for these slow recognitions (in January 1949 and January 1950, respectively) was that the solution of the so-called Jewish Question carried much less weight than that of the 'Indonesian Question'. It was of paramount importance to the government to keep its colony, the Dutch East Indies, under the wings of the Kingdom and there was fear that a recognition of the Jewish state would damage the relationship with the Indonesian independence movement and, as such, with the predominantly Islamic population. The assumption was that they would show solidarity with the struggle of other Muslims, i.e. the Palestinian Arabs. That was the position of the *Katholieke Volkspartij* [Catholic People's Party] (KVP), but also of the leaders, and the party leadership in particular, of the social democratic PvdA [Labour Party] – the two parties that had formed a Roman/Red coalition. When both France and England decided to recognise Israel *de jure*, the Netherlands could no longer opt out.[31]

The PvdA represents a good example of how, in an early stage, Israel – then still Palestine – could be the divisive element between Jews and non-Jews, even if they agreed on many other issues. Jews had a long track record within the Dutch social democratic and labour movements. A typical example is that after the war, for a brief period, the PvdA had a Palestine Committee. Its (Jewish) socialist Zionist PvdA members squarely opposed non-Jewish party brass. An important obstacle was determining the position with regard to England, which had been Palestine's mandatory since the First World War. The dominant feeling among PvdA leaders was a sense of gratitude towards England as one of the allied parties that had liberated the Netherlands. They also strongly identified with the ruling British Labour Party, which firmly opposed the foundation of a Jewish state. Criticism of Labour's whimsical behaviour and a passionate speech by the Zionist and Marxist Sam de Wolff, mentioned in previous chapters, about the important role of the socialist movement in Jewish Palestine, also for Arab farmers, failed to have an impact. Although everybody agreed about the rights of Jews to have their own state, there was a watershed between those who wanted to achieve this at any cost and those who had some reservations: if the foundation of Israel would lead to a Third World War or to a lengthy war between Jews and Arabs: in that case 'a decision that favoured the

30 Soetendorp, *Het Nederlandse beleid*, 50.
31 Gans, *De kleine verschillen*, 670-672.

Jews had to be ... avoided'.[32] It was a case of clashing priorities and loyalties. Meanwhile, protests by indignant and disappointed PvdA members about their party's, in their view, objectionable *Realpolitik*, weren't much use for the time being either.

Even before the war, communism throughout the world, including the Netherlands, had declared Zionism as a branch of the horrendous imperialism. The fact that the Soviet Union – and, in its wake, the Dutch communist party (CPN) – was the first country that recognised Israel, had mainly to do with political-strategic motives. For Israel, the communist world represented an enormous reservoir of potential East European immigrants; conversely, Israel offered the Soviet Union the prospect of getting a foothold in a Middle East dominated by the British and other Western 'imperialists'. In this period, Czechoslovakia was the main weapons supplier to the Jewish state.[33] But in 1951, when Israel converted to the West (partly because financial support from the United States proved to be essential), the Soviet Union and its satellite states resumed their previous anti-Zionist attitude.

Even a convinced social democrat such as the then Prime Minister Willem Schermerhorn (1894-1977), who was, in principle, well-disposed towards Zionism, had his reservations. After all, the times had changed. He did not use the term 'colonialism', but in 1946 he did draw a telling parallel by saying that in the Dutch East Indies 'the white race' had probably become too weakened to survive in an 'awakening Asia'. And with regard to Palestine: the Jews should have started that project forty years earlier. In the meantime, 'the Arabs had become too developed to force a Jewish Palestine upon them, against their will'.[34] In *Het Joodse vraagstuk*, Slotemaker de Bruine writes,

> the plan for a renewed occupation of the former tribal land Palestine, which is rooted in the antisemitic approach of Western guest populations, is, despite all this, also an expansion of Western colonial power in a West-Asian style.[35]

32 *Ibid.*, 701-702. See also the isolated position of the Jewish social democrat Lena Lopes Dias, the first secretary of the Women's Union of the PvdA; she unsuccessfully appealed to the board of the PvdA to send a congratulations telegram to Israel: *ibid.*, 694-695.

33 *See* Peeters, *Gezworen vrienden*, 46-49.

34 Gans, *De kleine verschillen*, 683-684. Apparently, Schermerhorn was not aware at that moment that the Zionist movement had been active for much more than forty years.

35 Slotemaker, *Het Joodse vraagstuk*, 178.

The importance of good relations with the Arab world also played a role. In August 1948, PvdA Minister of Transport, Public Works and Water Management, Hein Vos (1903-1972), had felt pressured by KLM into banning flights to Israel. The reason was that the Egyptian government had threatened that if the route remained open, no Dutch aircraft would be allowed to land in Egypt.[36] So understanding and approval went hand in hand with doubts, fundamental criticism and giving in to economic priorities.

On 29 November 1947, the partition plan submitted by the United Nations Special Committee on Palestine (UNSCOP) was accepted by a majority vote in the United Nations. After a lot of hesitation, the Netherlands eventually also voted in favour. A very important factor for a 'yes' vote was the fact that the United States, the new world power without whose support the Netherlands would be powerless with regard to the developments in Indonesia, backed the partition plan.[37] The plan entailed the foundation of both a Jewish and a Palestinian state; for the time being, the city of Jerusalem would remain under international supervision. The Palestinian Arabs rejected it: the foundation of a Jewish state was unacceptable for them, as it was for the entire Arab world. The Zionist organisations and the Jewish population in Palestine did accept the plan, but not wholeheartedly, because they, from their part, had also opposed a partition of Palestine, and called for a much larger part of Palestinian territory for the future Jewish state. The Zionist movement – also in the Netherlands – was divided. Some believed that they should be, above all, satisfied that there would be a Jewish state at all, no matter how small. Opponents insisted on their entitlement to an undivided bigger Israel. The latter were forced to back down; the pragmatists had the upper hand.[38] In the war that started after the withdrawal of the English army and the subsequent Israeli declaration of independence, Israel managed to expand its territory beyond the established borders. The Arab armies that had launched the attack were defeated. There was no peace agreement – but there were separate armistices. The term 'armed peace', used to describe the postwar situation, is an euphemism, considering, among other things, the number of violent border incidents.

When the Netherlands *de jure* recognised Israel in 1950, relatively late, this was not related to any sense of guilt. The nation's recognition was – unlike the people's recognition – not a sincere one. The government had no other option but to follow its allies. In 1956, during the Suez Crisis, the

36   Gans, *De kleine verschillen*, 701-702.
37   Soetendorp, *Het Nederlandse beleid*, 193.
38   Gans, *De kleine verschillen*, 642-644, 690-691.

situation was different. Indonesia had become irrevocably independent and no longer constituted an obstacle. Israel was a reality – albeit one under threat – and the Netherlands became one of its biggest supporters.

The Suez Crisis: the Netherlands is shifting

After turning to the West in 1951, Israel had been sucked into the Cold War. Prague had hit back in November 1952 with trials against Rudolf Slánský and other party leaders, mainly of Jewish descent. They were accused of having contacts with Israel and Israeli diplomats – i.e. with American and Zionist 'agents'. Slánský, former party secretary, and ten others, were hanged. A few months later, in 1953, the so-called Doctors' plot was discovered in the Soviet Union. A group of predominantly Jewish doctors were allegedly planning to poison Stalin and other party top brass. Here communist anti-Zionism mixed with antisemitism, though the Dutch Communist Party strongly rejected this accusation of antisemitism.[39] Hungary, East Germany and Bulgaria followed suit and arrested Jews who were accused of, among other things, contacts with the Joint Jewish Distribution Committee, or Joint.[40] Israel was now unequivocally part of the Western camp.

In the autumn of 1956, two events of global magnitude vied for political and public attention. On 29 October, Israel attacked Egypt. England and France followed suit a few days later, as the result of a secret agreement. On 4 November the armies of the Warsaw Pact invaded Hungary to end the Hungarian Revolt against the Stalinist regime. In July 1956, Nasser had nationalised the company that managed the Suez Canal and whose profits mainly benefited foreign shareholders. England (Egypt's former coloniser and until recently militarily based in Egypt) and France (Nasser supported the Algerian independence movement) considered this an affront. The same goes for the Netherlands, which at that time was at loggerheads with its wayward former colony.[41] Anti- and postcolonial motives got entangled with Cold War motives.

39 Bernard Wasserstein, *Het einde van een diaspora. Joden in Europa sinds 1945* (Baarn: Ambo, 1996; orig. *Vanishing Diaspora. The Jews in Europe since 1945*. Cambridge, MA: Harvard University Press, 1996), 59-62; Igor Cornelissen, *Paul de Groot. Staatsvijand nr. 1* (Amsterdam: Nijgh & Van Ditmar, 1996), 112-114.

40 *See* Gans, *De kleine verschillen*, 226-227; Peeters, *Gezworen vrienden*, 54-56. After Stalin's death diplomatic relations between the Soviet-Union and Israel were restored.

41 As the Dutch government refused to hand over the sovereignty of New Guinea, Indonesia had unilaterally cancelled the debt repayment agreement.

Meanwhile, the Soviet Union was arming Egypt, again via Czechoslovakia. The United States, however, refused to respond with arms deliveries to Israel, which had the most urgent motives for the attack. At an increasing speed, the border area between Egypt and Israel, from Gaza, was hit by Palestinian attempted murders, backed by Egypt, using 'permanent warfare' tactics. Israel retaliated, if it didn't take the initiative itself.[42] Critics condemned Israel's attack as a disproportionate reaction. The United States, eager to prevent both the start of a new armed conflict (so close after the Korean War) and the foundation of a Soviet power base in Egypt, played the spoilsport. France, England and Israel bowed to the pressure and pulled out their armies.[43]

In the Netherlands, news reports about the Middle East were overshadowed by news about Hungary. After all, Hungary was closer to home and, here, the Cold War manifested itself in a more striking manner. But this didn't mean that the Suez Crisis had no impact – especially on the positioning of the Dutch government regarding Israel. The Netherlands sided with Israel, England and France. This position was, according to the political scientist Robert Soetendorp (b. 1944), mainly due to the fact that the Soviet Union now squarely opposed Israel, having also severed its diplomatic ties with the Jewish state. Furthermore, KVP Minister of Foreign Affairs Joseph Luns (1911-2002) and Schermerhorn's successor, PvdA Prime Minister Willem Drees (1886-1988) both drew a parallel between the 'strained nationalism' and the break-up of international agreements by Indonesia and Egypt. The Dutch press was quick to compare Nasser with Hitler.[44] Meanwhile, there was, once again, division and feelings of doubt, in parliament and cabinet. The criticism focused on Dutch support of the British/French conduct vis-à-vis Egypt, which was driving a wedge in the Atlantic alliance (NATO had been founded in 1949) and had a 'colonial flavour'.[45] This scepticism was nowhere to be seen in the case of Israel. When the UN General Assembly started to discuss if it would also have to take steps against Israel, Drees formulated the opinion, broadly supported by Dutch politicians, that Israel's action was to be judged as 'defensive', possibly as 'excessively defensive', he added.[46] The Dutch population was less outspokenly positive than their representatives: 42% supported Israel's

42   See Peeters, Gezworen vrienden, 79. There were also upcoming American elections.

43   For the Suez Crisis, see Soetendorp, Het Nederlandse beleid, 59-71.

44   Ibid., 73. See also Peeters, Gezworen vrienden, 95.

45   Ibid., 76. The fact that France and England had both vetoed a resolution submitted by the US asking Israel, among other things, to withdraw to the 1949 borders, was seen as very shocking, see, e.g., Algemeen Handelsblad, 31 October 1956.

46   Peeters, Gezworen vrienden, 76. See also De Telegraaf, 10 November 1956.

actions; 24% didn't. But those percentages were still almost diametrically opposed to people's views on the French/British conduct, supported by 24% and rejected by 47%.[47]

Had guilt now set in? According to Soetendorp, the Dutch decision-makers were led by neither pro- nor anti-Israel feelings, nor by pro- or anti-Arab feelings, nor by 'the moral indebtedness to the Shoah'. Everything revolved around what the government saw as securing its own national interests.[48] Later, Soetendorp put this vision somewhat into perspective. The Dutch felt more affinity with Israel as a democracy in a hostile environment than with the authoritarian regimes in the neighbouring Arab countries. But on top of that, their sympathy was also 'undoubtedly ... to some extent' inspired by feelings of guilt about the large number of murdered Jews.[49] Soetendorp, however, does not set a starting point for this sense of guilt. Furthermore, he does not refer to decision-makers, but speaks of 'a large segment of the Dutch public'. The historian Fred Grünfeld (b. 1949), specialising in conflict studies, has challenged Soetendorp's position that the persecution of the Jews was not a guideline for the position of the Dutch government, but he avoids the terms sense or awareness of guilt. He writes that the Dutch decision-making process regarding Israel did not only take into account pro-Israel feelings among Dutch Jews, but was mainly based on 'sparing the feelings of Jewish fellow citizens as much as possible'. This latter intention was, according to Grünfeld, part of the postwar Dutch political culture and rooted in the Shoah. As a result, there was a 'high level of sensibility among decision-makers towards the wishes of the Jewish community'.[50] Grünfeld also refrains from assigning a starting point to this sensibility. In any case, he does not pinpoint it in the 1950s. In his *Nederland en het Nabije Oosten* (1991), Grünfeld looks at the period between 1973 and 1982, marked by, respectively, the October War and Israel's invasion of Lebanon.

In view of the weapons embargo on the entire Middle East, imposed by the United States, France and England, in the Tripartite Agreement of 1951, while in the same year the arms supply from Czechoslovakia to Israel choked, the Netherlands became involved in arms deliveries to the Jewish state. Still, in principle Foreign Affairs pursued a balanced relationship with the Middle East, as witnessed by an ammunition delivery to Egypt,

---

47   In other European countries there were less supporters, *see ibid.*, 81. For the analysis of and critical reflection on the value of these kinds of opinion polls, see Grünfeld, *Nederland en het Nabije Oosten*, 33.

48   Soetendorp, *Het Nederlandse beleid*, 205-206.

49   Soetendorp, 'The Netherlands and Israel', 697.

50   Grünfeld, *Nederland en het Nabije Oosten*, 45.

planned for 1953. That was, as Luns put it, 'a pro-Arab gesture'. And not without reason: 'Due to the alleged pro-Israel attitude of the Netherlands we are suffering under the Arab boycott, [technology company] Philips for example', Luns wrote to his secretary general.[51] In late 1955, Dutch arms supplies to Israel became more extensive and systematic. In May 1956, the then Minister of War, C. Staf, noted that the Dutch contribution to Israel's armament was possibly the largest of all countries. The Dutch position had repercussions, as Luns had noted – not only for Philips. In 1956, four Dutch companies were put on an Egyptian blacklist due to alleged trade relations with Israel.[52]

Arms deliveries, trade relations, the foundation of a Chamber of Commerce for Israel. Another crucial aspect of the 'special relationship' between the Netherlands and Israel was the affinity that had meanwhile emerged between the PvdA and the ruling Labour Party in Israel, embodied by the close and friendly relations between Prime Minister Willem Drees and his counterpart David Ben-Gurion (1886-1973). In August 1948, Drees had, albeit reluctantly, accepted that it was not yet time to recognise Israel.[53] Drees was born and raised in pre-war Amsterdam and had many contacts and friendships in Jewish socialist circles. He had an early sympathy for Zionism, having been a hostage in Buchenwald for some time in 1940-1941. Back in the Netherlands he became active in the resistance. According to one of his close collaborators Drees had developed 'a passion for Israel'. It was Drees who in 1953, defying the reservations at Foreign Affairs, pressed ahead with his plan for the Netherlands to represent Israel's interests in Moscow, after the Soviet Union had cut off diplomatic ties with Israel.[54] Not only was Drees strongly engaged with the Jewish cause, to him Israel was also a socialist role model. Drees, like many others, was enormously inspired by the powerful position of the Israeli Labour Party and union, including kibbutzim, the work and living community rooted in socialist and communal ideas.[55] According to former Minister of Defence Bram Stemerdink (b. 1936), the Labour Party leaders were part of the PvdA 'family', and the 'special relationship' between

---

51 Peeters, *Gezworen vrienden*, 77. The arms delivery to Egypt eventually fell through: Egypt said the ammunition was too outdated. It was then, ironically enough, sold to Israel.

52 *Ibid.*, 90-92. Peeters gives an extensive and as accurate as possible overview of the Dutch weapon supplies to Israel up until 1973: *ibid., passim.*

53 Gans, *De kleine verschillen*, 701.

54 Peeters, *Gezworen vrienden*, 57-61, 69.

55 *See, e.g.,* the articles about the kibbutz during the Suez Crisis in: *De Telegraaf*, 6 and 7 November 1956, in the framework of the series 'Dit is Israël', *see also, De Telegraaf,* 8 November 1956.

the Netherlands and Israel dated back to a tacit agreement between Drees and Ben-Gurion: 'If you need us, just let us know'.[56]

So was Drees a philosemite? You could say he was, in the unproblematic meaning of the word. The characterisation of someone who feels the urge to compensate for concealed aggression, does not seem fitting here. Karp and Sutcliffe's description – the idealisation of Jews or Jewry – however, does match Drees. The question is how realistic his image of Israel was. In the foreword of *Voordat ik het vergeet* [Lest I Forget] (1957), a collection of stories about Amsterdam's pre-war Jewish quarter by the social democrat, journalist and popular author Meijer Sluyser (1901-1973), Drees praised Sluyser's atmospheric description of the Jewish population 'who generally lived in harsh conditions, but managed to get through it *good-humouredly*'.[57] Of course, the reality was different. Furthermore, it was Drees who, with the Committee named after him, excluded Jews in hiding from the *Wiedergutmachung* funds, which were specifically intended for them.[58]

With regard to Israel, the motto 'You can count on us' was not on paper, but would nevertheless determine Dutch policy for a long time – often behind the scenes of the political stage.[59] In 1960, the Israeli Minister of Foreign Affairs Golda Meir said, on the occasion of a visit by the, by then former, Prime Minister Drees that Israel was pleased to count the Netherlands among its best friends.[60] Four years earlier, in November 1956, when UN resolutions were submitted condemning Israel for the slow pull-out of its troops from Gaza and the surrounding area, the Netherlands abstained from voting. During a PvdA demonstration meeting, party chairman Evert Vermeer said '... that the sympathy of the entire Dutch population lies with the small state of Israel'.[61]

This statement, however, should be taken with a large pinch of salt. If indeed 24% of the Dutch population opposed Israel's attack on Egypt (and 34% had no opinion), Vermeer was far too absolute.[62] Nevertheless, public counter-voices were rare: in general Israeli self-defence and security counted as decisive. There were signs of slight hesitation in *Het Parool*, which, while

---

56 Peeters, *Gezworen vrienden*, 67, 104.

57 Gans, *De kleine verschillen*, 819 (italics added). M. Sluyser, *Voordat ik het vergeet* (Amsterdam: Het Parool, 1957).

58 Hinke Piersma, *Bevochten recht: politieke besluitvorming rond de wetten voor oorlogsslachtoffers* (Amsterdam: Boom, 2010), 92-97. *See* chapter 5.

59 Peeters, *Gezworen vrienden*, 67.

60 *Ibid.*, 108.

61 *Ibid.*, 101.

62 Soetendorp, *Het Nederlandse beleid*, 81.

understanding that Israel had started the attack from a very distressing position, due to arms supplies from 'Moscow' to Egypt, doubted whether the situation justified a war.[63] *De Volkskrant* was more outspoken about its doubts. Israel had always, albeit reluctantly, taken the position that a preventive war was out of the question. Now, it had exactly done that, without putting conclusive evidence on the table that there was a threat of an imminent Arab attack. One *Volkskrant* columnist stated that, this way, Israel was definitely not contributing to maintaining world peace, and putting the sympathy it enjoyed as 'threatened state' at risk.[64]

This standpoint was, in turn, benevolent compared with the comment by the left-wing socialist and peace activist Jan Hendrik van Wijk (1907-1981) in *De Derde Weg* [The Third Way], the journal of the homonymous peace movement. In his article 'Jungle politics' Van Wijk particularly condemned the power politics of France and England, but he did not spare Israel either. That country had, as far as he was concerned, started an unauthorised war and had unacceptable refugee policies. Furthermore, it participated in the bedlam of retaliation, which so typified the Middle East: 'If you terrorise my farmers from Gaza then I will attack Gaza.' He accused the Dutch government of using double standards. While opposing in all possible manners the Russian coup in Hungary, it did not show any sign of supporting the overwhelmed Egyptians.[65] It was a comparison the government had strongly rejected before.[66] For the socialist Zionist Sam de Wolff the *Derde Weg* article was a reason to cancel his membership. The views of Van Wijk and his sympathisers did not find many willing ears.[67]

Turning point 1967 – double loyalties

Right from 1945 onwards, it had been tempting to compare Jews, especially those in Israel, and later Israelis with Nazis – as mentioned in chapter 3. But at first this rarely happened. The year 1967, the year of the Six-Day or June

63   *Het Parool*, 30 October 1956.

64   *De Volkskrant*, 3 November 1956.

65   Gans, *De kleine verschillen*, 787.

66   *See De Telegraaf*, 10 November 1956.

67   *See, e.g.*, Ron Leijser, 'Derde Weg, christelijk antimilitarisme en pacifistisch-socialisme.' In: Joost Divendal et al. (eds.), *Nederland, links en de Koude Oorlog: breuken en bruggen* (Amsterdam: De Populier, 1982), 99-116 contains an illuminating article by Ron Leijser about the Third Way: www.historischnieuwsblad.nl/nl/artikel/26099/de-derde-weg.html; Paul van der Steen, *Historisch Nieuwsblad* 9 (2009).

War, was a turning point. From then on the relationship with Israel gradually became a lot more complex, and dissenting voices were getting louder. But certainly not immediately. The Dutch government had recognised the state of Israel relatively late, but fully supported Israel during the Suez Crisis in 1956, and counter-voices had been rare.[68] In 1967, initially, the connection between the Netherlands and Israel manifested itself many time more openly and enthusiastically – both among the government and the population.

Even before it became clear that Israel was going to win the war, the government sided with Israel; it saw the Arab states as the real aggressor.[69] More so than in 1956, the population also sided with Israel. As described above, there was a sticker campaign, mass public demonstrations of support and far-reaching – tax deductible – financial support initiatives.[70] This time, an opinion poll showed that 67% sided with Israel and less than one-half percent with the Arab states. In the Netherlands there was significantly more sympathy for Israel than in the United States, England and France. This affection did have some limitations. While 49% was of the opinion that the Dutch government should actively support Israel, 41% wanted the government to remain neutral.[71]

Hundreds of volunteers signed up to go to Israel and personally support the country. They were mainly pupils and students, doctors and nurses, predominantly Jews, but probably also non-Jews.[72] In different batches they travelled, first from Amsterdam to Paris, and from then on to Israel. On 12 June 1967, two days after Israel's victory, the Dutch Zionist Union closed applications. Meanwhile, only a minority had reached Israel.[73]

68 *See also* chapter 3.

69 *See, e.g., de Volkskrant*, 7 June 1967. Only the Boerenpartij voted against the resolution adopted by the House of Representatives that the existence of Israel had to be guaranteed. *De Telegraaf*, 7 June 1967. For the Boerenpartij *see* chapter 4.

70 It was all over the newspapers, *see, e.g., Het Parool* and *Trouw*, 6 June 1967; *Het Parool*, 7 June 1967; *de Volkskrant*, 9 and 12 June 1967. The swastikas painted on the mess hall of the Dutch Zionist Students Organisation (NZSO), including a letter stating, among other things, 'Egypt will overcome', was an exception – like the woman collecting money for Israel who was hit by a 'foreigner' shouting 'Nasser': *NIW*, 2 June 1967, resp. *Het Parool*, 10 June 1967.

71 In the United States, England and France sympathy for Israel stood at respectively 55%, 50% and 58%, with sympathy for the Arab countries at 4%, 5% and 2%: Soetendorp, *Het Nederlandse beleid*, 99.

72 This last remark cannot be stated with full certainty, but the names of the interviewees in the diverse papers do give that impression.

73 Meanwhile, 70 volunteers had left with another 400 signed up: *de Volkskrant*, 12 June 1967. See also *Trouw, Het Parool, de Volkskrant*, 6 June 1967; *Trouw*, 8 and 9 June 1967; *Het Parool*, 9 June 1967.

Illustration 10   Volunteers for Israel, 5 June 1967

Photographer unknown / Anefo / Nationaal Archief

Volunteers for Israel, 5 June 1967. An impression of an almost 'merry-going-to-war' ambiance but also a sign of the far-reaching solidarity with Israel as 'David' in its struggle against 'Goliath'. Cameras are clicking from all sides in order to capture the historic moment.

The sociologist Abram de Swaan (b. 1942), who in the previous year had positioned himself as a strong supporter of assimilation – that is, if one was not a religious Jew nor left for Israel – and lived in New York at the time, had registered. In 2005, looking back, he put his motivations in perspective: 'Luckily, the hostilities had finished by the time I was able to fly out. Since then, I have been a supporter of the evacuation of occupied territory.'[74] The 19-year-old Job Cohen (b. 1947) – who many years later would become mayor of Amsterdam – had serious doubts about whether or not to go to Israel

74   Abram de Swaan, 'Anti-Israëlische enthousiasmes en de tragedies van het blind proces', *De Gids* 168 (2005), 349-367: n. 2. See also Hans Reijzer, 'De Swaans dans rond het Joodse sentimentalisme.' In: Annet Mooij et al. (eds.), *Grenzeloos nieuwsgierig. Opstellen voor en over Abram de Swaan* (Amsterdam: Bert Bakker, 2007), 251-260: 254. For De Swaan's pro-assimilation position, see Abram de Swaan, 'Het joods sentimentalisme betrapt', *NIW* (*Niweau*), 27 November 1964. *Niweau* was a monthly insert of the NIW, 'for young people'.

and join the fight. 'During the Six-Day War I had strong hesitations about whether to go there to help. A sense of: I should be there if that country goes to hell.'[75] There were more left-wing and generally non-Zionist oriented Jews who found themselves following the developments of the war in the Middle East with fear and trembling. Realising that they were apparently, unknowingly, relying on the existence of a Jewish state as a safety guarantee for when things got dangerous; Herzberg called every Jew without Israel an 'uncovered cheque'. The realisation that feelings of commitment, consolation and anger were at stake, sometimes struck unexpectedly.[76]

Grünfeld considered what he described as 'the Jewish community' as a 'pro-Israel group'. The question remains of course what the meaning of 'the Jewish community' was or should be.[77] What is certain is that a majority of the Dutch Jews who knowingly saw or manifested themselves as Jewish, whether or not religiously or Zionistically organised (there were relatively few of them), saw the existence of Israel as something of existential importance, were very sympathetic (or at least respectful) towards the country, went there to visit family etc. – there were many gradations available on this point. This could, but certainly did not have to, lead to the mentality of 'Israel, my country right or wrong'. There were Jews who struggled with double or even multiple loyalties or identifications: you could be Jew, Dutch, left-wing or right-wing and engaged with Israel. Ambivalent feelings in abundance. There were also dissidents in more outspoken Jewish, including Zionist, circles. After 1967, groups such as the Critical Zionists and, later, the Socialist Zionists (sz) emerged within socialist Zionist circles calling for an active Israeli peace policy, such as the willingness to territorial concessions

75   Colet van der Ven, 'Ik vond Cohen genoeg', NIW, 19 September 1998; Hugo Logtenberg and Marcel Wiegman, Job Cohen, burgemeester van Nederland (Amsterdam, 2010).

76   In an interview with Piet Pireyns in Vrij Nederland (5 October 1974), Herzberg said: 'Without the state of Israel we are defenceless. Then every Jew, anywhere in the world, becomes an uncovered cheque': Arie Kuiper, 'Inleiding.' In: Abel J. Herzberg, Zonder Israël is elke jood een ongedekte cheque. Essays selected and introduced by Arie Kuiper (Amsterdam: Querido, 1992), 9-19: 9. The term became, in a (slightly) changed form, an expression of its own as 'uncovered cheque' and 'blank cheque'. See also David Wertheim, 'Hypotheek op een ongedekte cheque.' In: Hetty Berg and Bart Wallet (eds.), Wie niet weg is is gezien. Joods Nederland na 1945 135-147: 138. Selma Leydesdorff et al. (eds.), Israël een blanco cheque? (Amsterdam: Amphora Books, Van Gennep, 1983), 9. For the change in attitude and awareness among (social democratic) Jews referred to here: Gans, De kleine verschillen, 842-869.

77   Grünfeld, Nederland en het Nabije Oosten, 45. Grünfeld describes the Jewish Community as '30,000 Jewish Dutch'; his figures are based on counts done in the late 1970s.

and negotiations with PLO, the Palestine Liberation Organization, led by
Yasser Arafat (1929-2004).[78]

In an interview by the starting Jewish journalist Ischa Meijer (1943-1995)
with his renowned and controversial colleague Renate Rubinstein (1929-
1990), in December 1967, both the interviewee and interviewer showed
their true colours by being ambivalent about Israel and the Dutch response
to the Six-Day War. Meijer's question what Rubinstein thought about 'the
mass hysteria that has broken out in the Netherlands as a result of the
Israeli war' speaks for itself.[79] Rubinstein was very alert when it came to
antisemitism. In 1963, after a personal confrontation with an extreme case
of verbal antisemitism, including Holocaust denial, in a bar, she had even
launched the idea of setting up an 'assault and discussion group' to deal with
'manageable, but not legally chargeable cases of antisemitism'.[80] However,
she was highly critical about Israel and outspoken about the fact that she
did not appreciate Zionism, 'or any other form of segregation'. In addition,
she tended, as always, to take a strong position against antisemitism 'in
favour of Wiesenthal's practices' – a formulation by Meijer, referring to the
man who managed to track down, among others, Adolf Eichmann.

The reason for the interview was Rubinstein's recently published and
controversial, at least in Jewish circles, book *Jood in Arabië, Goi in Israël* [Jew
in Arabia, Goy in Israel] (1967). The title reflects her position as an outsider,
albeit a strongly engaged one. Rubinstein said that it was easier for her to
identify with an Israeli intellectual than with an Arab one – but this did not
soften her strong criticism of Israel. The NIW lashed out against Rubinstein
in the person of former chief editor Jo Melkman, now living in Israel as
Jozeph Michman (1914-2009) and working as head of the department of
Culture of the Ministry of Education. He said the book contained errors,
even lies, that it was sloppy and opportunistic. He proclaimed among others
the frequently used standpoint that the Arab countries deliberately kept
the refugee problem intact. Furthermore, Michman's criticism was very *ad
feminam*, alleging that Rubinstein's doubts regarding Israel were directly
related to her identity struggle as a 'half Jewess'. It is okay to criticise, but

---

78 *See* Gans, *De kleine verschillen, 897;* Maarten Jan Hijmans, 'Nogmaals: de Socialistische
Zionisten', *Joodse Wachter,* February 1977.

79 Ischa Meijer, 'Het zionisme is geen acceptabele ideologie', *De Nieuwe Linie,* 2 December 1967.

80 Renate Rubinstein, 'Actie', *Vrij Nederland,* 25 May 1963. In a later column, 'Actie (2)', she
concluded, partly following readers' responses, that the plan had more disadvantages than
advantages: *Vrij Nederland,* 22 June 1963, NIOD, KB II, 307 A.

in times of need, it is important to be able to rely on a 'natural solidarity'.[81] Michman's accusation fitted into the tried recipe of accusing the 'Jewish heretic' of self-hatred.[82]

The NIW acted as *the* platform which proudly followed Israel and defended it against criticism. All the more remarkable is the tone about Rubinstein versus Michman in a letter to the editor by the upcoming philosopher Beate Keizer-Zilversmidt (b. 1942), who is a typical example of an increasingly radicalising Jewish activist. After 1982, Keizer-Zilversmidt briefly joined the Dutch branch of *Shalom Achshav* (Peace Now), then the Jewish-Palestinian Dialogue group. Later, in 1987 she joined peace initiatives in Israel such as *Women in Black* and *Down with the Occupation*. Eventually, she joined the peace and action group *Gush Shalom*.[83] In 1968, Keizer took note of the fact that the opponents agreed on their stance against antisemitism: on this topic both recognised exactly what it was about. According to Keizer the problem was mainly that most Jews had not figured out yet where the line between 'neurotic self-loathing and healthy self-criticism' lay.

> Some immediately call everything self-hatred, thus showing also neurotic self-love, based on a fear that makes sense but is unhealthy. Others sometimes use norms that are too strict when it comes to self-criticism and respond very emotionally to accusations of self-hatred.[84]

Keizer herself was enthusiastic about Rubinstein's book and maybe, she wrote, she occupied the same position on the 'self-loathing – narcissism scale'. So Keizer describes Jewish narcissism as 'neurotic self-love', emanating from an understandable but unhealthy fear. As mentioned before, Jewish narcissism can also be characterised as a Jewish self-image determined by two extremes: suffering and pride. In this case suffering, caused by

---

81   J. Melkman, 'Jodin in Israël', *NIW*, 16 February 1968. Rubinstein served him a reply: 'Antwoord aan dr. Melkman', *NIW*, 22 March 1968. Rubinstein had a German-Jewish father who was killed by the Nazis. For the argument of keeping the refugee issue alive, *see also* chapter 3. For Michman, *see also* chaper 5.

82   Gans, *Gojse nijd & joods narcisme*, 61-62. More extensive information about the phenomenon of Jewish self-hatred: Gans, *De kleine verschillen*, 204-222, 878-879. Michman has written extensively about Jewish-Dutch history, see Evelien Gans, *De weg terug. Het kantelend beeld van de joodse historicus Jaap Meijer (1912-1993)* (Amsterdam: Amsterdam University Press, 2003), 12-13.

83   Emails sent by Beate Zilversmidt to Evelien Gans, 12 February 2015.

84   B. Keizer, 'Ingezonden', *NIW*, 29 March 1968.

antisemitism and persecution of Jews, and pride about Israel – as compensation, consolation and counterweight.[85]

Keizer also addresses the phenomenon of Jewish self-hatred. In short, this concept refers to Jews who internalise antisemitic stereotypes and prejudices thereby pointing them against themselves, but also against other Jews and Jewry. Like antisemitism and philosemitism, it is an elastic concept, which is by definition prone to manipulation. Keizer is aware of this. She distances herself from the mechanism of 'calling everything immediately self-hatred' and, as such, from an, in her view, unnecessarily excessive polarisation. Self-hatred – just like self-love or narcissism – she provides with the predicate 'neurotic'; self-criticism, on the contrary, with 'healthy'. That Keizer, indeed, looks at the question from a Jewish perspective, is implicitly included in her formulations. Criticism (of Israel, of other Jews) here joins 'self' criticism – a stronger identification with everything Jewish, is hard to imagine. Furthermore, she talks of an explainable fear. So she takes the fear among Jews – that Israel would be crushed – serious. She also calls the fear unhealthy; it is unclear whether she believes that is because the fear is rooted in war traumas and bad for the mental state of mind, or disproportionate considering the actual balance of power in the Middle East.[86]

Early June 1967, few would have known that Israel, despite the threats it was facing, was in good militarily shape; there were hardly any reports on this matter. The image of David versus Goliath prevailed, at least during the first days of the war.[87] Most people were undoubtedly led by what they had read and heard in the run-up: threatening, bloodthirsty language used by Nasser and his sympathisers. After the war, the Red Cross came under fire for having too easily given in to demands by many donors to make their blood available only to Israel – and not to victims on the Arab side. Director Alfred van Emden, himself a camp survivor, defended himself by pointing to, among other things, the clear prospects of 'Israel being crushed'.[88]

85 Gans, *Gojse nijd & joods narcisme*; see also chapter 1 and 5.
86 *See, e.g., Trouw*, 6 June 1967. Keizer wrote her letter ten months after the Six-Day War.
87 *See, e.g., de Volkskrant*, 6 June 1967.
88 *De Volkskrant*, 14 June 1967. The Red Cross also supplied blood to the 'Arab side', but it came from a different supply consisting of blood explicitly donated for Arab victims. The organisation was authorised to accept 'selective supply'. It also assumed that the Arab countries would be supported by the 'communist countries'. For a cartoon about the issue: *de Volkskrant*, 10 June 1967. See also *Het Parool*, 8 June 1967. For A. van Emden (1909-1993) *see* Ben Schmitz, *Van Goede doelen en loterijen. Een biografie van de stichting Algemene Loterij Nederland* (Nijmegen: Valkhof Pers, 2009).

The publisher and book trader Johan Polak (1929-1992) admitted in 1970 that he was 'very pessimistic'. 'You know, my fear sometimes is that Israel will be wiped off the map.' When it came down to it, no one would help Israel, he feared.

When Israel will have disappeared from the map and another few million Jews have been killed, a few committees will probably be set up, which will commemorate the dead Jews from Israel with a few wreaths at the National Monument.[89]

Polak expressly recognised 'the rights of the Palestinians', adding, 'There is also a fair amount of discrimination in Israel'. Polak was explicitly not the 'Israel my country right or wrong' type. He was one of the many Jews who drew various maps in their heads – only to reject them again later. Maybe a Palestinian state in Trans- and Cisjordan – and then later a federation? Or back to the pre-1967 borders, but with the exception of the Golan Heights and Jerusalem? Polak never made any patronising remarks about the Arabs. He was anything but a hawk. But his solidarity with Israel was unquestionable; he certainly did not seek 'de-Zionisation'. 'After all, there are also people who are not like De Swaan and Renate Rubinstein', he told Ischa Meijer.[90]

His attitude earned him a letter with a death threat signed by 'El Fatah'. In 1968, Polak, together with, among others, the – also Jewish – economist and social democrat Arnold Heertje (b. 1934), had founded *Democratisch Appèl*. The initiative was intended as a counterweight against the opposition group *Nieuw Links* [the New Left], which had also been founded from within the PvdA, and particularly against the New Left's ideas about foreign politics – for example, with regard to Israel.[91] Unlike many of his political friends who had joined DS'70 (a more conservative splinter party of the PvdA) – varying from Willem Drees Jr to Meijer Sluyser – Polak did not leave the PvdA. His engagement with Israel went hand in hand with a big concern about antisemitism. Since the *'hakenkruiskladderij'* [swastika tagging] in 1959 and 1960, Polak had started to put together a 'huge clippings archive': 'For a while, there was a real revival of antisemitism ... not just in

89   Robert J. Kopuit. 'Uitgever Johan Polak: Voor mij is het niet nodig Israël van de kaart te vegen', *NIW*, 31 July 1970.

90   Ischa Meijer, 'Uitgever Johan Polak', *De Nieuwe Linie*, 25 February 1967.

91   G. Voerman, 'Een geval van politieke schizofrenie. Het gespleten gedachtengoed van DS'70', *Jaarboek 1990 Documentatiecentrum Nederlandse politieke partijen* (Groningen 1991), 92-114; http://pub.dnpp.eldoc.ub.rug.nl/root/DNPPjaarboeken/1990/.

Germany, but here as well, in fact everywhere.'[92] For Polak, Israel, the Shoah and postwar antisemitism were strongly interwoven. He was possibly a Jew for whom – in the style of Herzberg – life without Israel looked like an uncovered cheque.

In the same year that Polak went public about the existence of his clippings archive, there was a discussion in the NIW about how far one could or should go in criticising Israel. Not that far, most thought: 'one shouldn't wash one's dirty linen in public'; 'the best coaches are in the sands'; the unity of the Jewish people cannot be put at risk'; no 'Jewish betrayal'. Sometimes the debate heated up, because there were also opposing voices: 'Is Israel a land of Popes, i.e. infallible?', one dissident wonders. He warned against self-censorship and the demonisation of anyone who expressed criticism. Nine years after Verhagen's article in *Propria Cures* (see chapter 3), the young psychologist – and future professor – Alfred (Freddy) Lange (b. 1941) wrote: 'If you keep accusing people of antisemitism long enough they need a lot of patience to avoid becoming a bit antisemitic.'[93] Another reader remarked that there are different ways to support Israel. Criticism can actually have a positive effect. A solution has to be found for the Palestinians.[94]

In their letters, opponents used the expression 'nuanced thinking'. It is an expression that gained a special meaning in this period of political-semantic merry-go-round. The New Left used the term to indicate that they wanted to break open the rigid political frameworks and ideas. It was not only the time of the Six-Day War, but also of Vietnam and Cuba; a new generation wanted to break immediately with the admiring and dependent attitude towards the United States. Get rid of the Cold War mindset, no more imperialism. Opponents of the New Left like Meijer Sluyser spoke scornfully of 'nuanced [subtle] thinking': it was a ridiculous political concept which concealed double standards. How could a critical approach to Israel be combined with a breathless admiration for left-wing dictatorships?[95] In the most extreme case, nuanced thinking was equalled with antisemitism. That is what Abel Herzberg did during a meeting in Leiden, in late June 1967, when he said: 'He who still wants to think in a nuanced manner, is an antisemite!'[96]

92   Robert J. Kopuit. 'Uitgever Johan Polak', *NIW*, 31 July 1970.

93   Freddy Lange, 'Is Israël een land van Pausen, d.w.z. onfeilbaar?', *NIW*, 9 January 1970.

94   Joop Bromet, 'Kritiek op Israël: ja/nee?', *NIW*, 16 January 1967. *See also NIW*, 16, 23 and 30 January 1970.

95   Gans, *De kleine verschillen*, 831.

96   Arie Kuiper, *Een wijze ging voorbij: het leven van Abel J. Herzberg* (Amsterdam: Querido, 1997), 501. Herzbergs statement was only referred to in 1974, but follows on his remarks which did make the papers during the teach-in in question, in 1967.

As was so often the case, Jews again struggled with their various loyalties. An illustrative example is a remark Paul Spier, leader of the first batch of Dutch volunteers in Israel, made to a member of the leftist Zionist association Hashomer Hatzair. 'I simply don't understand how as a Jew you can still be left-wing, when you see that all Russia and China are doing is egging the Arabs on against Israel.' A young woman in the group, a trainee nurse, lived in Israel when she was young. It had left her with a negative and stereotypical image of Arabs: they are 'cowardly' and 'jealous'.[97]

Reports in 1967 zooming in on the stories of the Palestinian refugees, were initially rare in the Netherlands. It was typical that, of all broadcasters, it was the VPRO who took the lead in this. In the late 1960s this liberal Protestant broadcaster, managed by ministers, went through a cultural revolution and became a left-wing breeding ground for engaged and ground-breaking radio programs.[98] When VPRO journalist Leo Kool interviewed inhabitants of the West Bank, shortly after the occupation, showing their stories and anger, it caused a huge outcry. The programme was accused of being 'biased and distorted'.[99] Some people cancelled their VPRO membership; the same thing happened at the *Humanistisch Verbond* [Humanist Society] when it published photos of the occupied territories.[100]

Fear, as Beate Keizer had pointed out, was explicable, but not healthy. Herzberg had sleepless nights during the Six-Day War – but again, sometime later, about the course of Israel which, in his view, was increasingly drifting in the direction of an 'ordinary militaristic nation state'. Meanwhile, he was unable to live with all the criticism the country triggered. In 1969 he sided with the well-known right-wing oriented foreign affairs commentator G.B.J. Hiltermann (1914-2000). In his AVRO radio programme Hiltermann had called *de Volkskrant* 'openly antisemitic, at least anti-Israel' due to its reporting about Israel, after which the newspaper sued him. Herzberg himself described the mentality of *de Volkskrant* journalists as follows: 'Today the Jews are making this life, which isn't easy as it is, even a little bit harder; in the past they did so simply by their existence, and today by their stubborn persistence to continue to exist.' These and

97 *Het Parool*, 6 June 1967.
98 *See* Huub Wijfjes, *Journalistiek in Nederland 1850-2000. Beroep, cultuur en organisatie* (Amsterdam: Boom, 2004), 339-340.
99 Peeters, *Gezworen vrienden*, 148.
100 *See, e.g.*, Gans, *De kleine verschillen*, 844-845.

similar statements cost him his longstanding warm relationship with *de Volkskrant*.[101]

1967 was a year of paradoxes.[102] After 1945, sympathy with Israel dominated and counter-voices were rarely heard, although ambivalent feelings were always lurking around the corner. The Dutch government had switched from a reticent, even rejecting, attitude towards Israel, motivated by its own political interests, to a warm embrace. Philosemitism and a sense of guilt were indeed present, but both constituted by definition an unstable basis in a country where there was also certainly no lack of antisemitism. In 1967 there was a solidarity with the threatened Israel and relief and euphoria after Israel's victory. At the same time, 1967 sowed the seed for a growing distance. The Palestinians, in their position as underdogs and with their ambitions, became more visible, just like the Israeli occupation policy. The image of a left-wing kibbutz paradise gradually disintegrated. Initially, only marginal anti-Zionist groups voiced criticism, but gradually a sense of discomfort would hit many people. A similar statement can be made about the Dutch sense of guilt regarding the Jews. It had not even been explicitly defined yet and already dissenting voices were being heard. Had the victims in the meantime not turned into perpetrators?

---

101 Kuiper, *Een wijze ging voorbij*, 498, 516. The incident between *de Volkskrant* and Hiltermann resulted in several court cases; *de Volkskrant* won in appeal: *ibid.*, 525-528. *See also* Grünfeld, *Nederland en het Nabije Oosten*, 122-123, and n. 316.

102 *See* Evelien Gans, 'De politiek van het joods gevoel.' In: Marita Mathijsen (ed.), *Hartstocht in contrapunt* (Amsterdam: De Bezige Bij, 2002), 193-209: 208.

7 Transnational Left-wing Protest and the 'Powerful Zionist'

Remco Ensel

The rise of left-wing anti-Zionism in Europe and the United States has been extensively addressed in the historiography about antisemitism. In his analysis of left-wing anti-Zionism in Germany, Gerhard Hanloser even states, 'Israel and the Left – one might think everything has been told about this topic.'[1] But that's quite overstated when you look at the Netherlands, in particular with respect to postwar developments. Here, as elsewhere in Europe, dissenting voices could be heard from the early beginnings of Zionism. Before the war anti-Zionism was a common position within Dutch Jewish circles. The prevailing critique actually was a leftist rejection of Zionism based on the assumed incompatibility of nationalism with international solidarity and the improvement of the lot of the Jewish proletariat.[2] In his comprehensive work *A Lethal Obsession*, Robert Wistrich (1945-2015) describes in great detail how anti-Zionism was also part of twentieth-century Soviet communism. In this tradition, anti-Zionism was a form of anti-bourgeois and anti-capitalistic social criticism, but could also serve as thinly veiled antisemitism with Jews playing the part of class enemies, cosmopolitans and imperialists.

The postwar generation claimed these different left-wing anti-Zionist traditions and made its own interpretation. In this respect David Cesarani's statement that the 'fundamental [postwar] pro-Zionist, pro-Israel posture [of socialists in Great Britain] was undermined by the emergence of the New Left and the generation of 1968' can be generally applied.[3]

---

1   Gerhard Hanloser, 'Bundesrepublikanischer Linksradikalismus und Israel – Antifaschismus und Revolutionismus als Tragödie und als Farce.' In: Moshe Zuckermann (ed.) *Antisemitismus, Antizionismus, Israelkritik. Tel Aviver Jahrbuch für deutsche Geschichte* XXXIII (2005), 181-213.

2   For the different pre-war positions, *see* Evelien Gans, 'Are Zionist socialists bad socialists? A 1929 Amsterdam left-wing polemic about Zionism.' In: Jozeph Michman (ed.), *Dutch Jewish History*, Vol. III (Assen, Maastricht: Van Gorcum, 1993), 321-338 and more extensively Evelien Gans, *De kleine verschillen die het leven uitmaken: een historische studie naar joodse sociaal-democraten en socialistisch-zionisten in Nederland* (Amsterdam: Vassalucci, 1999).

3   *See also* chapter 6 of this volume on the New Left. Robert Wistrich, 'Left-wing Anti-Zionism in Western Societies.' In: Robert Wistrich (ed.), *Anti-Zionism and Antisemitism in the Contemporary World* (Basingstoke: MacMillan, 1990), 46-52 and Robert Wistrich, *A Lethal Obsession. Anti-Semitism from Antiquity to the Global Jihad* (New York: Random House, 2010); David Cesarani,

In an early French critique, Jacques Givet, *nom de plume* of Jacques Vich-
niac (1917-2004), connected the views of *La Gauche contre Israel* [The Left
against Israel] with the qualification of *néo-antisémitism*. In 1974, Arnold
Forster and Benjamin R. Epstein (leaders of the Anti-Defamation League
of B'nai B'rith) came up with the same term, 'New anti-Semitism', to coin
the alleged close connections between critique of Israel, anti-Zionism and
antisemitic stereotyping. The term was as contested at its introduction in
the early 1970s as it was at its reintroduction after 2000.[4] On the one hand
the characterisation of antisemitism was rejected because it would block
any substantial debate about the conflict; according to this interpretation
the charge of antisemitism should be seen as a contrived weapon to stifle
protest. The argument can of course still be heard today. On the other hand
the concept of 'new' antisemitism would be inappropriate because the
ideology of hate and the stereotypes behind some of the anti-Zionist and
anti-Israel criticism were hardly new. A further development was to add an
Arab, even Muslim, connotation to the term 'new antisemitism', as was done
by the Arabist Bernard Lewis (b. 1916) in an article in 1986. In this chapter
we will explore these issues and focus on manifestations of antisemitic
stereotyping, in particular those that have to do with the alleged violent
nature and lust for power of Israelis.[5]

The New Left was the outcome of the search by postwar Western European and American youths for a new engagement with the world, which led
to quickly spreading views on the Third World, the West and its imperialism.[6]
The search by these intellectuals in the making coincided with a boom in

'Anti-Zionism in Britain, 1922-2002: Continuities and Discontinuities.' In: Jeffrey Herf (ed.)
Anti-Semitism and Anti-Zionism in Historical Perspective. Convergence and Divergence (London,
New York: Routledge, 2007), 114-158.

4   Jacques Givet, *La Gauche contre Israël? Essai sur le néo-antisémitisme* (Parijs: Jean-Jacques
Pauvert, 1968; republished as *The Anti-Zionist Complex* (Englewood, NJ: SBS Pub, 1982); Arnold
Forster and Benjamin R. Epstein, *The New Anti-Semitism* (New York: Mc-Graw-Hill, 1974); Bernard
Lewis, 'The New Anti-Semitism', *The New York Review of Books* (April 1986) and Bernard Lewis,
'Muslim Anti-Semitism', *Middle East Quarterly* (June 1998). An early adopter of the term is Robert
Wistrich: 'Anti-Zionism as an Expression of Anti-Semitism in recent years.' Lecture delivered
to the study circle on World Jewry in the home of the President of Israel, 10 December 1984.

5   The discussion is complex and intense. For an historical perspective *see* Yehuda Bauer, 'Beyond the Fourth Wave: Contemporary Anti-Semitism and Radical Islam', *Judaism* 55, 127 (2006),
55-62; Timothy Peace, 'Un antisémitisme nouveau? The Debate about a "New Antisemitism" in
France', *Patterns of Prejudice* 43, 2 (2009), 103-121.

6   For the New Left's reactions *see*: Isaac Deutscher, 'On the Israeli-Arab War', *New Left Review* I
(1967), 44 and Fawwaz Trabulsi, 'The Palestine Problem: Zionism and Imperialism in the Middle
East', *New Left Review* I, 57 (1969). *See also* Mark T. Berger, 'After the Third World? History, Destiny
and the Fate of Third Worldism', *Third World Quarterly* 25, 1 (2004), 9-39.

student numbers. In his study *Postwar* (2005), Tony Judt (1948-2010) described how well-educated baby boomers had started to rebel against the 'old' Left of their parents' class struggle which did not really appeal to them and which also no longer directly affected them. Ideas about economic inequality were repackaged as to better fit the middle class. The old struggle against repression and power inequality was now projected onto the relations between Western Europe and the Third World, using a new selection of canonical texts ('the young Marx'). Anti-Zionism was fitted into this growing engagement with worldwide repression, i.e. Third-Worldism or *tiers-mondism*. Judt, slightly derisorily, referred to this engagement as 'a predilection for the exotic'. In the Netherlands, the sociologist Abram de Swaan, who in 1967 unsuccessfully tried to register as a volunteer (as we saw in the previous chapter), said more or less the same thing in 1968: '"Solidarity with the Third World" is a must-have for all political outfits that want stay up to date.'[7]

In the Netherlands too, the changing approach to the Middle East conflict can be explained by looking at the momentum of 'June 67' and 'May 68'. What is missing in the historiography is the postcolonial dimension of the protests. In the 1960s, for instance, Moroccans moved to Western Europe as postcolonial migrants and that experience was included in their collective actions. There is no need to explain this first-generation activism in an 'orientalist' way, as a cultural oddity, inasmuch as it can be traced back to a shared intellectual corpus of left-wing works, including those by the Martiniquan psychiatrist and writer Frantz Fanon (1925-1961), the French philosopher Jean-Paul Sartre (1905-1980), the Moroccan politican Mehdi Ben Barka (1920-1965) and the French Arabist Maxime Rodinson (1915-2004). The latter had published an influential article about Israel as a *'fait colonial'* in *Les Temps Modernes*, the famous journal of Sartre and Claude Lanzmann (b. 1925). According to Rodinson the conflict was not the outcome of a national emancipation struggle or the fulfilment of a religious promise, but the legacy of a colonial project. This explanation of Israel's existence fitted into the anti-imperialist atmosphere which had become *en vogue* worldwide and was also starting to influence the Dutch debate about Israel, Palestine and the Jews.[8]

---

7   Tony Judt, *Postwar, A History of Europe since 1945* (New York: Penguin Press, 2005); Abram de Swaan, 'De linkse oppositie. De stijl op zoek naar een situatie', *De Gids* 131(1968), 28-39.

8   Maxime Rodinson, 'Israel, fait colonial?' *Les Temps Modernes* (*Le conflit Israélo-Arabe*) 253 bis (1967), 17-88 and Maxime Rodinson, *Israel. A Colonial-Settler State?* (New York: Monad Press, 1973). On Fanon *see* Remco Ensel, 'Postcolonial Memories. Frantz Fanon in/on Europe.' In: Marjet Derks, Martijn Eickhoff, Remco Ensel and Floris Meens (eds.), *What's Left Behind. The Lieux de Mémoire on Europe beyond Europe* (Nijmegen; Vantilt, 2015), 199-206.

The apparently sudden political activism of second-generation migrants during the Palestinian Second Intifada of 2000 is rooted in the activism of the first generation, even though the mobilisation strategies and ideological commitment are different.[9] The transnational protest culture of the 1960s also helps to explain the rapid socialisation of Moroccan migrants in the Dutch protest and remembrance culture of the Second World War. What *was* different from their Dutch counterparts, however, was the way in which labour migrants articulated their own fate as a plaything of unequal global economic relations, in protests against Israel and during commemorations in which the racism of that era (i.e. Nazi antisemitism) was translated into contemporary xenophobia in the Netherlands. Furthermore, in contrast to the New Left generation, the class struggle remained an urgent and current issue for migrant workers.

Migrants and Dutch representatives of already existing left-wing activism joined forces against Israel as an imperialistic bridgehead of the West. That usually went well, but occasionally these partners in protest clashed. The 'slippery slope of antisemitism', as a minute taker of the *Nederlands Palestina Komitee* [Dutch Palestine Committee, or NPK] once described it, was always lurking. But there was also the ongoing threat, at least in the eyes of the Palestine Committee, that others would play 'the antisemitism card' to deflect 'legitimate criticism'.

The emergence of a left-wing protest movement

In June 1967, the Middle East conflict was catapulted into the Dutch public debate. Support for Israel was strong in the Netherlands and at times demanding. Civil servants, for example, paid a quarterly contribution of 0.5% of their salary.[10] The Netherlands had been slow to recognise Israel. 'Warm feelings' and the subsequent 'special relationship' only developed after the 1956 Suez Crisis and around 1967, respectively.[11] The press frequently hinted at the threat of destruction. There was a lot of support, but the cliché that

9   *See* chapter 14.
10   R.B. Soetendorp, *Pragmatisch of principieel. Het Nederlandse beleid ten aanzien van het Arabisch-Israëlisch conflict* (Leiden: Martinus Nijhoff, 1982), 100, with objection by the Catholic Union.
11   *See* chapter 6 for a discussion of the Dutch-Israeli relations. *See also* Soetendorp, *Pragmatisch of principieel*, 72 and René Deelen, 'Voor altijd verbonden. Een onderzoek naar de invloed van de Holocaustherinnering op de Nederlandse geopolitieke relatie met Israël' (MA thesis, History Politics and Parliament, Radboud Universiteit, 2015).

the Netherlands stood 'shoulder to shoulder' with Israel was exaggerated. The Dutch Arab Circle, founded in 1955, for example, organised lectures and debate evenings and there were lively debates in small venues long before 1967. Journalist Musa Suudi (1920-1989), one of the Palestinians who had settled in the Netherlands, also joined the debate.[12] Another prominent figure was Mahmoud Rabbani (1934-2002), who had fled his birthplace Haifa in 1948 and became a successful businessman and consul of a number of Gulf States. Rabbani was an activist, lobbyist and one of the initiators of the Palestine Committee. Up until the mid-1970s, Palestinian activism was predominantly the work of individuals like Rabbani and Suudi. The 'Palestinian community' of refugees and exiles, organised in the Palestinian Association, had its coming out during the Lebanon War in the early 1980s.

In 1963, a debate with Suudi in the newly opened Anne Frank House derailed. Mrs Woltjer-Van der Hoeven, co-founder of the Dutch Arab Circle played the main part. In 1948 in Cairo she had witnessed the war that started after the founding of Israel. Back in the Netherlands, Woltjer-Van der Hoeven had been given lectures about 'The Palestinian Question' since 1950. In 1967, she was 'delighted' with the rising students' activism. Nevertheless, as the chair of the Amsterdam Student Association and one of the founders of the Palestine Committee, Bertus Hendriks (b. 1942), noted, 'She was doing her own "thing" ... and she also thought we were a bit left-wing, but "that was forgivable" because we were still supporting the cause.' The 1963 debate in the Anne Frank House turned into a rhetoric battlefield. Woltjer was accused of using 'impure emotionality in her terminology', Suudi gave long monologues and, when everybody started talking at the same time, someone shouted: 'This is not the Waterlooplein' [the square which before the war hosted the Jewish market, now a daily flea market]: 'Then everybody starts shouting at the same time. Someone says that his father was a merchant on the square and an honourable person ..., the chairman says it's disgraceful. Then apologies are exchanged. The show goes on. Mrs Woltjer resumes her lecture ....'[13]

12   Born in Jerusalem, Musa Suudi worked as a journalist in London. He came to work for the Dutch *Wereldomroep* [Radio Netherlands Worldwide]. Suudi had a Dutch wife; their son Radi Suudi became a teacher, journalist and activist in his own right (I thank Radi Suudi).

13   Interview Ensel-Hendriks, 15 November 2011; Jos van der Lans and Herman Vuijsje, *Het Anne Frank Huis, Een biografie* (Amsterdam: Boom, 2010). A report in F.N., 'Emoties laaiden op tijdens forum over de Arabische vluchtelingen', *NIW*, 15 February 1963. Letter to the editor by J.E. van de Wielen, 'Wel protest', *NIW* 102, 6 (21 October 1966). The lectures by Mrs Woltjer reached parliament in 1966 (*Aanhangsel tot het Verslag van de Handelingen der Tweede Kamer*, zitting 1966-1967, 19).

It was a true pandemonium of different tones and unfortunate word-ings. But was there any substance to it? Many years later, one participant pinpointed his ideological turning point here '(of all places)' in the Anne Frank House: 'Until that day I was, as a socialist who had experienced the war as a boy, very pro-Israel, a safe haven for the Jews and a socialist experi-ment. But the debate heated up due to the presence of several Palestinian refugees. And that opened my eyes.'[14] And this was just one socialist making a U-turn. Up till then European socialists had been siding with Israel. In the late 1960s there was another U-turn under the New Left, this time led by students from Amsterdam and Nijmegen, united in student associations.[15]

In the 1960s, students in the Netherlands gradually became convinced that the aim of student associations was not only to entertain or represent the interests of their members, but also to join the public debate as a union, a syndicate. In 1969 the future chairman of the Palestine Committee, Bertus Hendriks, was one of the leaders of the occupation of the *Maagdenhuis*, the administrative centre of the University of Amsterdam. This was the Dutch version of the student protests in Paris and Berkeley. Local issues and atten-tion for global imperialism merged together in the protests. In France, but also in francophone North African countries, the politicisation of students had started much earlier. There, it was the protest against the Algerian War (1954-1962), both as a foreign and national affair, which marked a decisive moment in student activism.

The intellectual climate during the Algerian War provided exceptionally fertile ground for theories about colonialism and the Second World War. In the Algerian debate, ideas about colonialism and Nazi terror touched each other.[16] In the Netherlands the Algerian War resonated as well. A small group closely followed the conflict. The Jewish writer and resistance fighter Sal Santen (1915-1998), whose family had been killed during the war, actively joined the public debate. From a radical left-wing (Trotskyist) conviction

---

14   Quote about this or a similar meeting: reaction from Dick Fopma on www.anjameulenbelt. nl, 21 January 2010.

15   For the remarkable (and still relevant) anti-Israeli U-turn of Trotskyists (named after the Jewish leader Leon Trotsky who rejected Zionism but recognised current antisemitism in Europe and the Soviet Union), *see* Werner Cohn, 'From Victim to Shylock and Oppressor: The New Image of the Jew in the Trotskyist Movement', *Journal of Communist Studies* 7, 1 (1991), 46-68: Leon Trotsky, 'On the Jewish Problem', a 1945 collection of writings, Leon Trotsky Internet Archive; www.marxists.org).

16   About the impact of Algeria *see* Robert Young, *Postcolonialism. An Introduction* (Oxford, UK, Malden, MA: Blackwell Publishers, 2001) and Michael Rothberg, *Multidirectional Memory. Remembering the Holocaust in the Age of Decolonization* (Stanford, CA: Stanford University Press, 2009).

he became involved in forging money and IDs for Algerian fighters, using knowledge acquired during his wartime resistance activities. After his arrest, Sartre and De Beauvoir, among others, signed a protest letter to the Dutch government.[17] The poet Simon Vinkenoog (1928-2009) made a documentary for the first ever fundraising show on television, intended for Algerian refugees in Morocco. And the first Dutch solidarity committee ever was set up: for the Algerian fighters. At the time, in the 1960s and early 1970s, the Krasnapolsky Hotel behind the National Monument on Dam Square became an arena for debates. In the 1960s journalist, poet and resistance hero H.M. (Henk) van Randwijk (1909-1966) gave a talk about 'colonial relations'. Socialists and 'left-wing Catholics' felt particularly attracted to the emerging anti-colonial Third World perspective. Lawyer, socialist politician and – in his own words – 'very Catholic boy' George Cammelbeeck (1919-1997), for example, read Sartre during Mass. He had been involved in the resistance, was loyal to Algeria and many years later became co-founder of the Palestine Committee.[18] By then, the main issue had become state violence in Israel.

In the Netherlands, students of the Catholic University of Nijmegen toyed with the idea of a students' union, which in turn was picked up by members of the students' union ASVA in Amsterdam.[19] Palestine was not a popular topic among these globalists *avant la lettre*. The regimes in Southern Europe and the war in Vietnam, that's where the *real* engagement was located. Likewise, there was limited knowledge of the Middle East. During the entire 1960s, the region had not featured on the radar of ASVA's foreign affairs committee. And also after the Six-Day War of 1967, there was still resistance within ASVA against the idea of addressing the 'unpopular issue' of the Palestinian question: 'Let's do something that's "safer", like Southern Africa or NATO.'[20] Few students wanted to touch the hot potato 'Palestine'.

17 About Santen and Algeria: Marcel Menting, 'Verslonden door de revolutie. Het politieke leven van Sal Santen (1915-1998)' (MA thesis, Political history, Radboud Universiteit, 2007).
18 The fundraising initiative was in 1959. *See* Niek Pas, *Aan de wieg van het nieuwe Nederland. Nederland en de Algerijnse Oorlog, 1954-1962* (Amsterdam: Wereldbibliotheek, 2008). Cammelbeeck: Jan 't Hart, '"Rooie advocaat" schudde gevestigde orde wakker', *de Volkskrant*, 7 June 1997.
19 The enthusiasm among students in Nijmegen for syndicalism and social equality was soon associated with their Catholic non-elitist backgrounds (which made them reluctant to join the students' unions and promoted ressentiment about the hierarchy). *See* Frank A. Pinner, 'Student Trade-Unionism in France, Belgium and Holland: Anticipatory Socialization and Role Seeking', *Sociology of Education* 37, 3 (1964), 177-199. The thesis was picked up by the Dutch sociologist C.J. Lammers and eleborated by Hans Righart in *De eindeloze jaren zestig. Geschiedenis van een generatieconflict* (Amsterdam, Antwerp: De Arbeiderspers, 1995).
20 ASVA seminar on 19, 20 and 21 January 1973.

There was a knowledge deficit but also a lack of sensitivity for the Arab perspective. On the other hand, there was a lot of sympathy for Israel as the home of Holocaust survivors and as a state with a 'utopian socialist' signature. However, these sympathies started to tilt around 1967. Using his subscription to *Le Monde*, ASVA chairman Bertus Hendriks read into the Middle East and was promptly labelled Middle East expert among fellow students. He later became the Middle East correspondent for the *Wereld-omroep* [Radio Netherlands Worldwide] and public service broadcaster NOS. But that was in the late 1980s. On 5 June 1967, the day the Six-Day War started, he was hitchhiking along a French motorway. On his way home from a syndicalist conference he spotted the front page of *France-Soir*: *Les Egyptiens attaquent Israël*.[21] He would later come to understand this as a typical case of Israeli disinformation, but at the time the only thing on his mind was to ring home to discuss the matter with his fellow ASVA student syndicalists. When he arrived home, the discussion continued both intensively and extensively. The outcome was a statement which, while recognising the state of Israel, also hinted at sympathy for the Arab view on Israel as an 'artificial state' built on feelings of guilt.

The statement triggered a row: 'The world was too small.' Hendriks was almost thrown out by his constituency 'because just as today you go to Thailand or Australia after secondary school, back then you would go to a kibbutz. Half of the students had worked in a kibbutz.'[22] Nevertheless, the pro-Palestinian voice was getting increasingly heard, thanks to the students, the activism of Palestinian refugees and Arab students, and an active group of academics with knowledge of and experience in the Arab world and with a predominantly Catholic background.

There are several connections between anti-Zionism and Nijmegen. A number of students and academics (Arabists and theologians) were affili-ated with the Catholic University of Nijmegen. In June 1967, the university journal published a column by Jaap van Ginniken (b. 1943) in which he commented upon the alleged connection between the Dutch attitude towards Israel and the collective shame about 'the lack of resistance' against the persecution of the Jews. By rhetorically asking, 'Why not a

21   Marcel Liebman spoke about *France-Soir* in the same way to indicate the pro-Israeli atmosphere. *France Soir* remains a recurring reference in later observations: Marcel Liebman, 'Antisemitisme en antizionisme – een buitengewoon listig amalgaam', Marxists Internet Archive, 2009, French original in *Mai* 10 (1970), Alexis Berg and Dominique Vida, 'De Gaulle's lonely predictions', *Le Monde diplomatique* (June 2007) and 'Même de Gaulle était isolé ...', *Le Monde Diplomatique* (June 2007).
22   Interview Ensel-Hendriks, 15 November 2011.

Jewish state founded in Germany?', Van Ginniken knew he would be accused of antisemitism: 'Complacent people who are not willing to debate will hasten to label the following as antisemitic muckraking.' He was right, especially after a letter to the editor by a (Jewish) student was headlined as 'the smouse that roared'. In 1983, when in the heat of the Middle East conflict and terrorist bombings in Europe, the resurgence of antisemitism was debated, the influential journalist Martin van Amerongen (1941-2002) remarked with irony how the Dutch Jew had nothing to be afraid of, that is, if he is sensible enough to avoid the city of Nijmegen. To Hendriks these insinuations by his opponents were all very tiresome, and more to be seen as a kind of 'Pavlovian conditioning': 'a Catholic boy from Oss [a small town near Nijmegen], ah, what else can you expect'.[23]

The Palestine Committee was founded in 1969 in these circles of old academics and young students. To prepare themselves to join the organisation, a number of candidate members travelled through the Middle East, on the initiative of Mahmoud Rabbani and at the expense of the Arab League. Thanks to their travel companion Piet Nak (1906-1996), everywhere they went the group was welcomed with open arms: 'Only Nasser had no time'. Nak had been one of the organisers of the famous February Strike in Amsterdam in 1942. He received the Israeli honorary title of 'Righteous among the Nations' and was awarded a medal from the Israeli Yad Vashem memorial, which he demonstratively sent back after the Six-Day War.

The Palestine Committee was founded in a pub on the Leidseplein in Amsterdam in 1969. But it soon fell apart again. The breaking point was the weight of the anti-imperialistic perspective. Not all members of the established generation could handle the newly-found paradigm. For example, to Nak it was no use ('What has so-called "worldwide imperialism" got to do with it?'), so he left.[24] After a restart, the Committee set off again with a programmatic text which defined Israel as a bridgehead of the West. This became the anti-imperialistic voice used by the Committee in the 1970s

23   Jaap van Ginniken, 'Palestina of Israël', 'Palestijns Dagboek II' and 'Naar aanleiding van...', *Nijmeegs Universiteitsblad*, 27, 28, 29 (9, 16, 23 June 1967) and m.m.d., 'Nijmeegse humor', *NIW* 43, 7 July 1967; Martin van Amerongen, 'Een schijngestalte uit een ver (en fout) verleden.' In: Henk Rouwenhorst (ed.) *Koersbeweging. De zes Zeemanlezingen uit 1997* (Nijmegen: Nijmegen University Press), 84-95. On Van Ginniken: https://en.wikipedia.org/wiki/Jaap_van_Ginneken; Interview Ensel-Hendriks, 15 November 2011. On Van Amerongen *see also* chapter 8.
24   Annet Mooij, 'Nak, Pieter Frederik Willem (1906-1996)', in: *Biografisch Woordenboek van Nederland*. (www.historici.nl/Onderzoek/Projecten/BWN/lemmata/bwn6/nak); Max Arian, 'Profiel Piet Nak. Verzetsman en dwarsligger', *De Groene Amsterdammer*, 13 May 2000.

and 80s to create alliances with the Catholic organisation Pax Christi and left-wing migrant organisations.

Morocco, France, the Netherlands

On 14 May 1970, exactly 22 years after the foundation of Israel and after a three-year preparation period, the Amsterdam students' union ASVA finally managed to organise a three-day conference about the Middle East conflict. The University of Amsterdam had refused to host the event, citing the, allegedly, one-sided view of the conference. According to the University Board, 'Israel's viewpoints' would not get the attention they deserved. Or was the real reason the presence of too many 'critical Jews' on the list of participants, as the organisers underlined? Two prominent Jewish publicists, among whom the journalist Renate Rubinstein, author of the controversial book *Jood in Arabië, Goi in Israel* [Jew in Arabia, Goy in Israel] (1967; see chapter 6), felt pressured and pulled out at the eleventh hour. ASVA moved the conference to the aforementioned Krasnapolsky Hotel on Dam Square. The students had yet to claim 'freedom of speech'.[25]

The student conference was an initiative by the aforementioned Hendriks, who was chairman of ASVA in 1967 but had meanwhile become an active member of the Dutch Palestine Committee. Keynote speakers at the conference were the Belgian writer Nathan Weinstock (b. 1939), author of *Le Sionisme contre Israel* (1969), and Maxime Rodinson whose article in *Les Temps Modernes* in particular had been an eye-opener for Hendriks.

So, on 14 May 1970, the anniversary of both Israel (1948) and the Dutch Palestine Committee (1969), former student leader Hendriks and Rodinson sat side by side at the Krasnapolsky Hotel. Rodinson's lecture concluded with a Q&A session. In the back of the room, a young man stood up to criticise Rodinson's reluctance to act. Rodinson's position was that although Israel was indeed a colonial legacy, one could now only resign to this irreversible fact. Israel was a *fait colonial accompli*. That was unacceptable for the critic. Rodinson turned to Hendriks and whispered that he recognised this type of criticism as *'une critique de gauche'*. The critic in question was Mohamed Rabbae (b. 1941), a student who had fled Morocco in 1966 and rose to become a Dutch MP in 1994. Rodinson replied that the Arabic version of his article had taught the Arabs to stop viewing the conflict as a clash of civilisations, religions or race, but as a fight against imperialism. Not a clash of civilisations, but part of a worldwide class struggle. Still, we cannot turn back the clock, unfortunately. Israel was here to stay. But that analysis did not satisfy Rabbae. This injustice required collective action, which would arise among the Moroccan labour migrants who, in the early 1970s, organised themselves in the *Komitee Marokkaanse Arbeiders Nederland* [Committee for Moroccan Workers in the Netherlands, KMAN]. After the Six-Day War, pro-Palestinian activism in the Netherlands consisted of cooperation between the Palestine Committee and KMAN.

To Hendriks, the focus on imperialism – inspired by Rodinson's key text – must have been a revelation, but in Rabbae's Morocco there was nothing new about it. In Morocco, before 1967, anti-Zionism was already seen as an anti- and postcolonial struggle. In 1966 Mohamed Rabbae was one of only 5,000 Moroccans in the Netherlands. In the early 1970s, when KMAN was founded, that number had risen to 70,000. Three quarters of the so-called 'guest labourers' came from the Rif, a mountainous region in northern Morocco.[26] They had left a country that was unable to offer them a livelihood and with which they had an ambivalent relationship. After his father's unexpected death in 1961, King Hassan II emerged as a dictator who left no room for debate, let alone liberalisation. Politicians were murdered, exiled, imprisoned or disciplined. The inhabitants of the Rif region, for the most part Berber-speaking, heirs of the Spanish protectorate and the anti-colonial rise of Abd el-Krim, did not feel represented by the government and the political parties seated in Rabat. This resulted in an uprising that was harshly repressed, which would have contributed to a further alienation. Elsewhere in the country there were also protests. The Moroccans had seamlessly replaced anti-colonial protest with protests against the King and his policies.

It was from this *culture insoumise*, urban resistance and state violence, that Mohamed Rabbae arrived in the Netherlands in 1966 – after a massive student demonstration in March 1965 which had once again been repressed – and became politically active. Other educated migrants – including Mohammed Khojja, Abderrazak Sbaiti and Ahmed Lamnadi – founded KMAN in 1974. The Committee moved into a squatted warehouse, which

---

26   Data in: Carlo van Praag, *Marokkanen in Nederland: een profiel* (The Hague: NIDI, 2006), 3.

also housed the Palestine Committee which had been active for five years.[27] Abdou Menehbi became chairman. Menehbi had already been politically active in Morocco. As a student he had joined the 1965 protests in Larache. Later, he became active as a trade union 'worker' and as a 'guest worker' in Paris he continued on the same footing. These must have been exciting times for the large Maghreb community in the 18th arrondissement near Boulevard Barbès. Menehbi joined all the demonstrations whose participants enjoyed a certain protection as the marches were led by Sartre in the front. He familiarised himself with the common revolutionary texts, but was aware of the separation between the 'intellectuals' and the 'workers' within the Left. In particular, Menehbi was involved in the migrant organisation *Association des Marocains en France* (later *Association des Travailleurs des Maghrébins de France*) [Association of Maghrebian labourers in France], founded by the Moroccan politician Mehdi Ben Barka (1920-1965). The then 23-year-old Menehbi organised 'anti-racism and pro-Palestine demonstrations' in Paris and continued doing so in the Netherlands. A picture of Ben Barka hung above his desk at the KMAN office.[28]

The first Moroccan activists – Rabbae, Khojja (who arrived in the Netherlands in 1974), Sbaiti (1970) and Menehbi (1974) – all came from the same coastal region (the cities of Mohammedia, Kenitra, Tanger and Larache, respectively) and so they were not from the Rif; they were all around 20 years old. Menehbi wasn't the only migrant with France on his mind to eventually settle down in the Netherlands. Two years after Menehbi, Mustapha Mejjati, who later joined the communist CPN, made the same switch, from Ben Barka's *Association* to the Dutch KMAN. One of the early insiders, Khadija Arib (b. 1960), who was to become a social democratic parliamentarian and Chair of the Dutch parliament, described KMAN as 'a very politicised organisation' with a small group of academic men at the core – although that certainly did not apply to the 'worker' Menehbi – who had ended up in the Netherlands via France. In this male-dominated environment Arib became active as a 'fierce' participant of the 'ongoing discussions about the fight against capitalism and the oppression of women'. In Paris she had

---

27 Ineke van der Valk, *Van migratie naar burgerschap. Twintig jaar Komitee Marokkaanse Arbeiders in Nederland* (Amsterdam: IPP, 1996), 42 and the biographical profiles in Omar Bouadi et al. (eds.), *De vele gezichten van Marokkaans Nederland* (Amsterdam: Mets & Schilt, 2001).

28 Annemarie Cottaar, Nadia Bouras and Fatiha Laouikili, *Marokkanen in Nederland. De pioniers vertellen* (Amsterdam: Meulenhoff, 2009). On Ben Barka: Ben Barka, Bachir (ed.), *Mehdi Ben Barka en héritage. De la tricontinentale à l'altermondialisme* (Paris, Casablanca: Éditions Seyllepse, Tarik Éd., 2007) and Mehdi Ben Barka, *Option révolutionnaire au Maroc. Suivi de Écrits politiques 1960-1965* (Paris: Maspéro, 1966).

already acquired a stack of left-wing literature to prepare herself. In this environment of 'jeans ... long hair and beards', Arib would meet her husband to be, an activist from the Moroccan student movement who ended up in the Netherlands, via France, when the repression intensified.[29] KMAN addressed the class struggle, organised protests against the Moroccan regime, supported Third World thinking and sympathised with the liberation struggle of the oppressed around the world.

KMAN was active, but the size of its constituency remains somewhat unclear, partly because, due to the repression from Morocco, its member records were secret and not disclosed. Collective actions occurred through interaction between left-wing students, political exiles and migrant workers. The former two groups were many times smaller in the Netherlands than in France. KMAN focused on the labour and constitutional position of guest workers, but also on the Middle East. Mobilisation would have been harder for more distant issues. In pamphlets KMAN tried to connect the different issues with each other in one all-encompassing anti-capitalistic and anti-imperialistic frame. This also included anti-Zionism. This could clash when, for example, KMAN wanted to use the May Day meetings to protest against Israel and found no enthusiasm for this among migrant organisations or labour unions such the Turkish HTIB or the Polish Solidarność. The organisation thus continued to build on what was common in Morocco. Anti-Zionism had become part of daily life in Moroccan society in the 1960s; it was engrained in every political ideology and belonged to the *répertoire classique* of the culture of protest.[30]

Also in Morocco a young generation had started to toy with new ideas about culture, politics and society. *Lamalif* was a platform for Third World thinking with attention for Palestine. The magazine published articles about pro-Palestinian solidarity in Europe, about migrants in France and an interview with Rodinson.[31] The magazine's format fitted in with the *tiers-mondism* that was popular in the setting of the Tricontinental Conferences of non-aligned countries in Cairo and Havana and which was expressed in the work of Frantz Fanon and Mehdi Ben Barka. In 1943, Ben Barka was the youngest signatory of the famous declaration of the anti-colonial Istiqlal Party and later a founder of the left-wing splinter-group UNFP. The

29   Khadija Arib, *Couscous op zondag. Een familiegeschiedenis* (Amsterdam: Balans, 2009), 126-130.

30   Mounia Bennani-Chraïbi, *Soumis et rebelles: les jeunes au Maroc* (Paris: CNRS, 1994), 271-272.

31   Zakya Daoud, *Les années Lamalif. 1958-1988. Trente ans de journalisme au Maroc* (Casablanca: Tarik, 2007) and Éditorial, 'La guerre, La paix et le reste, *Lamalif* (June-July 1967), 16-19.

newspaper *Libération* was the party's mouthpiece. For the politician, Israel was the product of a global elite (not necessarily Jewish) capable of imposing its will and silencing the postcolonial voice. Israel was something strange in the region: Western, modern and not a Third World country.[32]

An unusual left-wing voice in Morocco was that of Abraham Serfaty (1926-2010), Moroccan, Arab nationalist *and* Jew, anti-colonialist under the French administration and political dissident during the regime of Hassan II. Serfaty was arrested several times and between 1974 and 1991 was continuously in prison under dreadful conditions.[33]

In 1969, Serfaty published in the literary magazine *Souffles* the essay *'Le judaïsme marocain et le sionisme'* [Moroccan Judaism and Zionism].[34] Serfaty wrote his piece in the wake of the *aliyah*, the large-scale Jewish-Moroccan emigration that really took off from 1961.[35] Families and communities were torn apart and in Israel, Oriental Jews had been accepted reluctantly and put at a disadvantage compared to European Jews. According to Serfaty, Judaism was historically anchored in Moroccan history and culture, while Zionism was a colonial lie. There had never been inherent marginalisation, exclusion or discrimination. Due to French colonialism, the *Alliance Israélite* and the anti-Jewish legislation of Vichy France, the Jews had become detached from the Islamic population with whom they had always lived in a symbiosis.[36] Serfaty was part of an intellectual tradition which tried to reconcile the Jewish identity with Marxism. In order to establish his position after 1967, he

32   Ben Barka, *Mehdi Ben Barka en héritage*. In 1962 Liebman described Ben Barka in *Les Temps Modernes* as one of the most 'resolute opponents' of Zionism. In 1965 Ben Barka was kidnapped in Paris and killed. A year later the Cuban President Fidel Castro lauded him as a martyr of the fight against imperialism. 'At the Closing Session of the Tricontinental Conference', 15 January 1966. Radio transmission translated by the US Government: Foreign Broadcast Information Service via www.marxists.org.

33   Serfaty was cofounder of the Marxist movement *Ila 'l-Amam*. *See* Marguerite Rollinde, *Le mouvement Marocain des droits de l'Homme: entre consensus national et engagement citoyen* (Paris: Karthala, 2003), 190-194.

34   Based on *Souffles* (4, 16-17, 1969) and a collection of interviews: Abraham Serfaty and Mikhaël Elbaz, *L'Insoumis. Juifs, Marocains et rebelles* (Paris: Ed. Desclée de Brouwer, 2001); Issandr El Amrani, 'In the Beginning There was Souffles', www.bidoun.org. Magazine no. 13 ('Glory').

35   Abraham Serfaty, 'Le judaïsme marocain et le sionisme', *Souffles* 4, 16-17 (1969), 24-37. On the migration history: Michael M. Laskier and Eliezer Bashan, 'Morocco'. In: Reeva Spector Simon, Michael Menachem Laskier and Sara Reguer (eds.), *The Jews of the Middle East and North Africa in Modern Times* (New York: Columbia University Press, 2003), 471-504.

36   The French Jewish *Alliance Israélite* was founded in 1860 to promote the advancement of the Jews in the Middle East: Michael M. Laskier, 'Aspects of the Activities of the Alliance Israelite Universelle in the Jewish Communities of the Middle East and North Africa: 1860-1918', *Modern Judaism* 3, 2 (1983), 147-171. In 1961 Morocco closed a deal with Israel about the emigration.

re-read the long-neglected *The Jewish Question* by Karl Marx, the literature of the Jewish socialist *Bund* and the remarkable anti-Jewish work (published in French with a foreword by Rodinson and in English with a foreword by Nathan Weinstock) of the Belgian Trotskyist Abram Léon (1918-1944) who had been murdered in Auschwitz.[37] This literature provided him with anti-Zionist argumentation: Israel is a repressive state and the Palestinians are fighting a liberation struggle. Like other *gauchistes* Serfaty was outspoken about Rodinson's acceptance of Israel: it was unacceptable.[38] Serfaty distinguished himself in his Marxist analysis by being able to make clear how he, as a Jewish Moroccan, was hurt by Zionism. The old, familiar world of Moroccan Judaism had been wiped out.

Whereas in his famous *Réflexions sur la question juive*, Sartre saw 'the Jew' as a figment of the antisemite's imagination, Serfaty and the Tunisian-Jewish writer Albert Memmi (b. 1920) recognised the existence of a Jewish social world and cultural identity. According to Memmi, however, Israel was the solution to save this almost lost world, while Serfaty claimed Israel had been responsible for the destruction of the authentic North African Jewish culture.[39]

KMAN in the Netherlands was anti-Zionist in the way Ben Barka and Serfaty were: populist and radically left-wing and, hence, in favour of the Marxist FDLP and not the nationalism of the better known Palestinian Liberation Organisation (PLO).[40] Ben Barka and Serfaty were icons of the anti-Zionist protest movement. Once, when KMAN was accused of antisemitism, chairman Menehbi countered by pointing to 'the Jewish Moroccan Abraham Serfaty': political prisoner, but above all 'one of the most important representatives of the Moroccan people'.[41] Serfaty was 'really a symbol for the progressive forces in Morocco for radical change', said Menehbi in an interview.[42] It must be said that Serfaty also acted as a testimony of KMAN's benevolence. His nostalgia about the once peaceful relations between

37 Léon wrote *La Conception matérialiste de la question Juive* (Paris: EDI, 1968), in English: *The Jewish Question. A Marxist Interpretation* (New York: Pathfinder, 1970). *See* Cohn, 'From Victim to Shylock and Oppressor'.

38 Serfaty and Albaz, *L'Insoumis*, 214-219.

39 Seth L. Wolitz, 'Imagining the Jew in France: From 1945 to the Present', *Yale French Studies* 85 (Discourses of Jewish Identity in Twentieth-Century France) (1994): 119-134; Albert Memmi, *Portrait d'un Juif* (Paris: Gallimard, 1962-1966; an early Dutch translation of the first volume appeared in 1964: *Portret van een Jood. De impasse*. Amsterdam: De Bezige Bij, 1964).

40 Interview Ensel-Menehbi, 8 April 2011.

41 IISH KMAN Archive, A. Menehbi, press release 10 October 1989. The press release mentions 'Servaty'.

42 Interview Ensel-Menehbi, 8 April 2011.

Islamic and Jewish neighbours can still be heard among first-generation migrants.[43]

Paradoxically, its association with Serfaty could also backfire against KMAN members. Because of Serfaty, royalist migrants, united top-down from Rabat in the *Amicales* movement, frequently accused them of being anti-national and pro-Jewish: once again it was deemed necessary to introduce 'the Jew'. This had already started in Morocco. The right-wing nationalistic voice already had an anti-Jewish undertone in Morocco. In 1967, newspapers such as *L'Opinion* and *El Ahlam* ran an outright hate campaign against indigenous Jews. In June 1967, during a period of two weeks, *L'Opinion*, the newspaper of the independence party *Istiqlal*, published excerpts from *The Protocols of the Elders of Zion*. Right-wing newspapers denaturalised Jews and portrayed them as the fifth pillar.[44] Now in the Netherlands not only (*'the cursed Jew'*) Serfaty was symbolically denaturalised, but so were his sympathisers. This is all the more remarkable when it is realised that Serfaty was the only Jew in 1967 to have received a nationalistic pat on the back because of his fundamental anti-Zionism.[45] In the 1990s Serfaty visited the Netherlands twice, at the invitation of KMAN.

The experiences with Jewish life and Zionism in Morocco, as well as with the international debates on Israel, the local hate campaign and the publications by Serfaty and others, all prepared politically active migrants to join in the Dutch protest culture.

Activism and allegations of antisemitism

In the 1970s, the Palestine Committee and KMAN formed the heart of pro-Palestinian protest in the Netherlands. There were nuanced, sometimes crucial differences between the activists in terms of language and opinions, but there was consensus on the position that the conflict was the legacy of an imperialist initiative. To eludicate these differences and similarities, we shall discuss several meetings and incidents between the late 1970s and

---

43   For an incisive study on this issue in Morocco *see* Aomar Boum, *Memories of Absence. How Muslims Remember Jews in Morocco* (Stanford: Stanford University Press, 2013).

44   This is extensively addressed (based on archival research in Morocco) in Remco Ensel, *Haatspraak. Antisemitisme – een 21ᵉ-eeuwse geschiedenis* (Amsterdam: Amsterdam University Press, 2014) ; *See also* Sion Assidon: Zineb El Rhazoui, 'Sion Assidon: je ne suis pas le dernier des Mohicans', http://voxmaroc.blog.lemonde.fr, 18 December 2010. *See also* Malte Gebert and Carmen Matussek, '"Selbst wenn sie under Land verlassen würden…" Die Adaptation der Protokolle der Weisen von Zion in der arabischen Welt', *Jahrbuch für Antisemitismusforschung* 18 (2009), 67-87.

45   Together with other Moroccan Jews, Serfaty published an anti-Zionist pamphlet in 1967.

the late 1980s. In 1970s, for example, the Palestine Committee attended a 'Moroccan rally,' with a strikingly large number of 'Fatah shawls' and a Moroccan *moussem* with a 'central place' for Palestine.[46] Both organisations also endorsed UN resolution 3379 (1975) which branded Zionism as racism. The importance of the conflict went beyond the region. 'Palestine' symbolised a global struggle and Israel was the symbol of the powerful West.

Despite this basic consensus, there were many things that could go wrong in the day-to-day practice of activism. The different organisations were not fully aligned, had different constituencies and maintained different networks.[47] Things went wrong in, for example, 1980, on the *Day of International Solidarity with the Palestinian People*. A PLO delegation was present in Utrecht and the popular 'progressive Moroccan music group' Nass el Ghiwane performed. The event was organised by the Palestine Committee, the Palestinian Association and KMAN. But most of the around 3,000 visitors were Moroccans. Outside, KMAN was handing out bilingual leaflets which it had written together with French, Belgian and German organisations for Moroccan workers, but without consulting the other organisations. It was a call for resistance against the 'colonial and Zionist occupier' because of the 'racist and Zionist reality and the colonial character of the state of Israel', and the 'international propaganda by Zionism'.[48] Further, Zionism, as an expansionistic ideology also aimed to 'become an international power' and to achieve this aim it collaborated with 'the most racist and fascist regimes', which was 'made a taboo' by the mass media. This went a lot further than the Palestine Committee's message about the aftermath of Western colonialism.

The Palestine Committee did not think in terms of a (worldwide) Zionist conspiracy. It sometimes referred to mass murder and genocide, but tried to take into account the sensitiveness surrounding references to Nazis and the Shoah in the Netherlands. It subsequently struggled with collaboration with organisations that wanted to make more generous use of the rich source of powerful genocidal words and images, such as swastika, Nazi, razzia, concentration camp, genocide etc. There was, however, also a sense in the Committee that the 'opposition party' was unfairly blocking a debate about the conflict by referring to the Holocaust. Every year, for example, the City of Amsterdam rejected a request by the Palestine Committee to organise a street collection for

46   'Fatah shawls', in: IISH NPK Archief 2 map 1969-1980: minutes national board meeting, 8 September 1978; 'moussem', in: IISH NPK Archief 12 map 1983: minutes, 6 May 1984.

47   IISH NPK Archief 12 map 1983: Toine van Teeffelen, Report of 'oriënterend gesprek Palestina Komitee – Palestijnse Vereniging', 6 May 1983.

48   The meeting was held on 29 November 1980 (pamphlet in CIDI documentation 102-103 and IISH NPK Archief 6 map 1879-1981: minutes meeting, 9 December 1980).

its medical fund. Jews in Amsterdam might be offended when confronted with the street collection, was the City's explanation. It was all the more annoying that it was a reference to the Shoah which led to a unique prosecution.

The case on the judge's desk had taken place at the Breda branch of the Palestine Committee in May 1980; yet there was also a connection to the Moroccan community. A group of young enthusiasts had started selling postcards door-to-door around the time of Remembrance of the Dead on 4 May, commemorating those who were killed during the Second World War. The postcards contained political cartoons made by the Syrian-German artist Burhan Karkutli. They included a drawing of a soldier split in half, representing a Nazi on the left and an Israeli on the right. A second symmetry was found on a card with a portrait of Premier Begin stressing his Great-Israel aspirations, with next to him Hitler and his Great-German fantasy. The branch had been offering the cards, at 25 cents apiece, in at least two locations, including Breda's multicultural centre. That was an interesting location because 'there is a lot of interest for the activities of the committee within the Moroccan community'.[49] So what was happening here was that this still young branch, composed of five active members, had started to use postcards, magazines and posters to recruit new members among the migrant community.

The artist Karkutli (1932-2003) had led a wandering life in Syria, Latin America and Western Europa.[50] Born in Syria, Karkutli had always identified himself as a Palestinian. The central theme of his first exhibition, in 1958, was the bombing of Hiroshima and caused an immediate outcry. The drawings were confiscated by the Syrian secret service. Karkutli's career is marked by legal challenges to publish and present his drawings, in West Germany, East Germany, Switzerland and eventually also in the Netherlands. Karkutli gave visual comments on contemporary politics by visualising war violence: the verbal provocations, the physical violence and the catastrophic consequences for ordinary people. Aiming to reach a wide audience, he distributed his art via postcards and posters *'die bei europäischen Studenten ebenso populär sind wie in palästinensischen Flüchtlingslagern'* [which are as popular among European students as they are in Palestinian refugee camps].[51] At the same time of the Dutch trial, Karkutli's iconography also caused a stir in Mexico, Venezuela and Germany (Frankfurt).

---

49   On the cards: IISG NPK Archief 26, 6 map 1979-1981 and map 1980-1981.
50   'Burhan Karkutli', Wikipedia; 'Von Schuhgeschäften, unsichtbaren. Frauen und Revolutionären Interview mit dem palästinensischen Künstler Burhan Karkutli'', www.ila-bonn.de/artikel/254karkutli.htm (interview Gert Eisenbürger and Gaby Küppers).
51   Harald Bock, 'In Memoriam', 27 December 2003, Das Pälestina Portal www.arendt-art.de/deutsch/palestina/Stimmen_Palaestina/burhan_karkutli.htm

Two drawings by the artist Burhan Karkutli sold as postcards by a local branch of the Dutch Palestine Committee, became the subject of a long criminal case for collective offense, i.e., antisemitism, in 1980-1982.

Illustration 11   Postcard with a drawing   Illustration 12   Postcard with a drawing
                   by Burhan Karkutli, 1980   by Burhan Karkutli, 1980

IISH Archive Dutch Palestine Committee   IISH Archive Dutch Palestine Committee

The board of the Palestine Committee distanced itself from the postcards, but the damage had already been done. The newly founded antisemitism monitor STIBA (Foundation for the Fight against Antisemitism) had reported it. Its founder, the American Richard Stein (b. 1936), may have been inspired by the pro-active approach in the United States (as, for instance, reflected in the Anti-Defamation League of B'nai B'rith; see chapter 8).

The judge ruled in favour of the prosecutor on the basis of group defamation, article 137e of the Criminal Code. Even though the postcards did not contain explicit 'Jewish symbols', the judge sympathised with the 'feeling' of some witnesses that Israel is the land where Jews can always go to and which they see as 'the country that has welcomed many survivors of the genocide'. One witness confirmed that Israel is more than a state. It is the homeland for all Jews, and on the Begin/Hitler postcard Israel represented all Jewish people.

The Palestine Committee did not agree with being labelled as antisemitic, however, stating this was only the case 'if people are insulted on the ground of them being Jewish'. Although this does refer to the wording of the Criminal Code article on group defamation, this could also be interpreted as an extremely literal view on racism and antisemitism, one that disregards the meaning of symbols. The argument corresponded with the more usual position that criticism of Israel has nothing to do with Jews and that those who claim such an interpretation unfairly play the 'antisemitism card'. The board did reject the postcards initiative, but only because, in this particular case, it concerned 'emotional and less nuanced criticism'.[52]

Throughout the years, the verdict has remained the subject of debate. A recurring objection was that it was about people with an Israeli nationality and not about Jews. Furthermore, it was not about criticism or insult 'on the basis of' race or ethnicity (see chapter 8 on the introduction of the concept of 'race' in the Criminal Code). At the most, members are touched by it, but that is not a punishable consequence. There is no suggestion of inferiority or anything similar. There is no suggestion that *Jews* are inherently violent. The use of the swastika is however crucial. This symbol, it was said, was used to recall a 'racial theory and antisemitism and that affects the dignity of a race'. So a swastika was insulting even without an explicit reference to Jews. The postcard campaign can then be considered group defamation because, due to the Israeli connection, the Jewish and, as such, antisemitic connotation of the swastika becomes relevant. So, even though in this case it may not be possible to say that Jews as a group are demonised as Nazis (because it is, after all, about Israelis), one can say that ascribing such hateful symbolism particularly offends Israelis as Jews.[53]

The Palestine Committee argued that even if Begin was Jewish and even if Jews felt offended, still nothing was said *'on the ground of them being Jewish'* (as is required by the article on group defamation). However, the Hitler/ Nazi comparisons mainly acquired a meaning in the knowledge that Israel, the soldier and Begin have a Jewish identity. That is exactly what handed the analogy its symbolic power. Another problem was the way in which the Shoah was used against Israel by portraying Israel as a Nazi country striving for world hegemony (from Hitler to Begin) as a central preoccupation. This, of course, ties in with the stereotypical strive for world power, for example as

52 IISH NPK Archief 26 map Breda: Statement NPK 17 November 1980 and *de Volkskrant*, 11 november 1980.

53 *See* Esther H. Janssen, *Faith in public debate. An inquiry into the relationship between freedom of expression and hate speech pertaining to religion and race in France, the Netherlands and European and international law* (PhD thesis, Universiteit van Amsterdam, 2014) and Marloes van Noorloos, *Hate Speech Revisited. A Comparative and Historical Perspective on Hate Speech Law in the Netherlands and England & Wales* (Cambridge: Intersentia, 2011).

laid down in the forged document *The Protocols of the Elders of Zion*.[54] For the close relationship between Israel and Jewry in the cartoons, we can also point to the timing of the door-to-door selling, i.e. close to Dutch Remembrance of the Dead on 4 May. This timing, which would reoccur in later incidents, shows the interwovenness with the Dutch remembrance and commemoration culture of the Shoah. It also indicates an awareness that the historical context of symbols – which not only include the swastika or the ss symbol, but also historical references (such as Hitler's aim for world hegemony) – determines their meaning in concrete linguistic expressions. This means that, within the historical awareness that Jews have been the victims of a genocidal mass murder, one can state that it is offensive and unjust to compare Jewish victims with 'their' henchmen (Hitler, Nazis). But it is also rhetorically effective. It fits into the pattern of zooming in on the victimisation of Palestinians, perhaps even hijacking it from the victims of the Jewish genocide and, in the process, portraying the Jews as the ultimate perpetrators, from *victim* to *victimizer*.

The court case also showed that in the Netherlands, 'being Jewish' had become partly associated with being committed to Israel. The fact that Israel as an identity marker had become a factual experience in the decade following 1967 had not yet sunk in. By now it had.[55] The postcard campaign also showed how Israel was starting to be viewed as a powerful state, even as a threat to world peace. This interpretation in the early 1980s refers to similar interpretations which circulated immediately after the foundation of Israel and which continue to resonate today.[56]

---

54   *See supra* on the Protocols in the Moroccan newspaper *l'Opinion*. In general: Norman Cohn, *Warrant for Genocide. The Myth of the Jewish World-Conspiracy and the Protocols of the Elders of Zion* (New York: Harper & Row, 1967).

55   Compare Samuel Ghiles-Meilhac, 'Les Juifs de France et la guerre des Six Jours: solidarité avec Israël et affirmation d'une identité politique collective', *Matériaux pour l'histoire de notre temps* 4, 96 (2009), 12-15.

56   *See, e.g.*, the statements by the historian Arnold Toynbee in his *A Study of History* (1935-1961) and the debate in 1961 with Yaacov Herzog (ambassador to Canada and brother of Chaim Herzog) and the poem by the German writer Günter Grass 'Was gesagt werden muss' (2012) in which he, like Toynbee, connects the threat to world peace with Israel's control over nuclear weapons. Yaacov Herzog, *A people that dwells alone. Speeches and writings of Yaacov Herzog* (London: Weidenfeld and Nicolson, 1975). Arnold J. Toynbee, 'Jewish rights in Palestine', *The Jewish Historical Quarterly* 52, 1 (1961), 1-11 and Solomon Zeitlin, 'Jewish rights in Eretz Israel (Palestine)', *The Jewish Historical Quarterly* 52, 1 (1961), 12-34. Toynbee and the postwar debate with the Dutch historian Pieter Geyl (which would influence the German *Historikerstreit*) is discussed in Remco Ensel, 'Pennestrijd. Public historians Geyl en Toynbee debatteren in de schaduw van de Holocaust (1948-1961)', *Ex Tempore* 34, 2 (2015), 145-157 [a special issue on mass violence and the public historian].

Israel, state of perpetrators; Jews, a people of perpetrators

A series of antisemitic bombings in Paris, Antwerp and Vienna was a major concern in the early 1980s.

Illustration 13   Photo of the laying of a wreath for the victims of an antisemitic bombing in Paris, 14 December 1980

Rob C. Croes / Anefo / Nationaal Archief

Over the years, representatives of Moroccan migrant organisations and Jewish organisations frequently clashed over the rules of public protest, while at the same time cooperating closely in several instances. On 14 December 1980, Ronny Naftaniel (CIDI, Centre for Information and Documentation on Israel) and Abdu Menehbi (KMAN, Committee for Moroccan workers in the Netherlands) laid a wreath for the victims of the antisemitic bomb attack in Rue Copernic, Paris, 3 October 1980. The swastika on the side was applied (and scrubbed off) a few hours before the start of the ceremony.

Illustration 14   Photo of the protection a synagogue receives, 21 October 1981

Marcel Antonisse / Anefo / Nationaal Archief

An Amsterdam synagogue receives protection during the bomb attacks in Antwerp, Vienna and Paris, 1980-1981 (21 October 1981). Note the simple police car in comparison with contemporary extensive procedures, measures and material to protect Jewish institutions and gatherings.

The early 1980s marked a turning point in the discourse about Israel and the Holocaust. The Jewish genocide was canonised, the concept of the Holocaust had become commonplace. It even became part of popular culture. For example, it entered the football stadium, in the form of anti-Jewish slogans and chants (where it was targeted at the football club Ajax, which was portrayed as Jewish (see chapter 11). There were also more well-reasoned contrasting voices. Was the Holocaust not too prominently positioned in the remembrance culture? And how did Jewish suffering relate to the suffering now inflicted by Israel upon the Palestinians? These 'reasonings' already existed, but started to grow louder. In the protest, Israel became a perpetrator state and, in its wake, sometimes the Jews became a people of perpetrators. This became particularly evident during the Lebanon War. The postcards initiative of the Palestine Committee in 1980 can thus be seen as part of a trend to exploit the symbolism of the Holocaust and turn 'the Holocaust against the Jews'.[57]

The massacre in the Palestinian refugee camps in Sabra and Shatila in 1982 constituted a dramatic reference point. This massacre in Southern Lebanon took place on 16, 17 and 18 September 1982, during the war in Lebanon. Christian militias, controlled by the Israeli army, moved into residential areas for a three-day killing spree. Israel's involvement, embodied by Defence Minister Ariel Sharon, in the massacre was not direct but still significant. It created the opportunity, supplied the means and did not intervene when news emerged about what was happening in the camps.[58]

According to the historians Helena Lindholm Schulz and Juliane Hammer, 'Sabra and Shatila' definitely cemented the conception of Palestinian victimisation in an unprecedented way.[59] The *Nieuw Israëlietisch Weekblad* (NIW) mainly stressed the bankruptcy of Begin's government. In its articles the weekly magazine for the Dutch Jewish community expressed concern about Israel's politics and status. It also pointed out that by showing determination and allowing a mass protest of 400,000 people one week after the tragedy, Israel had particularly demonstrated its strength as a democracy. The events marked the transition of small-scale actions to a solid peace movement. But meanwhile, the tragedy *had* taken place, with or without democracy or peace movement, and this made the NIW remarks rather gratuitous. Dutch pro-Palestinian activists took an ambivalent view of Israeli peace activists who called themselves Zionists, anyway; to them, Zionism and peace activism were mutually exclusive.

57   As expressed by Evelien Gans, *See* chapter 1.

58   *See* William L. Cleveland, *A History of the Modern Middle East* (Boulder, CO: Westview Press, 2001); Colin Shindler, *A History of Modern Israel* (Cambridge: Cambridge University Press, 2008), 179; a summary of the authorised report: 'Final Report of the Israeli Commission of Inquiry into the events at the Refugee Camps in Beirut', *Journal of Palestine Studies* 12, 3 (1983), 89–116. Also Robert Fisk ('The Israelis let the killing continue after the massacre was over'; Robert Fisk, 'The forgotten massacre', *The Independent*, 15 September 2002) and Odd Karten Tveit were quick to report about the mass killing.

59   Helena Lindholm Schulz and Juliane Hammer, *The Palestinian Diaspora. Formation of Identities and Politics of Homeland* (London, New York; Routledge, 2003).

At the end of the 1970s and the early 1980s the public discourse about Israel changed considerably and from different segments of society. Dutch Jews of the second generation, immigrant and leftist demonstrators all had their own media channels. On September 25, 1982 they walked together in one demonstration against the murderous violence in Sabra and Shatila.

Illustration 15   Photo of a demonstration against the mass murder in Sabra and Shatila, 25 September 1982

Rob C. Croes / Anefo / Nationaal Archief

'Jews against the Israeli invasion and massacre.' Demonstration, 25 September 1982, against the massacre at Sabra and Shatila. Jews protested but they also pointed out that the mass protest in Israel a week after the tragedy demonstrated the country's resilience as a democracy.

**Illustration 16   Photo of a demonstration against the mass murder in Sabra and
Shatila, 25 September 1982**

Rob C. Croes / Anefo / Nationaal Archief

'Wir haben es nicht gewusst.' Demonstration, 25 September 1982, against
the massacre at Sabra and Shatila. Note in the background the banners of
the Turkish organisations HTIB and Dev(rimci) Sol. Another banner at the
demonstration spoke of the Israeli 'solution' to the conflict: *Endlösung*.

The year of Sabra and Shatila was filled with protest. The Palestine
Committee collaborated with KMAN, the Turkish HTIB and the Palestinian
association. On 15 and 17 July there were demonstrations in Utrecht and
Amsterdam against the 'imperialistic war' under the slogan 'Israel out of
Lebanon now!'. Radi Suudi (b. 1957), son of the above-mentioned Musa Suudi,
was one of the participating activists. The 12 June demonstration got out of
hand. The Israeli airline El Al received a (false) bomb threat, and protestors
marched on its office. Thereupon the office of the Palestine Committee
was set on fire and two members were beaten up by unknown persons. The
perpetrators were never caught. There were clearly counterforces in operation. The police blocked forty pro-Israel protestors. According to the police
the 'deliberate' use of around 50 children at the head of the pro-Palestinian
march, which had 1,000-2,000 participants, constituted a problem. The
protestors were getting 'increasingly emotional' but the presence of the

children prevented interventions by riot control units. One member of the units, however, managed to speak to the protestors 'in Arabic' and restore calm.[60]

In addition to being a topic for debate, the events in Sabra and Shatila also became a recurring reference in the portrayal of Israel (under Prime Minister Menachem Begin and Defence Minister Ariel Sharon) as a violent state. Sharon was fired after the results of an investigation were made known, but twenty years later he would return as Prime Minister and play a key role in the Second Intifada. Far into the twenty-first century banners with the name and portrait of Sharon as the personification of Israel were carried through the streets of Amsterdam.

The focus of one of the first proposals for protest, a petition, was on the Zionist instead of the Israeli army and on 'genocide': 'We the undersigned protest at the genocide carried out by the Zionist forces in Lebanon.'[61] A week after the events there was a demonstration in Amsterdam 'in response to the recent massacre in West-Beirut'. The march, led by a banner saying 'Stop the massacre of Palestinians', went from Museumplein to Beursplein, where it was awaited by a number of speakers. In Maastricht, there was a silent march and there was another rally in Tilburg. The events would later be commemorated yearly. Another meeting was centred on the screening of *Kafr Kassem* (Borhan Alaouié, 1975), a film about a massacre in a village near Tel Aviv in 1956. The film had caused a polemic before when Jewish organisations labelled it as an antisemitic pamphlet. In order to address this criticism, which it interpreted as an attempt to silence pro-Palestinian activists and cover up the massacre, in 1978 the Palestine Committee organised a viewing with a debate. Now, five years later, *Kafr Kassem* fitted in with Sabra and Shatila.[62]

In Nijmegen, a visit by President Chaim Herzog (1918-1997), who had actually been invited because of his role in the city's liberation in 1944, did not go down well. 'Liberator in 1944 – Occupier in 1984', was the slogan: 'Not to mention the fact that his visit coincided with the days on which a massacre was committed in Sabra and Shatila two years ago.'

Israel, Zionism and state violence became synonymous. Palestinian victimisation gained recognition. Tariq Shadid, a doctor and son of a

60   Based on newspaper clippings of *Het Parool, De Groene* and *Het Algemeen Dagblad*, 15 July 1982.
61   Flyer in IISH Archive Palestine Committee.
62   G. Philip Mok, 'Palestina Komité verspreidt gif', *Elseviers Magazine*, 29 April 1978; IISH Archive NPK 2 map 1969-1980: Press release Palestina Komitee, 18 April 1978.

Palestinian exile who later became famous under the stage name Doc Jazz, said that Sabra and Shatila had opened his eyes:

> Sabra and Shatila was a turning point in my awareness of my Palestinian identity .... At that time I was still in secondary school in the Netherlands and deeply shocked by the news. It had an enormous and lasting impact on me. I remember getting into a fight when one of my classmates provocatively said that it was the Palestinians' own fault. They had no place in Lebanon anyway.[63]

It wasn't until after the Second Intifada in 2000 that he emerged as a protest singer and started his 'musical Intifada' against the Zionist 'racist ideology like National Socialism' and 'Übermensch philosophy'.

At the time of Sabra and Shatila there was a folk music band in Nijmegen called 'Volluk' [The People] which acquired some fame with 'very left-wing lyrics'. After having performed the song *'Sabra en Chatilla'* for a year, it was put as the opening track on the record *Het laatste vooroordeel* [The final prejudice] (1983). The song stood up for the suffering of the Palestinian people by making a comparison with the Holocaust:

> *In Auschwitz en in Maribor* [i.e. Sobibor], *Dachau en Treblinka*
> *Stierven dezelfde mensen als in Sabra en Chatilla*
> *Maar laat het doodsgeschreeuw van zes miljoen Joden*
> *het geschreeuw niet overstemmen van [die] 1500 Palestijnse doden.*
>
> ...
>
> The same people died as in Sabra and Shatila
> But let the death cries of six million Jews
> not drown out the cries of [those] 1,500 Palestinian dead.

The song also deals with Jewish victimisation:

> *Verdrukt, gestampt en uitgemoord, vervolgd in oost en west / Het Joodse volk werd eeuwenlang overal weggepest.*
>
> Crushed, stamped upon and massacred, persecuted in east and west / For centuries the Jewish people have been chased away everywhere.

63   www.docjazz.com/index.php/nl, 12 September 2011.

Unfortunately, they have not learned anything from this suffering:

Maar heb ik 't nou toch verkeerd en hebben zij geen les geleerd / Ten koste van het volk van Palestijnen.

Or am I wrong and have they not learned a lesson / At the expense of the Palestinian people.

The song ended with the slogan *'de volkerenmoord in de Libanon is het ware gezicht van het zionisme'* [the genocide in Lebanon is the true face of Zionism].

The intention clearly was to make a comparison between the Holocaust and Israeli violence. Jews had once been victims, but had not learned their lesson. The CIDI organisation, founded in 1974, to represent the interests of Jews in the Netherlands and to lobby on behalf of (though not in the service of) Israel, made an urgent appeal to the record company to take this record off the shelves.[64] The band was horrified about the fuss. They had 'after hearing about the events made a spontaneous association with the Holocaust'. The song only stated that terrible things had also happened in the past: 'It is not about numbers, but about people. Even one dead is too many.' It is about 'criticism of the Israeli government' and by talking about antisemitism 'any criticism is made impossible'. As argued above, this latter remark about antisemitism was frequently used and had become a cliché line of defence (from the Netherlands to Morocco). Doc Jazz would even include it in one of his songs fifteen years later: 'He who disagreed was immediately [branded] an antisemite / The taboo was unbreakable, justice? ... that was not an issue'. Yet Volluk, and others, had exaggerated the impossibility to criticise Israel; there was actually a lot of criticism of Israel. Or as the sociologist De Swaan said: 'Criticism of Israel has never been a taboo.'[65]

Volluk's argument looked more like a fig leaf to cover their own *faux pas* and dismiss Jews as whiners. It came up with the familiar reasoning that Israelis, as Jews, should know better: Auschwitz was, in Henryk Broder's

---

64 'Antisemitische text; LP uit handel genomen', *Limburgsch Dagblad*, 15 October 1983 and 'Nijmeegse popgroep beledigt Joodse "Volluk"', *Limburgsch Dagblad*, 29 October 1983; column 'Assie', 27 February 2009 and 'Reünieconcerten van folkgroep Volluk', 15 September 2005, *www. folkforum.nl*. The song was at least played one more time in 1987 on a local radio station in Nijmegen as introduction to an interview with Palestine Committee member Ben Alofs about his experiences in Lebanon.

65 IISH NPK Archief, 16 map 1983: Brief van Volluk. Abram de Swaan, 'Anti-Israëlische enthousiasmes en de tragedie van het blind proces', *De Gids* 168 (2005), 349-367 about the argument that 'it's time someone said it'.

words, used as a form of Holocaust education or 'education camp'.[66] The song took a very quick leap from talking about the involvement of the state of Israel to addressing Jews as survivors of the Holocaust. In addition, the song presented Zionism as a mystifying ideology that is finally being revealed. The unmasking revealed 'the true face', a genocidal ideology.

While Volluk's song can be seen as an example of left-wing pro-Palestinian protest, the above-mentioned Moroccan folk band Nass el Ghiwane can serve as an example of Moroccan protest music. In this period, Nass el Ghiwane was quite popular in the Netherlands. The band played several times at poetry and music festivals between 1980 and 1987 and during KMAN events. Sometimes they were refused a visa due to 'Hassan II's involvement', but that may also have been due to the chaotic organisation, for which they only had the KMAN to blame. Shocked by the images of Sabra and Shatila, the members of the popular band wrote the protest song *Sabra wa Chatilla*. It became one of their most popular songs and after the launch of the CD and the internet it got a second and third life during the Second Intifada. The song has certainly been performed at concerts in the Netherlands and was distributed via cassettes:

> *Oh world, there is a murderer among you*
> *Oh world, among you is victorious scorn*
> *Like the seas, the tears of children disappear*
> *Their lives are with God*
> *Oh world ....*
> *The world has remained silent*
> *The Zionists have been able to do what they wanted*
> *in Sabra and Shatila*
> *The big massacre*[67]

The Palestinian victimisation was called upon by connecting it to the heartless violence of the Israelis and Zionists who were called child murderers. This trope of Israeli soldiers as child murderers would return in future protest. The song mentions the bystander role, but 'the Jews' and the Holocaust were left out. Again, it showed that the association of Zionism

---

66 Henryk Broder, *Der ewige Antisemit. Über Sinn und Funktion eines beständigen Gefühls* (München: Fischer Taschenbuch Verlag, 1986) In: Gans, *Gojse nijd & joods narcisme. Over de verhouding tussen joden en niet-joden in Nederland* (Amsterdam: Arena, 1994), 45-46.

67 Translation: Rachid Alouad Abdallah. The song stresses the arrogance of the Israeli Defence Forces.

as a violent ideology and 'Zionists' as heartless and violent, and sometimes genocidal, had become a topos in the representation of Israel and its army.

The topoi of Israeli violence and cruelty stayed, just as the violence itself returned in waves. The motive however was bolstered by later events, such as the call to break the bones of Palestinian rebels attributed to Yitzhak Rabin. The battle was shifting to the Palestinian territories, the Gaza Strip and the West Bank under Jordan rule. The First Intifada – the second one was in 2000 – lasted from 1987 to 1991 and was accompanied in the Netherlands by a new cycle of demonstrations.

During the First Intifada Jewish institutions regularly received hate mail – sometimes signed and with a newspaper clipping included – in which Jews were held accountable, using all the familiar stereotype descriptions, for the violence of Israel: 'We do not aim to kill? The umpteenth lie of Judaism ... Greetings from Arafat.' Comparisons were made with Nazi Germany ('even worse than the ss', 'Jewish fascist thugs') or the killing of children was referred to: 'a new child murder of Bethlehem .... These are acts of cruelty.' The Jewish National Fund received their ad back with the following text: 'Why have you not stolen enough already? Have you not turned Palestine enough into an Apartheid state? Your democracy is a joke. Discrimination, exploitation.'[68] The hate and resentment emerging from these notes sometimes had an authentic antisemitic charge using notions of the protest repertoire we have described above. All these writings showed that attributing reckless and genocidal violence and the authors' use of the Holocaust to stress perpetratorship and remove the victimisation of Jews were already deeply imbedded in the public domain.

What was special about the regular protest of the Palestine Committee and KMAN was the newspaper they published on the occasion of the First Intifada. The newspaper caused a stir since its content included everything anti-Zionism had to offer during 1967-1988, such as news about demonstrations and background information about Israel and the Zionist project. At the last minute the Committee realised that the contents of the newspaper went too far and subsequently pulled out. In one surviving copy the name in the colophon has been crossed out, in another copy it hasn't. The tone of the newspaper was secular and left-wing. It specifically focused on Hassan II as a bad genius: 'It was he who opened the gates of Morocco for Zionist conferences.' This was a reference to the King's moderate attitude. Apart from that, what did readers learn from this newspaper?

68 Correspondence: CIDI documentation.

Zionism is the ideological core of the colonial and racist undertaking called Israel. While criminals and adventurers founded the Unites States and South Africa, the Jews founded Israel (and it cannot be ruled out that 'European and American criminals' were involved here as well).

Zionism is a threat to the worldwide people's struggle. Zionism is an all-encompassing project: the 'Zionist aim is to first dominate the entire region and then the whole world .... Everywhere in the world Zionists want to be in control. Those who challenge their power or criticise Zionism are destroyed.'

There is a close relation between Zionism and Nazism. See Fanon. Nazi Germany was an alibi for the Zionist colonial project and 'Zionism has also inherited a lot from Nazism/Fascism due to the historical didactics that binds them.' 'Fanon has put forward sufficient arguments for that in his book *The Wretched of the Earth*.' The 'Zionist state' has a 'fascist nature'.

Zionists have a habit of stealing babies for adoption. The foundation of the state was made possible by this practice and time and again 'new flesh' is required.

Before and after the Second World War Zionists set up media institutes in various countries to disseminate their propaganda.

Zionists distrust anybody who is not a Jew.

In the printed text Israel had been manually placed within double brackets. The authors had made lavish use of the hyperbole as a stylistic tool. It had become an outright antisemitic pamphlet. That was also the opinion of an adviser hired by KMAN. A spokesperson of the Palestine Committee said that it wasn't intended to be antisemitic but 'that it could be interpreted as such'. KMAN admitted that they could have been more subtle, but assumed the story about the babies was commonly known. In a stinging column, the publicist Anet Bleich (b. 1951) portrayed the newspaper as a contemporary imitation of *The Protocols of the Elders of Zion*. She would, however, take a lenient view if, in this time of rising tensions, this was to remain a one-off.[69] In a way, the incidental character of the newspaper

---

69   Anet Bleich, 'Gruwelsprookjes uit naam der solidariteit', *De Groene Amsterdammer*, 13 July 1988. The spokesperson for the Palestine Committee was Toine van Teeffelen.

was relative. The newspaper's tone fitted in with an established practice of framing the conflict in terms of Zionism as an imperialistic, world peace-threatening, racist and violent (and fascist) practice. More incidental in this Dutch culture of protest were the representations of Jews as misanthropic, reclusive, conspirators excitedly planning child murder, among others, and out for world domination. All the classical stereotypes in a nutshell. The Intifada newspaper put common notions to the utmost extreme while adding some new ingredients to the protest vocabulary.

After 1967, anti-Zionism with a postcolonial flavour increasingly became the central topic of a Dutch protest movement. The Palestine Committee noticed 'that the term Zionism sounds positive or neutral to many Jews and Israelis', but these (pro-Israel) 'subjective interpretations' were of no use to them.[70] They wished to refer to the visible and tangible Israel, instead of the 'fantasy' projected by 'Zionists' in Europe onto contemporary Israel. Zionism was nothing but a colonial ideology of oppression and racism. Perhaps we could – by ironically referring to the socialist catchphrase of that time – call the Intifada newspaper an expression of *real* or *actually existing* anti-Zionism, i.e. mainly consisting of a list of antisemitic stereotypes. But that would be an exaggeration. Incidents during protests in the 1980s more than once linked up with the passionate manner of protest among migrants. Still it seems that the Intifada newspaper in its public expression of a blend of anti-Zionist and antisemitic tropes was an exception. The protest movement of the late 1960s to 1990s was well-organised in 'committees' and 'migrant', 'peace' and 'solidarity' organisations. Mobilisation proceeded along the channels of these movements. There were particular differences regarding ideology, protest vocabulary and repertoire, but these were mostly contained by an ongoing dialogue between representatives of the organisations involved. The newspaper however did hold a gloomy promise for the (Second Intifada) protests in 2000, a little over ten years later, when use of media, ideological commitment and patterns of identification would change.

70 Documentation CIDI: 'Map Palestina Komitee'.

8   Israel: Source of Divergence

Evelien Gans

As chapters 6 and 7 showed, the year 1967 already contained all the contrasting (including future) elements in attitudes towards Jews and Israel: on the
one hand sympathy, idealisation and unconditional solidarity, and on the
other condemnation, aversion and demonisation. In both tendencies, Jewry,
the Shoah and Israel are usually seen as one single package. The temptation,
in the case of Israel, to turn victim into perpetrator, often turned out to be
irresistible, as we have seen in chapter 3 when tackling a fake interview
in a 1969 issue of *Aloha*, the most popular magazine among the rebellious
youths, which portrayed Anne Frank as a racist 'Arab hater'. The supposed
interview was a manifestation of what has been called the 'fatal triangle'
between criticism of Israel, anti-Zionism and antisemitism; all three can
function as separate issues, but they can also overlap and get intertwined.[1]
Since 1967 Israel no longer above all generated a mix of enthusiasm, compassion, doubt and ambivalence, but instead a lasting source of divergence:
between Jews and non-Jews – and among Jews. This chapter primarily
focuses on the so-called *niet-Joodverklaring* [literally: 'non-Jew declaration';
i.e. a statement that so and so was not a Jew] and, as such, on a policy of the
Dutch government and administration which facilitated antisemitism due
to economic interests. Furthermore, it will become clear that the previous
attitude of prominent Jews à la Abel Herzberg – 'antisemitism is a problem
of civilisation of the non-Jew'[2] – would, during the 1970s, turn into a both
legally and activist directed anti-antisemitism, particularly among younger
generations of Jews.

---

1   For the concept of the fatal triangle *see* Evelien Gans, 'Volgend jaar in Jeruzalem', *Vrij
Nederland*, [a historical essay on Zionism in a special issue on Israel: 'Is Israël mislukt? Joodse
Nederlanders over een verloren droom'] 5 April 2003; Evelien Gans, 'De almachtige jood. Hedendaags antisemitisme', *Vrij Nederland,* 29 November 2003; English version: 'The omnipotent
Jew. Antisemitism today', *Engage Online*, March 13, 2006: www.engageonline.org.uk/blog/article.
php?id=294# ; Evelien Gans, '"The Jews" as products of globalisation", *Engage Journal* 2, May 2006:
www.engageonline.org.uk/journal/index.php?journal_id=10amp;article_id=34&article_id=37;
Evelien Gans, 'Hamas, Hamas, All Jews to the gas', 99; Gans, 'They have forgotten to gas you', 90.
2   *See* chapter 5.

The 1973 oil boycott and the 'non-Jew Declaration'

In 1985, Richard Stein (b. 1936), chairman of the Foundation for the Fight
against Antisemitism (STIBA), looked back with some astonishment on
what Jews in the Netherlands had swallowed in terms of antisemitic abuse,
without taking any action. In his compilation *Veertig jaar na '45. Visies op
hedendaags antisemitisme* [Forty years after '45: Observations on contemporary antisemitism] (1985), a STIBA initiative, Stein took stock of the why,
what and how of the five-year-old foundation. Stein was an American Jew
who had been working in the Netherlands as a concert pianist and piano
teacher since around 1969.[3] The foundation was set up in the late 1970s by
a group of Jews who were active in various Jewish organisations and had
noticed that, due to a number of gradual changes, latent antisemitism in
the Netherlands had been rudely awakened from its slumber: economic
recession, no longer a 'tolerant society', but one with a 'foreigner problem'
(Stein probably mainly referred to the arrival of Moroccan and Turkish
labour migrants), the rise of the neo-Nazi *Nederlandse Volks-Unie* and far-
right *Centrumpartij* (see chapter 4) and, last but not least, the deterioration
of relations between the Netherlands and Israel.[4]

It must be said that Stein's conclusion that relations between the Netherlands and Israel had worsened, was quite exaggerated. However, it was true
that the Netherlands and Israel were less close than they had been after the
Dutch recognition of the Jewish state, culminating in the period starting
with the outbreak of the Six-Day War. The Netherlands had become more
critical of Israel. And 1973 was a year in which relations shifted following yet
another war in the Middle East, one that is known under three names: Yom
Kippur War, October War and Ramadan War. Israel was still occupying the
Sinai and Nasser's successor, Anwar Sadat, after several years of a 'war of
attrition' and diplomatic interactions decided to break the status quo and
force a change in the territorial situation, via a war with, mainly, tactical
intentions.[5] In this he succeeded. The Israeli secret service had not seen
the Arab offensive coming and had, therefore, failed. All of a sudden, Israel
proved more vulnerable than it had previously imagined. The fact that the
Egyptian (and Syrian) attack had been launched on the most important

---

3   *De Stem*, 22 November 1980. For Richard Stein, *see also* chapter 7.
4   Richard Stein, 'Nabeschouwing: Nederlands antisemitisme en de strijd tegen ideeën', in:
Veertig jaar na '45. Visies op het hedendaagse antisemitisme. Introduced by Prof Dr L. de Jong
(Amsterdam: Meulenhoff Informatief, 1985), 278-329: 281.
5   Robert Soetendorp, *Het Nederlandse beleid ten aanzien van het Arabisch-Israëlisch Conflict
1947-1977* (Meppel: Krips Repro, 1982), 123.

Jewish holiday, Yom Kippur, which that year fell on 6 October– hence the Israeli name – was all the more demoralising.

Initially, both the Egyptian and Syrian armies managed to break through the Israeli defence lines and there were heavy losses on both sides. But after just under a fortnight Israel managed to push back Egypt and Syria.[6] Subsequently, there was an interim agreement in the form of a 'disengagement accord' for the area around the Suez Canal. That was a concession by Israel in the sense that it agreed with a partial withdrawal without a signed peace agreement. Egypt, in turn, temporarily accepted that the Jewish state had only given up a relatively small area.[7]

Four days before a UN resolution put an end to the fighting, which both sides accepted, the Arab League sent a telegram to all Arab governments asking them to impose an oil embargo against the Netherlands. This followed on a recent embargo against the United States for being the most important arms supplier to Israel. It was clear why the Netherlands, in contrast to some other EEC countries, which faced partial cutbacks, was hit by a complete embargo.

Since 1948 and particularly since 1967, the country had a reputation as a pro-Israel bastion. In the UN it systematically voted against resolutions which demanded a complete withdrawal from the occupied territories and it had a different interpretation of resolution 242: Israel had to pull out of 'occupied territories' – not out of 'the' occupied territories. That way, the Netherlands had, time after time, also within Europe, blocked a solution to the conflict. In October 1973, things had got even worse – from the Arab perspective. The Dutch government had immediately and unilaterally branded Egypt and Syria as the aggressors. Defence Minister Henk Vredeling (1924-2007) and Deputy Minister Bram Stemerdink (b. 1936) supplied arms to Israel. These were, however, top secret supplies which not even the cabinet knew about.[8] Stemerdink also publicly attended a solidarity manifestation for Israel while the mayor of Amsterdam was involved in fundraising initiatives for Israel.[9] For the Arab world, a line had been crossed.

However, the Dutch government – since May 1973 led by the social democratic Prime Minister Joop den Uyl (1919-1987) – was not willing to give in to Arab pressure. It maintained its position that Israel should,

---

6   F. Grünfeld, *Nederland en het Nabije Oosten: de Nederlandse rol in de internationale politiek ten aanzien van het Arabisch-Israëlisch conflict 1973-1982* (Deventer: Kluwer-Deventer, 1991), 57.

7   Soetendorp, *Het Nederlandse beleid,* 133.

8   Peeters, *Gezworen vrienden,* 186ff; Maarten Jan Hijmans, 'De geheime hulp aan Israël', *NIW,* 28 March 1997.

9   Soetendorp, *Het Nederlandse beleid,* 141-142.

indeed, withdraw, but only behind safe borders, which were to coincide, approximately, with those from before 1967. In addition, one condition was that Israel's sovereignty (like that of the other countries involved) would be recognised. The Palestinian question was still, essentially, treated as a humanitarian refugee issue.[10] When the boycott was implemented, Den Uyl announced a car-free Sunday to save oil.[11] But it wasn't long before the government changed its position. On 7 November it supported a joint declaration by the EEC countries, which also included, as a peace agreement condition, the need for Israel to put an end to its post-1967 territorial occupation. Furthermore, the legitimate rights of the Palestinians were to be taken into account. Opponents believed that the Netherlands, and the EEC as a whole, had bowed its head to the Arab blackmail. The government insisted that it had not essentially changed its position. But in reality it had shifted. The implicit message was that border corrections were not an option for Israel, and the term 'refugees' was not used in relation to the Palestinians.[12]

Among the population, sympathy for Israel initially remained at a high level, around 73%. But the new key terms of government policy were 'balanced policy' and 'impartiality'. From now on, the starting point were the legitimate demands of *both* parties. A striking example was that the Netherlands doubled its financial contribution to UNWRA (United Nations Relief and Works Agency for Palestine Refugees in the Near East) in 1974.[13] The changed Dutch position was undeniably a result of the oil boycott. Western Europe had meanwhile become very dependent on oil as an energy source, and the Arab countries were the main supplier. If the Netherlands was to settle in more comfortably and safely within the European Political Collaboration (EPC), it had to abandon its *Alleingang*. The new motto was to avoid isolation.[14]

In addition, more room became available for what were seen as legitimate Palestinian demands and wishes. Step by step the government was heading towards recognition of the Palestinian right of self-determination and the

---

10   *Ibid.*, 135, 144.

11   Grünfeld, *Nederland en het Nabije Oosten*, 73; Peeters, *Gezworen vrienden*, 219-220.

12   Soetendorp, *Het Nederlandse beleid*, 145-147.

13   *Ibid.*, 150*ff*; Grünfeld, *Nederland en het Nabije Oosten*, 155.

14   *Ibid.*, 138-140, 202-204. The United States supported the Netherlands by founding the International Energy Agency (IEA). The oil boycott of the Netherlands ended on 10 July 1974; first by Algeria, then the other Arab countries followed suit. This was not because they believed the Netherlands had become less pro-Israel, but for the benefit of a desired relation with the European Community: Grünfeld, *Nederland en het Nabije Oosten*, 134, 152.

foundation of a Palestinian state.[15] In 1977, the European participants of the Euro-Arab Dialogue, including the Netherlands, still refused to recognise the PLO as the legitimate representative of the Palestinian people, but they all condemned the Israeli settlement policy.[16] In November 1975, the UN had adopted the controversial 'Zionism is racism' resolution 3379.[17] For several reasons the year 1977 too was significant with regard to the relations in and towards the Middle East. First and foremost, in Israel, the appointment of Menachem Begin of the right-wing Likud party as Prime Minister marked the end of the uninterrupted monopoly of power of Israeli social democrats. It was Begin who at the time had led the troops who had executed the massacre in the Palestinian village Deir Yassin. Under his premiership, the already ongoing settlement policy moved up a gear and was scaled up. Meanwhile, peace negotiations between Israel and Egypt were underway. A 1977 poll in the Netherlands showed that at least 43% of the population believed that the Palestinians were entitled to their own state. At the same time, the level of sympathy for Israel remained high.[18] The exact opposite was the case with regard to the level of appreciation of the Arab states, which remained very low despite, or possibly because of, the oil boycott.[19]

The private sector, on the other hand, made the best of a bad bargain. The boycott had a lasting effect on businesses at an invisible level. Companies that had business relations with Israel were blacklisted by the Arab League's Central Boycott Office. Quite a few companies did not want to run that risk. 'Petrodollars' had become an established term: trade relations with

15   If the government believed Israel's entitlement to safe border was not (sufficiently) taken into account, the Netherlands abstained from voting or voted against, but in the latter case never anymore as the only country: Grünfeld, *Nederland en het Nabije Oosten*, 153-155.

16   *Ibid.*, 167.

17   UN resolution 3379: '... Zionism is a form of racism and racial discrimination.' The resolution was revoked in 1991 with Resolution 46/86.

18   I.e. among, respectively, lower educated, less lower educated, average educated and higher educated rising from 43 to 49, 50 and 51%. This was an opinion poll conducted by NIPO for the Working Group Israel: 'Nederland onveranderd in sympathie voor Israël', *NIW*, 15 April 1977.

19   On this final issue Soetendorp and Grünfeld agree. Otherwise, they focus on different things, partly because they rely on different opinion polls, partly because of different interpretations. Soetendorp stresses that the 67% pro-Israeli support in June 1967 fell to 40% in November 1973 and a year later to 37% – the percentage of neutral respondents, however, rose from 26% in June 1967 to 51% in November 1973: Soetendorp, *Het Nederlandse beleid*, 151-152. Grünfeld states that the absence of a question about a neutral position led to a sharp rise of the pro-Israel position: in that case it would be 73% in October 1973 and 72% in November. He therefore concludes that sympathy for Israel remained fairly stable: Grünfeld, *Nederland en het Nabije Oosten*, 131. It may well be that this difference also includes the increased support for the Palestinian position which emerged from the 1977 NIPO poll: 'Nederland onveranderd in sympathie voor Israël'.

the Arab world hugely expanded during the 1970s in terms of size and value.[20] In addition to blacklists, the League also used other restrictive measures, such as the negative goods statement: a certificate stating that not a single part of a company's specific product came from Israel. In theory, these conditions related to Israel. In practice, the Dutch blacklist primarily contained companies with Jewish owners, most of which did not even maintain trade with Israel.[21]

On top of that the 'non-Jew declaration', as it soon became generally known, was introduced; it can be defined as 'a statement that you are Christian and have no ties with Israel'.[22] Businesses were asked if they had any Jewish managers. A 'yes' could result in being blacklisted. Employees were expected to prove that they were 'non-Jews', using certificates of baptism, notarial deeds or population register extracts. Jewish employees were not welcome in Arab states. Jaap van Wesel, a Jewish journalist who was to accompany the then Minister of Foreign Affairs Max van der Stoel (1924-2011) during his visit to Saudi Arabia in 1975, was refused a visa. Upon which Van der Stoel cancelled his trip.[23]

From 1974 onwards there were parliamentary questions about the issue, but except for one, the government brushed them all off. That was no longer possible when Ronny Naftaniel (b. 1948), deputy director of the CIDI, founded in 1974, denounced the practices in black and white. In his *Zwartboek* [Blackbook] *De Arabische boykot en Nederland* (1978), he listed a number of companies, including, for example, Philips, which complied with the conditions set by the Arab League's Central Boycott Bureau (and also a few companies which refused to comply). Allegedly, every year around 7,000 boycott statements were legalised.[24] Furthermore, and this was even more startling, Naftaniel revealed that the Dutch government was providing structural support. Some Arab countries wanted the negative goods statement to be not only legalised with a signature of a Chamber of Commerce,

20   Between 1970 and 1975 exports to the Arab League rose by 314% and imports by 191%: Ronny Naftaniel, *De Arabische boykot en Nederland: een zwartboek met feiten en documenten over de houding van het bedrijfsleven en overheid onder Arabische druk* (The Hague: CIDI, 1978), 41; Grünfeld, *Nederland en het Nabije Oosten*, 187. Grünfeld states that the entire question deserves a 'separate dissertation': *ibid.*, 51, n. 166.
21   Naftaniel, *De Arabische boykot en Nederland*, 21.
22   M.T. Josephus Jitta-Geertsema and J.H. Sanders, *Antisemitisme in Nederland*. WVC Literatuurrapport nr. 20 (The Hague: Ministerie van Welzijn, Volksgezondheid en Cultuur, 1983), 23.
23   *De Volkskrant*, 31 January 1981; *Het Parool*, 4 February 1981.
24   Naftaniel, *De Arabische boykot en Nederland*, 17. For an overview of the parliamentary questions since 1974: *ibid.*, 34-36. The figure 7,000 was mentioned by a spokesperson of the Rotterdam Chamber of Commerce, in October 1977: *ibid.*, 23.

but also with one of the Ministry of Foreign Affairs. And so the ministry did. Every day, officials of the ministry's legalisation department signed such statements, thereby effectively legalising the boycott at state level.[25] Furthermore, the ministers of Foreign Affairs and Economic Affairs, Max van der Stoel and Ruud Lubbers (b. 1939), had said that they were unable to obstruct the authorities of the Chambers of Commerce, and didn't believe concerted EEC measures would make any sense: anyway, such measures would never be unanimously accepted.[26] With regard to their latter claim, they probably did have a valid point though. Although there were also anti-boycott movements in other EEC countries, such as England and France, Europe did not exactly excel in determination – even though there were legal instruments available. So it was with good reason that Naftaniel and his sympathisers urged the Netherlands to take the lead, even though they were not very optimistic about the outcome.[27]

The publication of the *Blackbook*, in February 1978, triggered a wave of parliamentary questions. But the government braced itself. It announced, via a new Minister of Foreign Affairs, C. van der Klauw (1924-2005), that the Netherlands did not recognise the Arab boycott and that it did not wish to take any steps which would suggest recognition.[28] That was a fallacy. The government refused, in other words, to set up an inquiry. This did not satisfy the permanent Committee for Trade Policy and, in its wake, the House of Representatives. In April, a special committee, with representatives of almost all political parties, was set up to investigate the issue. Because both the government and employers' associations were dragging their feet, various Jewish organisations meanwhile decided to set up an Anti-Boycott Committee (ABC). The Committee pursued legal measures and passed on information to the new Parliamentary Committee. The government, in turn, now stated that it attached great value to a solution at an international level. It was important to prevent Dutch businesses from being in a disadvantaged position compared to businesses elsewhere in the European

---

25 Naftaniel, *De Arabische boykot en Nederland*, 23-24. See also Ralph Pluim, 'Reacties van de Nederlandse overheid op het Zwartboek van Ronny Naftaniel', March 2011 (unpublished paper; personal archive Evelien Gans). I thank Ralph Pluim.

26 Naftaniel, *De Arabische boykot en Nederland*, 35-36.

27 *Ibid.*, 39. For an overview of the international anti-boycott movement, parts of EEC cartel legislation relevant to the boycott and the so-called non-discrimination condition: *ibid.*, 27. The United States was the front runner with regard to legislation.

28 Questions asked by Members of Parliament and the answers provided by the government, sent in on 10 February 1978, 1-2.

Community.[29] According to Van der Klauw and his colleagues little could be done at national level: there were not enough figures available about the size and implementation of the Arab boycott.[30]

One year after publication of the *Blackbook*, in February 1979, the Parliamentary Committee published its report, which included several important findings. The declaration of the Arab League's press office that the boycott only targeted sympathisers of Zionism was incorrect. It was impossible to prove that all those blacklisted had such sympathies. So the League, de facto, made a distinction between Jew and non-Jew.[31] In practice, there also appeared to be 'gentlemen's agreements' between Dutch entrepreneurs and Arab authorities. In these cases, companies secretly agreed not to voluntarily post Jewish employees abroad. Many Dutch companies had conformed themselves to the Arab boycott conditions. The situation was exacerbated by the erratic application of the conditions; companies preferred to play it safe, cutting off, for example, contacts with Israel. Generally speaking, there had been – actually, already since the 1973 oil boycott – an ongoing decline in foreign investments in Israel.[32] KLM bowed to the Arab boycott by using two flight schedules: one for the Arab world, which did not mention Israel, and another for the rest of the world. Furthermore, in 1980 it was still issuing 'non-Jew declarations', to be replaced by 'non-Israel declarations' after the law was changed in 1981. In practice, however, they continued to affect mainly Jews.[33]

The biggest blow to the government was the enquiry's finding that it had indeed played a role itself in keeping the trade boycott in place. The Ministry of Foreign Affairs had hardly, or not at all, responded to companies which had alerted it to the existence of the boycott. Furthermore, the Minister had meanwhile confirmed that the staff at his department legalised trade

29 Report of a verbal meeting, approved on 4 April 1978, 14986, 'De Arabische boycot en Nederland, Tweede Kamer der Staten Generaal, Zitting 1977-1978', 4-7.

30 Ronny Naftaniel, *Nieuwe feiten over de Arabische boykot en Nederland: elf originele dokumenten en achttien kranteartikelen die de invloed van de Arabische boycot op het Nederlandse bedrijfsleven aantonen* (The Hague: CIDI, 1979), II.

31 The same was argued in Naftaniel, *De Arabische boykot en Nederland*, 21.

32 *Verslag van de bijzondere commissie voor het voorbereidend onderzoek naar de Arabische boycot en Nederland*, approved on 1 February 1979, 14986, 'De Arabische boycot en Nederland', Tweede Kamer der Staten-Generaal, Zitting 1978-1979: 6, 11-12, 20, 51.

33 Jitta-Geertsema and Sanders, *Antisemitisme in Nederland*, 24. See also 'Motie van de heer Nijhof, Behandeling van de stukken betreffende de Arabische boycot en Nederland (14 986) 10[de] zitting, 23-10-1979', 469.

documents with negative goods declarations.[34] The Ministry of Economic Affairs had published an import and export vademecum with information about the Arab boycott. Contrary to previous denials, the ministry also had a 'black list' of Dutch companies.[35]

Even though the report exposed the government's beating about the bush and its sole focus on national economic interests, Van der Klaauw and associates were still putting up resistance. In May, the Minister announced that the ministry would first conduct its own inquiry after all. The *Algemeen Dagblad* called it a disgrace. After all, there was already a well-documented inquiry report on the table; it seemed that the government was trying to hide internal division. Especially with regard to the 'non-Jew declaration' the government should have spoken in 'a clear language': 'The tension between political courage and economic fear is clearly palpable.'[36] In June 1979, Naftaniel published a sequel to the *Blackbook*, a publication dubbed *Witboek* [Whitebook], containing new facts and documents about the impact of the Arab boycott in the Netherlands. It mentioned, for example, that the head of HR of a consultancy firm in Scheveningen had reported that it did business with various Arab countries, and that it was just a fact that these imposed demands on their trade partners. Hence, unfortunately, it was unable to employ Jews.[37] The director of *Werklust* [Working spirit], a hydraulic machinery company, confirmed that exports to Iraq required signing a declaration that they had no business relations with Israel. That was not a problem, because it was correct. The same applied to the contested statement: '"Non-Jew declarations" for technicians posted abroad are not required. They are not Jewish.'[38]

A different issue was that of municipalities, notaries and churches issuing, upon request, documents which mentioned the applicant's religious orientation. These documents did not, by definition, serve as 'non-Jew declarations', but they could and sometimes did serve as such. On this issue, the government had intervened before. On 1 May 1975, the Minister of Justice, Dries van Agt (b. 1931), had ordered notaries to stop issuing 'non-Jew

---

34 *Verslag van de bijzondere commissie voor het voorbereidend onderzoek naar de Arabische boycot en Nederland*, 22.

35 *Ibid.*, 25; Naftaniel, *De Arabische boykot en Nederland*, 21. Meanwhile, Van Aardenne had replaced Lubbers as Minister of Economic Affairs.

36 *Algemeen Dagblad*, 22 May 1979, NIOD, KB II 454A.

37 *Utrechts Nieuwsblad*, 17 February 1979; Naftaniel, *Nieuwe feiten over de Arabische boykot*, Bijlage, nr. 12.

38 *Algemeen Dagblad*, 10 February 1979 Naftaniel, *Nieuwe feiten over de Arabische boykot*, Bijlage, nr. 18.

declarations', referring to the International Convention on the Elemination of All Forms of Racial Discrimination signed on 7 March 1966 in New York.[39] With reference to this same treaty, Interior Affairs Minister W. de Gaay Fortman (1911-1997) pointed municipalities to the inadmissibility of issuing details about religious orientation to 'be used during business trips to the Middle East'.[40] But in 1977 he went one step further. That year, the Israel Committee Netherlands (ICN) conducted a survey among all Dutch munici-palities to enquire if they provided information which indicated if someone was Jewish or not. The ICN assessed 8.3% of the responses as 'relatively negative'. There were 24 municipalities (3.3%) which issued declarations for commercial purposes without asking for further explanation. In addition, some municipalities (2.8%) said they did not refuse them *a priori*, but looked at requests on a case-by-case basis; 2.2% said they provided information for official purposes and mental care.[41]

The ICN had submitted a request to the Minister to impose a full ban on the issuance of religion-related information, and the Association of Dutch Municipalities (VNG) supported the initiative. According to VNG, under the current regulations abuse was still a real risk, and was indeed common in more than three percent of the municipalities. The ICN stressed that 16% of the municipalities had not bothered to respond, mostly in the provinces of Limburg and South Holland. In Limburg, with its predominantly Catholic population, non-response was at 31.3%; in South Holland, particularly in the region with a relatively high number of people working in Arab countries, an 'even 26%'.[42] In October 1977 De Gaay Fortman issued the desired complete ban for municipalities.[43] It was difficult to get a grip on the issuance policies of churches considering the 'organisational structure of Dutch churches', Van Agt told the Parliamentary Committee. The committee itself had noted that there were still churches – albeit a limited number – which

39   *Verslag van de bijzondere commissie voor het voorbereidend onderzoek naar de Arabische boycot en Nederland*, 19.
40   'Gemeenten verboden afgifte verklaringen van niet-jood', *NIW*, 21 October 1977.
41   Renate Katz, 'Aantal gemeenten geeft toch ariërverklaring af', *NIW*, 23 September 1977. *See also* Naftaniel, *De Arabische boykot en Nederland*, 20.
42   Allegedly, in Dordrecht, Alblasserdam, Oud-Alblas, Hardinxveld-Giessendam, Giessenburg, Molenaarsgraaf, Bleskensgraaf and Wijngaarden: Katz, 'Aantal gemeenten geeft toch ariërverk-laring af', 23 September 1977; *see also* 'Gemeenten autonoom bij afgiftebeleid', *ibid.*
43   *Verslag van de bijzondere commissie voor het voorbereidend onderzoek naar de Arabische boycot en Nederland*, 19. He did this on the grounds of article 90, clause 4 'Besluit Bevolkingsboek-houding' – an exception was made for that same article 90, clause 2, in case of church-related membership administration: 'Gemeenten verboden afgifte verklaringen van niet-jood', *NIW*, 21 October 1977.

issued 'Christian declarations'.[44] The 1983 report *Antisemitisme in Nederland* [Antisemitism in the Netherlands] by the Ministry of Welfare, Public Health and Culture (WVC) also established that there were still Reformed church councils which bowed to requests for a 'non-Jew declaration'.[45]

In his *Blackbook*, Naftaniel had launched the concept of 'new Aryan declarations'.[46] The term had already been circulating in Jewish circles for some time, and also caught on elsewhere.[47] That wasn't surprising. The House of Representatives officially referred to the non-Jew declarations; from there, it was only a small step to the Aryan declaration of 1940. The *Blackbook* also contained other references to the Second World War and the persecution of the Jews. Naftaniel had been hoping for a 'sort of February Strike mentality'; but what he found was the 'deeply rooted mercantile mentality' of the Dutch. With regard to the legalisation of the negative goods declarations he spoke of a '"peculiar" example of collaboration of the Dutch government'.[48] It was difficult to determine to what extent the frame of reference of the persecution of the Jews played a role in the effectiveness of the broadly supported protest. In any case, on 2 November 1979, the cabinet approved a proposal criminalising 'making a distinction based on race and origin in relation to work and business'; in 1981 it was incorporated in the Criminal Code as article 429c. From now on 'non-Jew declarations' were legally forbidden. As opposed to group defamation (article 137c, dating back to 1934) which was classified as a *misdaad* [misdemeanor], article 429c was labelled as a lesser infringement, i.e. an *overtreding* [offense]. The two articles, however are connected by the concept of 'race'. In 1971, influenced by the United Nations International Convention on the Elimination of All Forms of Racial Discrimination (1965) and the European Convention on Human Rights (1970), article 137c was modified to include defamation 'based on race, religion ...'. It thus seemed logical eight years later to include 'race' in article 429c as well. 'Race' however remains a complex and controversial

44 *Verslag van de bijzondere commissie voor het voorbereidend onderzoek naar de Arabische boycot en Nederland*, 20. See also Naftaniel, *De Arabische boykot en Nederland*, 34.

45 This was a breach of the decision by the Reformed Synod and therefore the Reformed provincial church assembly in Utrecht wanted to have the ban on issuing baptism statements in the challenged context, included in its regulations: M.Th. Josephus Jitta-Geertsema and J.H. Sanders, *Antisemitisme in Nederland*. WVC Literatuurrapport nr. 20, (The Hague: Ministerie van Welzijn, Volksgezondheid en cultuur 1983), 34-35.

46 Naftaniel, *De Arabische boykot en Nederland*, 13.

47 Katz, 'Aantal gemeenten geeft toch ariërverklaring af'. See, e.g., *De Telegraaf*, 22 January 1977. See, e.g., *De Telegraaf*, 22 January 1977; *Vrije Volk*, 23 February 1979; *De Waarheid*, 26 October 1979

48 Naftaniel, *De Arabische boykot en Nederland*, 17, 23.

concept, to put it mildly. To be punishable, expressions should pertain to 'what is characteristic for a group, namely their race ...', but it also necessary for abuses to be effective because of victims belonging to that race. 'Race' was conceived as a wide-ranging concept, as it is today, to refer to 'ethnicity', 'origins', colour of skin or nationality. Still it is surprising and awkward indeed that Jews should be understood as a race, in order to criminalise antisemitism. The Criminal Code allows for Israel criticism because it does not refer to characteristics of the Jews as a 'race'. But what if, as the Arab League did, distinctions between 'Israelis', 'Zionists' and 'Jews' are disregarded? Dutch companies and, in their wake, the government had actually endorsed the Arab League with regard to 'Zionists' and 'Jews'. Strictly speaking the cabinet had tolerated, and facilitated, an antisemitic policy, for economic motives and assisted by local governments, notaries and churches – i.e. making a distinction between Jews and non-Jews, whereby Jews, due to their origin, were put at a disadvantage. Neither the *Blackbook* nor the *Whitebook* characterised this government policy as 'antisemitic', but they did call it 'unjust' and 'hypocritical'.[49] They did, however, allude to it using metaphors such as Aryan declaration, February Strike and collaboration.

'Antisemitism' was not the main preoccupation of the different action groups which sprung up after 1973 emphatically supporting the Jewish state. They constituted a counter-reaction to the phenomenon, described as follows by *Vrij Nederland* journalist Martin van Amerongen (1941-2002):

> Within a few days it has become clear that the "We-are-behind-Israel"sentiments of a not insignificant part of the Dutch public opinion are regulated by the thermostat of the central heating.[50]

Van Amerongen openly positioned himself as being part of the 'Left', in the same way as he would later confidently manifest himself as 'half Jewish'. In 1973, he lashed out against the right-wing press and right-wing political parties: initially, their love for Israel had known no boundaries, now there was suddenly a lot of sympathy for the Arabs, who were up until recently described in 'racist language' as 'camel herders'. The Right was very keen to

---

49 Naftaniel, *Nieuwe feiten*, VII.
50 Martin van Amerongen, 'De vrienden van Israël krijgen koude voeten', *Vrij Nederland*, 10 November 1973'. In: Martin van Amerongen, *De muichelmoordenaar. Artikelen en polemieken* (Amsterdam: De Arbeiderspers, 1978), 173-179: 175. The journalist J.M. Bik wrote: 'We don't support Israel, we don't support the Palestinians, we support our own car': 'Vrije Encyclopedie van het conflict Israël-Palestina', www.vecip.com: www.vecip.com/default.asp?main=25 (consulted 17 December 2015).

blame the left-wing government, with Van der Stoel as their scapegoat, for having committed a diplomatic and, most importantly, costly blunder as a result of their unilateral and emotional pro-Israel approach.[51]

A different approach: Jewish organisation and action

Martin van Amerongen was not the type of person, or Jew, to organise himself in a Jewish context. But others were, such as *Werkgroep Israël* [Working Group Israel], *Actie Comité Israël* [Israel Action Committee], CIDI, *Anti-Boykot Comité* [Anti-Boycott Committee] and *Israël Comité Nederland* [Israel Committee Netherlands] (ICN). There was a determined will to act, especially, but certainly not exclusively, among Jews. The Israel Action Committee was a Jewish ad-hoc committee, founded in 1974 in the aftermath of the October War by the *Nederlandse Zionistenbond* [Dutch Zionist Union] (NZB), established in 1899. The committee collected money, enrolled volunteers for Israel and organised demonstrations.[52] But according to the NIW, the Israel Committee Netherlands, which had organised the survey among municipalities (to determine how widespread the issuance of non-Jewish certificates was), consisted of non-Jews and 'baptised Jews'. ICN sought to be the 'voice and action centre' of a large part of the Dutch population, which was 'either manifestly or latently and potentially united in solidarity with the Jewish people and the Jewish state' – but until recently unable to express its solidarity in an effective way. In its press release, the Committee announced that it would mainly disseminate information, but not shy away from 'tough action', if necessary, albeit within legal limits. It explicitly located the fault line in the year 1973: especially since the Yom Kippur War and the oil boycott '... the relativising element regarding the state of Israel's legitimacy has increased to a problematic extent'.[53] Of the many post-1973 pro-Israel groups that were based on a Protestant idea, the ICN had grown to become by far the most influential one with the most members.[54] No doubt a Christian-based form of philosemitism had something to do with

---

51 Van Amerongen, 'De vrienden van Israël krijgen koude voeten'. See also 'Kuifje in Zwitserland *of* Beter een halfjood dan een lege dop.' In: Van Amerongen, *De muichelmoordenaar*, 266-290: 290.

52 Grünfeld, *Nederland en het Nabije Oosten*, 113.

53 'Nieuwe Israël-groep in het geweer om met harde actie te overtuigen', *NIW*, 21 June 1974.

54 Grünfeld, *Nederland en het Nabije Oosten*, 46. For the specific reproaches of the 'right' against Den Uyl's left-wing government and its non business-minded, naive pro-Israel policy *see*; Peeters, *Gezworen vrienden*, 231-234.

this: a fusion of the (Old) People of Israel and the (Promised) Land of Israel. According to the ICN the world had not always pursued the preservation and protection of Israel with due care and consultation, and that's why it was 'not worthy of housing the Jewish people among other peoples'.[55]

The above-mentioned Anti-Boycott Committee was founded in 1978 to do what its name implied: take action against the Arab boycott. It had an official set-up with an advisory committee including, among others, the secretary-general of the Reformed Synod, the Professor of Economics Jan Pen (1921-2010) and a many other prominent Dutch. But the active members were from B'nai B'rith, the NZB and the Working Group Israel. They were able to do what the Parliamentary Committee was not, for example unexpectedly asking difficult questions during shareholders' meetings of large companies such as Ballast Nedam and Ogem. And as a result of these experiences with companies working in the Middle East, Naftaniel did eventually use the predicate 'antisemitism', albeit cautiously. It was shocking to him,

> how much hidden antisemitism then emerges. Shareholders are afraid that they will receive a few pennies less dividend per share if their company rejects the Arab boycott demands.[56]

Naftaniel was a linchpin within the pro-Israel movement, which had blossomed in the wake of the oil boycott. Initially, he had been part of the Working Group Israel, founded in December 1973 and mainly consisting of students. Within the pro-Israel spectrum, they were the most critical of the policies of the Jewish state and supported a two-state solution – at that time still a highly controversial view. The Working Group's message was that Israel's right to exist and the Palestinians' right of self-determination did not rule each other out: both could and had to be realised.[57]

The Working Group did not have an easy time: there were many board changes, the number of members grew, but the number of active members

55   'Nieuwe Israël-groep in het geweer'.
56   M. Kopuit, 'Anti-boykot comité gelijk met parlementair onderzoek gestart', NIW, 2 June 1978. The B'nai B'rith association was the Dutch branch of the American organisation B'nai B'rith, founded in 1843, which offers mental, social and material assistance to predominantly Jews. The Dutch branch consisted of three departments (lodges) at the time: Mau Kopuit, 'Bnee Beriet neemt bestrijding van het antisemitisme serieus', NIW, 25 July 1980. See also J. Michman et al. (eds.), Pinkas. Geschiedenis van de Joodse gemeenschap in Nederland (Amsterdam: Contact, Nederlands-Israëlitisch Kerkgenootschap, 1999), 382, 508.
57   Grünfeld, Nederland en het Nabije Oosten, 50. For one of the Working Group's activist initiatives against alleged antisemitism, see chapter 9.

remained small, and – as was true for all groups seeking a compromise in 'the conflict'– the Working Group regularly found itself caught between two fires. Talks with the Dutch Palestine Committee, founded two years after the Six-Day War, collapsed. The eventual dissolution of the group had mainly to do with the shift to the right in Israel related to the arrival of Begin. That also put the Working Group in a tight corner. It struggled to identify with the policies of Begin's government, but it was emotionally hard to act against these policies 'because the "love for Israel" came first'. The focus increasingly shifted to the rights of the Palestinians, which disturbed the balance of the original goals.[58] Members either moved to CIDI or joined the *Shalom Achshav* (Peace Now) organisation.

As mentioned above, CIDI was founded in 1974, less than half a year after the Working Group Israel. It supported a two-state solution and opposed Israel's settlement policy. Because of that, the organisation was criticised by the much more conservative NZB. Yet, it was not a surprise that CIDI acquired a reputation as the mouthpiece of the Jewish state and the Israeli embassy. It focused on influencing public opinion and policies regarding Israel, and – like the Working Group Israel – its primary loyalty was towards the Jewish state. Thanks to the *Blackbook*, CIDI had positioned itself with a bang on the political scene, with its standard bearer Naftaniel growing into the most important and influential Jewish spokesperson with regard to Israel. The media found their way to CIDI, particularly Naftaniel – and vice versa. The same was true for politicians, including government representatives.[59]

The opposite was true for the Dutch Palestine Committee, which struggled to get a foothold, as we have seen in the previous chapter. Its requests for government subsidies were rejected. The main argument for these rejections was the fact that the Palestine Committee unconditionally backed PLO's position and in 1973 had called for the foundation of 'a democratic Palestine, in which Jews and Arabs can live together as equal citizens in peace with neighbouring countries'.[60] So, no recognition of Israel's legitimacy. Time and again, this was the decisive factor – with the government, the majority of the political parties and public opinion, as well as with the pro-Israel movement. Both NZB and CIDI opposed contacts between government officials and PLO. In the late 1970s Jan de Koning (1926-1994), the Minister

58 'Inleiding' to Archive Working Group the Netherlands Israel, 1354, inv.nr. 118, Amsterdam City Archives: nr. 18. *See also* Grünfeld, *Nederland en het Nabije Oosten*, 51
59 As examples of CIDI's critical stand against Israel's annexation of the Golan Heights, Grünfeld mentions the expulsion of Palestinian mayors and the invasion in Beirut: Grünfeld, *Nederland en het Nabije Oosten*, 51, 189-190.
60 *Ibid.*, 47-50, 115.

for Development Aid, on a number of occasions refused to subsidise the Palestine Committee because it was a 'club aimed at destroying the state of Israel'. In 1979 he stated that the state of Israel offered Jewish citizens 'a certain security'. He did not want to be responsible for having that security put up for discussion again.[61] A possible 'security' of the Palestinians had little or no importance for De Koning.

The rejection by the PLO – and the Palestine Committee – of Israel as a Jewish state had a boomerang effect and was crucial to the other side's refusal to recognise the PLO as the (only) legitimate representative of the Palestinian people. Another breaking point was the Palestinian terror. In the 1970s the PLO and other Palestinian liberation organisations had been responsible for a long list of deadly terrorist attacks, both in Israel and beyond – of which we shall only mention a few. In 1970 a Swiss Air airplane was blown up in Zürich; in 1972 there was the infamous hostage taking of the Israeli sports team during the Olympic Games in Munich – which ended in a bloodbath; in 1974 there was an attack on a school in Ma'alot (Israel); in 1976 an Air France airplane headed from Tel Aviv to Paris was hijacked by Palestinian and German terrorists and forced to fly to Entebbe Airport in Uganda. There, Jewish passengers were separated from non-Jewish passengers.[62] In 1978, a group of Palestinians from El Fatah, the armed branch of the PLO, travelled from Lebanon to Israel to hijack a bus.

The fact that the PLO and its sympathisers only wanted to recognise Israel if Israel recognised the Palestinians' right of self-determination, while Israel only wanted to negotiate with the PLO if it recognised Israel's legitimacy, was a deadlock cast in concrete.[63] The first crack appeared in 1988, against the backdrop of the First Intifada (Palestinian Uprising), when Yasser Arafat declared an independent Palestinian state. He also declared that the Palestinian National Charter (which included the destruction of Israel) had become obsolete, thereby recognising resolution 242. Only after strong American pressure was Arafat willing to explicitly renounce terrorism.[64] It is not a coincidence that in that same year the Dutch Ministry of

---

61   Ibid., 48-49, 190.
62   Idi Amin's Uganda sympathised with the hostage takers. After a week the Israeli army intervened and managed to liberate all but three Jewish hostages (the non-Jews had been allowed to leave the plane).
63   Grünfeld, Nederland en het Nabije Oosten, 191.
64   These and the other most controversial issues, namely the foundation of a Palestinian state entirely covering historical Palestine and the rejection of a two-state solution, were not definitively withdrawn by Arafat until the 1993 Oslo I Accord. Hamas demanded a reintroduction of these articles in 2004: Colin Shindler, A history of Modern Israel (Cambridge: Cambridge

Foreign Affairs donated 1.2 million guilders to the medical aid organisation 'Palestine Red Crescent Society', while in previous years the City Council of Amsterdam had even banned collections for this organisation.[65] But the push to look at the Israeli-Palestinian conflict with slightly different eyes had already been given earlier. Looking back, Bertus Hendriks, former chairman of the Palestine Committee, said that at the time of the October War the committee had made no illusions about what it was able to obtain from the government. Yet he had noticed a change: 'The oil embargo set people thinking about the conflict.'[66]

1979 was the year of the *Whitebook* about the Arab boycott, of draft legislation abolishing distinctions between race and origin in professions and businesses, and of De Koning's statement about Israel being a safe haven for Jewish citizens. And, last but not least, of the peace agreement between Israel and Egypt, as the culmination of Sadat's historical visit to Jerusalem in 1977 and, in its wake, the signing of the Camp David Accords. They involved Egypt recognising Israel's legitimacy, Israel pulling out of the Sinai and promising the Palestinians autonomy – but not an independent state. Hence, the Palestinians rejected the agreement and El Fatah, PLO's military branch, and similar organisations continued their armed struggle and terror attacks against Israel.

1979 was also the year in which the American, internationally released, TV series *Holocaust* was broadcasted in the Netherlands. The series did not only generate positive responses. The chairman of the far-right and antisemitic *Nederlandse Volks-Unie*, Joop Glimmerveen, remarked that, at the exact moment that the *Endlösung* of the Jewish question by mass destruction of Jews in gas chambers had been proven a propaganda lie, international Jewry and its followers had had the astonishing nerve to produce and broadcast 'such a film insulting all Germanic people'.[67] Apart from the far right, most viewers were deeply impressed – 'Phone network

---

University Press, 2008), 209, 324. An important background of the breakthrough in 1988 was also that King Hussein of Jordan cut the administrative and legal ties with and responsibilities toward the West Bank; that put an end to the so-called Jordan option: the idea of Palestinian autonomy in direct solidarity with Jordan. For a more extensive analysis of the above developments *see* Shindler, *A history of modern Israel*, 204-226.

65 Grünfeld, *Nederland en het Nabije Oosten*, 49-50. A few years earlier, in 1982, the PLO had been granted permission to set up an information office in The Hague: Réne de Bok, 'Nieuw PLO-kantoor in Den Haag', *Elseviers Magazine,* 13 November 1982, 17-21. The massacre in Sabra and Shatila by Phalangists, supervised by the Israeli army, had put an end to the hesitations in the Netherlands.

66 Grünfeld, *Nederland en het Nabije Oosten*, 115-116.

67 Quoted in *De Tijd*, 27 April 1979, NIOD, KB II, 2152 B. *See also* chapter 4.

overloaded after Holocaust III', the headline of the newspaper *Het Vrije Volk* read. But there were also negative reactions, declaring that it was unnecessary to dig out that history again.[68]

Furthermore, in 1979 there was an incident and a controversial radio programme, and in 1980 there was a political action, all three related to Israel, which triggered a heated debate about whether these were cases of antisemitism. The incidents taking place in 1979 and 1980 have partly been discussed in detail in the previous chapter or will be discussed in the next.[69] We should, however, mention them here briefly in order to explain the foundation of the STIBA. In 1979, a contingent of Dutch troops was dispatched to Lebanon to join the UN peace force UNIFIL (United Nations Interim Force in Lebanon). In Lebanon a civil war raged between, roughly speaking, Christians, led by the Phalangists, and the Muslim population, seeking support from Palestinian militias. These militias – particularly El Fatah, PLO's armed branch – had been driven out of Jordan during the infamous Black September in 1970, seeking refuge, with many refugees tagging along, in Lebanon where they constituted an important force. In 1976, Syria invaded the neighbouring country in order to stabilise the situation. That same year, the Syrian intervention was enforced by the Arab countries at the Conference in Cairo.[70] There were scores of military confrontations at Israel's northern border. From March 1978 onwards, Israel, in response to the Palestinian bus hijacking organised from Lebanon, which had left 38 passengers dead, occupied a strip in southern Lebanon, closely collaborating with the Christian Lebanese militias, headed by the deserted major Sadad Haddad who was fighting against the PLO in the southern region of Lebanon and wanted to found his own state of 'Free Lebanon'.

In this minefield the lightly armed Dutch UNIFIL battalion, together with a number of other participating countries, was expected to form a buffer between Israel and the PLO and its allies. It was a particularly difficult task. Among other things, the troops faced violent conduct by the Israeli army which also regularly offended them. By behaving as it did, Israel made itself anything but popular. That much became clear in a report about 'Our boys in Lebanon' by the journalist Lieve Joris in the *Haagse Post* of 23 June 1979, in which several soldiers made hostile comments about Israel. Some of them

68 *Het Vrije Volk*, 30 April 1979; *de Volkskrant*, 25 April 1979 and *Het Parool*, 27 April 1979.
69 *See* chapters 7 and 8.
70 *See, e.g.*, Hassan Krayem, 'The Lebanese Civil War and the Taif Agreement': http://ddc.aub.edu.lb/projects/pspa/conflict-resolution.html.

also made antisemitic remarks about 'the Jews' in which the image of the 'gas chamber' re-emerged. It caused a national scandal in the Netherlands.[71]

But not everybody seemed to bother. For instance, the journalist Willem Oltmans (1925-2004), who was both famous and notorious in the Netherlands – and abroad – and maintained some bizarre alliances, for example with the Iraqi dictator Saddam Hussein and the notorious far-right Dutch ('black') widow Florrie Rost van Tonningen, wondered on the radio 'why one would not have the right to be anti-Israel or anti-Jewish, but would be allowed to loudly support anti-communism or anti-Sovietism'.[72] Oltmans clearly did not understand that 'anti-Jewish' does not belong on this list. On the contrary, he added that he felt sorry for 'the pathological projections of Jews, because on all fronts they are busy becoming the victim of their deviations'.[73] Oltmans would continue to reject Israel's right to exist and to make antisemitic statements right up until his death.[74]

Of a completely different nature was a series of radio programmes, broadcast by the VPRO in October 1979, about the position of the Palestinians in Israel and Lebanon. The broadcaster also extensively reported on Israeli torture practices, and not everybody believed or accepted this. The broadcasts led to outright reactions from Jewish side and the main question that emerged formed the motto of a radio debate, organised due to all the commotion, entitled 'Critical or antisemitic'?[75] Finally, in 1980, a few days after the 4 May Remembrance of the Dead, a local branch of the Palestine Committee started a campaign involving the distribution and sale of postcards with images comparing Israel with Nazi Germany, and Begin with Hitler (see previous chapter).

These issues led to a lot of commotion and, in the case of the postcards, to a court case. In that same year the aforementioned Richard Stein founded

71   Lieve Joris, 'Onze jongens in Libanon. "Die stomme joden hebben in het jaar 3000 nog oorlog", *Haagse* Post, 23 June 1979. Peters, *Gezworen vrienden*, 249-250. For the various UN peace forces until 1978: Grünfeld, *Nederland en het Nabije Oosten*, 215, n. 32; *See also* chapter 9.

72   For Florrie Rost van Tonningen, see more extensively chapter 4.

73   Willem Oltmans, 'Anti-Joods?', *Elseviers Magazine*, 21 July 1979. Willem Oltmans, *Memoires 1979-B* (Breda: Papieren Tijger, 2011), 97-99.

74   *See, e.g.*, 29 April 2002: Interview with Willem Oltmans, 'Amerika heeft gewonnen': www. battl.nl/oltmans29042002.html; Jaap de Wreede, '"Bin Laden is mijn held van deze tijd." Publicist Willem Oltmans kan het dwarsliggen niet laten', *Reformatorisch Dagblad*, 24 May 2003.

75   weblogs.vpro.nl/radioarchief/2009/01/09/kritisch-of-antisemitisch-de-palestijnse-kwestie-in-1979. For an extensive case study *see* chapter 9.

STIBA.[76] Unlike earlier founded organisations, STIBA primarily focused on the fight against antisemitism.

Where can we position STIBA? CIDI staff adhered to the rule of law, as did STIBA. Some Jews did not. As a result of the generally increasingly critical Dutch position regarding Israel, but especially of the series of (alleged) antisemitic incidents, a number of young Jews set up the action group Jewish Defence League. Its mentor was the journalist Hans Knoop (b. 1943) – famous for, among other things, having managed to track down the Dutch war criminal and former SS member Pieter Menten after his escape, in 1976.[77] A spokesperson of the League, medicine student Charlie Nenner (b. 1951), said that after the broadcasting of *Holocaust* many people had wondered why the Jews had not stood up for themselves.[78] It was a similar reflex as the one following the Eichmann trial: why did the Jews not put up resistance?[79] The Jewish Defence League positioned itself on the right side of the political spectrum; both Knoop and Nenner were members of the Dutch branch of Begin's *Heroet*, the most important party within the Israeli Likud. If needed, the League was willing to respond to (alleged) antisemitism with physical violence, and so it did – for example by invading/occupying the VPRO studio.[80]

Basically, STIBA can be seen as the 'legal' branch of the, short-lived, Jewish Defence League. In fact, in his writing Stein demonstrated sympathy for the League: it had selected targets which were indeed guilty of antisemitism in the advertising and public sphere. The League had undertaken initiatives accompanied with 'certain breaches of the law', but not with 'physical violence'.[81] In 1985, Stein would stress again that it was a

76　That had been decided a year earlier: Richard Stein, 'Nabeschouwing: Nederlands anti-semitisme en de strijd tegen ideeën.' In: *Veertig jaar na '45. Visies op hedendaags antisemitisme.* Introduced by Prof Dr L. de Jong (Amsterdam: Meulenhoff Informatief, 1985), 278-329: 281.

77　For Pieter Menten, *see, e.g.*, I. Schöffer, 'Menten, Peter Nicolaas (1899-1987)', *Biografisch Woordenboek Nederland* (BWN) *1880-2000*: www.historici.nl/Onderzoek/Projecten/BWN/lemmata/bwn4/menten. For a razor-sharp profile of Knoop by his first cousin, Martin van Amerongen: Van Amerongen: 'Kuifje in Zwitserland'. *See also* Hans Knoop, 'Over citaten en stenen', *NIW*, 29 June 1979. Knoop repeated this statement in: G. Philip Mok, '"Groeiende anti-semitisme beu". Joodse knokploeg opgericht', *Elseviers Magazine*, 7 July 1979.

78　Ischa Meijer, 'Allemaal symptomen', *Haagse Post*, 14 July 1979.

79　*See* chapters 2 and 15. The group can be considered a precursor of the later formed Jewish youth group, which became active in 1989, following the so-called Fassbinder case, under the motto: unlike the previous one, this generation of Jews will stand its ground; *see* chapter 12.

80　*See* chapter 9.

81　But, Stein underlined, the JDL had not recruited any members with a criminal background and some members were still involved in the protection of synagogues and other Jewish institutions: Stein, 'Nabeschouwing', 327 (n. 23).

traditional misconception to think that the term antisemitism only applied to overt discrimination and violent incidents. It was also a battle against 'the ideas which make discrimination acceptable'. Mental violence was a deed in itself; the Jewish victims at the time were not only killed by gas, bullets, hunger and ill-treatment but by 'ideas, partially polemic, partially stereotypical' as well.[82] Stein thus adopted the position, challenged to this day but true to the definition of Helen Fein, that there was more than the political and redemptive antisemitism of the late nineteenth century and that of the Nazis. Antisemitism had not ended 'with Auschwitz', he hence wrote.[83]

Educational programmes were necessary, but education could not replace confrontation. STIBA was making a name for itself with publications and legal proceedings, opposing what they considered a 'traditional, conservative, even passive attitude among Jews' – and the passivity of non-Jewish government officials. This is where two opposing approaches seriously clashed. STIBA did not want anything to do with the NIW whose editor-in-chief, Mau Kopuit (1930-1992), told the foundation that it made a mountain out of a molehill; there was no antisemitism in the Netherlands worth mentioning. Furthermore, it was 'the disease of the non-Jewish world', which could not be defeated, especially not by Jews. If STIBA put salt on every antisemitic slug, inherent to Christianity, Kopuit wrote, people might be numb in the unlikely event of having to act against 'real antisemitism'. Too much action and publicity would also increase fears in the Jewish community.[84] Stein's position was exactly the opposite: 'Jews can, may and must do something against antisemitism.'[85]

So, again, the question was: What is 'real' antisemitism? There was a lot of animosity back and forth. STIBA even filed a complaint against the NIW at the Council for Journalism in relation to the twisting and hiding of information about the foundation's activities. Publicist, writer and filmmaker Philo Bregstein (b. 1932) rightly notes that the clashes represented the uncertainty

82   Richard Stein, 'Nabeschouwing: Nederlands antisemitisme en de strijd tegen ideeën.' In: *Veertig jaar na '45. Visies op hedendaags antisemitisme.* Introduced by Prof Dr L. de Jong (Amsterdam: Meulenhoff Informatief 1985) 278-329: 281, 294. The compilation contained an extensive obituary of Ben Sijes by Simon Speijer and articles by both Bauer and Wiesenthal.

83   *Ibid.,* 296. *See also* chapter 16. For Helen Fein, *see* chapter 1.

84   Mau Kopuit, 'Antisemitisme', *NIW,* 25 July 1980. *See also* Philo Bregstein, 'De Nederlandse paradox.' In: Philo Bregstein and Sjoerd de Jong, *Antisemitisme in zijn hedendaagse variaties* (Amsterdam: Metz & Schilt, 2007), 102-132: 117, 246 (n. 18).

85   *Ibid.,* 289, 324 (n. 10).

and contrast in Jewish circles about how to respond to antisemitism.[86] STIBA and the Centre for Information and Documentation on Israel (CIDI) also didn't get on at all. Just as STIBA had outlived the Jewish Defence League, the foundation itself was outlived by CIDI, which is still very much active, and at the time quickly began to address the fight against antisemitism. In 1983, it started an (ongoing) series of annual reports about antisemitic incidents in the Netherlands; it also initiated legal proceedings regarding (alleged) antisemitism. But at the time, STIBA beat CIDI to it. Active members such as Richard Stein and Simon Speijer (1924-2004) believed CIDI was as meek as a lamb. In an interview in 1980, Speijer had indignantly quoted a lament by the now CIDI director Ronny Naftaniel, who, according to him, had said that Jews were 'very easily offended'. But that did not mean, according to Speijer, that others had the right to offend them.

> We don't want to be hurt anymore. The Jew has let himself be offended for too long. We are standing up for ourselves. Yes, call STIBA the watchdog, the terrier of the Jewish community in the Netherlands.[87]

This interview fragment as well as the title of the interview ('"We won't be hurt anymore": STIBA declares war on antisemitism') clearly describe STIBA's driving forces. The usual Jewish experience of being hurt and the (alleged) usual response of tolerance is now finally replaced by a raised fist that will dispel both practices. As such, STIBA's approach squarely opposed that of Kopuit, heir of Abel Herzberg and Salomon Kleerekoper, two Jewish veterans who had studied antisemitism more than twenty years earlier, back in 1962. Antisemitism, they contended, was the problem of a lack of civilisation of non-Jews; you can complain at home, but no public whining: that is beneath Jewish dignity. And if you can't stand it, just move to Israel.[88] Speijer and Stein strongly rejected this principled Zionist approach. They refused to see themselves as guests in a host country. STIBA's goal was a society 'that is also accessible to minorities'. This was not merely a slogan. Stein and associates also tackled racism in a more general sense, taking a stand against, for example, the discrimination against Roma and Sinti in the Netherlands.[89] On another occasion Stein stated that although they

86 Bregstein, 'De Nederlandse paradox', 117.
87 *De Stem*, 22 November 1980; in the article Naftaniel is quoted as reported.
88 *See* chapter 5. *See also* Kopuit, 'Antisemitisme'.
89 At the time, Stein spoke of 'gypsies' instead of Roma and Sinti: 'Wij laten ons niet meer kwetsen'. The term 'hurt' is remarkably often used in the interview. For example, STIBA put pressure on the government not to evict a group of 100 'gypsies': STIBA. *Stichting Bestrijding*

were fighting against anti-Zionism, they did want to continue to live as Jews outside of Israel.[90] In that sense, Stein was a Jew with the confident message that life in the 'Diaspora' was not subordinate to life in Israel.[91]

STIBA's first achievement was the launch of legal proceedings against the above-mentioned 'postcard campaign' by a branch of the Palestine Committee which eventually resulted in victory for Stein and associates.[92] The question basically revolved around the fatal triangle of criticism of Israel, anti-Zionism and antisemitism. This was something the prosecutor seriously struggled with in 1980, asking for a 'detailed explanation of concepts like antisemitism and anti-Zionism'. For Richard Stein, however, this theme was not a difficult one. In the 1980 interview he said that for the first time in Dutch Jewish history a group of Jews tackled, both in legal and political terms, antisemitism and anti-Zionism. He went on to describe those two phenomena as respectively 'insults against Jewry and against Israel'.[93] So, basically, STIBA not only focused on the fight against antisemitism, but also against anti-Zionism, which it defined as 'insults of Israel'. That was a very broad definition.

In 1985, Stein also included the category 'criticism of Israel' in his 'Nabeschouwing' [Summing-Up]. He believed that this newly introduced concept was above all clouding the issue. After all, it had become clear that criticism of the Jewish state contained 'all prejudices ever used against the Jewish people in the Diaspora'. Meanwhile, Israel was described as 'inexorable' and 'expansionist' like people once talked of the '"ruthless power of Jewish bankers and loan sharks", accusing them of causing war out of power hunger and, in particular, out of revengefulness(!)'.[94] Here, Stein equalled not only anti-Zionism, but also criticism of Israel, to antisemitism. This was an extreme point of view, one that was both increasingly common and challenged internationally. In 1980 he had said: 'I don't have to accept being hurt. And it is up to me to decide when I feel hurt' – a very personal

Antisemitisme / Foundation for the Fight against Antisemitism. Overview of Activities. January 1981 – September 1982, 7. See also Stein, 'Nabeschouwing', 288.

90   Mau Kopuit, 'Bnee Beriet neemt bestrijding van het antisemitisme serieus', *NIW*, 25 July 1980.

91   For 'diaspora nationalism' of, *see, e.g.*, the Jewish historian Simon Dubnow (1860-1941): Evelien Gans, *Jaap en Ischa Meijer. Een joodse geschiedenis 1912-1956* (Amsterdam: Bert Bakker, 2008), 155-156.

92   Stein, 'Nabeschouwing', 287, 324 (n. 8). Incidentally, Ronny Naftaniel – initially a member of STIBA for a short period before quickly leaving again – was one of the witnesses for the prosecution in this case.

93   'Wij laten ons niet meer kwetsen'.

94   Stein, 'Nabeschouwing', 282-283.

interpretation of antisemitism.[95] However, he then continued by saying: 'Which is not to say that we wish to *a priori* silence any criticism of Israel.' That turned out to be an empty promise. The anti-Zionist movement's tendency to lump together Zionism, Israel and Jewry was reflected in an organisation like STIBA, which declared antisemitism, anti-Zionism and criticism of Israel, by definition, an inextricable tangle. Stein gave the threat of antisemitism in the Netherlands too much weight, identifying a climate in which it had become 'fashionable' again to make anti-Jewish expressions: 'The pre-deportations climate is becoming palpable again.' Richard Stein was possibly the first in the Netherlands suffering from 'alarmism'[96] or 'anti-antisemitic enthusiasm'.[97] In his *Nabeschouwing* (1985) he did not mention the massacre in the Palestinian refugee camps Sabra and Shatila in 1982, committed by Phalangist militias supervised or tolerated by the Israeli army. The massacre, as mentioned in previous chapters, would lead to a new turning point in Dutch-Israeli relations.

Nevertheless, Stein had accomplished that no one should accept 'the Star of David being turned into a swastika'. In that sense STIBA had made history: the equation between, on the one hand, 'Jew', Zionist or Israeli and, on the other, Nazi became an offence punishable by law. And that was not all. On other fronts STIBA had also denounced what it saw as antisemitism, where possibly by subjecting it to legal judgment – particularly when it believed that there wasn't sufficient protest.[98] For example, it had a keen eye for antisemitism in Christian and theological circles – often referred to as anti-Judaism. For instance, it launched legal proceedings against the Catholic critical journal *De Bazuin*, which had called for the abolishment of a religion like the Jewish one, and against the Reformed pastor Daan

---

95   'Wij laten ons niet meer kwetsen'.

96   For a critical approach of the paradox of both the danger of an 'alarmist' view on antisemitism (being obsessed by it, exaggerating it, using it as a political agenda) and of playing down or denying the seriousness or even existence of contemporary antisemitism (calling it 'alarmist') *see* Robert Fine,'Fighting with Phantoms: Contribution to the debate on antisemitism in Europe', *Patterns of Prejudice*, 43, 5, (2009), 459-479: 469-471.

97   For the concept of anti-antisemitic enthusiasm (inspired by the concept of 'anti-Israeli enthusiasms', coined by the sociologist Abram de Swaan), *see* Evelien Gans, 'Anti-Antisemitic enthusiasm and selective philosemitism: Wilders, the PVV', on the website of the *Jüdisches Museum Berlin*: www.jmberlin.de/antisemitism-today/Gans.pdf and Evelien Gans, 'Anti-Antisemitischer Enthusiasmus & selektiver Philosemitismus: Geert Wilders, die PVV und die Juden', *Jahrbuch für Antisemitismusforschung* 23 (2014), 95-104. *See also* Epilogue.

98   Stein mentions three incidents which led to both agitation and debate, making a charge, as far as he was concerned, redundant: Stein, *Nabeschouwing*, 295-296. He referred to the twice-occurring equation between Nazism and Zionism/Israel (*see* chapter 9) and an antisemitic comment against the liberal Rabbi Awraham Soetendorp.

van der Meulen. The latter had expressed his support for the so-called Christian Palestinians. Within that framework Van der Meulen had made classical antisemitic statements during a meeting of the so-called Dutch Arab Circle in 1980. He said Jews had money, influence and a hold on the press. And that, therefore, the Palestinian problem received no attention in the Netherlands. But he also wondered what the Jews had learned from the Holocaust, looking at their fighting methods in Lebanon. Nothing, apparently: 'They use the Holocaust, to move people, yet they have not learned anything from the Holocaust.'[99] The lawyer J.E. Doek was disappointed about the acquittals in both cases: it meant that – unlike the expressions by the infamous right-wing extremist Glimmerveen – 'the more subtle type of antisemite' walks free.[100]

Moreover, STIBA challenged (the Catholic) Prime Minister Lubbers after his 'reprehensible expressions' in 1983 regarding the law demanding companies to report boycott-related demands, like the non-Jew declaration. The cabinet was in no rush about that law, according to Lubbers, but saw itself, after 'frequent protests' forced to express its regret.[101] STIBA also got involved in the issue, which has been regularly brought up since 1945, regarding the demand, by both animal protection organisations and the far right, to ban Jewish ritual slaughter and the export of kosher meat – a topic we will look into in the Epilogue.[102] Finally, STIBA was the first organisation to oppose antisemitism in Dutch sports and football in particular. It managed to get the famous sports journalist Mart Smeets convicted by the Council for Journalism because in an article about a basketball game of the Israeli club Maccabi he had used stereotypes such as 'Jewish chauvinism', 'rich Zionist sources' and 'Jewish annual fair'.[103] Stein invoked the fact that in 1980 STIBA was the first organisation to have approached the Royal Dutch

99 Ibid., 297. See also Prof Dr J.E. Doek, 'Recht en antisemitisme. Is de strafwet een papieren tijger?' In: Veertig jaar na '45, 168-193: 182, n. 26 on p. 319). Van der Meulen was not convicted: the judge ruled that 'intention' was not proven. For the antisemitic articles in De Bazuin, see Doek, 'Recht en antisemitisme', 182, 320 (n. 31). See also Jitta-Geertsema and Sanders, Antisemitisme in Nederland, 33-35: this book makes an inventory of various antisemitic expressions in the Christian sphere.

100 Doek, 'Recht en antisemitisme', 185-186. STIBA also instituted legal proceedings against the infamous antisemitic couple Goeree and against a number of Catholic and Protestant clergymen: Stein, Nabeschouwing', 326 (n. 22).

101 Ibid., 297, 327 (n. 24). In 1984 Lubbers also issued a contested joint statement with Kuwait that Israel should pull out of the territories which it had occupied after 1967. Stein subtly noted that the Lubbers family owned an important share of the Hollandia-Kloos company in Kuwait.

102 Ibid., 297.

103 Ibid., 297, 327-8 (n. 25).

Football Association (KNVB) and board members of various professional football clubs with the aim of combatting antisemitic slogans. This had led, he wrote, to an improved situation. Stein's claim was, as later became apparent, premature.[104]

It was Stein who, with great amazement, would look back on Abel Herzberg's statement (quoted in chapter 5). 'This éminence grise of the Dutch Zionist Union' had allegedly said that antisemitism was the disease of the non-Jewish world; 'the non-Jews suffer from it, the Jews suffer under it'. Stein also quoted Herzberg's famous words from 1962, '… and if the gentlemen want to be antisemites, then let them do as they please.'[105]

With Stein, STIBA and also CIDI, this era was over. Opinions still differed about how to approach the fight against antisemitism, but the fact that Jews had to oppose it, also publicly, was no longer the subject of debate. Eventually, philosemitism went on the wane.

104 *See* chapter 11.
105 *See* chapter 4.

9   'The Activist Jew' Responds to Changing Dutch Perceptions of Israel

Katie Digan

The 1970s were a time of change in Dutch public opinion on the Middle East. A survey conducted by NIPO and *Elseviers Magazine*, published on 6 September 1979, concluded that 91% of the Dutch supported the right of the Palestinians to have their own state. This meant a significant difference with a similar survey conducted two years earlier, when the score had been 43%.[1] The same survey showed a link between Dutch political preferences and the willingness to open a dialogue with the Palestine Liberation Organization (PLO).[2] Supporters of the Labour Party (PvdA) and Democrats (D66) were more open to such a dialogue than those supporting the more right-wing Liberals (VVD) and Christian Democrats (CDA).[3] Sympathy for the Palestinians was considered a typically left-wing stance in the Netherlands, as siding with the underdog. The Palestinians were increasingly seen as oppressed, a displaced people, and as being discriminated against by Israel. The 1970s in the Netherlands saw a rise in sympathy for the Palestinian case, combined with criticism of Israeli politics, accusations of abuse and torture by Israeli authorities and the questioning of the legitimacy of Israel as a state.

In chapters 6 and 8, Evelien Gans writes about the complicated relations between the Netherlands and Israel, and antisemitism and Israel. Before the 1970s, Dutch public opinion about Israel was generally positive and supportive (see chapter 6). The Dutch did not just support Israel in spirit, but also financially and even physically. During the 1967 Six-Day War, the Dutch donated millions of guilders to the Israeli case through fundraisers, as well as blood and even manpower in the form of voluntary medical and military personnel.[4] These donations came from private initiatives and were

---

1   *Elseviers Magazine*, 6 September 1979.
2   The PLO was founded in 1964 with the intention of liberating the Palestinian people. By 1979 it was recognised as the legitimate representative of the Palestinian people by the United Nations. However, it was considered a terrorist group by Israel (and the United States) until 1991.
3   *NIW*, 21 September 1979.
4   The volunteers applied for work in Israel at the Dutch Zionist Organisation [*Nederlandse Zionistenbond*]. So many people applied that there was a waiting list, which was closed when 400 people were still waiting to be assigned. *See Het Vrije Volk*, 12 June 1967.

further organised by churches and local organisations. The Dutch government helped out by granting tax breaks to individuals and companies that
donated.[5] People drove around with bumper stickers on their cars declaring,
'We stand behind Israel!'. Dutch newspapers featured full-page advertise-
ments stating, 'Israel needs two things: money and blood' – together, of
course, with a bank account number to allow their readers to meet those
needs. The Dutch support for Israel was outwardly strong and personal. It
would be unfair to say the Dutch were anti-Palestine, but Palestinians – as
an autonomous national group with agency, not as a passive group things
merely 'happened to' – were simply not in the public picture.

As the amount of criticism of Israel in the Dutch media grew in the
1970s, so did increasing suspicion about the loyalties of the Jews in the
Netherlands. Oftentimes, all Jews, regardless of their nationality or political
preferences, were seen as supporters of Israeli politics. Criticism of Israel
therefore easily translated into criticism of Jews. As a result, Dutch Jews
were somehow held responsible for what happened in Israel and a dangerous
slippery slope between legitimate political criticism and antisemitism took
shape. This slippery slope was one of the causes of several public debates in
the Dutch media. Navigating between legitimate criticism of Israeli politics
on the one side and flat-out antisemitism on the other, the discussions
about Israel were muddled and tainted by a perceived interchangeability of
'Israel' and 'Jews'. It resulted in Jewish sensitivities regarding critical reports
on Israel as well as a framing of Israel within a well-established context of
Jewish stereotypes. Unsurprisingly, these differing viewpoints clashed, and
especially the postwar generation of young Dutch Jews made their protests
public. In this chapter, we will discuss three instances of Dutch Jews publicly
protesting reporting on Israel that they considered anti-Israel or antisemitic.
Through these case studies, we will attempt to show the rise of Jewish
activism as a response to the changes in Dutch public opinion on Israel.[6]

Today this, tomorrow that...

In 1975, the VPRO (*Vrijzinnig Protestantse Radio Omroep*), a liberal Dutch
national broadcasting company known for its controversial and anti-
establishment programming, aired a TV series about the conflict in the

5   *Leeuwarder Courant*, 7 June 1967.
6   This activism evolved into organisations such as the CIDI and STIBA in 1974 and 1980, as
described by Evelien Gans in chapter 8.

Middle East. The series was commissioned by the *Nederlands Palestina Komitee*, a Dutch pro-Palestine activist organisation.[7] As part of this series, the VPRO made a film about the pro-Israel lobby in the United States, showing interviews with lobbyists and politicians and filming pro-Israel charity events.[8] The programme suggested and alluded to an idea of a powerful pro-Israel presence in American politics. The broadcast was announced in the VPRO magazine *Vrije Geluiden* [Free Voices], accompanied by a cover featuring a customised American flag adorned with stars of David.[9] The programme received critical reactions. Columnist Leo Derksen, a polemical writer for the right-wing populist newspaper *De Telegraaf*, called it 'nearly antisemitic'.[10] His colleague Wim Jungmann (1913-2000), who had been a journalist for illegal resistance newspapers during the Second World War, wrote that he thought Goebbels would have enjoyed the film.[11] The VPRO responded to the criticisms with astonishment, saying they could not help it if people drew antisemitic conclusions from their programme. Anyone who thought a TV programme about Jewish lobbies was stereotypical was antisemitic for making that connection, they stated.[12] A 'cheap argument', journalist Philip van Tijn (b. 1940) wrote.[13] The displeasure with the VPRO and their TV broadcast was not limited to news articles and letters. On the night of 6 November 1975, a group of activists stuck posters on the VPRO building, featuring the American/Stars of David flag next to a Syrian antisemitic cartoon of someone being strangled by a Star of David. The poster was captioned *'vandaag dit... morgen dat'* [today this... tomorrow that], referring not only to a causal relation between the two images, but also to the title of a well-known VPRO television show.

The action was not anonymous. It was immediately claimed by a group called *Werkgroep Israël* [Working Group Israel], represented by chairman Ronny Naftaniel. Naftaniel (b. 1948, a young Dutch Jew who as CIDI director would later become one of the most well-known Jewish activists in the Netherlands) (see chapters 7 and 8). The action was supplemented with an open letter in the *Parool* newspaper, explaining why the group had targeted the VPRO and what the group's mission was. Naftaniel described

7 *NIW*, 4 November 1975.
8 *Het Vrije Volk*,15 November 1975.
9 *De Volkskrant*, 8 November 1975.
10 *De Telegraaf*, 23 November 1975.
11 *Het Parool*, 7 November 1975
12 As cited by Philip van Tijn. In Dutch: 'door zo'n programma demagogeren mensen zichzelf', *Vrije Volk*, 15 November 1975.
13 *Het Vrije Volk*, 15 November 1975.

the American flag cover as reminiscent of the infamous Russian antisemitic hoax *The Protocols of the Elders of Zion*.[14] He further explained that action against the VPRO was not taken because their programme was anti-Israel, but because it alluded to the old (he did not use the word 'antisemitic') myth of a 'global Jewish conspiracy'.[15] The head of the VPRO TV broadcast Arie Kleijwegt (1921-2001) replied that he had never heard of *Werkgroep Israël* (which was later refuted by Naftaniel) and that he did not understand the consternation. He stated that he thought the broadcast was 'heart-warming' because it 'showed how much Jews in America are helping Israel'.[16] The poster action was titled a 'Jewish protest' in the Dutch newspapers, firmly framing the protest as a Jewish reaction rather than a political or pro-Israel one.[17] It was the first of its kind in the Netherlands, an action organised by Dutch Jews protesting a synthesis of the representation of Israel in Dutch media and antisemitism.

'We could have fitted in those other four million Jews too ...'

On 23 June 1979, an explicit headline graced the cover of the moderately left-wing Dutch weekly *Haagse Post*. 'Our boys in Lebanon: "Those dumb Jews will still be fighting in the year 3000"', it was written in red letters on a photo of soldiers in United Nations tanks. The article, written by journalist Lieve Joris (b. 1953), documented in detail the situation of the Dutch military men who served in the United Nations Interim Force in Lebanon (UNIFIL), sent there to restore Lebanese authority after the Israeli invasion (and withdrawal) in 1978. The article was filled with anti-Israel and antisemitic quotes from the soldiers. 'In the Netherlands, you always hear about how the Palestinians do this and that, and after a while you think: bunch of terrorists. But then you come here and you come around'.[18] They admit to feeling 'nothing but negative' about Israel because 'they have seen too much of Israel'.[19] One soldier adds to the conversation, 'they only made one mistake in 1945: they should have kept the gas chambers open, we could have fitted

14   *De Volkskrant*, 8 November 1975. For Ronny Naftaniel and for the Working Group Israel, *see* chapter 7 and 8.
15   *Het Parool*, 13 November 1975.
16   *De Volkskrant*, 8 November 1975.
17   *Nederlands Dagblad*, 8 November 1975.
18   'Onze jongens in Libanon', *Haagse Post,* 23 June 1979.
19   *Ibid.*

in those other four million Jews too'.[20] A Dutch lieutenant stationed in one of the observation posts described how some of the soldiers stationed in Lebanon were either pro-Israel or had no strong feelings about Israel before they came to Lebanon. 'Some of them said, We have to beat the Palestinians and Israel is *the* country. Now that they are here and most trouble comes from the other side, that idea simply gets turned around.'[21] The lieutenant further expressed sympathy for the Palestinian cause and talked about how Israel was bombing refugee camps as revenge for Israeli victims.

Less than two days after the article was published, the offices of the *Haagse Post* were vandalised in the middle of the night. Stones wrapped in paper with the words 'stupid Jews' and 'war' were thrown through the windows.[22] Afterwards, the Netherlands National Press Agency (ANP) received a call from a man claiming he belonged to a group of Jewish young men who had thrown the stones.[23] These young Jews spoke to various media outlets about their action, emphasising that they felt it was time that Jewish protests became physical. Referring to examples of anti-Jewish bombings in foreign countries they criticised what they called 'the traditional Jewish response' of 'words instead of deeds'.[24] Responses to both the article and the act of vandalism were mixed. *Haagse Post* editor Bert Vuijsje (b. 1942) called the trashing of the office a case of 'shooting the messenger' and emphasised that the magazine had published the quotes of others, not their own.[25] The Dutch Jewish weekly *Nieuw Israëlietisch Weekblad* (NIW) published a reaction stating they too felt it was wrong to attack the *Haagse Post* and to use violence, but that they understood both the frustration of the Jews and their wish to act on those feelings. They characterised it as a consequence of young Jews who felt they were not heard and could not get their point across via the regular channels.[26] The *Haagse Post* article and reactions led to official apologies to Israeli representatives from Defence Minister Willem Scholten and Foreign Affairs Minister Chris van der Klaauw, as well as a promise to better educate the men who would be sent to the Middle East.[27]

20 *Ibid.* For more about the 'gas chamber' trope, *see* chapter 2.
21 *Ibid.*
22 *NIW,* 29 June 1979.
23 *De Telegraaf,* 26 June 1979.
24 *NIW,* 29 June 1979.
25 *Ibid.*
26 *Ibid.*
27 *Elseviers Weekblad,* 30 June 1979. This reaction is an illustration of the new Dutch 'balanced policy' with respect to the Israeli-Palestinian conflict; Ben Schoenmaker and Herman Roozenbeek (eds), *Vredesmacht in Libanon. De Nederlandse deelname aan UNIFIL 1979-1985* (Amsterdam: Boom 2004), 175-176. *See* chapter 8

KATIE DIGAN

But perhaps one of the most striking reactions to the UNIFIL affair was an interview by the by now well-known Jewish journalist Ischa Meijer with Hans Knoop (b. 1943) and Charlie Nenner (b. 1951).[28] Knoop, a journalist who had risen to prominence for his role in the exposing and arrest of war criminal Pieter Menten, and Nenner, a medical student, announced the founding of the Jewish Defence League 'Af Paäm' (Hebrew for 'never again'). The league, not to be confused with the American Jewish Defense League ('our goals are the same but our situation is very different'), was a second attempt by Knoop to rally Dutch Jews to organise their own security force. A previous attempt ten years earlier had stranded due to a lack of interest, 'the climate in the Netherlands was different from what it is now'.[29] Knoop stated the league was not violent, but added, 'My name is not Jesus, I do not turn the other cheek. I am not principally opposed to the use of violence.'[30] Knoop predicted a negative response to the league in the Dutch Jewish press. 'The Dutch people are very servile. The Dutch Jews are very Dutch .... People think you can only combat antisemitism with strongly worded letters'.[31] Especially after the broadcast of the American TV series *Holocaust*, Knoop and Nenner said, Jews wanted to get proactive and 'no longer [be] passive'.[32] He described the league as an anti-establishment group that would certainly be condemned by 'proper' Dutch Jews. 'I am not so proper, if that propriety has to conceal something improper', Knoop added.[33] The article ended when Knoop left and Nenner, who had kept mostly silent up to that point, hastened to add, 'I just wanted to say, I do care about propriety. When we heard the responses to our action against the *Haagse Post* one of us said, "and I even tried to throw [the stones] carefully, so I would not do too much damage".'[34]

28 *Haagse Post*, 14 July 1979. Ischa Meijer, '*Allemaal symptomen*', *Haagse Post*, 14 July 1979. For more about Ischa Meijer, *see* Evelien Gans, *Jaap en Ischa Meijer. Een Joodse geschiedenis 1912-1956* (Amsterdam: Bert Bakker, 2008) and Evelien Gans, 'Next Year in Paramaribo: Galut and Diaspora as Scene-changes in the Jewish life of Jakob Meijer.' In: Yosef Kaplan (ed.) The Dutch Intersection: *The Jews and the Netherlands in Modern History* (Leiden / Boston: Brill, 2008), 369-387.

29 *See also* chapter 8.

30 *Ibid.*

31 *Ibid.*

32 On 'the meek Jew' *see* chapter 3.

33 *Haagse Post*, 14 July 1979.

34 *Ibid.*

The UNIFIL affair ended a bit anticlimactic when it turned out the Jewish activists had accidentally broken the windows of the wrong office. They promptly reimbursed the owners for the broken windows.[35]

The VPRO radio broadcasts

On 10 October 1979, the VPRO returned to the scene when they aired the second episode of a three-part series about the Middle East. The first episode, which had been broadcast a week earlier, had already gained controversy. According to the presenter introducing the second episode in a mockingly ominous and dramatic voice, 12 people had cancelled their subscriptions to the VPRO after the broadcast, whereas 83 others had joined. Moreover, the presenter spoke of people gathering in front of the studio, and how he would keep listeners up to date on the numbers of new subscriptions and cancellations during the broadcast. The Israeli embassy had also responded to the previous episode, calling it a bunch of lies.[36]

The first episode, broadcast on 3 October, was made by Ronald van den Boogaard (b. 1945) and Roel van Broekhoven (b. 1950) and had featured interviews with various people living in (or visiting) Israel and the West Bank. In the programme, the journalists talk about the Palestinians who have fled Israel, stating that 'most of them now live in refugee camps'.[37] A Dutch woman living in East Jerusalem and married to a Palestinian tells the interviewers that people in her neighbourhood were being chased away by the Israeli army to make room for another settlement. She also says that she cannot get a driving licence because 'she is not a Jew'.[38] The actual theme of the episode seems to be the, quickly intensifying, discrimination of Palestinians by Israel. A mayor of a West Bank town, a proponent of an independent Palestinian state, compares the Israeli occupation of the West Bank with '40-45', i.e. the Second World War.[39] Then the programme turns to interviews with Palestinians who have been imprisoned in Israeli prisons. The topic changes to torture and abuse. A Palestinian girl, Sonia Nimr, who was incarcerated in an Israeli prison for membership of an illegal organisation, tells a sickening story about how a fellow inmate had been

35 *Tammoez*, 27 July 1979.
36 Villa VPRO, 10 October 1979, recording available on: weblogs.vpro.nl/radioarchief/2009/01/09/kritisch-of-antisemitisch-de-palestijnse-kwestie-in-1979/
37 *Ibid.*
38 *Ibid.*
39 *Ibid.*

beaten, tortured and raped with a stick by guards. Later on, she says, the prison guards brought in the prisoner's father and tried to force father and daughter to have intercourse. The stories are horrific and detailed. It quickly becomes clear why the broadcast got emotional reactions.

The second episode of the Middle East series was made by Gerard Jacobs (b. 1953) and Roel van Broekhoven. It takes place in Lebanon. Jacobs and Van Broekhoven discuss their views on the Israel-Palestine conflict, commenting that the Israeli media only speak of Palestinians as 'terrorists'. Israelis are also terrorists, they say. They ominously comment that five years earlier, it was impossible to speak of the Palestinian lot in the Netherlands without being called an antisemite. But, they say, things have changed. The episode is a dark documentary of refugees in Lebanon. The journalists paint a harrowing picture of Israeli bombings in Lebanon, dead and wounded children and abandoned children's shoes in the streets. Back in the studio the presenter updates the VPRO subscription count: 167 new members and 6 cancellations. Then the programme suddenly changes. Presenter Kees Slagter:

> What is going on here? A couple of men just entered the studio. What is going on? Listeners, right now a few people have ran in and destroyed a tape of the broadcast. We will have to do something very strange. Is it impossible to continue the episode? The tape is completely destroyed. They took the tape.[40]

Live on air, a few men had entered the studio and destroyed the episode tape. Anyone who was listening to the VPRO at that moment had witnessed the interruption, not knowing what exactly was going on. As the men in the radio studio scrambled to improvise the rest of the time slot designated to the Lebanon episode, Van Broekhoven gave a phone interview about the interruption on a different radio station.[41] He told the interviewer that two men had come into the studio during the broadcast and destroyed the tapes with a pair of scissors. It was in itself a small act of vandalism, but the beginning of a big public discussion about criticising Israel, antisemitism and the difference between the two.

---

40   Transcript of VPRO, 10 October 1979, radioarchief/2009/01/09/kritisch-of-antisemitisch-de-palestijnse-kwestie-in-1979/
41   *Dingen van de Dag*, 10 October 1979.

Reactions in the press

Almost immediately, the action was claimed by the Jewish Defence League, again represented in the media by Hans Knoop.[42] Knoop had not been present during the VPRO action, but claimed he did speak to the men who did it. He said the League members were not afraid of being arrested, because 'concentration camp Auschwitz is no longer in use'.[43] The 'invasion' of the VPRO studio by the Jewish men attracted considerable media attention. As is often the case in media matters regarding antisemitism or Israel, many newspaper readers felt compelled to write in their world view on Jews or Israel, as well as actual reactions to the action. The action at the studio and Hans Knoop's subsequent comments in the media were not widely applauded in the Jewish communities in the Netherlands. The main criticism was that violence or vandalism was never an appropriate reaction to journalism, not in the least because of the freedom of press.

The Jewish Defence League was, as Knoop had predicted earlier, often ridiculed and rejected in the Dutch press. Many newspaper articles alluded to a new organisation of Jews in the Netherlands, a club of mostly young men who had started a strong-arm defence league of Dutch Jews, mentored by Knoop. Newspapers suggested implicitly or explicitly that this Dutch group was linked to the American Jewish Defense League, which, since its establishment in 1968, by 1979 had already grown from a vigilante club to a terrorist organisation with dozens of violent attacks to their name.[44] It was perhaps this assumed connection that gave the Dutch Jewish club a sensational image. Knoop himself gave several interviews and wrote letters to newspapers about the action. In *de Volkskrant* of 12 October 1979, Knoop characterised the men and their activist group as young people who 'drew lessons from the past', in an article titled 'Jewish youths let go of passivism'. He continued, 'In 1939, people also said: What is going on in Germany will not happen here. The league wants to show everyone that the Jewish community has changed. They will no longer react indifferently to all forms of antisemitism'.[45] Newspaper *Trouw* quoted members of the Defence League saying, 'After 2000 years of persecution it no longer makes sense to just talk'.[46] The recently established Centre for Information and Documentation

---

42 *Dingen van de Dag*, 13 October 1979.
43 *Ibid.*
44 Global Terrorism Database: Jewish Defence League.www.start.umd.edu/gtd.
45 *De Volkskrant,* 12 October 1979.
46 *Trouw,* 11 October 1979.

on Israel (CIDI) explained the frustration of the young Jews as a wish to join forces to defend themselves 'like so many other groups'.[47] Some newspaper readers wrote letters pointing to the change in the public opinion of Israel. Some did so thoughtfully, noticing the shift in attention from supporting Israel to the fate of the Palestinians.[48] Others were less nuanced. One reader pointed out a common side-effect of this shift, saying, 'Anyone who no longer supports Israel in every way is accused of antisemitism'.[49] Yet another reader abandoned nuance altogether and warned against the clouding of judgment by 'the history of the fate of the Jews' when it comes to 'political facts and new injustices'.[50]

The many strong reactions to the radio episode prompted the VPRO to organise a live TV debate quickly after the broadcast. The debate was led by the Jewish journalist Joop van Tijn (1938-1997). The participants were a divided group consisting of Ronald van den Boogaard, Rabbi Awraham Soetendorp (b. 1943), *Haagse Post* editor Bert Vuijsje, Hans Knoop, Ronnie Naftaniel and the publicist Anton Constandse (1899-1985). The title of the debate was 'Critical or antisemitic?' and was announced to tackle the issues surrounding the UNIFIL affair and the VPRO radio program.

Things are not going very well. Knoop, who gets the first turn, immediately accuses the VPRO of slander, lack of basic journalistic ethics and of supporting the PLO.[51] He says the VPRO 'shouldn't be petty about some Jewish youngsters who have had enough' and 'cut a few tapes with scissors'. Joop van Tijn and Ronnie Naftaniel take a more moderate approach and point out errors in the episode (this will be discussed later in this chapter). The topic quickly turns to the legitimacy of the existence of Israel as a state, and this is where things go inevitably sour. Anton Constandse challenges the United Nations resolution of 1947 and calls the Zionists 'terrorists'. Suddenly Naftaniel says,

> You know, what I find so peculiar, Mr Constandse, is that it is always the non-Jews who decide whether something is antisemitic or not. I think that if there is one group that knows if something is antisemitic, it is the Jews. I don't think that you, as a non-Jew, can be the judge of that.[52]

47 *Algemeen Dagblad*, 12 October 1979.
48 *De Volkskrant*, 9 October 1979.
49 *De Volkskrant*, 12 October 1979.
50 *De Groene Amsterdammer*, 17 October 1979.
51 Recording of TV debate VPRO 14 October 1979, private collection of Ronald van den Boogaard.
52 *Ibid.*

Constandse responds that he was a resistance fighter during the Second World War, and that stating that the Jews belong in Palestine would be a case of 'reaping the harvest of the Nazis'. Knoop helpfully adds that he has visited Palestinian refugee camps during the Six-Day War and has seen the Arab translation of *Mein Kampf* in almost all schools. Van Tijn bravely tries to redirect the debate to the main topic and asks Vuijsje if the UNIFIL article in the *Haagse Post* makes it seem like Dutch UNIFIL soldiers are antisemitic. Vuisje answers, but is soon interrupted by Constandse, who takes the debate to a new low, stating that 'we should ask these Jews here, are you Israeli or Dutch?'

This reaction could be branded a Dutch tradition: confusion and worry about the 'Dutchness' of Dutch Jews and questions of loyalty.[53] 'These Jews?' Van Tijn responds, 'they are not here as Jews!' 'Actually, maybe I am glad that the *Haagse Post* printed those antisemitic remarks', Knoop comments drily, 'at least it makes it clear once again that anti-Zionism, antisemitism and anti-Israel cannot be distinguished from one another'. Soetendorp tries to steer the debate back on track and says that the conflict between Israel and the Arab world is 'not a case of justice against injustice, but justice against justice'. He calls for an investigation into the torture allegations in Israel, but warns against dangerous tendencies in critical reporting about Israel. Constandse is then heard shouting in the background (perhaps because they turned off his microphone), 'Israelis are the Nazis of the Middle East!' At this point the debate can only be called one big argument. It takes a while for the topic to get back to the radio broadcast and Van den Boogaard tries to explain that he sees the invasion in the VPRO studio as a violation of freedom of speech. Shortly after, Van Tijn announces that they are out of time and the debate is over.

Unsurprisingly, the debate did not do much to clarify things or further the discussion. If anything, the responses to the VPRO-affair got more heated. Afterwards, the NIW reported that Rabbi Soetendorp, seen by many as the moderate voice in the debate, had got antisemitic threatening phone calls after the TV broadcast.[54] In an interview, historian Mozes Gans (1917-1987) called Rabbi Soetendorp foolish for reporting these threatening phone calls to the newspapers. 'If I got a phone call like that ..., I would not tell anyone. By telling the newspapers you add to the polarisation'.[55] In the same interview Gans said of the reactions to the VPRO affair, 'The problem is that

---

53   For more about the 'double loyalties' of the Dutch Jews, *see* chapter 6 in this book.
54   *NIW,* 19 October 1979.
55   *Het Parool,* 20 October 1979.

people expect Jews to act more dignified than non-Jews'.[56] His response signifies an important trend in the backlash against the Jewish activists. The action was turned against the Jewish community. The Jewish writer Abel Herzberg, characterising the League of 'reeking of fascism', wrote to the NIW, 'the whole Jewish community will be held responsible for the future developments'.[57] Another reader wrote how he has many non-Jewish friends who had called Hans Knoop 'a cultivator of antisemitism'.[58] Journalist Frans Happel wrote in the newspaper *Goudsche Courant* about the action of the League, saying it would 'only encourage antisemitism'. Regarding the TV debate he added that 'the Jewish side too often suggests antisemitism'.[59] W.L. Brugsma (1922-1997), a journalist who reminded his readers that he had been a resistance fighter during the war and had survived several concentration camps, warned in an article called 'Karate' that groups such as the Jewish Defence League might encourage the association between anti-Zionism and antisemitism.[60] An article in newspaper *Trouw* too warned against counterproductive effects of condoning the 'invasion' of the VPRO studio. By supporting this group as a reaction to antisemitism 'they might reinforce slumbering racism'.[61]

The VPRO got its own share of letters and phone calls responding to the radio and TV broadcasts, both supportive and critical. One letter writer wrote in to thank the VPRO for their show. He had lived in Israel and had seen discrimination against non-Jewish citizens there.[62] Another man urged the VPRO to keep their chin up and applauded them for being a model for freedom of speech.[63] Some letter writers, however, pulled out all the antisemitic stops to voice their displeasure with the 'weak' response of the VPRO to the protests from Dutch Jews, who according to them, controlled the Dutch media. 'You have let yourself be cornered by the Jews, who dominate the Netherlands (and other countries). The Jews terrorise not just the Palestinians, but the civilians of all countries where they have once again risen to the highest ranks'.[64] 'One thing is clear now to the Dutch people', someone else wrote, 'we are only allowed to listen to and watch what the

---

56 *Ibid.*
57 *NIW,* 26 October 1979.
58 *Ibid.*
59 *Goudsche Courant.*
60 *Haagse Post,* 27 October 1979.
61 *Trouw,* 13 October 1979.
62 Letter from the private archive of Ronald van den Boogaard, 15 October 1979.
63 *Ibid.,* 20 October 1979.
64 *Ibid.,* October 1979.

Jews dictate'.[65] The antisemitic letter writers were also gravely concerned about the 'anti-Dutch attitudes' of Jews living in the Netherlands. 'You do understand', one of them warned, 'that these Jewish thugs led by the Dutch-hating Hans Knoop, will continue on. The more Dutch people they terrorise, the more they will be in the picture, looking pitiful'.[66] Another concerned citizen wrote a helpful tip to the VPRO to refrain from using the word 'Jew' at all – as it was 'too fraught with emotions' – but to speak of 'the Israelis'. Furthermore, it would be wise if the broadcaster let Jews (she apologised for the use of this word) do the criticising when it came to Israel, as 'it is much more difficult to accuse *them* of "antisemitism"!'[67]

Errors and omissions

As mentioned before, during the TV debate Van Tijn and Naftaniel raised some issues about errors and inaccuracies in the programmes. They were not the only ones. Especially given the shocking nature of the accusations, the VPRO can be (and was) accused of being careless with their sources. The VPRO responded to the accusations partly by addressing them on the radio, partly by publishing a pamphlet about the radio series, citing their sources and providing transcripts of interviews.[68] They stood by the programmes despite their errors. Some mistakes or omissions were cleared up. For instance, Ronnie Naftaniel pointed out that the journalists had said in the first episode that 'most Palestinians now live in refugee camps'. This was untrue and later rectified by Van den Boogaard on the radio. Another inaccuracy, pointed out by Joop van Thijn, was the editing of the interview with the Dutch Ludwina Janssen who had been imprisoned in Israel on charges of espionage and aiding an enemy organisation. Janssen had caused a media storm in the Dutch press when in 1976, aged 23, she was arrested at Tel Aviv airport scoping out the security situation for the extremist Popular Front for the Liberation of Palestine.[69] Janssen was released from prison after having served half of her sentence in 1979, and not long after she gave an interview to Ronald van den Boogaard about her time in prison. However, in the final edit of the program Janssen only talked of being *accused* of crimes

65 *Ibid.,* 15 October 1979.
66 *Ibid.*
67 *Ibid.,* name and date unknown.
68 Ronald van den Boogaard and Roel van Broekhoven, *De Palestijnen. Brochure naar aanleiding van de radioserie* (1979).
69 *De Waarheid,* 24 September 1979.

against the Israeli state without admitting guilt. A small omission at first
glance, but within the context of stories of unfair imprisonments such a
minor oversight can easily fall into a pattern. A selected transcript of the
interview was published in the VPRO pamphlet of the radio broadcast, which
showed that Van den Boogaard did ask Janssen about her crime and Janssen
admitted to it (though she refused to talk about her time with the Popular
Front and described her espionage as 'looking around a bit at an airport').[70]

However, the mistakes made in the research concerning torture and
abuse of Palestinian prisoners in Israel were far more explosive. The
journalists misquoted reports of severe abuse and torture, claiming they
found them in Amnesty International reports, while the quotes actually
came from a report written by the Middle East Research and Action Group
(MERAG).[71] MERAG was a pro-Palestine action group based in the United
Kingdom, whose other publications included *The Candid Kibbutz Book*
(1978), a pamphlet detailing the locations of settlements. While this does
not automatically discredit the contents of the report, it was written from a
decidedly different point of view than the principally non-political Amnesty
International. This mistake was rectified in both the third episode and the
pamphlet.[72] The pamphlet however also included more specific details of the
sources that accused Israel of systematically torturing Palestinian prisoners.

Torture and abuse in Israel

The allegations of Israeli officials abusing or torturing Palestinians were
not entirely new. Amnesty International had accused Israel of mistreating
Arab prisoners in 1970.[73] The allegations included using electroshock and
putting out cigarettes on prisoners. In 1975, Amnesty International also
released a report accusing the Israeli and Syrian governments of violating
the Geneva Convention on the treatment of the prisoners of war.[74] The report
was written after an investigation done by independent researchers,

70 Ronald van den Boogaard and Roel van Broekhoven, *De Palestijnen* (Hilversum: VPRO, 1979),
36.
71 Middle East Research and Action Group, *Over de Israelische Bezette Gebieden (West Bank
en Gaza)*, 8 July – 18 August 1974.
72 Van den Boogaard and Van Broekhoven, *De Palestijnen*.
73 *De Tijd*, 2 April 1970.
74 *Jewish Telegraphic Agency*, 10 April 1975.

including a Dutch physician, interviewing and examining former prisoners.[75] The report, however, stated that 'absolute proof' of systematic abuse
could not be obtained.

Nearing the end of the 1970s, the number of allegations of Israeli abuse of
Arab prisoners grew. In 1977 the *Sunday Times* published an extensive report
entitled 'Israel tortures Arab prisoners', written by their own investigative
team.[76] The report contained details of horrific abuse, including sadistic
humiliation, sexual assault, physical torture and even beatings of wives in
front of their imprisoned husbands. The *Times* alleged that these abuses
were part of a deliberate policy, used not only to get prisoners to confess,
but also to deter Arabs 'in the occupied territories that it is least painful
to behave passively'.[77] The report also stated that, by getting confessions
from tortured prisoners who will admit to anything, the military courts
were able to imprison people as convicted terrorists rather than political
prisoners. The United Nations General Assembly Security Council discussed
the report, where the Israeli representative denied the allegations.[78] The
Israeli embassy in London also called the findings in the report completely
false.[79] The *Sunday Times* report gathered little attention in the Dutch press,
apart from some brief mentions in the foreign news sections. In 1979, *The
Washington Post* published more torture allegations. The story, again, came
from the *Sunday Times*, but their offices were closed in 1977 due to a labour
dispute and the journalists had therefore brought the story to *The Washington Post*.[80] The source of the information was a cable message between
the American Consulate in Jerusalem and the United States Department
of State. The message, known as 'Jerusalem 1500', was sent in May 1978 by
consular worker Alexandra Uteev Johnson. Johnson wrote that she had
gathered from first-hand testimonies that 'Israeli torture of Arab prisoners
may be a widespread and even common practice'.[81] A second cable written
by Johnson was sent from Israel on 30 November that same year, designated
'Jerusalem 3239'. This time the report was preceded by a message written

---

75   Amesty International, *Report of an Amnesty International mission to Israel and the Syrian
Arab Republic to investigate allegations of ill-treatment and torture,* 10-24 October 1974.
76   *Sunday Times*, 19 June 1977.
77   *Ibid.*
78   http://unispal.un.org/UNISPAL.NSF/0/15CF2F2B3798A5C68525636F006719AA Yearbook of
the United Nations, Office of Public Information United Nations, New York, 31 December 1977.
79   *Nieuwsblad van het Noorden*, 4 July 1977.
80   *The Washington Post*, 7 February 1979.
81   *Jerusalem 1500*, 31 May 1978, http://en.wikisource.org/wiki/File:Jerusalem_1500.pdf. The
source was classified in 1978, but subsequently released in full in 2008.

by the deputy principal officer of the American consulate in Jerusalem, stating that while the consulate did not necessarily stand behind every part of the report, 'the weight of evidence points to the validity of her general conclusion'.[82] The report itself documents 14 cases of abuse and concludes that 'physical mistreatment is systematically used on many Arab security suspects interrogated in the West Bank'.[83] Two months later, Johnson was 'relieved of her post', which prompted the leak of the cables by 'sources anxious to get official attention for her stories of mistreatment'.[84] The allegations of The Washington Post, together with the denial of the allegations by Israeli Minister of Justice Schmuel Tamir, again only appeared briefly in the Dutch newspapers.[85]

The allegations of 1975 and 1977 differed significantly from earlier accusations. First and foremost, rather than isolated incidents or 'excesses', the abuse was characterised as commonplace and even deliberate policy. Secondly, it cast a shadow of doubt on the Israeli treatment of Arab suspects, not just convicted political prisoners. Third, the Sunday Times typified the abuse not just as a way of getting confessions, but also as an instrument to frighten and oppress all Arabs living in Israeli territory. It was mostly these reports and their consequent conclusions (as well as their own interviews) that the VPRO based their allegations of systematic torture on. During the TV debate, Van den Boogaard stated that the purpose of detailing torture allegations in their broadcast was not to attack Israel, but to show that aberrations take place in any situation of war, and that 'Israel, Jews, are no worse or better than anyone else on this world'.[86] Knoop, in response, argued that many Palestinians claimed to be tortured to avoid retribution from their peers after confessing. He also stated that the Sunday Times apologised to Israel after publishing their report.[87]

The friction between the rise of Jewish activism and the newly critical Dutch public opinion on Israel in the 1970s was based less on political views and more on a highly flammable conceptual blend of Israel and Jews, of anti-Israel sentiments and antisemitism. The different combinations of these concepts were used both to disqualify legitimate disapproval of Israeli politics or policies – like the mistreatment of prisoners – as antisemitic,

82 Jerusalem 3239, 13 November 1978.
83 Ibid.
84 The Washington Post, 7 February 1979.
85 Nieuwsblad van het Noorden, 9 February 1979.
86 Recording of TV debate VPRO 14 October 1979, private collection of Ronald van den Boogaard.
87 Details of this apology were not mentioned and we have not been able to find them. As far as I know, the Sunday Times stands by its report.

and to mask actual antisemitism as anti-Israel or pro-Palestinian opinions. The slippery slope between the two ends proved difficult to navigate, and in many ways this has remained the case ever since. The critical views on Israel in the Dutch media continued and reached a high in 1982 with the Sabra and Shatila massacre, which significantly diminished the Dutch pro-Israel predominance.[88]

---

88   *See also* chapters 7 and 8.

10 Turkish Anti-Zionism in the Netherlands

From Leftist to Islamist Activism

Annemarike Stremmelaar

On 13 April 2002, a demonstration was held in Amsterdam in protest at Israeli military operations in the West Bank. Under the heading 'Stop the war against the Palestinians' it drew approximately 20,000 people, a huge number by Dutch standards. Observers were struck by the numbers of Turkish-Dutch and Moroccan-Dutch protesters; one of them even spoke of a demonstration with 'a distinct Islamic character'. A Turkish-born Muslim activist was of a different opinion: most protesters were Dutch. Although impressed by the large crowd with people of all persuasions who marched 'as one body', he was disillusioned by the number of 'our Turkish Muslims' present. Not that Palestine was a Muslim issue, according to him, but those who considered themselves Muslim should be the first to take it up. He found himself demonstrating alongside Turkish and Kurdish leftists whom, he confessed, he preferred over the apathetic and gutless conservative Turks. At least these leftists knew how to side with the oppressed against imperialism.[1] This lament illustrates the strong anti-Israel protest tradition among Turkish leftist activists in the Netherlands, which still continued at a time when Palestine had come to be seen as a Muslim issue.

In the 1970s and 1980s, protesting against Israel was largely a leftist affair in the Netherlands. Demonstrations against Israel featured representatives of various leftist parties and organisations, including leftist migrant associations. This changed in the 1990s, when religiously inspired organisations introduced novel frames and forms of protest. For a small number of Muslim organisations the Israeli-Palestinian conflict became an important issue which could also be used to mobilise their followers. This shift reflected

---

1   Zeynel Abidin Kılıç, 'Yazıklarolsun, yazıklarolsun', *Doğuş*, May 2002, 16. On the demonstration and the surrounding debate see Evelien Gans, '"Hamas, Hamas, All Jews to the gas." The history and significance of an antisemitic slogan in the Netherlands, 1945-2010.' In: Günther Jikeli and Joëlle Benayoun (eds.), *Perceptions of the Holocaust in Europe and Muslim communities. Sources, comparisons and Educational Challenges* (Dordrecht: Springer, 2013), 85-103: 85-86; Jessica ter Wal, *Moslim in Nederland. De publieke discussie over de islam in Nederland: een analyse van artikelen in de Volkskrant 1998-2002* (The Hague: SCP, 2004), 78-86: 80.

the advent of political Islam in the Middle East in the 1970s and 1980s. The first signs of this change were observed in the Netherlands a few years after the Iranian Revolution of 1979.

In Turkey itself, antisemitism was an integral part of religious-nationalist and ultranationalist ideologies.[2] With the arrival of Turkish migrants in the Netherlands these ideologies came to be represented locally. From the start of labour migration from Turkey to the Netherlands in 1964 until 1975 about 63,000 Turkish migrants settled in the Netherlands, the majority foreign labourers. From about 1975 onwards migration largely consisted of migrants' spouses and families, resulting in the presence of 120,000 Turkish migrants in 1980, which would grow to 190,000 in 1990.[3] Contrary to general belief, Turkish migrants were not unskilled and unqualified labourers from the lowest social strata and the most backward areas of the country. Turkish immigrants in the Netherlands came from almost all Turkish provinces, especially from the central part of the country and some cities on the Black Sea coast. About half of the Turkish migrants were of urban origin and their level of education and professional skills were high compared to the average educational level of the labour force in Turkey. Turkish migrants were employed mainly in the industrial sector.[4]

Initially, the life of Turkish migrants in the Netherlands centred around work, but as their residence continued, they set up their own organisations and associations. Turkish associational life in the Netherlands mirrored social and political bifurcations in Turkey in being dominated by organisations based on political or religious orientation. These organisations reproduced social distinctions between higher and lower classes, urban and rural backgrounds, and secular and religious orientations existing in Turkey. Many associations, such as the communist HTIB, the ultranationalist MHP, and the religious-nationalist Milli Görüş, were counterparts of political parties in Turkey, though these ties were usually informal, due to a Turkish law prohibiting official branches of parties abroad. Political activism among Turkish migrants was intensified by the arrival of political refugees in

2   Jacob M. Landau, 'Muslim Turkish attitudes towards Jews, Zionism and Israel', *Die Welt des Islams* 28, 1/4 (1988), 291-300 and the fourth chapter of Rifat Bali, *Musa'nın evlatları, Cumhuriyet'in yurttaşları* (Istanbul: İletişim, 2001), 221-450.
3   In 2000 there were 309,000 residents, of whom at least one parent had been born in Turkey, 178,000 first-generation migrants, and 131,000 second-generation migrants. Source: Centraal Bureau voor de Statistiek, www.cbs.nl.
4   Ahmet Akgündüz, 'Een analytische studie naar de arbeidsmigratie van Turkije naar West-Europa, in het bijzonder naar Duitsland en Nederland (1960-1974)', *Sociologische Gids* xl, 50 (1993), 352-385.

periods of political upheaval in Turkey, such as after the military coups of 1971 and 1980. Until the beginning of the 1980s most initiatives of political organisations were directed at the situation in Turkey. Only when it became clear that many migrants would not return to Turkey, were the social needs of migrant families with regard to, for example, housing, education and the labour market, raised as an issue.[5]

Whereas in Turkey, antisemitism was a constant feature of nationalist ideology, there are few traces to be found of such manifestations of anti-semitism in the Netherlands. In their first decades Turkish organisations in the Netherlands did not make any antisemitic statements. They were, however, responsible for the first registered incidents in the 1980s and 1990s. The little evidence about antisemitism within Turkish circles in the Netherlands seems to have been disregarded. In 1986, the scholar in Islamic studies Jacques Waardenburg surmised that Turks would be less affected by anti-Jewish attitudes than Arabs. Around the same time the Dutch convert Abdulwahid van Bommel (b. 1944), who was well-informed about the Turkish Muslim community, expected such radicalism from Surinamese rather than from Turkish (or Moroccan) Muslims.[6] It wasn't until 2000 that antisemitism within Turkish communities in the Netherlands became apparent, but at that point antisemitism had already been framed as an issue of the Moroccan-Dutch population.[7] This hidden antisemitism in Turkish circles is matched by a lack of academic research on the topic, especially in its historical dimension. This is not only the case in the Netherlands, but also in Germany. Moreover, this can also be related to the paucity of academia's treatment of antisemitism in Turkey itself.[8] This chapter gives an account of manifestations of antisemitism within Turkish communities, tracing these back to different ideological trajectories. This chapter shows that manifestations of antisemitism emerging from Turkish organisations in the Netherlands were, overall, related to anti-Zionist activism. This activism

5   Liza Mügge, *Beyond Dutch Borders: Transnational Politics among Colonial Migrants, Guest Workers and the Second Generation* (Amsterdam: Amsterdam University Press, 2010), 149-180.

6   'Uitspraken Moslims schokken Joden', *Israël Nieuwsbrief* 4 (1986); Ben Haveman, 'Anti-joodse bomdreiging "werk van een gek"', *de Volkskrant,* 25 October 1985.

7   *See* chapter 14.

8   Notable exceptions are the publications of Jacob Landau and Rifat Bali, mentioned above. Recent years have witnessed an increased interest in the history of the Jews in Republican Turkey, resulting also in studies of antisemitism, for example Hatice Bayraktar, 'Türkische Karikaturen über Juden (1933-1945)', *Jahrbuch für Antisemitismusforschung* 13 (2004), 85-108; Marc David Baer, 'An Enemy Old and New: The Dönme, Anti-Semitism, and Conspiracy Theories in the Ottoman Empire and Turkish Republic', *Jewish Quarterly Review* 103, 4 (2013), 523-555.

was primarily directed against Israel, but sometimes also included anti-Jewish discourses.

Turkish leftist anti-imperialism: Israel as an outpost of American imperialism

In the 1970s and 1980s, protests against Israel regularly featured Turkish and Moroccan migrants of leftist persuasion. Leftist Turkish migrants were mainly organised in HTIB, the Turkish Workers Association in the Netherlands (*Hollanda Türkiyeli İşçiler Birliği*). HTIB had been founded in 1974, in the same year as the Moroccan KMAN, by migrants sympathising with the Communist Party in Turkey (TKP). The activities of the TKP, which was banned most of the time, were mainly based outside of Turkey. Although HTIB was Moscow-oriented and Marxist it also included sympathisers of other leftist groups.[9]

In Turkey, left-wing activism had been flourishing from the late 1960s, when ideological, political and personal differences led to fierce struggles within the leftist camp. As a result, the Left had splintered into increasingly extremist groups which were advocating the use of violence. Their violence was answered by equally extremist right-wing nationalist groups which had come to the fore in the late 1960s and 1970s. The fight was unequal, though. Not only were the leftists outnumbered by the rightists, the latter were also being protected by the police and security services. Moreover, the extreme-right-wing MHP was in government between 1975 and 1978.

At the beginning and again at the end of the 1970s the violent clashes between extreme-leftist and extreme-right-groups in Turkey amounted to a civil war. This made the Turkish military decide to seize power on the grounds of the perceived threat to the democratic order, first on 12 March 1971 and again, almost a decade later, on 12 September 1980. Both coups resulted in a period of military rule, the banning of all political parties and the prosecution of thousands of activists.

As radical left movements were outlawed, most of them continued their activities in exile or illegally in Turkey itself. Due to the increasing

---

9   On HTIB and other Turkish leftist organisations in the Netherlands *see* Liza M. Nell,'The shadow of homeland politics: Understanding the evolution of the Turkish radical Left in the Netherlands', *Revue européenne des migrations internationales* 24, 2 (2008), 121-145. This discussion of HTIB is furthermore based on its journal *Gerçek* and the HTIB archive at the International Institute of Social History (IISH).

population of Turkish workers and refugees, Europe became the main exile base for leaders of illegal left parties in the late 1970s and 1980s. Mirroring internal and ideological divides in Turkey, a wide spectrum of radical leftist groups continued their activities in exile, mobilising workers for their party in Turkey and establishing their own networks with members throughout Europe. This was particularly true of Germany. But also in the Netherlands where HTIB was just one of a myriad of radical leftist Turkish organisations such as the Turkish Revolutionary Path (*Devrimci Yol*) and Revolutionary Left (*Devrimci Sol*).

Until the mid-eighties, HTIB, like other Turkish migrant organisations, was tied up in fighting the Turkish regime through demonstrations and publications. But although Turkish politics were at the forefront of their attention, HTIB's activists saw Turkey as only one front in a global struggle for liberation from oppression and exploitation, a struggle they themselves were involved in as workers and migrants. In a perspective dominated by the Cold War, the world was divided between regimes and parties acting on behalf of 'the people', and the forces of fascism, imperialism and capitalism. Global history was a sequence of people being victimised in fascist massacres, whether it was Hitler's German fascism which had sent several peoples to the gas chambers in order to establish the hegemony of German capital – neither National Socialism nor Jews were mentioned here – or Israeli attackers killing the Arab inhabitants of the village Deir Yassin in 1948, or Sukarno's regime in Indonesia in 1965, or the ultra-right-wing Greek Cypriot paramilitary EOKA-B killing Turkish-Cypriot villagers at the time of the Cyprus crisis in 1974.[10]

The main evil forces of imperialism were the United States and NATO, both of which were vehemently opposed by HTIB. It viewed Israel as an outpost of American imperialism in the Middle East that was only able to defy the opposition from the neighbouring Arab countries thanks to American military support. This view translated itself into declarations of solidarity with 'the justified struggle of the Palestinian Arab people against Israel'.[11] HTIB's affinity concerned first of all the leftist Palestine Liberation Organization (PLO). The recognition of the PLO, at an Arab summit in October 1974, as the representative of the Palestinian people, and of Arafat as its leader was welcomed in HTIB's journal, with the characteristic title *Gerçek* (The Truth), as an event which would bring an end to the American

10 *Gerçek*, 10 September 1974.
11 *Ibid.*, 15 June 1974.

and Israeli portrayal of 'heroic freedom-fighters' as 'anarchist or terrorist'.[12] Similarly, HTIB opposed Egypt's improving relations with Israel and the United States from 1974 onwards, arguing that this rapprochement would result in Israel definitely appropriating the occupied territories and gaining legitimacy worldwide.[13]

HTIB's support for the PLO may be explained from the ties which existed between extreme-leftist groups in Turkey and Yasser Arafat's Fatah, the largest faction within the PLO. In Turkey, the involvement of extremist Turkish leftists in the Palestinian struggle went beyond declarations of solidarity. A few hundred leftist students were trained in PLO training camps in Jordan, where they went in the years after the Six-Day War of 1967, in order to fight against 'American imperialism' rather than the Israelis. Several of the Turkish militant activists who engaged in violent activities such as urban guerrilla warfare in the late 1960s and early 1970s had trained in Fatah military camps in Jordan.

Turkey's most famous leftist militant, Deniz Gezmiş (1947-1972), had been trained in a military camp before returning to Turkey to set up a revolutionary group called Turkish People's Liberation Army (*Türkiye Halk Kurtuluş Ordusu*). In 1971 he was responsible for kidnapping four American technicians working for the US air force in Turkey and robbing several banks. He was sentenced to death for attempting to overthrow the constitutional order. Another notorious Turkish leftist militant, Mahir Çayan (1946-1972), was involved in a mortal terrorist attack on the Israeli consul in Istanbul in May 1971. The revolutionary leftist group involved, the Turkish People's Liberation Front (*Türkiye Halk Kurtuluş Partisi-Cephesi*, THKP-C), claimed its purpose was to demonstrate solidarity with the Palestinians, but apparently the consul had been giving Turkish security forces the names of Turkish militants trained in Palestinian camps. In January 1980 the Marxist-Leninist Armed Propaganda Group (MLSPB), a splinter group of THKP-C, claimed to have murdered the head of the Istanbul office of Israel's airline El Al.[14]

In the Netherlands, HTIB was soon integrated in the routines and rituals of established leftist parties and organisations. Throughout the seventies

---

12   'kahraman fedailerine ... anarşist, terrorist gibi sözler', *Gerçek*, 10 November 1974.

13   *Gerçek*, September/October 1975.

14   Robert W. Olson, 'Al-Fatah in Turkey: its influence on the March 12 coup', *Middle Eastern Studies* 9, 2 (1973), 197-205; Sabri Sayari, 'The terrorist movement in Turkey: Social composition and generational changes', *Conflict Quarterly* (1987): 21-32; Nur Bilge Criss, 'A short history of anti-Americanism and terrorism: The Turkish case', *The Journal of American History* 89, 2 (2002), 472-484.

and eighties HTIB joined the Dutch Communist Party (CPN) and other leftist migrant organisations in their protests against any manifestation of fascism or imperialism. In the 1980s, Moroccan and Turkish migrant activists, organised in KMAN and HTIB, would be regular associates in demonstrations against Israel. In the Netherlands, HTIB occasionally declared its solidarity with the Palestinian cause, but it was clearly an issue of secondary importance.[15] In the 1980s, HTIB participated in demonstrations against Israel organised by the Dutch Palestine Committee (NPK). In July 1982, HTIB participated in the demonstration against the Israeli invasion of Lebanon, as did KMAN and the Turkish revolutionary Dev-Sol; these organisations were also expected to provide stewards responsible for maintaining order during the protest.[16] After the massacres of Sabra and Shatila in September of that same year, another demonstration through the city of Amsterdam drew, according to observers, 3,500 protesters, 'a negligible number of mainly Turks and Moroccans, but more than ever before'.[17]

Five years later, during the First Intifada, when Palestinians protested against the Israeli occupation, Turkish leftist activists, including the 'Dutch branch of the Communist Party of Turkey', again joined demonstrations against Israel in December 1987 and in May 1988.[18] In his speech on the occasion of International Workers' Day celebrations on 1 May 1988, a representative of HTIB addressed the dire situation of the peoples in the Middle East. This was only a few weeks before the Iraqi regime of Saddam Hussein launched a chemical attack on the village of Halabja which killed thousands of the Kurdish inhabitants. The speech voiced abhorrence at the murder of the Palestinian and the Kurdish people. Whereas the attacks on Kurds by the Iraqi regime were called mass murder and genocide, the word 'mass' before murder had been crossed out in the case of the Palestinians, suggesting some sort of discussion had taken place about the use of these terms. Moreover, the phrase 'Hitlerian methods' used in the Turkish text to describe the Israeli treatment of Palestinians was missing in the Dutch version.[19] The appropriate choice of slogans and catchphrases to be used

15   In 1977 Palestine was mentioned in the speech for International Workers' Day, but in subsequent years it was not, while in March 1979, 'Long live the Palestinian people's fight for freedom' was one out of 25 slogans. Archive HTIB, IISH, No. 265, 411.
16   Archive Palestine Committee, IISH. I thank Remco Ensel for showing the references to HTIB in the NPK archive.
17   Mau Kopuit and Tamarah Benima, 'Libanese gebeurtenissen klieven joodse gemeenschap", *NIW*, 1 October 1982.
18   'Demonstratie tegen optreden Israël', *De Waarheid*, 24 December 1987.
19   Archive HTIB, IISH.

in the struggle against Israel had, over the years, been a topic of debate. These discussions had been fuelled among and between the NPK and KMAN by accusations of antisemitism levelled against both organisations. But while KMAN diverged every so often from the guidelines set by the NPK, HTIB seems to have gone along with the NPK. In 1982 HTIB produced a Turkish translation of the pamphlet made by the NPK, while KMAN produced its own pamphlet because it found the NPK's too soft. When KMAN used the same phrase 'Hitlerian methods' during a demonstration in July 1982, this became an issue because the NPK had stipulated that no comparisons between Nazism and Israel were to be made.[20] Characteristically, the criticism brought forward by HTIB during the evaluation of the demonstration was directed against the Turkish extreme-leftist Dev-Sol, which had set an American flag on fire.[21]

Turkish anti-communism in the Netherlands: Zionists as enemies of the nation

HTIB was well-versed in the vocabulary of Hitler and Nazism, but usually reserved it for its adversaries on the right, the Turkish ultranationalist Nationalist Action Party (MHP). Like other Turkish parties, the MHP and its youth organisation the 'Grey Wolves' had supporters in the Netherlands.[22] HTIB strove to hinder these activists as they were organising themselves in the Netherlands. Right-wing and nationalist activists came to Europe especially after the coup in 1980, when anti-terrorist campaigns in Turkey were no longer limited to left-wing activity, but also targeted the MHP and the Grey Wolves. From the emergence of right-wing Turkish organisations in the Netherlands, left-wing associations sought to prevent these from establishing themselves in Dutch society, protesting against them, organising activities and taking up office. Thanks to their connections to a large pool of leftist activists they had been fairly successful.

Throughout the 1970s and 1980s, HTIB was campaigning for a ban on the Grey Wolves, mustering substantial support for its opposition to right-wing

---

20   Remco Ensel, *Haatspraak. Antisemitisme – een 21ᵉ-eeuwse geschiedenis* (Amsterdam: Amsterdam University Press, 2014), chapters 3 and 4; the 'Hitlerian methods' are mentioned on page 124. *See also* chapter 7.

21   Minutes of NPK meeting 22 July 1982, archive NPK, IISH.

22   *See* Annemarike Stremmelaar, 'Sharing stories. A history of multicultural war remembrance in the Netherlands', to be published in: Philipp Gassert, Alan E. Steinweis and Jacob Eder (eds.), *Holocaust memory in a globalizing world* (Göttingen: Wallstein 2015) (under review).

activity. Turkish right-wing organisations had difficulty in establishing themselves, as their legitimacy was questioned by leftist organisations and their supporters. The efforts of leftist organisations to counter right-wing Turkish activism in the Netherlands directed itself against its fascist and nationalist character. Antisemitism, if it were a trait of Turkish nationalist activism in the Netherlands, did not attract particular attention.[23]

In Turkey, anti-communism was at the core of right-wing activism, both in its nationalist and conservative-religious shades. The distinction between right-wing and left-wing orientation replicated that between pious Muslims and secularists; thus, the Right criticised the Left as god-less. Classical antisemitic stereotypes of Jews as atheist and immoral were used in this context to vilify 'communism' and anything left of centre.[24] In the Netherlands, however, such antisemitic stereotypes do not seem to have been publicly used, although antisemitic statements could be found in Turkish nationalist and religious-nationalist publications distributed in the Netherlands.[25] Turkish nationalists in the Netherlands filled their propaganda primarily with anti-communist slogans. Surviving nationalist pamphlets do not refer to Jews, Zionism or Israel, but they do confirm the staunch anti-communist stance of the Turkish extreme-right. Enmity against Greeks and Armenians was probably more important at a time in which there was crisis over Cyprus in the 1970s and Armenian terrorist attacks on Turkish diplomats in the 1980s.[26]

The first documented manifestation of antisemitic stereotyping among Turkish migrants in the Netherlands can be placed in the context of political

23   In treatments of the Grey Wolves in the Netherlands there is no mention of antisemitism, see for example Stella Braam and Mehmet Ülger, *Grijze Wolven: een zoektocht naar Turks extreem-rechts* (Amsterdam: Nijgh & Van Ditmar, 1997); Anti-Fascistische Actie Nederland and Onderzoeksgroep Turks extreem-rechts, *'Ik sterf voor jou, Turkije'. Turks extreem-rechts in Nederland* (Utrecht: Alert! & Onderzoeksgroep Turks extreem-rechts 2009).

24   Rıfat N. Bali, *Musa'nın evlatları, Cumhuriyet' in yurttaşları* (Istanbul: İletişim, 2001), 257-259, 341-344.

25   Will Tinnemans, *Een gouden armband: Een geschiedenis van Mediterrane immigranten in Nederland (1945-1994)* (Utrecht: Nederlands Centrum Buitenlanders, 1994), 149-150, gives two examples of antisemitic phrases in the nationalist, MHP-oriented journals *Tercüman* and *Yeniden Milli Mücadele* distributed among Turks in Germany in 1972-1973. These were prob-ably taken from the anti-fascist brochure *De Grijze Wolf en de Halve Maan: Turks fascisme en rechts-extremisme in Europa* (Utrecht: Sektie Publikaties Buitenlanders van het Nederlands Centrum Buitenlanders, 1980). The religious-conservative ideology of the MSP was disseminated in Turkey as well as in Europe by its newspaper *Milli Gazete*, on which see Esther Debus, *Die islamisch-rechtlichen Auskünfte der Millî Gazete im Rahmen des ' Fetwa-Wesen' der Türkischen Republik* (Berlin: Klaus Schwarz, 1984).

26   See a number of Turkish nationalist pamphlets held in the HTIB archive at the IISH.

antagonisms between right-wing and left-wing migrants. The document, dating from 1982, was a ballot paper in Turkish to be used in the election of new board members for the Turkish Culture Centre (*Türk Kültür Merkezi*), a club for mainly right-wing Turkish migrants in Amsterdam.[27] It contained a list of candidates selected by two organisations: the Islamic Youth Organisation (*Islamcı Gençlik Teşkilatı*) and the World Islamist Union Organisation (*Dünya İslam Birliği Teşkilatı*) which were active in the local Selimiye Mosque and Aya Sofya Mosque respectively. These organisations were part of the burgeoning movement of political Islam, in which Islam provided not only a religious, but also a political identity and ideology. In Turkey, this development had resulted in the founding of a political party, the National Order Party (MSP), by Necmettin Erbakan (1926-2011) in 1969. In the Netherlands, this ideological movement, which also became known as *Milli Görüş* (National View), also had supporters who organised themselves around mosques. The two organisations were probably both part of this group.[28]

The election pamphlet instructed attendees of the club to vote for the recommended candidates, the 'Muslim Turkish brothers' whose names were listed and who would 'serve you most beneficially and justly': 'Dear brother, use your vote absolutely diligently so that our own culture will not fall into the hands of Zionists or communists, or others who are harmful for you.' A second pamphlet explicated that 'the path in which the Muslim Turk believes is the path of God and the Quran. Communists and Zionists definitely do not believe in Islam. Can believers and unbelievers be one?'

The pamphlet thus depicted Zionists and communists as enemies of the community, defined as Turkish and Muslim and as prying on cultural and religious values. They were unpatriotic, immoral and atheist. These were stereotypical characterisations of both communism and Zionism within Turkish rightist political discourse, which were now used against left-wing Turkish migrants. Whoever drew up the pamphlets used 'Zionist' as synonymous with 'Jew' in order to brandish his opponents as 'Jewish' and therefore as a threat to national culture. A similar use of the stereotypical identification of left-wing political ideology and Jews was applied to HTIB's

---

27   The two election pamphlets of 21 February 1982 are in the archives of the Centre for Information and Documentation on Israel (CIDI), an organisation seeking to protect the interests of Israel and Jews in the Netherlands. A later election pamphlet held in the IISH does not refer to Zionists: HTIB archive, No. 378.

28   For the early history of Milli Görüş in the Netherlands *see* Nico Landman, *Van mat tot minaret: de institutionalisering van de islam in Nederland* (Amsterdam: VU uitgeverij, 1992), 121-122.

'Moroccan counterpart', the leftist KMAN, which was also brandished as 'Jewish'.[29]

The idea that Jews would not be loyal to the nation was a classical antisemitic stereotype, as was the association of Jews with leftist political ideologies; both were also connected to the stereotype of Jews as immoral. Antisemitic stereotypes of the Jews as instigators of modern intellectual currents as wide-ranging as communism, capitalism and atheism started circulating in the Ottoman Empire from the late nineteenth century, soon after their inception in (Christian) Europe.[30] These stereotypes had gained currency in Turkey in the course of the twentieth century, where from the 1960s onwards they were increasingly used by the Right against their opponents on the Left. In the hands of right-wing publicists, antisemitic images of the Jews as representatives of modernity, the West and atheism became fuel to denounce leftists whom the former considered impious, immoral and too Western oriented. Although the word 'Jew' (*Yahudi* in Turkish) was also used, 'Zionist' and 'Zionism' were often used with all the same negative connotations. This had the advantage of disguising the antisemitic intent, while adding the negative connotations surrounding the state of Israel and the Protocols of Zion.[31]

A sign of the evolution of organised 'anti-Zionism' in Turkey can be found in the foundation of a Turkish Association for Combating Zionism (*Türkiye Siyonizmle Mücadele Derneği*) in 1968 by nationalist-conservative publicists and activists, parallel to existing associations for combating communism. The association called Zionism the political arm of world Jewry, and repeated stereotypical associations of Zionism with communism and freemasonry – three international phenomena which it considered a threat to the nation, but with Zionism being the force behind the other two. The association was to 'fight destructive and corrosive ideas and currents, first

---

29 See Ensel, *Haatspraak*, chapter 3.

30 See for the first stereotype Erhard Stölting, 'Sechzehntes Bild; "Der Verräter."' In: Julius Schoeps and Joachim Schlör (eds.), *Antisemitismus. Vorurteile und Mythen* (München: Piper, 1995), 218-228; for the second *see* Peter Niedermüller, 'Zwei und zwanzigstes Bild; "Der Kommunist."' In: Schoeps and Schlör (eds.), *Antisemitismus*, 273-278; and André Gerrits, *The Myth of Jewish Communism: A Historical Interpretation* (Frankfurt: Peter Lang, 2009); for the third stereotype, *see* Joachim Schlör, "Der Urbantyp." In: Schoeps and Schlör (eds.), *Antisemitismus*, 229-240. On the advent of antisemitism in Ottoman lands see Özgür Türesay, 'Antisionisme et antisémitisme dans la presse ottomane d'Istanbul à l'époque jeune turque (1909-1912)', *Turcica* 41 (2009), 147-178; Marc D. Baer, *The Dönme: Jewish Converts, Muslim Revolutionaries, and Secular Turks* (Stanford, CA: Stanford University Press, 2010); Baer, 'An enemy old and new'.

31 Landau, 'Muslim Turkish attitudes towards Jews, Zionism and Israel.' On the print history and reception of the *Protocols see* Bali, *Musa'nın evlatları*, 316-340.

of all Zionism, to protect the national culture and customs and spiritual, religious and moral values.'[32]

Two antisemitic quotations found in Turkish ultranationalist journals distributed in Europe appealed to the same stereotype of a Zionist-communist cooperation.[33] In the election pamphlets these stereotypes were used against Turkish leftists who were well represented in Amsterdam in the early 1980s, overshadowing other Turkish migrant organisations. For a long time, leftist organisations, although representing a minority of migrants, held a dominant position in the field of migrant affairs and in the social welfare sector. Many of the Dutch employees in the welfare sector had leftist sympathies and little understanding for religion. Leftist migrants usually also had higher educational levels than other migrants and considered the latter provincial and illiterate, reinforcing the latter's sense of isolation and exclusion and discrimination.

HTIB was criticised by other Turkish organisations for presenting itself as the voice of all Turks in the Netherlands, while not representing the majority. In 1984, a representative of a Turkish religious federation complained that the municipality of Amsterdam only had eyes for leftist organisations: 'The Turkish Marxist group HTIB … is in terms of supporters 25 times smaller than the largest and moderate Islamic Turkish organisations. But in Amsterdam they get 25 times as much subsidy as moderate Islamic organisations.'[34]

The political cleavage would manifest itself in the struggle over the editorial profile of the Turkish-language journal *Haber*. Journalists quit working for *Haber* when its board, consisting of a majority of conservative Turks, began censoring left-leaning writings, for example a story written by the Turkish socialist novelist Yaşar Kemal. After the right-wing take-over, the journal acquired a more nationalist and pious character. A joke about Arafat may have appealed to all readers, irrespective of their political orientation, and testifies to the self-evidence of pro-Palestinian partisanship. The joke took the form of a fake news report about Yasser Arafat visiting Amsterdam to ask the city for help to end the Israeli occupation. Arafat had been trying for fifteen years to get rid of the Israelis, while the municipality of Amsterdam had succeeded in throwing house squatters out of their buildings within 15 days.[35]

32 Bali, *Musa'nın evlatları*, 257-269.

33 Tinnemans, *Een gouden armband*, 149-150; a longer quotation is to be found in the anti-fascist brochure *De Grijze Wolf en de Halve Maan: Turks fascisme en rechts-extremisme in Europa* (Utrecht: Sektie Publikaties Buitenlanders van het Nederlands Centrum Buitenlanders, 1980).

34 *Haber,* 31 August 1984; Tinnemans, *Een gouden armband*, 151-154, 274.

35 *Haber,* 25 February 1984.

The Turkish election pamphlets referring pejoratively to Zionists were produced by a group which also identified itself with the ideal of political Islam through their name 'Islamist Youth Movement'. The documents served as evidence of Muslim antisemitism in an official report on antisemitism in the Netherlands published in 1983. The report had been commissioned by the Ministry of Welfare, Public Health and Culture at a time when there was concern about manifestations of antisemitism after Israel's invasion in Lebanon in 1982. The authors saw excessive criticism of Israel as one important form of antisemitism, among others, but also identified religious antisemitism in Protestant and Catholic circles. What was new was that they also mentioned the presence of antisemitism among migrants of Muslim faith, stating that with the rise in the number of Muslims antisemitic propaganda had also begun to be issued by Muslims. In addition to the election pamphlets mentioned above, the report also referred to two publications in Dutch in which Jews were called 'unworthy' and 'straying off the path ordained by God'.[36]

The quotations in the report came from Muslim Moluccans and from *Qibla*, a journal published by Dutch converts to Islam, not from the large Moroccan and Turkish Muslim communities. The same was true for subsequent antisemitic statements by Muslim communities reported in the Dutch press. In October 1985 a representative of the Surinamese World Islamic Mission Netherlands, Mohamed Idris Lachman, complained that Jews were in charge in the Netherlands, especially in Amsterdam, where 'all day long one would hear Jewish songs on the radio'. His comments smacked of jealousy, a form of 'goyish envy': unlike for Muslims they would do anything for Jews. But his animosity concerned Israel just as much as Dutch Jews. He foresaw that Israel's display of power would create so much hate among Muslims in the Netherlands that it would only be a matter of time before bombs would go off in Amsterdam, The Hague and Rotterdam, like they had done in Brussels, Paris and London. Not even six months later, a representative of the Hussaini Mission Nederland, a small Pakistani Shia organisation, similarly complained that Jews always want 'more and

36 M.T. Josephus Jitta-Geertsema and J.H Sanders, *Antisemitisme in Nederland.* WVC literatuur-rapport 20, (Rijswijk: WVC, Hoofdafdeling documentatie en Bibliotheek, 1983), 35. Jos Teunissen, 'Psycholoog Jaap Sanders: Leeft het antisemitisme op? Ik geloof er niets van', *Het Vrije Volk,* 8 June 1984; Peter Schumacher, 'Ministerie van WVC terughoudend met verspreiding van rapport antisemitisme', *NRC Handelsblad,* 12 May 1985. For the report in question, *see also* chapters 7 and 8.

more' and to 'dominate the other', and that destroying humans was 'in their blood'.[37]

In these years, the emergence of radical and antisemitic views within Muslim circles in the Netherlands was attributed to financial connections with foreign countries such as Iran, Saudi Arabia, but particularly Libya. Fear of Iranian influence was, as yet, in the background. In 1984 the city of The Hague first discovered Iran's antisemitic and anti-Zionist propaganda when the Iranian consulate-general organised an exhibition on the occasion of the fifth anniversary of the Iranian Revolution. It took more than one intervention to discard all antisemitic material; after a first complaint some offensive content was still on display.[38]

In the 1980s and 1990s, antisemitic sentiments within Muslim circles rarely surfaced: during the First Intifada, protests against Israel late 1987 and early 1988 were still a leftist affair.[39] Only in the course of the 1990s, after the Rushdie Affair (1989) and the First Gulf War (1990-1991), would Muslim mobilisation lead to more sustained Islamic anti-Zionist activism.[40]

From leftist to Islamic anti-imperialism

A first sign of the turning tide was a demonstration of supporters of the Turkish nationalist MHP against the Soviet invasion in Afghanistan on 5 January 1980 in front of the Soviet embassy in The Hague. The demonstration was a clear indication of the MHP's anti-communist agenda. The pro-Soviet Communist regime of Afghanistan had called in the help of the Russian troops to provide security at a time of factional strife and to assist in the fight against the mujahideen rebels – Islam inspired guerrillas. HTIB felt the need for a counter-demonstration because it supported the Soviet intervention, but also because it was confronted with the prospect

37 'Uitspraken Moslims schokken Joden', *Israel Nieuwsbrief,* 27 February 1986; Ben Haveman, 'Anti-joodse bomdreiging "werk van een gek"', *de Volkskrant,* 25 October 1985; 'Fikse boete wegens beledigen joden', *Algemeen Dagblad,* 15 October 1988; 'Boete geëist tegen voormalige voorzitter stichting Welzijn voor Moslims', *NIW,* 4 November 1988. For the two organisations involved, the Surinamese 'World Islamic Mission Nederland' and the Pakistani Shii 'Hussaini Mission Nederland', *see* Landman, *Van mat tot minaret,* 223-227, 240-241. For goyish envy, *see* chapter 2.
38 '"Beledigend" materiaal van Iran expositie weggehaald', *Algemeen Dagblad,* 11 February 1984; 'Antisemitisch materiaal verwijderd van Iran-expositie; Rabbijn dient klacht in over expositie Iraanse ambassade', *de Volkskrant,* 17 February 1984.
39 On anti-Zionist activism during the First Intifada, *see* chapter 7.
40 On the effect of the Rushdie Affair *see* chapter 15.

of a right-wing Turkish demonstration. It tried to get the demonstration banned by organising a picket-line in front of the police station in The Hague and demanding that the demonstration be forbidden. To their dismay, the protesters were left unhindered by the Dutch authorities whereas their own protest was terminated by the police.[41]

What was remarkable was not so much HTIB's loyalty to the Afghan regime, as its effort to refute the Afghan armed resistance's claim to be fighting on behalf of the same people HTIB had declared solidarity to. As was argued in *Gerçek*, the resistance fighters were mistakenly called 'Muslim guerrillas' – the term 'mujahedeen' was not used – although they had 'nothing to do with Muslims' and were 'only abusing the religious sentiments of the people', a phrase usually applied by the secularist Turkish regime for any political claim referring to Islam. The 'counterrevolutionaries', to use the journal's vocabulary, were mercenaries paid by wealthy Americans and Chinese, a clear sign that they were instruments of imperialism. As if that was not enough proof that the American support for the Afghan resistance was meant to dominate the people in the region, not to free or empower them, *Gerçek* repudiated the US posturing as saviour of the Muslims as symbolic of the hypocrisy of imperialism. How could the United States act as saviour of the Muslims when it had ruthlessly attacked the most holy place of Islam, the Kaaba in Mecca, in, even worse, collaboration with 'Zionist Israel'?

This accusation referred to the seizure of the Grand Mosque in Mecca by Islamist extremists denouncing the Saudi regime on 20 November 1979, an event which shocked many in the Muslim world, especially since it took place during the annual Hajj pilgrimage. The occupation ended after two weeks when security forces attacked the mosque, resulting in the death of hundreds of pilgrims. Only slowly, it became clear what exactly had happened, who had been the insurgents and how many people had been killed. At the same time, Khomeini insinuated that American imperialism and Zionism were behind the events, leading to anti-American protests in various Muslim countries, including Turkey. HTIB saw no harm in repeating this conspiracy theory.[42] This illustrates the ideological confusion created by the upsurge of political Islam. Starting in Iran and Afghanistan, but increasingly in other Muslim countries as well, popular movements claimed to speak out on behalf of the same 'people' as the Left did. However, these

---

41 'Omstreden betoging', *De Telegraaf,* 7 January 1980; 'Turkse "Grijze Wolven" betogen voor Sowjetambassade', *De Waarheid,* 8 January 1980.
42 *Gerçek,* May 1980.

did so not in the name of class struggle and social revolution, but in the name of Islam.

Nevertheless, both aimed at liberating people from imperialist oppression. Political Islamic ideology was deeply shaped by leftist ideologies.[43] As from the 1970s, Khomeini (1902-1989) depicted society as consisting of two antagonistic classes: the oppressed and the oppressors. In doing so, he was borrowing from ideologists of political Islam such as the Iranian revolutionary and sociologist Ali Shariati (1933-1977). In the early 1960s Shariati had translated Franz Fanon's *Les damnés de la terre* [The wretched of the earth, 1961] transforming Fanon's postcolonial revolutionary thinking into an understanding of Islam as prescribing a specific political ideology and regime. The oppressors, Khomeini argued, had always favoured unjust, satanic and tyrannical rule, while the oppressed were struggling for a just and Islamic government. This discourse, which evolved as a religious translation of an originally leftist discourse, proliferated in the years after 1979, first in the Middle East, but soon also in Europe.[44]

The Rushdie Affair first made the impact of the Iranian revolution being felt in the Netherlands. Salman Rushdie's *The Satanic Verses,* published in 1988, led to protests in India, Pakistan, Bangladesh, the UK and Turkey, because it was found to be blasphemous. In February 1989, these protests acquired new impetus when Ayatollah Khomeini issued a religious ruling calling on Muslims to kill Rushdie and his publishers. When plans were made for its publication in Dutch, Muslim representatives in the Netherlands did not expect much opposition. Muslims organisations preferred legal action and protests 'in a reasonable manner' over 'book burning and other medieval methods of censorship'. They had not reckoned with the mobilisation of Muslim protesters for two demonstrations, one in Rotterdam, organised by an organisation of Pakistani Muslims, and one in The Hague.[45]

Both demonstrations included all the scenes Muslim organisations had feared: the burning of Rushdie's book and portrait, protesters calling for his death, carrying Khomeini's portrait. The demonstration in The Hague featured Turkish activists and followers of Cemalettin Kaplan, a radical Turkish preacher who took Khomeini as an example. These followers had

---

43 As pointed out by Olivier Roy, *The Failure of Political Islam* (London: IB Tauris, 1994), 4-6.

44 Ervand Abrahamian, *Khomeinism: Essays on the Islamic Republic* (Berkeley: University of California, 1993), 47-51.

45 'Justitie onderzoekt "De Duivelsverzen" op godslastering', *Leeuwarder Courant*, 18 February 1989. *See also* Ensel, chapter 14 in this book, and *Haatspraak*, 166-174.

distributed an anonymous pamphlet calling on Muslims to demonstrate against Rushdie, resulting in a turn-out of 5,000 people, which was quite a lot given the fact that the Muslim federations rejected the call.[46] This showed the potential of mobilising a politicised Islamic identity.

Islamic antisemitism: Jews as enemies of Islam

Three years later, in March 1992, the same group staged a demonstration that was equally noteworthy as the one against Rushdie, attended by a combination of bearded, veiled and juvenile protesters carrying portraits of Khomeini and Khamenei (b. 1939) and burning flags. Abdulwahid van Bommel, the aforementioned Dutch convert to Islam and director of a Muslim organisation called the 'Muslim Information Centre', was well-informed about the various Turkish Muslim groups active in the Netherlands. He identified its organisers as the same group which had demonstrated against Rushdie, and referred to them as a 'small Turkish splinter group with connections in Germany' whose spiritual leader was called 'the Turkish Khomeini'.[47] Three hundred protesters had been demonstrating in front of the Israeli embassy for the liberation of Jerusalem and the Palestinians from oppression by Israel. Most protesters were Turkish migrants living in the Netherlands or Germany, but there also seem to have been migrants of Arab or Iranian background. The protesters marched to the Israeli and American embassies , as well as to the seat of government and parliament at the Binnenhof. They called for the destruction of Israel, Zionism and America, and burnt a portrait of the Israeli Prime Minister Shamir and an Israeli flag. Protests against Israel were nothing new, but this one was different as it was organised in the name of Islam. The new character of the protest manifested itself in its focus on Jerusalem as a sacred city of Islam which should be brought back under Muslim rule.

The Iranian inspiration of the demonstration was obvious. Protesters carried portraits of the deceased Ayatollah Khomeini and his successor Khamenei, and flags of the pro-Iranian Lebanese militant organisation Hezbollah. In addition, it was held on 'Quds Day', the last Friday of the month of fasting Ramadan, an event invented by Ayatollah Khomeini. In August 1979, only months after his ascent to power, he introduced Quds Day,

46   Landman, *Van mat tot minaret*, 134; 'Islamieten tieren over Duivelsverzen', *Het Vrije Volk*, 4 March 1989.
47   Abram, 'Moslims distantiëren zich van protest in Den Haag.'

after the Muslim name of Jerusalem, as a demonstration of international solidarity with the Palestinian people. He had been the first to call for the liberation of Jerusalem and Palestine, not just as Muslim territory, but as holy land. Khomeini made the struggle against Israel and Zionism a central and religious issue.[48] This meant a new understanding of the conflict in the Middle East as one between the adherents of Islam and Judaism, instead of the Israeli and Arab nations. Making the conquest a religious duty for all Muslims fitted well with Khomeini's export of the revolution and turned Palestine from an Arab issue into a universal Muslim one. It may have been one of the most successful elements of the Islamic revolutionary ideology to be exported. It was also a way of transcending the Shia-Sunni divide; Quds Day was and is celebrated in several Muslim countries, also by Sunni Muslims, for example in Turkey. Internationally, the repertoire of the demonstration is remarkably similar.[49]

Despite its Iranian inspiration, the demonstration was organised by officials of the local Vahdet Mosque in The Hague. These were followers of the aforementioned Cemalettin Kaplan (1926-1995) who himself resided in Cologne.[50] Kaplan had been a religious official in Turkey and active within Necmettin Erbakan's party until the military coup of 1980. After the coup, he moved to Germany, where he continued his political and religious activities for the party. Soon, however, he would break away from the organisation because his ideas were at odds with those of the party leadership in Turkey and in Germany. In 1983, he left the organisation and established himself in Cologne. Over time, his movement changed more and more into a sect, increasingly dissociating itself from the outside world. This resulted in the proclamation of a government in exile and in the self-appointment of Kaplan to caliph in 1994 – hence his nickname 'Caliph of Cologne'.[51]

48   On the anti-Zionist stance of the Iranian regime of Khomeini and Khatami, see Henner Fürtig, 'Die Bedeutung der iranischen Revolution von 1979 als Ausgangspunkt für eine anti-jüdisch orientierte Islamisierung', *Jahrbuch für Antisemitismusforschung* 12 (Berlin: Metropol, 2003), 73-98; Meit Litvak, 'The Islamic Republic of Iran and the Holocaust: anti-Semitism and anti-Zionism.' In: Jeffrey Herf (ed.), *Anti-Semitism and Anti-Zionism in Historical Perspective: Convergence and Divergence* (Abingdon: Routledge, 2013), 250-267.

49   'Politie beschermt ambassade Israël tegen betogers', *Trouw*, 28 March 1992; 'Moslim-protest in Den Haag', *De Telegraaf*, 28 March 1992; 'Joodse organisaties protesteren tegen islamitische actie', *NRC Handelsblad*, 1 April 1992.

50   An announcement for Quds Day 1993 was issued by the 'The Hague branch of the Islamic movement', part of movement. On Kaplan's organisation see Landman, *Van mat tot minaret*, 128-134.

51   Werner Schiffauer, *Die Gottesmänner. Türkische Islamisten in Deutschland. Eine Studie zur Herstellung religiöser Evidenz* (Berlijn: Suhrkamp, 2000), 126-128.

The split within the organisation was the result of a radicalisation of its followers in Germany after the 1980 coup in Turkey. With the banning of all political parties, Islamic politics in Turkey seemed to be at a dead end. At the same time, there was the feeling of a global Islamic awakening as an Islamic popular movement had brought down the regime in Iran. Kaplan fed into an unfolding revolutionary enthusiasm. He challenged the legitimacy of the engineer Erbakan at the helm of the Islamic movement in Turkey, claiming that only a religiously educated person like himself was entitled to its leadership. The path of parliamentary politics, as followed in Turkey, was doomed to fail, as the Turkish Republic itself was illegitimate. His message was revolutionary: he aspired to overthrow the Turkish Republican regime and establish an Islamic state like in Iran. As the anthropologist Werner Schiffauer has argued, this radicalism was, in many ways, a product of the migration: people could be more radical than in Turkey, for whatever they said was ultimately inconsequential. Moreover, in the Diaspora the idea of an Islamic state acquired its own meaning: it was connected with the hope to overcome the torn life abroad in a true homeland.[52]

Kaplan's outlook was as internationalist as it was revolutionary: he foresaw a revolution of Muslims worldwide. Kaplan's international outlook manifested itself in displays of solidarity with the Islamic popular movements in Bosnia, Afghanistan and especially Palestine.[53] For Kaplan, the Israeli occupation of Palestinian lands was the prime example of how imperialism dominated and humiliated Muslims worldwide. By identifying an American-Israeli alliance as Islam's number one enemy, Kaplan followed Khomeini in his defiant posture against the United States.[54] Like the Iranian regime, which had blamed the Rushdie Affair on an American-Zionist conspiracy, Kaplan and his followers resorted to conspiracy theories about Jewish and Zionist influence in American and Turkish politics in order to explain political events around the world.[55]

In Germany, a large number of communities accepted Kaplan's authority; there the movement collapsed after Kaplan's death, in 1995, due to

---

52   Schiffauer, 'Die Islamische Gemeinschaft Millî Görüş' (2004), available on www.cie.ugent.be/CIE2/schiffauer1.htm.

53   Fulya Atacan and Schiffauer testify to the centrality of the issue of Palestine among Kaplan's followers. Fulya Atacan, *Kutsal Göc. Radikal Islamcı birgrubun Anatomisi* (Ankara: Bağlam, 1993), 91-93; Schiffauer, *Die Gottesmänner*, 116-118.

54   Schiffauer, *Die Gottesmänner*, 126-127.

55   Atacan, *Kutsal Göc*, 120. Articles in the organisation's journal imply not only that Mustafa Kemal Atatürk had connections to Judaism, but also that he was involved in preparations leading to the foundation of the state Israel. Schiffauer, *Die Gottesmänner*, 116-119.

inner strife; it was banned in 2001 for anti-constitutional activities. In the Netherlands, the movement only played a marginal role. At its height, it amounted to a dozen associations, but at one point there was only one group left. Its isolation was augmented by the fact that other Turkish and Muslim organisations excluded it from assemblies and gatherings, like they had ignored its call for protest during the Rushdie Affair.[56] Kaplan had been visiting congregations in the Netherlands in the beginning of 1985, but in 1987 there seems to have been a peak in activity. In a sort of forerunner to the Quds demonstration, protesters had been seen protesting in The Hague in May of that year calling upon Muslims 'to kill the Jews'.[57] In December of that same year some 150 adherents met in Tilburg, and in February 1988 there was another meeting near Rotterdam.[58]

A pamphlet for the demonstration of 1993 shows the Iranian inspiration of Kaplan's followers.[59] It referred to Khomeini's call for the liberation of Jerusalem and his statement that every Muslim should prepare himself to fight Israel. Echoing the words of Khomeini, Muslims should reclaim Jerusalem not just for the Palestinians' sake, but in order to be saved themselves. Jerusalem was a holy city because, according to the canonical account of Mohammed's life, he initially chose Jerusalem as prayer direction, before changing this to Mecca. Jerusalem was 'the homeland of the Islamic community worldwide'.

The pamphlet held Muslims themselves responsible for the dire situation of Palestine: Muslim leaders had failed to keep their promise to save the occupied lands, and Muslims themselves were following false deities and fighting each other, resulting in the fragmentation of the Islamic community by heathen ideologies such as nationalism, capitalism, communism, liberalism and secularism. The plight of Muslims, according to the pamphlet, was their living in servitude and humiliation: 'the honour and dignity, pride and integrity of millions of Muslims all over the world was trampled'. The humiliation consisted not only in the victories of Israel over

56   Landman, *Van mat tot minaret*, 132-134; Thijl Sunier, *Islam in beweging. Turkse jongeren en islamitische organisaties* (Amsterdam: Het Spinhuis, 1996), 240, n.34; the yearly reports of the BVD.

57   On 22 May 1987 protesters identified as 'Muslims' demonstrated in the city centre of The Hague with banners in Dutch and Arabic; a note about the demonstration is held in the CIDI archive.

58   'De opmars van Khomeiny de Tweede', *Amigoe,* 13 August 1988.

59   A Turkish-language call for the demonstration on Quds Day on 19 March 1993, held in the CIDI archive.

its Arab opponents in 1956 and 1967, but more in particular in the Israeli occupation of territories which were central to Islam.[60]

In a binary view not only of the Israeli-Palestinian conflict, but of global politics, the pamphlet put oppressors against the oppressed and called upon the oppressed to raise their voice against the tyrants. This was an Islamic version of viewing Jews and Zionists in terms of perpetrators and oppressors and Palestinians as mere victims. The vocabulary of the oppressors and the oppressed was the contribution of political Islamic ideology as formulated by Khomeini.[61]

The demonstration caused concern because of the unknown spectre and because of the slogans calling for the end of Israel and Zionism. Newspaper readers expressed their shock and aversion over the slogans used by the protesters which reminded them 'of pre-war Germany and Iraq and Iran in the eighties'.[62] Jewish organisations addressed not only the Dutch Islamic Council, but also Minister of Foreign Affairs Van den Broek, asking the latter to protest with the Iranian government against 'the Islamic threats of Israeli targets'.[63]

There was reason enough to be concerned. Only ten days earlier there had been a suicide attack on the Israeli embassy in Buenos Aires, probably by a Lebanese Shia group called Islamic Jihad Organisation. Moreover, only a week earlier the national security service (BVD) had, for the first time in its existence, published a report on the security threats to Dutch society. This listed fundamentalist Muslim groups and highlighted the role of Iran in exporting fundamentalist and revolutionary radicalism. It warned of 'the potential for conflicts between minority groups in our country' which could lead to disturbance of the public order and even to bloodshed.[64]

---

60   Bernard Lewis attributes antisemitism in the Arab world to the outrage caused by the victories of Israel over its Arab opponents in 1956 and 1967, whose previous humility as protected but inferior residents made their triumphs especially humiliating. Bernard Lewis, *Semites and Anti-Semites: An Inquiry into Conflict and Prejudice* (London: Weidenfeld and Nicolson, 1986), 191, 194, 204, 239.

61   Atacan, *Kutsal Göç*, 114; Schiffauer, *Die Gottesmänner*, 126-127. Instead of Khomeni's *mostazafin* and *mostakberin* the pamphlet used the equivalents *mazlum* and *zalim*, which likewise had their origin in Arabic but were much more commonly used in Turkish.

62   Letters from L.P. van Mierlo (Helmond), 'Leuzen", *NRC Handelsblad*, 4 April 1992; and Jan Gerrit Dercksen (Bennebroek), 'Betoging", *Trouw*, 3 April 1992.

63   CIDI press announcement dated 30 March 1992, CIDI archive.

64   *Ontwikkelingen op het gebied van de Binnenlandse Veiligheid: Taakstelling en Werkwijze van de BVD*. 's-Gravenhage: Binnenlandse Veiligheidsdienst, Ministerie van Binnenlandse Zaken, 1992.

The warning was, in part, based on the reactions in the Netherlands to the American invasion in Iraq. The war and related developments in the Middle East had led to an intensification of identification processes in the Netherlands. Some people of Muslim background had felt they were perceived differently; others reported an increase in discrimination. A number of Islamic and Jewish representatives had taken the initiative for an interreligious dialogue to quell fears of Muslim-Jewish tensions. Now these fears resurfaced.[65]

Representatives of Muslim organisations hurriedly denounced the demonstration. The Dutch Islamic Council, through Coşkun Çörüz, distanced itself from 'all actions offensive to the Jewish community', while the aforementioned Abdulwahid van Bommel declared that 'a Shia leader operating from Iran has no right to discredit the Muslim community in the Netherlands'. Moreover, Van Bommel denounced the way the protesters were described as 'Muslims' instead of 'fundamentalists' suggesting 'a broad involvement of the Muslim community, which fortunately does not exist'.[66] One year later, the Dutch Muslim Council was prepared and issued a press statement, distancing itself from the demonstration and lamenting its negative effects on the 'reputation of ordinary, quiet Muslim citizens'.[67]

Quds Day seems to have been organised in The Hague yearly from 1991 onwards drawing a fluctuating number of protesters. At its height, in 1993 and 1996, 1,000 protesters joined, whereas in 1998 they numbered only seventy.[68] The demonstration had international appeal in two ways. Protesters were of different backgrounds: not only Turkish, but also Lebanese, Iraqi, Moroccan and Egyptian. Also, not all of them came from the Netherlands, but some also from Belgium and particularly Germany, where Kaplan's organisation had its European headquarters.[69] In Germany, Quds Day was organised in the 1980s in Bonn until 1995, from then on in Berlin. In Germany, Iranian

65   R.A. Levisson, 'Knipoog naar de actualiteit', *NIW*, 10 January 1992; Golfoorlog wakkert racisme tegen moslims en joden aan',*Nederlands dagblad*, 22 January 1991; 'Racistische gevoelens worden versterkt door Golfoorlog', *Het vrije volk*, 21 January 1991; 'Dialoog met Islam komt onder druk'', *Leeuwarder Courant,* 25 January 1991.

66   Çörüz later became parliamentarian for the Christian Democratic Party (CDA) (2001-2012). 'Joodse organisaties protesteren tegen islamitische actie'', *NRC Handelsblad*, 1 April 1992; Jan Goossensen, 'Op het randje'', *Hervormd Nederland,* 9 May 1998.

67   *NIW*, 26 March 1993.

68   Jan Goossensen, 'Op het randje'', *Hervormd Nederland,* 9 May 1998.

69   Many Turkish associations in the Netherlands had connections to European headquarters in Germany. Mügge, *Beyond Dutch Borders*, 104, 179. For an illustration of the ties, *see* 'Onder de loep: Turkse posters', *Brabants Dagblad*, 8 April 1999.

activists seem to have played a prominent role, although there were also Turkish, Iraqi and Afghan protesters.[70]

The repertoire of protest as displayed during the demonstration was constant through the years. Threats and curses were directed against Zionism and Zionists, in addition to Israel, the United States and their heads of state. The call to kill the Jews, which was heard in 1987, was not reported after that. From the beginning the authorities were confronted with the question to what extent the slogans and images used were to be tolerated, resulting in extensive monitoring by the police. Ahead of the demonstration, a process of negotiation emerged during which the organisers and the police established the boundaries of what was acceptable. In 1995, the police prevented protesters from burning the American or Israeli flag, and forbade the slogans 'death to Israel' and 'death to Rabin'.

In 1995, protesters carried posters and pamphlets which showed the Dome of the Rock in Jerusalem in the clutches of an octopus adorned with a Star of David. Ronny Naftaniel, director of CIDI figuring in several chapters of part II of this book, had pointed these out to the police. He found the image clearly antisemitic, as the octopus was the Nazi symbol for global Jewish power. The police found the image merely 'on the edge', because 'the Arabic text was not offensive'. For members of the organising Vahdet Mosque, the octopus was a symbol of Zionism; it was not their intention to hurt Jews and they would not want to be considered antisemites.[71]

Although the legal actions of CIDI did not lead to prosecution, they did lead to political interventions: in 1995 and 1996 questions were raised in parliament which explicitly mentioned the antisemitic character of slogans. Thereafter, the demonstration was followed with possibly even more scrutiny, which, according to some observers, was due to the stricter policy of the new mayor, Wim Deetman (b. 1945). In 1997, the police set a rule that written texts and verbal slogans should be in Dutch. As this demand turned out to be hard to enforce, the police also brought interpreters to

70 Udo Wolter, *Beispiel Al-Quds-Tag. Islamistische Netzwerke und Ideologien unter Migrantinnen und Migranten in Deutschland und Möglichkeiten zivilgesellschaftlicher Intervention* (Berlin, 2004); Klaus Holz and Michael Kiefer, 'Islamistischer Antisemitismus Phänomen und Forschungsstand.' In: Wolfram Stender, Guido Follert and Mihri Özdogan (eds.), *Konstellationen des Antisemitismus* (Wiesbaden: VS Verlag für Sozialwissenschaften, 2010), 109-137: 118.

71 Algemeen Nederlands Persbureau (ANP), 'Moslims protesteren tegen Israël", 24 February 1995; Anja Sligter, 'Joods centrum vermoedt kwade opzet achter octopussymbool tijdens moslimdemonstratie", *de Volkskrant*, 4 April 1995; R. Pasterkamp, 'Verbazing over beledigen joden", *Reformatorisch Dagblad*, 21 March 1995.

translate on the spot.[72] CIDI's director Ronny Naftaniel and another staff member were usually present to check slogans and images. Naftaniel had been closely following anti-Israel discourse and protest for antisemitic elements. CIDI had been involved in the discovery of 'Muslim antisemitism' from the beginning, by bringing instances and documents to the attention of authorities or media, and would continue to do so in the years to come.

Other images used fitted the anti-Israel protest tradition, in calling Israel, America and their heads of state Peres, Shamir, Clinton 'murderer', a conventional way of denouncing heads of state. However, the protesters went further reviving stereotypical associations of Jews with blood by also calling them 'child killer', 'vampire' and 'terrorist'.[73] A pamphlet distributed in 1993 spoke of the bloody boots and the blood-shedding of the Zionist Jews who were 'swarming the lands of Islam spewing blood'. A flyer in 1996 linked Israel and blood visually portraying the Dome of the Rock on top of a map of Israel dripping with blood, while one of the organisers declared that the Dutch government should take a stance against the Israeli police 'breaking children's bones and raping women'.[74]

In the Netherlands, associations of Israel with massacre and genocide had come into use after the 1982 massacre in the Palestinian refugee camps of Sabra and Shatila in Beirut, which were under surveillance by the Israeli military commanded by Ariel Sharon. Numerous civilians, mostly Palestinians and Lebanese Shias, were killed by a Lebanese Christian militia. The stereotype of Jewish bloodlust and cruelty which manifested itself as blood libels in medieval Europe survived in changing formations until the twenty-first century. In Turkey such stereotypes had increasingly been expressed in the form of child murder accusations since Camp David. But also in protests in the Netherlands imagery and vocabulary of bloodthirsty Israeli's were used.[75]

Although the demonstrations for Quds Day became a marginal phenomenon, the understanding of the Israeli-Palestinian conflict as an issue of

---

72   ANP, 'Moslims protesteren tegen Israel', 24 February 1995; Anja Sligter, 'Joods centrum vermoedt kwade opzet achter octopussymbool tijdens moslimdemonstratie', de Volkskrant, 4 April 1995; ANP, 'Demonstratie tegen Israël in Den Haag', 16 February 1996; ANP, 'Moslims demonstreren tegen Israelische regering', 7 February 1997; Jan Goossensen, 'Op het randje', Hervormd Nederland, 9 May 1998; ANP, 7 January 2000.

73   A list of slogans used for Quds Day in 1996 is held in the CIDI archive.

74   'Protest moslims tegen Jeruzalem', Het Parool, 17 February 1996.

75   On the association of Jews with blood see Christina von Braum, 'Blut und Butschande. Zur Bedeutung des Blutes in der antisemitischen Denkwelt.' In: Schoeps and Schlör, Antisemitismus. Vorurteile und mythen, 80-95. Debus, Die islamisch-rechtlichen Auskünfte der Millî Gazete, 21.

animosity between two religions was lasting. In 2000 this would manifest itself as a dominant frame for anti-Israel protest, both in the Netherlands and elsewhere. The division of the world between tyrannical oppressors and oppressed Muslims would often remain implicit. It did not need an explicitly political expression but sometimes found one, as in the case of radicals such as Mohammed B., who murdered Theo van Gogh, or the adherents of Milli Görüş.[76] For these Zionism posed a global menace to Islam and humanity at large, but the God of Islam was on the side of the oppressed and promised a just world in which the tyrants would be punished.

76 *See also* chapters 12 and 16.

Part III
The Holocaust-ed Jew in Native Dutch
Domains since the 1980s

11 'The Jew' in Football

To Kick Around or to Embrace

Evelien Gans

Following one of the leitmotifs in this volume, namely how and why the Shoah was turned against 'the Jew', one inevitably lands in the football domain too. 'The Jew' has always been an issue in Dutch football, also before the outbreak of the Second World War. But it did not end with the war. Since the 1980s, the antisemitic identification of Jews with gas and gas chambers, which started in Dutch society directly after 1945, has become common in the 'football world' – not only in the Netherlands.[1] It should be mentioned that there is an ongoing debate about whether one should use the term 'antisemitism' in this context, or rather rely on terms such as 'rivalry', 'vandalism' and 'provocation'. This chapter will analyse both the phenomenon itself and the debate. It will also address the role of the (alleged) Jewish image of the world famous Amsterdam football club Ajax and its supporters. What is their part in the game? And how did Jews themselves, in and outside of the stadium, react to on the one hand the supposed Jewish image of Ajax, and on the other anti-Jewish chants, slogans and banners? In this chapter we start with a football scandal in 1982 and will then kick the ball backwards through history right up to the present again.

Jewish football players are 'Jewed'

On 2 May 1982, FC Utrecht supporters, on their way to a match against Ajax, took at least two remarkable banners with them. One showed a capital J, a Star of David and a swastika and the word 'Death'. The other one was written in rhyme:

Hé Adolf	Hey Adolf
Hier lopen er nog elf	Here's another eleven
Als jij ze niet vergast	If *you* won't
Doen we het zelf[2]	*We* will gas them to heaven

---

1   *See* chapters 1 and 2.
2   *Het Parool,* 7 May 1982.

Initially, the police denied having spotted the banners. *Het Parool* then published a photo showing a police officer looking at the first banner. The commander, standing directly below the second banner in the Ajax stadium in Amsterdam, said that police non-intervention had been a 'matter of weighing up the benefits and risks'. It was clear that the police considered order maintenance more important than tackling antisemitism.[3]

Anti-Jewish expressions in and around Dutch football stadiums have always been the subject of heated debates. Were – and are – these expressions not, first of all, provocations, intended to tease and provoke football rivals, opponents – in this case Ajax, known as a 'Jewish club' – and hit their weak spot? Were *Ajacieden* (Ajax fans) such role models? Is this really a case of antisemitism? The year 1982 was, as mentioned above, certainly not the start of anti-Jewish expressions in Dutch football. They already occurred before the war. In fact, there is a clear continuity, albeit that the vocabulary, images, extent and focus have shifted in a remarkable way.

In pre-war Amsterdam there were five, relatively small, predominantly Jewish football clubs, including *'Wihelmina Vooruit'* [(Queen) Wilhelmina Ahead] and AED (*Allen Eén Doel*) [All One Goal]. Most clubs were directly related to the neighbourhoods where the players lived. AED players, for example, lived in the old Jewish quarter. Regularly there were serious incidents, involving anti-Jewish insults and fights, mostly during matches outside of the city, but occasionally also in Amsterdam. AED, the most outspoken Jewish club, had a reputation for being 'hot-headed' and was most frequently 'Jewed'. Players fought back against their opponents, wielding rakes and shovels, and against players who were NSB members and who would call them 'bloody Jews'. The club won the title three times.[4]

Ajax, which played at the top, did not have more Jewish players than other football clubs playing at the same level. So it was certainly not a Jewish club, although it already partly had that image before the war. That was mostly due to geographical factors. Amsterdam was in a sense a 'Jewish city' because during the interwar period almost 10% of the population was Jewish; most Jews lived in the old Jewish quarter near Waterlooplein and in East

3   *Ibid.*, 3 and 7 May 1982.
4   Evert de Vos, '"Verliest den moed toch niet". Joodse voetbalclubs in Amsterdam 1908-1948' (MA thesis, Universiteit Leiden, 2000), 21-22, 27-29, 59. *'Gejood'*: being called a Jew. AED won the title in the lower divisions of the football league, in the so-called *Onderbond* [minor league]. There were also Jewish football clubs in The Hague, Utrecht and in the province of Friesland: *ibid.*, 19-20. I thank E. de Vos. *See also* Franklin Foer, *How Soccer Explains the World. An Unlikely Theory of Globalization* (New York: Harper Perennial, 2004), 77. There were also Jewish football clubs in, for example, Berlin, Budapest, Prague, Innsbruck and Linz: Foer, *How Soccer Explains the World*, 68.

Amsterdam. The Ajax stadium was also located in East Amsterdam – albeit in a far corner – so the share of Jewish supporters was relatively high. In addition, the club welcomed Jews, including Jews from outside of Amsterdam. Another very important factor was that fans of visiting teams from outside of the city took the train to Weesperpoort Station, travelling eastwards from there. So they ended up in the heart of a Jewish neighbourhood full of Jewish vendors peddling their wares in the streets and inside the stadium. 'So they soon said: we are going to the Jews.'[5] Opponents teasingly called Ajax a 'club of noses'.[6] According to the British investigative journalist Simon Kuper (b. 1969), even before the war Ajax was sometimes 'Jewed'.[7] So the route to the Ajax stadium, right through neighbourhoods with buzzing Jewish street life, played a defining role in Ajax's pre-war image. Furthermore, according to Kuper, there was indeed a certain Jewish culture, due to, for example, the (Jewish) neighbourhoods, theatres and cafés where titles and club parties were celebrated.[8]

As we know, most of the Jews in the Netherlands were murdered during the war – as were most of the Jewish football players. The attitude of the *Nederlandse Koninklijke Voetbal Bond* [Royal Dutch Football Association] (KNVB) during the German occupation was cooperative; and the same applied to the board of Ajax. At any rate, the Dutch sport sector in general, including the football industry, did little to stand up for their Jewish players or members. In the autumn of 1941, Ajax, like all other football clubs (and many other associations and organisations which had nothing to do with sport), expelled their Jewish members. For this reason the names of those who had been murdered quite often did not feature on commemorative plaques put up at various clubs after the war.[9] Surviving Jewish sportsmen and board members often had to struggle after the war to reclaim their former positions – as was, more

5   Evert Vermeer, *Het Parool*, 23 October 1999, referred to in Daniel Benjamin Einhorn, 'Super-joden? Een onderzoek naar de herkomst en implicaties van het joodse zelfbeeld bij sommige Ajax-supporters 1900-2011' (MA thesis, Vrije Universiteit Amsterdam, August 2011), 31. Relevant is also the passage in Einhorn, 'Superjoden?', 8-34. I thank D.B. Einhorn.

6   Evert Vermeer, *95 jaar Ajax, 1900-1995* (Amsterdam: Luitingh-Sijthoff, 1995), 96.

7   Simon Kuper, 'Ajax, de joden, Nederland', *Hard Gras. Voetbaltijdschrift voor lezers* 22 (March 2000), 13.

8   Kuper, 'Ajax, de joden', 11-17. Kuper opposes the Ajax historian Evert Vermeer, who stated (*Het Parool*, 23 October 1999) that Ajax 'did not have a Jewish culture at all' before the war. *See also* Simon Kuper, *Ajax, the Dutch, the War. Football in Europe during the Second World War* (London: Orion, 2003), 18.

9   Kuper, 'Ajax, de joden', 70, 72, 89-90. Rob van Ginkel, *Rondom de stilte. Herdenkingscultuur in Nederland* (Amsterdam: Bert Bakker, 2011), 165.

generally, the case for Jews reclaiming their former houses or jobs.[10] Dutch antisemitism, which had seen a rise during the occupation, also manifested itself in football. As mentioned in the Introductory Essay, in 1947 the KNVB felt the need to organise a course for referees on how to tackle antisemitism on the football pitch. In October 1947, *Onze Revue* [Our Revue], Wilhelmina Vooruit's club magazine, wrote about 'growing antisemitism in football'.[11]

Three small old Jewish clubs picked up the ball again, positioning themselves even more prominently as 'Jewish' than their predecessors had done. They were also more keen to pick a fight in case of antisemitic incidents and were, hence, part of the group of Jews which literally did not tolerate anti-Jewish expressions, by going on the attack or reporting these incidents.[12] During the war, Ajax had kept playing, without Jewish players. After the war, Ajax's image *and* self-image were at least as complicated as before 1940, both in a positive and negative sense. In 1947, people started calling Ajax a 'Jewish club' again, like before, but this may also have been a force of habit, without intent to insult, according to a former supporter.[13] The comment in an Amsterdam café, however, just after the war, that the 'Noses' had returned on Amsterdam's pitches, sounded explicitly hostile.[14] For Jewish survivors, Ajax remained the most attractive football club, because of a certain tradition, as a meeting point – although there were, as far as we know, no Jewish Ajax players.

Jewish image, self-image and antisemitism

The absence of Jewish players ended in the late 1950s when two of them joined Ajax's first team, Sjaak (Sjakie) Swart (whose father had played for

10   Kuper, 'Ajax, de joden', e.g. 70-71. Informal Ajax networks did save Jewish players. De Vos, 'Verliest den moed toch niet', 13; Susan Smit, 'De bal bleef rollen. Ajax binnen voetballend Amsterdam tijdens de Tweede Wereldoorlog' (MA thesis, Nieuwe en Theoretische Geschiedenis, Universiteit van Amsterdam, 1997): www.ethesis.net/ajax/ajax.htm. André Swijtink, *In de pas. Sport en lichamelijke opvoeding in Nederland tijdens de Tweede Wereldoorlog* (Haarlem: De Vrieseborch, 1992); for the postwar situation: 328*ff*, and De Vos, 'Verliest den moed toch niet', 51-55, 71. *See also* the Introductory Essay.
11   De Vos, 'Verliest den moed toch niet', 54, 60, 70-71. *See also* chapter 1.
12   *Ibid.*, 47-50, 54-55. *See* chapter 5.
13   Piet Walraven in Smit, 'De bal bleef rollen', Interview with P. Walraven, March 1997.
14   Lecture by W.L. Brugsma on the occasion of the presentation of the book *Daar praat je niet over. Kinderen van foute ouders en de hulpverlening*, Nederlands Instituut voor Zorg en Welzijn, Utrecht, 2 June 1993 (unpublished). I thank Margriet-Marie Govaart. The witness in question, W.L. Brugsma, was a prominent journalist, a former member of the resistance and a survivor of concentration camp Dachau.

AED before the war) in 1956 and Bennie Muller in 1958. They were both born two years before the war and many of their family members had been murdered. In 1959, Salo Muller joined the club as masseur (as a small boy he had survived the war at eight hiding addresses; his parents were gassed; after the war he was sent by the rowing club Amstel to the 'Jewish' club Poseidon). Other important Jewish 'characters' were property and hotel developer Maup Caransa, born in the old Jewish quarter, and Leo Horn, former referee and resistance fighter, now turned textile magnate. They became funders and service providers of the club. The starting capital, however, was raised by the Van der Meijden brothers, two non-Jewish collaborators who built bunkers during the war and now continued to co-fund Ajax. In 1964 the Jewish Jaap van Praag became chairman of Ajax's board.[15] War-related issues were always delicate and contradictory. If necessary, Van Praag would start a fight, when confronted with antisemitic comments, but he was friends with the Van der Meijden brothers – something Salo Muller couldn't bear. At first the former bunker builders were refused Ajax membership due to their war past. But later on Van Praag offered them a membership. Jaap van Praag was succeeded by his son Michael who, in turn, was succeeded by Uri Coronel, who was chairman from 2008 to 2011. They were all Jews, or of Jewish descent.[16]

Muller and Swart became prominent players. Kuper describes how something like a Jewish sub-culture started to develop among both Jewish and non-Jewish Ajax players and people in their direct environment: Muller used to bring Amsterdam Jewish *ossenworst* to matches, non-Jewish players were looking forward to his 'Yiddish sausage', everyone was telling Jewish jokes, also about Jews and goyim. Subtle allusions, some themes remained taboo, though. Salo Muller set up a music band with several other Ajax players; as a matter of principle, he didn't work on Yom Kippur, Day of Atonement. The later world-famous non-Jewish Ajax player Johan Cruijff had quite a few Jewish in-laws. Wim Suurbier and Ton Pronk both married a Jewish woman.[17]

15   Kuper, 'Ajax, de joden', 100-110. According to the Jewish law, Sjaak Swart and Michael van Praag are not Jewish because they have a Jewish father, not a Jewish mother. Nevertheless, Swart's first name in his passport was Jesaia: *ibid.*, 111. Bennie Muller had a Jewish mother. *See also* Kuper, *Ajax, the Dutch, the War*, 178-192.

16   Michael van Praag in Kuper, *Ajax, the Dutch, the War*, 114; For Uri Coronel, see *Het Parool*, 18 April 2008. About Jaap van Praag, *see* Menno de Galan, *De trots van de wereld. Michels, Cruijff en het Gouden Ajax van 1964-1974* (Amsterdam: Arbeiderspers, 2006), 72-77, and Marga van Praag and Ad van Liempt, *Jaap & Max. Het verhaal van de broers Van Praag* (Amsterdam: Nijgh & Van Ditmar, 2011), 178. I thank Willem Wagenaar.

17   Bram de Graaf, *Voetbalvrouwen. De glorietijd van het Nederlandse voetbal 1970-1978* (Amsterdam: Ambo, 2008) (Maja Verkaart with Suurbier). *See also*: http://nl.wikipedia.org/wiki/Anton_Pronk. (consulted 29 April 2014). 'Sjaak Swart received antisemitic letters. Luckily,

So there was a certain Jewish sub-culture, a number of Jewish networks – but certainly not a Jewish majority: not a Jewish club. There was also antisemitism. Both Sjakie Swart and Bennie Muller were 'Jewed'. Salo Muller was sometimes called a *'pleurisjood'* [pleuritis Jew] – at FC Den Haag (from 1996: ADO), and by a supporter of Groningen club GVAV. When he went to see the club's medic John Rolink with a serious stomach ache, the diagnosis was: 'You and your weak Yiddish stomach .... Like you all have, you Jews.' It turned out he had acute appendicitis.[18]

Ajax starts to make a name for itself and during the 1960s becomes probably the best-paying Dutch football club.[19] The first major incident which reaches the press takes place in January 1965. Goalkeeper Jan Jongbloed, of local rival DWS, calls Bennie Muller 'dirty pleuritis Jew', Muller wants to beat him up, but restrains himself. The players are pulled apart. That is, at least, the most credible version of the incident. Ajax's board lodges a complaint with the KNVB; Chairman Jaap van Praag expresses his hope that this initiative will result in a ban on 'these kinds and, of course, also other kinds of insults' on the football pitch. Jongbloed is handed a two-game ban.[20]

In 1965 the influential Dutch sports journalist Nico Scheepmaker writes an article about the issue in *Vrij Nederland* with the telling title 'Antisemitic football' in which he explains that it is a structural problem. In an earlier match, one of Jongbloed's teammates had insulted Muller in a similar way; Muller and Swart are often targeted. Jewish football players at other clubs, such as Otto Polak, have the same experience. When, after one such incriminating game, the referee, whilst enjoying a soda, refuses to take the issue further, Polak angrily overturns the referee's table, including his soda.[21] Scheepmaker readily admits that name-calling and intimidation are commonplace and that Muller wasn't a goody-goody himself. But there is a difference between calling someone names and calling them 'dirty rotten Jew', says Muller. Just as Ajax's Surinamese players are often verbally abused with comments like 'Hey blacky, go back to your own country'. That

they're anonymous', *NIW*, 6 June 1969. Ajax player (and later coach) Frank de Boer married a Jewish woman. '*Ossenworst*' is a typical Amsterdam sausage, made from raw beef and rooted in the Jewish kitchen.

18   Kuper, 'Ajax, de joden', 112, 116. Conversation with Salo Muller, Remco Ensel, 22 January 2015, Holocaust Memorial Day, Vrije Universiteit, Amsterdam.

19   Kuper, *Ajax, the Dutch*, 181-182.

20   Kuper, 'Ajax, de joden', 112. Jongbloed said that Muller gave him a punch and upon which he shouted '*krijg de pleuris*'. See also *De Telegraaf*, 19 January 1965: NIOD, KB 307B.

21   Nico Scheepmaker, 'Antisemitisch voetballen', *Vrij Nederland*, 23 January 1965. Jongbloed's incriminating teammate was, allegedly, DWS player Arie de Oude.

also happens to Surinamese players elsewhere, according to Scheepmaker. These things take place outside of the referee's earshot and are part of a more general psychological warfare of teasing and nagging. Scheepmaker hopes that from now on referees will act more strictly. 'Despite all excesses, antisemitism, thank God, is still taken seriously in the Netherlands.'[22]

But antisemitism, and racism, on and around the pitch, in the dressing rooms and among supporters, does persist. A year later, the social democratic broadcaster VARA aired a radio programme in which listeners heard a Rotterdam Feyenoord supporter shouting antisemitic insults in a bar before his club's match against Ajax.[23] So it is even more ironic that in 1970 an Egyptian newspaper writing about Feyenoord's successes does not mention the family name of the team's captain, Rinus Israël, in the photo caption.[24] In that same year – three years after the Six-Day War – the Israeli-Palestinian conflict also enters Dutch football. This time, the protest against the Israeli occupation policy focuses on Ajax. The club receives several threat letters signed by El Fatah Europe. One letter threatens with attacks on the club's building and stadium: 'This Jewish, imperialist sports complex will be destroyed by us sooner or later.' Another letter, addressed to Sjaak Swart, reads: 'They forgot to gas you and your parents ....'[25]

In 1969, Sjaak Swart had reported to the *Nieuw Israëlietisch Weekblad* (NIW) about the antisemitic letters which he, Bennie Muller and Jaap van Praag were receiving. Muller could fill an archive with them. Luckily the letters are anonymous. 'I would rip their heads off', said Swart. He added that on the pitch he is mainly called 'dirty rotten Jew' by opponents of clubs which risk relegation. Swart called it 'envy'. If he was right, it was a typical case of goyish envy. A trainee police inspector who wrote the thesis *Antisemitisme langs de lijn* [Antisemitism on and off the pitch] (1985) agreed with him: the players in question would, possibly, have been able to affect the course of the game to their club's advantage.[26] But the referee 'never hears anything', according to Swart. He himself would not fight, but his father had thrown a few punches on the ADO stands when someone shouted: 'Those Jews should

22   *Ibid.*
23   *Het Parool*, 14 January 1966; *Vrij Nederland*, 15 January 1966.
24   *NIW*, 13 November 1970.
25   Jurryt van de Vooren, 'Anti-joodse dreigbrieven bij Ajax. Heftige dreigementen in 1970', 10 March 2009: www.npogeschiedenis.nl/nieuws/2009/maart/Anti-joodse-dreigbrieven-bij-Ajax.html, Jurryt van de Vooren, 'Antisemitische dreigbrieven voor Ajax', 22 March 2011: www.sportgeschiedenis. nl/2011/03/22/antisemitische-dreigbrieven-voor-ajax.aspx (both consulted 27 February 2015).
26   P.M.W. Melsen, 'Antisemitisme langs de lijn' (Thesis for the Police Academy, Apeldoorn, 1985), 27. I thank Ralph Pluim.

be kicked out.' When asked, Swart replied that he was not very involved in Jewry, but that almost all his friends were Jewish and that he thought Israel was a great country. One of the letters he received was not anonymous, but signed by 'that Nazi' Paul van Tienen. 'If you could, you would personally kill those guys.' Swart had taken this letter to Loe de Jong, the historian and director of the *Rijksinstituut voor Oorlogsdocumentatie* [State Institute for War Documentation (RIOD)].[27] Van Tienen was, indeed, a former Dutch Nazi and SS soldier, who having absconded remained politically active after the war. He was also the first public Holocaust denier in the Netherlands.[28]

The Shoah enters the stadium once and for all

Before and after the Second World War, 'the Jew' had been an issue in Dutch football. In the early 1980s this took a new turn when the Shoah and the Middle East Conflict entered the stadium.

Illustration 17   Photo of a Feyenoord football fan

Michael Kooren / Hollandse Hoogte

'110% Anti-Nose'. A Feyenoord (Rotterdam) fan shows his T-shirt in the Feyenoord-Ajax match, 16 March 2003.

27 'Sjaak Swart kreeg antisemitische brieven', *NIW*, 6 June 1969. Unfortunately, the letter has been lost. For Loe de Jong and the RIOD, *see* chapters 2 and 3.
28 *See* chapters 4 and 5.

Illustration 18   Photo of a Feyenoord football fan

Arie Kievit / Hollandse Hoogte

'King of the Gas station'. A Feyenoord Rotterdam fan shows his '110% anti-Ajax' T-shirt in the UEFA Cup final against Borussia Dortmund, 8 May 2005. Note the link between 'the Jew' (Ajax) and gas.

Such a fusion of football antisemitism and extremist right-wing or neo-Nazi politics was rare in this period. But in the early 1980s, so-called football vandalism, including its antisemitic component, took a new turn. The banners mentioned at the start of this chapter illustrate this. Hooliganism, large-scale violence between supporters of rival clubs, became a well-known phenomenon, at an international level. In the case of Ajax, however, the shape and content went well beyond the verbal abuse of individual Jewish players ('dirty rotten Jew') and Ajax as a collective ('those Jews/that Jewish club'). Also in football, the Shoah was now turned against (alleged) Jews – in particular football players but also Ajax and their supporters. And once again, 'gas' and 'gas chamber' played a central role. 'Dissing' became 'hissing'.

The 1982 incident, in which Hitler was asked to gas 'those eleven [Ajax players]', had a short but powerful history. In December 1980, Feyenoord

Illustration 19   Photo of a stand with Ajax fans

Michael Kooren / Hollandse Hoogte

Fans of Ajax Amsterdam wave the flag of Israel in the Ajax-Feyenoord match,
3 March 2002.

supporters sang: 'I recently saw Ajax standing in front of the gas chambers.'[29] During the Ajax-FC Utrecht match in April 1981, antisemitic slogans were shouted and there was a banner on display which read 'Ajax Jews stink'. That same month saw the debut of the banner 'Death to all Jews' at the match of Ajax vs. the Rotterdam club Sparta. A Feyenoord slogan read: 'Jews and dogs not allowed in De Kuip stadium'.[30] Hissing sounds – escaping gas – could first be heard around this time. In January 1981 an anonymous letter was sent from Rotterdam to Ajax, which deserves to be printed in full:

Adolf Hitler / Hij is weer herboren / onze hitler / Nu komt gauw weer / de gaskamer weer open / voor jullie rot / JODEN in Amsterdam / en omstreek. vooral / de AJAX tuig / leve onze grote / Vriend Hitler / Hoera Hoera (gevolgd door Davidster, hakenkruis en SS-teken) / leven duitsland 1940-1945 GAS, GAS, GAS, GAS /leve de grote / GAS / KAMERS / IN. ONS. LIEVE / DUITSLAND / EN GROTE. / BRANDOVENS / Zieg Heil / Hiep Hoera / Hi[l]tler[31]

Adolf Hitler / He is born again / our hitler / Now soon comes back / the gas chamber open again / for you rotten / JEWS in Amsterdam / and surroundings. especially / the AJAX scum / long live our big / Friend Hitler / Hooray Hooray (followed by Star of David, swastika and SS symbol) / long live germany 1940-1945
GAS, GAS, GAS, GAS /long live the great / GAS / CHAMBERS / IN. OUR. BELOVED / GERMANY / AND BIG. / FURNACES / Zieg Heil / Hip Hooray / Hi[l]tler

This was certainly no Standard Dutch but the message was clear. Should such letters, slogans and banners be taken seriously? STIBA, the Foundation against Antisemitism mentioned in previous chapters, thought they should, and started its first campaign against antisemitism and racism in football in December 1980.[32] Six months earlier, the *Amsterdams Initiatief Tegen Fascisme, Racisme en Antisemitisme* [Amsterdam Initiative Against

29   R.A. Pieloor, B. van de Meer and M. Bakker, *F-side is niet makkelijk! Over vriendschap, geweld, humor, Amsterdam en Ajax* (Utrecht: Het Spectrum, 2002), 95, referred to in Einhorn, 'Superjoden?', 61.

30   Melsen, 'Antisemitisme langs de lijn', 27; *Het Parool, See also* Ralph Pluim, '1981: een keerpunt in het antisemitisme in Nederland?', June 2011 (unpublished paper; personal archive Evelien Gans). Feyenoord's stadium is called 'De Kuip'.

31   Januari 1981, CIDI Archive.

32   Kuper, 'Ajax, de joden', 138; *Het Vrije Volk,* 27 December 1980. For STIBA *see also* chapters 7, 8 and 9.

Fascism, Racism and Antisemitism] had already sent a letter to Ajax's board. Among other things, it reported the jingle *'Het is een jood, het is een miet, het is een Ajacied'* [It's a Jew, it's a sissy, it's an Ajax fan]. It rhymes nicely in Dutch and homophobia was popular. The fact that – as in the past and as elsewhere, whether or not deliberately – Jewry and homosexuality ('perversion', 'decadence') were linked together and forged into the stereotype of the perverse Jew (or: Ajax supporter), seems somewhat farfetched in this case.[33] Yet both are conceived as the Other – as 'queer'. The organisation urged Ajax to prevent scenes like those seen in English stadiums involving the British far-right 'National Front'.[34]

But it was only a year later, in May 1982, following the photos published in *Het Parool,* that the government and the judiciary were no longer able to pass on the hot potato. Up until then there had only been parliamentary questions,[35] and the average response of most football clubs had been that their supporters 'were too stupid to understand what they were saying'.[36] The youths in question took a different view. In May 1982, *Het Parool* interviewed several FC Utrecht supporters. It turned out that they were angry at the press and the Anne Frank House for ruining the atmosphere by calling them fascists or racists. Which they weren't. For them, Ajax had simply always been a 'Jews' club', just as they were considered a 'peasants' club' by Ajax. In 1978 they had started to produce 'Jew banners'. It was understandable that older people, who had experienced the war, got angry. But they were not 'Jew haters'. And the press had better keep quiet. Now what will happen is that every club will start making Jew banners, not because they have anything against Jews, 'but because of the publicity they will get'.[37]

A few months earlier, in late 1981, *Vrij Nederland* journalist Leonard Ornstein (b. 1955) had been embedded in various FC Utrecht supporter groups, including a group of around 28 hardcore fans. Most were aged between 18 and 24. A quarter of them were unemployed; some worked as roofers, welders, clerks, plumbers or bakers; there were also some pupils, a few (former) students and a community worker.[38] In his comprehensive

---

33   For pornographic antisemitism *see* chapter 12.

34   *Het Amsterdams Initiatief tegen Fascisme, Racisme en Antisemitisme* to the Board of Ajax, Amsterdam, 26 June 1981, CIDI Archive.

35   *See, e.g., Trouw,* 10 April 1981. See also *Het Vrije Volk,* 9 June 1981; *Het Parool,* 17 and 23 June 1981.

36   Kuper, 'Ajax, de joden', 138.

37   *Het Parool,* 7 May 1982.

38   Leonard Ornstein, 'De FC Bunnikzijde. "Overal waar we komen, maken we er een zooitje van"', *Vrij Nederland,* 9 January 1982 (separate insert), 2-22.

report Ornstein also lets the youths who produced the 'Ajax Jews stink' banner have their say. Why had they done so? And, again, the answers he got are the same as today's, 35 years on: an inconsistent mix of football rivalry, the image of Amsterdam as a 'Jewish city' and antisemitic stereotypes.

'Amsterdam is a Jewish city. Ajax, to us is basically a Jew club.' They hated Ajax even more than they hated Feyenoord. The hatred is against Ajax, not against Jews. There were rich Jews behind the scenes at Ajax. Where has the money gone after the very profitable sale of Cruijff and Neeskens? Do they know what Jews are, Ornstein asks. People with their own religion – who were already persecuted in the year 500, did not have access to education and therefore ended up working in trade. On those points Jews are 'other people' – that's it. So there is some fragmented knowledge. This is also apparent on another occasion. One year earlier they had made a banner that read *'Für Juden verboten'* [German for: Forbidden for Jews]. In the train on the way to a game they had sung: 'We are on a Jew hunt'. And what about the murder of six million Jews then? There were mixed responses. At first jolly ('Dik always says: there is a good side to that, too'); Dik himself said he had nothing against Jews, but hasn't any personal experience. In hindsight, most of them didn't 't really like 'those antisemitic expressions', nor being called antisemitic. The conversation then moved on to the topic of foreigners, particularly Turks and Moroccans. Apart from one or two, they all thought those are dirty and stupid, and that they steal jobs from the Dutch. And regarding those 'blacks': they were are all on the dole and driving around in Mercedes cars. There was an easy solution for lack of housing and unemployment: kick all the foreigners out of the country, said Sybrand. Community worker Michiel, also FC Utrecht supporter, has adapted himself, otherwise he couldn't continue the life he lives. He does not believe that 'the boys' vote for the far-right party leader Glimmerveen, although they say they do.[39]

So it is not that strange that the aforementioned trainee police inspector questions that latter statement. In his thesis, which is based on a wide range of sources, he records how STIBA chairman Richard Stein explains the – pre- and postwar – Jewish image of both Ajax (the departure of the Muller brothers and Swart, in the 1970s, did not change this) and Amsterdam: it is here that half of the Dutch Jews live and where there is still 'real Jewish life', this is where various Jewish institutions are based, and where the

---

39 Ornstein. 'De FC Bunnikzijde', 21-22. The names of the interviewees are not their real names. For Glimmerveeen, *see* chapters 4 and 8.

mayor is Jewish. So the 'anti-Ajax supporters' struck a nerve.[40] Unlike other
researchers of football vandalism, Melsen questions the – according to
him – too easy assumption that the anti-Jewish slogans fall into the same
category of 'labelling' as calling FC Utrecht supporters 'peasants', or that we
should show restraint, and that not the police but society itself should find
a solution for the conflict. He is more inclined to endorse the conclusion of
De rechterkant van Nederland [The Right Wing of the Netherlands] (1983).
This study found that, although those singing antisemitic slogans primarily
do so to shock the opponent, they are definitely not free from antisemitic
sentiments. They also form a fertile feeding ground for 'real' antisemitism.
Among other things, Melsen points to the slogan

Auschwitz, Auschwitz	Auschwitz, Auschwitz
was een Jodenkamp	was a Jew's camp,
al die Joden aan de kant,	all those Jews out of our way
rettetrettetet	ratatat

The fact that the supporters also had prejudices against other minorities,
made them susceptible to the approaches of fascist and racist organisations
looking for new recruits among their ranks.[41]

The reasons behind the 1982 turn

In the 1980s the Dutch government and community initiatives became
more alert to anything that reeked of 'racism'. It is not for nothing that the
Amsterdam Initiative Against Fascism, Racism and Antisemitism pointed
its finger at England, the birthplace of hooliganism. One of the targets *and*
participants of hooliganism was the London club Tottenham Hotspur: the
Spurs. Just like Ajax, they were not a Jewish club, but they did have a Jewish
image. There were many Hassidic Jews in the area where the club is based
and a significant number of their supporters were Jewish. And they were
as violent as any other English football club. In 1974 the Spurs performed
an important rite of initiation in the Netherlands when their supporters

40   Richard Stein quoted in Melsen, *'Antisemitisme aan de lijn'*, 32. For Richard Stein *see, e.g.,*
chapter 7 and 8.
41   *Ibid.,* 30-32; 49-50; 76. Other researchers mentioned are H.H. van der Brug and M. Marseille,
who published about football vandalism and the police psychologist Frans Denkers: *Trouw,*
11 May 1982.

unleashed a proper battle in Rotterdam against their Feyenoord opponents (200 injured).[42] Since the late 1970s, the National Front had been actively recruiting members in British stadiums and distributing Nazi literature. There were racist chants against black players and antisemitic chants against the Spurs: 'Hitler's gonna gas them again ....'[43] A close relationship developed between *Ajacieden* and Spurs, who call themselves 'Yids' and 'Yiddo![44]

In the Netherlands, the May 1982 antisemitic slogans, and the wave of strong criticism in the press of the phenomenon itself and the lack of strong action by the riot police (ME), resulted in those carrying banners being prosecuted. Melsen notes that in the course of the 1980s police policy became stricter. Guilty verdicts often involved an educational or moral penalty, such as being 'sentenced' to visit the former transit camp Westerbork and the Anne Frank House.[45] Wim Polak, mayor of Amsterdam and, as such, head of police, ordered an investigation into the lack of police intervention, but reached the conclusion that measures against the ME were not required.[46] Six months later a Feyenoord supporter was sentenced to donate money to the Second World War foundation *Stichting 1940-1945* after shouting antisemitic slogans.[47]

Why were the years 1980-1982 a tipping point in the sense that the Shoah was widely used against an (allegedly) Jewish club and its supporters? There

---

42   Foer, *How Soccer Explains the World*, 79; Ramón Spaaij, *Understanding Football Hooliganism. A Comparison of Six Western European Football Clubs* (Amsterdam: Amsterdam University Press, 2006), 192-193.

43   Spaaij, *Understanding Football Hooliganism*, 244; Peter Brusse, 'Tweemaal 45 minuten "Sieg Heil, Sieg Heil"', *de Volkskrant*, 21 March 1981, referred to in Pluim, '1981', 19. About antisemitic actions against the Spurs, also in Lyon: *de Volkskrant*, 22 February 2013.

44   For the diverse and contradictory use of the term 'Yids', in divergent football contexts, *see* Emma Poulton and Oliver Durell, 'Uses and meanings of "Yid" in English football fandom: A case study of Tottenham Hotspur Football Club', *International Review for the Sociology of Sport* (2014), 1-20; published online, 16 October 2014: http://irs.sagepub.com/content/early/2014/10/15/1012690214554844 (consulted 11 June 2015). I thank Emma Poulton; Gabriele Marcotti, 'Star of David, For Entertainment Only', *The Wall Street Journal*, 11 November 2012: www.wsj.com/articles/SB10001424127887324439804578112891365453074; see also chat on Spurs website, 'Why are Spurs fans called yids?', 20 March 2012: www.shelfsidespurs.com/forum/threads/why-are-spurs-fans-called-yids.27184/ (consulted 1 February 2015); On Ajax and the Spurs: Pluim, '1981', 21.

45   Melsen, 'Antisemitisme langs de lijn', 60-62; Rob Witte, *'Al eeuwenlang een gastvrij volk': Racistisch geweld en overheidsreacties in Nederland (1950-2009)* (Amsterdam: Aksant, 2010), 80-81.

46   *NRC Handelsblad*, 4 May 1982; *Het Parool*, 4 and 14 May 1982; *Algemeen Dagblad*, 15 May 1982.

47   *NRC Handelsblad* and *Vrije Volk*, 16 December 1982. The Foundation '40-'45 is an institute providing services to resistance fighters, victims of persecution and civilian war victims from the years 1940-1945.

are three obvious reasons. First, the rise of the (international) phenomenon of hooliganism: supporters who felt they had to protect the honour of their club at all costs and to mentally and physically hit their rivals as hard as they could. Ajax's hardcore fans – and their followers – are, for their part, anything but peaceful. They fight as hard as their rivals, calling them 'peasants' or telling Feyenoord fans that they will bomb Rotterdam (Rotterdam was heavily bombed by the Nazis in May 1940).[48] An unprecedented mass fight between Feyenoord and Ajax hooligans in 1997 left one dead.[49]

Second, in the Netherlands, and elsewhere, attention for the murder of the Jews slowly moved towards the centre of public memory in the form of press attention, remembrances of the dead, the erection of monuments, historiography about the Second World War and lessons at school. That led to some resentment and irritation. The Holocaust was associated with the elite and that demanded rebellion: 'the hooligans became uncooperative'.[50]

Finally, things were anything but calm in the Middle East. In June 1982, Israel invaded Lebanon and in September of that year, the massacre in Sabra and Shatila took place. Feyenoord supporters started carrying Palestinian flags; and Ajacieden flags of Israel – with the Star of David. Previous chapters have also referred to the crucial year of 1982; the Dutch government and public opinion reacted negatively to Israel's role in Lebanon. In Israel there were mass demonstrations against government policies and against Defence Minister Ariel Sharon in particular. A combination of the latter two factors seems to have led to aversion to 'the Jew' both as victim and as perpetrator – 'posing' as a victim: a connection that will extend far beyond football.[51]

The political element introduced into the stadiums by the clubs' respective flags, was (and is) largely superficial. The same is true for the Jewish identity which Ajax supporters seem to embrace. In response to anti-Jewish slogans, supporters have adopted the epithets 'Jews' and 'Super Jews' as badges of honour. This is particularly the case among hardcore fans (F-side and, from 2001 onwards, Section 410), but also among other supporters. Earlier on, Spurs supporters had done the same. After being called 'Yiddo!'

48 Evelien Gans, 'Over gaskamers, joodse nazi's en neuzen', 142; Evelien Gans, 'On gas chambers, Jewish Nazis and Noses.' In: Peter Rodrigues and Jaap van Donselaar, (eds.), *Racism and Extremism Monitor. Ninth Report* (Amsterdam: Anne Frank Stichting, Universiteit Leiden, 2010), 74-87: 81: www.annefrank.org/ImageVaultFiles/id_12537/cf_21/Monitor9UK.PDF.
49 *NRC Handelsblad*, 24 March 1997. The victim was Carlo Picornie, an old guard Ajax hooligan.
50 Kuper, 'Ajax, de joden', 139.
51 Evelien Gans, 'It is antisemitic – no, it isn't. The public debate on antisemitism and the Holocaust in the Netherlands.' Paper presented at the IIBSA symposium 'Perceptions of the Holocaust and Contemporary Antisemitism', Berlin, 31 May 2011. *See* chapter 1.

they started calling themselves 'Yids' and 'Yiddo!'.[52] This way, both sides got involved in a curious dance around a presumed Jewish self-image and image – between alleged philosemitism and antisemitism. But *was* this really alleged antisemitism? And *was* this philosemitism?

The Gordian knot of antisemitism and an artificial Jewish self-image

This chapter will conclude with an attempt to answer these questions, including, as a final chord, the clash between ADO and Ajax in 2011. In the meantime, anti-Jewish slogans remained a weekly recurring practice. Supporters shouting these slogans were sometimes given conditional fines or ordered to write an essay about their visit to the Anne Frank House or Westerbork.[53] In 1986, FC Den Haag (now ADO) supporters walked around in Amsterdam South (with a relatively large Jewish community) shouting slogans like *'Wij gaan op jodenjacht'* [We're on a Jew hunt] en *'Joden, wij komen'* [Jews, we are coming for you]. Mayor Polak's successor, Ed van Thijn (b. 1934), the third Jewish mayor in line since 1967, considered if FC Den Haag supporters could be banned from Amsterdam.[54] The chairman of the club refused to apologise, but did ask the hardcore fans of his club to stop singing antisemitic songs. He then played down this request by stating that the songs were a result 'of the fact that Ajax clearly presents itself as a Jewish club'. Furthermore, Van Thijn's response had been 'excessively emotional'.[55] A typical case of *blaming the victim*, accompanied by the stereotype of the hypersensitive, if not hysterical, Jew.

52   John Efron, 'When is a Yid not a Jew? The strange case of supporter identity at Tottenham Hotspur.' In: Michael Brenner and Gideon Reuveni (eds.), *Emancipation Through Muscles. Jews and Sports in Europe*, (Lincoln: University of Nebraska Press, 2006), 242-244; Poulton and Durell, 'Uses and meanings of "Yid".

53   *NIW*, 24 June 1983; *de Volkskrant* and *NRC Handelsblad*, 30 June 1983.

54   A. Kosto, 'Het voornemen van Van Thijn', *Elseviers Magazine*, 13 August 1986; *NRC Handelsblad*, 5 September 1986. The first Jewish mayor of Amsterdam was Yvo Samkalden (1967-1977), followed by Wim Polak (1977-1983), then by Ed van Thijn (1983-1994) and thereafter by Job Cohen (2001-2010). In-between Van Thijn and Cohen the non-Jewish mayor, Schelto Patijn (1994-2001) was in function. For a brief comment on the phenomenon of Jewish mayors in postwar Amsterdam: Gans, *Gojse nijd & joods narcisme,* 76. Job Cohen was, in 2010, succeeded by (the non-Jewish) Eberhard van der Laan.

55   Kuper, 'Ajax, de joden', 139-140. For the stereotype of 'the nervous Jew', *see also*: Christina von Braun, 'Der sinnliche und der übersinnliche Jude.' In Sander L. Gilman, Robert Jütte, Gabriele Kohlbauer-Fritz (eds.), *'Der Schejne Jid'. Das Bild des 'jüdischen Körpers'in Mythos und Ritual* (Wien: Picus Verlag, 1998) 97-108: 104.

The all-round Jewish sports journalist Frits Barend (b. 1947), a watchdog of antisemitism and racism on the pitch, in the written press, on the radio and on TV, was told that he was oversensitive or even 'paranoid'.[56] On some occasions, Barend had been sometimes overalert and had been forced to apologise.[57] On the part of his antagonists, he himself was 'watched' as well. When PSV (Eindhoven) won the top league title in 1988, a group of PSV supporters raised their right hands upwards chanting 'He is a cancer Jew' to Barend and his non-Jewish colleague Henk van Dorp.[58] The same thing happened before a Feyenoord-Ajax match, when they were seated in the press section of the Feyenoord stadium. During the cup final between Ajax and FC Den Haag, in June 1987, Barend and Van Dorp recorded antisemitic songs and jungle sounds.[59] During another match against Ajax, FC Den Haag put up a banner which read *'Groet aan* [Greetings to] *Rost van Ton-ningen'* – which was probably not intended as an ode to the most virulent antisemitic Dutch National Socialist within the NSB (Meinoud), but rather as one to his 'Black Widow' (Florrie), figurehead of the far right.[60]

The argument of those saying that the incriminating supporters themselves are also being verbally abused, and that they don't target 'real' Jews, evaporated when FC Den Haag supporters made violent threats in front of houses with a menorah behind the window. The club was subsequently temporarily banned from Amsterdam.[61] Feyenoord then took over and a number of its supporters were fined in 1988 after shouting and chalking 'Ed van Thijn, Jewish swine' and 'death to the Jews' on walls.[62] Hissing sounds became a regular feature; the same goes for the 'political' slogan 'Hamas, Hamas, all Jews to the gas'. Such incidents resulted in tougher policies. In 2002, Mayor Van Thijn's successor, Job Cohen, would send all FC Utrecht

56 *de Volkskrant,* 7 October 2000. *See, e.g.,* the website www.antisemitisme.nu (R. Ensel, E. Gans., I. Gusc, A. Stremmelaar) www.antisemitisme.nu/wij-gaan-op-jodenjacht-analyse en www.antisemitisme.nu/wij-gaan-op-jodenjacht-reacties. For publications by Frits Barend, see *Ajax' roemruchte Europacup* (Amsterdam: Born, 1971); *Ajax' 2ᵉ roemruchte Europacup* (Amsterdam: Born, 1972); (with Henk van Dorp) *2 x 45 minuten: [interviews met Johan Cruijff ... et al.* (Baarn: Thomas Rap, 1978); with Manon Colson (eds.), *De Nederlandse sportliteratuur in 80 en enige verhalen* (Amsterdam: Prometheus, 2013)

57 *See, e.g., de Volkskrant,* 3 September 2005.

58 Email Frits Barend to Evelien Gans, 28 February 2014.

59 Email Frits Barend to Evelien Gans, 1 March 2015. Bananas were also thrown towards the goal of the black goalkeeper Stanley Menzo.

60 *See e.g.,* the TV programme *Andere Tijden,* 18 November 2013. I thank Willem Wagenaar. *See also* chapters 4 and 8.

61 Kuper, 'Ajax, de joden', 140.

62 'Voetbalsupporters bestraft voor beledigen joden', *NIW,* 1 January 1988.

supporters back following antisemitic slogans in the train to Amsterdam.[63] In 2009, Job Cohen and his colleague in Rotterdam, Ahmed Aboutaleb (b. 1961), both prominent members of the Labour Party (PvdA), decided to ban visiting supporters for a five-year period during Ajax-Feyenoord matches. The same decision had already been taken in 2006 for Ajax-ADO matches.[64]

In relation to a case in 2009 against a supporter from The Hague who was arrested for chanting 'Hamas, Hamas, all Jews to the gas', the Supreme Court brought in a remarkable verdict. The defendant's lawyer had stated that the slogan concerned was used 'frequently, particularly in football and is part of our society's culture'. Additional arguments were that the suspect did not have the intention to offend anyone, and that the chant had not been aimed at a specific person. The judges rejected the defence on all counts. The fact that the slogan was frequently used did not mean that it was part of the 'culture of our society'. The efforts made by 'football authorities' to stamp out these and similar slogans in stadiums pointed to the contrary. The slogans had been shouted in the public domain and had caused feelings of humiliation or shock. That did not require 'people of Jewish descent' actually being present in the crowd. The court therefore ruled that it had twice been proven that the suspect had deliberately insulted 'Jews because of their race, religion or beliefs'.[65]

The verdict also requires some ironical, or rather cynical, comment. Did the lawyer not have a point when he claimed that the incriminating slogan – also during anti-Israel demonstrations – has become part of the 'culture of society'? For sure, but that did not make it less criminal. It is important to recall the philosopher Judith Butler's statement that insults especially become powerful – and punishable – when they contain a traumatic history, like the Holocaust.[66] That is definitely the case here.

---

63   *Trouw*, 24 February 2002. *See also* 'Antisemitic Incidents from Around the World – A Partial List January –June 2010', *Journal for the Study of Antisemitism* 2, 1 (2010), 7. That happens again in a similar situation in 2010: RTV Utrecht, 'Weggestuurde FC Utrecht-fans terug in Utrecht', 28 January 2010: www.rtvutrecht.nl/nieuws/230948 (consulted 29 February 2015).

64   Voetbalzone.nl, 'Ajax en Feyenoord hebben tot 1 mei om kritische Aboutaleb te overtuigen'5 April 2013: www.voetbalzone.nl/doc.asp?uid=185224 (consulted 2 March 2015); 'Ajaxsupporters niet welkom bij ADO Den Haag', *Metro*, 26 September 2012: www.metronieuws.nl/sport/2012/09/ajax-supporters-niet-welkom-bij-ado-den-haag (consulted 3 March 2015).

65   LJN: BI4739, Supreme Court, 08/00424, 15 September 2009. I thank Willem Wagenaar.

66   Padu Boerstra, 'Woorden zijn soms ook daden', *Filosofie Magazine* 3 (2007). www.filosofie-magazine.nl/nl/artikel/5166/woorden-zijn-soms-ook-daden.html. Judith Butler, *Excitable Speech: A Politics of the Performative* (New York: Routledge, 1997) *See also* Tzvetan Todorov, *Les morales de l'histoire* (Paris: B. Grasset, 1991), quoted in Dick van Galen Last, 'Wetenschapsbeoefening en revisionisme.' In: Jaap van Donselaar, Teresien de Silva and W. Sorgdrager (eds.), *Weerzinwekkende*

A poignant detail is that the judges did not address something else that was brought up during the trial, though not as an explicit charge. In the trial dossier plain clothes police officers testify that, when several uniformed colleagues walked past the 25 ADO Den Haag supporters in question (including the suspect on trial), this group shouted 'Jews' to the policemen.[67] In a 2012 report on antisemitism (not specifically related to football) the researchers distinguish between *intentional* antisemitism (antisemitism aimed at Jewish targets and/or people) and *unaimed* antisemitism (antisemitism not specifically aimed at Jewish targets and/or people). With regard to 'unaimed' antisemitic swearing, by far the most incidents (72%) involved insulting or verbally abusing an officer on duty, particularly the police. The police officers involved did not have a Jewish background themselves. In all cases the swear words 'cancer Jew', 'cancer Jews' or 'dirty cancer Jews' were used, sometimes in combination with other insults.[68] Actually, this aspect recalls the definition of antisemitism by Dik van Arkel, which states that antisemitic manifestations can take place 'irrespective of whether they are direct or indirect, intended or not'.[69] The police officer as 'the Jew' – this time stereotyped as representative and protector of the government and the establishment[70]

In March 2011, when ADO unexpectedly won their home game in The Hague against Ajax while ADO supporters chanted 'Hamas, Hamas, all Jews to the gas', ADO let it all hang out during a party at their club house. ADO player Lex Immers sang along with the ADO supporters: 'We are on a

wetenschap. Holocaustontkenning en andere uitingen van historisch revisionisme (Amsterdam: Anne Frank Stichting, 1998), 31. *See* chapter 1.

67   *Ibid. See also* chapter 15 and 18.

68   For example in the case of 'cancer homos': Bas Tierolf and Lisanne Drost, *Antisemitisme 2012*. Poldis thematic study (July 2013), 10-11. According to Tierolf and Drost people who on the basis of their appearance are recognised as 'Muslims' or 'non-western immigrant' are also often addressed in similar terms. However, according to them, antisemitism seems to occur relatively much more frequently. This is definitely the case when you consider that the Dutch Jews who are recognizably Jewish (e.g., by wearing a yarmulke), make up only a small group in the Netherlands. So, the non-intentional form of antisemitism occurs relatively frequently.

69   Dik van Arkel, *The Drawing of the Mark of Cain, A Socio-historical Analysis of the Growth of Anti-Jewish Stereotypes* (Amsterdam: Amsterdam University, Press 2009), 77; *see* chapter 1.

70   Jews as authorities do occur in, for example, rap songs: chapter 14 and Remco Ensel, *Haatspraak. Antisemitisme – een 21ᵉ-eeuwse geschiedenis* (Amsterdam: Amsterdam University Press, 2014), 239-243. The Poldis Antisemitism study report a total number of suspects (perpetrators) of 1,360. Most suspects are male (1,218) and the average age of the perpetrators is 25. With regard to ethnic background most suspects (almost 70%) have a Dutch ethnicity; 3% a Moroccan ethnicity and 6% a Turkish ethnicity: *ibid.*, 6. Calling police officers 'Jews' is perhaps a widespread European phenomenon which requires further research.

Jew hunt', the others joined in. A teammate gave a raised-arm salute. Then, they started singing a popular anti-Ajax song:

Jood, jood schop hem dood	Jew, Jew, kick him, don't save it
Tot hij sterren ziet!	Until he sees stars!
Wat voor sterren?	What kind of stars?
Jodensterren!	Stars of David!
(possibly followed by: *KK ajacied!!*)[71]	(possibly followed by KK ajacied!!)

With mobile phones now widespread, footage soon started circulating on the internet and a row followed. Immers apologised and received a four-match ban; the coach, who did not sing along, but stood next to Immers and did not intervene, was banned for one match.[72]

For thirty years the recurring question has been whether these are expressions of yobbism, provocation or antisemitism. The same debate was held around 1960 after youths ('rascals', 'brats') had painted swastikas and damaged Jewish cemeteries.[73] And now again – to this day – with regard to anti-Jewish expressions in football stadiums and on football clubs' websites. A first reflex seems to be to quickly play an incident down or deny that there is an antisemitic dimension to it. The question returns in a recent study into radicalisation among youths in school, which seems to focus on extreme-right and Muslim pupils. The title of the report (2010) also nicely applies to young football supporters: 'Adolescent, difficult or radicalising?'[74]

A recurring refrain is that Ajacieden solicit the anti-Jewish slogans because of their nickname, '(Super) Jews': 'As long as Ajacieden keep using this nickname, the provoked counter-chants cannot be antisemitic, even

71 Erik Schumacher, 'Blond antisemitisme', *Hard//hoofd. Online tijdschrift voor kunst en journalistiek*, 11 April 2011: http://hardhoofd.com/2011/04/11/blond-antisemitisme/ (consulted 9 February 2015); and Robin Qfoxx, 26 December 2006 on www.youtube.com/watch?v=5tQ9qV91L4M (consulted 9 February 2015). 'KK ajacied' literally means 'Cunt Cancer Ajacied'.

72 'Lex Immers op Jodenjacht in het ADO Supportershome', YouTube, uploaded by BlackopsHDService, 21 March 2011; *Elsevier*, 23 March 2011; *NRC Handelsblad*, 18 July and 3 August 2011; *Haarlems Dagblad*, 27 October 2011. Robert Vuijsje, 'Je roept gewoon niet: we gaan op Jodenjacht. Vanwege de geuzennaam Joden bezoek ik de wedstrijden van Ajax niet meer', *de Volkskrant*, 23 March 2011; 'Lex Immers op Jodenjacht in het ADO Supportershome', YouTube: www.youtube.com/watch?v=cCFgY6xyI98, 21 March 2011.

73 Witte, *Al eeuwen lang een gastvrij volk*, 59-60; see chapters 4 and 5.

74 Ine Spee and Maartje Reitsma, 'Puberaal, lastig of radicaliserend? Grensoverschrijdend gedrag van jongeren in het onderwijs' ('s-Hertogenbosch: KPC groep 2010).

though they do contain all the hallmarks'.[75] That debate also heated up after the Immers case. It is a fallacy. At one time, the Ajacieden took on 'Jews' as their badge of honour in response to the antisemitic accusations of their opponents. What's more important is that responding to 'Jews' with 'the gas chamber', is an antisemitic abuse – a perverse verbal link which has been made since 1945.

Furthermore, these slogans are contagious; 'Jew' has become a swear word, also in schools. The slogans constitute a breeding ground for (latent) antisemitism.[76] In 2013, the populist right-wing broadcaster PowNed wrote the following about Ajax on its website: 'Jews have too much money'.[77] It has not been proven that supporters have no antisemitic prejudices; various statements show they have. For example, in an interview with the most talkative young man of a group of Ajax opponents, the author was told, among other things, that 'Hamas Hamas ...' had nothing to do with the Second World War, but only with football; that his own grandfather had hidden Jews in his house, and that his own mother had to be hospitalised, because as a child she had been suffering from fear and tensions because of Jews hiding in her house; that Ajax was indeed a Jewish club, because they were rich, and they had Jewish chairmen like Michael van Praag; Jews were rich anyhow; Israel did things that were worse than the Nazis. He had been there twice and thought it was horrible how they were treating the Palestinians; Israel decided what the United States did; Israel was the centre of the world.[78] So, his argument contains nearly all contemporary antisemitic stereotypes in a nutshell. The actual victims are those giving a hiding place to Jews; Jews are rich; 'Jews to the gas' has nothing to do with the war; criticism of Israel and anti-Zionism turn into demonisation.

Another source – interviews with several ADO Den Haag 'hooligans' – also reveals that one of them actually knew 'a lot' about the Second World War and the persecution of the Jews, but directly associated this with Israeli actions against the Palestinians, in casu (in 2010) the Israeli invasion in Gaza. In general, the supporters did not want to play down 'the Jewish suffering' during the German occupation, but they thought it was more important that in Israel 'today, certain parallels can be drawn with former Nazi Germany'. And: '[The Jews] have seized a piece of land and made it fertile, while it was

75   de Volkskrant, 26 August 2013. For earlier reports, see Algemeen Dagblad, 5 May 1999; NRC Handelsblad, 17 March 2000.
76   See Kuper, Ajax, de joden, 142-145.
77   www.powned.tv/nieuws/sport/2013/08/joden_hebben_te_veel_geld_af.html, 30 August 2013 (consulted 26 February 2014).
78   Discussion Evelien Gans with X., 12 May 2010, De Balie, Amsterdam.

not only theirs'. Followed by the statement that the persecution of the Jews was a very sad thing for the Jews, but 'that they should have put up more resistance during the war, like the rest'.[79]

Having said that, the (non-Jewish) hardcore Ajacieden, particularly the F-side, with their artificial (Super)Jews are keeping the football 'war' alive. But not just them. During the 1990s, less fanatical, even 'occasional' supporters and crowds have started shouting 'Jews', identifying themselves with the alleged Jewish identity of Ajax – even if it is during one match only.[80] The 'we feeling' (even if only for a short while) obviously plays a crucial role in sports and football. Feyenoord fans have been heard saying that it's easier to change one's 'bit of skirt' than one's club. Moreover, club feeling has a lot to do with family feeling.[81] Actually, the football domain can function as a 'civil' or 'secular' religion. The scholar of international relations and humanities – and of soccer (the term used in North America) – Tamir Bar-On (b. 1967), quotes the Mexican writer Juan Villoro who called football 'a secular religion', and the filmmaker Pier Paolo Pasolini who spoke of 'the last sacred ritual of our time'. Bar-On himself states with respect to Mexico: 'Soccer is Mexico's pagan religion for all social classes ....'[82]

But why is it so attractive for non-Jewish supporters to adopt an artificial Jewish identity? This question cannot be answered satisfactorily only by pointing to the 'nickname' motive as a reaction against antisemitism. Amsterdam is a 'Jewish city', supporters say, and 'it gives a warm feeling'.[83] That sounds quite sentimental. Moreover, although there was a large Jewish population before the war, and today Amsterdam is the centre of Jewish life in the Netherlands, Jews still make up a very small minority of its population.

79 Wytske Oyevaar, 'Antisemitisme in voetbalstadions. Een onderzoek naar de racistische spreekkoren en liederen van voetbalhooligans' (Assignment within the framework of the UvA course Contemporary Antisemitism. Lecturer: Evelien Gans, 9 August 2010; unpublished paper), 13-15. I thank Wytske Oyevaar.

80 M.A. van Bemmel, '"We are Superjews, Ajax is the name." A study of identity of Ajax supporters' (MA thesis, Universiteit van Amsterdam, 20 August 2012), 59. Following the sociologist Richard Giulianotti, Van Bemmel mentions four different types of spectators: 'supporters, followers, fans and flâneurs'. So the latter categories also feel involved. I thank Martijn van Bemmel. Conversation with Tim Staal, Amsterdam, 26 June 2014.

81 Conversation with R.J. Spek, Amsterdam, 5 June 2015; Email of F.J. Spek to Evelien Gans, 9 June 2015.

82 Tamir Bar-On, 'El Tri: 'A pagan religion for all', The Washington Post, 4 June 2014; Tamir Bar-On, The World Through Soccer. The Cultural Impact of a Global Sport (Lanham, MD: Rowman & Littlefield, 2014), 83.

83 Remark by dedicated Ajax supporters during: 'Stadsgesprek: Superjoden!', among others with: Frits Barend, Janneke van der Horst, John Jaakke and Yves Gijrath, De Balie, Amsterdam, 15 November 2012.

Calling Amsterdam a 'Jewish city' is incorrect and seems a bit of a flirtation with a remarkable past that was destroyed, and a present that still appears to be appealing. What about the 'warm feeling'? Probably it is attractive to identify, to some extent, with 'the Jew'. Jews have an 'interesting' and dramatic history – even today. Not a day goes by without news about the Jews in the papers, on television or internet. It can be seductive to identify oneself with that history and this turbulent present. Shared 'pride' – shared 'suffering'.

In turn, Jewish Ajax supporters – not hooligans – often tend to have an ambivalent approach: proud of the successful achievements of an (alleged) Jewish club, 'their' Ajax; not so pleased with the antisemitic reactions this identity triggers. A light form of Jewish narcissism. Initially, Ajax chairman Uri Coronel (1946-2016) was not bothered by the Israeli flags. 'Before it started triggering annoying reactions by other supporters, I actually quite liked it. Ajax was ours.'[84] The fascination of the, largely invented and contradictory, self-image of a 'Jewish club' among Ajax supporters, is underlined by the fact that in 2013 two documentaries were produced about this topic – not so much on football antisemitism.[85]

It is also no wonder that both the alleged Jewish image and self-image of Ajax leads to confusion and heated debates in Moroccan-Dutch communities. The Moroccan Ajax player Mounir El Hamdaoui was told by Ajax fans that he was 'not a Jew' and, hence, not a 'real Ajax player'. Some Moroccan Dutch put up a barrier between their affection for Ajax and their dislike of Israel. Others, Ajax opponents, among whom also fans of a Moroccan football club in Rabat, were outright negative ('as a Moroccan, how can you play for that 'Jew club?!'), started referring to the Palestinians, or came up with antisemitic stereotypes such as, 'If someone is screwing you, that person is a Jew', and references to fraud and stinginess.[86] So the football domain acts as a parallel world in which ethnic origin, local connections, different identifications and loyalty apparently play their own game.

---

84   Gans, *Gojse nijd & joods narcisme*. Uri Coronel, referred to in *Haarlems Dagblad*, 27 October 2011. See also *de Volkskrant*, 4 June 2012; 'Stadsgesprek: Superjoden!', with: Frits Barend, Janneke van der Horst, John Jaakke, Yves Gijrath, De Balie, Amsterdam, 15 November 2012. *See also* next footnote.

85   They are, in succession, *Ajax! Joden! Amsterdam!* by Frans Bromet (60 min., 2013) (in which the author of this chapter is also interviewed) and *Superjews* (2013) by Nirit Peled. *See* Carine Cassuto, 'Op zoek naar de Superjood', *NIW*, 16 August 2013 and *NRC Handelsblad*, 28 February 2014.

86   Ensel, *Haatspraak*, 230-232.

After the remarks by ADO football player Immers and his buddies, there arose, once again, a discussion in the press whether 'they are just saying something' or whether football-related antisemitism had never been systematically tackled. The 'noses' slogans are old, according to *NRC Handelsblad*.[87] ADO player Immers with his 'Jew hunt' was strongly criticised ('antisemitism!') and equally strongly defended ('everyone says these things, and then they pick on him!'). Many debates were held, both in the regular press and on the internet. There is no shortage of antisemitic outbursts. For example, in response to the, misguided, proposal by the tiny, but very activist, group Federative Jewish Netherlands (FJN), which is rather isolated within the Jewish community. FJN demanded that Immers convert a possible fine into a donation to the next of kin of the parents and three of the six children of an Israeli family who had recently been murdered by two Palestinian brothers. Under the motto that the Palestinian perpetrators had also gone 'on a Jew hunt'. If Immers refused, FJN would press charges.[88]

Reactions ranged from many accusations – not surprisingly – of 'blackmail', to equally many comments about Jews and money: 'Just ordinary money wolves those Semites'; 'As usual, it's about the money. Lewmann Bros [sic], Madoff, Goldman Sachs ....' An outright ideological statement like: 'Is that what Henry Ford meant with his book "The International Jew"'? So-called Holocaust fatigue: 'after every wrong comment right away ... play victim', and: 'All that moaning, it was 70 years ago'. And a combination of, on the one hand, a dislike of the Jew as a victim and, on the other, a political stance in which 'the Jew' has become 'perpetrator':

> The Palestinian committed an act of resistance against the occupier and repressor. The Jews should stop picking the victim role while acting like occupiers and repressing other people, how hypocritical can you be?[89]

These statements are only a few small waves in a choppy ocean: 'Do Jews enjoy travelling? Hail hail, to Auschwitz by rail!', and: 'Never a dull moment, with those whining curls'.

But just as much as after the incidents in 1982, and in 1987/1988, the government and KNVB tightened the leash a bit more. Clearly, Ajax's F-side

---

87   *NRC Handelsblad*, 5 September 2011.
88   *De Telegraaf*, 24 March 2011.
89   Reactions to the article in *De Telegraaf* of 24 March 2011, on: www.telegraaf.nl (consulted 7 April 2011. 'Lewmann Bros' obviously meant 'Lehman Brothers'. Henry Ford was a convinced antisemite. I thank Paul Damen.

(and the same is true with respect to hardcore supporter groups of other clubs) do represent, in the literal and figurative sense, a significant power base for the boards. Nevertheless, (Jewish) Ajax chairmen like Michael van Praag and Uri Coronel, and successive mayors of Amsterdam, have tried to convince the Ajax followers to stop using their 'nickname'. CIDI had previously made a similar appeal.[90] To no avail; after all, shouting 'Jews' is not an offence. The results of (secret) talks between on the one hand Job Cohen and his successor Eberhard van der Laan and, on the other, diehard Ajax supporters remain as yet shrouded in mystery.[91]

Supporters with antisemitic slogans, however, are tackled more systematically. During the 2014 football season, the KNVB issued 662 stadium bans. In 2011, BAN was founded: an organisation specifically focused on the fight against antisemitism in football. In 2011, among other things, the foundation filed a complaint against ADO, and it also put pressure on the KNVB following other incidents, including chants – also by Ajax supporters. BAN's 'media adviser' is Hans Knoop, who has also figured in previous chapters.[92] The Immers case, however, did not result in prosecution – not even after the above-mentioned FJN had initiated legal proceedings.[93] The judge did rule that ADO's board was to prevent a repeat and halt the match in case of similar outbursts.[94] The club subsequently invested a lot of money in setting up CCTV cameras in the ADO stadium; arrests have been made based on CCTV footage.

90 'Stop gebruiknaam "Joden"', 23 March 2011 www.telegraaf.nl/telesport/voetbal/ajax/9339501/ referred to in: Einhorn, 'Superjoden?', 71-73. Open letter CIDI (3 March 2009), referred to in: Van Bemmel, '"We are Superjews, Ajax is the name,"'107. I thank Martijn van Bemmel. (Secret) talks have started between the City of Amsterdam and the Ajax board and supporters, see Het Parool, 2 January 2012.

91 See, e.g., Het Parool, 13 May 2011; de Volkskrant, 4 June 2012; David Laakman, 'Van der Laan wil af van Jodenleus bij Ajax', NRC Handelsblad, 13 May 2011: www.nrc.nl/nieuws/2011/05/13/ van-der-laan-wil-af-van-joden-leus-bij-ajax/ (consulted 2 March 2015).

92 For BAN, see, e.g., Kemal Rijken, 'Welles-nietes tussen BAN en ADO', NIW, 5 August 2011; NRC Handelsblad, 18 July and 3 August 2011; Haarlems Dagblad, 27 October 2011; NIW, 20 April 2012. For Hans Knoop see chapters 8 and 9.

93 See, e.g., www.uitspraken.rechtspraken.nl: ECLI:NL:GHSGR:2012: BW4468 (2 May, 2012). In 1999 Feyenoord player Ulrich van Gobbel who, during his club's title-winning ceremony, had shouted 'Who doesn't jump is a Jew', was also not prosecuted by the judiciary. Van Gobbels' behaviour was considered 'unsuitable and unwise, but not discriminating': Trouw, 30 April 1999; NRC Handelsblad, 18 June 1999. Ajax supporters, on the contrary, shout: 'Who doesn't jump is not a Jew': www.youtube.com/watch?v=atwv3mD29yI (consulted 28 May 2015). I thank Willem Wagenaar.

94 LJN: BR4406, Voorzieningenrechter Rechtbank 's-Gravenhage, 398200 / KG ZA 11-812, 9 August 2011, referred to in: Manfred Gerstenfeld, 'Anti-semitism on the Dutch Soccer Fields and Beyond', 7 September 2011: http://tundratabloids.com/2011/09/anti-semitism-on-the-playing-fields-of-dutch-football.html (consulted 4 March 2015).

In 2013, the club received the CIDI Respect Award for its revised policies.[95] Early February 2015, the Dutch Parliament discussed the introduction of even harsher measures, for example against first-time hooligans disturbing public order . One of the ideas on the table is the introduction of 'regional bans'.[96]

In 2013 the Anne Frank House commissioned a study into antisemitism in secondary schools through interviews with teachers. It revealed that pupils with a Moroccan (10%) or Turkish (8%) background were overrepresented in the case of anti-Jewish manifestations within the framework of the Israeli-Palestinian conflict or, as it is neutrally referred to, 'the events in the Middle East'. A very remarkable finding is that in almost two-thirds of the recent incidents the 'perpetrators' have a native Dutch background, and that they are predominantly involved in offending Jews within a football context (i.e. in 64% of the cases). In addition, pupils of all backgrounds call each other (and in one instance a teacher) 'Jew' ('"Jew" means "bad" to us, you see?'). In addition, the teachers who were interviewed, more often witness abusive comments about Islam (75%) and homosexuality (85%) than about Jews and the Holocaust. They consider – an interesting fact in itself – anti-Jewish expressions within the framework of football as 'the least serious type of incident'.[97]

In conclusion, antisemitism in football has, just like the Israeli-Palestinian conflict, become globalised. The case of Tottenham Hotspur has already been mentioned, but there are similar situations – in other national contexts – for instance in Germany, Poland, Belgium, Italy and also in Israel.[98] Some anti-Jewish expressions are so subtle that they are difficult to

95 See, e.g., de Volkskrant, 26 August 2013; Nederlands Dagblad, 8 November 2013.
96 NRC Handelsblad, 3 February 2015.
97 Eva Wolf, Jurriaan Berger and Lennart de Ruig, 'Antisemitisme in het voorgezet onderwijs', Panteia. Research to Progress (Projectnr. C10000, Zoetermeer, 8 July 2013), 7-8, 13, 23-25, 31. Antisemitic expressions occurred more often at lower-level secondary school than at higher-level secondary school: ibid., 19. See also Het Parool, 12 July 2013; de Volkskrant, 13 July 2013. In de Volkskrant (4 June 2012) 'an Ajax supporter and Amsterdam policy adviser' also stated that in football homophobia was a bigger problem than 'the alleged antisemitism'.
98 Florian Schubert, Rechtsextreme Fans beim Bundesligafußball. Ihre Strategien und die Maßnahmen der Vereine – Eine Fallstudie am Beispiel des HSV [Right-wing fans at German professional soccer league: Their Strategies and theme asures of the Clubs – a case-study based on the Hamburger Sport Verein (HSV)] (Saarbrücken: VDM-Verlag Dr. Müller, 2009); Florian Schubert, 'Antisemitismus in Fußball-Fankulturen.' In: Martin Endemann et al. (eds.), Zurück am Tatort Stadion: Diskriminierung und Antidiskriminierung in Fußball-Fankulturen (Münster: Die Werkstatt, 2015). On Poland: Johanna Podolska, Staszek Goldstein and Andrew Tomlinson, 'Something fishy in the town of Lodz. The word "Jew" is an insult for soccer fans, but is it anti-Semitic?', Fanatismo. One-off magazine on today's fanaticism, May 2011, (initiated by Castrum Peregrini, Amsterdam), 40-43. There have been contacts between ADO and the Polish league club Legia Warszawa since 1984. Legia supporters also shout 'Hamas, Hamas, Joden aan het gas' or a

grasp, let alone punish, and only recognisable by 'insiders'. There was a lot of activity on the websites of fanatic ADO supporters after the Immers case. The suggestion to start calling Ajax 'FC Ter*neuzen*' [FC Ter*noses*], is not very original. The comment on the proposal by an Amsterdam city councillor to take Lex Immers and his coach to the Anne Frank House – they 'want Lex to bow for those c****r people' – is simply rude. The Anne Frank House is a target anyway: they would like to 'run amok' there. A certain columnist called 'Billy Odol' was more cunning. He wrote about the Immers case under the title 'The peeled shrimp' and called the KNVB the KNJB – Royal Dutch *Jewish* Association. This is where the Jewish conspiracy comes in. And the peeled shrimp? Odol referred to a circumcised penis. He suspected that Ajax players are forced to get circumcised. This is one of several examples where the dividing line between 'Ajax Jews' and 'real' Jews disappears. An (Ajax) Jew is someone with a big nose and a circumcised penis.[99] Or with a yarmulke. When, in Rotterdam, a Jew with a yarmulke walked past a group of Feyenoord fans, they said 'Hey, cancer Ajacied'. The man in question had nothing to do with Ajax, was not wearing an Ajax shirt or anything else related to Ajax.[100] Jew equals Ajacied and vice versa.[101] Finally, the 'peeled shrimp' reference leads us straight into the world of pornographic antisemitism, which is not only present in football.[102]

German version: 'Juden ins Gas', particularly aimed at Widzew, a club with a Jewish image. *See* http://legia.com/www/index.php?akt=7570 and www.youtube.com/watch?v=ZYAQW4zL8ko (consulted 19 April 2011). I thank Iwona Gusc. Maciej Kozlowski, *Naród Wybrany. Cracovia Pany. Z wielokulturowej historii poskiego sportu* (Warszawa-Krakow: Nigdy Wiecej, 2015) (with an English summary: 78-79). Due to their racism and antisemitism UEFA hands out numerous fines and punishments to this extreme-right bastion; on 19 February Ajax beat Legia 1-0 in Amsterdam, in the absence of Legia supporters: *NRC Handelsblad,* 21/22 February 2014. On Italy and rival clubs in Rome: www.thelocal.it/20131206/football-fans-use-anne-frank-in-anti-jewish-dig-against-rivals (consulted 26 February 2015). In 2010 the Israeli football club Hapoel Tel-Aviv started singing a song to their local rival Maccabi Tel-Aviv which included: 'Put Maccabi in the chambers .... So put Maccabi in the chambers, fill them with gas ...': Adam Keller, 'If you are Racists, You Lose!', www.Salem-News.com, 11 January 2011 (consulted 5 February 2015). On 11 and 12 June 2015, an international conference on football-related antisemitism was held in Amsterdam: 'Tackling anti-Semitism in professional football', Amsterdam Arena, organised by the Anne Frank House. One of the papers presented was: Evelien Gans, '... Cause Jews burn the best: Football Antisemitism. The different historical manifestations of an ever-existing phenomenon in the Netherlands'.
99   Erik Schumacher, 'Blond antisemitisme', *Hard//hoofd. Online tijdschrift voor kunst en journalistiek*, 11 April 2011. Billy Odol was a contributor of the (now-closed) website haguesityfirm.nl. *k****rvolk* means 'cancerpeople'. I thank Erik Schumacher.
100 Van Bemmel, '"We are Superjews"', 54 (n. 98).
101 *See also* chapter 14.
102 *See* chapter 12.

12   Pornographic Antisemitism, Shoah Fatigue and Freedom of Speech

Evelien Gans

The previous chapter on football antisemitism concluded with a reference to an internet column titled 'The peeled shrimp', in which it was suggested that players of Ajax, the Amsterdam club with a 'Jewish' image, got themselves circumcised.[1] This can be construed as a form of pornographic antisemitism. The fascination for and aversion of the Jewish circumcised penis has been around for centuries. This chapter starts by briefly addressing the history of the image of 'the Jew' as perverse, and will then elaborate relatively recent Dutch cases.

The juxtaposition of three phenomena in football – 'Shoah fatigue' or *Schlusstrichbedürfnis*, 'a desire to provoke' and 'pornographic antisemitism' – would also manifest itself in a completely different social context: in the columns of the widely cherished *enfant terrible* Theo van Gogh (1957-2004). In 1984 this filmmaker and columnist published a notorious antisemitic pamphlet, resulting in a string of lawsuits. These judicial confrontations touched upon two urgent topics in the 1980s public debate: the question of unrestricted freedom of speech and recurring recriminations of an alleged Jewish monopolisation of suffering. These topics remained on the agenda, engaging various followers of Van Gogh, or kindred spirits, including the painter Ronald Ophuis (b. 1978), as shown in two of his controversial paintings.

The Netherlands into which columnist and filmmaker Theo van Gogh was born no longer exists. Van Gogh was someone who strongly rejected multiculturalism, particularly when it came to facilitating professing the faith of Islam, a religion he frequently came to refer to in pornographic terms. This grandson of the brother of the world-famous painter Vincent van Gogh became known worldwide for entirely different and very sad reasons: in 2004 he was killed by the Dutch Islamist Mohammed Bouyeri (b. 1978).

---

1   Erik Schumacher, 'Blond antisemitisme', *Hard//hoofd. Online tijdschrift voor kunst and journalistiek,* 11 April 2011.

A short history of pornographic antisemitism

There are quite a few Dutch expressions and children's verses in which 'the Jew' figures, to put it mildly, as someone deviant, also from a physical and sexual perspective. The expression 'Jew it' was used to tell smokers to cut off the top of their cigar.

Trek je vaders laarzen aan!	Put on your dad's boots!
Moeder, die zijn me te groot.	Mother, they're too big to fit.
Snij er dan een stukje af!	Then cut something off!
Moeder, 'k ben geen jood.[2]	Mother, I'm not a Yid.

Already in the Greek and Roman era the Jewish circumcised penis was a source of both fascination and disgust; it was seen as ugly, as a symbol of mutilation and separatism, but also as a symbol of obscenity and horniness. Jews were, reportedly, extraordinarily 'potent'.[3] So there was a dubious but at the same time intriguing 'Jewish sexuality': what do those circumcised have in common from which the non-circumcised are excluded? Over the course of the centuries various stereotypes also developed about Jewish women, ranging from the 'exotic and pretty Jewess' and *'la belle juive'* to *'das jüdisches Mannweib'* and the Jewish prostitute.[4]

We know that the court Jew Joseph Süss Oppenheimer (1698-1738), Jud Süss in short, financier and economic reformer of Charles Alexander, Duke of Württemberg, acquired a lot of influence and privileges. After the duke's death he was brought down by his opponents and brutally killed. What is less known is that his interrogators, mostly Lutheran Pietists in pursuit of a pious and moral life, seem to have been obsessed with Süss' sexual

2   Evert Werkman, 'Het woord JOOD in onze woordenboeken', *Het Parool,* 13 February 1965.

3   Pieter van der Horst, *Joden in de Grieks-Romeinse wereld. Vijftien miniaturen* (Zoetermeer: Meinema, 2003) 29; Peter Schäfer, *Judeophobia. Attitudes Towards the Jews in the Ancient World* (Cambridge, MA: Harvard University Press, 1997), 99-102.

4   Sander Gilman, *The Jew's Body* (New York, London: Routledge, 1991), 76; *see* there especially Gilman's chapter 'The Jewish Psyche. Freud, Dora, and the Idea of the Hysteric', 60-103; Sander Gilman, *Jewish Self-Hatred: Anti-Semitism and the Hidden language of the Jews* (Baltimore: Johns Hopkins University Press,1986), 243-245, 267, 258; Paula Hyman, *Gender and Assimilation in Modern Jewish History. The Roles and Representation of Women* (Seattle, London: University of Washington Press, 1995), 134. *See also* A.G. Gender-Killer (eds.), *Antisemitismus und Geschlecht. Von 'effiminierten Juden, maskulinierten Judinnen' und andere Geschlechterbildern* (Münster: Unrast, 2005), and Gabrielle Kohlbauer-Fritz, '"La belle juive" und die "schöne Schickse".' In Sander L. Gilman, Robert Jütte, Gabrielle Kohlbauer-Fritz (eds.), *'Der Schejne Jid'. Das Bild des 'jüdischen Körpers' in Mythos und Ritual* (Wien: Picus Verlag, 1998) 109-121: 109.

life, bombarding him with questions on this very point.[5] Two centuries later, Goebbels' propaganda film *Jud Süss* further inflated the stereotype of the Jew as a libidinous womaniser to a perverse rapist and committer of *Rassenschande*. At the same time, the Jew fails as a man: in the film, when his carriage tips over, a woman has to come to his rescue.[6]

That Jews were, allegedly, both 'horny' and 'not real men', also emerges from the connection that has been made between Jews, perversion, effeminacy and homosexuality. Sander Gilman has written an entire book about the history of antisemitic images and rhetoric with regard to the Jewish body: *The Jew's Body* (1991). The chapter 'The Jewish Nose' explains that since ancient times, people have made a direct connection between noses and genitals, mainly the penis, in particular with regard to their size. At around 1900, doctors and psychoanalysts, including Sigmund Freud, assumed that people's noses and genitals were made of the same tissue. In racist and Nazi antisemitism the usual pattern was turned around in the sense that the size of the Jewish nose, portrayed as hideously huge, was not hinting at a presumed enormous potency, but a reference to the circumcised, hence 'deformed', Jewish penis. All this did not, however, stand in the way of the threatening image of the *jüdischen Geistes* [Jewish intellect], the stereotype of the Jewish intellectual.[7]

Opposite stereotypes, as mentioned before, tolerate each other well.[8] So 'the Jew' was seen as feminine, effeminate – and homosexual. There exists a whole collection of critical literature, with George Mosse as pioneer, on the supposed connection between Jewishness and homosexuality; the subject forms a study of its own.[9] In contrast, however, 'the Jew' was also a cunning

5   Süss had also had relationships with Christian women. Although that was no longer forbidden, it went against the prevailing traditions and morals and may have caused offence. The detailed questioning however mainly does point in the direction of the hidden and forbidden lusts of the Pietists – i.e. a matter of projection.

6   Evelien Gans, 'The Feuchtwanger-effect. Jud Süss as a testing ground for philosemitic and antisemitic stereotypes.' Paper presented at the symposium 'The many guises of Jud Süss', Menasseh ben Israel Institute, Amsterdam, 10 & 11 May 2012; Susan Tegel, *Jew Süss. Life, Legend, Fiction, Film* (London: Continuum, 2011), 33-34, 46.

7   Gilman, *The Jew's Body*, 188-192; Von Braun, 'Der sinnliche und der übersinnliche Jude', 105.

8   See chapter 1.

9   See also chapter 14. George Mosse, *Nationalism and Sexuality: Respectability and Abnormal Sexuality in Modern Europe* (New York: Howard Fertig, 1985); George Mosse, *The Image of Man: The Creation of Modern Masculinity* (New York and Oxford: Oxford University Press, 1996); Matti Bunzl, *Symptoms of Modernity: Jews and Queers in Late-twentieth-century Vienna* (Berkeley and Los Angeles: University of California Press, 2004); Stephen Frosh, 'Freud, Psychoanalysis and Anti-Semitism', *Psychoanalytic Review*, 91, 3 (2004): 309-333; David Baile, 'The Discipline of Sexualwissenschaft Emerges in Germany, Creating Divergent Notions of the Sexuality of

seducer and rapist of 'Aryan' women. And of French women – and men too. In one of his antisemitic pamphlets the author Louis-Ferdinand Céline (1894-1961) writes that French women loved the frizzy hair of the Jews who also had 'such remarkable dicks'. With their 'long rotten fake dick' they were also going to 'fuck five hundred million Aryans in the arse! French, from now on you are fucked in the arse by the Jews!'[10] Jews in their familiar twilight position, neither man nor woman, or with a Janus face: both at the same time. And by definition perverse. The connection between sex and money also fitted them perfectly. This again ties in with a debate on the question of whether, in addition to the Hollywood film industry, the Jews did not also specifically control the porn industry.[11]

From the 1980s onwards the Holocaust denier Ditlieb Felderer and his associates started publishing pure Holocaust porn, known as 'pornocaust', in magazines like *jewish information | jüdisch information* and *Bundesprüf-stelle* (BPS). They distributed their writings from Sweden, where the far right and neo-Nazis had found a refuge immediately after the war; the Dutchman Paul van Tienen also attended several meetings there at the time.[12] A piquant detail in this context is that, in the late 1950s and early 1960s – basically before the Holocaust became a public issue, starting to receive a lot more attention only since the Eichmann trial (1961) – Holocaust porn also became popular in Israel. But it was an entirely different type of porn compared to that produced by Felderer and his associates. The Israeli pocket series *Stalags* featured voluptuous sadistic female SS guards in a concentration

European Jewry.' In S. Gilman and J. Zipes (eds.), *Yale Companion to Jewish Writing and Thought in German Culture 1096-1996* (New Haven: Yale University Press, 1997), 273-279; Sandrine Sanos: *The Aesthetics of Hate. Far-Right intellectuals, Antisemitism, and Gender in 1930s France* (Stanford: Stanford University Press, 2012); Daniel Boyarin, Daniel Itzkovitz, and Ann Pellegrini (eds.) *Queer Theory and the Jewish Question* (New York: Columbia University Press, 2003). I thank Stefan Dudink.

10   Solange Leibovici, 'Het pornografisch antisemitisme', *De Groene Amsterdammer*, 17 May 1995.

11   There are both serious and antisemitic publications and items about Jews and/in the porn industry. *See, e.g.,* Lawrence Schimel (ed.), *Kosher Meat* (Santa Fe, NM: Sherman Asher, 2000); Nathan Abrams, 'Nathan Abrams on Jews in the American porn industry', *Jewish Quarterly* 196 (Winter 2004), 27-30. But on many sites and blogs Abrams' analysis and words are distorted into the stereotype of the 'perverse' and 'money grabbing' Jew, *see e.g.* on the website of Holocaust denier David Duke, 'Jewish Professor Boasts of Jewish Pornography used as a Weapon Against Gentiles', February 26, 2007: http://davidduke.com/jewish-professor-boasts-of-jewish-pornography-used-as-a-weapon-against-gentiles/ (consulted 5 July 2015). It is crucial here, just as with respect to the Jewish money trade, to make a distinction between a historical and socio-economic analysis and a stereotypical approach.

12   *See* chapter 4.

camp raping a captured Allied pilot, who then escapes and takes revenge by raping his tormentors in turn.[13]

Revisionist magazines like BPS were also sold in the Netherlands. In this chapter, the focus is on the pornographic drawings rather than on the denial of the authenticity of both Anne Frank's diary and the existence of gas chambers. The drawings show, for example, an old Jewish man, with a 'Jewish nose', big balls and a long stretched out penis with a little bow, standing in front of an old saggy woman, and saying: 'Kuck mein liebling – Dr. Mengele hat das einmal mehr geschaft!' [Look my darling – Dr Mengele has managed it again!] The caption mentions, among other things, that pensioners in Auschwitz also had everything they needed; they were given a new erection.[14] The magazine also features a sexually insatiable Jewish woman, Beate Klarsfeld (named after the well-known French-German-Jewish journalist and Nazi hunter Beate Klarsfeld-Künzel). Again, the setting is Auschwitz. The woman appears to enjoy having sex with 'Dokter Broszat' – a reference to the German Holocaust historian Martin Broszat (1926-1989). It also suggests Jews had sex in the gas chambers.[15] Moreover, it contains a circumcised erect penis with 'Arbeit macht frei' written on it, and an anonymous Jewish woman engaged in a threesome with Nazi hunter Simon Wiesenthal (1908-2005) and Ignatz Bubis (1927-1999), the chairman of the German Zentralrat der Juden. The woman in question is afraid that they will find her hidden treasures: 'Hoffentlich finden Sie nicht mein Gold drinnen in meinen kleinen Pussy [I hope they won't find my gold in my small pussy].'[16] Again: sex, money, women – and Jews.

13 See Trouw, 20 May 2009; Isabel Kershner, 'Israel's unexpected spinoff from a Holocaust trial', The New York Times, 6 September 2007. See also the documentary by Ari Libsker, Stalags: Holocaust and Pornography in Israel (2007). Earlier, Auschwitz surviver Yehiel Feiner De-Nur, under the pseudonym Ka-Tzetnik 135633, wrote Beit Habubot (1953), translated as House of dolls (New York, Simon and Schuster, 1955), a novel about a Jewish brothel in Auschwitz (the existence of which is strongly contested by historians). At the Eichmann trial Yehiel Feiner De-Nur made a deep impression with his testimony.

14 Bundesprüfstelle für Jugendgefährdene Schriften (BPS), 318, 3, 1981: NIOD, 10.8 Rev (Revisionisme).

15 Jüdisch information, 650, 11, 1993; BPS, 640, 6, 1993; Beate Klarsfelds Zeugnis, Pornocaust, 606, 7 (1994).

16 BPS, 10031, July 1994; Ibid., 639, 3, 1993.

Political (in)correctness, 'the perverse Jew' and freedom of speech

Now, we can safely assume that Theo van Gogh never read these magazines; and his knowledge of the history of the Jews or antisemitism appears to have been rather superficial. Nevertheless, his pornographic antisemitism seems to fit into a tradition. What was relatively new, was the connection he made with the Shoah – with Treblinka and barbed wire – and with a Jewish, circumcised ('thought') police. It started with *'Een Messias zonder Kruis'* [A Messiah without Cross], a piece written in 1984, against the Jewish author and filmmaker Leon de Winter in which Van Gogh, among other things, refers to De Winter as 'circumcised' – a frequently recurring theme.[17] It's not clear if Van Gogh's own (medical) circumcision as a small boy played any role in this.[18] The non-Jewish Van Gogh grew up in the posh village of Wassenaar near The Hague, the seat of Dutch government, in a prosperous family with a history of war resistance activities. The uncle he was named after, had been shot by the Germans. That Van Gogh, as a youngster, grew into a troublemaker, is not relevant here. Instead, we focus on showing what he has written about (and particularly against) Jews, and later Muslims (his pornographic and sexist tirades against women and his anti-black racist outbursts are not explicitly addressed here).[19] We also look into his role in the debate about the freedom of expression. His dissatisfaction was not exclusively, but frequently and systematically, wrapped up in pornographic terms – always very usable for someone one can describe as a professional provocateur.

Van Gogh had a charming side and, long after his dead, a solid loyal circle of friends, even though, during his life, friendships sometimes abruptly changed into strong enmities.[20] He was a man with multiple faces. On TV,

17   Theo van Gogh, 'Een Messias zonder kruis (Enige kanttekeningen bij Leon de Winter)', *Moviola – een tijdschrift tot Rust and Vreugde in film and cultuur* 1 (1984).
18   Theo van Gogh, 'Lof der besnijdenis', *Metro*, 8 October 2004.
19   With regard to Van Gogh's sexism: see e.g. the words he uses to describe women who disagreed with him: 'grave cunt', 'pygmy in heat', 'fatty', 'menopaused drag battered by life' etc.: Gans, *Gojse nijd & joods narcisme*, 84; and 'chatterboxes': referred to in *Trouw*, 3 November 2004. On the other hand, he expressed a wish to return in a next life as a 'pregnant woman': Theo van Gogh, 'Zelfportret', *HP/De Tijd*, 4 June 2004. Nor did Van Gogh hesitate to voice anti-black racism. For example, he called the Dutch mixed-raced journalist and writer Stephan Sanders a 'racistische beroepsneger' [racist professional negro], idem, 'Een procesverbaal', 16 November 1999: www.theovangogh.nl/stuk42-99.htm (consulted 6 July 2016).
20   *See, e.g.,* Jan Kuitenbrouwer, 'De 150 hatelijkheden van Theo van Gogh', *NRC Handelsblad*, 30 October 2014; Andreas Kouwenhoven, 'Hij stortte graag zijn gal over je uit', *NRC Handelsblad*,

usually on Amsterdam's local channel AT5, where he earned a reputation as an interviewer, he publicised his lack of confidence in the multicultural society and his resentment of Islam too. But his TV appearances usually were devoid of any direct insults.[21] In his talk shows on the local channel of his home town Van Gogh could be disarming, and forthright. His films (based on other people's scripts) equally lacked any tasteless insinuations, or anti-Jewish or anti-Muslim stereotyping. His feature film *Cool* (2004) was about young criminals, with real-life offenders featuring in the main roles, some of whom were of Moroccan descent. Van Gogh also directed *Najib and Julia* (2001), a TV series about a 'Romeo and Juliet' intercultural romance between a 'Moroccan' boy and a 'Dutch' girl. The scriptwriter of the series revealed that Van Gogh did not want the romance to have an happy ending.[22] In his numerous columns however, Van Gogh showed no restraint. For this complex mixture, a film producer depicted Van Gogh as a Jekyll & Hyde.[23]

Van Gogh's debut as a filmmaker was the, unsubsidised, low-budget film *Luger* (1982), which won plaudits, but also drew strong criticism due to its violent character: for example, he instructed the main character, a psychopath, to stick the barrel of a gun into a woman's vagina.[24] In that same period, Leon de Winter (b. 1954) was starting to become a popular author and his third novel, *La Place de la Bastille*, was turned into a movie. Both the writer and the filmmaker, Rudolf van den Berg (b. 1949), were Jews from the postwar Jewish generation.[25] In the novel and the film the main character is a Jewish man whose parents and twin brother have been gassed, and who struggles with his Jewish identity, for a while cherishing the hope that the murder of his brother is based on a misunderstanding. Both the novel and film were a success.

Van Gogh seemed to find this success hard to stomach. In the same year in which the movie came out (1984) – and De Winter started appearing

---

30 November 2014.

21 With at the least one exception: see note 153.

22 Justus van Oel, *Mijn jaren met Van Gogh* (2005): www.justusvanoel.nl/asp/detail_overig. asp?id=1468 (consulted 1 June 2015). For the filmmaker Theo van Gogh, Emile Fallaux, 'Een groot filmer zou hij worden', *NRC Handelsblad*, 5 November 2004.

23 *NRC Handelsblad*, 1 February 1993. *See also* Max van Weezel, '2/11. Theo van Gogh 1957-2004', *Vrij Nederland*, 6 November 2004.

24 Incidentally, what caused most indignation was a scene with two small cats in a working washing machine: *NRC Handelsblad*, 1 February 1993. Theo van Gogh was rejected by the Film Academy on the basis of the submission of a video in which a former slave pushes the legs of two wine glasses in his master's eyes: Jannetje Koelewijn, '"Ik ben niet begonnen." Vrije meningsuiting volgens Theo van Gogh', *NRC Handelsblad*, 6/7 November 2004.

25 Rudolf van den Berg (direction), *Bastille* (drama, 91 min., 1984).

in talk shows – Van Gogh wrote his *'Messias Zonder Kruis'*. According to Solange Leibovici (b. 1946), a literary theorist who is trained in psycho-analytical analysis, the title suggests De Winter is a man who 'is actually a woman', which exposes Van Gogh's desire to castrate his rival.[26] The text is rude, vulgar – pornographic and antisemitic. As to the adequacy of the two latter characteristics the debate still rages.

Among other things, Van Gogh lets De Winter read out the text of an animation about 'two copulating yellow stars in a gas chamber'. Just like Felderer, he is suggesting that the sexual hunger of Jews had lasted right up until the gas chamber. Van Gogh is disgusted because De Winter allegedly uses 'the stench of the crematoria' to 'add some aroma' to his own tasteless product, *Bastille*. Van Gogh also appears preoccupied with the circumcised penis, which he projects on De Winter: 'Out of their age-old solidarity with Israel, my father and mother circumcised me at the age of four and since then I now and then like to get a grip on my, eh... "Jewish identity".'[27]

In his article, Van Gogh repeatedly accuses De Winter of exploiting the murder of the Jews, 'because although you are bleating on about your "identity" as a private concern, you are really only advertising with 6 million victims'. In his article Van Gogh links the stereotype of the perverse Jew to 'the Jew' who is always greedy for money – in this post-Holocaust era by profiting from his own suffering and identity, and those of his parents and ancestors. The article is filled with terms like 'hawking', 'sales pitches', 'commercial', 'showing off', 'ongoing flow of money' and 'merchandise'. Van Gogh's motive seems to be partially based on goyish envy. '[Even if I wanted to] I cannot boast about deported uncles and aunts, grandfathers and grandmothers ....' Van Gogh himself is named after his uncle Theo, who was shot for his resistance activities. But, he says, that does not give him the right to promote his film *Luger* over 'the dead body of his family'.[28]

In brief, it seems as if Van Gogh blames 'the Jew', personified in De Winter, to have a story, a dramatic history – and because of that an identity – which others lack, or don't want to reflect upon in fiction and non-fiction. In response to another affair, De Winter used the term 'thematic jealousy' to

---

26 Leibovici, 'Het pornografisch antisemitisme.' The word *'Kruis'* [Cross] simultaneously refers to the crucifixion of Jesus (of which the Jews were also allegedly guilty) and the Christian sign of the Cross, but also to the (sometimes vulgarly intended) physical 'crotch'. Leibovici's interpretation partly seems to refer to that of Freud who, among others, stated that the circumcised penis raised the fear of castration among non-Jews: Gans, *Gojse nijd & joods narcisme*, 25; *see also* chapter 1.

27 Van Gogh, 'Een Messias zonder kruis'.

28 *Ibid.* Much later, Van Gogh returned to this aspect of his family history.

describe the phenomenon.[29] So here was a case of professional and thematic envy and, on top of that, an allusion to De Winter as a 'stranger'. Why, Van Gogh wondered, had Leon not moved to Israel, 'the most backward province of America ...', if he felt so estranged from his own culture here?[30] Van Gogh never disassociated himself from his diatribe. On the contrary, he would later republish it in a number of compilations.[31]

Actually, Van Gogh continued to use similar prose in a long series of columns in various newspapers and magazines. In September 1993, in two successive columns in *Folia*, the magazine of the University of Amsterdam, he attacked what he considered to be the 'politically correct' Dutch justice system and, again, Leon de Winter. He wrote, for example, about 'Feldwebels of the circumcised police'. Further on he let Leon de Winter's former lover whisper in his ear: 'Tonight to Treblinka, darling'. Upon which she 'grabs a piece of barbed wire and wraps it around Leon's cock'.[32] Elsewhere he calls Richard Stein of the *Stichting Bestrijding Antisemitisme* (STIBA) the 'unpaid chief inspector of the circumcised police'.[33]

At least as relevant are, of course, the reactions in the Netherlands to Van Gogh's inflammatory words. In a large number of legal proceedings, starting in 1985, Van Gogh was alternately convicted and cleared of group defamation (i.e. article 137c of the Criminal Code). The series of legal and appeal cases against and by Van Gogh, which regularly found their way to the Supreme Court, the highest Dutch judicial body, constitute a complicated tangle. It is remarkable that during one of the lawsuits the lawyers in question frequently use the term 'pornography' (Van Gogh himself spoke of 'sick jokes') in a judicial context as opposed and related to the factors 'freedom of expression' and 'context'. In a verdict of the Supreme Court on 11 December 1990, the judges referred to an article by the philosopher and literary critic George Steiner (b. 1929) about literature as art and pornography. In this case the court ruled about the incriminating article that 'its discriminating character ... persists'.[34]

---

29   *NRC Handelsblad*, 19 December 1992; Gans, *Gojse nijd & joods narcisme*, 13.
30   *See also* Theo van Gogh, 'Snif, Snif. Ruikt het hier naar antisemitisme?', *Moviola*, 2, 1985.
31   In: *De Weldoener* (1988) and *Mijn favoriete graftak (en ander onheil)* (1989).
32   Theo van Gogh, 'Rubriek: Wassenaarse brieven over onderwijs, kunst and wetenschap. A correspondence between Boudewijn Büch and Theo van Gogh', *Folia*, 10 and 17 September 1993:
33   Theo van Gogh, 'Een columnist die voor Sonja Barend zwicht.' In: Theo van Gogh, *Er gebeurt nooit iets*, (Amsterdam, Antwerp: Veen, 1993). This is a compilation of columns published between 1991 and 1993, 30-33: 31. See also: Van Gogh, 'Lof der besnijdenis'. For Richard Stein *see* chapter 8.
34   Hoge Raad, 11 December 1990, nr. 257, 472-480. George Steiner, 'Woorden van de nacht.' In George Steiner, *Verval van het woord* (Amsterdam: Athenaeum-Polak en Van Gennep, 1990),

Van Gogh was also engaged in an endless polemic with the well-known and widely respected writer, and, as a columnist, equally controversial Hugo Brandt Corstius (1945-2014), who, following De Winter, tagged Van Gogh with the epithet 'The Eternal Antisemite'. In the same year that Van Gogh published his pamphlet against De Winter, Brandt Corstius became part of a row because he had, in one of his columns, compared Finance Minister Onno Ruding (b. 1939) with Eichmann, because of his harsh policy against people on benefits.[35] Actually, Brandt Corstius spoke, in the very same column, of 'a fearful parallel between the persecution of the Jews and that of people on benefits: the sheep-like servility of the majority of the victims'.[36] So here Brandt Corstius spoke of 'the passive, servile Jew'. Up till now this latter remark of his has not raised any reaction; it went totally unnoticed. Van Gogh and Brandt Corstius operated in a period when there seemed to be an explosion of extremely polemical columns, sometimes downright insulting. Leon de Winter also happily joined in.[37] Columnists were all trying to outdo each other: a fine case of Dutch journalistic machismo.[38]

Against those who strongly criticised Van Gogh, there were those who cherished him as an *enfant terrible* and as the embodiment of an all-encompassing, principled freedom of speech. In the early 1960s, the both political and playful protest movement Provo had already made an issue of the right to freedom of expression. But back then the social context was constituted by the still very conservative, imperious authorities at both the local and national level.[39] In the 1980s the type of narrow-mindedness against which Provo had protested – fossilised administrative relations, a serious lack of democracy in schools and universities, taboos on sex and drugs – was history, even though the police reacted to a re-emerging squat

83. *See also, e.g.*, Hoge Raad, 11 Februari 1986, nr. 122, 173-176. It is stated here: The case again ended up at the Supreme Court, 11 December 1990, RR no. 257 and at the Court of Amsterdam, 26 January 1993, RR no. 309, red. In 1993, when Van Gogh republished 'Messias zonder Kruis' in his volume *De Weldoener*, he was acquitted: Court of Amsterdam, 26 January 1993, no. 309, 644-646. I thank Willem Wagenaar.

35   Quoted in: Aleid Truijens, 'Hugo Brandt Corstius 1945-2014', *NRC Handelsblad*, 1 March 2014. That is why the Dutch government refused to give him the prestigious literary award P.C. Hooftprijs, which a jury had awarded him. Eventually, he did receive the prize, three years later.

36   Quoted in: Truijens, 'Hugo Brandt Corstius'. *See also* chapter 13.

37   During the 1994 election campaign Leon de Winter called the social democratic politician Hedy d'Ancona a 'masturbation queen': Gans, *Gojse nijd & joods narcisme*, 84.

38   *See, e.g.*, Gans, *Gojse nijd & joods* narcisme, 84.

39   For Provo *see* Eric van Duivenvoorden, *Rebelse jeugd. Hoe nozems en provo's Nederland veranderden* (Amsterdam: Nieuw Amsterdam, 2015); Willy Lindwer, *Rebelse stad* (Documentary, 2015); *NRC Handelsblad*, 9/10 May 2015. Provo was dissolved in 1967.

movement, in a familiar harsh way.[40] Van Gogh did not take part in any of these socio-political movements. Instead he and his followers kept hammering away at the right to freedom of expression, stressing it was or should be defined as an 'absolute' right. 'One and indivisible', as Van Gogh put it in quasi-religious terms.[41] This development was accompanied by a dance around the concept of political (in)correctness.

Political incorrectness and correctness are Siamese twins. Political incorrectness only exists at the grace of its mirror image, rival and counterforce, political correctness, which it constructed and launched. The concept first appeared in the late 1980s in the United States, as a rhetorical weapon of the neoconservatives against left-wing politicians.[42] In a similar way antisemites had, one century earlier, branded their opponents as philosemites.[43] Those profiling themselves as 'politically incorrect' protested against what they declared to be 'politically correct': counterproductive simplifications and hypocritical taboos that are upheld for the sake of social peace and quiet – when actually debate and polemic would be more appropriate and urgent. Theo van Gogh would become the uncrowned Dutch king of both freedom of speech and political incorrectness.[44] In view of the contemporary public debate in the Netherlands, Van Gogh has succeeded in bringing the message across that it is 'politically correct' to be 'politically incorrect'.

40   See, e.g., Eric van Duivenvoorden, Een voet tussen de deur: geschiedenis van de kraakbeweging (1964-1999) (Amsterdam: De Arbeiderspers, 2000).
41   Theo van Gogh, 'Voor gojim verboden', and 'Ik d-d-d-dreig u', in Van Gogh, Er gebeurt nooit iets, 26-30: 28 and 117-122:118; Van Gogh, 'Prinses Lama', in: Theo van Gogh, Allah weet het beter (Amsterdam: Xtra, 2003), 22 February 2002, 163-165: 164; Gans, Gojse nijd & joods narcisme, 84.
42   Ariane Manske, 'Das ist doch nicht normal, oder doch? Kontext und Funktion der U.S.-amerikanischen PC-Diskussion der 90er Jahre und warum Barack Obama PC ist.' Paper presented at Internationale Tagung: 'Political Correctness. Aufforderung zur Toleranz oder Selbstzensur? Geschichte und Aktualität eines kulturellen Phänomens', Amsterdam, 11-12 December 2008. See also: Ariane Manske, Political Correctness und Normalität. Die amerikanische PC-Kontroverse im kulturgeschichtlichen Kontext (Heidelberg: Synchron Wissenschaftsverlag der Autoren, 2002).
43   See chapter 5.
44   Theo van Gogh, 'Het knuisje van oom Vuijsje.' In: Van Gogh, Er gebeurt nooit iets, 93-96: 93; Van Gogh, 'Tot hier heeft Allah ons gebracht.' In: Van Gogh, Allah weet het beter, 2 July 2001, 83-86: 83. A former cameraman on Van Gogh's first movie Luger said in 2005 that they had just wanted to make a film that seemed to be 'as politically incorrect as possible': Sietse Meijer, 'Theo moest en zou. The Making of Luger', VPRO gids, 17-23 September 2005; see also www.cinema.nl/nff-2005/artikelen/2173616/theo-moest-en-hij-zou#comments (consulted 18 March 2015). In an interview the author described Van Gogh as a 'free speech fetishist': 'De grens van assimilatie verlegt zich keer op keer.' In: Bart Top, Religie en verdraagzaamheid. 10 gesprekken over tolerantie in een extreme tijd (Kampen: Ten Gave, 2005), 47-60: 60.

Sympathisers, followers, counter-voices – pornographic Islamophobia and murder

Initially, Theo van Gogh was referred to as the 'Fassbinder of the Lowlands' – Rainer Werner Fassbinder (1945-1982) being the talented, famous but also provocative and controversial German film director.[45] Van Gogh was no direct participant in the Dutch equivalent of the Fassbinder affair, in 1987, but he made his position very clear, several years later. The Dutch Fassbinder affair, too, fitted into the climate of political incorrectness and irritation about an alleged Jewish monopolisation of suffering. The affair is not very well-known outside the Netherlands, but that did not make it less intense. Fassbinder's controversial play *Der Müll, die Stadt und der Tod* [Garbage, the City and Death] contained, among other roles, the nameless character of 'The Rich Jew'. That created ill-feeling, considering the long history of this stereotype. Moreover, the character seemed based on Ignatz Bubis (1927-1999), at that time a project developer in Frankfurt.

However, a strong case can be made to claim that with this rather sloppy play, Fassbinder had, first of all, made an interesting attempt to represent a duality in the figure of 'The Rich Jew after Auschwitz' with a Janus face again: as a symbol and tool of social change (first money trade and capital-ism, now speculation and project development) *and* as a scapegoat (for the pernicious effects of this social change).[46] 'The Jew' is difficult to criticise because of his post-Shoah victim status, but still remains the outsider against whom, eventually, one may discharge any feelings of discontent. Second, in his play Fassbinder does indeed seem to put German secondary antisemitism or *Schuldabwehrantisemitismus* on the stage. For example, in the play a former Nazi can be heard saying: 'He sucks us dry, the Jew. Drinks our blood and makes sure we are wrong, because he is a Jew and we carry the blame.[47]

45   Guido Franken, 'Theo van Gogh – l'enfant terrible', Neerlands Filmdoek, 15 April 2006 (consulted 21 January 2016); Mark Moorman, 'Theo van Gogh was een lastpost met een heftig filminstinct', *Het Parool*, 1 November 2014.
46   Gans, *Gojse nijd & joods narcisme*, 37-38; Gans, 'Ischa Meijer, De soldaat van Oranje en de Fassbinderaffaire', 164-165.
47   R.W. Fassbinder, *Het vuil, de stad en de dood*, vert. en nawoord door [translation and afterword by) Gerrit Bussink (The Hague: BZZTôH, 1986), 43. This is the title of the play in Dutch. For a subtle and positive interpretation of the Rich Jew in the play, *see* Anat Feinberg, 'Ein missglückter Versuch: Klaus Pohls Jud Süss-Drama.' In: Hans-Peter Bayderdörfer and Jens Malte Fischer, in cooperation with Frank Halbach (eds.), *Judenrollen. Darstellungsformen im europäischen Theater von der Restauration bis zur Zwischenkriegszeit* (Tübingen: Max Niemeyer Verlag, 2008) 189-198: 192. I thank Robert Jütte.

However, in the Netherlands, opponents, ranging from historian Loe de Jong to Jewish youths of the action group *Alle Cohens aan dek* [All Cohens on deck], did not care about these nuances. Especially for the young (often: 'third') generation it was clear that this time they would stand their ground as Jews: 'people will have to get used to combatant Jews'.[48] Whereas mainly, though not exclusively, Jews campaigned against the alleged antisemitic character of the play, trainee director Johan Doesburg and his followers invoked the right of freedom of expression, while protesting against the 'dictatorship' of Jewish suffering. Doesburg (b. 1955), however, knew very well, as emerged from a leaked application form in which he describes why he wanted to produce this particular play, that, considering the numerous actions and demonstrations which had prevented the performance of the play in Germany, there inevitably was going to be a 'fuss' in the Netherlands as well. He had been even disappointed by the quality of the play.[49] Nevertheless, he did not, beforehand, approach any Jewish organisation. What he actually did, once the bombshell had been dropped, was making a statement that he had been aware of 'the hypersensitivity sticking to Jewish affairs like resin to a conifer'. That did not strengthen his case, neither did his lack of historical awareness.

He said he *did* understand why the performance in Frankfurt, in the country of the 'perpetrators', had caused problems: this was because in that city so many Jews had been 'destroyed'. Moreover, every older German was a potential perpetrator.[50] But why here? Apparently, at that moment, Doesburg did not realise that the number of Jews deported from Amsterdam and subsequently murdered was many times higher than the number of Jews deported from Frankfurt – and that this certainly hadn't involved only Germans, but also Dutch officials and civilians. In the end, there was only one private performance with an audience that consisted mainly of representatives of the theatre sector and 'the Jewish circuit'.[51]

48   *Vrij Nederland,* 28 November 1987, referred to in: Gans, *Gojse nijd & joods narcisme,* 35.

49   *De Fassbinderkrant,* Theaterschool, 29 February 1988, quoted in: Gans, *Gojse nijd & joods narcisme,* 36-37.

50   *De Volkskrant,* 23 November 1987, *see also* NIW, 6 November 1987 and: Gans, *Gojse nijd & joods narcisme,* 8-9, 34-38. Moreover, Doesburg did give the Rich Jew a name, *i.e.* A.

51   *See, e.g.,* Loek Zonneveld, 'Het citatenkerkhof. Kroniek van R.W. Fassbinders "Het vuil, de stad en de dood", 1975-2002.www.loekzonneveld.nl/2004/fassb01.htm; Loek Zonneveld, 'Fassbinder, het geniale monster. Bij wijze van Inleiding.' In: Rainer Werner Fassbinder, *Het vuil, de stad en de dood / Rainer Werner Fassbinder* (Translated from German by Gerrit Bussink) (Utrecht: Signature, 2002), 7-16.

Pornographic elements did not play any role in this affair. But Jewish narcissism did: often enough Jewish campaigners had not read the play, but were still convinced that they, and Jews in general, were being subjected to antisemitism.[52] Their opponents, on the other hand, in different degrees, gave vent to their 'Shoah fatigue'. Doesburg himself showed, moreover, a certain degree of opportunism, expressing his hope of raising a dust in the above-mentioned application form, and not only 'cultural' but 'historical incorrectness' as well. In Muslim circles the 'Fassbinder affair' became a symbol of the impossibility of saying or writing anything against or about 'the Jews', while anything goes when it comes to Muslims.[53]

Theo van Gogh would interview Johan Doesburg in his television programme in 1994, seven years after the affair. He tried several times to draw Doesburg out by phrasing his questions in provocative terms: 'Hadn't the occupation of the stage by the Jewish activists not been a 'fascist way of acting'? And should the lack of response from the theatre community not be construed as 'an NSB-like silence'? Doesburg, who in the meantime had become older and wiser, answered he used such terms very sparingly and left them to the responsibility of Van Gogh. Political incorrectness emerged in Van Gogh's jeers against all possible individuals, including, mainly left-wing, politicians, particularly when he suspected them of acting opportunistically. But initially Jews were his main target. In a sense Van Gogh rebelled against the same 'taboo' as the football hooligans: making negative remarks about Jews.[54] Likewise, at a time when, in the early 1980s, the Shoah became a central focus of public memory and culture, Van Gogh too turned the Shoah against the Jews, making use of one of the genres at his disposal, the column. Columns became his ideal playground to launch his aggression. It would be boring to list all examples of Van Gogh's *Spielerei* with antisemitic stereotypes. It is more interesting to signal a turning point in 1994. Then, after having been being criticised in *Gojse nijd & joods narcisme* [Goyish envy & Jewish narcissism] (1994) because of his antisemitic stereotypes against Leon de Winter and other Jews, Van Gogh in a column in *Folia* vented the suspicion that the author 'in her wet dreams ... often gets fucked by Dr Mengele'.[55] This was, again, a manifestation of pornographic

---

52   For Jewish narcissism: Gans, *Gojse nijd & joods narcisme*; Gans, 'They have forgotten to gas you', 81*ff*; *see also* chapters 1, 5, 6, 18.

53   Ensel, *Haatspraak*, 170, 177; Gans, *'They have forgotten to gas you'*, 81. See Epilogue.

54   *See* chapter 10.

55   Gans, *Gojse nijd & joods narcisme*, 70*ff*; Gans, They have forgotten to gas you', 85, 95 (n. 11); Theo van Gogh, *Folia. Weekblad voor de Universiteit van* Amsterdam, 10/17 September 1993; November 1994 (no titles). The author in question was myself.

antisemitism and of sexism. It took a while, but then his remark caused such a row that *Folia*'s editorial staff, which had initially conjured up freedom of expression as a license to write, was forced to apologise – upon which an angry Van Gogh absconded. But even then Van Gogh did not fall from grace, but remained popular in several social circles as well as a source of inspiration. This was, for example, the case for quite a few intellectuals who, even while acknowledging his occasionally 'tasteless' approach, saw in him most of all a pioneer who said what others thought too but just lacked the courage to say. Van Gogh continued his crusade elsewhere; but usually not for long. He eventually found a stage on his own blog *De Gezonde Roker* [The Healthy Smoker] and in the free daily *Metro*. There was a certain change as he shifted his main focus from Jews to Muslims.

Van Gogh certainly had followers and sympathisers. In 1992, the editors of the, still existing, provocative Amsterdam student magazine *Propria Cures* (*PC*)[56] believed that Leon de Winter had gone too far, both in commercial terms and with regard to content, in a commercial for his latest novel *De ruimte van Sokolov* [Sokolov's universe] (1992) (published by the bookstore chain Libris). That was partly because of his appearance in a tuxedo, surrounded by small glittering Stars of David. The *PC* editorial staff decided to put De Winter in his place by making a composite picture in which he is situated, wearing a tuxedo, in a mass grave (probably near Vilna in Poland), with a human bone in his hand: 'Every writer is at Libris, and where am I'. Leon de Winter responded in the press and successfully sued *PC*. But the 15,000-guilder fine *PC* was forced to pay, was quickly raised by sympathisers of the magazine. Theo van Gogh explicitly expressed his solidarity by suggesting a new composite picture with the well-known Jewish talk show host Sonja Barend, smiling in a concentration camp: '*Morgen gezond weer op*' [Rise and shine tomorrow], with which she always used to finish her show.[57] In 1993, in an obscure magazine, *Reactie* [Reaction], editor-in-chief Bart Croughs (b. 1966), pioneer of the New Right – with a great passion for political incorrectness, up till now – accused Jewish writers of being busy looking for 'their own Holocaust'.[58]

In the Groningen University student magazine *Nait Soez'n*, also in 1993, editor-in-chief Peter Middendorp (b. 1971) let a fake professor talk about a

56 *See* Gans, *Gojse nijd & joods narcisme*: 'Theo van Gogh als fenomeen', 70-85, and for *Propria Cures* also chapters 2 and 4.
57 Theo van Gogh, 'Voor gojim verboden', 29.
58 Quoted in: *NIW*, 1 October 1993; René Zwaap, 'De opstand der incorrecten', *De Groene Amsterdammer*, 17 January 1996. Croughs also accused both Leon de Winter and journalist/writer Daphne Meijer of exaggerating antisemitism.

'sexually transformed' Anne Frank who lived in Argentina. When a fictitious spokesperson of the Jewish community accuses him of antisemitism,
he responds by saying: 'That dirty filthy fucking cancer Jew doesn't know
what he is talking about'.[59] After a while, his exasperated co-editor started
answering calls from indignant readers by saying: 'We can't take every
Jew into account'.[60] Middendorp himself said he had wanted to raise the
question whether the 'Jewish genocide can be prostituted to justify the
human rights' violations by the Israeli state'.[61] Here criticism of Israel is
completely derailed, as it is described in terms of 'Jewish genocide' and
'prostitution' – and in terms of sex and money too.[62] *Nait Soez'n* was seized
and the editorial staff suspended.

Ten years after the murder of Van Gogh, in November 2014, Peter Middendorp got the opportunity to write a comprehensive article about his
visit, in 1993, to Van Gogh, whom he used to admire a lot and obviously still
does.[63] Today, Middendorp is a writer and an established columnist for the
daily *de Volkskrant*. In a column on 2 May 2015, he expressed his annoyance
about the placement of a cattle carriage in transit camp Westerbork, because
it may not have been 'original'. The question whether so-called Holocaust
material must be 'authentic' is, indeed, a serious point of debate. But Middendorp wrote that it was a 'lie in the landscape'. 'From Westerbork people
were not transported to the camps in cattle carriages but in normal trains.'[64]
There was a big uproar, not without reason. Half of the trains in question
consisted of goods and cattle carriages and the other half of normal trains.
An example of the latter type will also be put on display.[65] The editorial staff
of *de Volkskrant* apologised, removed the column and then left it to Peter
Middendorp to personally apologise extensively.[66] The fact that Middendorp
was subsequently indeed 'forced to bite the dust', was widely appreciated; *de
Volkskrant* called his reaction a 'much-needed, open-hearted and humble'
column.[67] Though Middendorp's apologies certainly give a sincere impres-

---

59 'Anne Frank leeft nog', *Nait Soez'n*, January 1993. For an earlier fake interview, with Anne
Frank herself, *see* chapter 2.

60 *de Volkskrant*, 1 November 2014.

61 *Universiteitskrant Groningen (UK)*, 11 December 1993.

62 A theme which regularly features in Gilman's *The Jewish Body*, 121-124, 126-127.

63 *de Volkskrant*, 1 November 2014.

64 *Ibid.*, 2 May 2015.

65 *See, e.g., Nieuwsblad van het Noorden*, 2 May 2015.

66 *de Volkskrant*, 2 May 2015 and in the paper version: *de Volkskrant*, 4 May 2015.

67 *See, e.g.,* RTV Drenthe: www.rtvdrenthe.nl/nieuws/peter-middendorp-diep-door-stof-na-
volkskrant-column ; *de Volkskrant*, 9 May 2015.

sion, his omission – not checking the historical facts – shows that 'Shoah fatigue' can easily arise.

Ronald Ophuis is a case in itself, if only because he is a painter and not a writer or columnist. A visual artist known also outside the Netherlands, Ophuis (b. 1968) is fascinated by all possible forms of violence: from executions, bloody miscarriages and the genocide in Srebrenica to rape. Hence, he is sometimes referred to as 'the painter of the horrific'. This may also involve an element of political passion, but, as the documentary *Painful Painting* (2012), about him and his work, suggests, also arousal, sensation, perhaps even light sadism. 'Violence appears to eroticise him.'[68]

Five years before the murder of Van Gogh, Ophuis painted Birkenau I (1999), followed, a few years later, by Birkenau II (2003). A lot has been written about Ophuis' artistry, often in words of praise, occasionally with doubts about his 'good taste'.[69] But the term 'antisemitism' has never been used in relation to his 'Birkenau's'. On the two paintings two Jewish male prisoners (recognisable by their yellow stars and striped clothing) are raping a fellow female (in the second painting possibly male) prisoner in an empty barracks. Ophuis usually gets away with his focus on the (worn-out) theme that 'victims' can become 'perpetrators'. In order to further intensify this, to him important, theme, he had applied yellow stars to the 'raping victims'.[70] Apart from the fact that these paintings again publicise the myth that Jews cannot or will not control their hunger for sex in the most horrific circumstances, the scene is also wide off the mark from a historical, physiological and psychological perspective. Birkenau, part of the big Auschwitz complex, was a camp where Jewish prisoners who had not already been sent to the gas chambers during the first selection worked in degrading conditions until they were ready to be gassed after all. Apart

---

68   Catherine van Campen (direction), *Painful Painting* (documentary, 53 min., 2011); Niels Bakker, 'Webfilm: Painful Painting', *De Filmkrant*, 2 February 2012. *See* for the work of Ophuis: http://www.ronaldophuis.nl/.

69   *See, e.g., Trouw,* 5 September 2000. In his interesting essay *Waanzin in de literatuur* [Madness in literature] (Amsterdam: CPNB, 2015), 8, the literary reviewer and non-fiction writer Pieter Steinz simply refers to Ophuis as a shock artist. Robert Roos, 'Ophuis tart de goede smaak', *Trouw* 5 September 2000; Huub Mous, 'Wie is er bang voor vernietiging?, ' 6 September 2015, with a link to 'Birkenau 1': www.huubmous.nl/2015/09/06/wie-is-er-bang-voor-vernietiging/ (consulted 22 January 2016); Ernst van Alphen, 'Pijnlijke schilderijen', *De Witte Raaf*, Edition 125, January-February 2007: www.dewitteraaf.be/artikel/detail/nl/3153; Hilde van Canneyt, 'Interview met Ronald Ophuis', Gesprekken met hedendaagse kunstenaars, Amsterdam, 12 May 2011: http://hildevancanneyt.blogspot.nl/2011/07/v-behaviorurldefaultvmlo.html.

70   Catherine van Campen, *Painful Painting.'* Documentary about Ronald Ophuis, broadcast on 31 January 2012.

from the heavy work and the working hours, deprivations like hours-long roll calls, abuse, hunger and diseases were of such a scale that there was no room anymore for libido. Yet, a Birkenau II was painted. A case of both cultural and historical 'incorrectness'.

Each time, these kinds of incidents led to statements that at stake was the area of tension between 'tastelessness and freedom of opinion'. In such cases legal proceedings were rejected.[71] On the other side of the spectrum one finds the Jewish writer Marcel Möring (who Van Gogh called 'Marcel Göring'[72]) who, with regard to Van Gogh, clearly spoke of antisemitism, expressing his concern about the fact that no Gentile writers had stood up for Leon de Winter after the composite picture in PC. Möring (b. 1957) wrote – and this is valid today as well – that freedom of expression can never be absolute, because slander and racism are punishable. No preventive censorship, said Möring, but any text could, might or should, indeed, be assessed with respect to its lawful or unlawful character. In his response Möring lifted the discussion to a more general level by stating that in the Netherlands the question of how to get rid of the country's immigrants, instead of how to deal with them, was increasing; the taboos on racism and antisemitism were more and more seen as 'soft nonsense from the 1970s'.[73] Möring wrote his article in December 1992. In 1994 Van Gogh made his statement about Mengele, which grew into an 'affair'.

This will have been one of the reasons that Van Gogh started looking for a new main target: Muslims and Islam. Other, at least as relevant, factors were the cultural and political climate as described by Möring, the temptation for Van Gogh to break another taboo – namely that of the idea and practice of the multicultural society, which he cursed, and the lack of public criticism of undesirable manifestations of Islam – and, finally, the attention such a role would give him. Apart from anything else, Van Gogh was an attention junk; a friend said that Van Gogh's need for attention 'bordered on the maniacal'.[74] A direct, personal motive seems to have been his impression that his little

71   Gans, *Gojse nijd & joods narcisme*, 80.
72   Theo van Gogh, 'Wie niet voor Jezus heeft gestudeerd.' In: Van Gogh, *Er gebeurt nooit iets*, 6-7:6. Van Gogh enjoyed calling Jews NSB members, camp bullies etc.: *ibid.*, 21, 49.
73   *NRC Handelsblad*, 11 December 1992.
74   Eva Rovers, 'De scherpe rand van ironie. Hoe de dorpsgek een duivelse spotter werd', *De Groene Amsterdammer*, 23 October 2010. The friend in question was Roeland Hazendonk, *see* Epilogue.

Illustration 20   The cover of 'Allah knows best', a collection of columns by Theo van Gogh, January 2004

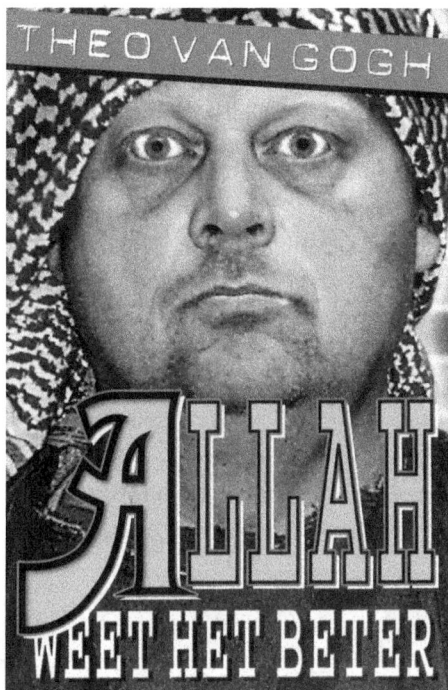

'Allah knows best.' Theo van Gogh on the cover of a collection of his columns, January 2004. Later that year, the film director and columnist was killed.

son Lieuwe was not getting enough attention in primary school because of all the 'immigrant' or Moroccan or Turkish pupils in his class.[75]

Van Gogh saw himself as 'preacher of the nihilistic community' and 'professional infidel'.[76] In his columns he frequently lashed out against Muslims, whom he consistently called 'goat fuckers'. This was occasionally

75   Theo van Gogh, 'Lang leve de racist!', *HP/DeTijd*, 24 March 1995 (Incidentally, in this article Van Gogh also says he does not think it's a good idea to remove children from school that are from parents that don't have a legal status), and Van Gogh, 'Eigen schuld dikke bult', 20 October 1995, *ibid*. Van Gogh said in *Trouw* (22 November 2004): 'Faith is the source of all evil.'

76   Theo van Gogh, 'Brief aan Bea Irik', 14 December 2000, and 'Allah weet het beter', in: Van Gogh, *Allah weet het beter*, 37-38: 38; 9-16:14.

alternated with 'young immigrant camel fuckers, pigmented faggots'.[77] This time a form of pornographic Islamophobia, which was also present in how he referred to the Belgian-Lebanese Dyab Abou Jahjah (b. 1971), then leader of the controversial Arab European League (AEL), which would regularly operate on the border of anti-Zionism and antisemitism. Van Gogh called Abou Jahjah 'the prophet's pimp' – and Mohammed himself 'that goat fucker from Mecca'.[78] Nowadays Abou Jahjah is the leader of the anti-colonialist, anti-discrimination Movement X, founded in Belgium in 2014, which claims to fight for civil rights and radical democracy. When the chairman of the right-wing New Flemish Alliance (N-VA), Bart De Wever (b. 1970) in his capacity as mayor of Antwerp, raised the security measures for Jewish institutions during the Jewish holidays because of the jihadist attacks in Brussels, Abou Jahjah called him a *'zionisten-pijper'* [literally, Zionist cocksucker].[79] Thus, ironically, Abou Jahjah acted in Van Goghs' spirit: pornographic antisemitism.

Van Gogh's insults of Muslims – and Jews – are not restricted to pornographic metaphors. This can be illustrated by his numerous references to various Jews as NSB members and by his response to the cancellation of the

77   Van Gogh, 'Brief van Bea Irik aan Theo van Gogh', 24 January 2001: Van Gogh, *Allah weet het beter*, 48-49: 49.

78   Theo van Gogh, 'Leve de islam', *HP/De* Tijd, December 1995; *Trouw*, 3 November 2004. Ensel, *Haatspraak*, 188, 203; Gans, 'On gas chambers, Jewish Nazis and noses', 83-84. Mohammed Benzakour, *Abou Jahjah. Nieuwlichter of oplichter? De demonisering van een politiek rebel* (Amsterdam/ Anwerp: L.J. Veen, 2004), 144. The journalist and writer Max Pam (b. 1946), a close friend of Van Gogh, has looked into the history of the Dutch word *'geitenneuker'* [goat fucker], related to Muslims, in the Netherlands. He demonstrates the term was already used before Van Gogh. Pam however ignores the systematic and casual use of the term by Van Gogh (using it not only with respect to Islamists, but to Muslims in general, something which Pam denies), the stereotypical and pornographic aspect of the term – i.e. referring to the sexually needy and primitive Muslim – and, finally, the link to Van Gogh's pornographic connection between 'the Jew' and sexual perversity: Max Pam, 'De geschiedenis van het woord "geitenneuker"', *The Max Pam Globe*, 28 January 2016: www.maxpam.nl/2014/11/geschiedenis-van-het-woord-geitenneuker/. For the AEL *see also*: chapter 14.

79   Christophe Callewaert, 'Movement X wil museum Europa afstoffen', *DeWereldMorgen. be*, 7 October 2014: www.dewereldmorgen.be/artikel/2014/10/07/movement-x-wil-museum-europa-afstoffen (consulted 11 July 2016); 'Verhoogde veiligheidsmaatregelen in Antwerpen blijven van kracht (fotoverslag)', *Joods Actueel*, 28 May 2014: http://joodsactueel.be/2014/05/28/verhoogde-veiligheidsmaatregelen-in-antwerpen-blijven-van-kracht-na-aanslag-fotoverslag/; https://twitter.com/bdlumey/status/475568377625583616 (both consulted 12 July 2016). When he was criticised, Abou Jahjah promised this would never happen again and changed his term into 'zionistenknechtje' [servant of the Zionists]: Harm Ede Botje and Jaco Alberts, 'Abou Jahjah, tien jaar later', *Vrij Nederland*, 8 August 2014. For Abou Jahjah *see also*: Ensel, *Haatspraak*, 188-189, 203.

opera *Aïsja en de vrouwen van Medina* [Aïsja and the women of Medina], written by the Algerian writer Assia Djebar (1936-2015), which was to be performed by the *Onafhankelijk Toneel* [Independent Theatre] in Rotterdam. The opera was said to be insulting to Muslims, and the ban was, indeed, controversial. Van Gogh wrote: 'The SA is marching again, this time in a veil'.[80]

Ironically, Theo van Gogh and his former arch-enemy Leon de Winter had, unintentionally, grown closer to each other. De Winter, who eventually became a spokesperson of alarmed conservative Jews in the Netherlands, positioned himself as a staunch defender of Israel, who warned against the danger of the Arab world and Islam.[81] Van Gogh declared that he fully supported President Bush and his attack on Iraq. If it were for the UN, Saddam would still be in power and 'Israel wiped away'. And along the same lines as De Winter he drew a parallel with the 1930s: 'It is a kind of nightmare, it's Hitler Germany 1938: you look at it and there is nothing you can do.'[82] Van Gogh also became a great admirer of Pim Fortuyn (1948-2002), the articulate, witty and populist right-wing politician who quickly became popular with a unique combination of both anti-Islam and anti-establishment rhetoric and libertinism (confidently bringing out his homosexuality), and putting the Dutch political landscape on its head. In fact, both Van Gogh and Fortuyn wanted to prove that criticising Islam or the multicultural society was a taboo. They wanted to break that taboo – in their own provocative, respectively destructive way. Fortuyn called Islam *'een achterlijke cultuur'* [a backward culture], said the Netherlands was 'full', and campaigned to have the principle of non-discrimination removed from the constitution.[83] Van Gogh baptised him the 'Holy Baldy'.[84]

---

80   About the ban *see, e.g.*, Fleur Bokhoven, 'Gysbreght and Aïsja. Censuur: zaak van of taak voor de overheid' (Research Master Kunst-, religie- en cultuurwetenschappen, Universiteit van Amsterdam, 2006-2007); http://cf.hum.uva.nl/bookmaster/gysbrecht/censuur.htm#2.1: Aïsja: Het zingen het zwijgen opgelegd (consulted 23 February 2015); *De Volkskrant*, 31 January 2006; Paul Steenhuis, 'Aïsja: de verboden sterke vrouw', *NRC Handelsblad*, 1 December 2000; Theo van Gogh, 'Propaganda', 30 January 2001, in: *Allah weet het* beter, 55. In Rome the opera was performed without problems.

81   For this development *see, e.g.*, David Wertheim, 'Hypotheek op een ongedekte cheque. De betekenis van Israël voor de Nederlandse-joodse schrijvers Abel Herzberg, Leon de Winter en Arnon Grunberg.' In: Hetty Berg and Bart Wallet (eds.), *Wie niet weg is, is gezien. Joods Nederland na 1945* (Zwolle: Waanders, 2010), 134-147: 139-142.

82   Theo van Gogh, 'Vooruitgang', *Haagse Post/De Tijd*, 24 March 1994.

83   *De Volkskrant*, 9 February 2002. Also referred to in Bas van Stokkom, *Mondig tegen elke prijs. Het vrije woord als fetisj* (The Hague: Boom Juridische Uitgevers, 2008), 46.

84   Van Gogh, 'Allah weet het beter', in: Van Gogh, *Allah weet het beter*, 9-16:12. Yoeri Albrecht and Thijs Broer, 'Ik hou niet van verlossers. Theo van Gogh 1957-2004', *Vrij Nederland*, 6 November 2004.

In 2002 Fortuyn was killed by the animal activist Volkert van der Graaf (b. 1969). It was a political murder; Van der Graaf said in court he wanted to finish the increasing power of Fortuyn, whom he saw as a danger to society, especially the weak.[85] In the emerging political climate after the murder – captured in the tagline 'the bullet came from the Left' – Van Gogh declared on television that the Left had got what it had worked on. 'The man who would have won the elections has been finished off, and that's it.'[86]

Van Gogh can be seen as an 'Enlightenment fundamentalist'. As someone who paved the way for Fortuyn by systematically pushing the boundaries of freedom of expression, because of his fervent anti-establishment approach and superficial Islam bashing, turning to Islamophobia. Fortuyn, in turn, can be seen as a precursor of the populist, extreme Islamophobic politician Geert Wilders. Hence, Van Gogh played an important role in what came to be known as the debate about the 'Islamisation' of the Netherlands or Europe. Fortuyn never criticised Jews. Van Gogh went on with it, albeit less pronounced. He gave the Jewish mayor of Amsterdam, Job Cohen (b. 1947) – to him the ultimate embodiment of multiculturalism – the part of a modern Judas, calling him, among other things, an 'NSB member by nature'. It was Cohen who was bringing the Muslims into the country: 'Of all swindlers who are trying to sell us the Fifth Column of the goat fuckers .... Cohen is the most cunning'.[87]

The film pamphlet *Submission*, directed by Van Gogh based on a script by VVD politician and Islam critic Ayaan Hirsi Ali (b. 1969) intended to expose anti-women practices in Islam and Muslim circles, sealed his fate. The images of Quran texts written on naked and abused female bodies in the television film *Submission* were extremely provocative. They resulted in defensive responses and did not, as intended – or so it was suggested – lead to debates in Muslim circles; as such, *Submission* was counterproductive. In this case, it even had a deadly outcome. As far as we know, Hirsi Ali was the real target of the attack, but she had been living under police protection for some time, because of her threatened status. At an earlier stage, Van Gogh had been threatened as well, and had received some protection. But at this very moment he did not really worry, or even

85 'Levenslang voor Van der G. zou unicum zijn', *NRC Handelsblad*, 2 April 2003. Louis Cornelisse, 'Volkert houdt iets achter', *Trouw*, 30 June 2003. By 'weak people' Van der G. meant for example refugees, Muslims and recipients of disability benefits.

86 Femke Halsema, *Pluche. Politieke memoires* (Amsterdam: Ambo/Anthos, 2016), 107.

87 Theo van Gogh, 'De boel bij elkaar houden', *Metro*, 13 March 2004; Van Gogh, 'Onze burgemeester', Van Gogh, *Metro*, 22 October 2004.

refused protection. On 2 November 2004, Theo van Gogh was killed on the street in Amsterdam by Mohammed Bouyeri, a Moroccan-Dutch young man, featuring in both previous and following chapters, who had become a Muslim extremist. The letter he left on Van Gogh's body was not only drenched with accusations against Hirsi Ali, other Islamic apostates and the depraved West, but also against the large number of Jews who, allegedly, controlled politics and considered non-Jews as non-humans. All of that was supposedly supported by the Talmud. In a cynical twist, there was one target which Bouyeri shared with Van Gogh, albeit from a different perspective: mayor Cohen, who 'supports an ideology in which Jews are allowed to lie against non-Jews'.[88] Here we have 'The Jew' Cohen with a Janus face: as an accomplice *and* enemy of Islam.

The political murder of Van Gogh obviously sent a shockwave through the Netherlands, as had been the case after the assault on Fortuyn. The latter had been committed by a 'native' Dutch. This time the executer was a Moroccan-Dutch, a Muslim. The murder raised a storm of indignation[89] – though there were certainly mixed feelings too.[90] A lot of attention was paid to the (supposedly) dangerous gap dividing Moroccans and, more generally, Muslims and the 'others', and the assumed threat of Muslim

88   *See, e.g.*, M. de Kessel, 'Tango met de Dood. Over Mohammed Bouyeri's *Open Brief aan Hirsi Ali.*' Lecture at the symposium *'It takes two to tango: Religie in de publieke ruimte'*, Erasmus Universiteit Rotterdam, Faculty of Philosophy, 21 September 2005; Ensel, *Haatspraak,* 271*ff.* Both Van Gogh and Bouyeri have certainly used dubious websites to make their respectively anti-Islam and anti-Jewish statements: Bernard Hulsman, 'Getto's op het web. Op internet heeft elke groep zijn eigen waarheid', and 'Khomeiny en de geitenneukers', *NRC Handelsblad,* 8/9 January 2005.

89   *See, e.g., NRC Handelsblad,* 2 November 2004. 'Herhaal Submission elke dag op de televisie.' Letters to the editor, *de Volkskrant,* 6 November 2006, Connie Palmen, 'Moord. In memoriam Theo van Gogh 1957-2004', *Vrij Nederland,* 20 November 2004. For a critical analysis and con-textualisation of the killing: Jannetje Koelewijn, 'Ik ben niet begonnen', *NRC Handelsblad,* 6/7 November 2004. There were too many shocked, indignant and furious articles and letters in the regular press to list here; they are in the personal archive of the author.

90   There were also those that didn't care, or believed Theo van Gogh had more or less provoked his own death. Others rebelled against his 'canonization', *see* notes 193 and 194. There were, for example, mixed feelings among Dutch Muslims: Rachid Majiti and Ahmed Dadou, 'Weg met mea-culpa-media-Marokkanen', *NRC Handelsblad,* 11 November 2004; Laura Schot, 'Zeggen wat je denkt', *NIW,* 26 November 2004; Marjolein van Trigt, 'Afgebrand door Van Gogh', *Babel. Maandblad van de faculteit der Geesteswetenschappen* 13, 3 (November 2004), 4-5.The Somali-Dutch Mohammed B. (not to be confused with the murderer of Van Gogh), who went to Syria to fight with IS, openly welcomed the murder, in 2004, on a digital forum: 'Good riddance': André Kouwenhoven, 'De blinde jihadist komt uit Groningen', *ibid.,* 28 May 2015.

terrorism. The murder of Van Gogh was world news.[91] On Dam Square in Amsterdam thousands of people gathered to honour the 'advocate of the free word'. Elsewhere in the country mosques were set on fire. Princess (now Queen) Máxima praised Van Gogh as a 'champion of the free word'.[92] Van Gogh's friends put two goats on the stage in the venue where the victim was commemorated. The word 'goat fucker' was included in the 2005 edition of the authoritative Van Dale dictionary. The demand by a small group of Muslims to ban the announced sequel of *Submission* – an exception: until then Muslims had exercised restraint with respect to starting legal procedures as a reaction to anti-Muslim utterances like those by Van Gogh – was not granted by the judge. Among other things, the litigating Muslims were offended by Hirsi Ali's references to the prophet Mohammed as a 'paedophile'; she said that Muslim men were unable to control their 'sensual urges, like billygoats'. That came rather close to Van Gogh's goat fuckers. In *Mondig tegen elke prijs. Het vrije woord als fetisj* [Independent at all cost. The free word as fetish] (2008) the sociologist and philosopher Bas van Stokkom (b. 1953) wrote he was disappointed that the government had deemed it unnecessary to take the initiative and prosecute Van Gogh for his qualification 'goat fuckers'. This would have given the Muslim population a sense of inclusion and protection.[93]

Immediate responses, directly after the murder, like that of the famous Dutch poet and writer Remco Campert (b. 1929), were an exception. Campert instantly challenged the adoration of Van Gogh. He thought that someone who had written, 'What's that caramel smell? Today they are burning Jews with diabetes', should not enter history as a hero of freedom of speech. In

---

91   Foreign journalists who travelled to the Netherlands to report about the political murder, were sometimes baffled about the things the victim had been allowed to say and write about Jews and Muslims, *see, e.g.*, Peter Waterman, 'Saint Theo', *Risq. Review of International Social Questions*, 9 November 2004; 'Theo van Gogh, un profilo', *Rekombinant. linee di fuga dal pensiero binario*, Indymedia.nl, 15 November 2004; 'Speak now or forever rest in peace... The Netherlands: Death of Theo van Gogh – Free speech fundamentalist', *Index for free expression*, 19 November 2004; Christopher Caldwell, 'Faith and Death', *The New York Times*, 10 September 2006, review of Ian Buruma, *Murder in Amsterdam. The death of Theo van Gogh and the limits of tolerance* (New York: Penguin Press, 2006), translated into Dutch as: *Dood van een gezonde roker* (Amsterdam/ Antwerp: Atlas/Contact, 2006). Buruma doesn't touch on the theme of antisemitism. In the Arab world the murder hardly raised any attention – if one had seen *Submission*, one probably would have sympathised with Mohammed B.: Hassan Daoud, 'Een moord zonder echo', *De Groene Amsterdammer*, 14 January 2005.

92   Koelewijn, 'Ik ben niet begonnen'.

93   Van Stokkom, *Mondig tegen elke prijs*, 46-47, 55.

general, this remark was not appreciated.[94] Although Campert certainly wasn't and wouldn't be the only critical voice,[95] that is, however, exactly what would happen.[96]

94 Remco Campert, 'Gemengde gevoelens', de Volkskrant, 3 and 5 November 2004.
95 See, e.g., the above-mentioned article by Koelewijn, 'Ik ben niet begonnen'; Frits Abrahams, 'Terug', NRC Handelsblad, 11 November 2004; the writer Arnon Grunberg in his weekly, public correspondence with Professor in Economics, Arnold Heertje, 'Vreedzame broeders', Het Parool, 6 November 2004.
96 See Epilogue.

Illustration 21   Photo of Jews being forced to leave their house

Photographer unknown / NIOD archive / Imagebase

Jews, forced to leave their houses, on their way to be deported to transit camp Westerbork. Behind the small group in front, some people on the pavement are watching. Daily life seems to go on as usual.

13 *Historikerstreit*

The Stereotypical Jew in Recent Dutch Holocaust Studies

Remco Ensel and Evelien Gans

A postwar history of antisemitism and representations of 'the Jew' includes the historiography of the Second World War and the Shoah. In the postwar Netherlands Abel Herzberg and particularly Jacques Presser and Loe de Jong slowly and partly – there would always be opposition[1] – managed to get their historical views adopted through their publications and, in the case of De Jong, also through his prominent role in the media. Their views, incidentally, didn't always correspond.[2] But from the mid-1960s, through communication with a substantial readership and a television audience that was susceptible to the subject, the Shoah would very gradually become a central part of the history of the Second World War. Before that, the persecution of Jews was a minor topic in the public debate and historiography. The 'national story' of occupation, collaboration and resistance was the main area of concern, the Jewish perspective was neglected.[3] Even so, experiences of Jewish persecution during *and* after the war did get recorded in the form of verbal and written testimonies, and in 1940's and 1950's, in the publications of respectively Sam de Wolff, Willy Kweksilber and Abel Herzberg – none of them being historians.[4]

---

1   See Conny Kristel, 'Survivors as historians: Abel Herzberg, Jacques Presser and Loe de Jong on the Nazi Persecution of the Jews in the Netherlands.' In: David Bankier and Dan Michman (eds.), *Holocaust Historiography in Context. Emergence, Challenges, Polemics & Achievements* (Jerusalem: Yad Vashem, Berghahn Books, 2008), 207-226.

2   See chapters 2 and 3.

3   Frank van Vree, 'Iedere dag en elk uur. De jodenvervolging en de dynamiek van de herinnering in Nederland.' In: Hetty Berg and Bart Wallet (eds.), *Wie niet weg is, is gezien. Joods Nederland na 1945* (Zwolle: Waanders, 2010), 57-72: 70. *See also* Frank van Vree, 'De dynamiek van de herinnering. Nederland in een internationale context.' In: Frank van Vree and Rob van der Laarse (eds.), *De dynamiek van de herinnering. Nederland en de Tweede Wereldoorlog in een internationale context* (Amsterdam: Bert Bakker, 2009), 17-40; Frank van Vree, *In de schaduw van Auschwitz. Herinneringen, beelden, geschiedenis* (Groningen: Historisch Uitgeverij, 1995).

4   Ido de Haan, *Na de Ondergang. De herinnering aan de Jodenvervolging in Nederland, 1945-1995* (The Hague: Sdu, 1997), 17-20. Sam de Wolff, *Geschiedenis van de Joden in Nederland. Laatste Bedrijf* (Amsterdam: Arbeiderspers, 1946; H. Wielek (pseudonym of W. Kweksilber), *De oorlog die Hitler won* (Amsterdam: Amsterdamse Boek- en Courantmij. N.V., 1947) and the still well-known book of Abel Herzberg, *Kroniek der Jodenvervolging, 1940-1945* (Amsterdam: Querido, 1950). For Herzberg *see also* part I, chapter 7, and hereafter.

From the late 1980s, the Shoah was a focal point of collective memory in the Netherlands – and elsewhere in the West. From a symbol of Jewish suffering, 'Auschwitz' developed into a universal symbol of persecution and annihilation. As a result, Jewish survivors to a certain extent lost ownership of their history.[5] In the same paradoxical manner – albeit in a different context – the Jewish testimonies at the Eichmann trial had not necessarily led to more empathy, but rather had been experienced as painful.[6]

The academic representation of the Shoah is not disconnected from perceptions in society. Through their work and authority historians intervene in society, but they themselves are influenced by the overall cultural-historical developments of their time.[7] This is evident in the case of the historiographical shift that J.C.H. (Hans) Blom (b. 1943), one of the successors of De Jong as director of the Netherlands Institute for War Documentation (NIOD) (1996-2007), brought about with his inaugural lecture in 1983. Blom made an appeal to abandon the narrative framework of (heroic) resistance versus collaboration that had come to determine postwar historiography. In his opinion, such a framework amounted to a judgmental attitude labelling wartime behaviour as either 'right' or 'wrong' that does not suit historians. Incidentally, the moralising perspective to which Blom referred, was not primarily related to the Shoah. In the nation-oriented context of resistance and collaboration, the Shoah only played a minor role. As mentioned above, in the first decades after the war there was virtually no academic debate on the persecution of Jews in the Netherlands, on the high percentage of Dutch Jews who were murdered or on the involvement of the authorities and 'bystanders'. All these questions – including the role of antisemitism – actually were among the research topics proposed and initiated by Blom. In his inaugural lecture, Blom also drew attention to forms of 'contact, deliberation and collaboration with the occupiers' which he called 'accommodation', following the historian E.H. Kossmann (1922-2003), to distinguish it from collaboration and resistance: cooperating with and implementing the policies of the occupier, including the persecution policy, without any ideological conviction.[8]

5   Frank van Vree, 'Iedere dag en elk uur', 71.
6   De Haan, *Na de Ondergang*, 180-181. *See also* chapter 3.
7   For some of the features of public debates on mass violence, such as the remarkable key role of non-academic media, *see* Remco Ensel, 'Slag of Stoot: Over het strijdtoneel van het historisch debat', *Ex Tempore* 34 (2015), 86-94.
8   E.H. Kossmann, *De Lage Landen 1780/1980. Deel II 1914-1980* (Amsterdam, Brussels: Elsevier 1986), 177. The changes in perspectives that Blom mentions included a history of the state of mind during the occupation, attention to continuity rather than discontinuity and the setting of

Blom's appeal for a historiographical turn tied in with the 'scientification' of the Second World War historiography he had appreciated in the work of, among others, the German historian Martin Broszat (1926-1989). Broszat argued in favour of more attention to the people's perception of their daily life and experiences, and of not too much isolating the Second World War from the periods before and after, a perspective which, incidentally, was severely criticised by Saul Friedländer.[9] Broszat's perspective seemed to match Blom's point of view, which he conveyed time and again, that unlike 'the public', professional historians should refrain from showing emotion and giving meaning to the more or less 'objective' facts of history.[10]

In his overview of the historiography of the Holocaust Ido de Haan noted, that the historical oeuvre of respectively Herzberg, Presser and De Jong was

the Dutch war history in an international comparative framework. Some of the most discussed publications of J.C.H. Blom were: J.C.H. Blom, *In de ban van goed en fout? Wetenschappelijke geschiedschrijving over de bezettingstijd in Nederland* (Bergen: Octavo 1983); J.C.H. Blom, 'The persecution of the Jews in the Netherlands in a comparative international perspective.' In: Jozeph Michman (ed.), *Dutch Jewish History II* (Assen, Maastricht: Van Gorcum, 1989), 273-289. J.C.H. Blom, 'The persecution of the Jews in the Netherlands: a comparative Western European perspective, *European History Quarterly* 19 (1989), 333-351. Together with R.G. Fuks-Mansfeld and I. Schöffer, Blom edited *Geschiedenis van de joden in Nederland* (Amsterdam: Balans, 1995) which was also published in an English-language version: *The History of the Jews in the Netherlands* (Portland Oregon: Littman Library of *Jewish Civilisation, 2002*). *For the bibliography of Blom until 2002: Kristel (ed.), Met alle geweld, 293-308.* For Hans Blom *see* also chapter 2.

9   Blom, 'In de ban van goed en fout.' In: J.C.H Blom, *In de ban van goed en fout? Geschiedschrijving over de bezettingstijd in Nederland* (Amsterdam: Boom, 2007), 9-29: 20-24. Incidentally, the historian Saul Friedländer strongly criticised Broszat when the latter started claiming, from 1986 onwards, that there was such a thing as 'a mixture of conformism and non-conformity' in the attitude of the Germans (did this not ultimately result, according to Friedländer, in empathy for everybody?) and Broszat's plea to study the Third Reich like any other period: Martin Broszat and Saul Friedländer, 'A controversy about the historicization of National Socialism', *New German Critique* 44 (1 April 1988), 85-126; Martin Broszat and Saul Friedländer, 'Um die "Historisierung des Nationalsozialismus": ein Briefwechsel, *Vierteljahrshefte für Zeitgeschichte* 36,2 (1988), 339-372; Peter Baldwin (ed.), *Reworking the Past: Hitler, the Holocaust, and the Historians' Debate* (Boston: Beacon Press, 1990); Evelien Gans, 'Iedereen een beetje slachtoffer, iedereen een beetje dader. De Nederlandse *Historikerstreit* over de grijze oorlog', *De Groene Amsterdammer,* 28 January 2010; and Evelien Gans, 'Eigentlich waren doch alle ein bisschen Täter *und* Opfer... Nivellierungstendenzen und sekundärer Antisemitismus im Geschichtsbild des niederländischen Historikers Chris van der Heijden.' In: Nicole Colin, Matthias Lorenz and Joachim Umlauf (eds.), *Täter und Tabu. Grenzen der Toleranz in deutschen und niederländischen Geschichtsdebatten* (Essen: Klartext, 2011), 33-47. For Saul Friedländer *see also* chapters 1, 15 and hereafter.

10   Blom, *In de ban van goed en fout?* About Broszat: Torben Fischer and Matthias N. Lorenz (ed.), *Lexikon der 'Vergangenheitsbewältigung' in Deutschland: Debatten- und Diskursgeschichte des National-sozialismus nach 1945* (Bielefeld: Transkript, 2007).

characterised by 'an almost total lack of historiographical debate' about the validity of their approach and interpretation.[11] This might have been true for the academic world but it was certainly not the case for the general public. Criticism in academia was not abundant, but it was not entirely lacking.[12] And actually, since Herzberg, Presser and De Jong began to make room, in their work, for the perspective of the victims – for the persecution of the Jews – these historians can be seen to have been part of a historiographical turn as well.[13] They furthermore made a point of not writing exclusively for 'specialists'.[14] The regular press and several magazines published about 'the great three' – also critically, such as an article on Loe de Jong's television serial *De Bezetting* [The Occupation] (1960-1965) by the 'star reporter' and writer Renate Rubinstein. She fulminated against the television serial which preceded De Jong's elaborate magnum opus *Het Koninkrijk*, and reproached him exactly for reducing complex war experiences to the dichotomy of resistance vs. collaboration.[15] As mentioned in chapter 2, Herzberg, Presser and De Jong, were 'experts by experience'. This aspect was welcomed, but also sharply criticised, for example because, it allegedly led to an emotional writing style and choice of words. Especially Presser was reproached for applying a (supposedly) weak methodology and for failing to contextualise his findings in the international historiography. For instance the historians Hermann von der Dunk, Yvo Schöffer and Jaap Meijer stated that the historical and scholarly quality of Presser's *Ondergang* (1965) had been severely damaged by his emotional approach, the introduction of his own 'personage' and his identification with the victims. They found his analysis of the Jewish

11   De Haan, *Na de ondergang*, 38.
12   The historians Hermann von der Dunk, Yvo Schöffer and Jaap Meijer – Meijer most sharply – criticised Presser's *Ondergang* with respect to his far-reaching identification with the victims and his one-dimensional negative analysis of the role of the Jewish Council: Kristel, *Geschiedschrijving als opdracht*, 246-249; A systematic critic of De Jong's oeuvre was Jan Rogier in his *De geschiedschrijver des Rijks en andere socialisten. Politieke Portretten I* (Nijmegen: SUN, 1979).
13   De Haan and Blom deny this turn: De Haan, *Na de ondergang*, 41.
14   Madelon de Keizer, 'Inleiding.' In: Madelon de Keizer (ed.), *Een dure verplichting en een kostelijk voorrecht. Dr. L. de Jong en zijn Geschiedwerk* (The Hague: Sdu Uitgeverij, 1995), 7-20: 12.
15   R. Rubinstein, 'Deugd, ondeugd, deugd', *Opinie, veertiendaags orgaan van de Partij van de Arbeid*, 19 March 1965; see also Van Vree, *In de schaduw van Auschwitz*, 80. In his written work, *Koninkrijk*, De Jong is in fact more subtle. For other critics of De Jong's *Bezetting*, see the documentary *Vastberaden, maar soepel en met mate* [Firmly, supply but with moderation] (1974) by Henk Hofland, Hans Keller and Hans Verhagen (prod. Maud Keus), and reactions to and effect of Presser's *Ondergang: ibid.*, 82. See also De Haan, *Na de ondergang*, 38. For Renate Rubinstein *see also* chapters 3, 6 and 7.

Council biased.[16] De Jong too was outspokenly negative with respect to the Jewish Council.[17]

Blom's inaugural lecture in 1983 bore fruit, and received both praise and criticism.[18] But though his appeal to 'scientify' the historiography of the occupation led to new lines of research, it did not put an end to the labelling of right and wrong. After the year 2000, a long and intense debate started as a result of two historical publications on the Second World War and the persecution of the Jews and the way these were addressed after the war. The debate appealed to Blom's change in perspective, but the questions and concerns of the previous moral framework remained relevant.

In 2001 the journalist/publicist and historian Chris van der Heijden (b. 1954) published *Grijs verleden* [Grey Past], in 2011 followed by his dissertation *Dat nooit meer* [Never again]. Van der Heijden first disapprovingly established that thinking about the war in terms of right/wrong still prevailed in Dutch society. He then translated Blom's attention to accommodation into an appeal for a 'grey' perspective, focusing on the pragmatism of the Dutch population under German occupation. Van der Heijden's rejection of a moralising approach that was fraught with the burden of the Shoah – even though his own work also included moralism – was combined with criticism of the alleged central role of the Shoah in the perception of history and intended to create room for other groups of victims. We will focus on elements in the work of Van der Heijden which we distinguish as expressions of secondary antisemitism, i.e. as expressions of the conviction that the legitimate desire to draw a line under the past and move on to normalisation is heavily obstructed by the frantic attention to the Shoah.[19]

In 2012 the historian Bart van der Boom (b. 1964) published a study that was also inspired by Blom's lecture: a history of the mindset of common citizens during the years of occupation, this time not to point out their accommodating attitude or 'grey' perceptions, but rather to once again demonstrate how these ordinary citizens were very much aware of the

---

16   *See* Kristel, 'Survivors as historians.'

17   Evelien Gans, 'Formalisme, lafheid en nalatigheid', *De Groene Amsterdammer*, 29 October 1997. Blaming the Jewish Council in considerable measure could feed the illusion that the Jews themselves could have done more to rescue themselves.

18   For the fruit, *see, e.g.,* Guus Meershoek, *Dienaren van het gezag*; Gans, 'Gojse broodnijd', and many other publications. Blom has been the supervisor of exceptionally many doctoral students. For criticism *see, e.g.,* Gjalt Zondergeld, 'Continuïteit en discontinuïteit in de moderne Nederlandse geschiedenis. De these van J.C.H. Blom nader bezien', *Kleio, tijdschrift van de Vereniging van Geschiedenisleraren in Nederland* 25, 8 (1984), 1-6.

19   For secondary antisemitism *see* chapters 1 and 2.

divide between right and wrong.[20] In *'Wij weten niets van hun lot.' Gewone Nederlanders en de Holocaust* ['We know nothing of their fate.' Ordinary Dutchmen and the Holocaust] (2012) Van der Boom partly targeted Van der Heijden's grey perspective, but the book actually shares Van der Heijden's perspective with regard to a fascination for the issue of guilt. Also in common is the topos of 'the Passive Jew' as a crucial factor in the outcome of the persecution policy as well an underestimation of the fundamentally different position of Jews as victims. It is for the occurrence of these topos – explicitly not that of (secondary) antisemitism – that we discuss the work of Van der Boom in this chapter.

In light of the complex shifts in historiography following Blom's speech, Maarten Brands, one of Blom's former colleagues at the University of Amsterdam, argued that in his attempt, in 1983, to move away from the 'moralising perspective', Blom had left 'a few doors' open 'which caused a draught that ruffled up files'.[21] Giving meaning, emotion and personal engagement still appeared to be closely entwined with historical research, despite Blom's appeal for professional distance.[22] This is part of the reason for the importance of focusing on both works in this chapter: contrary to De Haan's complaint about 'the lack of a serious impact' of historians in the public debate, the publications of Van der Heijden and Van der Boom prompted a long debate with a wide variety of engaged contributions, covering, for example, the question as to how to organise the annual 4 May Commemoration. The visions of these two historians with regard to the alleged passivity of the Jews during the war, to the *'nivellering'* [levelling] of victims, perpetrators, bystanders and accomplices, and to the absolving of guilt, are by no means disconnected from their 'readership'.[23]

20   Van der Boom was inspired by Hans Blom, who, in his turn, was inspired by Broszat's *Stimmungsgeschichte* of Bavaria during the war: Martin Broszat et al., *Bayern in der NS-Zeit. Herrschaft und Gesellschaft im Konflikt* (München: Oldenbourg, 1979).

21   Maarten Brands, 'Beslagen buitenspiegels. Over de grenzen van zelfreflectie.' In: Conny Kristel (ed.), *Met alle geweld. Botsingen en tegenstellingen in burgerlijk Nederland* (Dedicated to J.C.H. Blom on the occasion of his sixtieth birthday) (Amsterdam: Balans, 2003), 34-47: 43-47.

22   As Blom cautiously acknowledged in retrospect (in his valedictory lecture): J.C.H. Blom. 'Een kwart eeuw later. Nog altijd in de ban van goed en fout'. In: Hans Blom, *In de ban van goed en fout? Geschiedschrijving over de bezettingstijd in Nederland* (Amsterdam: Boom, 2007), 55-179.

23   De Haan, 'The paradoxes of Dutch history'.

Chris van der Heijden: Never again

Although Chris van der Heijden never became active in university circles, his *Grijs verleden* [Grey Past] came as a bombshell, and the term *'grijs'* became a historic brand name for 'the war', in academia and among the general public. After the success, criticism and praise, Van der Heijden wrote, among other things, *Dat nooit meer* [Never again] (2011), a dissertation about the aftermath of the Second World War based on a large number of war-related issues and controversies.[24] This time, he did seek academic recognition and he found two prominent promoters to guide him: Hans Blom and Ido de Haan. The latter called Van der Heijden the most influential historian of his time when the book was published.[25] With regard to Blom, it looked like Van der Heijden had like a true sorcerer's apprentice set off with Blom's lecture and historiographical shift. That same Blom, whose attitude was described in a biographical article as one of always looking for balance, for 'the middle of the circle', supported the two publications despite Van der Heijden's divergent radical stance.[26] Likewise, he would also support Bart van der Boom's work, which we will discuss later.

Yet there do seem to be substantial differences in perspective between Blom and Van der Heijden. First, Blom had called upon his fellow historians to abandon the motif of giving meaning and making judgments, because it sits in the way of asking new scholarly questions, disclosing alternative domains of research and perspectives. Van der Heijden, on the contrary, interpreted the war almost exclusively in terms of accommodation and a lack of clear moral divisions. Second, Blom looked at the right/wrong perspective in light of the focus on resistance versus collaboration. But Van der Heijden, as Blom recalls in his review of *Grijs verleden*, mainly looks at the right/wrong (or black/white) perspective in connection to the alleged increasingly central place of the Holocaust since Presser's *Ondergang* (1965). That's why, after Blom's predominantly positive review of *Grijs verleden*, the

---

24 Chris van der Heijden, *Grijs verleden. Nederland en de Tweede Wereldoorlog* (Amsterdam, Antwerp: Contact, 2010); Chris van der Heijden, *Dat nooit meer: de nasleep van de Tweede Wereldoorlog in Nederland* (Amsterdam, Antwerp: Contact, 2011).

25 In Bob Moore, 'The war that won't go away', *BMGN* 128, 2 (2013), 73-80. The critic Arjen Fortuin referred to *Grijs verleden* in a retrospective as 'the most important Dutch war book of this decade ... [and] not because it is that good.' Arjen Fortuin, 'Een ander moreel oordeel propageren. De Oogst van het Decennium: "Grijs verleden" (2001) van Chris van der Heijden', *NRC Handelsblad*, 12 July 2010.

26 Conny Kristel, 'J.C.H. Blom of het midden van de cirkel.' In: Conny Kristel (ed.), *Met alle geweld: botsingen en tegenstellingen in burgerlijk Nederland* (Amsterdam: Balans, 2003), 275-292.

above-mentioned Brands wrote that, although it was commendable that Blom had opposed the 'prevailing Manichaeism of thinking in "right" and "wrong"', by doing so he was, occasionally and unintentionally, joined by 'those who would like to see "wrong" behaviour excused or trivialised'.[27] Blom dismissed this connection in his valedictory speech.[28]

Van der Heijden's defence of his PhD thesis was a remarkable event because of the way he ostentatiously disregarded academic conventions, and because of the fierce criticism that was expressed both publicly and behind closed doors: there was an unprecedented amount of disagreement within the dissertation's defence committee, which was even reported in the press, something quite unique.[29] As with *Grijs verleden* at the time, the reviews ranged from praise to harsh criticism.[30] The dissertation failed to bring Van der Heijden any closer to the academic community. The Dutch weekly *De Groene Amsterdammer,* however, still regularly publishes articles which carry the same message as his books, and he is a regular guest on radio and television.[31]

Here we mainly look at instances of secondary antisemitism in the work of Van der Heijden. Evelien Gans introduced this term in the Netherlands

27   Maarten Brands, 'Beslagen buitenspiegels,' 43-47; J.C.H. Blom, 'Grijs verleden?', *BMGN* CXVI, iv (2001), 483-489.

28   Blom. 'Een kwart eeuw later. Nog altijd in de ban van goed en fout', 55-179.

29   *NRC Handelsblad*, 4 November 2011.

30   For critical reviews: Ewoud Kieft, 'Fouten na de oorlog' and 'Dat nooit meer', *NRC Handelsblad,* 28 October and 4 November 2011; Elsbeth Etty, 'De erfzonde van de linkse kerk', *ibid.,* 1 November 2011; Ronald Havenaar, 'Een grenzeloze passie voor grijs', *Vrij Nederland,* 5 November 2011; Dienke Hondius, 'Modderige mierenhoop. Chris van der Heijden: dat nooit meer', *De Groene Amsterdammer,* 2 November 2011. For positive reviews: Paul Scheffer, 'De lange schaduw van de bezetting', *de Volkskrant,* 29 October 2011; Hans Renders, 'Eigenlijk was bijna iedereen fout', *Het Parool,* 2 November 2011. References and reviews in English: Friso Wielenga, 'Tale after Tale after Tale. The lost chance of a great project', *BMGN* 128, 2 (2013), 90-99; Koen Aerts, 'A Belgian view of (the debate on) "Dat nooit meer" – "Never Again"', *BMGN* 128, 2 (2013), 81-89. In: Robert van Voren, *Undigested past: The Holocaust in Lithuania* (Amsterdam: Rodopi, 2013), 113: *Grey past* is determined to be a 'detailed and balanced view' and the perspective is adopted: 'From black and white to shades of grey' (p. 113) and chapter eight; Frances Gouda is very sceptical in 'Divided memories of World War II in the Netherlands and the Dutch East Indies: Sukarno and Anne Frank as icons of Dutch historical imagination.' In: Daniel Chirot, Gi-Wook Shin and Daniel Sneider (eds.), *Confronting memories of World War II: European and Asian Legacies* (Seattle: The University of Washington Press, 2014), 105-134.

31   Chris van der Heijden, 'Het laatste appèl. Het verhaal van een foto', *De Groene Amsterdammer,* 27 April 2011; Chris van der Heijden, 'Onnozele geiten. Auschwitz door de lens van de SS', *De Groene Amsterdammer,* 20 February 2013; Chris van der Heijden, 'Waarheidsversneller', *De Groene Amsterdammer,* 9 October 2013; Chris van der Heijden, 'Waar is hun menselijkheid?', *De Groene Amsterdammer,* 8 April 2015.

in an article published in *De Groene Amsterdammer* in 2010, *'Iedereen een beetje slachtoffer, iedereen een beetje dader'* [There's a bit of victim and a bit of perpetrator in everyone], based on a critical reading of several of Van der Heijden's publications. Dienke Hondius (b. 1960) is one of the few people in Dutch academia who, like Gans, thinks that the concept of secondary anti-semitism applies to Van der Heijden's work. In a comprehensive analysis the historian Frances Gouda characterised Van der Heijden's grey perspective as 'a highly revisionist trend' and considers Gans' earlier characterisation of secondary antisemitism to be 'well-argued and documented'.[32] Unlike in Germany, people in the Netherlands generally think it is not done, to say the least, if not completely inappropriate to label a learned colleague's work as (secondary) 'antisemitic'.[33] Since people, also in this intellectual milieu, often still automatically, or instinctively but unjustly, identify antisemitism with Nazi antisemitism, they feel as if they would be calling a colleague a 'Nazi'. In our opinion 'antisemitism' is a multi-layered and variable phenomenon as we intend to make clear in this volume.[34] Taking a view instead that it functions as a 'showstopper', an end to all discussion – following some of the comments we have received – would deny researchers using secondary antisemitism as an analytical concept. The qualification of secondary antisemitism relates to the way in which Van der Heijden's work undermines Jewish victimhood, contains perpetrator-victim reversal and comprises an accumulation of anti-Jewish post-Holocaust stereotypes.

32 Gouda, 'Divided memories of World War II, 111-112. Evelien Gans, 'Iedereen een beetje slachtoffer, iedereen een beetje dader', *De Groene Amsterdammer*, 27 January 2010; Hondius, 'Modderige mierenhoop'.

33 *See* chapter 2 for an interpretation of the concept of secondary antisemitism. Historian Juliane Wetzel used the term in 2012 to interpret the poem *'Was gesagt werden muss'* by German writer Günter Grass (1927-2015). It is said to revolve around 'antisemitic clichés' and the projection of guilt and shame. Grass had served in the Waffen-ss, among other positions: Juliane Wetzel, 'Die Täter-Opfer-Umkehr', *Der Freitag*, 22 April 2012 (www.freitag.de/autoren/der-freitag/die-tater-opfer-umkehr). *See also* Evelien Gans, 'Het waarom van de weerstand in academisch-intellectuele kring tegen het uitdelen van het stempel "antisemitisme"', NIOD researchers lunch (unpublished), NIOD, 5 September 2011. For a recent radio appearance:, on 5 May 2015: www.werkgroepherkenning.nl/chris-van-der-heijden-op-radio-npo-1/.

34 Robert Fine, 'Fighting with Phantoms: A Contribution to the Debate on Antisemitism in Europe', *Patterns of Prejudice* 43, 5 (2009), 459-479: 460, n. 2. *See also* chapter 1.

Ad hominem?

The sense of *Schuldabwehrantisemitismus* also plays a role in the characterisation of Van der Heijden's work. It was initially not widely known, but
after a fierce and personal public dispute between Van der Heijden and
his former friend, the Jewish writer Leon de Winter and De Winter's wife,
Jessica Durlacher, also a novelist, it became clear that Van der Heijden was
the son of a former Dutch SS officer.[35] In his book *Israël. Een onherstelbare
vergissing* [Israel. An irreversible mistake] (2008), Van der Heijden would
explicitly refer to this heritage as a child of parents who stood at the 'wrong'
side. Actually, he appealed to this background, stating that he was one of
those most involved: 'Partly as a result of my heritage I have been reading
and writing about the war my whole life and have tried time and again to
understand what went wrong at the time and why'.[36]

   The mnemonic community of 'children of wrong parents', organised in
Stichting Werkgroep Herkenning [Recognition], of which Van der Heijden is
the most prominent member, has become an active group which regularly
expresses its opinions in public. Recently, *Kinderen van foute ouders. Hun
verhaal* [Children of wrong parents. Their story] (2014) was published, in
which Chris van der Heijden portrays himself alternately as fellow victim,
historian and psychologist writing about the intense fear and anger: 'As a
child of wrong parents you never get rid of such emotions, just like you can
never get rid of the feeling of guilt and shame'.[37] During a debate about *Grijs
verleden* Van der Heijden compared himself to Blom. It was 'not entirely by
accident that Van der Heijden and Hans Blom were both defined by the
war because of a wrong family member'. Afterwards, it was pointed out

---

35   Van der Heijden and De Winter have co-authored the book *Handleiding ter bestrijding
van extreem-rechts* (Amsterdam: De Bezige Bij, 1994). When Van der Heijden wanted to give
Grijs verleden to his father the friendship turned to hostility that became a public battle in *Vrij
Nederland*, spring 2001. See also *NRC Handelsblad*, 10 June 2002 and *Trouw,* 30 June 2001. There
seems to exist an interesting, though not complete 'fatal triangle' between Theo van Gogh, Chris
van der Heijden and Leon de Winter. De Winter and Van Gogh were enemies, but, ideologically,
got closer – *see* chapter 12; Van der Heijden was intensely befriended with Leon de Winter, but
they became 'enemies'. Van der Heijden has ignored the 'Van Gogh affair' (the rows with respect
to Van Gogh's antisemitic and war-related abuses) as well as the 'Fassbinder affair'. Leon de
Winter wrote a novel in which Theo van Gogh figures prominently: *VSV* (Amsterdam: De Bezige
Bij, 2012).
36   Chris van der Heijden, *Israël. Een onherstelbare vergissing* (Amsterdam/Antwerp: Contact
2008), 23.
37   Van der Heijden also writes: 'I see myself as a historian – not as a child of.' Characterisation
by the critic David Barnouw, review of Chris van der Heijden, *Kinderen van foute ouders. Hun
verhaal* (Amsterdam: Atlas Contact, 2014), 11, *BMGN* 130, 1 (2015), review 14.

that this was a false comparison. In the case of Van der Heijden it was his *father*'s membership of the Waffen-SS, in Blom's case it was his *grandfather* who was a 'minor case of collaboration'.[38] Blom's *father* had been active in the resistance.

A recurring element in the debate about Van der Heijden's work is the reproach that critics would have unfairly and maliciously tied Van der Heijden's vision to his father's role in the war.[39] Bob Moore even called 'the *ad hominem* charges about why he has chosen his subject material' one of the main aspects in the debate.[40] It should be noted, however, that Van der Heijden effortlessly refers to Loe de Jong's Jewish identity in his interpretation of De Jong's work, just as he labels other historians as 'Jewish'. However, apart from the fact that Van der Heijden himself makes, publicly, much of his personal background, it is, contrary to Moore's assumptions, not just a matter of a choice of subject, but also and particularly of interpretations and choice of words in *Grijs verleden* and in the long series of other publications.

The literary critic and writer Joost Zwagerman (1963-2015) states Van der Heijden's works contains a hidden personal quest, which is not expressed by the author.

> While mocking his opponents' 'sentimentality' he appears to be blind to the inevitable after-effect of his own emotional quest [for an answer to the question how someone like his father could be so blind, in Van der Heijden's own words, 'to participate in a system that is so revolting'].[41]

Although in academic circles it is rather uncommon to mention one's own personal history and involvement, it is naive to deny those factors do play a

38 Margreet Fogteloo, 'Grijsdenken. Het zwart-witdenken over de Tweede Wereldoorlog heeft afgedaan', *De Groene Amsterdammer*, 6 May 2005.
39 The reproach of ad hominem arguments emerged as a result of *Grijs verleden* well before the publication of Gans' essay 'Iedereen een beetje slachtoffer, iedereen een beetje dader'. *See for* example Carl Friedman who speaks of slander and witch hunt: 'Heksenjacht', *Trouw*, 30 June 2001; Rob Hartmans calls the link to his father's war past 'total nonsense': 'Who's afraid of grey, black and white', *De Groene Amsterdammer*, 7 April 2001. Later on Koen Aerts wrote, in 'A Belgian view of (the debate on) 'Dat nooit meer' – 'Never Again'', *BMGN* 128, 2 (2013) 81-89, about slander and calls the referral to the personal past 'not very constructive or intellectually honest.' Gans' essay consists of an interpretation of the work of Van der Heijden. Subsequently she relates Van der Heijden's references to his father to the analysis of Alexander and Margaretha Mitscherlich on the incapacity to grieve: *Die Unfähigkeit zu trauern. Grundlagen kollektiven Verhaltens* (München: Piper, 1967).
40 Moore, 'The war that won't go away.'
41 Joost Zwagerman, 'De eeuw van zijn vader', *de Volkskrant*, 11 April 2001.

role in one's work. According to the historian Saul Friedländer the research into the war and the persecution of Jews by his own Jewish generation gains a 'special drive' through personal involvement.[42] This also applies to following generations.[43] Transgenerational transference is a recognised psychological phenomenon.[44] In this same context Friedländer also noted that every historian 'can deal objectively with that past when [he or she] becomes aware of the place where he or she stands ... and then accept his subjectivity and even use it, up to a point, in your way of writing history ... but very clearly and very explicitly.'[45] This implies transparency and self-reflection. But unquestionably, a personal involvement is of no value, in this professional context, if it is not supported firmly by convincing, verifiable and discerning foundations and argumentation. As noted by Zwagerman, self-reflection is missing in the case of Van der Heijden. Instead, there is lasting resentment. Two years after the murder of Theo van Gogh he wrote:

> despite Pim [Fortuyn], Theo and the global 'clash of civilisations', the Second World War is still the most crucial event in recent Dutch history. And it is still looked at unequally, least of all from the perspective of the half a million Dutch people who, at the time, cooperated with the Germans in some way.[46]

42   Saul Friedländer, *Nazi-Duitsland en de joden, deel 1: De jaren van vervolging 1933-1939* (Utrecht: Het Spectrum, 1998), 13; Saul Friedländer, *Nazi-Duitsland en de joden, deel 1 en deel 2: De jaren van vernietiging* (Amsterdam: Nieuw Amsterdam, 2007), 15.

43   Comment by Evelien Gans: My work is certainly not disconnected from my Jewish background which is, I assume, well-known by those who read my work, for instance, because of the forewords in my publications and the various interviews I have given. However, in my historical work I have to the best of my knowledge always substantiated my arguments, reference material and analysis as accurately as possible. Van Gogh (*see* chapter 12), Van der Heijden and Van der Boom have all pointed to my Jewish identity; the first two in a manner that was outright insulting and antisemitic.

44   *See, e.g.,* E. de Wind, 'Transgenerationele overdracht.' In: *Kinderen van de oorlog: opstellen naar aanleiding van een lezingencyclus, georganiseerd in de periode januari-april 1986 door de RIAGG's Centrum/Oud-West Amsterdam en Zuid/Nieuw-West Amsterdam, in samenwerking met de Stichting ICODO te Utrecht* (1987), 9-2. Petra Aarts, 'Transgenerationele oorlogsgevolgen: gesprek met prof.dr. D.J. de Levita, ICODO-info, 1991, vol. 8, episode 2 (July), 18-26; F.A. Begemann, 'Transgenerationele traumatisering: klachten bij kinderen van oorlogsgetroffenen.' In: F.A. Begemann, *Arbeidsongeschiktheid en traumatische (oorlogs)ervaringen* (Utrecht: Icodo, 1993) 49-66; Gonda Scheffel-Baars, 'Transgenerationele traumatisering: problemen bij de naoorlogse generatie', *Bulletin Stichting Werkgroep Herkenning* 23, 3 (2008), 19-23.

45   Saul Friedlander in: Frank Diamand, *When memory comes – a film about Friedländer* (2012).

46   Van der Heijden, 'Vertel het hele verhaal van de oorlog'.

All in all, Chris van der Heijden is a living paradox. He is deeply entwined in the historical perspective of the Second World War and the Shoah, the dominance of which he challenges. His work can be seen as the expression of a trend in which new victim groups claim recognition by referring to the Shoah, often resulting in victim competition. Van der Heijden's clear rejection of 'the war' as a moral benchmark contrasts with his own unremitting preoccupation with that same war. Van der Heijden repeatedly shows that he wants to do away with the memory of the Shoah, but at the same time his writings display a strong preoccupation with it, even when in these same writings that preoccupation is projected onto 'the Other'.[47]

The issue of the historian's personal background was again a central theme of the debate in 2012-2013 about Bart van der Boom's book *Wij weten niets van hun lot*. This time, the paradox was related to the fact that Van der Boom rejected the *ad hominem* argument, while using it at the same time. As a result of criticism by Gans and Ensel, Van der Boom himself brought up Gans' Jewish father by stating that it should not matter for the tenability of the positions that the father of historian Chris van der Heijden was a member of the SS, Gans' father was 'Jewish' and that Van der Boom's father was 'very friendly and optimistic'. With this disparate characterisation of three fathers, Van der Boom stated that he, as opposed to Gans and Van der Heijden, had no transgenerational involvement in the Second World War. Devoid of personal involvement, Van der Boom seemed to claim the position of an 'objective' historian. In an interview he declared that he wasn't Jewish and 'and as far as I know, I have no relatives who were very good or very evil. This is not personal. Call it an intellectual interest.[48] Van der Boom seems to put himself – and probably, the 'ideal' World War Two historian – in the third category of actors during the war, that is, that of the bystanders.

Reflection on the war and the Holocaust forces each one of us to seek a balance between distance and involvement, between discovering connections and recognising that there are limits to interpretation, between maintaining your stance as a historian and engaging in dialogues with 'others'.[49]

---

47 Gans, 'Iedereen een beetje slachtoffer'.

48 *Reformatorisch Dagblad*, 28 November 2012.

49 Remco Ensel and Evelien Gans, 'We know something of their fate. Bart van der Boom's history of the Holocaust in the Netherlands': https://independent.academia.edu/Remco Ensel and https://independent.academia.edu/EvelienGans. *See* Dominick LaCapra, *Representing the Holocaust. History, Theory, Trauma* (Ithaca: Cornell University Press, 1994), 63-66 on the necessity of subject positions connected to the practice of scholarship that cannot be reduced to reified oppositions of mourning or commemorating.

Schlussstrichbedürfnis

The essence of Van der Heijden's vision is captured in the first two opening sentences of *Grijs verleden:* 'First there was the war, then the story about that war. The war was terrible, but the story made the war even worse.'[50] This is a remarkable statement, because does that mean that 'the story about the war' made the persecution of the Jews worse than it was? Van der Heijden's strongly relativist opening lines are, basically, the thrust of all his publications on this topic. This includes the title of his dissertation *Dat nooit meer* [Never again], which alludes to *Nooit meer Auschwitz* [Auschwitz Never Again], but which, combined with the subtitle *De nasleep van de Tweede Wereldoorlog* [The aftermath of the Second World War], refers to the way the Shoah was dealt with after the war. The Dutch word for 'aftermath' [*nasleep*] is not neutral. It has a negative connotation: it refers to an unpleasant consequence of a previous event. If you look at it that way, the dissertation points to the first lines of *Grijs verleden,* published ten years earlier: 'The war was terrible, but the story made the war even worse.'

Although Van der Heijden regularly refers to the Shoah, his work – not just *Grijs verleden* – lacks an analysis of this mass murder. The Shoah is merely described in vague terms as if it were a natural disaster: 'that one unimaginable phenomenon', 'the most memorable' or 'dramatic' or 'repulsive' event of the Second World War, 'the unparalleled fact that no one knew how to deal with – and that no one does still'.[51] Although he himself does: Van der Heijden demonstrates – as did the like-minded German Ernst Nolte (b. 1923) who ignited the *Historikerstreit* in Germany in the 1980s – that 'enough is enough'. Van der Heijden displays a *Schlusstrichbedürfnis* in several ways. It surprised him that the war had stood 'like a block of concrete in the middle of our country's history for so long'.[52] Van der Heijden explicitly describes himself as 'historically incorrect'. This is, like 'politically incorrect' – see Theo van Gogh and his supporters – employed as a badge of honour.[53] His article *De oorlog is voorgoed voorbij* [The war is over for good] (2003) is in line with Nolte's *Die Vergangenheit die nicht vergehen will* [The past that

50 Van der Heijden, *Grijs verleden*, 9. *See also* Gans, 'Iedereen een beetje slachtoffer'.
51 Chris van der Heijden, 'Van zwart, wit en grijs. Oorlog en mensbeeld.' In: Louis Paul Boon et al., *Hij was een zwarte. Over oorlog en collaboratie* (Amsterdam: Meulenhoff, 2003), 69-83: 73, 82; Van der Heijden, 'Fout en foutjes', *Vrij Nederland*, 3 March 2001; Van der Heijden, *Israël. Een onherstelbare vergissing*, 99. For the mud and the grey landscape, *see also* Van der Heijden, *Grijs verleden*, 412 and 'De oorlog is voorgoed voorbij', *Vrij Nederland*, 26 April 2003.
52 Chris van der Heijden, *Grijs verleden*, 12.
53 Idem, 'Het einde van de historische correctheid', *Vrij Nederland*, 6 December 2012.

won't go away] (1986) and the speech called the *Paulskirchenrede* that the
German writer Martin Walser (b. 1927) gave in 1998, when accepting the
Friedenspreis des Deutschen Buchandels [the Peace Prize of the German
Book Trade].[54]

Walser expressed his discontent with the way the Shoah was commemorated ('I notice that something inside me is opposing this permanent show
of our shame') and referred to this, according to him, over-attention, as 'the
exploitation [*Instrumentalisierung*] of our shame for current goals. Always
for the right purpose, for sure. But yet the exploitation of ... Auschwitz is not
suitable for becoming a routine-of-threat, an always available intimidation
or a moral club [*Moralkeule*] or also just an obligation.' In anticipation, so
to speak, of Van der Heijden's description of the war as 'a block of concrete'
that is annoyingly barring the way, Walser specified his discontent by
contemptuously stating that because of the Holocaust Monument in Berlin
the centre of the capital has been turned 'into concrete with a nightmare,
the size of a football pitch. Turning shame into monument.'[55]

Van der Heijden's reproach of the exploitation of the Shoah – in the context
of the lawsuit against the Ukrainian war criminal John Demjanjuk in 2009
– relates to former victims and their surviving relatives who are allegedly
artificially keeping the 'War' alive with their 'hunt for compensation' and
their 'moral' based on 'grief' and 'reasons of the heart'.[56] In his dissertation
he writes that the Shoah has '*burdened* the international community with
the moral duty to do all it can to avoid a recurrence', because of the central
and universal meaning it has obtained.[57] This is once again an expression
of *Schlusstrichbedürfnis*. In this context he refers to the leading historian
Tony Judt (1948-2010) who, with some scepticism, called the Shoah 'the

54 Ernst Nolte, 'Die Vergangenheit die nicht vergehen will. Eine Rede, die geschrieben,
aber nicht gehalten werden konnte', Frankfurter Allgemeine Zeitung, 6 June 1986; www.
friedenspreis-des-deutschen-buchhandels.de/sixcms/media.php/1290/1998_walser.pdf: '*Die
Betonierung des Zentrums der Hauptstadt mit einem fußballfeldgroßen Alptraum.*' Ludger Jansen,
'Alles Schlußstrich – oder was? Eine philosophische Auseinandersetzung mit Martin Walsers
Friedenspreisrede', *Theologie und Philosophie* 80 (2005), 412-422.

55 *See* previous note.

56 Chris van der Heijden, 'Moordenaars onder ons', *De Groene Amsterdammer*, 27 November
2009. *See also* Van der Heijden, 'Het einde van de historische correctheid', *Vrij Nederland*,
6 December 2012; Van der Heijden, 'De oorlog is voorgoed voorbij', *Vrij Nederland*, 26 April
2003; Nolte, 'Die Vergangenheit die nicht vergehen will'.

57 Van der Heijden, *Dat nooit meer*, 605. Italics added.

best possible entrance ticket to Europe'. But Judt by no means used terms such as 'burden'.[58]

The passive Jew

While the processing of the war is the central theme of *Dat nooit meer*, in *Grijs verleden* Van der Heijden outlines his vision of the Second World War. Coincidence plays the key role in that vision; free will or choice are completely secondary.[59] The resistance did not amount to anything,[60] the NSB only became antisemitic under pressure from the German Occupation and was, initially, a pretty normal political party[61] whose ideology was only a 'disposable product',[62] the average Dutch citizen tried to live on for better or worse (the so-called 'muddling on scenario'), and the Jews were persecuted and murdered.

Van der Heijden deals with the situation of the Jews during the Occupation mainly from the perspective of a member of a local Jewish Council, and from an alleged passive Jewish position. He states twice that the large majority had 'resigned' themselves to being deported, labelling the *species hollandica judaica,* not only as obedient inhabitants of a well-lubricated, civilised and 'happy' society, but also as 'the root cause of the success of the German extermination policy'.[63] This is a masterly example of blaming the victim.

58 Tony Judt, *Postwar: A history of Europe since 1945* (New York: Penguin Press, 2005), 803; Gans, 'Anti-Antisemitischer Enthusiasmus', 101.

59 Van der Heijden, *Grijs verleden*, 15; Gans, 'Iedereen een beetje slachtoffer'.

60 For a head-on critique on this aspect, *see* D. Verkijk, *Die slappe Nederlanders of viel het toch wel mee in 1940-1945?* (Soesterberg: Aspekt, 2001).

61 Chris van der Heijden, 'Die NSB – eine ganz normale politische Partei? Ein Plädoyer für historische Korrektheit jenseits der Political Correctness.' In: Nicole Colin, Matthias N. Lorenz and Joachim Umlauf (eds.), *Täter und Tabu: Grenzen der Toleranz in deutschen und niederländischen Geschichtsdebatten* (Essen: Klartext, 2011), 25-31: 27; Chris van der Heijden, *Joodse NSB'ers: De vergeten geschiedenis van Villa Bouchina in Doetinchem* (Utrecht: Begijnekade 18 Uitgevers, 2006), 26. *See also* Chris van der Heijden, 'Vertel het hele verhaal van de oorlog en betrek de NSB erbij', *NRC Handelsblad*, 9/10 December 2006. This article triggered several very critical reactions by historians, *see* Herman Langeveld, 'Beeld van de NSB behoeft geen bijstelling', and Peter Romijn, 'Er is volop aandacht voor de NSB', both in *NRC Handelsblad*, 12 December 2006.

62 Van der Heijden, *Grijs verleden*, 197.

63 *Ibid.*, 225, 230, 233-234. Van der Heijden forgets to put 'succes' between quotation marks, a professional deformation researchers and authors specialising in the Second World War and the Shoah should be alert about.

Whereas in *Grijs verleden* 'the Jew' featured as a 'meek lamb' and 'semi-collaborator' (i.e. as member of the Jewish Council), in *Joodse NSB'ers* [Jewish Members of the NSB, the Dutch National Socialist Party] (2006) the author makes the transition to 'full collaborator'.

Initially, Jews were allowed to join the NSB and a small number did. In 1934, they were banned from assuming party roles. In 1937 the NSB officially embraced racist antisemitism, but there had already been a virulent anti-semitic current from the start. From 1933 onwards vigorously antisemitic articles started to appear in the Dutch National Socialist press.[64] Actually, party leader Anton Mussert (1894-1946) had been making very violent comments about Jews right from the start, albeit initially 'only' against left-wing and foreign Jews.[65] From 1938 onwards he routinely produced the usual antisemitic stereotypes. In *Joodse NSB'ers* Van der Heijden zooms in on a handful of former Jewish NSB members who, under protection of party leader Mussert, are put up in a villa during not even three months, until they, too, are deported.[66] The drift of his booklet is that Jews could also be 'wrong' and that the NSB, Mussert in front, was less antisemitic than assumed. It is a failed attempt to obtain rehabilitation. During the German occupation the NSB was anything but an organisation with 'a ceremonial role', as Van der Heijden claims.[67] NSB members were, for example, well represented among the so-called 'Jew hunters'.[68]

Van der Heijden has also joined the debate about Israel and the conflict with the Palestinians. In *Israël. Een onherstelbare vergissing* (2008) 'the Jew', respectively, 'the Zionist', or Israeli-in-the-making, has evolved into a 'perpetrator'. The ambiguous title is deliberately confusing. 'Should every history which makes victims in the present from now on get the subtitle 'irreparable mistake?', the historian Amanda Kluveld (b. 1968) wondered.[69]

---

64 See Jozeph Michman, Hartog Beem and Dan Michman, *Pinkas. Geschiedenis van de joodse gemeenschap in Nederland* (Ede/Antwerp: Kluwer, 1985), 162-163.

65 Robin te Slaa and Edwin Klijn, *Ontstaan en opkomst van de Nationaal-Socialistische Beweging, 1931-1935* (Amsterdam: Boom, 2009), 249-256, 713.

66 Van der Heijden, *Joodse NSB'ers.*

67 Idem, *Grijs verleden*, 209. For criticism of his vision, see Tessel Pollman, *Mussert & Co. De NSB-Leider en zijn vertrouwelingen* (Amsterdam: Boom, 2012), 17.

68 Ad van Liempt and Jan H. Kompagnie, *Jodenjacht. De onthutsende rol van de Nederlandse politie in de Tweede Wereldoorlog* (Amsterdam: Balans, 2011). See also Josje Damsma and Erik Schumacher, *Hier woont een NSB'er. Nationaalsocialisten in bezet Amsterdam* (Boom: Amsterdam, 2010); Josje Damsma, *Nazis in the Netherlands: A social history of national socialist collaborators, 1940-1945* (Academic dissertation, Universiteit van Amsterdam, 2013): http://dare.uva.nl/record/1/395531.

69 Amanda Kluveld, '60 jaar Israël is tijd voor een kus', *de Volkskrant*, 14 May 2008.

Van der Heijden's booklet was a political pamphlet which, between the lines, compared the Shoah to the Nakba, the catastrophe as it unfolded for the Palestinians in 1948. He also played down the impact of the Shoah on the foundation of Israel which, as he suggested, was actually redundant: 'When Israel was founded, the Shoah had already happened, after all.'[70]

In *Dat nooit meer* Van der Heijden continues along the same lines. Although the book addresses the postwar period, this PhD thesis, as mentioned above, can also be interpreted as an academic remake of *Grijs verleden*. Even though the reviews were more unanimous in their criticism, most failed to pick up the continuity between the two books. The historian Friso Wielenga, for example, wrote a very dismissive review of *Dat nooit meer* in the authoritative BMGN – *Low Countries Review* and stated that, although *Grijs verleden* also had its critics, the latter book 'unquestionably was an important and useful contribution to the discussion of the period of occupation'.[71] He failed to mention the joint framework of both studies.[72]

The historian Dienke Hondius, however, *did* notice. She pointed out that, actually, together with *Dat nooit meer*, also *Grijs verleden* was admitted the doctor's degree and so, as well, 'the relativist perspective on WW2 and the memory of it'.[73] This repetition of moves emerges from, among other things, Van der Heijden's statement that in the first fifteen years or so after the liberation it was, indeed, difficult to discuss the war. What he, at the same time, judged positively, was that people were not, as it were, stuck in it. That changed during the 1960s. Precisely in the 1960s, of all eras, when society changed so dramatically 'people could have easily turned their backs to the most recent history. That wasn't the case. On the contrary. People deliberately looked for it. The question is: Why.'[74]

In *Dat nooit meer* Van der Heijden describes how the 'good' versus 'wrong' thinking, which *Grijs verleden* challenges, started in the postwar Netherlands. He mainly emphasizes how the war started to serve, particularly for the Left, as a political-moral framework of 'good' and 'bad' to be used against the political establishment, and how the victim's (read: mainly Jewish) perspective became overpowering.[75] The war, but particularly the Shoah, were artificially polished. Van der Heijden refuses to acknowledge that

70   Van der Heijden, *Israël. Een onherstelbare vergissing*, 102. For more details: Gans, 'Iedereen een beetje slachtoffer'; Gans, 'Eigentlich waren doch alle ein bisschen Täter *und* Opfer.'
71   Wielenga, 'Tale after Tale after Tale'.
72   *ibid.*
73   Hondius, 'Modderige mierenhoop'.
74   Van der Heijden, *Dat nooit meer,* 329.
75   See *Ibid.*, 15-16, 329-331, 414*ff*, 446*ff*, 605, 703-724.

people were 'finally' ready for it (instead of, what he had suggested, turning their backs to it). In *Grijs verleden* he had already aimed his displeasure at the Jewish historians Presser and De Jong who, at this time of all times, when the Netherlands finally seemed to become a modern country, had started 'a repetition of the war through words and images', with a 'tense representation' of 'good' and 'wrong' in a society that could really use the war as a unifying event.[76]

It is, by the way, not surprising that the extermination of the Jews, also beyond the historical context, as Friedländer wrote, 'has become, to many, the ultimate yardstick by which to measure all evil in a century of genocide and mass murder'.[77] The fact that this is and has been abused is subject to criticism and research (also in this book).[78] Van der Heijden, however, is less interested in what happened during the war (the subject of *Grijs verleden*) and what happened *to* the war after the war (the subject of *Dat nooit meer*), then in proving that people have kept the war, with the Shoah as the biggest crime, artificially alive on the basis of, predominantly, opportunistic motives. In this process, a specific group of wartime actors, the 'wrong' Dutch – and their children – were allegedly sacrificed as scapegoats for this dominant moralising perspective, without leaving any space for *their* lasting suffering.

Levelling and 'the guilty bystander'

As mentioned before, the notion of *'nivellering'* [levelling] in Holocaust historiography refers to the reduction of the existing differences in circumstances, emotions, dilemmas and motives between Jews and non-Jews, victims and bystanders.[79] This concept indicates that people with divergent

---

76 Idem, *Grijs verleden*, 10. *See* most recently Chris van der Heijden, 'En behoed ons voor het kwade. De Tweede Wereldoorlog – De oorlog als sociaal houvast', *De Groene Amsterdammer*, 15 April 2015.

77 Saul Friedländer, *Nazi-Duitsland en de joden*, deel 1: *De jaren van vervolging 1933-1939* (Utrecht: Het Spectrum 1998), 14 and vol. 2: *De jaren van vernietiging* (Amsterdam: Nieuw Amsterdam, 2007), 15. Van Vree, *In de schaduw van Auschwitz*, 109.

78 *See, e.g.*, the phenomenon of Jewish narcissism, chapters 5, 6, 7, 11, 12. Gans, *Gojse nijd & joods narcisme*, 46-48, 112*ff*, 126-142; Gans, 'De strijd tegen antisemitisme is verworden tot ideologie tegen moslims', *NRC Handelsblad*, 8 January 2011; Gans, 'Verbaal misdrijf' (reaction to the article of rabbi Evers 'Job Cohens onmogelijke vergelijking', *NIW*, 24 December 2010), *NIW*, 7 January 2011; Susan Glenn, 'In the Blood? Consent, Descent, and the Ironies of Jewish Identity', *Jewish Social Studies* 8, 2/3 (2002), 139-152. *See* Epilogue.

79 Gans, 'Iedereen een beetje slachtoffer.'

connections to the genocide are put under a single denominator without further problematisation, and without adequate reflection on the different positions and attitudes of perpetrators, bystanders, collaborators and victims.[80]

In 2012 the historian Bart van der Boom of Leiden University won the honourable Dutch Libris History Prize. This annual price is awarded to the best popular history book of the year by a jury of historians associated to universities, journalists and other cultural sector stakeholders. Complaints about the awarding of prizes are more than common, but in this case the protest went further and lasted longer. Triggered by an essay by Gans and Ensel in *De Groene Amsterdammer,* the book became the subject of an intense debate in the Netherlands, which was layered and diverse, partly because the participants were not only historians and other scholars. In view of the contributions in newspapers and journals, letters to the editor, email correspondences and face-to-face conversations, many felt engaged in this debate.[81] The historian Jaap Cohen (b. 1980) was right when he called it a Dutch *Historikerstreit.*[82] Ensel and Gans (the authors of this chapter) certainly couldn't count on approval only; apart from fierce reactions on the part of Van der Boom (and Van der Heijden) they were criticized of being, for example, too strict with regard to the role of antisemitism, or of playing down the relevance of Van der Boom's main questions and themes.[83] In

80 Remco Ensel and Evelien Gans, 'We know something of their fate.'
81 *See,* however, for an early critical review, Ed van Thijn and Ies Vuijsje: Anne Burgers, 'Ed van Thijn: "Boek Van der Boom misleidend"', *Historisch Nieuwsblad,* 7 May 2012: www. historischnieuwsblad.nl. The personal archives of both Gans and Ensel contain several emails with, for example, letters to the editor that were not published.
82 Jaap Cohen, 'Hoe cruciaal is onwetendheid?', *NRC Next,* 3 April 2013. The term had been used before in the heading which *De Groene Amsterdammer* (27 January 2010) used for a critical reading by Evelien Gans of Chris van der Heijden's work: 'Iedereen een beetje slachtoffer, iedereen een beetje dader. De Nederlandse Historikerstreit over de grijze oorlog.' The historian Christina Morina has made an overview of the debate: 'The "Bystander" in recent Dutch historiography', *German History* 32, 1 (2014), 101-111. At the same time, Morina did not seem to feel at home in this debate: 'Van der Boom wrote and spoke about the book ... in a bellicose spirit ..., and the tone in his critics' statements is often sharp and bellicose as well .... Engaging in lively academic controversies is, of course, our core business, but thus far, the book's actual contribution to the issues at hand seems to be obscured by the smoke stirred in public controversy.' Almost all the topics, however, which she mentions further on in the article, were addressed in the debate.
83 Some academics thought the debate was not very useful. Frits Boterman, *Duitse daders. De Jodenvervolging en de Nacificatie van Nederland (1940-1945)* (Amsterdam: Arbeiderspers, 2015), 44. Abram de Swaan called the debate at first 'a silly discussion': Abram de Swaan: 'Achter deze discussie gaat een schuldvraag schuil', *NRC Handelsblad,* 1 February 2014. But later on he retracted this statement: Abram de Swaan, 'Klaag niet alle Nederlanders aan om de Holocaust en pleit ze ook niet allemaal vrij', *NRC Handelsblad,* 14/15 June 2014. *See also* Frederik van Gelder,

our analysis of *Wij weten niets van hun lot* we focus on the evocation of the stereotype of the passive Jew (as introduced in chapter 3 of this volume) and the concomitant rhetorical strategy of 'blaming the victim'. The stereotype of the passive Jew is an important part of his thesis on the rehabilitation of the bystanders, i.e. the so-called 'ordinary Dutchmen' of the subtitle.

Van der Boom's core research question is: what did 'ordinary Dutchmen' know about the fate awaiting the Jews and at what stage? That 'fate', the Holocaust, is defined in the book as 'death upon arrival' in the gas chamber. On the basis of 164 diaries as source material, Van der Boom concludes 'there was no knowledge regarding the fate of the Jews, there were only rumours and suspicions and fears .... The widespread notion that bystanders knew enough about the Holocaust [to take action], but did not much care, is untenable.'[84] With his book, Van der Boom aims to give short shrift to the 'myth of the guilty bystander', allegedly propagated by historians, columnists and others, and which he supposes to dominate the vision of the Holocaust: 'Bystanders ... consciously allowed the Holocaust to happen, remaining passive or lending a hand.' Van der Boom argues this 'myth' is generally accepted in 'international historiography', referring to the work of the historians Saul Friedländer and Dan Stone. In his 'authoritative and nuanced overview', Stone writes of the 'shocking extent of collaboration and antisemitic initiative in occupied Europe'. 'In this view', as Van der Boom argues, 'the Holocaust was not a Nazi project, not even a German project, but a European project – or, if one wants to include American bystanders: a Western project.'[85] His reasoning is then that *if* non-Jewish 'ordinary' Dutch, but also accomplices like policemen, railway staff and civil servants working in the registry office, had known about 'it', they would have adopted a less

---

'Commemoration, a philosophical view': www.amsterdam-adorno.net/fvg201303_crescas_ENG. html; Ido Abram: 'Wat wisten Joodse en niet-Joodse Nederlanders tijdens "de" oorlog? Volgens historicus Bart van der Boom niet genoeg om adequaat te kunnen handelen.' *Kol Mokum*, September 2012; Leo Frijda, 'Ik ben het er niet mee eens dat het boek van Van der Boom, zoals Evelien Gans en Remco Ensel ... betogen, past in de trend van nivellering van daders, omstanders en slachtoffers: www.crescas.nl/site/blog/webcolumnfrijda/ (consulted 25 February 2013).

84 Bart van der Boom, 'Ordinary Dutchmen and the Holocaust: a summary of findings'. In: Peter Romijn et al. (eds.), *The Persecution of the Jews in the Netherlands, 1940-1945* (With an introduction by Wichert ten Have). (Amsterdam: Vossiuspers UvA / NIOD, 2012), 45-49.

85 Bart van der Boom, *'Wij weten niets van hun lot.' Gewone Nederlanders en de Holocaust* (Amsterdam: Boom, 2012), 218. Saul Friedländer, *Nazi Germany and the Jews. The years of extermination* 1939-1945 (New York, 2007), xxi, 190; Dan Stone, *Histories of the Holocaust* (Oxford: Oxford University Press, 2011), 16-17, 53.

passive position.[86] Now, there was nothing to blame the bystanders for, said Van der Boom – 'our grandparents', he specified in an interview.[87]

The debate about the book generated a great deal of criticism about Van der Boom's approach and conclusions. After all, there is a lot to be said against the concepts and definitions that have been used, for example, 'the Holocaust' ('Death upon arrival'), thus reducing the Holocaust to a murder technique: the gas chamber; 'knowing' or 'knowledge' ('subjective certainty').[88] Who *could*, except for a few, know about the gas chambers? But many, if not all, knew about the preceding processes of discrimination, segregation, robbery, humiliation – and deportation. Notably, Ido de Haan in his review refrained from an explicit judgment, whereas his own writings provide sufficient grounds for considerable criticism. In *Na de Ondergang* (1997) De Haan did not waste any words about the level of understanding concerning the maltreatment and humiliation of the Jews: many were witnesses to their often futile cry for help. 'Auschwitz' should not be made the catchword of what had happened, because the persecution of the Jews happened around the corner, on every doorstep and in front of one's house.[89] That was, however, precisely what Van der Boom did.

Just like there was disapproval of Van der Heijden's selective use of sources, so Van der Boom was criticised for his one-dimensional reading of war diaries. The Dutch historians Arianne Baggerman (b. 1959) and Rudolf Dekker (b. 1951), both known for their studies of diaries and other 'ego-documents', have pointed out that autobiographies and diaries cover up as much as they reveal. What does the author leave out? Moreover, many diaries are ambiguous. Finally, a diarist can use his diary to present himself as he pleases. Van der Boom, as he explicitly argues, never bothers with the caveat, familiar in scholarly circles, regarding the use of diaries for research, opting instead for a so-called 'carefree approach'.[90]

---

86   *See also* Bas Kromhout, "We hebben het niet gewusst". Bart van der Boom over *Nederlanders en de Holocaust*", *Historisch Nieuwsblad* 21 (May 2012). Van der Boom, *Wij weten niets*, 414-415.

87   Kromhout, 'Nederlanders hebben het niet gewusst', *Historisch Nieuwsblad*, 24 April 2012. *See also* Gans and Ensel, 'Wij weten iets van hun lot', I & II.

88   Van der Boom, *Wij weten niets*, 377, 100.

89   Ido de Haan, *NRC Handelsblad*, 4 May 2012; *id.*, *Na de ondergang*, 14.

90   In their contribution to the debate, Baggerman and Dekker wrote: 'It is actually incomprehensible that someone who has studied 164 diaries still believes that such texts are unmisted mirrors of what the writers thought and felt.' Garbarini calls diaries "improvisational texts". This characterisation opens the possibility that diaries have a function in the explanation and legitimisation of behaviour, of personal inability and unwillingness. Arianne Baggerman and Rudolf Dekker, 'Egodocument als bron', *De Groene Amsterdammer*, 24 January 2013; Alexandra Garbarini, *Numbered days. Diaries and the Holocaust* (Ann Arbor: Yale University Press 2006),

Van der Boom reached one of his main conclusions, stating that 'many Jews' did not go into hiding because they did not know about 'it', based on an, according to him, plausible assumption. This is, however, as speculative, Van der Boom acknowledges, as the conclusion that if the bystanders had known about 'it', they definitely would have done more. He furthermore assumes there is a relationship between the lack of knowledge and the lack of action among bystanders.[91] These bystanders would have calculated that not acting was better both for themselves and for the Jews. For there was a chance to survive 'Poland', while hiding Jews meant risking arrest and deportation, leading to a deportation as a so-called *'strafgeval'* [a case for punishment], and thus, directly to death. Van der Boom's argument consists of a number of sub-theses. People were not indifferent, but quite involved with the fate of the Jews. Neither bystanders nor collaborators knew the Holocaust was taking place.

It seems that, in his reactions to the strong criticism, Van der Boom has abandoned the weakly founded thesis about the connection between the bystanders' lack of knowledge and lack of action – in his book presented as one of the most important conclusions. This can be inferred from later interviews and replies, in which Van der Boom tends to stress the connection between the Jews' lack of knowledge and their reluctance to go into hiding. But this is done without the admittance that his former thesis regarding the bystanders and the thesis with regard to the Jews, was built on quicksand.

In the debate the argument about not going into hiding plays a key role. As said, many Jews are assumed not to have gone into hiding out of ignorance and out of fear for punishment on discovery, as is argued in the book. To the objection that there were huge problems of a practical, social and emotional nature as regards going into hiding, Van der Boom's repeated reply is: 'But there were Jews who *could* have gone into hiding, but didn't or only after long hesitation. Of this, I give dozens of examples.'[92] There is a

17. Van der Boom, *Wij weten niets*, 116. *See also* Willem Melching, *Hitler. Opkomst en ondergang van een Duits politicus* (Amsterdam: Bert Bakker, 2013), 226-227.

91   For a very critical approach of this supposed link, *see*: Mary Fulbrook, *A Small Town Near Auschwitz. Ordinary Nazis and the Holocaust* (Oxford: Oxford University Press, 2012); *see also* Jaap Cohen''s review of this book: *NRC Handelsblad*, 21 November 2013.

92   Van der Boom adds the crucial explanation 'because they were afraid of the punishment that would follow': Fabian van Semang, 'Wij weten niets van hun lot. Een nieuwe benadering van de Jodenuitroeiing in Nederland [interview with Bart van der Boom]', *Sporen van herinnering, Pedagogie en Geschiedenisoverdracht* 2, 6 (2012), 2-4. *See, e.g.*, blog Van der Boom, 17 May 2013; blog FAQ, question 11.

problem with this reply, as it puts people who did not go into hiding and those who eventually did, under the same denominator. Unfortunately, the book doesn't contain any example of Jews who did not go into hiding out of ignorance or fear.[93] Thus, the book only offers people who wanted to go into hiding but could not find a place, people whose motivation remains unclear or whose stated motivation points in another direction. Moreover, Van der Boom doesn't mention the information, to be found both in ego-documents of resistance fighters and in historiography, that it was most difficult to find hiding places for Jews. 'Many times', the historian researcher Ben Sijes (1908-1981) wrote, 'people were met with closed doors'.[94] A former resistance fighter says that it was extremely hard to find hiding places for Jews: 'Only one time in ten we were lucky.'[95]

Van der Boom believes that his book offers an important key to an understanding of the fact that so many Jews were deported from the Netherlands and murdered. His argument supposedly explains the 'obedient behaviour' of the victims, and the passivity of the bystanders (which he challenges). The argument that bystanders would have acted, had they known, is not based on his findings but, as Van der Boom has explicitly stated, inferred from his 'optimistic world view' and 'the laws of logic'. Van der Boom calls those who do not agree with his optimism 'misanthropic', people who turn bystanders into 'monsters'.[96]

93   Of the 164 diarists, 53 were Jewish; 34 diarists went into hiding and 19 did not. Of these latter, eight don't mention anything about their motives. Seven Jewish diarists who did not go into hiding 'could, according to their own words, have gone into hiding'. That applies to Claartje van Aals: 'If I no longer have Arno [who was refused by her father to go into hiding together], I do not care about the rest anyway'; and it applies to Gertrud van Tijn: 'I was fully determined to experience everything, up to the very end.' Van Aals worked in a psychiatric institution where, the night before the institution would be deported, half of the staff ran away. Van Tijn thought (eventually correctly) that her place on the so-called Palestine list would save her. Van der Boom, *Wij weten niets van hun lot*, 395-396.

94   Member of the RIOD (the former name of today's NIOD). Ben Sijes, 'Enkele opmerkingen over de positie van de Joden in de Tweede Wereldoorlog in Nederland', *Jaarboek van de Maatschappij der Nederlandsche Letterkunde te Leiden*, 1973-1974 (Leiden, 1975), 14-38: 35. *See* Jacques Presser, *Ondergang. De vervolging en verdelging van het Nederlandse Jodendom* (2 vols. The Hague: Nijhoff, 1965) II: 255; Loe de Jong, *Het Koninkrijk der Nederlanden in de Tweede Wereldoorlog* VII (The Hague: Staatsdrukkerij, 1976), 463; Moore, *Slachtoffers en overlevenden*, 215-216. De Haan, *Na de ondergang*, 13. *See also* chapter 2.

95   Bob van Amerongen, quoted in: Loes Gompes. *Fatsoenlijk land. Porgel en Porulan in het verzet* (Amsterdam: Rozenberg, 2013), 58. With a DVD of the documentary *Fatsoenlijk land* (2013) by Loes Gompes and Sander Snoep (Lumen films, 60 min.). *See also* Ensel and Gans, 'We know something of their fate'.

96   Van der Boom, *Ordinary Dutchmen and the Holocaust*, 46-47. 'Misanthropic' in Bernard Hulsman, 'Doe het niet, zou je willen schreeuwen', *NRC Handelsblad*, 12 July 2013.

All these points, including the one-sided conceptualisation and reading, have frequently been raised in the debate. The earlier-mentioned historians Baggerman and Dekker assumed that Van der Boom was suffering from a 'tunnel vision' when he read the diaries, a qualification which is substantiated by including his previous work in the analysis. The same conclusions had already, and with great certainty, been formulated by him in various previous publications, without the benefit of reading a large number of diaries. Back then it was also crystal clear to him that people really had not 'gewusst'.[97]

Within the context of this volume it is important to look at these critical notes in the context of the specific vision of the Shoah that Van der Boom's book conveys. By lumping people together who find themselves in very different positions with relation to the German occupier – a case of 'nivellering' [levelling] – Van der Boom's work relates to that of Van der Heijden's. The same applies to the propagation of 'the myth of Jewish passivity' when speaking of 'obedience'.[98] Considering that Van der Boom also received a lot of praise, we might infer that we are dealing with a broadly supported view on the Holocaust. Even though both authors have been criticised because of this aspect, critics have refrained from using the term nivellering [levelling]. Sometimes, however, they reach the same conclusion. The aforementioned historian Wielenga, for instance, stated about Van der Heijden's Dat nooit meer:

Typical of taking too far the grey view that comes of this, is the very unfortunate order of the summary of the 'groups deeply affected by the war …: resistance, forced labour, collaborators, Jews, political prisoners …'.[99]

Ido de Haan, the co-promotor of Dat nooit meer, had written the following about Grijs verleden:

97   In a 1997 book review, for example, he corrects the author of a local war history: 'But everything – from the reluctance of many to go into hiding to the good-humoured cooperation of the Dutch authorities – points to the fact that in the Netherlands almost nobody realised that the aim of the deportations was not forced labour, but a certain death. It does not fit into our collective guilt, but it is true: we really did not know [nicht gewusst].' Bart van der Boom, Review of J.J. Huizinga, 'Friesland en de Tweede Wereldoorlog', de Volkskrant, 3 January 1997.
98   Richard Middleton-Kaplan, 'The Myth of Jewish Passivity.' In: Patrick Henry (ed.), Jewish Resistance Against the Nazis (Washington, D.C.: The Catholic University of America Press 2014), 3-26.
99   Wielenga, 'Tale after tale after tale', 94; Van der Heijden, Dat nooit meer, 24 (italics added).

By overextending the reach of this concept, as well as polemically applying it equally to all participants in this history, from Dutch members
of the SS to Jews reacting to the threat of deportation, Van der Heijden
ended up in the position, which Saul Friedländer identified as the weak
spot of Broszat's plea for normalization, that it was ultimately hard to
distinguish between the apologetic narratives of Andreas Hillgruber
and Ernst Nolte.[100]

By comparison Guus Meershoek, the author of a study about the police
during the war, wrote that 'Van der Boom's explanation for the behaviour
of non-Jews – provided it cuts any ice – cannot be transposed to that of the
Jews'.[101] But that's exactly what happens in *We know nothing of their fate*.

It has already been noted that Van der Boom partly rejected the perspective of *Grijs verleden*. However, this only refers to one issue, i.e. that Van
der Boom, unlike Van der Heijden, does not believe that 'ordinary Dutch
people' muddled on for better or for worse. No, the majority of them were
explicitly anti-German – although usually not in terms of behaviour, but in
disposition.[102] In practice, however, as also noted before, there are striking
similarities between Van der Boom's and Van der Heijden's approach. As
an illustration we might refer to Blom, who previously embraced Van der
Heijden's work, and subsequently wrote a jubilant statement for the back
cover of Van der Boom's book. In Van der Boom's *'stemmingsgeschiedenis'*
[history of moods], Blom recognised the appeal he made during his oration
to map people's perceptions during the occupation, in particular as Broszat
had done in his investigation of the *Stimmung* of the German civilian
population in Bavaria.

What are those similarities between the works of Van der Heijden and
Van der Boom? First, like Van der Heijden Van der Boom underlines the
myth of 'Jewish passivity' and obedience. When Van der Boom describes
the behaviour of the Jews, he does so under the banner of 'obedience'. In
the final chapter, the behaviour of the Jews, as can be deducted from the

---

100 Ido de Haan, 'The paradoxes of Dutch history. Historiography of the Holocaust in the
Netherlands.'In: David Bankier and Dan Michman (eds.), *Holocaust historiography in context.
Emergence, challenges, polemics & achievements* (Jerusalem: Yad Vashem, Berghahn Books,
2008), 355-276: 369.
101 Guus Meershoek, 'Een aangekondigde massamoord. Wat wisten Nederlanders van de
jodenvervolging?', *De Groene Amsterdammer*, 30 January 2013. For Guus Meershoek, *see also*
chapter 2.
102 Van der Boom, *Wij weten niets*, 144-146; idem, *'We leven nog.' De stemming in bezet Nederland*
(Amsterdam: Boom 2003).

diaries, is discussed under the section heading 'Behaviour: the logic of obedience' [*Gedrag; de logica van gehoorzaamheid*]. The fact that only a few Jews (210) escaped from Westerbork while, allegedly, it had been easy, is explicitly interpreted by him as a 'deliberate choice against resistance'.[103] Without mentioning that escapes led to severe repercussions for those left behind.[104] The many forms and graduations of Jewish resistance – apart from going into hiding – remain beyond Van der Boom's field of vision. In reality, many Jews took part in resistance activities.[105] About the relatively and absolutely high number of suicides among Jews from May 1940 onwards, also in the transit camp Westerbork, Van der Boom only mentions that this did not necessarily point to specific knowledge of the Holocaust, but that it only confirms that they, with reason, 'took a dim view of the future'. He fails to acknowledge that suicide can also be interpreted as a final attempt to take control.[106] Jewish doctors struggled with the question whether they wanted or were allowed to meet requests for poison by their patients.[107] Like many Dutch historians, Van der Boom rejects the 'psychological factor'. Repression, suppression, denial. Why should one repress, suppress or deny what one couldn't know? Suppression was a 'superfluous hypothesis'.[108] On this point – the supposed irrelevance of suppression and denial – he was not only contested by Ensel and Gans, but also, very firmly, by the sociologist and psychiatrist Abram de Swaan.[109] Like De Swaan, the sociologist Rineke

103 Idem, *Wij weten niets*, 397-398; 401. Van der Boom states this on the basis of three Jewish diarists.

104 In 2015 it was discovered that precisely because of that a small group of Jews had prepared to escape from the actual train itself, by sawing a hole in the bottom of the carriage using small smuggled saws; their attempt was successful: *NOS journaal*, 12 April 2015: http://nos.nl/artikel/2029889-zaagje-redde-gevangene-kamp-westerbork.html

105 *See, e.g.*, Ensel and Gans, 'We know something of their fate'. *See also* chapter 3.

106 Van der Boom mentions suicide, going into hiding and escape in the same breath: *Wij weten niets*, 377 and 144-146. For Jewish suicide in the Netherlands during the war: Wouter Ultee and Ruud Luijks, 'De schaduw van een hand. Joods-gojse huwelijken en joodse zelfdodingen in Nederland 1936-1943.' In: H. Flap and W. Arts (eds.), *De organisatie van de bezetting* (Amsterdam: Amsterdam University Press, 1997), 55-76; Karin Dangermond, 'Het heft in eigen handen: Joodse zelfmoorden in Nederland tijdens de Tweede Wereldoorlog', *Misjpoge* 25, 1 (2012), 4-12.

107 Hanna van den Ende, *'Vergeet niet dat je arts bent'. Joodse artsen in Nederland 1940-1945* (Amsterdam: Boom 2015), 10.

108 Van der Boom, *Wij weten niets van hun lot*, 385. Van der Boom spoke also of a 'debatable psychoanalytical theory': Gans and Ensel, 'Wij weten iets van hun lot'.

109 De Swaan, 'Achter deze discussie gaat een schuldvraag schuil', and: De Swaan, 'Klaag niet alle Nederlanders aan'. *See also* note 279. About 'compartimentalisation': Abram de Swaan, *Compartimenten van vernietiging. Over genocidale regimes en hun daders* (Amsterdam: Prometheus/Bert Bakker, 2014), 249. Rineke van Dalen, 'Een late kritiek', blog 'Kundig in het midden', http://rinekevandaalen.nl/en-nog-veel-meer/een-late-kritiek/ (consulted 2 December 2015).

van Dalen (b. 1947), very critical of Van der Boom's book, argues emphatically for a multidisciplinary approach.[110]

A second similarity between Van der Heijden and Van der Boom is their lack of knowledge or their playing down of Dutch antisemitism. An example in the case of Van der Heijden can be found in his characterisation of the prominent NSB member and radio propagandist Max Blokzijl (1884-1946), the first postwar death penalty victim. In prison, awaiting the final verdict, Blokzijl kept a diary, quoted by Van der Heijden. He quotes him both incorrectly and selectively, reproducing, without reflection, Blokzijl's own statement that he was not an antisemite.[111] He characterises Blokzijl's statements about the *'nationale onbetrouwbaarheid'* [national unreliablility] of the Jews as a 'critical attitude' towards Jews instead of identifying it as an anti-Jewish stereotype.[112] And he leaves out other blunt antisemitic remarks by Blokzijl such as the undesirability of *'een oligarchie van het joodsche grootkapitalisme'* [an oligarchy of Jewish big business], and the observation that, now that the German occupation was over, it was again mainly Jewish artists who were performing in Dutch theatres and concerts halls. The press would soon also be dominated by Jews, according to Blokzijl.[113]

Van der Boom, too, referred to Blokzijl's fate as the first postwar convicted war criminal before the firing squad. He did so in an article about the cemetery where, during the war, resistance fighters were executed and, after the war, Blokzijl and Mussert – both more 'demonstratively than fairly', thus Van der Boom – and the traitor Anton van der Waals (1912-1950) plus the highest SS man in the Netherlands, Hanns Rauter (1895-1949). Van der Boom looks ahead and puts this diverse group of executed in one category when he writes:

Future, more disengaged generations may see a common tragedy in this varied collection of executed: people sucked into the maelstrom of the

---

Rineke van Dalen, 'Een late kritiek', blog 'Kundig in het midden', http://rinekevandaalen. nl/en-nog-veel-meer/een-late-kritiek/ (consulted 2 December 2015). Abram de Swaan does the same in: *Compartimenten van vernietiging*, 249.

111 Gouda speaks of Van der Heijden's 'deceptive deployment of historical evidence', in: 'Divided memories of World War II in the Netherlands', 111.

112 Van der Heijden, 'Die NSB – eine ganz normale politische Partei?', 28; idem, *Dat nooit meer*, 92-93.

113 Max Blokzijl, 'Dagboek', 20-21; 28-29: Archive NIOD, Amsterdam.

war, struggling to do the right thing or just to keep their heads above water.[114]

Like Van der Heijden, Van der Boom is not well-equipped to recognise and analyse antisemitism. When for instance one host describes two Jews in hiding who don't appear to have any money as 'parasites' in his diary, Van der Boom does not interpret this as an antisemitic stereotype.[115] He calls antisemitism in the Dutch interwar years a mild yet widespread phenomenon, and claims it was only a variant 'of the ambivalent feelings all groups in the pillarised Netherlands harboured against each other'.[116] That claim is incorrect. Antisemitism actually transcended pillarisation – and if anything it was a negative unifying phenomenon between diverse communities.[117]

When a diarist removes the things left behind from Jewish houses, she thinks the deportations are 'terrible', and she wonders what will be done to the Jews in Poland: 'After all, they are also people (although they will never be our friends)', she writes. 'Why don't they just put them in one area?' Van der Boom uses the terms opportunism and segregation here – not antisemitism. He does place the diary writer – together with several others – in his section 'Antisemitism', but mainly ascribes the increase, registered at the time, to an 'increased sensibility' on this subject among 'progressively minded contemporaries'. He prefers to speak of ambivalent feelings towards Jews.[118] In an interview Van der Boom admitted that *if* antisemitism had been 'a dominant sentiment' after the liberation, then this would discredit his thesis. But according to him the revival of antisemitism after the liberation has not been conclusively proven. His impression is that it is exactly the opposite. 'Since most people assume people abandoned the Jews during the war, we think that after the war they were inclined to treat the victims unkindly.'[119] Chapters two and three of this book try to demonstrate something else: i.e. a continuous process of mutual alienation,

---

114 Bart van der Boom, 'Den Haag: de Waalsdorpervlakte. Verzet en repressie in de Tweede Wereldoorlog.' In: Wim van den Doel (ed.), *Plaatsen van herinnering. Nederland in de twintigste eeuw* (Amsterdam: Prometheus, 2005), 122-133: 132-133; *see also* Ensel and Gans, 'Wij weten iets van hun lot II'.

115 Van der Boom, *Wij weten niets*, 407.

116 *Ibid.*, 402.

117 Ensel and Gans, 'Wij weten iets van hun lot II'.

118 *Ibid.*, 212; 206-207.

119 Kromhout, 'Nederlanders hebben het niet gewusst'.

including antisemitism, of Jews and non-Jews since the 1930s until after the liberation.[120]

Ordinary Dutchmen

Compared to what was available at the time when Hans Blom gave his inaugural lecture, we now have at our disposal a substantial body of in-depth, sometimes comparative, studies through which we are better equipped to come to grips with the process of exclusion and deportation of Jews, with the functioning of public authorities and the role of individual citizens. In themselves these studies do not provide an overarching narrative or an answer to the question as to how to integrate the Shoah into the history of the Occupation or twentieth-century Dutch history. A significant portion of the recent debates in the Netherlands may thus be construed as an ongoing quest for a common narrative in which shared experiences, personal choices, large-scale processes and individual decisions all have their distinct place. A comprehensive history of the Shoah, such as written by Saul Friedländer, has yet to be written.

Both Van der Heijden and Van der Boom however did signal in their respective books a master narrative in the historiography of the Second World War, in both cases one with which they strongly disagreed. Van der Heijden stressed the ongoing framework of right vs. wrong, Van der Boom started from the 'generally accepted' thesis of the guilty bystander. In fact, although their narratives differ, the question of guilt is a common denominator. The work of Van der Heijden revolves around collaboration and *individual* guilt. Van der Heijden includes the Jews as victims under the banner of 'the grey past' he claims to observe. This leads to a far-reaching blurring of 'good' and 'wrong' with Jews as obedient victims or collaborators. Van der Boom explicitly starts from the question of *collective* guilt, or rather 'our' collective guilt.

We conclude this chapter by taking a closer look at the collectivity Van der Boom addresses in his book. The personal and possessive pronouns 'we' and 'our' refer to the Dutchmen and -women whom Van der Boom identifies as 'ordinary'. In his study, he speaks unabashedly of 'we' Dutchmen. On the first page it is said that 'we Dutchmen' are still occupied with the

---

120 Remco Ensel and Evelien Gans, 'The Bystander as a non-Jew.' Paper presented at the Conference *Probing the Limits of Categorization: The "Bystander" in Holocaust History*, 24-26 September, German Studies Institute Amsterdam.

question why so many Jews were killed because 'it immediately touches upon our identity'. From the book it appears that the nation is embodied in the 'ordinary' or 'average' Dutchman, the same ordinary Dutchman who was blamed wrongfully as bystander. As referred to earlier, Van der Boom stated: 'It is quite a strong statement to say about our grandparents that they thought it was OK that their Jewish neighbours were killed.'[121] In *'We weten niets van hun lot'*, it seems as if Van der Boom seeks liberation and redemption from the guilt for which 'we', the Dutch nationals (and not just the so-called collaborators), were wrongfully blamed.[122]

The concept of 'ordinary Dutchman' can be traced back to the common term 'bystanders', as introduced by Raul Hilberg. It is hardly the first time the concept of 'ordinary men' pops up in a book title, but what does it actually mean?[123] On the one hand we are dealing with a seemingly neutral left-over category – those who were not victims, perpetrators, resistance fighters or accomplices. On the other hand, however, the typification of 'indifference', which Van der Boom so fiercely challenges, also has been applied to them. To begin with, the term 'bystander' deserves more in-depth study; an initial attempt at that has been made in the study *Looking at the Onlookers and Bystanders* (2012), which, among other things, makes a distinction between 'passive' and 'active' bystanders.[124] This distinction also came up in the Dutch debate. Even non-Jews who, at first sight, were not actively involved in the persecution of the Jews, could, perhaps unintentionally or inadvertently, still have had their own share in it. Whether, as Meershoek writes in his contribution to the debate,

> it was the telephone engineer who came to disconnect the telephone connection of a Jewish family or the male nurse of the *GG en GD* [Municipal

---

121 Kromhout, 'Nederlanders hebben het nicht gewusst'.

122 *See also* Maarten Asscher, 'De doorwerking van de Shoah in de Lage Landen. Nederland: Drie vragen die niet weggaan', *Ons Erfdeel* 4 (November 2015), 42-50: 46.

123 A famous example is Christopher Browning's *Ordinary Men: Reserve Police Battalion 101 and the Final Solution in Poland* (New York: Harper Collins, 1992). For a critical approach, also of the widespread belief in the value of the Milgram experiment: De Swaan, *Compartimenten van vernietiging*, e.g. 250; De Swaan, 'Nooit meer Auschwitz lezing', Amsterdam, 21 January 2015; an English version is included in the same booklet.

124 Raul Hilberg, *Perpetrators, Victims, Bystanders. The Jewish Catastrophe 1933-1945* (New York: Aaron Asher Books, 1992); Michael Marrus, 'Acts that speak for themselves', *The New York Times*, 20 September 1993; Henrik Edgren (ed.), *Looking at the Onlookers and Bystanders. Interdisciplinary Approaches to the Causes and Consequences of Passivity* (Stockholm: The Living History Forum, 2012), e.g. 9. *See also* Epilogue.

Health Authority] who took bedridden Jews by ambulance to the train
.... These were ordinary Dutchmen and trusted organisations.

Meershoek also mentions

... the board members of a club who revoked Jewish memberships, the
housewife who stopped buying from a Jewish shopkeeper, the entrepre-
neur who, after a hint from the ministry, fired his Jewish employees,
the civil servant of the regional job centre who put unemployed Jews to
work in separate camps and, finally, the officials who collaborated in the
deportation? Were they not ordinary Dutchmen?[125]

In his analysis, Van der Boom's prime subject, the ordinary Dutchman,
constitutes an obfuscating category. Furthermore, and as already stated,
in order to make his point about the innocence of the bystander, Van der
Boom, just as Van der Heijden, needs to bring in the Jews as victims. He
explicitly does so by calling the Jewish diarists his 'control group', whereas,
as we argue, this actually comes down to using 'the (passive) Jew' as legitimation.[126] One of the Jewish diarists is Etty Hillesum (1914-1943). The
main title *'We know nothing of their fate'* is a phrase from her famous diary.
Van der Boom concentrates on the word 'know' in this phrase and ignores
what 'we', 'their' and 'fate' could mean. Through the personal pronoun
'we', the Jewish Hillesum is wrongfully used as the mouthpiece of ordinary
Dutchmen who, as bystanders, knew nothing of the fate of the Jews.[127] The
plural tense in the quote should be read differently: we, the left-behind
prisoners of Westerbork, we Jews, we who are also liable to be deported to
the East, we know not what fate awaits us there. And what about the word
'fate'? On the basis of her diary, it is clear that Hillesum knew something
of the fate of the deported, not everything, not nothing, but something. In
the quote, the word 'fate' is filled with threat and doom.[128] Furthermore,

125 Meershoek, 'Een aangekondigde massamoord.'
126 *Ibid.*, 313. Of the 164 diaries used by Van der Boom, 53 were written by Jews: that is a
disproportionately large number compared to the number of Jews living in the Netherlands.
David Wertheim, 'Wilders, Le Pen kapen de Joodse zaak', *NRC Handelsblad*, 13 November 2013.
International conference 'The Jew as Legitimation' in Amsterdam, August 2013, organiser: David
Wertheim (Menasseh ben Israel Institute, Amsterdam); idem (ed.), *The Jew as Legitimation.
Jewish–Non-Jewish Relationships beyond Antisemitism and Philosemitism* (under review).
127 *See also* 'The average Dutchman was much more afraid than reality warranted in hindsight':
Van der Boom, *Wij weten niets van hun lot*, 138.
128 Etty Hillesum, *Het werk. 1941-1943* (Amsterdam: Balans 2012; sixth rev. ed.).

Hillesum and her Jewish fellow citizens had been anything but 'ordinary' Dutchmen since the German invasion.

International research into the mechanism of leveling, by which categories such as bystander and ordinary citizen, Jew and non-Jew, are indiscriminately mixed, is deemed extremely desirable.[129]

---

129 *See* the criticism of the book by Gunnar Paulson, *Secret City: The Hidden Jews of Warsaw, 1940-1945* (New Haven, CT: Yale University Press, 2002), which, in a much more extreme way than in the Dutch historiography quoted above, blames the Jews for not having fled in large numbers to the other side of the city to find hide-outs among their Polish neighbours, in this context accusing them of 'racism' (34), suggesting the Jews had a 'collective death wish' (61-62), neglecting the despair that overtook the Jews (64) who had not been prepared to 'give it a go' (67). Also, in this case the Jewish perspective is disregarded (64). His critic Havi Dreyfuss states moreover that Paulson used his sources selectively: Havi Dreyfuss, *Changing Perspectives on Polish-Jewish Relations during the Holocaust. Search and Research. Lectures and Papers* (Jerusalem, Yad Vashem / The International Institute for Holocaust Research / Center for Research on the Holocaust in Poland, 2012), 55*ff.* I thank Dan Michman.

Part IV
Generations. Migrant Identities and Antisemitism in the
Twenty-first Century

14 'The Jew' vs. 'the Young Male Moroccan'

Stereotypical Confrontations in the City

Remco Ensel

The period 2000-2010 is marred by a number of headline-grabbing incidents involving mainly male youngsters, such as disrupting the 4 May Remembrance of the Dead, shouting 'Hamas, Hamas, all Jews to the gas' during demonstrations, and harassing Jews on the street. From the first news items in October 2000, 'the street' has played a role in the interpretation of these joint pro-Palestinian protests and anti-Jewish provocations. The commotion about the riotous atmosphere surrounding the demonstrations of the Second Intifada followed upon the growing attention, throughout the 1990s, for adolescents' 'deviant behaviour': annoying groups of young people gathering in the street, harassing people, causing disturbances in public transport and committing criminal offences. Over time, a number of larger urban 'violence spectacles' had occurred in Amsterdam. Referring to the Moroccan background of the youngsters, one of these, which took place in 1999 in the Amsterdam borough Nieuw-West ('New West'), has been listed as the only real race riot in the Netherlands.[1]

The incidents cannot be written off as typical youthful inappropriate behaviour, although this certainly explains part of the badgering. Here we consider the post-2000 incidents particularly as part of the troublesome identity politics of second-generation migrants. In France, the well-known publicist and historian George Bensoussan (b. 1952) has used harsh words in describing how society literally and metaphorically was losing ground to youths of North-African descent. Bensoussan considered verbal and physical public racism and antisemitism in schools and in the street the result of failed government policy in the postcolonial decades. The *banlieues* had become no-go areas where resistance to France's secular culture had

---

1   Spectacle of violence in Luuk Slooter, 'Wijkidentiteiten in voorstedelijk Frankrijk: Gevangen tussen misère en trots', *Migrantenstudies* 27, 1 (2011), 43-57; Margreet Fogteloo and Eduard van Holst Pellekaan, 'August Allebépleinvrees. Marokkanen in West, vijf jaar na de explosie', *De Groene Amsterdammer*, 20 December 2003; Frank Bovenkerk, 'Rassenrellen of criminaliteit?', *Migrantenstudies* 4 (1999), 255-270.

become the standard, where antisemitism was part of children's upbringing and where the word 'Jew' was an insult.[2] This and the following chapters are concerned with the Dutch urban culture of provocation and protest, and with people without routine access to broadcast and print media but with slogans and banners, songs, pamphlets, videos and internet postings at their disposal to bring their message across. More specifically we shall explore the face-to-face interactions in 'neighbourhoods of relegation', as the French sociologist Loïc Wacquant calls the deprived neighbourhoods in the Western world where 'a blemish of place is ... superimposed on the already existing stigmata traditionally associated with poverty and ethnic origin or postcolonial immigrant status'.[3] These are also the urban spaces, though not exclusively, where Jewish inhabitants were challenged by youngsters who themselves grappled with their 'hyphenated' Turkish- or Moroccan-Dutch identity.[4] It appears that in the first decade of the new century the stereotype of 'the Jew' once again got deployed in a politics of national and ethnic identities, a kind of goyish envy in a new key, thereby seriously affecting the daily lives of actual people. To make this tangible we shall take a closer look at various incidents recorded in the annual reports of a Dutch antisemitism monitor.[5]

Demonstrations

Around the turn of the century, antisemitism seemed a distant problem: 'I come across very little antisemitism in the Netherlands,' Tamarah Benima (b. 1950), editor-in-chief of the *Nieuw Israëlietisch Weekblad* (NIW) declared. 'Now and again I think, some people put the Jewish or the Israeli people on a very high pedestal. But society here is reasonably well-composed. For years now, the NIW has been receiving the same antisemitic letter, always sent by

2   Emmanuel Brenner (Georges Bensoussan), *The Lost Territories of the Republic* (American Jewish Committee, 2006; first French edition, 2002); Georges Bensoussan, *Antisemitism in French Schools. Turmoil of a Republic* (Jerusalem: Hebrew University of Jerusalem, Vidal Sassoon International Center for the Study of Antisemitism, 2004).

3   Loïc Wacquant, 'Territorial stigmatization in the age of advanced marginality', *Thesis Eleven* 91 (November 2007), 66-77

4   Remco Ensel, *Haatspraak. Antisemitisme – een 21ᵉ-eeuwse geschiedenis* (Amsterdam: Amsterdam University Press, 2014) and Heba M. Sharobeem, 'The Hyphenated Identity and the Question of Belonging. A Study of Samia Serageldin's *The Cairo House*', *Studies in the Humanities* 30, 1 & 2 (2003), 60-84.

5   The Monitor is put together by the CIDI, the Centre for Information and Documentation on Israel.

the same person. We no longer open it.' CIDI director Ronny Naftaniel seemed equally unimpressed: 'It is not massive and does not seem to be deep-rooted, and yet it does occur. Very constantly, like it has done for years.'[6] There was a certain resignation about the existence of a stable antisemitic foundation in society. Newspapers and CIDI's annual antisemitic incident reports, the antisemitism monitor, confirm this picture of relative resignation to the odd isolated incident, one year before antisemitism hit the front pages.

First we should point out that when we look at the antisemitism monitor 'relative peace' mainly implies that much continued as before. In the run-up to the Commemoration of the Dead in 2000, the editor of a university news bulletin said that he was done with the twentieth century: Jews are 'an arrogant, nagging people .... In the last century, something horrific happened, which I did not witness, but I still have to feel terrible about it ....' With his careless evocation of an antisemitic stereotype and the concomitant expression of a sense of 'Shoah fatigue', the editor clearly aimed to mimic the provocative style of Theo van Gogh, columnist and trendsetter of politically incorrect writing on the Shoah.[7] In a somewhat similar vein, the Second World War was also very much on the minds of the follow-ups of the *Alte Kameraden*, hardcore techno and metal fans, and skinheads. Each of these groups occasionally made the news, for making the Nazi salute, for defiling Jewish headstones in numerous places outside the major urban centres, or for commemorating either Rudolf Hess or Adolf Hitler.[8]

This was all annoying yet familiar territory. In the autumn of 2000, however, a new phenomenon became visible. On 28 September 2000, Israeli prime ministerial candidate Ariel Sharon paid a visit to the Temple Mount in Jerusalem, which instigated the uprising known as the Second Intifada. In the Netherlands, the frequency of antisemitic incidents rose. It seemed there was something new in the air. Many Muslims, or those who were increasingly identified as such, in the Netherlands closely followed the development of the Second Intifada. For 'Rachid, a 25-year-old Muslim' who

---

6   Margreet Bal, 'Laveren tussen het orthodoxe en het liberale Jodendom', *Trouw*, 24 april 1999; Charles Sanders, 'Er is nog volop antisemitisme', *De Telegraaf*, 9 January 1999; Tracy Metz, '"Ik heb altijd geleerd weerbaar te zijn." Ronny Naftaniel, jood van beroep en van overtuiging', *NRC Handelsblad*, 11 March 2000. In an interview by Remco Ensel, 15 July 2011, Naftaniel nuanced his views.

7   *See* chapter 12 on Van Gogh. The opinion piece by Piet Hein Peeters was published in *KuNieuws*, 7 May 2000 and was thus directly linked to the 4 May Remembrance of the Dead. The editor refused to 'push the writer into the corner of antisemites'. Still it is obvious the author represents Jews as a people in an adverse and stereotypical way.

8   CIDI Antisemitism Monitor 2000. For right-wing antisemitism *see* chapter 4.

participated in a demonstration linked to the Second Intifada on 14 October 2000, the most recurring image was 'that of the child who was killed, while his father begged them not to shoot'. Rachid was referring to the death of Muhammad al-Durrah, a twelve-year-old Palestinian boy who had become involved in a shootout in Gaza on 30 September 2000.[9] Through photos and songs, distributed on TV and via the internet, his death, the circumstances of which are heavily contested, would quickly become a key symbol of the new, violent confrontation between Israel and the Palestinians. People carried his portrait in the very first demonstrations. As a signifier of the Middle East conflict, the death of Muhammad al-Durrah came to bridge several ideological commitments and strategies of protest, ranging from 'old school' secular left-wing persuasions to new Islamist beliefs.[10]

Following a summer of mounting tension, the two weeks between Sharon's visit to the Temple Mount and the TV screening of al-Durrah's killing triggered the first pro-Palestinian protests of the new century. But the nature of the protests had changed. One newspaper reported that during the aforementioned Amsterdam demonstration organised by the KMAN, the Committee of Moroccan Workers in the Netherlands, on 14 October 2000, 'thirty Moroccan youths invoked Hitler' on one of the canals of Amsterdam. The KMAN said it was only 'adolescent misconduct'. Still, the organisation came under attack because of 'the anti-Jewish rabble-rousing'.[11] According to the KMAN the demonstration went smoothly, 'without a single incident …. The KMAN has nothing against Jews', while the only incident that did occur was blown out of proportion with malicious intent.[12] Subsequent demonstrations, however, where harsher. On 13 April 2002, on the occasion of the Israeli operation 'Defensive Shield', the KMAN and the Palestine Committee organised a demonstration in Amsterdam, the largest in years. 'Not regular', 'extreme form', 'intense', 'shocking', 'high-strung emotions' were some of the terms used by the city council in its evaluation of the demonstration.[13]

---

9   Yoram Stein, *Trouw*, 14 oktober 2000 ('De rabbijn verhaalt vandaag van het feest van de vrede'). Protests have been documented with the aid of CIDI documentation and local and national TV News (*AT5, NOVA, Buitenhof* and *Twee Vandaag*). I thank Gülsen Devre and René Deelen for their research into the iconography of banners.

10   *See* Remco Ensel, 'Singing about the death of Muhammad al-Durrah and the emotional mobilization for protest', *International journal of media and cultural politics*, 10, 1 (2014), 21-38.

11   Brieuc-Yves Cadat, Magenta.nl, *Amsterdams Stadsblad* Oost, 25 October 2000: 'KMAN-leider zit achter antisemitisme', 26 October 2000.

12   Press release KMAN, fax 27 October 2000 (CIDI documentation).

13   Memo on the occasion of the demonstration on Dam Square, 13 April 2002, City Council, 24 April 2002. Report of the meeting of the committee for General Affairs, 4 June 2002. Questions from Verhagen et al. with the answer from, among others, Minister Korthals, 2001-2001, no. 1249:

Even though the KMAN was held accountable for the misbehaviour of some participants, the demonstration mainly signalled the organisation's waning influence on the protesters.

Between 15,000 and 20,000 people walked through the city with slogans condemning Israel's policies and military violence, expressing support for the Palestinian struggle. Things got out of hand when a number of youths climbed the National Monument on Dam Square yelling, 'Hamas, Hamas, all Jews to the gas!'. An American man with a yarmulke was punched and had to take refuge in the Krasnapolsky Hotel on the square. Thus, three years after two representatives of two Jewish institutions had spoken of a relative peace, the quality newspaper *NRC Handelsblad* published an article with the headline: 'Jews call the shots in the Netherlands. The antisemitic world view of young Moroccans.'[14] What had happened?

The list of incidents that took place at post-2000 protests relating to the Israeli-Palestinian conflict shows that much remained the same, albeit in a more antagonistic form. There was still a fascination for Shoah analogies, genocide-related vocabulary and conflict in general – for which the sociologist Abram de Swaan coined the term 'anti-Israeli enthusiasm'.[15] This enthusiasm in denouncing Israel had gained momentum after the partial failure of the peace negotiations for Palestinian autonomy (the Oslo Accords) in the mid-1990s which had the effect of propelling Hamas and its religious frame as an alternative for the secular nationalist PLO. This turning point in Palestinian and Israeli politics indirectly led to the Second Intifada. The slogans on the banners, such as 'Jewish Nazi Terror 1948-1998 50 years', also signalled a change thwarting earlier KMAN /Palestine Committee resistance against using the analogy between Israel and Nazi Germany. Another banner read: 'Hitler could have been a Jew!' and there were banners combining 'Warsaw 1942' with a swastika and 'Gaza 2000' with the Star of David. Another slogan, 'Let the Jews stop moaning about the Second World War, They are not one jot better themselves', referred

'Action was undertaken against swastikas, photos of Hitler and texts and images that made the connection between Israel and/or Jews and/or Zionism with the Nazi regime, but also against otherwise discriminating or antisemitic slogans. Obviously, non-discriminatory texts aimed against the state of Israel and the government of that country were admitted because of the freedom of expression.'

14   Hans Moll and Hella Rottenberg, 'Joden maken de dienst uit in Nederland. Het antisemitische wereldbeeld van Marokkaanse jongeren', *NRC Handelsblad*, 14 June 2003.

15   Abram de Swaan, 'Anti-Israëlische enthousiasmes en de tragedie van het blind proces', *De Gids* 168 (2005), 349-367.

to the idea that the Jews were exploiting the Holocaust to hide their own perpetratorship.[16]

In January 2009, operation 'Cast Lead' in Gaza led to new demonstrations. During one protest meeting, on 3 January, against the 'Zionist genocide', Amsterdam rapper Rachid El Ghazoui aka *Appa* (b. 1983) addressed the crowd at the Museumplein with the slogan: 'I write my own laws and determine my own boundaries: fuck the system and fuck demonstrations'. In the 2014 Summer of Protest, with another military operation in Gaza underway ('Operation Protective Edge'), this slogan had changed into 'Fuck the Zionists, Fuck the Talmud.' One newspaper claimed Appa used 'tough street language'.[17] Back in 2009, Appa minutely explained the generational change, that is, the new protest of a new generation.

> It is time for a revolutionary fight, pay attention to the history I write /
> I am a visionary, this is the generation of the new revolutionaries / ....
> It is not too late, the truth is on the street, the biggest criminal organisation is the state / ....
> The propaganda paints us as the bad guys / because this life is more hypocritical than Israeli retaliatory actions
> Everywhere I see pain and blood and yet another child that must / go into battle for the murder of its parents, it cries out
> More Muslims are killed than Jews were in the Holocaust / They create fear of Islam and hatred against Muslims.[18]

In Appa's conflict model, it is the street vs. the state, 'us' against the Israelis, Muslims against the rest of the world. The Muslim 'genocide' and the Shoah cancel each other out. The street is ours, Muslims worldwide vs. Jews.

In another rap song, Appa, self-styled *straatfilosoof* [street philosopher], 'revolutionary armed with a pen' and rapper by profession, interprets the mindset of his generation. The first generation of immigrants had become stranded 'in a system that made them numb. / Of the desired cake, they only got crumbs,' the second generation fought 'against rage and impotence' in

16 *See* note 8.
17 *De Gelderlander*, 25 August 2014 ('Rapper Appa: op het randje voor Gaza').
18 '*Worden meer moslims vermoord dan joden tijdens de holocaust / Creëren angst voor de islam en haat tegen de moslims.*' This text is a combination of the text as spoken that day (according to footage on YouTube) and the original (Dutch) rap text (Appa, 'Revolutionair', 2008), www.songteksten.net), CD *Straatfilosoof* (2007).

a hostile Netherlands ('... who am I supposed to be: Dutch or Moroccan?')[19], haunted by bad press and anti-Muslim hatred. Or, as the lyricist says:

Of ben ik nu radicaal? Een losgeslagen extremist
Van Marokkaanse komaf, het standaard clichéverhaal

Or am I a radical? A rogue extremist
Of Moroccan origin, the standard cliché story[20]

Appa, who shows himself to be aware of the force of stereotypes and 'cliché stories', positioned two generations, each with its own experiences and frustrations, next to and opposite each other: 'Our generation has lost its way now ... but you cannot fool me ... under the umbrella of integration / lies the heart of all our problems: discrimination.'[21] Appa clearly wanted more than cake crumbs. 'I carry the pain of an entire people on my shoulders'. In his lyrics, Appa mixed this position of the victimised Dutch Muslim with the victimhood of the Palestinians.

One could say he was riding on someone else's coat-tails, but it is more interesting to see how Israel – once more – became part of Western European identity politics. Personal grievances, feelings of impotence and frustration, were communalised and became an issue in a political struggle, both in the Netherlands and in Palestine. The assumption that more Muslims or Palestinians were killed than 'Jews in the Holocaust' remains a recurring motif. The fight against the Palestinians and against the Muslims in the Netherlands was one single coordinated action by 'the devil' whose greatest accomplishment is not his hypocrisy, but the fact that everyone thinks he does not exist. With that, Appa concluded his rap. Did the rapper here refer to a demonic secret conspiracy and, if so, who was wearing the devil's clothes?[22]

---

19   Appa, 'Ya Rassi' (2009), www.songteksten.net and www.rapmaster.nl, CD *Straatfilosoof* (2007).

20   Appa, 'Kijk door m'n ogen' (2008), www.songteksten.net and www.rapmaster.nl.

21   Idem, 'Minister van Deportatie' (2006), www.songteksten.net and www.rapmaster.nl.

22   This line was supposed to have been uttered by the author of *The Protocols of the Elders of Zion*, Sergius Nilus: Svetlana Boym, 'Conspiracy Theories and Literary Ethics: Umberto Eco, Danilo Kiš and the Protocols of Zion', *Comparative Literature* 51, 2 (1999), 97-122: 105. The poet Charles Baudelaire wrote, 'La plus belle des ruses du diable est de vous persuader qu'il n'existe pas.' Baudelaire, 'Le joueur généreux' [The Generous Gambler]. In: Charles Baudelaire, *Petits poèmes en prose. Le Spleen de Paris* (Paris: Flammarion, 1969).

Rap and the social climate

Appa made use of a new protest repertoire, meanwhile denouncing the authority of established organisations and migrant representatives and turning 'old-fashioned' worldwide solidarity into an issue of local ethnic and national identity politics. His rap about the strife and struggle of the second generation was broadly felt. Here, we see another aspect of the post-2000 changes. New was the way in which Israel/Palestine and the Holocaust became embedded points of reference in all discussions about Jews, within the framework of primarily urban 'multicultural' tensions. This development illustrates another feature of De Swaan's sociological point of departure for the study of the impact of the Middle East conflict in Europe, that is, how a limited representation of a violent conflict always drags 'new parties' 'into the maelstrom', resulting in an inextricable tangle of 'ties that bind and blind'.[23]

This can be demonstrated by looking at the Dutch rap scene of these years. When the Moroccan-Dutch Mohammed Bouyeri killed Theo van Gogh, in 2004, the popular 'white' rappers Lange Frans and Baas B. added a tribute to Van Gogh to their song '*Zinloos*' [Senseless] (2004) about 'senseless violence', which had reached the Top Ten that very week.

> *Theo van Gogh nam nooit een blad voor zijn mond*
> *En laat dat de reden zijn dat ie vanochtend niet meer opstond*
> *Een aantal schoten, een mes en een brief*
> *Ik vraag me af wordt het ooit nog positief*

> Theo van Gogh always called a spade a spade,
> and that's the very reason why he is dead of late.
> A number of rounds, a knife and a letter,
> I wonder, will things ever get better.

In 2005, the duo wrote '*Het Land van ...* ' [The Country of ...] in which they took stock of the nation: *Kom uit het land van Pim Fortuyn en Volkert van der G. / Het land van Theo van Gogh en Mohammed B.*

---

23   De Swaan, 'Anti-Israëlische enthousiasmes.' The French version speaks of 'la tragédie d'un processus aveugle', in the abstract it says 'anti-Israeli furor: the tragedy of a blind process'. Abram De Swaan, 'Les enthousiasmes anti-israéliens: la tragédie d'un processus aveugle', *Raisons politiques* 4, 16 (2004), 105-124.

I'm from the country of Pim Fortuyn and Volkert van der G.
The country of Theo van Gogh and Mohammed B. ....
I come from the land of red, white and blue, of clogs and cheese.
Pillage the world, and we call it the Golden Age.

And integration is a magnificent word,
But if no one listens to you, it sure hurts.
I share my country with Turks, Moroccans and Chinese,
Antilleans, Moluccans and Surinamese.

One day we will all shine and we will sing a hymn
To the country I love so dear, at the stadium,
This is the country where I will overcome in the end.
This is for the Netherlands.

As a recipe against the state of confusion, the two rappers invoked a national multicultural imagined community made up of football, the Golden Age, the Dutch landscape and Dutch tolerance: *The country where I will stay, I really love it / Honestly.* Lange Frans and Baas B. belonged to the large group of young rappers who, after a brief stint of rapping in English during the 1990s, started rapping in Dutch.[24] Moroccan-Dutch rappers achieved a prominent position in this genre known as *Nederhop* but would increasingly be identified with their own sub-genre known as *Maroc-hop*.[25]

An important aspect of the hip-hop scene – woven into the lyrics, performances and public personae of the rappers – is the identity politics of both rappers and listeners. Rappers present themselves based on their roots, rapping in the first person singular, as if singing about their own experiences. Like elsewhere, rappers in the Netherlands also used ethnic labels: The New Immigrant Generation, the North African Alliance, Paramocro (i.e. angry *Mocro*, i.e. Moroccan-Dutch). Rappers Ali B. and Naffer went one step further by using an alias in reference to the stigma of the delinquent Moroccan-Dutch youths.[26] Rappers referred to themselves in hyphenated terms and their fans acknowledged the existence of Moroccan-Dutch

---

24 Jolan Douwes, 'RAP. Hollandse rap deukt, scheurt en beukt', *Trouw* 27 April 1995.
25 Miriam Gazzah, *Rhythms and Rhymes of Life. Music and Identification Processes of Moroccan-Dutch Youth* (Amsterdam: Amsterdam University Press, 2008).
26 Naffer is a police term for a North African suspect: Gazzah, *Rhythms and Rhymes of Life*. Ali B. developed into a celebrity, TV presenter and stand-up comedian. His 2016 show is titled *'Je suis Ali'*, obviously referring to the 'Je suis Charlie' slogan in response to the assault on Charlie Hebdo, January 2015 (*see* 'Epilogue').

(gangsta) rap. *Our gangsta shit hits home, I am a thug life Moroccan.*[27] The Maroc-hop genre was particularly characterised by playing with identities, authenticity and the motifs of the misunderstood 'I' against the rest of the world. In fact, it would be interesting to write a contemporary Dutch history based on rap songs. These Maroc-hop songs, full of references to a large number of incidents, show how the Netherlands struggled with the emancipation of its immigrants, with national identity, alienation, multiculturalism, xenophobia, violence and 9/11.

In this context, rapper Salah Edin (Abid Tounssi) (b. 1980) reacted to the rap song by Lange Frans and Baas B. with a variation in which he is a lot less unctuous about the Dutch social climate.

> *Het land van de hoogste percentage moslimhaters*
> *Het land dat is opgebouwd door onze vaders*
> *Het land dat ons ziet als gevaar en terreur*
> ....
> *Het land waar ik geboren ben maar waar kom ik vandaan*
> *Het land dat mij bestempelt als de Kutmarokkaan*

The country with the highest percentage of Muslim bashers
The country built up by our fathers
The country that sees us as a danger and a terror
....
The country where I was born but where am I from?
The country that marks me out as a fucking Moroccan.

The expression *Kut-Marokkaan* (literally 'Cunt Moroccan') – hyphenated, according to the Dutch standard dictionary Van Dale – became part of public language in 2002. Amsterdam alderman Rob Oudkerk (b. 1955) used the expression in a short altercation with mayor Job Cohen – to refer to the Moroccan-Dutch youth who were involved in public disturbances and petty crime – without being aware of an open microphone. The term was already part of Dutch slang – e.g. in 1995, a football player of Ajax Amsterdam used the term on the pitch – but Oudkerk's slip of the tongue made a highly abusive term acceptable. In one instance a judge at a hearing addressed a young suspect as *Kut-Marokkaan*. As it turned out, *K-Marokkaan* and *K(anker) Jood* became interconnected when in several violent incidents

---

27   DHC, 'Studiogangsters', www.songteksten.nl.

opponents expressed their anger by using exactly these terms.[28] Menachem Sebbag, a British rabbi of Moroccan origin posted in Amsterdam, explained how the two words familiarised him with Dutch society. On his way to the synagogue he was frequently yelled at. 'And then on my way home an older man who was walking beside me, said: "This is what it was like in '35 or '38", that was a real eye-opener .... Once when I was asked by a journalist, I responded: "I have pain in my neck here in the Netherlands. I walk on the streets and I am called a Bloody Jew. Then I turn around and someone calls me a Fucking Moroccan. So you know. I feel somewhat torn."'[29]

In response to 'K-Marokkaan', the term *Kaaskop* ('Cheesehead'), originally used to denote the regional identity of the *Hollanders*; i.e. the Dutch living in the western part of the country, was appropriated and increasingly used as an ethnic marker:

> These *Tattas* are all Sharons.[30] They only speak badly about us and other people. They think they are Tony Montana; that they have control over us and can handle everything. I live here too, so I want to be treated like everyone else. I don't want that spoiled by people like Ayaan Hirsi Ali, Geert Wilders or [Minister for Immigration and Integration] Rita Verdonk. I don't want to hear the whole time that I am a foreigner or that my ancestry is Moroccan. These are all things I already know, and I most definitely do not need to hear it from a Cheesehead.[31]

An editorial of the website 'We stay here!', jokingly said: 'It's not right to call a Moroccan youth of the second or third generation a *Kut-Marokkaan*. If you want to do it right, call him a *Marokkaanse Kut-Kaaskop* [Moroccan Bloody

---

28   'Rechter vindt "Kutmarokkaan" pedagogisch verantwoord', Ad.nl, 20 January 2011. One incident in 2003 took place when a woman died after having been wrongly accused of shoplifting and got subsequently beaten up. Some, not all, suspects were Moroccan-Dutch youngsters. In a statement mayor Job Cohen linked the incident to the problem schools face in teaching the Holocaust. 'Although we seem to be dealing with two distinct issues, they have much in common. In both cases the intimidation and violence of one party threatens the freedom of the other to move freely and to speak freely.' The second incident happened in 2012 when a referee died after being chased and beaten by the members of a visiting amateur youth football team. In both instances, *Kankerjood* en *Kut-Marokkaan* were the abusing terms. Charlotte Huisman, 'Ze weten het niet of het was de ander', *de Volkskrant*, 30 mei 2013. On Cohen: Hugo Logtenberg and Marcel Wiegman, *Job Cohen: burgemeester van Nederland* (Amsterdam: Nieuw Amsterdam, 2010), 141.

29   Interview Sebbag by Remco Ensel, 11 March 2011. Rabbi Menachem Sebbag was born in England, his father is from Morocco.

30   Tatta is slang voor Dutchman, originally Surinamese.

31   Yassine Zahraoui, 'Hoe racistisch is een Marokkaan', *NRC Next*, 14 October 2006.

Cheesehead] ....'[32] In response to the Oudkerk Incident, rapper Raymzter (Raymond Redouan Christiaan Rensen, b. 1979) wrote the more serious rap song 'Kutmarokkanen??!':[33]

> KUT MAROKKAAN, dat is wat ze zeiden.
> Ze willen ons zwart maken als ze over ons praten.
> We hebben ze niks gedaan en alsnog willen ze ons haten.
>
> Shit als dit kan mijn gedrag bederven.
> Als ik langs een vrouw loop en ik zie haar d'r tas verbergen.
> Maar mijn vader had het vast nog erger.
> Hij was een Berber, een gast uit de bergen.

> FUCKING MOROCCAN, that's what they said.
> They want to vilify us when they talk about us.
> We've done nothing and yet they want to hate us.
>
> Shit like this can spoil my behaviour.
> I walk past a woman and I see her hide her purse.
> But my father must have had it worse.
> He was a Berber, a guy from the mountains ....

Mohammed Bouyeri, the murderer of Van Gogh, could conceivably have written these lines or the aforementioned lines by Salah Edin.

Moreover, on the cover of his CD 'Nederlands Grootste Nachtmerrie' (2006), Edin posed as Bouyeri. This led to the inclusion of a picture of Salah Edin as Mohammed Bouyeri in Geert Wilders' anti-Islam film Fitna for which Wilders was prosecuted twice – with success in the case of the rapper. In 2011 Salah Edin released the CD WO II with song titles that all play with different meanings of World War Two and its lieux de mémoire such as 'Auxwitz' and 'Het Achterhuis' (referring to Anne Frank's Secret Annex).

---

32   'Hoe racistisch is een Marokkaan?', NRC Handelsblad 14 October 2006; 'Marokkaanse kut-kaaskoppen', https://wijblijvenhier.nl/1673/marokkaanse-kut-kaaskoppen/, 5 October 2008. Cheesehead has become increasingly politicized, as shown for instance by the publication of a collection of interviews about multicultural Netherlands by the Jewish author Robert Vuijsje: Kaaskoppen (Amsterdam: Van Nijgh & Van Ditmar, 2016).

33   Raymtzer, 'Kutmarokkanen??!', www.songteksten.net. Raymtzer was born to a Moroccan father and a Dutch mother, see chapter 17.

Illustration 22   Photo of rapper Salah Edin in a talk show, 27 March 2008

Truus van Gog / Hollandse Hoogte

Rapper Salah Edin ≠ Murderer Mohammed Bouyeri. Edin had posed as Bouyeri on the cover of his CD, which led to the inclusion of his picture in Geert Wilders' film *Fitna* for which the politician was prosecuted twice. Incidentally, the Danish cartoonist Kurt Westergaard had also objected to the inclusion of one of his cartoons in *Fitna*.

The CD also included the song, *'Als ik eens Nederlander was'*, in which the rapper dreams of being Dutch (which he really is).[34]

Maroc-hop produced several rap songs in which the topic of alienation and some sort of activist victimhood is linked to either the Middle East conflict, the Holocaust or to Jews. In the latter instance, 'Jews' may refer to a politician, the police or 'Dutch society' in general. The next category is constituted by songs that go beyond multiculturalism, protest and long-distance solidarity and directly express straightforward hate speech.

In 2002, *'Kankerjoden'* was uploaded to kazaa.com. The song's lyrics include lines such as:

---

34   Together with the release of the cd, photographer Moustapha Lamrabat, illustrator Franklin Westhoek and artist L'estoir (Esther Claus) organised a parallel art project 'Goudstikkers', named after the Jewish pre-war art dealer Jacques Goudstikker.

You Jews should know that I hate you.
I will visit you soon with a Kalashnikov.
You should know that I will finish you off.

The songwriter of 'Kankerjoden' was first identified as 'Moroccan' but turned out to be a Turkish-Dutch youth, while the rapper and presumed client was indeed Moroccan-Dutch. DHC, a rap formation from The Hague, which also wrote *Hirsi Ali Diss*, a hate rap against Ayaan Hirsi Ali, was responsible for the 9/11 rap *'Paf Paf Paf'* (also known as '11 September'):[35]

Good for them
now the blood flows on the other side
good for them
yeah, now you can see how it feels
fucking Jews, fucking Jews, we are coming to kill you.

There seems to be a symbiotic relationship between the rap songs and anti-semitic football chants. For instance, fans of the Belgian football club Club Brugge addressed fans of Anderlecht in the following terms: 'Fuck the Jews, those dirty Jews, the Bruges fans will come to kill you .... Hamas Hamas, all Jews to the gas.' Then the song goes on about a vulnerable twelve-year-old boy, an Anderlecht fan. The whole chant constitutes an odd redeployment of the aforementioned raps *'Kankerjoden'* and *'Paf Paf Paf'*, including the reference to the death of Muhammad al-Durrah, in the world of football.[36]

In 2000, the atmosphere in which these raps were composed was described in an influential, albeit alarmist, newspaper article by sociologist Paul Scheffer (b. 1954). The multicultural society had degenerated into a 'multicultural drama'. The title became a standard expression in Dutch. Scheffer predicted the advent of a generational conflict. Taking a psychological approach he argued young people despised their parents' past as immigrants, or 'guest workers':

They are angry with the society that abused their parents and with their parents who did not put up any resistance. I find it striking that many Moroccan youths feel victimised themselves. A victim feels abused,

---

35   The rap is attributed to DHC, but in *Rhythms and Rhymes of Life*, Gazzah stated that the Leidse Maffia or SWG was responsible. For the world of football *see* chapter 11.
36   http://hilarisch.skynetblogs.be/archive/2007/05/17/anti-rsca-moppen.html.

misunderstood, unsafe. They will have to shed their victim role in order
to find an identity.[37]

We may add this is not unlike the undertaking of the Jewish second generation in the 1970s and 1980s. Paul Schnabel (b. 1948), sociologist and former
director of the authoritative Netherlands Institute for Social Research, told a
slightly different story. In the Netherlands, there was a shared *A culture* with
an additional B level. This so-called A culture was 'the culture as expressed in
the constitution, containing the values and standards that have become self-
evident in modern, democratic societies'. The boundaries of the B culture are
delineated in 'social conflicts and debates'. Both widely quoted sociologists
laid the blame mainly on the culture of the immigrants. But while Scheffer
situated the emotional state of mind and concomitant social, generational
culture clash within the immigrant community, Schnabel counterposed an
idealised Dutch culture to an objectionable immigrant culture. Both statements (internal generational conflict and Dutch culture versus immigrant
culture) would co-exist and become entangled. In his study *Globalization
and National Identity*, sociologist Frank J. Lechner spoke of 'integration
fatigue' in the Netherlands. The 'catch-up nationalism', a persistent need to
recover a lost sense of community, as recognised by Lechner in the politics
of Fortuyn and his followers at the turn of the century, did not seem to fit
'in a country priding itself on not taking pride in its national culture'.[38]

Feelings of estrangement were thus living in different segments of society.
The rap lyrics illustrate one side of the story of the Dutch in the twenty-first
century. The songs and Bouyeri's early writings appeared at a time when
native Dutch people started to oppose 'immigrants', while these 'immigrants',
in turn, started to redefine their position, for example by rejecting concepts
such as *allochtonen* and *autochtonen* [immigrants and natives] which were
assumed to exacerbate social differences. Scheffer's image of a generational
struggle could thus also be construed as an emancipation struggle, a provocative, mutual and ambiguous quest for new collective identities and a struggle
for a new reading of hyphenated (Moroccan-Dutch) identities. Exemplary is
the rise of the Arab European League (AEL), an originally Belgian organisation
founded in 2000 by the Belgian-Lebanese Dyab Abou Jahjah (b. 1971). The

37   Paul Scheffer, 'Het multiculturele drama', *NRC Handelsblad*, 29 January 2000; Paul Schnabel,
'De multiculturele illusie', *de Volkskrant*, 17 februari 2000. *See* Paul Scheffer, *Immigrant Nations*
(Cambridge: Polity Press, 2011) including the chapter 'After the Multicultural Drama.'
38   Frank J. Lechner, *The Netherlands. Globalization and National Identity* (New York, London:
Routledge), xiv.

AEL was dedicated to two equally important causes: the struggle in Palestine against the 'Zionist entity' (i.e. Israel) and the struggle for the emancipation of Arab immigrants in Belgium and, later, in the Netherlands. In a *tour de force*, the movement tried to unite people who identified themselves as Muslim, Berber, Arab or Moroccan, in a more or less classical form of Arab nationalism. The AEL believed that this Arab identity was central to a European 'multicultural society'. In Belgium, the AEL was involved in the preparations for a trial against Sharon. During a debate in the Netherlands, chairman Abdou Bouzerda (b. 1978) refused to shake hands with CIDI director Naftaniel (since he was 'bankrolled by the Zionist entity').[39]

In 2006, the organisation was prosecuted following an 'unnecessarily hurtful' cartoon alleging that the Jews had artificially boosted the number of Holocaust victims to six million. The cartoon, drawn by Abdou Bouzerda and not Abou Jahjah, was intended to show that, while it was possible to insult Muslims and go unpunished – i.e. when the Danish newspaper Jylland-Posten published cartoons of the prophet Mohammed in 2005 and these cartoons also appeared in Dutch journals, this did not lead to prosecution in the Netherlands – Jews enjoy a protected status. The subtle distinction in the Dutch Criminal Code between group defamation (article 137c) in the case of Holocaust denial, and blasphemy (based on the almost derelict article 147 which was abolished in 2013) in the case of the cartoons, fell on deaf ears.[40] The belief in a 'double standard', or favouring the Jews, remained a motif in the immigration debate. It was an echo of the time of the Rushdie Affair, when Fassbinder's play *Garbage, the City and Death* was banned, while Rushdie's *The Satanic Verses* was not. Anne Frank was honoured, but the young Muhammad al-Durrah was not; shouting *Kankerjood*

---

39   Bouzerda has made a radical ideological u-turn distancing himself fully from the cartoons and dismissing antisemitism: Ally Smid, 'Ik weet nu dat Jodenhaat verkeerd is', *Trouw* 13 September 2009.

40   In Dutch law, *godslastering* [blasphemy] as an offence fell under article 147 of the Criminal Code. 'This article stipulates that "any person who publicly – orally, in writing or by means of portrayal – expresses himself in a manner insulting for religious feelings by means of scornful blasphemy" is liable to a maximum sentence of three months.' The article was to a large extent defunct but critics still argued its existence would hinder an open debate about religion (i.e. Islam). In 2007, after a heated debate, the government decided to maintain the article, but in 2014 the article was eliminated nevertheless. Holocaust denial, the subject of the AEL cartoon, fell under group defamation (article 137c). Thus far initiatives to criminalise genocide denial in a separate article have failed. *See* L.A. van Noorloos, *Hate speech revisited. A comparative and historical perspective on hate speech law in the Netherlands and England & Wales.* PhD thesis, Universiteit Utrecht, 16 December 2011: 181. In 2010-2011 Geert Wilders was charged with (and acquitted of) group defamation and inciting hatred against Muslims on the basis of articles 137c and 137d. The latter does not concern discrimination but hate speech: *haatzaaien*.

In reaction to the publication of the so-called 'Mohammed cartoons' in Dutch newspapers, the Dutch section of the Arab European League (AEL) published on its website cartoons which referred to Dutch Jews and the Holocaust, probably in an attempt to reveal the so-called 'double standard' in the legal rules on freedom of expression and desecration. A similar analogy was sought in an International Holocaust Cartoon Competition sponsored by an Iranian newspaper.

Illustration 23   Cartoon on the Holocaust by Abdou Bouzerda

Cartoon: Abdou Bouzerda, chairman of the AEL, 2006, 2008 / website AEL

'We have to get to 6,000,000 somehow.' 'I don't think they are Jews.' ('Auswitch').

Jews thus had artificially boosted the number of Holocaust victims to six million. The AEL was prosecuted (and, after a first acquittal, condemned) for group defamation (article 137c of the Dutch Criminal Code) because of the suggestion of Holocaust trivialisation.

Illustration 24   Cartoon on the Holocaust by Abdou Bouzerda

Cartoon: Abdou Bouzerda, chairman of the AEL, 2006, 2008 / website AEL

Pornographic antisemitism: 'Write this one in your diary, Anne!' The original title of the cartoon is 'Hitler goes Dutroux', hereby referring to the notorious Belgian serial killer and child rapist Marc Dutroux who was convicted in 2004.

is punishable, but saying *Kut-Marokkaan* is not, etc. As if the signal from their Holocaust-denial cartoon was not enough, the AEL also published a second cartoon in which 'we see Hitler in bed with Anne Frank and saying to her, "Write this one in your diary, Anne"'. According to Evelien Gans, it's 'a typical example of secondary pornographic antisemitism in which a sexual relation is suggested between the Jewish victim, or any Jew at all, and the Nazi: a perverted relation'.[41]

41   Evelien Gans, 'On gas chambers, Jewish Nazis and noses.' In: Peter Rodrigues and Jaap van Donselaar, (eds.), *Racism and Extremism Monitor. Ninth Report* (Amsterdam: Anne Frank Stichting, Universiteit Leiden, 2010), 74-87: 84.

The AEL made the new generation independent and politically active, in opposition to the 'masquerade' – as termed by Abou Jahjah – of the established 'spokespersons' of the 'immigrant community'. This revealed both a generational conflict and a crisis of authority. The new generation pushed aside any hint of a 'multicultural drama': instead of submission or sluggishness, it argued for mobilisation and activism. But Schnabel's perspective also comes to the fore, albeit with a twist; the AEL and others demanded a piece of the 'A culture' pie. In any case they apparently needed 'the Jew' in all his different stereotypical manifestations to succeed in their objective. Sometimes 'Jews' stand opposed to 'Muslims' or 'Moroccans', whereas in other instances 'the Jew' functions as a third party, *der Dritte*, positioned in-between the regular Dutch (whom they control) and the powerless Moroccan-Dutch.[42]

An anti-Gay and an anti-Jewish manifesto

Rap songs are one way of combining anti-establishment protest and anti-Jewish provocation. There are other ways as well. In November 2004, the month that Van Gogh was murdered, publicists of Elqalem.nl announced the publication of an anti-Jewish manifesto. This new website opposed the subsidised 'immigrant sites' (such as Maroc.nl, Marokko.nl and Maghreb. nl) and 'token immigrants' featuring in the media as 'immigrant representatives'. One such token immigrant was Ahmed Aboutaleb (b. 1961), now mayor of Rotterdam and then alderman of Amsterdam's city council, led by mayor Job Cohen at the time of the murder of Van Gogh. Aboutaleb was portrayed as an errand boy of the establishment and became the butt of criticism.[43] One of the founders of the website looked back on its launch: 'We noticed that the people representing the Muslim community in this debate [on multicultural society] were actually very docile. That they were easily out-argued .... I'm talking primarily about the politicians. We thought that someone like Aboutaleb was a perfect example of a ... uhm, "Moroccan House Negro."' The speaker is blogger Mohammed Jabri (b. 1975), who also made a name for himself as a writer of, for instance, *Hubal*, a novel about

---

42 On *Der Dritte*, see chapter 1 and Klaus Holz, *Die Gegenwart des Antisemitismus. Islamistische, demokratische und antizionistische Judenfeindschaft* (Hamburg: Hamburger Edition, 2005).

43 On internet use: Koen Leurs, *Digital Passages. Moroccan-Dutch youths performing diaspora, gender and cultural identities across digital space* (PhD Thesis, Utrecht University, 2012) and Albert Benschop, *Kroniek van een aangekondigde politieke moord. Jihad in Nederland*, www. sociosite.org.

the heathen idol of pre-Islam, and was planning the launch of a bilingual
Dutch edition of *The Islam Times.* Jabri received a Muslim education, reacted
against this, but then returned to Islam 'after a long quest'. Shortly before
the turn of the century, he became a 'practising Muslim'.[44] It was then that
he became known as one of Theo van Gogh's verbal opponents (because of
the latter's anti-Islamic statements), using the epithet 'pig' to refer to the
columnist who himself denoted Muslims, or Moroccans, as 'goat fuckers'.[45]

The greatest satirical feat of the website Elqalem.nl was the publication of
an anti-gay manifesto under the title 'No gay in the light of day'. This came
about through the familiar procedure of turning Geert Wilders' anti-Islam
statements into anti-queer statements. Uproar ensued. Jabri: 'There were
even questions in Parliament. I thought that was pretty cool. We definitively
got our point across.' Two Members of Parliament asked the cabinet to
pronounce upon 'the supposed right to state, for the purpose of provocation',
that 'heterosexuality should be standard in the public sphere. What is your
opinion on the words of the Amsterdam columnist M.R. Jabri "We stop at
nothing" in reference to the publication of the manifesto?[46]

After this anti-gay manifesto, the plan arose to do the same with the
Jews. Possibly, the anti-Jewish manifesto was meant as a radicalised version
of the 2003 manifesto *Koerswijziging.nl* [Change of Course.nl] signed by
fifty Moroccan-Dutch people, including Aboutaleb. The fifty signatories
were concerned about the prevailing nasty atmosphere since 9/11, with the
negative media image of Moroccans and Muslims and a 'stubborn stigma'
attached to young Moroccans: 'We urgently ask you not to keep focusing
on what goes wrong, but also to pay attention to and to build on what is
praiseworthy.[47] The staunch Jabri chose a completely different approach
from this rather timid manifesto of established Moroccan-Dutch.

In November 2004, thanks to the anti-gay manifesto, Jabri quickly became well-known in the Netherlands. Subsequently, he and his colleague
wanted to do the same trick once more: exaggerate stereotypes by using
recalcitrant language: 'Abdelhakim [Chouaati, his colleague] passed the
news on to some journalist who ran the story. All Abdelhakim had to say

44   This passage is based on an interview with Mohammed Jabri by Remco Ensel, 2010 and
Steven de Jong, 'Mohammed Jabri: "Allochtonen kunnen niet tegen kritiek"', *Politiek-digitaal*,
18 December 2005. The novel is not available, not even in the Royal Library (KB) in The Hague.
45   *See* chapter 12 on Theo van Gogh.
46   In Parliament, MPs Timmer and Van Heemst (both PvdA) posed questions to the Ministers
of Interior Affairs and the Deputy Minister of Health, Welfare and Sport about an anti-gay
manifesto on a Muslim website (Sent 10 November 2004).
47   Open Letter by Prem Radhakishun and others, published in *Spits*, 19 November 2008.

was *Anti-Jewish Manifesto* and hey presto, a full article on the front page of *de Volkskrant*.[48] Jabri had always remembered the commotion over the antisemitic statements by Professor Griff, one of the rappers of the American band *Public Enemy*, which made him realise that people were more sensitive about antisemitism than about homophobia. They agreed it was probably better to cancel the plan so as to avoid prosecution. The Anti-Jewish Manifesto was written, but never published: 'I also showed it to a Jew, and he said, 'Do it, this is satire.' But the title made it so heavy. We were all thinking, "Should we really do this …. " In the end we said, "We'd better not: afterwards, you cannot extenuate it."' And is the manifesto still somewhere on his computer? 'Yes, ha-ha, but you cannot have it. The text is not very exciting. When I read it again, I think to myself, "How low can you go, man. Now, I have so many more years of experience."'[49]

Insults

We leave our seat in front of our computer screen and take to the streets. New after 2000 was the hate felt at demonstrations in the street and in incidents involving face-to-face insults, reproaches and threats. Ideology became palpable in interpersonal contact. A shop owner in South Amsterdam said that she had been insulted in the street. 'In broad daylight, out of the blue, a Moroccan boy started shouting 'Dirty rotten Jewess.'' He went on and on. Nobody did anything. I have never experienced anything like it. The shock was enormous, I still have nightmares about it.'[50]

Jews were starting to get harassed in the streets, in class or in the school corridors, on their way to the synagogue, during commemorations and at other gatherings. Sometimes they were touched, their yarmulke was flicked off and, in some instances, they were (severely) beaten up. More often, they were shouted at, screamed at, insulted or given the Nazi salute. You can avoid rap songs, websites and demonstrations, but direct contact in the street is more unpredictable and more confronting. In fact, the very first report about the involvement of Moroccan-Dutch youths with the demonstrations in *Het Financieele Dagblad* of October 2000 already indicated that a combination of protest and provocation took place in the street, with adolescent young

---

48   Interview Jabri by Ensel, 2012. *Politiek-digitaal*, 23 December 2004.

49   *Ibid.*

50   *Algemeen Dagblad*, 24 December 2001. In reference to this and other incidents here discussed, CIDI talks of 'Real Life'incidents.

men as the perpetrators. This also happened elsewhere. In Paris, on the occasion of the huge riots in the so-called *banlieues*, one researcher made a connection between pro-Palestinian protest and the 'low-level intifada' against Jewish institutions.[51] One could compare this use of the concept of intifada with the way the politician Geert Wilders tried to put the social problems of multicultural cities on the agenda by coining the term 'street terrorists'.[52] In fact, the recorded incidents indicate that confrontations did indeed take place within the urban space. Amsterdam's 'multicultural urban problems' date back to the 1990s. After 2000, they sometimes acquired an anti-Jewish tone, although this was not always recognised as such. The locations acquired a significant role in the confrontations: the riots during the demonstration on 13 April 2002 happened in the centre of Amsterdam, involving youths from the 'suburbs' who had descended upon Dam Square in groups. Ethnic identities – from Moroccan-Dutch to Jewish – had become tied up with neighbourhood identities. 'Jews', which could mean just about anybody, served as a projection screen for the deep-felt frustrations about one's own position in society and a stigmatised collective identity.[53] What were the repercussions for the Jews in Amsterdam?

> On 25 April 2004, at 9:50 pm, the CIDI received the following email:
> *Subject: Moroccans*
> For your statistics.
> This evening, we were being Jew-called by a car full of Moroccans and had the usual insults aimed at our yarmulke.
> Let it be noted.
> Best regards,
> Frank family Amsterdam

This is an unusually succinct email. From the resigned tone of the opening phrase 'For your statistics', one might deduce that the sender did not expect

---

51   Robert S. Leiken, *Europe's Angry Muslims: The Revolt of the Second Generation* (Oxford: Oxford University Press, 2012).

52   Sylvain Ephimenco, 'Straatterrorist', *Trouw*, 12 November 2010.

53   For projection screen: *see* chapter 1 and Evelien Gans, '"The Jew" as a multifunctional projection screen.' Introduction at the international symposium *The Dynamics of Contemporary Antisemitism in a Globalizing Context*, Amsterdam, 12 mei 2010. On the Parisian riots, the debate and the fake antisemitic incident in the underground: Kay Adamson, 'Issues of Culture and Identity in Contemporary France: The Problem of Reconciling a Colonial Past with a Present Reality', *Sociology* 40, 4 (2006), 627-643. (2006), Jean Beaman, 'Identity, marginalization, and Parisian banlieues.' In: Mark Clapson and Ray Hutchison (eds.), *Suburbanization in Global Society* (Bingley: Emerald, 2010), 153-175; Slooter, 'Wijkidentiteiten in voorstedelijk Frankrijk'.

much from his report of the incident and saw it as his civic duty to file a
report. There are no further details about the contents of the hate speech.
Because of the succinct phrasing chosen, the verbal confrontation seems as
much a part of the Amsterdam Jewish life as the report of it. Mr Frank did
not waste many words or much time to write his email: he had just been
gejood [Jew-called], got home, switched on his computer and fulfilled his
perceived reporting duty. But on closer inspection, the phrasing appears to
be precise: the emphasis on 'a car full of Moroccans', the choice of 'Moroccans' in the subject line, the use of the perfect participle 'Jew-called', the
unspecified 'usual insults', the wordplay in 'aimed at our yarmulke'[54], and
the rather cynical and archaic 'Let it be noted' to stress the bureaucratic
nature of the reporting ceremony. All in all, the emotion that emanates
from the email is complex and well-managed.

Two months later, the CIDI received a longer report with a similarly
resigned tone: 'Shalom aleichem! I wish to report an antisemitic incident.
In general, I am used to being called names on a weekly basis, but now
and again there is an even more unpleasant experience.' Then, the sender
describes the incident.

> Today ... I was walking home from work. Since I am wearing a yarmulke,
> I am recognisable as a Jew. Two North Africans stop their car right next
> to me. These brave people, license number ..., open their window, make
> a pistol gesture with their fingers, and while the "shooter" produces
> shooting noises, the other one shouts, "Dirty bloody Jew".

The sender concludes: 'A nice start of the weekend. I no longer wish to
report these kinds of incidents to the police ....' The previous year, the same
person had already notified the media that, while he was waiting for the
train, a man of 'North African appearance' had told him: 'Bloody Jews, do
you wanna get beaten up?'.[55]

These kinds of direct confrontations, when people are identified and
addressed as Jews and conversely, when they think they recognise the
perpetrators as 'Moroccans' or 'North Africans', increased after 2000. The
two above-mentioned reports are from April and May 2004, a peak year.
The following years, the number of reports dropped. Earlier that year, on
5 January, a young man on his way to the synagogue in Amsterdam was
called a bloody Jew and had coins thrown at him. On 4 February, there was

54   In Dutch idiom 'an insult was thrown at my head' translates as 'to ballyrag'.
55   Aad Wagenaar, 'Nederland 2003: De nieuwe Jodenhaat', *Panorama*, 24 September 2003.

a rowdy atmosphere during a screening of *Shouf Shouf Habibi,* a popular movie about second-generation Moroccan-Dutch, and some visitors started shouting 'Jews Jews': 'Something that touched me intensely personally ...', one complainant wrote. The visitors also constantly shouted 'whore' to one of the characters on the screen.[56]

Just as 'Jew' and 'Gay' seem to be connected, so too are 'Whore' and 'Jew'. The cinema incident is similar to a radio broadcast of 7 December 2010 in which someone yelled *kankerjood* [bloody Jew] from a red Mercedes to a recognisable Jew who was talking to a reporter, and called the (female) reporter *kankerhoer* [bloody whore]. This incident again is similar to a situation in the same year in which Moroccan adolescents first addressed a girl on the street in East Amsterdam as 'whore' and subsequently, with a slow transposition of 'whore, whore' to 'Jew'. One might see this as a case of pornographic antisemitism.[57] Brenner reports on an incident in *The Lost Territories of the Republic:* 'In the same community in December 2001, a middle school teacher found this graffiti on her car: "Whore. Dirty Jew."' Lastly, there is the Dutch lawsuit in 2011 against a Moroccan man (born in Larache) who was charged, among other things, with calling a woman a 'Jewish whore' because of 'the killing of children in Palestine'.[58]

On 3 August 2004, on the occasion of an incident at a school, a complainant recorded what he and his daughter had experienced: 'My daughter cannot even leave the house on her own because she will be called a bloody Jew and similar things. Me, they only call "Jew". I cannot complain about that unless a negative adjective is added ....' One day, the words *K***rjood* ['C****r for the Jews'] had been sprayed on the wall. Since 'we are the only Jews in our neighbourhood, we know this is meant for us'. In November 2004, two 9 and 11-year-old children were chanted to by a passing boy saying, 'Jews, you should kill them'.[59]

56   Incidents based on the CIDI antisemitism monitor and email, 18 June 2004. Typos corrected.
57   *See* chapter 12.
58   Brenner is a pseudonym of George Bensoussan. Brenner, *The Lost Territories of the Republic*, 9; 'Arrest, gerechtshof 's-Hertogenbosch, 15 September 2011 (parketnummer 20-000510-10)'; 'Dit is de dag'. EO radio of 7 December 2010 (*Dit is de dag*); report research assistant, 2010.
59   CIDI documentation: email to CIDI, 5 May 2004; email to CIDI, 3 August 2004. I assume that the perpetrators did not spray stars but letters; email to CIDI, 3 February 2005; email to CIDI, 12 January 2004 and 13 January 2004. These reports were included in the antisemitism monitor on 2004-2005, some with less detail. I have never before come across the phrasing 'Jews, you *should* kill them' (in (rhyming) Dutch: 'Joden, je zou ze moeten doden,' and it sounds odd.

Experiences in West Amsterdam

Another report, from 10 January 2004, fits into the above-mentioned list. The informer was Erwin Brugmans (b. 1950), an inhabitant of the De Baarsjes neighbourhood in West Amsterdam. Walking back from a Sabbath lunch, he and two acquaintances passed a 'clearly recognisable' Moroccan man and a boy of around 10. 'At the sight of our kippah [skullcap]' the man started to yell, 'Dirty Jew, bloody Jew, death to all of you Jews.' The incident lasted one and a half minutes until the three had disappeared from the Moroccans' sight.

Brugmans has filed several reports, also due to his involvement in the synagogue in his Amsterdam neighbourhood. In the years after 2000, he regularly appeared in the press because of his active involvement in a project aimed at reconciling his neighbourhood around the Mercatorplein. In 2004, he helped organise a remarkable *MaJo* (Moroccans/Jews) football tournament on the Balboaplein, attended by local Jewish and Moroccan boys. Balboaplein is the square where famous footballers like Frank Rijkaard, Ruud Gullit and Driss Boussatta ('the first Moroccan to play for the Dutch national team') grew up. The tournament became world news and has since been organised several times. One day after the 15 January report, Brugmans was in a meeting with representatives of 'all religions', where he also reported the incident. Later that year, on 4 July, he was again the victim of a similar verbal attack. On his way to the synagogue, he passed four boys aged between 11 and 13 who immediately started to yell: 'Bloody Jews, you must leave here, death to you Jews ....' One boy made a 'cutthroat movement'. Brugmans addressed the boys, but this did not yield the desired effect. After the service, he reported the incident at the nearby youth centre, where he was welcomed with full consideration. Erwin Brugmans explains:

> I live here and I go to the synagogue. And on the way to the synagogue, I get insulted. I moved here in '86 and back then I already went to the synagogue, but I was not harassed by 'cultural ignorance' as I call it, or by Moroccan or Dutch people shouting abuse at me, 'Why do you need to do the whole Jewish shtick?' Sometimes it's an ordinary Dutchman, looking at it from the perspective of, 'Hey, Jews here, that's surprising'. I wear a kippah and, on the Sabbath, my decent clothes. And if we have a consulta- tion at the synagogue, as I am its representative in the neighbourhood, I wear a kippah, for the commemoration committee, the neighbourhood consultation or the interreligious consultation. Then I wear my kippah,

because it makes me feel good. And then people start making comments. For instance, 'Jews? Is there a synagogue near here?' Then I say, 'Yes, just around the corner.' 'Gee, to think we have Jews living in the neighbour- hood, well, well. You are an Ajax fan? And Israel and the Palestinians.' Then you have another one of those discussions. And I think to myself, 'Oh dear, here we go again.'

In the beginning [just after 9/11], I walked to the synagogue, here on the Hoofdweg, past the coffee shops [a café where you can buy hashish, RE], and they called me names, 'bloody Jew, rotten Jew, Palestinians, Hamas, Hamas, Jews to the gas.' They shouted all of that, I reported it, and the police said, 'We take this very seriously.' They went to the coffee shop and they said, if we get another complaint, you lose your licence and you will have to close down. It was very quiet for a while, and then it was, 'Hello, sir, Good morning, sir.' And I don't care what they think of me. But I have found that if you act like a scared Jew, if you crawl in a hole with your tail between your legs, and you let them get the upper hand, or if you leave and say nothing, or do not react, this gives them reason to think that they are strong and can condescend to you. Fight back with humour or with the police, or invite them, and you will find that a whole lot of things will go differently ....

Being Jew-called

'A password to madness. Jew. One little word with no hiding place for reason in it. Say "Jew" and it was like throwing a bomb.' Said Howard Jacobson's protagonist in his acclaimed novel *The Finkler Question* (2010).[60] In the public sphere of a city, you would expect people to be able to move about freely and anonymously. Leaving each other in peace is part of city life. It's an obvious aspect of urban life, but in practice, it does not equally apply to everybody. Some people are more invisible than others on the city streets.[61] Not all intrusions are equally unpleasant: people saunter along, flirt, make contact, greet or address people they don't know. Sociological studies have revealed that there is a pattern regulated by gender and ethnicity. Women and members of ethnic minorities are more quickly 'identified' in the street and robbed of their anonymous status. They are more quickly spotted and

60   Howard Jacobson, *The Finkler Question* (New York: Bloomsbury, 2010), 233.
61   *See, e.g.*, Steve Farner, *Whiteness. An introduction* (London, New York: Routledge, 2007), 38-40.

addressed as an anomaly compared to white males who can more easily move invisibly across the city, less often bothered by authorities, and are, therefore, not aware of the fact that their identity is also restricted by gender and ethnicity.

Addressing is central here. One of the informers wrote that some modes of address are limited to 'Jews', 'of which I cannot complain unless an expletive is attached to it ....' Indeed: what does it mean when someone shouts 'Jew' to a passer-by (or wishes him Shalom from a bench)? Does that in itself constitute antisemitism?

On the occasion of an incident in which children yelled 'Jews, Jews' at a funeral procession, one poster, called Hatert (i.e. 'Hater'), stated that he condemns the shouting of 'Jews', 'although I must admit that I would have no problem if people shouted "Moroccan" at me. But then I would shout back, "Yes!" And make a power sign.'[62] Justus, who calls himself an 'Indo' [Dutchman with Indonesian roots] also wrote that he would be proud to be called that way. 'But Jews often find occasion to think [something] is antisemitic ... a matter of racial insecurity, I'm afraid.' Others quickly responded to this post. When did people ever shout, 'Indos to the gas' at the stadium? Justus replies that other expletives are used and, furthermore, 'Let's be honest, Jews do not really go out of their way to be popular ....' This reply fits in with the classical antisemitic rant: Jews peddle their misery and overstate their victimhood.[63]

A complaint from the 2000 antisemitism monitor: 'While we are walking from the Frederik Hendrikplein to the Van Hallstraat, children call after us: "Jews, Jews'"; later, this becomes: 'Rotten Jews, rotten Jews'. This is neither a philosophic nor a linguistic treatise, but it is necessary to contemplate how the modes of address and reaction constitute or identify a subject and establish a relationship between two or more persons in the public domain. A mode of addressing people, even without the accompanying expletive, is a meaningful linguistic expression. One may ask here whether words are deeds (just as the question will later be treated of whether deeds are also words). The philosophers Louis Althusser (1918-1990) and Judith Butler (b. 1956) have called attention to the power of addressing people. What

---

62 Maroc.nl, 30 May 2011.

63 Maroc.nl, 31 May 2011. Jews are arrogant, violent, and they peddle their misery: 'The orthodox behave very haughty and think they are better, the Zionists don't do anything but use German methods to repress the Palestinians ..., they have not yet used the gas, but most of the other means they have. With that kind of actions, you do not make yourself loved as a Jew. And, finally, they have CIDI, which does nothing, but say how miserable the Jews are, that does nothing towards the furthering of fraternisation.'

happens when a police officer calls out in the street, 'Hey, you!'? When you decide to react by stopping, turning around or answering him, you enter into a relationship of the kind that an officer has with potential offenders. Thus, the mode of address directs the contact, restricts the opportunities to react and determines your identity within social exchange. The mode of addressing people in public pulls them out of their anonymity, classifies them and categorises them. When someone is addressed as a Jew, this yields a reaction – affirmative or negative – that demands an acknowledgement of the mode of address.[64] The mode of address also implies a set of ideas, maybe even a definite ideology, in this case pertaining to ethnic and national identities: a Self is constructed by addressing an Other.[65]

Furthermore, addressing a person concerns usage and words, and these have a history. The existence of the verb 'to be Jew-called' also indicates the awareness that something significant occurs here, a deed that has been performed before, one that needs no further explanation. The agents are, in Butler's words, primarily doers. The associations and the language that is rooted in history have a meaning that needs to be considered in assessing the deed. There is a difference between calling someone 'Zionist', 'Bloody Jew' or 'Jew', but in all three cases, it can be intended as hurting and experienced as hurtful. A word brings a number of histories in its wake, which colour the significance of the mode of address. Once, in his criticism of the policy of the right-wing Minister for Immigration and Integration Rita Verdonk, the social democratic politician Jan Pronk used the word 'deportation' (as would rapper Appa in the song *'Minister van Deportatie'* [Minister for Deportation]). This turned into a whole affair. Pronk defended himself by stating that he was not referring to the Second World War. Language historian Ewoud Sanders thought this was 'obviously a bogus argument. Pronk does not need to make that reference, it is already there.' At the end of the 1960s, the linguist Frida Balk-Smit Duyzentkunst wrote, in reference to the usage of 'deportation' by demonstrators in Amsterdam, how flippantly the postwar generation sometimes used these words, while for the war generation, the association with the war was still very much

64 Judith Butler, *Excitable Speech: A Politics of the Performative* (New York: Routledge, 1997) and John L. Austin, *How to do things with words. The William James Lectures delivered at Harvard University in 1955* (Oxford: Clarendon Press, 2004).

65 For a comparative attempt to apply speech acts theory into antisemitism studies, *see*: Remco Ensel and Annemarike Stremmelaar, 'Speech Acts. Observing Antisemitism and Holocaust Education in the Netherlands.' In: Günther Jikeli and Joëlle Allouche-Benayoun (eds.), *Perceptions of the Holocaust in Europe and Muslim Communities. Sources, Comparisons and Educational Challenges* (Dordrecht: Springer, 2013), 153-171.

alive. She took it very seriously: 'Conclusion? What the Nazis did to the Jews was not that severe. That is the way things works. Surreptitiously. The autonomous power of the word.'[66] Obviously people differ about the usage of words and concepts, their meaning is not fixed and they are certainly nobody's exclusive possession.

What about the word 'Jew'? The Dutch word *'Jood'* as mode of address has no evidently negative connotation. This is in agreement with Van Dale, the most prominent Dutch dictionary:

> Jood ... (derogatory) *In the past* used as an insult, with various additions, with a reference to certain (mainly bad) characteristics which prejudice sometimes attributed to Jews. [italics added]

In other words, Jew needs an adjective or 'addition' to become derogatory. But in that perspective, any word can become derogatory with an addition. Moreover, it is striking that from 1995 the lexicographer has placed the insults in the past, as if name-calling is behind us now. 'Funnily though, dictionaries are of little use in this kind of conflict,' Sanders added to his notes on 'deportation'. Indeed, the context, the usage in real-life situations is what counts, and even then, there will be different interpretations.

In Dutch, 'Jew' and 'Jewess' have more than one meaning or connotation. Sociologist Günther Jikeli (b. 1973) investigated the derogatory use of 'Jew' in French, German and English. *'Feuj'* is French slang for Jew and has the connotation of cowardly, weak and evil. More than other ethnic terms in French 'Jew' does not need an adjective to function as an insult.[67] Jikeli explains that this use of the word is just a joke, a thing between friends who can call each other 'Jew'. 'Queer' and 'Jew', but more so 'Jew', have the common characteristic that they can be used both for members and non-members of the respective category. A Jew is bad and anybody could be a secret Jew. 'Jew' has become a metaphorical insult, also in the Netherlands. This also applies to the Arabic language, where the word *yahūd*, in contrast to *Bani Israel,* has a negative connotation: evil, deceitful, cowardly and unstable.

---

66 Ewoud Sanders, *Allemaal woorden* (Amsterdam, Rotterdam: Prometheus, NRC, 2005), 99.
67 Günther Jikeli, 'Anti-Semitism in youth language: the pejorative use of the terms for "Jew" in German and French today', *Conflict & Communication online* 9, 1 (2010), 1-13. Ewoud Sanders and Rob Tempelaars, *Krijg de vinkentering! 1001 Nederlandse en Vlaamse verwensingen* (Amsterdam: Contact, 1998): 'While there were 61 compounds with jood- or joden- (Jew or Jews) in the most important dictionary, Van Dale, there were only 35 in 1992, and 32 in 1999.'

'As scared as a Jew' is a common expression in present-day Morocco, as anthropologists have claimed.[68]

Egging: 'In a hail of eggs to the synagogue'

Once out in the streets, we go from words to deeds. About twenty 'Arab boys' of 'approximately sixteen years old' are throwing stones at the synagogue in the Lekstraat in South Amsterdam. 'Just like on CNN.'[69] This incident occurred in Amsterdam on the aforementioned demo of 14 October 2000, during the Second Intifada, at the time of the large demonstration. It was clearly meant as a provocation, as a form of vandalism and threat in the infective, agitated atmosphere of the Second Intifada of the autumn of 2000. This time there were stones, the week before it had been an incendiary bomb – of unknown perpetrators – in a synagogue in Emmen.[70] Or was this mischief, 'acting out', playing Intifada?

With all the attention on statements that people are make or carry during demonstrations, it is often forgotten that many references to Jews, Israel and the Holocaust are utterances of a mere sentence, a short phrase, an image or a single word. Incidents can be even harder to assess. Consider the following example. A man and a woman meet in front of the woman's house in Watergraafsmeer, a 'gentrified' area in eastern Amsterdam. The woman is cleaning her windows, washing off egg contents and shells, visible marks of eggs that have hit the front of the house shortly before. The man is a passer-by who has immediately recognised from experience what has happened here. The two exchange experiences and the man asks the woman's surname (Polak). 'Damn,' he reacts. But is the name sufficient indication? Might the surname or the nameplate in Yiddish next to the front door have given occasion? The woman recounts that on several occasions

68 See Alegria Bendelac, *Mosaïque. Une enfance juive à Tanger (1930-1945)* (Casablanca: Wallada, 1992), 16; Kevin Dwyer, *Moroccan Dialogues. Anthropology in Question* (Baltimore: The Johns Hopkins University Press, 1982), 128. Emanuela Trevisan Semi, 'Double trauma and manifold narratives: Jews' and Muslims' representation of the departure of Moroccan Jews in the 1950s and 1960s', *Journal of Modern Jewish Studies* 9, 1 (2010), 107-125 and Aomar Boum, *Memories of Absence. How Muslims Remember Jews in Morocco* (Stanford: Stanford University Press, 2013). South Berber (*tashelhit*) has a word for 'Jew' in compound words that means cowardly (I am grateful to Dr Harry Stroomer for this personal communication). In general on ethnic identities in Morocco, Remco Ensel, *Saints and Servants in Southern Morocco* (Leiden, Köln: Brill, 1999), chapter one.

69 Peter Giesen, 'In regen van eieren naar de synagoge' [In a hail of eggs to the synagogue], *de Volkskrant*, 16 February 2015.

70 Yasha Lange, 'Joden bezorgd over reeks incidenten', *NRC Handelsblad,* 17 October 2000.

she has chased the same boys who threw the eggs, under the overpass to the other side of the tracks in a nearby lower-class neighbourhood. They turned out to be Moroccan-Dutch boys who were surprised to be pursued by a running mother. The woman wants to file a complaint. The result is an interesting experience. The police refuse to process the report, because it not worth mentioning. Is this a case of damage to property, of physical threat or insult? The first possibility seems exaggerated, the other two hard to prove. So the 'difficult to classify' case is dropped. The woman does, however, report the incident to the CIDI antisemitism monitor. The report is included in their 2000 annual survey: 'The windows of two families in East Amsterdam – one Jewish, the other one not – have for several months been regularly dirtied now, probably by Moroccan youths ....'[71] This instance, which occurred over a longer period and is not a single event, happened in November 2000, in the middle of the commotion of the Second Intifada.

'Throwing eggs was popular in 2000,' the annual survey of antisemitic incidents of that year stated: a Jewish clubhouse, a house featuring a small Israeli flag and a mezuzah were pelted. 'There was another complainant in Amsterdam who suspected Moroccan boys of pelting his house with eggs for antisemitic motives. This incident was not counted: upon arrest by the police, the offenders turned out to be Jewish.' The latter incident featured big in the newspapers. The police 'contradicted' the antisemitic character of the incident by publicly stating that the apprehended perpetrators were of Jewish descent: 'This is not a matter of antisemitism, but of mischief.' This statement naturally led to scornful and disgruntled reactions on the internet, raising the question of why it would be antisemitism if eggs are pelted at Jewish homes, and mischief when pelted at non-Jewish homes. In any case, the follow-up question might also be whether a more meaningful assessment might be reached than the qualification 'mischief'. This requires more detailed information about the exact relationship between perpetrator(s) and victim.

In 2005, throwing eggs was part of the commotion about street problems in the Amsterdam neighbourhood 'Diamantbuurt'. The periodical *Vrij Nederland*, which had been following the neighbourhood for years, reported on the riots and referred to Geert Wilders' questions in Parliament about an incident involving egg-throwing. Loitering youths called the inhabitants 'bloody Jews' and threw eggs against people's front doors. In his question to the Minister of Justice, Wilders also mentions the Nazi salute and urinating against front doors. Minister of Justice Donner added 'small stones

---

71 Based on a conversation with the female victim.

thrown against the windows'. Neither the Minister nor Wilders mentioned antisemitism, the Minister spoke of 'a series of relatively minor offences'.[72]

The phenomenon of egging is interesting because it is a good example of more frequent problems in street confrontations: the identification of perpetrator and victim is difficult and can rest on wrong assumptions. Sometimes the victim is in the dark about the meaning of the act aimed against him or her. The same can be said of the perpetrator of the deed. The perpetrator does his deed, for instance by making a statement, often without knowing the historical significance of his deed.

A second issue to consider is the connection between the literal meaning of a statement or a deed and the meaning attributed to it. This issue is certainly relevant for speech acts or actions that are performed in a face-to-face situation or that appear to copy a physical threat. In both cases, it is difficult to distinguish language and deed, to name the literality of the deed and to interpret its metaphorical meaning. An egg is thrown, and a person or his/her property is soiled. But what does this mean? An egg is not a stone and a stone is not a shoe, while a cake is not the same as a tea warmer stand, which is not the same as a Molotov cocktail. In the Netherlands, all of these objects have been famously thrown in protest at persons or objects and, because of that, have become the focus of both a deed and a public expression, in short, a performance.[73] Furthermore, who determines this meaning? Does the perpetrator determine the meaning of his deed ('It was only mischief', 'I did not mean it like that', 'It is not as serious as all that') or is the interpretation of the victim decisive? This is a recurring issue in the debate.

Egging is both common mischief and an equally common form of pro-test. In the latter case, it mostly targets authorities or the buildings they occupy. In the Netherlands, a number of subversive actions have taken place over the last few years. At the same time, the media have suggested that in the twenty-first century, egging has become a specifically urban, Moroccan or Muslim, form of action. Although there is no 'profile of the egger', one news item about the situation in the city of Gouda stated that it was 'predominantly Moroccan boys aged 8 to 13 who were throwing eggs at shopkeepers, customers or buses'. In 2005, in Amsterdam, egging was

72 Max van Weezel and Margalith Kleijwegt, 'Terug naar Amsterdam-West', *Vrij Nederland*, 29 October 2005.
73 In 2010, at the annnual parade of the Queen's 'Golden Carriage', an anti-royalist threw a tea warmer stand at the coach. More common is the practice of pieing as a political action: Pim Fortuyn in 2002, two months before his assasination, was pied which was afterwards framed as the overture to the actual assassination.

part of prolonged bullying of inhabitants. Both Job Cohen, as the mayor of Amsterdam, and Geert Wilders, as a Member of Parliament in his struggle against 'street terrorists', made statements as to this example.[74] But there are other examples in which the meaning of egging seems to be clearer. In the previous two years, the Danish cartoonist who made a Mohammed cartoon was egged, 'radical Muslims' disrupted a debate in Amsterdam by throwing eggs and shouting slogans such as 'Allahu Akbar' and Moroccan boys threw eggs and made insults at Minister Rita Verdonk. On 4 July 2012, four Muslims in Britain were convicted of pelting Jewish children in the street with eggs. They had purposely bought thirty eggs to throw at the children from their car. The judge explained the deed of the four as 'religiously aggravated harassment, alarm and distress by words and behaviour': when the car was slowed down, 'the men shouted, "Oi, Jews" and "Jews" while they drove past before throwing an egg, one of which hit a girl in the face'.[75]

Street culture

In 2007, the Dutch anthropologist Jan Dirk de Jong (b. 1976) published the study *Kapot moeilijk* [Damn Hard], based on extensive fieldwork among youths loitering in the Amsterdam New West borough. The study focuses on the internal group dynamics and hardly pays attention to confrontations with others. Hence, as a reader you get a good idea of the 'street culture', in which a sense of community, hanging out and loitering together play an important role and where verbal and (threats of) physical violence are part of their everyday repertoire. It also becomes clear that the youths have a strong territorial awareness: the feeling that the neighbourhood streets belong to the domain of the group members, but that the city centre is alien. In this regard, sociologist Loïc Wacquant (b. 1960) spoke of a 'territorial stigma' related to 'race, nation and religion'.[76] Both group and individual identity are formed by what the neighbourhood of origin has to offer. The boys themselves, sometimes unintentionally, supply the ammunition for this stigma. Now and again, the 'street culture' leads to excited or disturbing group behaviour at obvious places such as the beach, the cinema or the fair.

---

74 Camiel Driessen, 'Eieren gooien is de nieuwste kinderrage', *Dagblad De Pers*, 16 November 2009.

75 www.jihadwatch.org/2012/07; In their defence, a father stated that the boys had shouted 'oi, you' instead of 'oi, Jew'. The 'oi' could arguably be interpreted as a far-right symbol.

76 Wacquant, 'Territorial stigmatization'.

De Jong has described one such an incident at the fair. In his book, we read of 'impetuous behaviour' in the Ferris wheel, but only later, at a talk show, did the criminologist clarify what the troublemakers were shouting: 'We are the Jews from Amsterdam', recalling the denomination of the residents of Amsterdam as Jews as is common among football fans. This warrants the assumption that the fair was not in Amsterdam. In any case, the owner of the attraction was not amused. We may also assume that De Jong did not think the yelling important enough to include in his book.[77]

De Jong's study suggests that the public space is the battlefield where youths fight it out with each other, a world where you cannot cast down your eyes, but need to face the confrontation, a world where the socialist politician and Amsterdam alderman Ahmed Marcouch (b. 1969) is a traitor and where you approach life as a group.[78] Antisemitism – one of the main themes during the years of De Jong's research (1999-2006) – is strikingly absent from the study. We get no perspective on confrontations with people from other age categories, people who are not competitors, who do not share the 'street values', who do indeed cast down their eyes and walk an extra block when they see a group of loitering boys or do not even dare to leave their home (and hence walk their dog in the shower cubicle), who may well look down upon the youths, but who themselves are also addressed or insulted.

De Jong's main point was that it was not Moroccan culture, but rather street culture that explained the youths' behaviour. It is acquired behaviour, but it is acquired on the street. 'Street racism' – De Jong's words – is not typically Moroccan, not a 'deep-rooted ideology', but socialisation by peers.[79] Other commentators too would present the lack of 'deep-rooted' hatred as an excuse for deviant behaviour, including antisemitic statements. But what does it mean? The problem is that in, for example, De Jong's explanation of behaviour, street culture is in danger of becoming as strictly delineated and immutable as earlier interpretations of 'culture'. It may well be not 'typically Moroccan' to have a Pavlov reaction and to make a remark each time a man wearing a yarmulke passes. But the way in which ethnic identities – Moroccan-Dutch and Jewish – are the issue in confrontations in the street

77   J.D. de Jong, *Kapot moeilijk: een etnografisch onderzoek naar opvallend delinquent groepsge-drag van 'Marokkaanse' jongens* (Amsterdam: Aksant, 2007); interview *Pauw en Witteman*, 12 November 2007.

78   Marcouch used the term 'traitor' for people who know about an offence, but fail to inform the police, in Serge Markx, 'You are a traitor if you do not report criminal behaviour to the police', *West.Amsterdam.nl*, 3, 3 (21 March 2013).

79   Jan Dirk de Jong, 'Straatracisme is niet typisch Marokkaans', *de Volkskrant*, 15 May 2012.

is still intriguing. The youths *act* Moroccan when faced with people they frame as being *Jewish*. The same applies to gender: the boys *act* masculine and Moroccan by insulting a passer-by for being Jewish, feminine and not masculine. Group dynamics do indeed seem important in this process. The vast majority of the cases concerns one or more perpetrators as part of a group. You could say that the speech act, the addressing of a passer-by, is not only directed at the victim, but also at their own friends.

Whenever antisemitism is discussed in the Netherlands, we sometimes seem to be preoccupied with text exegesis and the interpretation of referrals to abstract processes or international conflicts thousands of kilometres from the Netherlands. But the experience of antisemitism is often quite sensorial: visible, audible and tangible. The sidewalk, which urban designer Jane Jacobs (1916-2006) once famously characterised as the core of urban community life, is where confrontations between passers-by take place. 'When people say that a city, or a part of it, is dangerous or is a jungle, what they mean primarily is that they do not feel safe on the sidewalks.'[80] Ironically, in 2002, in his quality of community worker, Mohammed Bouyeri, who was later to assassinate Theo van Gogh, had the following advice for this peers and co-religionists: 'Especially the elderly are not comfortable when they meet a large group. From my own experience, I know that most youths feel the need to gather together in the street. But as a Muslim, I would prefer to do so in accordance with the tenets of my faith.' That amounted to 'casting down the eyes ... answering the Salaam [i.e. the Muslim peace greeting], demanding good and combating evil'.[81] The message did not reach everyone, but it indicated the importance of (avoiding) eye contact.

In De Pijp, an area in Amsterdam near the aforementioned Diamant-buurt, on his way to the Gerard Dou synagogue, rabbi Menachem Sebbag was regularly shouted at: 'Nearly every week over a period of six months, I was shouted at or insulted. You could feel the eyes from afar. They spat and called me the worst possible names,' from 'dirty Jew' to 'Hamas, Hamas, Jews to the gas'.

Sebbag did not report one single time to the police but he did start to adapt his route: 'In some streets', he no longer 'walked on the right-hand side, but on the left-hand side', in order to avoid the Moroccan coffee shop. 'I sometimes even took the car.' But this is also defeat: 'They are looking for a confrontation. They love it when you walk round.' Sebbag also adapted his clothes: he stopped wearing his recognisably 'Jewish clothes' and started

---

80 Jane Jacobs, *The Death and Life of Great American Cities* (New York: Random House, 1961).
81 Written under the pseudonym Hassan B., 'Normen en waarden.doc.' (before 4 August 2002).

wearing a Moroccan headdress.[82] The sidewalk belongs to the youths, and there is no place there for 'whores', 'gays' and 'Jews'.

Like all stereotypes, that of 'the Jew' is conceived in confrontation. A stereotype of the emotional Jew, the weak-nerved Jew, scared and submissive, not masculine but feminine, has existed for a long time. This stereotype exists in European culture and also has a Moroccan counterpart. In Europe, nineteenth-century biological and medical racism supplied it with a foundation when the 'Jewish body' was fatally reduced to an essence: Jewish men who were physically and mentally feminine.[83] The 'racial insecurity' from which the Jews suffer according to an internet correspondent, refers to this image. The aforementioned Erwin Brugmans' call not to behave like a 'scared Jew' also references this cliché. This is the image of the Jew in the *galut*, the Jew in the Diaspora who, out of necessity, has adopted a submissive attitude and who will avoid confrontation. It also is the image of the 'Passive Jew'.[84] It's the attitude to which Israel was going to put a stop. But sometimes, the image resurfaces: 'The worshippers of the Sabbath service of last Saturday would rather not mention it. Better let sleeping dogs lie. Maybe, the abuse against the synagogue visitors will sort itself out. 'This may be a stupid attitude, to want to hide what is experienced as threatening,' a visitor of the synagogue at the Lekstraat in South Amsterdam says. Sometimes, there is resistance against the attitude of the 'scared Jew'. But Sebbag has also experienced that they positioned themselves in front of him, forcing him to walk around them. 'One time, a group advanced towards me. They said: "We are going to hit you." I answered: "Try me. I have a black belt in taekwondo."' The Moroccan-Israeli-Dutch Sami Kaspi also stated firmly: 'I always wear a kippah when I go outside. I have that courage. That's me. There is no need to be afraid. We have been afraid more than enough.'[85]

Brugmans contrasted the attitude of the West Amsterdam Jews with those of South Amsterdam. A serious incident had occurred involving a boy who 'had been attacked and hit, some four years ago. South Amsterdam was in shock over it. In West, we are not so easily startled. I sometimes say: "What is it you want, get the fuck off my street." They never expect that.' Subsequently, on the advice of an alderman, Brugmans was invited as an experience expert to share his expertise with South: 'And those South Jews

82   Interview Sebbag by Remco Ensel, 11 March 2011; CIDI monitor 2001.
83   Klaus Hödl, 'Masculinity.' In: Richard S. Levy (ed.), *Antisemitism: A Historical Encyclopedia of Prejudice and Persecution,* Volume 1 (Santa Barbara, CA: ABC-CLIO, 2005), 447-448. *See also* chapters 1 and 12.
84   As discussed in the chapters 2, 3 and 13..
85   Interview Kaspi by Remco Ensel, 2011.

go .... Don't we need security and police surveillance? And: Moroccans here and Moroccans there .... A pvv-like mindset [pvv being Geert Wilders' party]. And I go, *Ah, pfff.* Then I started to explain: this is about consultation ... and acting pro-actively when dealing with these youths, making reports, supporting each other. Why haven't you done anything? The sports club where the incident occurred hadn't done anything ....' And then these people from South said, "Yeah, but you West Jews ...." And I said, "Yeah, you South Jews. Why so pusillanimous? You can do something about this but you have to turn your mindset around. And then you can do something. I cannot convince you. You are stuck in your own thinking . I fully understand that. I also understand very well how you people think. I can say it. I am a Jewish man from West Amsterdam, from a synagogue who has seen one or two things." He had done so himself, *Stand still, look them in the eyes, and then out loud, slightly aggressive, shut up, shut up, walk on!*[86]

86   Based on interviews with Brugmans, Kaspi, Sebbag by Remco Ensel and conversations with a community worker from East Amsterdam.

15   Conspiracism

Islamic Redemptive Antisemitism and the Murder of Theo van Gogh

Remco Ensel

On 2 November 2004, at about 8.45 am, one 'angry Muslim' called Mohammed Bouyeri killed film director and journalist Theo van Gogh in the Linnaeusstraat in Amsterdam.[1] On Van Gogh's body, Bouyeri left a five-page written message that has become known as the 'Open Letter to Hirshi Ali'.[2] The letter, written almost two months before the murder, predicted the death of Hirsi Ali (b. 1969), at the time a Member of Parliament for the Liberal Party (VVD). She was also the *auctor intellectualis* of the short film *Submission* (2004), directed by Van Gogh.[3] The 'Open Letter to Hirshi Ali' is an intriguing source for 'Muslim antisemitism' in the early twenty-first century.[4] Like Bouyeri's numerous other writings, the letter is eclectic and idiosyncratic, a mix of religious and secular references to ideas from both the political left and right. The letter referred to the Quran, to earlier writings by Quran scholars and to internet texts by American antisemites. It was both

1   Robert S. Leiken, *Europe's Angry Muslims: The Revolt of the Second Generation* (Oxford: Oxford University Press, 2012).
2   Bouyeri (as well as Theo van Gogh) spelled Hirsi Ali as Hirshi Ali. Bouyeri's writings are ordered and numbered by Ruud Peters in *De ideologische en religieuze ontwikkeling van Mohammed B. Deskundigenrapport in de strafzaak tegen Mohammed B. in opdracht van het openbaar ministerie opgesteld voor de Arrondisementsrechtsbank Amsterdam* (May 2005) and *Overzicht teksten geschreven of vertaald door Mohammed B. Bijlage bij het deskundigenrapport 'De ideologische en religieuze ontwikkeling van Mohammed B.'* (May 2005). Also consulted were these and other source texts found in the seizure on the occasion of the Piranha investigation, on the basis of which the following report was drawn up: Roel Meijer, *Inhoud van de religieuze en ideologische documenten aangetroffen in het beslag van verdachten in het Piranha-onderzoek. Deskundigenrapportage opgesteld voor de Arrondissementsrechtbank Rotterdam* (2007).
3   *Submission*. Direction: Theo van Gogh, script: Ayaan Hirsi Ali, 2004. I thank Roel Meijer. *See also* chapter 12.
4   'Open brief aan Hirshi Ali.doc' in Peters, *Bijlage bij het deskundigenrapport*, no. 49. This Word file was made on 17 August 2004. The letter is also available via *Wikipedia*. In *Murder in Amsterdam. The Death of Theo van Gogh and the Limits of Tolerance* (New York: Penguin Press, 2006), Ian Buruma quotes and refers to the letter, but this contains a number of inconsistencies. The author probably mixed up several texts. For instance, Buruma states that Hirsi Ali had become a 'willing tool' in the hands of 'Zionists and crusaders' (Buruma, *Murder in Amsterdam*, 5), yet the words 'Zionist' and 'Zionists' do not feature in the file 'Open Letter to Hirshi Ali' but in 'Open Letter to the Dutch People'.

an explanation and a prediction, a declaration of war and a profession of
faith all rolled into one. In this chapter, the three themes of the letter – the
multicultural society, the Jewish conspiracy and Muslim eschatology – will
be used to describe a historical process through which Muslim antisemitism,
via a political mobilisation of enduring anti-Jewish representations, became
connected with the identity politics and the self of young immigrants in the
Netherlands (as introduced in chapter 14).[5] Especially male adolescents experienced their hyphenated identity (Moroccan-Dutch) as a stigma. Global
Islamism offered an escape route. By emphasising the Muslim identity,
the hyphenated identity was dissolved. Our point of departure here is that
the changing function and meaning of concepts such as 'Muslims' and
'Islam' should be taken into account in the analysis of expressions of Muslim
antisemitism in the early twenty-first century, such as Bouyeri's letter. In
general, it is striking how little, until the attacks in Brussels and Paris in 2014
and 2015, the antisemitism of jihadist Muslims has been taken seriously or
registered as a crucial ingredient of their ideology.[6]

Bouyeri's antisemitic letter

Bouyeri's letter reproached Hirsi Ali for a number of things – especially
for her attacks, as a lapsed Muslim, on Islam. To underpin this argument,
Bouyeri not only referred to the controversial short film *Submission*, but
also to a Dutch TV report in which Hirsi Ali asked pupils in a school yard
about their faith: 'For instance, you had the cowardly nerve to demand
from Muslim children at school that they choose between their Creator
and the constitution.'[7] It is striking that Bouyeri exonerated Hirsi Ali in two
ways. Firstly, her success was largely due to the weakness of the Muslim
community: '[The Muslim community, or Ummah] has neglected its task
of resisting injustice and has left evil to sleep off its hangover.' Luckily,

5   This was confirmed at one of the first presentations of these ideas: Remco Ensel, 'Plan
B. Het verlossingsantisemitisme van Mohammed B. en kompanen.' Paper for NWO congres
'Conflict and Security: Framing Conflict in Culture, Politics, and Science' (23 November 2011,
Utrecht). *See, e.g.,* Klaus Holz and Michael Kiefer, 'Islamistischer Antisemitismus. Phänomen und
Forschungsstand.' In: Wolfram Stender, Guido Follert and Mihri Ozadogan (eds.), *Konstellationen
des Antisemitismus. Antisemitismusforschung und sozialpädagogische Praxis* (Wiesbaden: VS
Verlag für Sozialwissenschaften, GWV Fachverlage GmbH, 2010), 109-138.
6   However, since 2000 there had been great attention to antisemitic incidents in general. *See*
chapter 14.
7   Jan Eickelboom and Monique Wijnants, 'De strijd van Ayaan Hirsi Ali', television programme
NOVA, 20 November 2004 (but the visit referred to dates back to 20 November 2003).

Muslim revival was at hand, Bouyeri confidently stated. Secondly, Hirsi Ali was only a tool in the hands of higher powers, an 'ally who hands the "gun powder" to others so that they do not have to dirty their hands'. As a 'soldier of evil' she is probably not even aware of these higher powers and their evil ideals, but Bouyeri is willing to point them out to her. This was nothing less than a Jewish conspiracy against Islam. A conspiracy spearheaded by the VVD, the liberal party which Hirsi Ali represented in parliament. Bouyeri identified party chair Jozias van Aartsen as Jewish and also the unnamed 'mayor of Amsterdam' (by which the social democratic politician Job Cohen was meant). Bouyeri talked about Hirsi Ali's 'chums', without specifically mentioning anybody. He did talk about the VVD as an infidel, devilish ('thaghut') party, about 'Jewish masters' and about the institutions shaping the Jewish conspiracy against Islam. Ultimately, this was the Dutch state, because '[i]t is a fact that Dutch politics are dominated by many Jews who are the product of Talmud dogma; as are your political fellow party members.'[8]

Bouyeri realised all too well that Hirsi Ali and, with her, all 'extremist infidels' would attach little value to his eschatological philosophies, but he was not going to wait to be proven right like some quietist believer. Instead, he adopted an activist attitude, but without the usual repertoire of resistance resources: 'No discussion, no protests, no parades, no petitions'. Violence is the only proper instrument: 'Only DEATH will distinguish the Truth from the Lie.'[9] With so much certitude, the thought arises – and is at one point stated literally – that there is a connection between the ink of religious scholars and the blood of martyrs. Apparently, violence alone was not enough. Bouyeri felt the need to explain himself in writing. Blood and ink became synonymous. Not without reason, his written and rhymed short testament is called 'Dipped in Blood'. The murder of Van Gogh and the letter left behind complemented each other.[10] Especially in hindsight, we can establish that 'Only DEATH' proved to be a premature and even pathetic exclamation. Bouyeri was captured with only minor injuries.

8   Evelien Gans has already pointed out the letter's antisemitism: Evelien Gans, 'Over gaskamers, joodse nazi's en neuzen.' In: Peter R. Rodriguez and Jaap van Donselaar (eds.), *Monitor racisme en extremisme. Negende rapportage* (Amsterdam: Anne Frank Stichting, Amsterdam University Press, 2010), 129-152.

9   This is a phrase derived from Al Qaida, according to Petter Nesser, *The Slaying of the Dutch filmmaker. religiously motivated violence or Islamist terrorism in the name of global Jihad?* FFI report. Norwegian Defence Research Establishment, 2005: 23.

10   *Martelaren* [Martyrs]. *De bouwstenen van naties door Shaykh Abullah Azzam Shaheed (rahmatulahi Alaih).*

From February 2002 onwards, Mohammed Bouyeri produced all kinds of texts, primarily distributed via the internet. Sometimes he acted as translator, sometimes as writer – but even then, he used existing texts. He translated some texts from English to Dutch ('I ask Allah to forgive me my shortcomings'[11]). This applies, for instance, to the books *The True Muslim*, under his pseudonym Abu Zubair, and to the hefty *Principles of a Fundamentalist* (no. 31), under his pseudonyms Abu Zubair and Muwahhid, which was partly written by the famous Pakistani theologian Abul Ala Mawdudi (1903-1979) with some phrases by Bouyeri himself.[12] Although he had attended a Quran School as a young boy, we may assume that Bouyeri, a native Berber speaker, was not able to directly translate Arabic texts into Dutch.

The writings were meant to be distributed. The significance of the texts appears from the verdict of the court from 2008, in the appeal case of Nouriddin El Fahtni, convicted for preparing a terrorist attack. The verdict mentioned that Bouyeri

> had handed out approximately 150 copies of 'To Catch a Wolf' in the street, that he had left the 'Open Letter to Hirshi Ali' – according to several statements also published on the internet – on the body of Van Gogh and that he has 'bequeathed' a memory stick in order for the files saved on it to be distributed among the rest of the Ummah and partly also across the whole world. The memory stick contained, for instance, the writings 'To Catch a Wolf', 'Obligation to Kill Those Who Curse the Prophet' and 'Dipped in Blood', as well as the open letters to the Dutch people, Hirsi Ali, Aboutaleb and the Muslim Ummah.[13]

The sociologist Albert Benschop (b. 1949) has painstakingly mapped the internet traffic of Mohammed Bouyeri/Abu Zubair, Bilal L. aka Aboe Qataadah, Omar A. aka Abu Nawwaar and others. Their texts about jihadist Islam were distributed via mainstream websites such as Marokko.nl and

11   Remark by Abu Zubair/Mohammed B. on the English/Dutch translation of Shaykh Hammoed Al Uqla Shuaibi, *Fatwa naar aanleiding van de gebeurtenissen op 11 september 2001*.
12   No. 31 in the numeration of Peters's annex. The available texts are diverse and it is not always possible to make a strict distinction between Bouyeri's own work, translations and adaptations. The collection of texts comprises passages from religious writings such as quotes from the Quran and texts by or derived from Ibn Taymiyya, Hassan al-Banna, Mawdudi, Sayyid Qutb, the Egyptian-British preacher Abu Hamza al Masri', the religious organisation Hizb al-Tahrir, publications of the British Azzam Publications and the website islamawakening.com.
13   LJN: BC4171, The Hague Court of Justice, 2200187106.

MSN groups. 'There was a promiscuous online exchange of texts and ideas.' Fellow-religionists gathered in so-called 'living room meetings' and in chat rooms to meet 'Islam scholars' to exchange knowledge and experiences and point out interesting writings to each other. Yehya Kaddouri (b. 1987), convicted in 2005 for the 'preparation of a crime with terrorist intent', sometimes received 'some links to radical websites …' from the young men of the *Hofstad Network*.[14] They had their own websites on MSN groups. 'Because it seldom took long for these sites to be removed or replaced again, I added Mohammed B. to my MSN chat account, in order for him to send me new links now and then. I had noticed his radical pamphlets …. For some time already, I had been aware of the pamphlet "How to Catch a Wolf" published on these sites.'[15]

The 'Open Letter to Hirshi Ali' is one of more than 50 texts that Islam scholar Ruud Peters has identified as written by Bouyeri. The open letter genre is a well-known phenomenon in the Dutch public media and is especially intended to vent an opinion. In such a case, the open letter is usually published in a newspaper or journal. The fact that Bouyeri left his letter on Van Gogh's body is idiosyncratic. But it cannot be equated with a 'suicide note'; that would rather apply to 'Dipped in Blood' (no. 53 on Peters' list), the second document that Bouyeri had on him at the time of the murder. For Bouyeri, the open letter was apparently an attractive format. His files contain open letters to then alderman Ahmed Aboutaleb, to the Dutch people, 'to the lying "aalim and imam"' (no. 51), 'to Muslim youth' (no. 55), 'to the Muslim Ummah' (no. 56) and to Geert Wilders (no. 57). In the Christian tradition, an open letter can also act as a religious document, in the form of the Epistles of the Apostles, but it is also a genre in Islam.[16] In 1973, the preacher and leader of the religious movement 'Al Adl wa Al Ihssane', Abdessalam Yassine (1928-2012), sent a pamphlet to the King of Morocco that might be considered a letter as it is written in the second person singular. Expecting to be killed, Abdessalam Yassine viewed his open letter as his will.[17]

---

14   Hofstadgroep is the name the Dutch secret service gave to a network of jihadists and terrorists. In 2008 the court dismissed existence of a criminal organisation (http://deeplink. rechtspraak.nl/uitspraak?id=ECLI:NL:GHSGR:2008:BC2576).

15   Albert Benschop, *Kroniek van een aangekondigde politieke moord. Jihad in Nederland* (Utrecht: Forum, 2005); Yehya Kaddouri, *Lach met de duivel. Autobiografie van een 'rotte-appel'-Marokkaan* (Amsterdam: Van Gennep, 2011), 77.

16   Henri Munson, jr., *Religion and Power in Morocco* (New Haven: Yale University Press, 1993).

17   Yassine was first imprisoned in a psychatric asylum and subsequently kept under house arrest.

The emergence of political Islam and the pre-eminence of 'The Jew'

Bouyeri's apparent belief in a Jewish conspiracy is part of a long tradition in the representation of 'the Jew' as a conspirator who, together with his co-religionists, rules the world for his own benefit.[18] As a topos, it is connected with other stereotypes, such as that of the Jew who hides his intentions and emotions, including his true faith.[19] It is also closely connected with the idea that through their control over mass media, Jews are able to bend the world to their will. During the twentieth century, 'the Jew' as conspirator was the most stubborn stereotype, also in relation to the debate about Israel – and to a lesser extent with the Holocaust. The specific antisemitic dimension of the 'fear of the power of small numbers'[20], leads us to speak of *conspiracism*.

During the last fifty years, particularly in the Arab world, 'theories' about a Jewish conspiracy have made significant progress, as can be seen from the unrelenting popularity of the *Protocols of the Elders of Zion*. This is the argument of Malte Gebert and Carmen Matussek's contribution to the *Jahrbuch für Antisemitismusforschung*.[21] According to the authors, 'In this country [i.e. Germany], nobody would give any credence to the idea that his Jewish neighbours are a direct threat to mankind', but in 'the Arab world', the twentieth-century 'ideological transfer' of European antisemitic thought has led to a conspiracy antisemitism that has started to circulate relatively independently of the Middle East conflict during the last few decades. This belief in conspiracies fits in with the early adoption in the Arab world of other European antisemitic topoi such as stereotypes of Jews as ritual killers and poisoners of wells.[22]

Within the Dutch context, we do not distinguish as sharply between 'the Arab world' and Western Europe as Gebert and Matussek do. The Netherlands has a marginal, but nonetheless solid, right-wing antisemitic tradition which includes publications of and references to the *Protocols*. The Netherlands is in no way sealed off from the outside world. During the last 15 years, particularly

18   Ernst Piper, 'Achtes Bild: 'Die jüdische Weltverschwörung.' In: Julius H. Schoeps and Joachim Schlör (eds.) *Antisemitismus. Vorurteile und Mythen* (München, Zürich: Piper, 1995), 127-135.
19   This is not unlike the publicity about the religious concept of *taqiyya* which supposedly allows Muslims to lie or hide their true intentions in case their religion is in danger. For the Netherlands, *see, e.g.,* Hans Jansen, 'Wat u moet weten over Taqiyya', www.geenstijl.nl, 12 April 2004.
20   Arjun Appadurai in Sindre Bangstad, *Anders Breivik and the Rise of Islamophobia* (London: Zed Books, 2014), 95).
21   Malte Gebert and Carmen Matussek, '"Selbst wenn sie unser Land verlassen würde..." Die Adaptation der Protokolle der Weisen von Zion in der Arabischen Welt,' in *Jahrbuch für Antisemitismusforschung* 18 (2009), 67-87.
22   Gebert and Matussek, '"Selbst wenn sie unser Land verlassen würde...", 71.

through video-sharing websites, thinking and speaking in terms of conspiracies, or conspiracism, has become a global phenomenon.[23] Furthermore,
immigrants have imported their ideas from their native countries into the
Netherlands and have passed them on to their children. From the Netherlands
they maintain contact with the rest of the world through various media
channels. The discourse about Jews, central to this chapter, seems to be the
result of the global religious adaptation of originally secular antisemitic
thought. The use of Islam as an alternative for nationalism and other secular
ideologies gained traction after the fiasco, at least from the Arab point of
view, of the Six-Day War (or June War) of 1967. From that time on, existing
religious notions made headway with small subversive movements seizing the
opportunity to mobilise students and 'wake up' the political establishment.
The Revolution in Iran (1979) and the murder of President Anwar Sadat of
Egypt (1981) are considered the key moments in this development.

After 1967, the secular anti-Western and anti-colonial narrative was
translated into a more explicit religious vocabulary. Rather than just a
symbol of economic inequality and political dependence, the West became
synonymous with decadence and moral decline. Just look at Western mass
media and the lifestyle of indigenous elites. According to this emerging
anti-Western discourse of injustice, Muslims were economically, socially
and culturally repressed and exploited. And Western global culture particularly prevented Muslims from living out their faith. In the early 1990s,
this discourse spread across Europe. Islam became a domestic matter, partly
due to the distribution of anti-Western material via cassettes and later
CDs, satellite television and the internet. For instance, the sermons of the
popular Egyptian Sheikh Abdal-Hamid Kishk found a listening ear in the
Netherlands, with others copying his preaching style. In one of his sermons,
he looks back on the time of the Six-Day War when he was imprisoned by
the secular regime of Nasser:

> I have often said the Jews were busy with preparations ... and on the day
> itself the Egyptian army chief was playing football .... The commander of
> the Israeli air force rightfully claimed that what has happened in Egypt,
> should be seen as the fulfilment of the Great Western Dream.[24]

23 Jovan Byford, *Conspiracy Theories. A Critical Introduction* (Houndmills: Palgrave MacMillan,
2011).
24 Abdal-Hamid Kishk, Sermon *al-masjid al-aqṣā al-asīr/* ('the Aksa Mosque, the prisoner of
war), 10 December 1977 (29 Dhu al-Hijjah 1397 AH), CD Al-Maghribia, Beni Mellal, Morocco.
Translation: Rachid Alouad Abdallah.

Even today, his sermons are for sale everywhere. In the Netherlands, the ideas of the earlier Egyptian preacher Sayyid Qutb (1906-1966) were spread by the aforementioned Moroccan preacher Abdessalam Yassine, who was inspired by him.[25]

Obviously, due to the colonial connection to Indonesia and Surinam, the Netherlands has had Muslim inhabitants for a long time. Moreover, from the very beginning of their stay, the first foreign workers made an effort to facilitate the celebration of their faith in the Netherlands. There were, for instance, initiatives to establish prayer rooms and to collectively celebrate religious rituals.[26] Nonetheless, the presence of Muslims remained implicit and Islam did not feature in any public debate. Not until the 1980s did the Netherlands witness Muslims politically organising and manifesting themselves as Muslims. The Rushdie Affair was the culmination of this process.[27]

The Rushdie Affair

A lot has been written on how the novel *The Satanic Verses* (1988), by the Anglo-Indian writer Salman Rushdie (b. 1947), impacted ideas about national identity and multiculturalism in Western Europe. Especially the anthropologist Talal Asad, the political scientist Malise Rutven and the writer Kenan Malik have shown how, in Great Britain, the affair put Muslims on the map as politically active citizens but also accelerated their exclusion from the national imagined community.[28] In hindsight, the writer Lisa Appignanesi called the affair a dress rehearsal for 9/11, and the political

25 Oussama Cherribi, *Imams d'Amsterdam. À travers l'exemple des imams de la diaspora Marocaine* (PhD thesis, University of Amsterdam, 2000), 111, 113, 181. An interview with Yassine is in François Burgat, *L'Islamisme au Maghreb* (Paris: Payot et Rivages, 1995), 71-74.

26 Annemarie Cottaar, Nadia Bouras and Fatiha Laouikili, *Marokkanen in Nederland. De pioniers vertellen* (Amsterdam: Meulenhoff, 2009).

27 For the development of the so-called 'faith communities', *see* Sophie Gilliat-Ray, *Muslims in Britain. An Introduction* (Cambridge: Cambridge University Press, 2010). *See* Inayat Bunglawala, founder and chair of Muslims4UK: 'Looking back to the autumn of 1988, I think it is perhaps no exaggeration to say that it was in the heat of the *Satanic Verses* affair that we first saw the forging of a consciously British Muslim identity in the UK.' In: 'Looking back at Salman Rushdie's The Satanic Verses', *The Guardian*, 14 February, 2012.

28 Benedict Anderson, *Imagined Communities. Reflections on the Origin and Spread of Nationalism* (London, New York: Verso, 1991); Talal Asad, *Genealogies of Religion. Discipline and Reasons of Power in Christianity and Islam* (Baltimore: Johns Hopkins University Press, 1993); Malisse Rutven, *A Satanic Affair: Salman Rushdie and the Wrath of Islam* (London: Hogarth Press, 1991); Kenan Malik, *From Fatwa to Jihad. The Rushdie Affair and its legacy* (London: Atlantic, 2009).

scientist Gilles Kepel (b. 1955) considered the murder of Van Gogh a hybrid of 9/11 and the 2009 attack in Madrid.[29] Kepel made his statement immediately after the murder of Van Gogh. They all particularly refer to the call for the use of violence and the anti-Western Muslim discourse.[30] From a different perspective, the Rushdie Affair can also be seen as a regular verbal protest and a struggle for the recognition of some form of 'Muslim citizenship'.[31] In this paradoxical development of national inclusion and exclusion, the construct of 'the Jew' played an interesting role.[32] For the first time, Jews were presented as counterparts of the marginalised Muslims.[33]

The commotion over *The Satanic Verses* started in 1988 and reached the Netherlands in the spring of 1989.[34] According to his critics, Rushdie had described the time of the prophet in a blasphemous manner. At the time of publication, the writer was already well-known in the world of literature. In 1981, one of his previous novels, *Midnight's Children*, had landed him the prestigious Booker Prize. In 1988, *The Satanic Verses* was also shortlisted for the Booker Prize and won the Whitbread Prize. The novels *Midnight's Children* (1981) and *Shame* (1983) had already led to small controversies in India and Pakistan. This prequel – British praise and Pakistani-Indian criticism – must have enhanced the sensitivity for *The Satanic Verses*. This time, Indian and Pakistani protests were transmitted to immigrant communities in Bradford, Great Britain. Khomeini's fatwa, on 14 February 1989, was the

---

29   Lisa Appignanesi in: 'Looking back at Salman Rushdie's The Satanic Verses', *The Guardian*, 14 February, 2012. Gilles Kepel, 'Radical Islamism in Europe', interview with Irshad Manji, Steven Emerson, and Gilles Kepel, *Aspen Alert*, Aspen Institute, Washington, D.C., Dec. 2004.

30   *See* Ian Buruma and Avishai Margalit in *Occidentalism. The West in the Eyes of its Enemies* (New York: Penguin Press, 2004).

31   This distinction returns in the question of whether we should call it the Rushdie Affair (putting emphasis on the fatwa) or the Satanic Verses Controversy, emphasising the perceived problematic character of the novel. Here we have opted for the 'Rushdie Affair' because the duration and the intensity of the conflict eventually focused on the writer, as is the case with Van Gogh and Hirsi Ali. For Muslim citizenship, *see* Barbara Daly Metcalf, 'Introduction: Sacred Words, Sanctioned Practices, New Communities.' In: Barbara Daly Metcalf (ed.), *Making Muslim Space in North America and Europe* (Berkeley, Los Angeles: University of California Press, 2002), 1-27.

32   The affair was hardly finished by 1990, as appears from Salman Rushdie, *Joseph Anton. A Memoir* (New York: Random House, 2012).

33   For an interesting and highly relevant interpretation of 'the Jew' in Rushdie's oeuvre, *see* Anna Guttman, '"People set apart": representations of Jewishness in the fiction of Salman Rushdie', *Ariel* 42, 3 (2011), 103-121.

34   *See also* chapter 10.

spark that ignited the affair.[35] In the Netherlands, protests only started after Khomeini's ruling, abroad months before. On 3 March 1989, organisers of a protest in The Hague stated, 'We strongly condemn the book and its writer who has purposely slandered our faith and our Prophet'.[36]

The transnational protest proved that immigrants, as Muslims, had gained access to the public sphere of debate and protest. The Netherlands became familiar with the concept of the fatwa, the religious sensibilities surrounding the prophet and for the first time experienced Muslims engaging in a debate. It soon became apparent that there was more at stake than the protest against the publication of a novel which none of the protesters had even read.[37] The protest echoed the resentment of the immigrants about their position in the national imagined community, like in Great Britain. There, the protesters demanded the amendment of existing blasphemy legislation so that Islam could no longer be desecrated with impunity.[38] Also in the Netherlands, the protests had a legal focus. An action committee, consisting of representatives of Turkish, Pakistani and Moroccan religious organisations, stated: 'We reject any call for murder, but we will use any legal opportunity the Dutch law provides to fight the slander of our religion.'[39] Their prominent lawyer Max Moszkowicz sr. (b. 1926) saw possibilities for a ban, using article 147 of the Criminal Code on scornful blasphemy, but he failed to achieve this.[40] Rushdie, himself active in the anti-racism

35   For a perspective from Bradford, see Zaiba Malik, We are a Muslim, please (London: Windmill Press, 2011). Knowledge of Islam was extremely limited. Even the publisher of Penguin India was completely taken by surprise when he was alerted about potential problems 'as I was, at the time, largely ignorant of the history of Islam and its sacred texts.' In Appignanesi , 'Looking back at Salman Rushdie's The Satanic Verses.'

36   IISH, Archief NOS Paspoort 19: Press release signed by, among others, Friends of Islam in the Netherlands, Turkish and Pakistani organisations, various Muslim organisations and the Committee of Moroccan Workers in Rotterdam (KMAN), the Association of Moroccan Immigrants in Utrecht and a similar organisation in Breda.

37   In the Netherlands, the question of whether it was important to have read the book was discussed by two prominent Moroccan immigrants, who later became Members of Parliament.

38   See, e.g., Paul Weller, A Mirror of our Times: The Rushdie Afair and the Future of Multicultural-ism (London: Continuum, 2009) and Faisal Devji in 'Looking back at Salman Rushdie's The Satanic Verses' and Pnina Werbner, 'Stamping the Earth with the Name of Allah: Zikr and the Sacralizing of Space among British Muslims.' In: Barbara Daly Metcalf (ed.), Making Muslim Space in North America and Europe (Berkeley, Los Angeles: University of California Press, 2002) 167-185: 181; see also 'British Blasphemy Laws and the Rushdie Affair', www.salmanrushdiearchive.com, May 2012.

39   IISH, Archief NOS Paspoort 19: Press release.

40   Bas van Stokkom, Henny Sackers and Jean-Pierre Wils, Godslastering, discriminerende uitingen wegens godsdienst en haatuitingen. Een inventariserende studie, Radboud Universiteit Nijmegen, 2006 Ministry of Justice, WODC. In 2010-2011, Max Moszkowicz's son, Bram

movement, was denounced, even by (previous) supporters of secular left-wing politics. In *From Fatwa to Jihad*, the journalist Kenan Malik acutely records this *Umwertung aller Werte* in the British immigrant community. Multicultural sensitivity mixed with resistance against Western arrogance and Muslim wrath. According to the protesters, the distribution of the novel showed the 'Western' lack of respect for Muslims' religious identity. In this conflict, according to the Dutch action committee, 'the Muslim community' was up against 'the Dutch community'. But let's not forget that it was also the beginning of a new split in the so-called *secular* migrant 'community' vis-à-vis the *Muslim* 'community'.

In the protest, Jews and Israel were represented in various ways. Various sources show that Jews served as a kind of imaginary opponent of Islam. According to a tried anti-colonial and anti-American recipe, Khomeini saw Rushdie's novel as part of a larger project of American, European and Zionist Islamologists. In this anti-Occidentalism, Rushdie was the Westerner in disguise.[41] By summoning non-Zionist Jews to protest, Rafsanjani, Iran's Speaker of Parliament, made it clear that he considered *The Satanic Verses* a Zionist project.[42] Emmanuel Sivan stated that in Egyptian 'cassette culture', Rushdie had become part of 'a Hollywood-based, "Judeo-Masonic" conspiracy to de-Islamise the Middle East with the help of movies, soap operas, and shampoo ads.' Preachers like Kishk depicted Rushdie 'as the last link in a long chain of "false Muslim conspirators", including, among others, Kemal Atatürk (said to have been a Jew masquerading as a Muslim) ....[43] Paul Weller, author of a study on the affair, wrote that many Muslims in Great Britain believed that the book was the product of 'an anti-Islamic conspiracy'.[44]

In Great Britain, some people also believed that the Jews were behind the publication, referring, first and foremost, to its Jewish publisher. The alleged Jewish connection explains why South Africa's *Weekly Mail* received

Moszkowicz, acted as Geert Wilders' barrister in the latter's court case for incitement to hatred and discrimination.

41   In the decade before the 1979 Revolution, a fascinating shift had taken place in Iran, from Occidentalism to anti-Occidentalism. *See, e.g.*, Mehrzad Boroujerdi, *Iranian Intellectuals and the West. The Tormented Triumph of Nativism* (Syracuse, NY: Syracuse University Press, 1996) and Ali Rahnema, *An Islamic Utopian. A Political Biography of Ali Shari'ati* (London: I.B. Tauris, 1998).

42   Malise Ruthven in Lisa Appignanesi and Sara Maitland, *Het internationale Rushdie dossier* (Amsterdam: Van Gennep, 1989), 160.

43   Emmanuel Sivan, 'Eavesdropping on radical Islam', *Middle East Quarterly* (March 1995), 13-24.

44   Weller, *A Mirror of our Times*, 61-63.

antisemitic mail after inviting Rushdie for a lecture, and why the famous Jewish-American writer Arthur Miller (1905-2005) declined to publicly support Rushdie.[45] The producers of the Pakistani film *International Guerrillas* (1990) made the boldest statement. A group of mujahideen sets out to find Rushdie who is the pivot of a Jewish-Israeli network. When one of the heroes is captured, Rushdie tortures him before handing him over to Israeli soldiers. The film turns Rushdie into 'the Jew' and subsequently depicts him stereotypically as a rich, Westernised, cosmopolitan and sadistic dandy frequenting nightclubs. It is ironic that, in view of the Rushdie Affair, the Dutch newspaper *De Telegraaf* voiced concern over the British Board of Film Classification's possible admission of the film, without mentioning its antisemitic connotations.[46]

In the Netherlands, the Jewish-Muslim opposition also played a part. One of the grievances of the Dutch action committee was de aforementioned 'double standard' the authorities supposedly use. In 1987, the planned performance of the play *Der Müll, die Stadt und der Tod* [Garbage, the City and Death] (1975) by the German director and screenwriter Rainer Werner Fassbinder (1945-1982) was banned after a row over the alleged antisemitic nature of the play.[47] A year later, during the First Intifada, a protest newspaper of immigrant organisations printed a picture of Fassbinder next to that of the Austrian President Kurt Waldheim (1918-2007), a highly controversial figure due to his Nazi past: thus, they were presented as the victims of the all-pervasive Jewish power. Another year later, the Fassbinder Affair returned during the Rushdie Affair. Why, the anti-Rushdie protesters wondered, did people now stand firm for freedom of expression, while they had demanded a ban of the performance of the play two years ago? In Great Britain, there were similar feelings of inequality and impotence when Jewish protests succeeded in banning Jim Allen's play *Perdition* (1987).[48]

All in all, the Rushdie Affair was the culmination of the rise of a politicised public Muslim faith community. In the Netherlands, a 1991 speech in Lausanne by VVD politician Frits Bolkestein (b. 1933), is often referred to as the first blow towards the eventual defeat of the multicultural ideal at the hands of politicians Pim Fortuyn, Rita Verdonk (b. 1955) and Geert Wilders. Less attention has been paid to the fact that this speech was mostly about

45   Christopher Hitchens, 'Assassins of the mind', *Vanity Fair*, February 2009.
46   'Rushdie's boek symbolisch verbrand', *De Telegraaf*, 4 March 2013.
47   *See* chapter 12 and Evelien Gans, *Gojse nijd & joods narcisme* (Amsterdam: Arena, 1987), 27-38.
48   Jim Allen (1926-1999). The play is about the contacts between Hungarian Zionists and the Nazis in the Second World War. Weller, *A mirror of our times*, 145.

'Muslims' and no longer about 'ethnic minorities'. This was part of a new vocabulary and directly inspired by the Rushdie Affair.[49]

In the 1990s, the publicist and politician Pim Fortuyn (1948-2002) – author of *Tegen de islamisering van onze cultuur* [Against the Islamisation of Our Culture] (1997) – touched a nerve with his discourse about the growing feelings of alienation among many Dutch people, the decline of Dutch identity and the role he assumed the 'Islamisation' of the Netherlands was playing in both these developments.[50] As discussed in chapter 12, in the 1980s and 1990s, Theo van Gogh was involved in a number of court cases due to his alleged antisemitic utterances, but later on, he followed in the footsteps of Fortuyn in his focus on Islam. Van Gogh's disgust of religious bigotry in a country that from the 1960s on had experienced a radical secularisation, was expressed, among other things, in a television series he directed, *Najib en Julia*. In 2003, Van Gogh stated that in this modern-day *Romeo and Juliet*, neither the 'Dutch' nor the 'Moroccan' milieu are depicted favourably. With respect to the Moroccan milieu he aimed to highlight the prevalent bigotry and hypocrisy: 'There is this father who recites lines from the Quran like he's some relict [fossiel] from the Stone Age .... They always talk about respect .... For instance when someone says: "He, show some respect for the Quran, you're not permitted to mock [the Scripture]. But, when you start to read all that's written in it on dissenters [*andersdenkenden*], you think: fuck off with your respect.' Thus in *Najib en Julia* 'you can see a Moroccan father watching television and remarking that Dutch broadcasting is in the hands of the Jews. In Moroccan circles, many people think that way ....'[51]

What about Bouyeri? Did he think so during the 1990s, when he became fascinated by 'the conflict between Israel and the Palestinians' and subsequently got his information exclusively from the Flemish broadcasting company VRT, 'because it approaches incidents in the Middle East much less from the Israeli perspective than the Dutch broadcasting companies'?[52]

---

49 The newspaper article spoke of 'minorities' referring to the older 'ethnic minorities'. Frits Bolkestein, 'Integratie van minderheden moet met lef worden aangepakt', *de Volkskrant*, 12 September, 1991.

50 Pim Fortuyn, *Tegen de islamisering van onze cultuur: Nederlandse identiteit als fundament* (Utrecht: A.W. Bruna, 1997).

51 Ad Fransen, 'Theo van Gogh: "Wat is er mis met geitenneuker"', *HP/De Tijd*, 28 October 2009. This article consists of a reproduction of an interview from 2003 in the same journal.

52 Jaco Alberts et al., 'De wereld van Mohammed B.', *NRC Handelsblad*, 9 juli 2005.

REMCO ENSEL

Youth culture and gender trouble

In chapter 10, Annemarike Stremmelaar highlighted the first registered Turkish-Muslim antisemitic incidents in the 1980s. In 1974, the first Moroccan mosque in the Netherlands, Al Kabir, opened its doors in Amsterdam; the Union of Moroccan Mosques (UMMON) was founded in 1977. Soon, there was an escalating conflict regarding the increasing influence of Saudi Arabia on Al Kabir. In the same period, there were similar problems at other new mosques. In 1985, the CIDI antisemitism monitor suggested that there was a connection between 'this increased influence [of Libyan and Saudi money] and the regular antisemitic statements by certain Muslim representatives in the Netherlands'. At Al Kabir, the quarrel about which direction to follow became tainted with antisemitism. This became apparent when, between 1990 and 1993, there was a wave of publicity surrounding the imam's advice to 'our youth' not to mix with the 'dirty Jews'.[53]

After the first indications of Muslim antisemitism in the last two decades of the twentieth century, the incidences increased in frequency after 2000.[54] In the Netherlands the most prominent result was Bouyeri's eschatological tract in which antisemitism was linked to the perspective of an ideal Muslim society. The religious battle underlying Bouyeri's act and his letter can also be understood in the light of the growing political significance of Islam and Muslims in the Dutch public sphere during the first decade of the twenty-first century. This battle also includes the campaign by Bouyeri's opponent Ayaan Hirsi Ali, the anti-Islam insults by Theo van Gogh, the anti-Islam and nationalist agendas of Pim Fortuyn and Geert Wilders, and the Christian Democrats' sermons about the Judeo-Christian heritage as the foundation of the Dutch nation. Actually, Theo van Gogh received his first death threats in 2003, before the film *Submission* and following the publication of a collection of essays entitled *Allah weet het beter* [Allah knows best].[55]

---

53 Based on (police) reports, collected in the IISH KMAN Archive (no inventory), a news item in *Het Parool*, 3 April 1993, the statements in a radio broadcast of 25 December 1992 as recorded in M. Rabbae, *Naast de Amicales ook de Ummon. De mantelorganisaties van de Marokkaanse autoriteiten in Nederland* (Utrecht: NCB, 1993), annex 24, 71 p. 37; *see* for 1978 'Ook Marokkaanse intimidatie op Salto', *Trouw* 12 December 1990.

54 *See* Remco Ensel, 'Singing about the death of Muhammad al-Durrah and the emotional mobilization for protest', *International journal of media and cultural politics*, 10, 1 (2014), 21-38 and chapter 14.

55 Theo van Gogh, *Allah weet het beter* (Amsterdam: XTRA Productions, 2003). *See* illustration 20, p. 333.

In the Netherlands, the divergent attitudes towards 'Islam' during the last 15 years were the preliminary result of a process that became visible during the 1990s and which led to a public collective Muslim identity. This process became apparent in the lives of Bouyeri and his friends. Mohammed Bouyeri was born in 1978 in the Domselaerstraat in East Amsterdam and grew up in the Hart Nibbrigstraat in West Amsterdam. Overtoomse Veld/ Slotervaart in New West was the neighbourhood run by city district chair (and later Member of Parliament) Ahmed Marcouch, who was surprised to find that the people in this area called outsiders Romans (*Rumi*), one of the terms people in Morocco use for foreigners. The neighbourhood saw itself as an 'Asterix village', the last remaining non-Roman fortress, located just outside Amsterdam's ring road. For them, the nearby Mercatorplein in Old West was a different country, while the city centre was a different continent, visited only on group expeditions. At a later age, Mohammed delivered the newspaper *NRC Handelsblad* in the proverbial *'Grachtengordel'* of South Amsterdam where the upper middle class and the intellectual elite live.[56] Like many boys his age, Mohammed visited the local mosque school to learn the principles of Islam and basic Arabic. The teacher was strict and used corporal punishment. Occasionally, on his way home 'native' inhabitants would shout at him that they could hardly wait for summer to arrive (when the immigrants would travel to Morocco). This is where Mohammed Bouyeri grew up and early on, some confrontations caused him to come into contact with the authorities.

At the beginning of the century Bouyeri was in his early twenties. The latent feelings of dissatisfaction that had led to the first and only Dutch race riot between youngsters and the police were strengthened by the attacks on the Twin Towers in September 2001 and the murder of Pim Fortuyn in May 2002 by the environmentalist Volkert van der Graaf. In 2000, the sociologist Paul Scheffer had published his influential article on how the multicultural society had degenerated into a 'multicultural drama'.[57] Scheffer's prediction about the advent of a generational conflict between first- and second-generation immigrants can also be found in Bouyeri's writings. In one of his first pieces, 'Jihad in Amsterdam-West', Bouyeri says that this generational gap was now so wide that parents and children were literally unable to understand each other, because they could no longer communicate in the same language. He proposed a step-by-step

56 Literally *Grachtengordel* denotes the Amsterdam ring of canals; the term however refers metaphorically to the intellectual and cultural elite of Amsterdam.
57 *See* chapter 14.

approach, with an important role for local imams, in order to reconcile the two generations. A year later, he had already passed this point, denouncing the imams as pillars of the establishment.[58]

The streets in Bouyeri's neighbourhood were named after painters from around the turn of century. The local high school was named after Piet Mondrian, the primary school after Marius Bauer. After a merger, the latter school, also attended by Mohammed, was, named Ru Paré. They explained the children that, during the Occupation, this artist 'had saved the lives of 52 Jewish children by supplying them with hiding addresses .... That is actually the reason why we have chosen this name. Ru Paré stands for: freedom and friendship, helping each other regardless of faith or race, living together.'[59] The reporter Margalith Kleijwegt (b. 1951) had spent some time in 'Mohammed B.'s neighbourhood' long before the murder for an article for the periodical *Vrij Nederland*. She visited the neighbourhood again right after the murder and was able to shed more light on the very particular downfall of one of its members: the neighbourhood was 'dismal ... families were isolated from all things Dutch' and children grew up, watching their parents struggle through life and feeling embarrassed for them.[60] To a certain extent, Bouyeri was the exception to this sombre perspective. He had done reasonably well at school and for a long time tried to make an effort for the neighbourhood and his peers. His earliest writing is an enthusiastic report of a meeting between youths and local politicians.

As we can deduct from his letter to Hirsi Ali and his other writings, Bouyeri's Moroccan-Dutch identity remained important. It entailed a constant focus on his father's foreign-worker status, but also on relationships between men and women. As a teenager, he clashed with his sister because of her contact with a boy. In the middle of his conversion process, he still launched a plan for the reorganisation of community work. His proposal to divide men and women was met with disapproval and led to disappointment, which forced Bouyeri to find other ways to realise his recently acquired social vision.[61] In 'Islam and Integration.doc' he addressed Muslim women: 'Society has dragged you into all sorts of discussions about integration, and now you have even become an issue for all sorts of false politicians who campaign on your behalf and present themselves as the liberators of the Muslim woman.' This is a clear reference to Hirsi Ali's agenda. As early as 2002, Hirsi Ali

---

58   'Jihad in Amsterdam-West', Amsterdam.doc, 27 October 2002, no. 4.
59   Website OBS Ru Paré [no longer available].
60   Margalith Kleijwegt, 'De buurt van Mohammed B.', *Vrij Nederland*, 13 November 2004.
61   'Islam en integratie.doc', 13 February, 2003.

was an important target for those who were more than vexed by her public interventions in the debate about the multicultural society and the position of Islam in the Netherlands. Six months before the murder, the rap song *Hirsi Ali Diss* by the rap formation DHC was distributed. In this rap, the politician is slandered and threatened. The striking line, 'You used to be a Muslim but now you are a Jew ...'[62], refers to Hirsi Ali's apostasy. It's unavoidable to draw a parallel with Rushdie's apostasy.[63] In the context of the rap text as a whole, 'the Jew' corresponds to the rap line 'You are a token immigrant'. The rappers were prosecuted for making threats, not for the anti-Jewish reference.[64]

Mohammed Jabri, internet writer and author of the 'Anti-Jewish Manifesto' (chapter 14), also targeted Hirsi Ali. In his opinion, the 'overrated amateur' Hirsi Ali had 'a secular, extremist agenda'.[65] Hirsi Ali's film *Submission* was about Islam, but primarily about the subservient position of women. Fifteen years earlier, during the Rushdie Affair, the specific issue of the desecration of the Muslim woman had already been an important yet little noticed matter (as argued by the anthropologist Marina Warner). Sexuality as prism for the representation of Islam played an important role in *The Satanic Verses* and in the controversy. This was also a factor in Van Gogh's statements, in his *Najib en Julia* and in *Submission*. The film showed naked female bodies and linked these to Quran texts. Van Gogh was the director, but more specifically the person who, as we saw above, called Moroccans 'goat fuckers' in his publications (collected in 'Allah knows best'). In his study about the murder, Ron Eyerman pointed to the importance of gender, in reference to the demolition of the patriarchate of the first-generation fathers and Mohammed Bouyeri's effort to win back a certain manhood through an individual act of violence.[66]

Protocols and Illuminati

Hirsi Ali was ultimately a pawn in a plan of an elite operating from behind the scenes. According to Jabri, Hirsi Ali was a 'puppet of secular extremists',

62 'Hirsi Ali wil rappers laten oppakken', *Trouw* 1 July 2004.

63 Weller, *A mirror of our times*, 65-67.

64 The police court issued a suspended sentence: 'Werkstraf voor rappers "Hirsi Ali-diss"', *de Volkskrant*, 27 January 2005.

65 Steven de Jong, 'Mohammed Jabri: 'Allochtonen kunnen niet tegen kritiek'', *Politiek-digitaal*, 18 December 2005.

66 Ron Eyerman, *The Assassination of Theo van Gogh: From Social Drama to Cultural Trauma* (Durham: Duke University Press, 2008). For the sexism in Van Gogh's writings *see also* chapter 12.

'a controlled robot'.[67] In conspiracism, as the psychologist Jovan Byford explains in his study, the plan is always more important than the puppets. So a conspiracy cannot be undone by eliminating a public figure. His or her place will automatically be taken by a new candidate puppet. In this perspective, the remark about Hirsi Ali in Bouyeri's letter ('a soldier of evil ... only an instrument of higher powers' and an 'ally who hands the "gun powder" to others') was conspiracy rhetoric. The letter contained yet another conspiracy topos. The Jewish conspiracy takes shape through the recruitment of non-Jews. These other powerful figures, who form a link in the conspiracy, are then often 'Judaised'.[68] This explains why in Bouyeri's letter, apart from Hirsi Ali, who had already been labelled a Jew, the chair of the VVD fraction, Jozias van Aartsen (b. 1947) was attributed the Jewish identity: apostate Muslims were Jewish, liberal politicians were Jews, the Dutch establishment was Jewish.

Around the turn of the century, the idea of a Jewish conspiracy became more widespread in the Netherlands. Gebert and Matussek have argued that conspiracy antisemitism was also vocal outside of the small circle of jihadists and outside of the Netherlands. And for the Netherlands, it was not a completely new phenomenon. For instance, the Netherlands also had a print history of the *Protocols of the Elders of Zion*, with the first Dutch translation published in 1928. Before that, Dutch people had easy access to the *Protocols* via English (Victor E. Marsden) and German (Gottfried zur Beek) translations of the 1905 Russian publication which were published after the First World War. Other translations followed. After the Second World War, new editions kept surfacing, including a Dutch adaptation in 2007.[69]

The by now standard evidence for the statement that, in the Arab-Muslim world, the *Protocols* circulate as a serious text, is the charter of the Muslim organisation Hamas, founded in 1988, which includes the *Protocols of the Elders of Zion* as source material for Jewish/Zionist evil. In 2004, the year of the anti-Jewish manifesto and Bouyeri's letter, there was commotion and a court case in the Netherlands regarding the availability of a Dutch version of *The Upbringing of Children in Islam* by the religious scholar Saudi Abdallah Nasih 'Alwan. This book refers directly to the *Protocols*:

---

67 De Jong, 'Mohammed Jabri'.
68 Byford, *Conspiracy Theories*, 73.
69 Robin de Ruiter, *De Protocollen van de wijzen van Sion ontsluierd* (Enschede: Mayra publications, 2007).

Illustration 25   Photo of graffiti thematizing Jews and media, Rotterdam, 2 June 2006

Peter Hilz / Hollandse Hoogte

Control of the media; the reappearance of an old stereotype: 'The National News is a Jewish Lie!' Graffiti on the wall of Rotterdam Hofplein railway station, 2 June 2006. Graffiti on the same wall included '9/11 was the work of the Israeli Mossad' and 'Bin Laden is a myth'.

In their *Protocols*, the Jews have vented these misguided opinions to spoil
people's professions of faith, as well as their conscience and intelligence.
The Jews have even gone as far as conceiving a plan for mankind, which
they have started to execute, by means of mass communication media,
radio and television programmes, Masonic bodies that they have founded
and by means of every treacherous spy and paid writer. Through their
cunning and evil, they were able to spoil people through general information, art, amusement parks, brothels, etc.[70]

The quoted text touches upon a number of stereotypes and on the belief in
a Jewish conspiracy. Jews are referred to alternately as Jews, Zionists and
Freemasons. In the passages, Christians ('crusaders' or 'jealous Christians')
and communists are mentioned in one breath, but only in the case of the
Jews do we extensively read about their will to and potential for power. Here,
we touch upon the stereotypical reproach that Jews strategically employ
the entertainment industry to stupefy the innocent and the ignorant and
to rock them to sleep. Bouyeri would also refer to this topos in his writings.

The 'discovery' of *Upbringing* led to a legal investigation which also
involved *The Road of the Muslim* (1964) by Abu Bakr Al Jazairi and the collection of fatwas by the medieval scholar Ibn Taymiyyah, *Fatwas of Muslim
Women*.[71] The latter two books were, for instance, for sale at the El Tawheed
Mosque in West Amsterdam, which was known as Salafist and frequented
by Mohammed Bouyeri and his childhood friend Samir Azzouz (b. 1986).[72]
In the previous year, the CIDI antisemitism monitor had found an English
edition of the *Protocols* on the shelves of the American Book Center on the
Spui in Amsterdam. The book was removed without much publicity.[73] Now
the case of Muslim literature was turned into an affair.

Upbringing belongs to the genre of translated classics and simple educational booklets that were distributed via shops or the internet.[74] *The Road
of the Muslim* was available in normal bookstores and several libraries.
Consequently, J.J. Witkam (b. 1945), curator at the Leiden University Library
and collector of Arabic antisemitic literature, reacted rather laconically
to the find: 'You could have found these booklets ten years ago also. It is

70 Copies of the pages from the books were consulted as part of the dossier of the CIDI .
71 P.C. Velleman, district court to R.M. Naftaniel, CIDI, 7 April 2005.
72 The documentation on which this chapter is largely based originates from the Piranha trial
where Azzouz was tried. I thank Roel Meijer.
73 'Antisemitisch pamflet even weg', *Trouw* 17 April 2003.
74 For Abdallah Nasih 'Alwan, *see* Gebert and Matussek, '"Selbst wenn sie unser Land verlassen
würde…", 85.

a genre of which there are thousands of books in Arabic. They are based on commandments in the Quran and on tradition. Banning them would be idiotic.' The last statement, put into legal wording, would eventually be the verdict of the judge. With a single exception: *Upbringing*. Curator Witkam's nuanced remark was understandable, but not entirely justified because the find of *Upbringing* did in fact point out a novelty. It indicated that there was a market for Dutch versions of these established booklets. The original Algerian handbook *The Road of the Muslim [Minhaj al-muslim]* by Abu Bakr Al Jazairi is from 1964; the copy in the mosque was a Dutch translation.[75] The fact that the book only appeared in Dutch in 1998-2000 (in three volumes), indicates that it catered to a new niche in the book market and fitted in with the rise of a new reading public. This also applies to *The Upbringing of Children in Islam* from 2004. The publications may, for instance, be connected to the above-mentioned increasing religious zeal from the 1990s onwards, to the growing wish to be able to read didactic texts in Dutch or maybe even to the increased need for didactic literature. In the latter case, this might indicate a more textual approach to faith transmission than before.

After 'extensive research' the District Attorney established that neither the *Fatwas of Muslim Women* nor *The Road of the Muslim* contained 'illegal passages': 'Although some passages may be perceived as insulting in themselves, they should be considered within a certain context. This concerns passages that are known as familiar expressions of a religious conviction, which cancels their illegal (i.e. insulting) character.' If one were to make these passages punishable, 'one should consequently also see the Quran as punishable'.[76] The Council for the Prosecution did find some passages in *Upbringing* punishable and held the publisher responsible. However, it would not pursue with the prosecution if all copies would be removed or stripped of the illegal passages.[77]

75   Date of the original edition: press release Contactorgaan Moslims en Overheid (CMO), 23 April 2004; Based on several newspaper articles and on the explanation accompanying the letter of the district attorney, P.C. Velleman, district court to R.M. Naftaniel, CIDI, 7 April 2005. The book quotations: CIDI documentation.

76   *Ibid.* In *De weg van de moslim,* this concerned homophobia.

77   One year after the district attorney's conclusion and two years after the commotion over the three books, the antisemitism monitor stated that *The Upbringing* was still for sale, with the words 'Jew', 'Jewish' and 'Jews' covered with correction fluid. This proved to be an insufficient guarantee for illegibility. Also, even with these three words obliterated, the antisemitic message of the passages remained perfectly understandable.

There are several versions of the Jewish conspiracy. The banker Baron Rothschild, the philosopher and economist Karl Marx, the biologist Charles Darwin and the psychiatrist Sigmund Freud are assumed to have played their part in a devilish, secular, financial, mental and sexual brainwash. The *Protocols* and other conspiracy fantasies are characterised by the Jewish disdain for non-Jews, the Jewish invention of the concept of 'antisemitism' to mask their plans, Jewish control over the mass media and their employment of stupefying means to spread corruption, lust and atheism.[78] We find these ideas both in the more ancient secular forms as well as in the Muslim forms of conspiracism.

A modern version is the 'Zio-American' conspiracy. In the same way that, during the Interbellum, the First World War provided the evidence of the *Protocols'* accuracy, the Six-Day War constituted the ultimate proof that the Jews had already started to implement their world-encompassing plan.[79] 35 Years later, 9/11 became the target of conspiracy theories. The 9/11 hoax is the idea that the plane attacks were staged to frame the Muslims as the perpetrators. On the internet, a plethora of clues are circulating to prove the correctness of this statement. For example, that on 9/11, all Jews who worked at the WTC supposedly took a day off. Bouyeri also subscribed to this in itself not Islamist statement. His earliest antisemitic statement seems to have been his remark to a friend, that 'in my opinion, the Jews were behind the attack'. This is an idea he shared with the Egyptian-Dutch Mohammed Abdallah, who broadcast his ideas about Geert Wilders and the Zio-American conspiracy to the world via a website in 2010-2011 and during a demonstration on the International Day for the Elimination of Racial Discrimination in 2011.

I am not the first to doubt the events of 9/11 …. The whole story is a movie written by the amateur George Bush, the execution and production of which were realised by Zio-Americanism, at the expense of Islam and the Muslims. The spinning and weaving of this scenario had been prepared a considerable time beforehand, with great precision and exactitude, as were the places to be destroyed. The aim was to make Islam and the Muslims responsible for the execution of the scenario, to show them in a bad light.[80]

78 Svetlana Boym, 'Conspiracy Theories and Literary Ethics: Umberto Eco, Danilo Kiš and the Protocols of Zion', *Comparative Literature* 51, 2 (1999), 97-122.
79 Illustrative are the title and the introduction (by Faëz Ajjaz) to the 1967 edition of *Protocoles des Sages de Sion. La vérité sur Israël, ses plans, ses visées, révélée par un document israélite.*
80 The acquaintance with Mohammed Abdallah started at a demonstration on the International Day for the Elimination of Racial Discrimination in 2011. This was followed by an interview at his house, May 2011.

Popular with Abdallah and others is the fifty-part internet series *The Arrivals*. The series also enjoys a certain popularity among Dutch pupils in post-secondary education. *The Arrivals* is an eclectic mix of various Muslim ideas, American right-wing ideas, the work of the Briton David Icke (who talks about Illuminati and the 9/11 hoax), the American antisemitic conspiracy fantasists Milton William Cooper and Tex Marrs, scenes from *The Matrix*, the Kennedy Zapruder film, and the film study *Reel Bad Arabs* by Jack Shaheen. The makers, one of whom uses the pseudonym 'The final day', probably originate from Kuwait. Accompanied by bombastic music, the series explains how a sinister group of Freemasons, Illuminati (with Rothschild as instigator) and Zionists is preparing the coming of the Antichrist. One participant commented on Youtube: 'Assalamoe aleikoum, I discovered these films a couple of days ago, while I was looking for answers about the situation in Palestine, and why other countries do not take action.' The chat room participant warns that the films are made by Shiites,[81] but once you can ignore that and the devilish music, you acquire a valuable insight into the 'global conspiracy': 'A battle between good and evil. An elite of powerful families and politicians that tries to rule the rest of the world through mind control.' Another zealot on the internet especially likes the eschatology: the *dajjal* [the most important false prophet to take on the returned Christ or Mahdi] will come, 'and this is unavoidable, as our beloved prophet has stated (*ʒalayhi assalat wa salam*): furthermore, he (our prophet) has said that especially the Jews will control him. He only has one eye and will work miracles to get the people to believe in him: Get ready to be shocked, educated and inshallah get ready to wake up ....'

Islamic redemptive antisemitism

We have tried to show how Bouyeri's thinking was connected to a broadly felt sense of dissatisfaction among young Muslims in Dutch society around the turn of the century, and to all kinds of notions regarding the assumed central role of Jews in Dutch and global society. By linking the letter to Bouyeri's other writings, we are able to present a more accurate determination of his vision of the Jews. This 'vision' can be called a kind of Islamic redemptive antisemitism. The concept of 'redemptive antisemitism' is, of course, derived from historian Saul Friedländer, who coined it to

---

81   That is, the adherents of a branch of Islam that confess to different regulations and beliefs than Sunni Muslims.

characterise the Nazis' antisemitism.[82] It describes an apocalyptic vision of an all-encompassing global conflict in which representations of Jews are the key element. In such an end-time expectation, the world is on the eve of an ultimate 'life-or-death struggle'. Redemption can only be found by getting rid of the Jews and 'the Jew'. Hence, redemption is the liberation of mankind from the grasp of the Jews who are working on their own devilish pact to rule the world. The achievement of the state of redemption is closely linked with activism, or more precisely, with violence. On the road to Judgment Day, an act of violence has a cleansing effect and is an inevitable element of the eschatology.

The End-Time Expectation

The overarching principle in Bouyeri's oeuvre is his belief in the end time. Throughout history, an eternal battle is being fought out between Good and Evil. This battle culminated in the colonial age. The 'history' of the conflict between Islam and the Infidels 'goes back centuries, back to the time when the Jewish tribes united against the Prophet Mohammed ... it is part of the underlying conspiracy in an effort to destroy Islam in the world.' Subsequently, the crusades came. Jews were at the basis of this struggle because of their refusal of the prophet's message which some accepted 'with the mouth' while not acting accordingly. Although the struggle between the crusaders and the Muslims has been going on for centuries, it cannot be denied according to Bouyeri that in the twenty-first century, this confrontation has reached a culmination point, 'a decisive battle between tyranny and justice; between infidelity and faith'. This was also the position of the above-mentioned Egyptian thinker Sayyid Qutb (who was executed by order of President Gamal Abdel Nasser) as explained in 'This is the Road'.[83]

The struggle has two sides. On the one side, we see the pious Muslims, excluded from power, on the other side, the 'world rulers' under the direction of America and Zionist Israel. The Netherlands, which is 'under the direction of Zionist Jews' ('who are in power in the Netherlands'), is part of the coalition of evil. Islam contains the promise of an ideal world. A sceptic will counter that this world is nowhere visible: 'In Muslim countries, there is chaos, corruption and misery. What are you talking about?'[84] But we are

---

82 *See* chapter 1. Saul Friedländer, *Nazi-Duitsland en de joden. Deel 1: de jaren van vervolging 1933-1939* (Utrecht: Nieuw-Amsterdam, 1998), 95-139.

83 Peters, *De ideologische en religieuze ontwikkeling van Mohammed B*, 3.

84 No. 31: 'Grondwet van een fundamentalist'.

dealing here with an eschatology, which means that the realisation of the ideal world is still in the future. Between dreams and reality, a conflict is played out that will develop into the definitive battle (*harmajiddun*), 'World War III'. This will be followed by the end time. In the first phase, everything old (i.e. the lies the authorities have been telling us for years) will be obliterated, in the second phase, 'everything ... will be newly defined'. The 'blessed September the eleventh [2001]' was an important turning point in the battle between good and evil.

The end time is preceded by the coming of the Mahdi (who will fight the *dajjal*, the devil or the false prophet). The effort, as expounded in 'Open Letter to the Dutch People'[85], to realise a Muslim state in which only faithful Muslims live or, possibly, where the infidels have gained the special right to live according to their own (non-)beliefs by means of a special tax (*jizyah*) ('Our Prophet, the Messenger of our Rabb, has ordered us to kill you until you worship only Allah or you pay Jizyah'). In Bouyeri's new world, Jews and Christians become *dhimmis* under the banner of Islam, as was once the case during the Caliphate. A variation on this, states that the jizyah should be abolished so that 'not a single Jew or Christian' will be left 'on Earth'.[86]

Bouyeri's texts largely fit in with what has been discussed here. The eschatology was more explicit. An ideal upside-down world will present itself in which Jews and Christians take a subservient position. No longer will the 'arrogant Jews' and Christians rule, but the true Muslims will take power. When 'Zionists and Crusaders' are mentioned ('the covenant of Zionists and Crusaders' regularly returns[87]), these terms can mostly be replaced by 'Jews and Christians'. Apart from this model for an ideal reality, it is striking that in the model of contemporary reality, Jews and Christians are not equally disqualified. Whereas Christians are mentioned as a category, Jews are featured as the 'Jewish-Zionist cabal'.[88] Jews constitute a group of individuals who collaborate to realise their global plan. This makes the role of the Jews more important and dangerous than that of the Christians.

Judaism is Evil and the Jews are behind all Evil

The Talmud features several times in Bouyeri's letter. However, he was not inspired by the actual texts, only by what is available about them on

---

85 No. 48: 'Nederland.com'('Open brief aan het Nederlandse volk').
86 *Ibid.* and mentioned in *Truly, Allah's Victory is Near*, translated by a friend of Bouyeri.
87 Based on Osama bin Laden, *Declaration of War to the Americans*.
88 No. 31: 'Grondwet'.

the internet[89], using a bad translation published on islamawakening.com. Michael A. Hoffman and Alan R. Critchley's *The Truth about the Talmud* (2002) supplies the foolishness on 'Judaism' that Bouyeri went on to use in his writings. Here we find that Jews do not consider goyim as human, that they are allowed to steal from them, that they are superior to them and may kill them according to their wish. Since Jews are not looking for a bad press, they attribute the texts as figments of 'Anti-Semites'. Luckily, a certain [unnamed] 'Hebrew University Professor has confirmed the hatred and racism contained in the Talmud.' These kinds of texts legitimise 'the mass killings of Palestinian [sic] citizens'.

The identification of the Jews with Evil also refers to their social role. In the texts, we recognise the aforementioned series of stereotypical associations of Jews with conspiracy by means of stupefaction, entertainment or other instruments of soft power and money.

The idea that the Jews soothe the goyim 'in a deep sleep' also belongs to the association of Jews with entertainment and mass media ('the Satanic media'). In the introduction to a text by Sayyid Qutb, Bouyeri states that 'the mob' seems to be 'hypnotised or stunned by the large media offensive'.[90] Democracy is also seen as a sop (a 'democratic fake-lollypop') and an attractive detour (the Netherlands as 'one giant democratic Pleasure Ground' is 'camouflage ... for the abattoir') and the greatest idol ('Hubal') of this age. The unsuspicious Muslim is enticed to drown in 'his own lusts'. The Jews are responsible for the democratic system and, moreover, supply their own entertainment. So, in this chain of associations, a characterisation such as 'democratic vampires' is fitting, as it typifies Jews not only as greedy, but also as bloodthirsty. In 'Open Letter to the Dutch People', Bouyeri talks of

89   For centuries, the Talmud has been an obvious target of suppression by the church. From the sixteenth century a new phenomenon occurred: quotes were picked – or made up – to show the malignant impact of Judaism. Jews are allowed to lie to non-Jews, to cheat and even kill (for ritual purposes). In later centuries, the duties and privileges taken from the Talmud were attributed to Jews as character traits. Key became the idea that the mysterious books contain something to discover. The hypocrisy of Judaism now was finally revealed! The volume *Entdecktes Judenthum* by Johan Andreas Eisenmenger appeared in 1711. In 1871, this book was picked up and expanded in *Der Talmudjude* by the Catholic priest August Rohling. The Talmud Jew was turned even more into an embodied stereotype. In 1890, a journal entitled *De Talmudjood* was sold in the south of the Netherlands (*see* Preface). The idea culminated in the Nazi propaganda and has not disappeared. *See* Joel Berger, 'Zweites Bild; "In der Synagoge".' In: Julius H. Schoeps and Joachim Schlör (eds.), *Antisemitismus. Vorurteile und mythen* (München, Zürich: Piper, 1995), 67-73 and Ronald Grosz, 'Der Talmud im Feuer der Jahrhunderte.' In: Jüdisches Museum der Stadt Wien (ed.), *Die Macht der Bilder. Antisemitische Vorurteilen und Mythen* (Wien: Picus, 1995), 111-116.
90   No. 28: 'Dit is de weg.doc'.

'democratic pillagers', thus bringing political and economic exploitation under a single denominator. Capitalism, politics and the entertainment industry are three equal institutions in the hands of the 'money vampires' and the 'democratic vampires' who, with their 'amusement policy', try to lead us astray and to maintain inequality in the world: 'The democratic system is nothing but a system that aims to enslave people to themselves, in order for a few bloodsuckers to capitalise and to subject these people to their will'.[91] In the name of democracy (but in reality 'democratic slavery'), global inequality is maintained.

Resentment and a sense of belonging

Mohammed Bouyeri acted like he did in an atmosphere of neo-nationalism, 'integration fatigue' and the growing popularity of a global collective Muslim orthodoxy. Soon after Bouyeri's arrest, others were arrested on suspicion of planning religiously motivated violence. The 'Hofstad Group' became the moniker for the network the authorities thought to have tracked down and with which Bouyeri was assumed to have been in contact.[92] Although in some aspects he had acted as a 'lone wolf', Bouyeri's statements were in line with those of the other arrested and convicted persons with similar Muslim backgrounds. His peers also framed the social, cultural and religious conflict in an anti-Jewish discourse. As for so many, for Bouyeri's friend, Samir Azzouz, who had travelled to Chechnya as a young jihadist, the anti-Jewish orientation was connected to Israel, but a more direct religious reference can also be gleaned from his biography (by Arjan Erkel who himself was imprisoned for almost two years in Dagestan): 'The judgment of Allah as regards the Jews [stories about many prophets, including those about the prophet Moses] is very clear to Samir. Allah gave them all they could desire, but they were ungrateful and therefore they have forfeited the right to the promised land of Israel.'[93] In 2011, after six years in prison, Nouriddin El Fahtni (b. 1982) looked back on his youth: 'In puberty, you are zealous, enthusiast ... you see things in black and white. Everything is fierce, simple and clear-cut. I said things like 'The Jews are the cause of

91   No. 27: 'De Ware Moslim groot.pdf'.

92   Jaco Alberts c.s., 'De wereld van Mohammed B.', NRC Handelsblad, 9 July 2005; Petter Nesser, The slaying of the Dutch filmmaker. Religiously motivated violence or Islamist terrorism in the name of global jihad? FFI report. Norwegian Defence Research Establishment, 2005; Albert Benschop, Kroniek van een aangekondigde politieke moord. Jihad in Nederland (www.sociosite.org.).

93   Arjan Erkel, Samir (Amsterdam: Balans, 2007), 42.

everything.[94] In his autobiography, Yehya Kaddouri, who had been arrested even before 2 November 2004 (i.e. the day of the murder of Van Gogh) on suspicion of planning an attack with a can labelled 'Jodenkoeken' (literally Jew Cookies, a regular brand in the Netherlands) filled with explosives, was most explicit about the 'Jewish war' that was his objective. Kaddouri 'hates' Jews. Not only Israelis are 'Jews', also other Dutch representatives of power: Jews are 'evil'. In prison, wardens angled for his opinion on Van Gogh's death: 'To me, they were bloody Jews, so I thought, What was I gonna tell them?'[95]

In France, on 19 March 2012, the 23-year-old Mohammed Merah committed an antisemitic attack on a Jewish school in Toulouse. Back in 1995, the 24-year-old Khalid Kelkal had committed an attack on a Jewish school in Marseille. The historian Robert S. Leiken calls this latter attack the first European home-grown Islamist (and antisemitic) attack.[96] There are several similarities between these offenders: both are young Muslim males with a North African background and previous convictions, who radicalise and possibly join the frontlines of the jihad. Both attacks are preceded by a break in the parent-child relationship, and often a break with their siblings. The offenders have attempted to 'approach the nation' – for instance as a social worker – but that ends in a feeling of rejection. Above all, they have an antisemitic world view which enables them to project their sense of exclusion onto the Jews. As far as we can tell, Mehdi Nemmouche, the perpetrator of the assault on the Jewish Museum in Brussels (on 24 May 2014), also fits this profile in several aspects.

The well-known, proverbially 'controversial' Swiss philosopher Tariq Ramadan (b. 1962) – who was Visiting Professor at Rotterdam Erasmus University between 2007 and 2009 – commented on the assault by Merah, arguing that his act should be understood as the result of the 'deformed image' of the Maghreb youth as 'the Other' in contemporary France. Merah's provocation closed the circle: he had lost himself in this deformed and degrading image to become irrevocably 'the Other'. The French had stripped Merah of his French identity which made him the victim 'of a social order that marginalises him and millions of others instead of recognising them as citizens with equal rights and opportunities'.[97]

94 Jutta Chorus and Ahmet Olgun, 'Op de thee bij de jongens van de Hofstadgroep', *NRC Handelsblad*, 10-11 September 2011.

95 Yehya Kaddouri, *Lach met de duivel*, 18-19, 67-68, 'bloody Jews': 64, 78.

96 Leiken, *Europe's Angry Muslims*.

97 Tariq Ramadan: 'Il faudra que la France comprenne que Mohamed Merah était un enfant de la France, non de l'Algérie', *Le Monde des religions.fr.*, 28 March 2012.

What Ramadan does not mention is how the subordinated and marginalised 'Other' finds a solution to his dissatisfaction and exclusion by committing an act of violence against another 'Other', who, in his imagination, is more powerful and responsible for his discomfort and impotence. So it appears that in the first years of the twenty-first century antisemitism and the figure of 'the Jew' as *der Dritte* has once again become the ideal weapon to express resentment and create a sense of belonging in the Netherlands as well as elsewhere.

16   Reading Anne Frank

Confronting Antisemitism in Turkish Communities

Annemarike Stremmelaar

In February 2013, a documentary shown on Dutch television triggered a prolonged debate on how to deal with antisemitism. The programme featured a Turkish-Dutch youngster stating loud and clear that he hated Jews. The statements made in the programme were a shock for many. 'This most unadulterated antisemitism ever seen on Dutch television', as one commentator called it,[1] became the subject of commentary and parliamentary questions and provoked international reactions as fragments of the footage went global on YouTube.[2]

The explicit anti-Jewish statements shown in the documentary *Onbevoegd Gezag* [Unauthorised Authority] were made in reaction to a reading from the Diary of Anne Frank, organised by a youth worker who lived in the city of Arnhem. He had started reading the diary with local pupils as a panacea against the antisemitism he had encountered in his environment. But in this case reading about the persecution of the Jews did not prevent youngsters from expressing their antipathy of Jews. On the contrary, the youngster who expressed his hatred of Jews said that by killing them Hitler had done a good thing. For some people this made the statements even more incomprehensible. If knowledge of the Holocaust did not help against antisemitism, what would?

An explanation for the lack of effect of Holocaust education on these youngsters was found in their background. The four boys featured in the documentary all came from Turkish families and were, presumably, Muslim. As newcomers – or rather children of newcomers in Dutch society – migrants were, apparently, not fully aware of the historical experience of the Holocaust and would, therefore, cross the boundaries of what was acceptable to say about it.[3] There was some surprise that the youngsters had

1   Max Pam, 'Ik haat Joden', *Het Parool*, 2 March 2013.

2   The first to do so were Elma Drayer, 'Het taboe op jodenhaat is verdwenen', *Trouw*, 28 februari 2013, and Max Pam, 'Ik haat Joden', *Het Parool*, 2 March 2013.

3   Maurits Berger, 'Meer dan antisemitisme: een botsing van trauma's', *NRC Handelsblad*, 5 August 2014, and the reaction by Remco Ensel, 'Als het antisemitisme is, moet je het ook zo noemen', *NRC Handelsblad*, 13 August 2014. *See also* IOT, 'Quickscan antisemitisme in de Turkse gemeenschap in Nederland', 2013.

a Turkish, and not Moroccan, background. Antisemitic incidents since the beginning of the Second Intifada in autumn 2000 had led to an identification of antisemitism with Muslims, migrants and Moroccans.[4] So far, the Turkish-Dutch had not been associated with antisemitism in the same way that Moroccan-Dutch youngsters had.

This raised the question whether the antisemitism which now manifested itself among Turkish-Dutch youth was a new phenomenon or, alternatively, if it had been there all along without being recognised or challenged. Some commentators found the reactions of those who had expressed their shock naive. Those who were surprised to find antisemitism in Turkish circles in the Netherlands had, to say the least, a short memory. There had been several cases of antisemitism in Turkish-Dutch circles from the 1980s through the 2000s. Most cases had been inspired by political Islam. Adherents of the Turkish mosque organisation Milli Görüş, in particular, had occasionally propagated antisemitic statements from 1998 onwards.[5] This had contributed to the identification of these cases as related to Islamic religiosity and one particular organisation, rather than to Turkish identity.Since the 1990s, but even more so after 9/11, public debate and policy regarding Turkish-Dutch and Moroccan-Dutch citizens had become very much focused on Islam.[6] This aspect was never far away in the reactions to the incident in Arnhem, but it was first of all framed as a Turkish case. Turkish-Dutch spokespeople rose to the challenge: representatives of an umbrella organisation of Turkish associations in the Netherlands, the IOT (*Inspraak Orgaan Turken*), denounced the antisemitic statements and announced an investigation into the dissemination of antisemitic attitudes within the Turkish-Dutch community.[7] Minister of Social Affairs and Employment Lodewijk Asscher (b. 1974) responded by announcing talks with the IOT about the steps to be taken. Thus both went along with identifying antisemitism as an issue of concern for Turkish communities and organisations in the Netherlands.[8]

The Moroccan-Dutch parliamentarian Ahmed Marcouch (b. 1969) argued that this was 'the first time that antisemitic sentiments in that community had manifested themselves so openly' and went as far as to suggest that Turks could learn a lot from Moroccan organisations in this respect, because the latter were already familiar with the prevalence of antisemitic ideas

4   As shown by Remco Ensel. See *Haatspraak*, chapters 1 and 14.
5   *See* chapter 10.
6   *See* chapter 10, and examples in IOT, 'Quickscan antisemitisme'.
7   Letter sent by the IOT to Minister Lodewijk Asscher, dated 11 March 2013.
8   Letter by the Minister of Social Affairs to parliament, dated 13 March 2013, Parliamentary Papers 30950 nr. 49.

among their constituencies and knew how to deal with them.[9] But not only the manifestations of antisemitism within Turkish-Dutch circles had been almost forgotten; the same was true for the efforts to counter these. From 2000 onwards, representatives of Islamic organisations had taken initiatives to establish contacts between Jews and Muslims during upsurges of antisemitism. This was especially true for Milli Görüş, so indeed there was some experience in confronting antisemitism in Turkish-Dutch circles. This chapter examines manifestations of antisemitism within Turkish-Dutch circles in the twenty-first century and the ways in which Dutch society and its Turkish-Dutch representatives dealt with them.

The discovery of antisemitism within Milli Görüş

In 1998, antisemitism within Milli Görüş in the Netherlands was publicly discussed for the first time. In June 1998, the Dutch public became acquainted with Milli Görüş when it organised a European meeting for its members in the Amsterdam ArenA, the stadium of football club Ajax.[10] The yearly mass gatherings Milli Görüş organised were themselves a clear sign of its political character, as they served as platforms to stage a collective identity of loyalty to the Turkish-Muslim nation and to political Islam.

What drew attention on 20 June 1998 was not only the 40,000 people who had come from all over the Netherlands, Belgium and Germany, but also the enthusiasm with which they hailed Necmettin Erbakan (1926-2011), chairman of the Welfare Party, banned by the Turkish Constitutional Court in February of that same year, as a 'saviour' and 'hero'. Dutch news media featured debates on the question of how desirable it was that an organisation which had been banned in Turkey be active in the Netherlands. In Germany, Milli Görüş was closely watched by the German security service (Bundesamt für Verfassungsschütz, BfV), which had branded the organisation 'extremist' and a 'wolf in sheep's clothing'. The leading figure of Milli Görüş' headquarters in Germany, Mehmet Sabri Erbakan (b. 1967), a nephew of Necmettin Erbakan, tried to dismiss prejudices by emphasising that

---

9   Danielle Pinedo and Sheila Kamerman, 'De minister is niet meer verrast als jongeren Hitler prijzen', *NRC Handelsblad,* 15 March 2013. *See* on Marcouch, Remco Ensel, *Haatspraak. Antisemitisme – een 21ᵉ-eeuwse geschiedenis* (Amsterdam: Amsterdam University Press, 2014), 262-263, and chapters 15 and 16.

10   Levent Tezcan, 'Inszenierungen kollektiver Identität. Artikulationen des politischen Islam-beobachtet auf den Massenversammlungen der türkisch-islamistischen Gruppe Milli Görüs', *Soziale Welt* 53, 3 (2002), 303-324.

Milli Görüş followers first of all wanted to be fully accepted as European citizens of Muslim faith.[11]

Milli Görüş officials in the Netherlands customarily contended that their organisation had no official ties with Erbakan and his political party in Turkey, both because of its history of bans and because of a Turkish law which forbade political parties to set up branches abroad. Such reassurances paled in the face of the massive shows of allegiance to Erbakan and his party.[12] The Dutch national security service (BVD) monitored Milli Görüş as the largest Islamic organisation in the Netherlands which propagated what at the time was called 'fundamentalism', political Islam. Although BVD's assessment of Milli Görüş varied over the years, on the whole it regarded Milli Görüş as moderate.[13] The suspicions harboured towards Milli Görüş were that it was fundamentalist and anti-democratic. Antisemitism was only one aspect of this, which hardly interested anyone except Jewish organisations. The first organisation to raise this issue was CIDI (Centre for Information and Documentation on Israel), which protects the interests of Israel and Jews in the Netherlands. It criticised the stadium's decision to rent the venue to Milli Görüş. According to CIDI, Milli Görüş was an extremist and extreme-rightist organisation, which, moreover, was known for its antisemitism.

Although there were no antisemitic statements during the event, which CIDI admitted, it pointed to antisemitic passages in the *Milli Gazete*, the organisation's mouthpiece in Turkey, which was also available in Germany and

11   ANP, 'Milli Gorus wil af van vooroordelen jegens islam', 4 June 1998; J. van Klinken and J. Visscher, 'Omstreden moslims. Turks-orthodoxe islamaanhangers in Nederland schuwen antisemitisme niet', *Reformatorisch Dagblad*, 25 July 1998. After the event in Amsterdam, representatives of the Amsterdam branch of Milli Görüş even suggested they could bring about a change in the relations between the German Milli Görüş organisation and the German authorities. For Erbakan and Milli Görüş *see also* chapter 10.

12   ANP, 'Ex-voorzitter Welvaartspartij Turkije in Arena als god onthaald', 20 June 1998.

13   See the annual reports of the BVD; *De Politieke Islam in Nederland*. Leidschendam: Ministerie van Binnenlandse Zaken, Binnenlandse Veiligheidsdienst, 1998. In May 1998, the growing interest in the phenomenon of political Islam led to the publication of a report which reviewed the Islamic organisations in the Netherlands. The BVD's attention focused on radical tendencies within Muslim organisations including Milli Görüş. For BVD's policies towards Islam *see* B.A. de Graaf, 'Religion bites: Religieuze orthodoxie op de nationale veiligheidsagenda', *Tijdschrift voor Religie, Recht en Beleid* 2 (2012), 62-80. Nico Landman, author of an academic study of Islamic organisations in the Netherlands (*Van mat tot minaret: De institutionalisering van de islam in Nederland*. Amsterdam: VU uitgeverij, 1992) rejected the term 'fundamentalist' because of its associations with violence and intolerance, which he neither saw nor expected within Milli Görüş. Instead, he preferred the term 'Islamist' to describe political Islam. *See* ANP, 'Milli Gorus: Turks moslimfundamentalisme in Nederland?', 11 January 1995.

the Netherlands. The newspaper had called Jews 'bloodsucking vampires' and Western countries 'tools of the secret Jewish world conspiracy'. Journalists followed CIDI and also made an issue of Milli Görüş' antisemitism using the same quotations. In defence, Mehmet Sabri Erbakan, from the organisation's headquarters in Cologne, argued that his uncle did not know the difference between antisemitism and opposition against Israel because Turkey had not lived through the Holocaust. But CIDI director Ronny Naftaniel refused to believe that Erbakan, who had studied in Germany, did not know what antisemitism was.[14]

Erbakan was certainly well-versed in the political use of antisemitic stereotypes; he used them when he first announced his own political party in 1969 and still did one year before his death in 2011. Zionism and Jews were pivotal in Erbakan's ideology as 'villain images'; they represented all the wickedness which stood in the way of the just social order and the national heritage Milli Görüş claimed to be defending: the evil forces of capitalism and communism, the United States and Europe, Christianity and the Church and the pro-Western and secularist state ideology of Kemalism. In short, the ideologies and lifestyles of the West. This enabled him to build on a Turkish nationalist and conservative tradition which branded the Jews as representatives of modernity and enemies of the nation, religion and the established social and moral order.[15]

When confronted with accusations of antisemitism in the summer of 1998, Haci Karacaer (b. 1962), Milli Görüş' spokesman in the Netherlands, emphatically denied there was any question of antisemitism, or fundamentalism or anti-Westernism for that matter. 'I get so tired,' he complained. 'We supposedly want to bring the state under Muslim rule. That is nonsense. We are inherently suspected because we are Muslims.' In the years to come, Karacaer became less defensive and began to recognise the prevalence of

14   'CIDI: 'Milli Görüş bijeenkomst misplaatst', www.cidi.nl; Harry van Wijnen, 'Wat niet hoort wat niet deert', NRC Handelsblad, 30 June 1998; Van Klinken and Visscher, 'Omstreden moslims'. See on the newspaper Esther Debus, Die islamisch-rechtlichen Auskünfte der Millî Gazete im Rahmen des 'Fetwa-Wesen' der Türkischen Republik (Berlin: Klaus Schwarz, 1984).

15   Little scholarly attention has been paid to antisemitism as an element of Turkish Islamist ideology. The exceptions are Jacob M. Landau, 'Muslim Turkish Attitudes towards Jews, Zionism and Israel', Die Welt des Islams 28, 1/4 (1988), 291-300, and numerous articles by Rifat Bali, 'The Image of the Jew in the rhetoric of political islam in Turkey', Cahiers d'Etudes sur la Méditerranée Orientale et le monde Turco-Iranien, 28 (1999), 2-10. Jacob M. Landau, Radical Politics in Modern Turkey (Leiden: Brill, 1974), 191; Rıfat Bali, Musa'nın evlatları, Cumhuriyet'in yurttaşları (Istanbul: İletişim, 2001), 281; Rıfat Bali, Cumhuriyet Yıllarında Türkiye Yahudileri: Devlet'in Örnek Yurttaşları, 1950-2003 (Istanbul: Kitabevi, 2009), 179. Werner Schiffauer, Nach dem Islamismus. Eine Ethnographie der Islamischen Gemeinschaft Milli Görüs (Berlin: Suhrkamp, 2010), 70-71.

antisemitic views within Milli Görüş. But the organisation he represented also transformed.

As the cultural anthropologist Werner Schiffauer (b. 1951) has shown, the development of Milli Görüş in Europe was always closely tied to the party's fortunes in Turkey. Milli Görüş emerged in Europe in the 1970s when Turkish migrants supporting Erbakan and his party started founding associations in the hope that Erbakan would develop Turkey in such a way that they would be able to return home.[16] In Europe, Milli Görüş evolved around mosques as its adherents strove to establish their own meeting places for prayer and congregation. It thus was both a political association and a religious community.[17] After subsequent parties founded by Erbakan had been closed down, the *Refah Partisi* (Welfare Party), established in 1983, managed to remain legal for more than fifteen years acquiring substantial electoral support. It reached the 10% election threshold in the 1991 national elections and the elections of 1995 made it the largest party in parliament, with Erbakan as Prime Minister. Supporters in Europe were enthused by this success. In the mid-1990s, Milli Görüş started to produce a new generation of officials who were well-versed in Dutch and moved easily in Dutch society. They offered the outside world an alternative to the first-generation migrants who had been dominating mosque boards and often spoke poor Dutch. These young activists responded to the increasing interest in Islam

16   Liza Mügge, *Beyond Dutch Borders: Transnational Politics among Colonial Migrants, Guest Workers and the Second Generation* (Amsterdam: Amsterdam University Press, 2010), 149-180; Schiffauer, *Nach dem Islamismus*, 76. On the history of Milli Görüş in the Netherlands *see* Landman, *Van mat tot minaret*, 117-127 and Thijl Sunier, *Islam in beweging. Turkse jongeren en islamitische organisaties* (Amsterdam: Het Spinhuis, 1996).

17   In Turkey these religious networks were illegal and evolved as oppositional movements aiming each in their own way to defend Islamic identity against forced secularisation. For an overview of Turkish religious networks *see* Landman, *Van mat tot minaret*; Gamze Avci, 'Religion, transnationalism and Turks in Europe', *Turkish Studies* 6, 2 (2005), 201-213; Ahmet Yükleyen and Gökçe Yurdakul, 'Islamic activism and immigrant integration: Turkish organizations in Germany', *Immigrants & Minorities* 29, 01 (2011), 64-85. In Turkey all mosques were subordinate to the government through a State Office for Religious Affairs (*Diyanet*), but in Europe it did not have this monopoly. In the 1980s, Diyanet became active in Europe in order to combat the leftist and Islamist organisations which were active in Turkish migrant communities. From then onwards, this Turkish public institution administrated, financed and staffed the majority of the Turkish mosques in the Netherlands. After Diyanet, Milli Görüş was the largest religious Turkish organisation, with about 35 mosques versus 150 mosques for Diyanet. On Diyanet *see* Jak den Exter, *Diyanet: een reis door de keuken van de officiële Turkse islam* (Beverwijk: Centrum Buitenlanders Peregrinus, 1990); Thijl Sunier et al., *Diyanet. The Turkish Directorate for Religious Affairs in a changing environment* (VU University, Utrecht University, 2011).

among the general public which became more aware of the presence of Muslims and Islam within Dutch society.[18]

The enthusiasm of the new Milli Görüş cadre was soon tempered by events in Turkey. Within two years of the electoral victory in December 1995, Erbakan had been pushed out of power by the military; in January 1998, the Welfare Party was closed down by the Constitutional Court in Turkey for violating the separation of religion and state, and Erbakan and several leading politicians were barred from active politics for five years. These developments resulted in a change of mood among Milli Görüş' supporters in Europe. The younger generation shifted their focus from Turkey to an activist outlook which was both more local and more internationalist. From a stable base in Europe, the communities should engage themselves for the global Muslim community. The new generation said farewell to the dream of an Islamic state and focused on living a Muslim life in Europe.[19]

Antisemitism had been part and parcel of Milli Görüş' ideology as formulated by Erbakan, especially in the form of antisemitic conspiracy theories. These had changed only slightly through the years; instead of Israel, Europe and the Catholic Church, the main evil force became an alleged American-Zionist alliance.[20] Little is known about the ways in which antisemitic stereotypes have been transmitted among Milli Görüş' supporters in Europe. In the 1980s and 1990s, preachers in associated mosques presented the idea of a worldwide conspiracy of the United States, the European Union and Zionism against Islam.[21] Werner Schiffauer has argued that the need for antisemitic explanations attributing all negative events to a single evil force diminished as a new generation stopped seeing Islam and the West as mutually exclusive entities.[22] This seems to hold true for the Netherlands as well. The change was not effectuated in one go, of course, resulting in contrasting and sometimes conflicting views on Jews and antisemitism. The divergent positions of two officials may serve as illustration. The first

---

18   See on this chapters 7 and 10; Will Tinnemans, *Een gouden armband: Een geschiedenis van Mediterrane immigranten in Nederland (1945-1994)* (Utrecht: Nederlands Centrum Buitenlanders, 1994), 355-359; Sunier, *Islam in beweging*, 129, 241, 242, 243; Rob Witte, *'Al eeuwenlang een gastvrij volk': Racistisch geweld en overheidsreacties in Nederland (1950-2009)* (Amsterdam: Aksant, 2010), 99-108.

19   Schiffauer, *Nach dem Islamismus*, 114; Günter Seufert, 'Die Millî Görüş Bewegung (AMGT/IGMG): Zwischen Integration und Isolation.' In: Günter Seufert and Jacques Waardenburg (eds.), *Turkish Islam and Europe: Europe and Christianity as reflected in Turkish Muslim discourse and Turkish Muslim life in the diaspora* (Istanbul, Stuttgart: Steiner, 1999), 295-322: 298-299.

20   See chapter 15 on conspiracy thinking.

21   Landman, *Van mat tot minaret*, 125-127.

22   Schiffauer, *Nach dem Islamismus*, 112.

of these, Haci Karacaer, would dominate the Dutch media as spokesman for Islam for almost a decade. The second, Zeynel Abidin Kılıç, addressed a Turkish-speaking audience, as editor-in-chief of the Turkish-language magazine *Doğuş* published in Rotterdam.

Two faces

Karacaer arrived from the Anatolian interior to the Netherlands in 1982, when he was twenty, following his father. He soon started working and held various jobs, including for the municipality of Amsterdam and a large bank. In 1994 he first manifested himself in public as spokesman for the Milli Görüş association Aya Sofya. As the association was striving to establish a mosque complex and social centre in the West of Amsterdam, it ran into a prolonged conflict with the local administration over the buildings plans. Through the negotiations and administrative and legal procedures he became well-versed in representing Milli Görüş in the Netherlands, and also learned to appreciate the workings of the Dutch state.[23]

In 1999 Karacaer became director of the northern of two federations which united Milli Görüş' associations in the Netherlands.[24] Under Karacaer's leadership, his federation became a popular cooperation partner. Dressing and speaking Dutch 'with nonchalance typical for Amsterdam' he became quite popular with the media who described him as someone 'expressing the Islamic sound Dutch politicians are waiting for'.[25] In the years after 2001, Karacaer's organisation was partner in projects in the field of gender relations, forced marriages, honour killings, organ donation, and

23   Haci Karacaer, 'Keulen locuta, causa finita', *NRC Handelsblad,* 19 May 2006. Werner Schiffauer has pointed out the effect of following 'the path through the institutions' on the perceptions of majority society for Milli Görüş in Germany, *Nach dem Islamismus,* 24. On Karacaer *see* Jurgen Maas and Annemarike Stremmelaar, 'Ik heb een missie.' Interview met Haci Karacaer.' In: Maurits van den Boogert and Jan Jonker Roelants (eds.), *De Nederlands-Turkse betrekkingen. Portretten van een vierhonderdjarige geschiedenis* (Hilversum: Verloren, 2012), 106-111.

24   The split between Milli Görüş Noord-Nederland in the north and the *Nederlandse Islamitische Federatie* (NIF) in the south was effected in 1997, due to practical reasons as well as ideological differences.

25   Yoram Stein, 'Als moslim hier gelukkig leven', *Trouw,* 28 September 2001. Between 1998 and 2002 Milli Görüş was the single most quoted Islamic and Turkish organisation in the national paper *de Volkskrant* as was Karacaer as its spokesman. Jessica ter Wal, *Moslim in Nederland. De publieke discussie over de islam in Nederland: een analyse van artikelen in de Volkskrant 1998-2002.* SCP-werkdocument 106d (The Hague: SCP, 2004), 14.

prevention of radicalisation. Such initiatives were conspicuously absent within the southern Milli Görüş federation.

Also on the issue of antisemitism there were marked differences in attitude among and within the various Milli Görüş associations, which came to light from the beginning of the Second Intifada in autumn 2000. Like elsewhere, people in the Netherlands were following the course of events, when on 29 September 2000, Palestinians started protesting in Israel and the occupied territories. As the Israeli state responded with military action resulting in violent clashes and numerous casualties, reports and images of the conflict filled the newspaper columns and the television screens. In several European countries people showed their solidarity with the Palestinians through demonstrations and other means. In the Netherlands several demonstrations against Israel were held through October and some of these resulted in verbal or physical violence against Jewish institutions and individuals.[26]

During a pro-Palestinian demonstration in The Hague on 6 October some of the 400 protesters were waving Israeli flags with swastikas. A week later, on 14 October, young people demonstrating against Israel in Amsterdam shouted, 'Hamas, Hamas, all Jews to the gas.' That day visitors of a synagogue in Amsterdam were harassed; later that month several other synagogues were molested.[27] Observers were struck not only by the anti-Jewish sentiments which spoke from such actions, but also the involvement of protesters identified as 'Moroccan' or 'Muslim'. Commentators debated whether Dutch society was witnessing a new kind of antisemitism, transmitted from the Middle East to the Netherlands via migrants and their descendants.[28] Soon, leaders of several Muslim organisations, including Karacaer, issued a joint

---

26 *See* for this demonstration also chapter 14 and Evelien Gans, '"They have forgotten to gas you." Post-1945 Antisemitism in the Netherlands.', In: Philomena Essed and Isabele Hoving (eds.), *Dutch Racism* (Amsterdam/New York: Rodopi, 2014), 71-100.

27 'Synagogen worden extra beschermd', *NRC Handelsblad*, 21 October 2000; 'Herdenking afgelast na incidenten bij synagogen', *Het Parool*, 24 October 2000; Arjan Paans, 'Nederlandse joden en moslims zeggen salaam en shalom', *Algemeen Dagblad*, 28 October 2000; Diederik van Hoogstraten, 'Verplaatste Intifada', *Elsevier*, 28 October 2000.

28 The anti-Israeli stance taken by citizens with family ties to North Africa and the Middle East was a phenomenon observed and debated in other West European countries as well. *See, e.g.,* Helga Embacher, 'Neuer Antisemitismus in Europa – ein historischer Vergleich.' In: Moshe Zuckerman (ed.), *Antisemitismus – Antizionismus – Israelkritik. Tel Aviver Jahrbuch für deutsche Geschichte* XXXIII, (Göttingen: Wallstein Verlag, 2005), 50-69.

declaration to distance themselves from any act of aggression or violence against Jews and to call for peace and calm.[29]

At the same time, in Rotterdam the Milli Görüş activist called Zeynel Abidin Kılıç went down a different path. As editor-in-chief of the local Turkish-language magazine *Doğuş* he expressed his desire to be 'a stone hitting the Jew in Palestine on the head'.[30] Rather than remaining silent, he wished to 'strike back' in response to the ongoing stream of gruesome reports and images from the Middle East. Characteristically, Kılıç's first opinion piece about the Intifada was written on the occasion of the death of the twelve-year-old Muhammad al-Durrah, who was killed on 30 September 2000 when caught in crossfire between Israeli and Palestinian forces. France 2 footage of the boy and his father hiding together went around the world in the following weeks and months, turning al-Durrah into a lasting symbol of Palestinian victimhood.[31]

Troubled by these images, which were printed adjoined to the text, Kılıç expressed all his feelings of anger, humiliation and dejection. Not intending to upset people by calling Jews murderers, as he wrote, he would refrain from satisfying his urge to scold and curse the Jews, and only mention a few points which were common knowledge about the Jews. What then followed was an enumeration of classic anti-Jewish stereotypes he would *not* use, culminating in the conclusion that the Jews were the single cause of all trouble in the world. Too bad, he added, that the people who were upset by antisemitism would not feel the same anxiety over the murder of a Palestinian boy.

The author pretended to refrain from using antisemitic language, or 'Jew-hatred', as he explained, but at the same time hostility against Jews was dripping from the lines. For example, in his warning that the occupied lands would become 'a bloody grave' for the Jews. When a reader accused him of antisemitism, Kılıç' indignantly retorted in the next issue of the journal that 'one cannot call Jews Jews!'. He explained he was 'enemy not

29 ANP, 'Moslimorganisaties afkerig van geweld tegen joden', 26 October 2000; 'Nederlandse joden en moslims samen tegen geweld', *Leeuwarder Courant*, 28 October 2000.

30 Zeynel Abidin Kılıç, 'Utanıyorum', *Doğuş*, November 2000, 16. The journal was published from 2000 onwards by a foundation affiliated to the southern Milli Görüş Federation NIF. It was distributed free of charge in the area of Rotterdam up to 2008. It appeared every one or two months; in the beginning it had a circulation of 180,000 which dropped to about 15,000 in 2004 when it stopped to be free.

31 On al-Durrah as a symbol of Palestinian victimhood *see* Remco Ensel, 'Singing about the death of Muhammad al-Durrah and the emotional mobilization for protest', *International Journal of Media and Cultural Politics* 10, 1 (2014), 21-38. *See also* chapter 14.

of the Jew, but of Zionism'. Being averse to Zionism was self-evident for him as it was a 'racist understanding turning the Middle East into a sea of blood'.[32] Kılıç, who distanced himself from classic antisemitic stereotypes of the Jew as representative of modern political ideologies and disturber of social peace and morality, embraced stereotypes linking Zionism and Jews to racism and cruelty.

The latter theme had been brought into criticism of Israel since the 1950s, but from the end of 2000 onwards was played out with more vigour than ever before.[33] In *Doğuş*, military actions in Israel were described with hyperboles such as 'genocide', 'mass murder', 'atrocity' or 'brutality', and Israel itself was called vampire and bloodsucker. Such terms were illustrated with pictures of dead children and of Sharon adorned with vampire teeth. Sharon, called 'the butcher of Lebanon', acted as the counterpart of the iconic victim Muhammad al-Durrah: he had turned Palestine into a sea of blood and said he would kill every child in Palestine.[34] In this way, medieval Christian anti-Jewish stereotypes proved to be alive and kicking in a contemporary, Turkish-Dutch, context. Israeli soldiers were accused of killing women, children and elderly; they would 'burn houses, riddle babies with bullets, crush cars with tanks, kill even animals, turn streets into pools of blood, torture youngsters, perpetrate genocide, burn mosques and churches'.[35]

From victims to perpetrators

During his editorship for *Doğuş*, which started in 1999, Kılıç repeatedly used antisemitic stereotypes in his writings. As far as we know, none of this antisemitism provoked any noteworthy response. Once, a reader criticised the way in which socialism had been described as an instrument in the hands of the 'Zionist monster', but the criticism was in defence of socialism not Zionism. Within the Ministry of Justice there was some displeasure when a portrait of Minister Rita Verdonk, criticised for her harsh stance towards migrants and Muslims, had been printed along with the image of a shouting Hitler.

32 Zeynel Abidin Kılıç, 'İnanç ve umudunuzu tüketmeyin!', *Doğuş*, December 2000, 3.
33 *See* chapter 14 in this volume.
34 Helga Embacher and Margit Reiter, 'Israel-Kritik und (neuer) Antisemitismus seit der Zweiten Intifada in Deutschland und Großbritannien im Vergleich.' In: Monika Schwarz-Friesel, Evyatar Friesel and Jehuda Reinharz (eds.), *Aktueller Antisemitismus – ein Phänomen der Mitte* (Berlin, New York: De Gruyter, 2010), 187-212. *Doğuş*, May 2002, 16, 19, 32, June 2002, 3.
35 *See* on this anti-Zionist tradition chapter 7.

ANNEMARIKE STREMMELAAR

Only once, legal repercussions loomed for *Doğuş* and its editor-in-chief, when an article on Anne Frank triggered the Anne Frank House in Amsterdam into action.[36] In an opinion piece, Kılıç had cast doubt on the authenticity of the Diary of Anne Frank, saying that 'the most important parts of the diary, those which smothered the whole world in tears', had been written with a ballpoint. The ballpoint, however, was only discovered after the war. This was a classic argument of Holocaust deniers, notably Robert Faurisson and Roger Garaudy, which can easily be disproved. It is based on a distortion of evidence of ballpoint ink on two separate sheets of paper mentioned in a German forensic report dating from 1980.[37] Kılıç argued that the diary was a 'lie of the Zionists', and a 'project to exonerate the Jews'. Without using the words Israel or Palestine, the author referenced Israel's occupation of Palestinian lands writing: 'Hit, kill, demolish, burn, occupy, murder, exterminate! .... And be innocent with one or two teardrops shed .... There are still many idiots who will listen to this humbug ....' He put the blame on the rest of the world for turning a blind eye on 'the crimes, massacres, expulsions and deaths perpetrated today [which] will put those days in the shade'.

In the article, Kılıç denied the genocidal character of the Holocaust, the Nazi attempt to annihilate the Jewish people; he had earlier written that he did not think that 'the Jews had faced an atrocity in the alleged manner'.[38] Kılıç needed to deny Jewish victimhood, as Jews could not be innocent victims because they founded the state of Israel and as such were perpetrators. This was a clear case of Holocaust denial and post-Holocaust antisemitism, as analysed by Deborah Lipstadt and Klaus Holz.[39] What moved the Anne Frank House into action, however, was the specific claim that the diary was a forgery. It was ready to press charges against the journal: in 1998, the Anne Frank House had won a case against the Belgian Holocaust denier Siegfried Verbeke (b. 1941), who had sent around a publication which challenged the authenticity of the diary. The legal verdict set a precedent in banning the distribution of such publications. Taking legal steps, however, seemed a disproportionate measure when no other means had been tried; moreover, reporting the publication to the police and seeking media

36 *Doğuş*, February 2005.
37 *The Diary of Anne Frank: The revised critical edition* (New York: Doubleday, 2003), 168, 170.
38 *Doğuş*, April 2000.
39 Deborah E. Lipstadt, *Denying the Holocaust: The Growing Assault on Truth and Memory* (New York, Toronto: Free Press, Maxwell Macmillan Canada, Maxwell Macmillan International, 1993); Klaus Holz, *Die Gegenwart des Antisemitismus. Islamistische, demokratische und antizionistische Judenfeindschaft* (Hamburg: Hamburger Edition, 2005).

attention might have 'undesired consequences'. After obtaining legal advice, the Anne Frank House decided to give the journal a chance to rectify. It consulted Haci Karacaer asking him to intervene and sent the journal a letter requesting a rectification. The addressees accepted this request and in August 2005 a small rectification appeared in *Doğuş* stating that there was no doubt that the diary was authentic and there had been no intention to hurt anyone. This way, the case was nipped in the bud.[40]

The Holocaust had been brought into criticism of Israel since the 1950s, but from the end of 2000 onwards the theme was played out with more vigour than ever before.[41] This was also not the first case of Holocaust denial Karacaer was confronted with. In November 2004, the chairman of a Milli Görüş youth club said in an interview it was not possible that 6 million people died during the Holocaust. When this became a news item, the young man claimed he had not said that, but given the timing, right after the murder of the film director and columnist Theo van Gogh by a radical Islamist, Karacaer saw no other option than discharging the young man from his function. He was disappointed as his association had been an active participant in commemorations of the Second World War since 1998. 'It was a slap in our face. All the work of five years all at once seems to have been for nothing.'[42]

Between two fires

In the eventful years after 2000 Karacaer would consistently engage in organising mutual Muslim-Jewish exchanges and meetings, at a time when the public debate on Islam and Muslims was polarised and the atmosphere surrounding these themes was extremely tense and negative. In addition to the terrorist attacks of 9/11, there were the American invasions in Afghanistan (2001) and Iraq (2003), and extensive military operations in Israel/Palestine (2002). In the Netherlands, there was a fierce public debate on Islam, with the public appearances of Ayaan Hirsi Ali, an outspoken critic

40 My account of the incident is based on the archives of the Anne Frank House in Amsterdam and personal communication with Haci Karacaer and former staff members of the Anne Frank House (Peter Rodriguez and Willem Wagenaar).

41 *See* chapter 14.

42 Coen Verbraak, "'Het wordt tijd om terug te slaan'", *Vrij Nederland*, 27 November 2004. *See* on the commemorations Stremmelaar, 'Sharing Stories. A history of multicultural war remembrance in the Netherlands', to be published in: Philipp Gassert, Alan E. Steinweis and Jacob Eder (eds.), *Holocaust Memory in a Globalizing World* (Göttingen: Wallstein, 2015) (under review).

of Islam, and the murder of film director and columnist Theo van Gogh in November 2004, as described in earlier chapters.

All these events fed into conspiracy theories explaining why Islam was under attack. A perusal of *Doğuş* in these years shows that the military interventions in the Middle East were perceived as proof of Jewish-Israeli control over the US; the alleged aim was the destruction of Islam and the oppression and massacre of innocent people in Palestine and other Muslim countries.[43] The attacks of 9/11, which Karacaer denounced in a press statement, led to an intensification of the ongoing debate on Islam and to acts of aggression towards Muslims, as well as Jews. Karacaer had heard conspiracy theories about the attacks, with people around him saying, 'Bin Laden couldn't have done it, America is behind it, Israel, the Mossad.'[44]

In November 2001, the intifada seemed to have been imported to Amsterdam, as a rabbi commented; a female Jewish singing group had been hurled with stones by Moroccan-Dutch youngsters when leaving the synagogue in the West of Amsterdam.[45] The impact of conspiracy theories was again to be noticed a few weeks before the American invasion in Iraq. Karacaer then feared for disturbances as Milli Görüş' supporters turned out to be susceptible to the idea that the invasion was an American-Jewish war against Islam.[46] He himself explained a few years later that he had come to the Netherlands as 'a real Super-Turk', suspecting plots everywhere, but had lost his mistrust of the West. Now he tried to explain that 'the world was more complex than that' and got easily irritated by conspiracy theories.[47]

Over the years, Karacaer would recognise the prevalence of antisemitic views within Milli Görüş. In December 2001, asked whether antisemitism was preached in his mosques, Karacaer denied that that was the case, but announced that he would check the book collection for antisemitic literature. Three years later, after the murder on Van Gogh in November 2004, he admitted: 'I am not going to paint a rosy picture: anti-Jewish sentiments are widespread in Muslim circles. Unfortunately, also within Milli Görüş.[48]

---

43 According to one article, the script for 9/11 had been written by the Americans; the result was a bad film called *Enduring Freedom*, but as with all films it would soon end and the bad guy would die: *Doğuş*, October 2001; *Doğuş*, November 2000, April, May, June, October, November 2001, May, June, July-August, September, November, December 2002, January 2003.

44 Yoram Stein, 'Als moslim hier gelukkig leven', *Trouw*, 28 September 2001.

45 *Ibid.*; Yoram Stein, 'Gezellig praten over jodenhaat en moslimangst', *Trouw*, 7 December 2001; Janny Groen, 'Intifada-taferelen in Amsterdams stadsbeeld', *de Volkskrant*, December 12, 2001.

46 'Vlam kan in pan slaan', *NRC Handelsblad*, 19 February 2003; *Trouw*, 15 January 2005.

47 Margalith Kleijwegt, 'Super-Turk wil de politiek in', *Vrij Nederland*, 18 March 2006.

48 Coen Verbraak, '"Het wordt tijd om terug te slaan"', *Vrij Nederland*, 27 November 2004.

The hindrances encountered in removing antisemitic content from Milli Görüş' premises illustrate the difficulties Karacaer and his fellow officials faced. They were able to get rid of antisemitic books that were on sale, but were still obliged to purchase Milli Görüş' journals, such as the *Milli Gazete*. These generated income for the headquarters in Germany; a ban would 'antagonise' the headquarters and be 'counterproductive' within the community.[49] The Milli Görüş executives in the European headquarters in Kerpen, near Cologne, were unhappy with the progressive statements made independently in Amsterdam: 'We were not allowed to associate with Jews and Christians, nor with homosexuals', said vice-chairman Kabaktepe.[50]

Karacaer was also the target of criticism from local members and officials who regretted or rejected his public statements on controversial subjects such as homosexuality.[51] The relation with Jews was one matter of dispute. 'A handful of people in my community say: I do not like Jews. They found a planned visit by a synagogue not a good idea.'[52] Karacaer himself commented on his hazardous position after the murder of Van Gogh in 2004. As he said, 'Young people often find me too progressive, too soft towards Dutch people and too critical of Muslims.'[53] Still, he stayed on until March 2006, when resistance to his policies had become insurmountable among the board members of his federation. It is no coincidence that one of the reproaches made occasioning his resignation was his positive attitude towards Jews.[54]

Karacaer's attitude towards the issue of antisemitism stood out when compared to that of his fellow Milli Görüş officials, as an incident occurring in June 2005 corroborates. That month the Dutch current affairs programme NOVA reported about an antisemitic Iranian-made soap series, 'Zahra's blue eyes', being sold in mosques, among them Karacaer's Aya Sofya Mosque. The soap series contained several anti-Jewish stereotypes; its main plot concerned an Israeli military commander ordering a Palestinian girl's eyes to be transplanted to his blind son Theodor, thus adapting the myth of

---

49   Koert van der Velde and Yoram Stein, 'Allemaal typisch Turkse retoriek', *Trouw*, 2 January 2002; Yoram Stein, 'Gezellig praten over jodenhaat en moslimangst'; Lodewijk Dros, 'AIVD wist van coup Milli Görüs', *Trouw*, 6 June 2007.
50   *Ibid.*
51   Flip Lindo, *Activiteiten en doelstellingen van Nederlandse organisaties gelieerd aan Milli Görüş.* Report (FMG: Institute for Migration & Ethnic Studies, 2008), 5.
52   *Trouw*, 15 January 2005.
53   The model sermon proposed by Karacaer for the Friday after the murder resulted in one mosque stepping out of the federation; Verbraak, '"Het wordt tijd om terug te slaan"'.
54   Interview with Karacaer, 2011.

ritual murder to the present time.[55] A Turkish-speaking journalist showed
in the programme how the series could be obtained in three mosques, in
the bookshop attached: in addition to Karacaer's mosque, the Iskenderpaşa
mosque in Rotterdam, belonging to the southern branch of Milli Görüş, and
a Diyanet Mosque in The Hague. Karacaer declared the film had not been
on sale in his mosque, but had been ordered by the undercover journalist
especially for the programme.[56] The series was first shown on the Iranian
television in December 2004 and afterwards available in Turkish in Turkey
as well as in the Netherlands and Germany.[57] The television programme resulted in parliamentary questions and a judicial investigation; the Minister
for Immigration and Integration, Rita Verdonk, called Islamic organisations
to task on the issue and CIDI asked for the film to be banned.[58]

Whereas Karacaer clearly distanced himself from the film, his colleague
in Rotterdam and surroundings declared the film was violent and emotional
but not antisemitic; it only contained 'artistic critique of the practices of the
Israeli armed forces against the Palestinian people'.[59] Newspapers reported
that Karacaer had banned the film from his mosques, whereas the southern
branch Milli Görüş refused to do so. In reality the difference was less clear-
cut. Karacaer wrote that he had not banned the film but found the film
unsuitable for screening in an educational setting. Board members of the
Rotterdam mosque said the same, although the official spokesman of the
southern federation declared it would not ban the film until there was a
judicial verdict that the film was antisemitic and thus illegal. During the
judicial investigation the film was no longer to be found in any of the three
mosques, so that its unlawful nature could not be established and legal
procedure came to an end.[60]

Karacaer's position was all the more difficult as authorities, politicians,
journalists and critics kept on scrutinising the organisation. Although the
Dutch security service BVD regarded Milli Görüş as moderate, suspicions
remained. Criticism came, among others, from citizens with a Turkish

55 The programme, NOVA, was broadcast on 18 June 2005 with Evelien Gans commenting on
three elements in the film: criticism of Israel, anti-Zionism and antisemitism.
56 Haci Karacaer, 'Prem verliest realiteit uit het oog', Het Parool, 24 June 2005.
57 Daniel Bax and Michael Kiefer, 'Sarahs blaue Augen', die Tageszeitung, 2 May 2006.
58 Letter by Minister Verdonk to parliament, 10 July 2006; Parliamentary papers, 2005-2006,
29 754, no. 75 2.
59 Press statement issued by the NIF, www.nifonline.nl, 28 June 2005.
60 Answers to questions from Rotterdam's council member J.C. Siemons, 2 August 2005; 'College
informeerde naar omstreden "Zahra's ogen",' Rotterdams Dagblad, 5 August 2005. Answer by
the Minister of Justice Piet Hein Donner to parliamentary questions, Appendix to Parliamentary
papers 2004-2005 no. 1439.

background and an awareness of the political cleavages within Turkey.[61] Again and again Karacaer and other Milli Görüş officials were questioned as to their stance towards the party in Turkey. The question raised was whether Milli Görüş' activities represented its 'true nature' or were only a façade to hide its 'real plans' of establishing an Islamic state.[62]

Critics in the Netherlands pointed to the German security agency (*Bundesambt für Verfassungsschutz*, BfV), which regarded Milli Görüş as a threat to the German constitution. That institution, the domestic security agency for the protection of constitutional order, interpreted diverging statements about, for example, antisemitism as proof that Milli Görüş was hiding its true convictions behind soft talk. Press statements in which Milli Görüş officials in Germany rejected antisemitism or accepted invitations for Jewish-Muslim encounters were dismissed as window dressing, whereas antisemitic utterances from the Turkish sister party, Erbakan's Saadet Party, were taken as an indication for anti-constitutional activities of the organisation in Germany. The suspicion of a double-faced strategy was based on the hesitation with which ties to the Turkish sister party were admitted. However, as Werner Schiffauer has convincingly argued, diverging opinions could also be taken as a sign of heterogeneity within the movement.[63] In his analysis these differences were a necessary corollary of the ideological flexibility and pragmatism with which Milli Görüş appealed to broader segments of the population; he has termed this ideological shade 'popular Islamism'.[64]

Such differences in outlook between more liberal and more conservative segments have been observed in both academic studies and official reports

61   Notable critics of Turkish background were Mehmet Ülger, Rafet Kabdan, and Lokman Uzel. Flip Lindo, *Heilige wijsheid in Amsterdam: Ayasofia, stadsdeel De Baarsjes en de strijd om het Riva-terrein* (Amsterdam: Het Spinhuis, 1999), 128-130; Van Klinken and Visscher, 'Omstreden moslims. ANP, 'Milli Gorus: Turks moslimfundamentalisme in Nederland?', 11 January 1995; Maurits Schmidt, 'De Schaduw van de Islam', *Het Parool*, 18 February 1995; Bas Blokker, '"Wij hebben de zaak onder controle"; Uzeyir Kabaktepe, voorman van Milli Gorus, stelt Nederland gerust', *NRC Handelsblad*, 5 September 1998; Mehmet Ülger, 'Soldaten van Milli Gorus tegen scheiding kerk en staat', *Trouw*, 22 January 2002; Yoram Stein, 'De titanenklus van Karacaer', *Trouw*, 24 January 2002.

62   The change of the board resulted in speculations about a take-over of Milli Görüş Noord-Nederland by the German headquarters. These, together with reports about financial transgressions, resulted in a study requested by the Dutch parliament about the ideological tendencies within the Amsterdam branch. Lindo, *Activiteiten en doelstellingen*, 46-47.

63   Werner Schiffauer, 'Verfassungsschutz und islamische Gemeinden.' In: Uwe E. Kemmesies (ed.) *Terrorismus und Extremismus – der Zukunft auf der Spur: Beiträge zur Entwicklungsdynamik von Terrorismus und Extremismus – Möglichkeiten und Grenzen einer prognostischen Empirie* (München: Luchterhand, 2006), 237-254: 241; Lindo, 'Activiteiten en doelstellingen', 39-45.

64   Schiffauer, *Nach dem Islamismus*, 136-149.

on Milli Görüş.[65] The study of antisemitism within Milli Görüş and the manner in which its representatives dealt with the issue confirms this interpretation. It also contradicts a rather simplistic view of Milli Görüş as a top-down run sect in which all members shared the same basic ideas about the world and the place of Jews in it.

Reading the Diary of Anne Frank

Despite the incidents and reports of antisemitism within Milli Görüş and other Turkish communities in the years before 2013, the display of anti-semitism in the documentary *Onbevoegd Gezag* [Unauthorised Authority] came as a surprise or even shock to many. The shock effect was, to some extent, due to the fact that the entire five-minute conversation, in plain Dutch, could be heard and seen on the screen. The footage which provoked so much discussion was part of a documentary series made by the public broadcasting organisation NTR about 'unauthorised authorities': individuals who know how to command respect in local settings where traditional authorities have lost their grip.[66] One such 'authority' was Mehmet Şahin (b. 1981), a PhD student in his early thirties who did voluntary work in 't Broek, a neighbourhood in Arnhem with mostly Turkish-Dutch inhabitants. Şahin himself was born and raised in Turkey and had migrated to the Netherlands at the age of sixteen. He had studied pharmacy and social geography and was doing a PhD when the documentary was broadcast. In his spare time, he assisted local families with administrative procedures and filling out forms, and helped local youngsters, many of Turkish descent, with their education.

Şahin was the main character in the documentary which was screened on Dutch television on Sunday afternoon, 24 February 2013. The broadcasting organisation presented the neighbourhood 't Broek as a deprived area. In 2007 the neighbourhood had been designated as one of forty problem areas targeted for special attention. In the following years the govern-ment was investing substantially in these neighbourhoods, many of them affected by high unemployment, poverty, public nuisance and crime. In 't Broek these investments did not lead to substantial improvements; in particular, residents were distrustful of authorities.[67] As Şahin explained

---

65 *See, e.g.*, the publications of Landman, Avci, and Lindo referred to above.

66 Janneke de Weerdt (direction), *NTR, Onbevoegd gezag: Kennis is macht* (documentary, 25 min, 2013).

67 *See* Kees Leijdelmeijer et al., 'Outcomemonitor Wijkenaanpak 2015', Leefbaarometer.nl.

in the documentary, this distrust was the reason he did not want to accept any subsidies for his work. The documentary portrayed Şahin during his voluntary work. One of Şahin's activities was reading the Diary of Anne Frank with youngsters as a way of tackling the antisemitic attitudes he had witnessed around him. When still in Turkey his cousin, a left-wing activist, had told him about Anne Frank and he had become fascinated with her story. In the Netherlands, he had read the diary in Dutch when he was learning the language, and had subsequently started reading it with pupils as part of his tutoring activities.[68]

The last minutes of the documentary show him at home discussing the Diary of Anne Frank with four youngsters, in the presence of his neighbours, a young couple. After reading one page aloud, Şahin urges the boys to comment. Then one of them starts by saying he was pleased with what Hitler had done. From there on, the conversation takes off, with Şahin, supported by the husband of the couple, trying to reason with the boy, who maintains that he hates Jews and that it was a good thing that Hitler had killed them. As Şahin argues that his view on Jews and the Holocaust is wrong, the other three boys back up their friend. The discussion finally results in Şahin accepting a fifty-euro bet that he won't be able to change their minds.

The footage for the documentary was shot in autumn, and the programme was aired for the first time on 24 February 2013. As commotion about the programme was setting off, the programme's editor-in-chief, Frans Jennekens, explained that he and his colleagues had discussed whether to show the footage. Astonishingly, in hindsight, the possible repercussions for Şahin or the four boys had not been a major consideration; for Jennekens, the most pressing argument against showing the footage had been that it contained 'pure discrimination' and that it would be shown on daytime TV. For that reason, a warning had been inserted immediately before the fragment announcing 'vehement antisemitic statements'. Jennekens had decided in favour of showing the fragment because he wanted the issue of antisemitism among Muslims – a taboo, as he said – to be out in the open. In his opinion, antisemitic sentiments were abundant and deeply rooted among many Muslims in deprived neighbourhoods. This had been known for ages, but politicians and social workers were too soft on those neighbourhoods to do anything about it. Jennekens chastised officials and the Anne Frank House in Amsterdam in particular for not commenting on

68 Interview with Mehmet Şahin, 2014.

the case. 'They did not want to get their fingers burnt because they found it too sensitive a subject.'[69]

Local, national and international repercussions

When the programme was announced, Şahin was introduced as someone who managed to achieve more than all social workers and professional agencies combined, because the locals did not see him as being part of the establishment, which they greatly distrusted. As it turned out, this distrust was turned against Şahin himself when his interview exposed four youngsters to the public.

The day after the broadcast, the fragment in which the four boys talk about Jews was put on the Dutch blog *GeenStijl*, which describes itself as 'biased, unfounded and needlessly offensive'. The footage was put online under the heading 'Shocking images. GingerTurk wants new Shoah' – the boy in question was red-haired.[70] Soon the news spread and the boys were targeted on the issue at school and in their neighbourhood. The boys and their parents were obviously upset and directed their displeasure against Şahin and his family. They blamed him for the broadcast, which had put the boys in a bad light.

In TV and radio interviews the following days Şahin tried to ease tensions by emphasising that the boys were still young and uninformed and, moreover, were repeating what other Dutch youngsters were saying. But on Saturday nobody showed up at his tutoring sessions. The neighbourhood sided with the boys and against Şahin. He was called names, intimidated and received death threats by email. That weekend, one week after the broadcast, it became known that the local Anti-Discrimination Office had reported the incident to the Public Prosecutor, which would examine whether the boys were to be prosecuted. This only added to the tensions in the neighbourhood. At which point the mayor urged Şahin to leave his house for his own safety. Together with his wife and two sons he stayed in a hotel for five days.

---

69 'Joods op zondag', Joodse Omroep, 3 March 2013. Spokesperson Maatje Mostart of the Anne Frank House claimed that the reason not to cooperate was that 'there was not enough space allotted to us to do justice to our analysis of this issue and our educational approach on this topic'. Almost two weeks later director Frank Leopold appeared on television together with Şahin. Frank Kromer, 'Overheid aan zet', *NIW*, 15 March 2013.

70 'Schokkende beelden. Gingerturk wil nieuwe Shoah', www.geenstijl.nl, 25 February 2013.

In the first ten days after the broadcast there had been some publicity, but media attention took off when on Friday 8 March it became known that Şahin had 'gone into hiding', as it was put. It would be an exaggeration to say that the Dutch media had kept the incident quiet, as the Israeli publicist Manfred Gerstenfeld claimed, but interest had indeed been limited.[71] Gerstenfeld's claim that it took the public action of the Simon Wiesenthal Center in Los Angeles for the broadcast to spark national attention is unfounded, however. The Center, a global NGO, devoted to combating antisemitism, made the headlines in the national paper *De Telegraaf* on Saturday 9 March 2015 when it sent an open letter to Dutch Prime Minister Mark Rutte (b. 1967) and demanded an investigation into antisemitic attitudes and measures against these attitudes. But the commotion peaked as it became known that the tutor had become the victim of intimidation. It was precisely this element in the affair that sparked national attention, not as Gerstenfeld argued, the action taken by the Simon Wiesenthal Center. A few days later, the Minister of Social Affairs Lodewijk Asscher declared that he found the antisemitic statements shocking and that he would visit Şahin.[72]

From Friday onwards local politicians had been asking the mayor of Arnhem to intervene and prevent further escalation. Meanwhile, the mayor was still steering clear of the affair declaring that she had advised Şahin 'to temporarily stay somewhere else to create peace for himself and his surroundings', and that she would not issue any statements while the case was being investigated. After the weekend, when city councillors raised questions in a council meeting, she finally announced that she would visit the neighbourhood at some point.[73]

Social democratic parliamentarian Ahmed Marcouch tried to mobilise support for Şahin in his neighbourhood, but admitted that 'tensions were tangible'. Marcouch himself had experienced similar social dynamics as he had taken a stand against antisemitism in Moroccan-Dutch communities. He commented that people were holding each other hostage, because the

71   Manfred Gerstenfeld, 'Onderzoek naar Jodenhaat in Nederland hard nodig', *Reformatorisch Dagblad,* 14 March 2013; idem, 'Dutch press tries to hide anti-Semitic incident', *Jerusalem Post,* 17 March 2013. For Gerstenfeld *see* chapter 5 and Epilogue.
72   The incident and footage of it had been published on several English-language websites devoted to issues of Judaism and antisemitism. *Arutz Sheva* (Channel Seven), an Israeli media network: Dutch Youngsters on TV: 'Too Bad Not All Jews Were Killed', *Arutz Sheva,* 5 March 2013; Aaron Kalman, '"Hitler should have killed all Jews", teens in Holland say', *The Times of Israel,* 7 March 2013.
73   Harry van der Ploeg, 'Krikke roept op tot les tegen antisemitisme', *De Gelderlander,* 12 March 2013.

Turkish-Dutch people who hated what had happened to Şahin were afraid
to express themselves.[74] His fellow party member Yasemin Cegerek, who
had a Turkish background, associated the resentment against Şahin with
anti-Kurdish sentiments among the local Turkish-Dutch population. 'The
atmosphere in the neighbourhood has been tense for months. Kurds, Alevis
and Turkish Christians feel threatened by nationalist Turks. Şahin is of
Kurdish descent'. In January, a local newspaper had reported about ethnic
tensions in the neighbourhood and questions had been asked in the city
council.[75]

Şahin had been on national television at least once before, to talk
about the repercussions of Turkish-Kurdish tensions in communities in
the Netherlands. On that occasion he had identified himself as Kurdish,
showing sympathy with the plight of the Kurds in Turkey and criticising a
Turkish organisation for its nationalist stance. If people had forgotten about
this, they were reminded in March 2013.[76] On several occasions Şahin had
criticised neighbours involved in local activities for being nationalist Turks.
Şahin's propensity to present himself as about the only educated member
of an otherwise ignorant and uneducated community had also been cause
for resentment.[77]

These political and social antagonisms all played a role in the hostility
against Şahin. But he was particularly blamed for having been instrumental
in putting the four boys in an unfavourable light on national television;
he had put 'vulnerable minors' on television without parental consent.
As minors, they were in his care, they were not only his pupils, but also in
his home; he should have guarded them even against themselves. Months
later, Şahin admitted that he had come to understand the parents. 'They
believed that I had only the best of intentions. Their sons were in the familiar
surroundings of my home during the recording. I blame myself that I have
not protected them.'

74 Janny Groen, 'Weinig steun bedreigde onderzoeker', *de Volkskrant*, 11 March 2013.
75 Ahmet Olgun and Guido de Vries, 'Koerdisch-Turks conflict smeult ook in Arnhem', *NRC Handelsblad*, 31 October 2007; 'Brand en bekladding moskee', *De Gelderlander*, 24 October 2011; 'Etnische spanningen in Arnhemse wijk 't Broek', *De Gelderlander*, 25 January 2013.
76 The programme was 'De halve maan', NTR, 28 October 2011; the organisation was the Turkish Youth Associations' Federation in the Netherlands (HTGF); for a reaction *see* www.gundem.be/tr/dunya/pkk-lilarin-ahlaksiz-suclamalari-hollanda-hukuku-karsisinda; reposted in March 2013 on the websites www.turkinfo.nl and http://habergelderland.com.
77 Hasan Bahara, '"Die Hitler, daar ben ik wel tevreden mee." Verstoten uit de Turkse ge-meenschap', *Groene Amsterdammer*, 4 September 2013; Son Haber, 'Arnhem tedirgin, Eroğlu tepkili (video)', 11 March 2013, www.sonhaber.nl/gundem/arnhem-tedirgin-eroglu-tepkili-video-h20236.html.

For many local residents it was difficult to conceive that Şahin had not foreseen the consequences of the broadcast. Rumour had it that the programme was a set-up; the boys had become victim of provocation and distortion. NTR editor Jennekens felt compelled to publicly defend the producers' integrity. Şahin was accused of using this opportunity to make a name for himself. A powerful exponent of this view was the chairman of the local Türkiyem Mosque, Veysel Eroglu, who even claimed that Şahin's move to another location because of threats was a 'filthy game' and that he needed psychological therapy.[78]

As opposition against Şahin was building up in the neighbourhood, he hardly received any public support from Turkish-Dutch organisations. A few individuals came to visit him privately. Two representatives of the umbrella organisation of Turkish associations in the Netherlands IOT visited Şahin at home. During this visit they received a call from Eroglu and decided to visit the Türkiyem Mosque as well. Chairman Eroglu was offended and aggrieved and gave them a hostile welcome. The two urged him to take a stand against the intimidations Şahin was a victim of. The next day, before Friday prayer, the imam called for calm and peace, but however that may be, Şahin was told by his father in law, who was in the mosque that Friday, not to come to the mosque for Friday prayer because his safety could not be guaranteed.[79] Months later, a local Turkish-Dutch politician admitted that the chairman should have called the statements unworthy of a Turk and Muslim. Nevertheless, he showed understanding for the chairman: 'One should find nuance in such a situation. I think that's what the chairman was trying to do. He needs to watch over his community.'[80]

A few Turkish and Muslim organisations issued statements about the case, distancing themselves from the boys' antisemitic statements. These statements were carefully worded, stressing that the incident did not reflect a Turkish or Muslim majority view of Jews. One statement blamed the media for stirring things up. There was no or scant mention of Şahin's plight. Obviously, Turkish officials shied away from siding with Şahin. Not a single politician or official of Turkish background was willing to join a TV debate

---

78 Son Haber, 'Arnhem tedirgin, Eroğlu tepkili (video)', 11 March 2013; Ali Bozdag, '"Ik denk dat Mehmet Sahin een psychologische behandeling nodig heeft",' *HaberGelderland*, 13 March 2013 (www.HaberGelderland.com); 'Bu kez de Arnhem'li Türkleri kışkırtıyorlar', Ufuk.nl, www.ufuk.nl/detay.asp?id=17957; Paul Bolwerk, '"Ophef over uitzending is afleidingsmanoeuvre," *De Gelderlander*, 15 March 2013.

79 Interviews with Şahin (2014) and Ahmet Azdural and Emre Ünver, director and chairman of the IOT, 2015.

80 Statements made during a radio broadcast on Radio 5, NTR, Dichtbij Nederland, 9 July 2013.

about the case.[81] Ali Özyürek, councillor for the local party Arnhems Belang criticised parliamentarian Marcouch for visiting the neighbourhood and calling upon local residents to support Şahin. 'What does the Labour Party want to achieve with such a visit?' According to Özyürek, the visit was only meant to win votes.[82]

Şahin felt isolated and abandoned by his neighbours, the authorities and politicians. The threats and insults stopped, but relations were not mended. People in his neighbourhood avoided and excluded him. He was hurt and paralysed after all the accusations and taunts. He saw the impact they had on his wife and two sons. It made life in the neighbourhood unbearable for him. Eventually, he decided to leave the neighbourhood where he had lived for years. This came at the price of having to say goodbye to all his cherished contacts: family, friends and neighbours. In 2015 he was still missing his old, conservative environment; for example he had not been able to go to the mosque for Friday prayers as there was no mosque in his new neighbourhood.[83]

Punish or educate?

The boys' antisemitic statements led to unanimous expressions of shock and rejection, but opinions differed on what course of action should be taken. What should be done with the four boys and what could be done to counter antisemitism? As the Public Prosecutor was investigating the case, people voiced their doubts as to the use of penalisation. Were the boys not also victims, if not of Şahin and the broadcasting company then of deprivation and discrimination, lack of education, the media and society at large? Had they not been punished enough? Would education not be a more effective tool?[84] The mayor of Arnhem, when asked what she was planning to do about the issue, answered that she wanted schools in Arnhem to actively fight discrimination, antisemitism and other hostilities. Unsurprisingly, some teachers and educators found this a rather easy way of putting the

81   NTR, 'De halve maan', Friday 8 March 2015.
82   'Racistische taal weerklinkt vaker', De Gelderlander, 12 March 2013.
83   Paul Bolwerk, 'Jeugdwerker ligt eruit in wijk', De Gelderlander, 12 March 2013; Janny Groen, '"Verketterd omdat ik de vinger op de zere plek heb gelegd",' de Volkskrant, 26 April 2013.
84   See, e.g., Dilan Yesilgöz, 'Alle vormen van discriminatie kennen één gemeenschappelijke deler', www.republiekallochtonië.nl, 5 March 2013.

responsibility elsewhere. Local teachers also said that they did not recognise the problem.[85]

When the discriminatory remarks made on television were reported to the Public Prosecutor, they had no choice than to investigate the case. Employees of the Anti-Discrimination Office in Arnhem had brought the case to the Prosecutor's attention, because the programme had been reported to them immediately after the broadcast. While some complainants thought that the programme contained hostility towards Jews, others found it hostile towards Turks or Muslims. After watching the fragment 'about thirty times', to see which statements were liable for punishment, the Anti-Discrimination Office forwarded the case to the Public Prosecutor.

It took the Prosecutor a few weeks to investigate the case and reach a decision. The outcome of their investigation was that one of the boys had voiced several antisemitic statements in breach of Article 137c of the Criminal Code. The Public Prosecutor argued that these comments were 'wholly unacceptable' and had caused a great deal of social unrest. Nevertheless, it decided to impose an educational sanction instead of putting the boys on trial, favouring a speedy settlement and bearing in mind that the boy was a minor, had apologised, and admitted to the police that his remarks were unacceptable. The other three boys had made no criminal statements and their cases were dropped.[86]

The tutor of the four youths, Şahin, was also heard as a suspect. People had filed complaints against him for two reasons: Şahin had elicited negative statements about Jews from the boys during the broadcast and a few weeks later he had insulted them during an argument on the street. There had been several emotional exchanges between the two sides, but Şahin had not formally filed a complaint with the police as 'he was alone against all the others'. The Prosecutor ruled that Şahin had not been involved in any criminal offence during the programme. However, he had committed an offence by insulting the boys and received a warning for this 'given everyone's responsibility to maintain peace in the neighbourhood'. This meant that if such an incident occurred again within the next year he would be prosecuted. The Public Prosecutor also stated that the police investigation had not revealed that punishable threats had been made against Şahin.[87]

---

85   'Turk of kaaskop hoor ik, nooit Jood', *De Gelderlander,* 13 March 2013.
86   Paul Anderson Toussaint, 'Ik haat Joden. Klaar', *Elsevier* 7 June 2014.
87   Press statement of the Public Prosecutor on www.om.nl/actueel/nieuwsberichten/@31708/onderzoek/.

The decision not to prosecute but to impose an educational sanction was incomprehensible for CIDI, the most outspoken and involved Jewish interest group in the case. Director Esther Voet was particularly annoyed that the Prosecutor had rapped Şahin on the knuckles. The day after the broadcast CIDI had announced that it would not report the case to the police in order not to complicate Şahin's position and activities.[88] But as the Public Prosecutor announced his decision to impose an educational sanction CIDI decided to start a legal procedure, after all, to force the Public Prosecutor to prosecute the boy. For Voet it was a matter of principle: 'We never go to court, but this is very serious. The attitude of the Public Prosecutor is one of papering over the cracks. The Prosecutor's decision is more harmful than the boy's statements. You get away with this while politics take it very seriously.' CIDI found 'some education' wholly insufficient and was afraid the case would set a precedent. Moreover, the boy would turn eighteen in two months.[89]

The legal procedure started by CIDI did not alter the course of events, and the Public Prosecutor confirmed that his decision was a 'tailored response directed at raising awareness' and 'preferable to a repressive response'. The boy had had a conversation with a rabbi and a youth worker about 'the background and the dangers of antisemitism and racism'; he had visited the Anne Frank House, where he attended a workshop and a presentation, and he went to Auschwitz. The officer of the Anti-Discrimination Office had pleaded to not bring the case to court and been involved in mediation between the Prosecutor and the boys. She argued that the boys had already suffered a lot in their environment. The boy who had made the punishable remarks, for example, had been suspended from school and lost his job.[90]

Other supporters of an educational sanction were rabbi Lody van de Kamp (b. 1948) and youth worker Said ben Sallem (b. 1971), who had teamed up in 2010. Rabbi van de Kamp had been the victim in an antisemitic incident in the district where Ben Sallem lived and worked. Together, they had been involved in Jewish-Moroccan dialogue in Amsterdam and activities for Moroccan-Dutch youngsters. Van de Kamp had become a vocal supporter of dialogue and education as a means to combat antisemitism. The Public Prosecutor had consulted Van de Kamp and Ben Sallem and asked them to help set up an educational programme for the boy. The envisaged end

88   A small activist Jewish organisation called FJN (*Federatief Joods Nederland*) announced it would complain with the police.

89   'CIDI eist vervolging Turkse jongen', *De Telegraaf,* 15 April 2013.

90   Anderson Toussaint, 'Ik haat Joden. Klaar.'

goal was the boy's social rehabilitation. The planned reappearance of the boy on television, to show the changes he had gone through, fell through because his family opposed it.[91]

Hating Jews, admiring Hitler

Only a few commentators tried to analyse the statements of the four boys. What do their statements represent? When you analyse the five-minute discussion, it turns out there is little in the boys' answers that is particularly, let alone exclusively, Turkish or Muslim. The conversation started off with the tutor asking who Anne Frank was and how she died, but soon one boy, the most adamant of the four, said, 'I am satisfied with what Hitler did with the Jews, to be honest.' When Şahin asked 'satisfied?' another boy said, 'Me too.' Then the first boy went on saying, 'What Hitler said about the Jews is that there will be one day when you will prove me right that I killed all the Jews. Yes, that day will come.' The youth worker and his neighbour tried to reason with the boys, objecting that even women, children and babies were killed by Hitler, and that there is a distinction between Jews and Israel. But the boys stood by their hate for Jews and came up with arguments to justify their hatred. 'The hatred for Jews is because they try to steal somebody's land innocent just like that', they argued, and they killed zillions of Palestinians. When asked, 'You think it is justified that Hitler killed millions of Jews?', the boys objected that 'you don't know if they are innocent'. 'Why would Hitler hate Jews then,' said one, 'he wouldn't kill a Jew for no reason.' The most outspoken of the boys bluntly said, 'As far as I am concerned, Hitler might as well have killed all Jews,' to which the other boys responded by laughing. Other replies to questions asked by the youth worker show that at least for one of the boys the word 'Jew' had extremely negative connotations. 'You don't have to know Jews to say something about them,' he said. In order to explain why 'Jew' is used to call people names he likened it to cancer, which is used as a cursing word in Dutch, 'Jew is the worst thing for us'.[92]

The antisemitic statements made during the discussion entailed hatred against Jews and equating Jews with evil. Moreover, justifying the Holocaust by claiming that Jews are committing the same crimes against Palestinians is an example of victim-perpetrator reversal, a regular element of postwar antisemitism, which we see here in one of its most frequent forms: conflating

91 Personal communication Lody van de Kamp, 2015.
92 NTR, *Onbevoegd gezag*, 24 February 2013.

the Jews of the Holocaust with today's Israelis. Finally, and probably most shocking, the boys asserted that it is perfectly acceptable to kill Jews.

Commentators connected the antisemitic phrases to the Muslim identity of the boys, by pointing out that, among Muslims, negative views of Israel may give way to or merge with antisemitic views. The boys themselves did not say much about the origins of their views, but they claimed that everybody at school, including native Dutch pupils, hated Jews. The interaction between the boys and their tutor is reminiscent of pupils' reactions to Holocaust education.[93]

The boys knew their basic facts about the persecution of the Jews: they knew who Anne Frank was, that she was Jewish and even that she died of typhus. One of the youngsters even sounded a bit offended when he said he had read all the books in primary school, and that he did not feel the need to be convinced. But the chronology is not right: one of the boys, when asked, 'You find it justified that Hitler killed millions of Jews?' answered, 'There are zillions of Palestinians … [killed].' As if that justified the killing of millions of Jews retroactively.

The remark 'zillions of Palestinians' also shows that young people have no idea of the scale of the Israeli-Palestinian conflict. In their view, Israel equals Jews, and Jewish 'is just bad', as one of the boys says.

These views on Jews are formulated in interaction with teachers and fellow students, as is evident in the television fragment. The sniggering laugh when making an offensive statement, the startled looks of other attendees, the embarrassment or shyness of the other youths holding their breath while waiting for the adult to respond. One of the boys half-heartedly distances himself from the statements saying 'extreme, extreme'. The argument is put forward that making these statements is 'freedom of speech' – a right increasingly invoked in public debate during the 1990s and 2000s.[94] Eventually, the others support a position which they called 'extreme' only a few minutes earlier. This illustrates that expressions of antisemitism depend as much on the dynamics of social interaction as on the rootedness of such ideas.

One commentator wrote that Hitler's alleged quote 'one day you will prove me right that I killed all the Jews' is frequently used in Islamist

---

93   On Holocaust education: Remco Ensel and Annemarike Stremmelaar, 'Speech Acts.' In: Günther Jikeli and Joëlle Allouche-Benayoun (eds.), *Perceptions of the Holocaust in Europe and Muslim Communities. Sources, Comparisons and Educational Challenges* (Dordrecht: Springer, 2013), 153-171.

94   *See* chapter 12 on Theo van Gogh, chapter 15 and the Epilogue.

propaganda. While conceding that it is unknown where the boy heard this quote, the commentator assumes it is quite likely he read it in Islamist propaganda rather than in neo-Nazi literature. The original source may be the so-called Bormann-Diktate, which Hitler supposedly dictated to his secretary Bormann in the final weeks of his life. The authenticity of this source is disputed, but that is of secondary importance here.[95] It would be interesting to know where the boy picked up this quote; so far it has been impossible to trace it back to either Islamist or neo-Nazi media. The quote seems to be one of many spurious quotations and rumours which pop up every so often on the internet or at school, without anyone knowing their source.

There are more elements in the interaction between tutor and boys that remind us of a school class situation. The same goes for the way the boys associate National Socialism with Israeli policies, without any sense of temporal, geographical or numerical dimensions of historical events. Or the emphasis on Hitler as the evil genius behind the Holocaust and incredulity at the idea that millions of Jews were murdered without them somehow bearing some guilt or responsibility. When they are told that the Jews have nothing to with what is happening in Gaza, one of the boys asks despairingly, 'But who are they then?'. Apart from the content of the discussion, the dynamics of interaction between tutor and boys is also similar to those seen in classrooms. This should not come as a surprise, as the youth worker was the boys' homework tutor. One internet commentator claimed that the boys' smirks and body language revealed a deeply-embedded hatred, but they look more like typical classroom exchanges about sensitive topics.[96]

Anne Frank as cause and cure

The two cases, 'Arnhem' and *Doğuş*, are quite different in many respects, as were the reactions. In Arnhem it was young male individuals who spoke their mind in plain Dutch. They voiced the stereotypes and forms of speech

95   François Genoud (ed.), *Hitlers politisches Testament. Die Bormann Diktate vom Februar und April 1945. Mit einem Essay von Hugh R. Trevor-Roper und einem Nachwort von André François-Poncet* (Hamburg: Albrecht Knaus, 1981), 64. Compare Peter Longerich, *Hitlers Stellvertreter: Führung der Partei und Kontrolle des Staatsapparates durch den Stab Hess und die Parteikanzlei Bormann: Eine Publikation des Instituts für Zeitgeschichte* (München: K.G. Saur, München, 1992), 6, and Ian Kershaw, *Hitler 1936-1945. Nemesis* (London: Allen Lane, 2000), 1024-1025.
96   Compare: http://fighthatred.com/2418/mehmet-sahin-a-dutch-muslim-doctoral-student-exposes-the-jew-hatred-of-dutch-turkish-muslim-youth/.

ANNEMARIKE STREMMELAAR

to be encountered in classrooms and on the internet when the Holocaust is an issue. Behind the speech patterns there was an argument to be found, one that is well-known and has gone global. In the case of Milli Görüş, antisemitic stereotypes and arguments were formulated on paper in Turkish amounting to an antisemitic world view. This world view could be related to Milli Görüş' ideological background, even though it was not shared by all its members.

In both cases, antisemitic hate speech was triggered by aversion against the memory of the Holocaust. This aversion was related to a black-and-white perception of the Israeli-Palestinian conflict and an image of Israel and Jews as perpetrators. As has been observed throughout this volume, both the Holocaust and Israel were turned against the Jews. The journal *Doğuş* did not deny the historicity of the Holocaust, but played down its significance through a reversal of perpetrator and victim roles. The Turkish-Dutch youngsters in Arnhem applauded the Holocaust, and this was, again, accompanied by assigning a perpetrator role to Jews in Palestine. The theme of the Holocaust in relation to Israel has been part of anti-Israeli activism almost since the foundation of Israel in 1948. However, as Remco Ensel has shown, it re-emerged in 2000 with new vigour and among new social groups: people whose families had migrated from Morocco and Turkey. Earlier antisemitic attacks against Israel from within Islamic organisations had turned 'the Jews' into perpetrators, but without referring to the Holocaust. The cases examined here featured one of the Holocaust's strongest icons, and moreover, a Dutch one: Anne Frank.

17 Holocaust Commemorations in Postcolonial Dutch Society

Remco Ensel

In the Netherlands, the Remembrance of the Dead on 4 May 2003 marked a turning point in the judgment of the problematic interpretation of the Holocaust among children of Moroccan immigrants. Disturbances at seven locations in Amsterdam led to a lot of commotion and a heated public debate, not only in Amsterdam, but throughout the whole country. The disturbances ranged from breaking the silence, chanting antisemitic slogans to destroying wreaths. One of the incidents was picked up by the national press under the heading of 'wreath football'. On some occasions, attendants of the commemorations brought in the conflict in the Middle East chanting slogans or distributing pamphlets.[1] 'New Antisemitism', as it controversially came to be called, seemed to have found an outlet at Holocaust and war commemorations.[2]

Resistance against Holocaust remembrance and education became a widespread phenomenon in Western Europe in the first decade of the twenty-first century, but the concept of secondary antisemitism had already been introduced in the late 1950s to describe the supposition that continued references to the Holocaust would obstruct a coming to terms with the past. Only by drawing a final line under the past, as historian Juliane Wetzel pointed out for Germany, 'could there be a normalisation of the relation between the Jewish minority and the majority society'. The Jews, however, 'force the Germans to continuously remember' their shameful past. The concept of secondary antisemitism also allows us to recognise the feelings of guilt and repression and their projection onto Jews in postwar Dutch society. In the early 1980s, Theo van Gogh spoke out against the '4 May industry' targeting, among others, Jewish writer Leon de Winter for thematising the war in his oeuvre and public persona. The same Van Gogh, however, was also concerned about antisemitism among 'Muslims' and 'Moroccans',

---

1   Minutes of the City Council Amsterdam: Answers to the written questions of the members H. Bakker, H.H.G. Bakker regarding the disturbance of the Remembrance of the Dead', 18 June 2003.

2   *See* on the concept of 'New Antisemitism', the introduction of chapter 14.

especially since, in his view, leftist multiculturalists were turning a blind
eye to the threat they posed to Western liberal society.[3]

Evelien Gans introduced the concept of secondary antisemitism in Dutch
historiography to refer to phrases, images and acts that express the feeling
that Jews exploit, possibly amplify, their suffering. 'Turning the Holocaust
against the Jews', as Gans put it, to exonerate bystanders, accomplices and
perpetrators results in behaviour ranging from disregard and denial to
verbal and physical vandalism.

You would expect first- and second-generation immigrants not to be
bothered by any suppressed feelings of guilt about crimes in which neither
they nor their parents or compatriots were implicated. They might, however,
have similar feelings about the 'disproportionate' attention for the past
sufferings of Jews and adhere to the idea that Jews deliberately try to keep
their sufferings at the centre stage so that people will overlook their own
wrongdoings. This is, of course, where the Middle East conflict enters the
argument. From this perspective, disturbing the annual Remembrance of
the Dead – incidentally misconstruing it as an exclusive remembrance of
Jewish victims – intentionally obliterates the memory of the Holocaust.

Another way to understand the incidents at the 4 May commemorations is by appreciating the polyphonic and multifaceted quality of all
'collective' remembrances. In his study of the simultaneous remembrance
of the Holocaust, slavery and colonial violence, literary historian Michael
Rothberg challenges the intrinsically competitive nature of remembering.[4]
Memory does not work by depriving others of their right to commemorate, but by borrowing, exchanging and adapting distinctive memories.
Rothberg's 'multidirectional' approach – even if it does not exactly deal
with ritualised public forms of remembrance – points to other aspects of
the 'disturbances', in particular to the use of slogans and flyers to raise
awareness about the sufferings of the Palestinians. It also helps to shift
the attention from isolated incidents to the long-term commitment of
immigrants to war commemorations. This chapter looks at three separate
commemorations in which the Holocaust was assigned a meaningful place

3   Juliane Wetzel, 'Antisemitism and Holocaust remembrance.' In: Günther Jikeli and Joëlle
Allouche-Benayoun (eds.), *Perceptions of the Holocaust in Europe and Muslim Communities.
Sources, Comparisons and Educational Challenges* (Dordrecht: Springer, 2013), 19-28. Evelien
Gans, '"Hamas, Hamas, all Jews to the gas." The history and significance of an antisemitic slogan
in the Netherlands, 1945-2010.' In: *Ibid.*, 85-103. *See* chapters 12 and 15.
4   Michael Rothberg, *Multidirectional Memory. Remembering the Holocaust in the Age of
Decolonization* (Stanford: Stanford University Press, 2009); Michael Rothberg, 'From Gaza to
Warsaw: Mapping multidirectional memory', *Criticism* 53, 4 (Fall 2011), 523-548.

and in which, in one way or another, first-generation migrants took part. The first part of the chapter provides the necessary context to recognise similarities and differences with the Remembrance of the Dead ceremony, which is addressed in the second part of the chapter.[5]

The 1941 February Strike, Postcolonial migration and Palestine

The February Strike refers to the general strike of 24 and 25 February 1941 planned by members of the Communist Party of the Netherlands (CPN) against the antisemitic terror and the first collective arrest (*razzia*) of Jews. Immediately after the war, the strike was annually commemorated in the old Jewish Quarter of Amsterdam, under the auspices of the city council, which also commissioned a commemorative statue. That statue, *De Dokwerker* [The Docker], is located on the J.D. Meijer Square where the first *razzia* took place (see Illustration 12). The city council, however, rather callously refused to grant permission to erect a Jewish monument on the same square (as was pointed out in a fuming opinion piece in the Jewish weekly NIW).[6] When, in the 1950s, the government allocated a series of memorial sites throughout the Netherlands, a proposal for a monument to the memory of the vanished Jewish community was rejected. Instead, it became mandatory that the Jewish Monument should propagate 'Jewish gratitude' for the fortitude and the bravery of their fellow-citizens. It took several decades before Jewish victims were first honoured in the form of public memorials. The monument which the city council had refused to place on the J.D. Meijer Square and which was supposed to express 'gratitude', is now located a few hundred meters from the square.

Today, the area around The Docker shows how the Holocaust has been gradually incorporated in the city's collective memory, from 'near denial' to public recognition.[7] Close to The Docker there are the Auschwitz Memorial (1977), the National Holocaust Memorial (1962), located in the former deportation centre 'Hollandsche Schouwburg', and a memorial honouring 'The resistance of Jewish citizens in 1940-1945' (1988), which became the site for the commemoration of the November 1938 pogrom, better known

---

5   This chapter is based on archival research (in the KMAN archive), interviews and observations at one neighbourhood war commemoration over a three-year period.

6   Van Ginkel for the 'fuming piece': Rob van Ginkel, *Rondom de stilte. Herdenkingscultuur in Nederland.* (Amsterdam: Bert Bakker, 2011).

7   'Nearly denial' in Rob van Ginkel, *Rondom de stilte.*

as the *Kristallnacht*. Two recent plans include a Wall of Names and the establishment of a Holocaust Museum in the same 'Jewish Quarter'.[8]

The gradual public recognition of the Holocaust characterises the history of public commemorations in the postwar Netherlands, but there were already many early forms of remembering including literature, ego-documents and semi-public commemorations, as well as 'the silent remembrance ... every day and every hour' in the private sphere.[9] The Dutch Auschwitz Committee was founded in 1956 and went against the grain when the Shoah was not yet part of the national commemorative culture. It began the commemoration of victims in a small circle. The commemoration only gradually evolved into a more structured and public event and, eventually, the building of an official monument, Auschwitz Memorial, in 1977.[10]

Another feature of the commemoration history is the transformation of the J.D. Meijer Square from a location for one specific commemoration into the main location for antiracist protests in general, ranging from the laying of a wreath for the victims of the antisemitic attack in Antwerp in 1981, various demonstrations against the extreme right in the 1980s and 1990s, to protests against Geert Wilders' Freedom Party (PVV) in the twenty-first century. Every gathering at the square – which has become a *lieu de mémoire* in its own right – conjures up memories of repression and resistance.

No sooner was a ceremony to commemorate the February Strike set up, than conflicts over how to interpret the strike emerged. The CPN, the self-proclaimed 'Party of the February Strike', wanted to commemorate the strike as an act of solidarity by labourers against fascism. The city council preferred to leave out the class dimension and interpret the strike as a spontaneous initiative of citizens standing up against flagrant injustice

8   May 2016 the Museum opened its doors. The Wall of Names probably will be located at the site of the aforementioned Jewish Monument. *See* chapter 2 for the post-liberation discussion on the question what to do with the Hollandsche Schouwburg, the theatre and former assembly point for deportation.

9   Frank van Vree, 'Iedere dag en elk uur. De jodenvervolging en de dynamiek van de herinnering in Nederland.' In: Hetty Berg and Bart Wallet (eds.) *Wie niet weg is, is gezien. Joods Nederland na 1945* (Zwolle: Waanders, 2010), 57-78. One of the best-known war poems was written in 1941 and partly refers to the February Strike. Jan Campert wrote *'De achttien dooden'* [The Eighteen Dead] to remember the execution of fifteen resistance fighters and three strikers on 13 March 1941. The poem was clandestinely published in 1943. Campert died in captivity in the Neuengamme concentration camp. His son, Remco Campert, is a well-known poet and writer in his own right.

10   The ideological background of the early Auschwitz memorial may have overlapped with the February Strike since there were several personal connections between the Auschwitz Committee and the CPN. *See* Maarten Bijl, *Nooit meer Auschwitz! Het Nederlands Auschwitz Comité, 1956-1996* (Bussum: Thoth, 1997).

against fellow citizens. In the Cold War climate, political parties didn't like to see the communists capitalising on their role in the strike.

The commemoration has always been linked to contemporary issues. The CPN believed 'political actualisation' was essential because 'not relating to the present would betray the fallen heroes'. A range of domestic and foreign topics were introduced at the annual commemorations. Numerous disagreements about the meaning of the strike and the content of the remembrance resulted in separate ceremonies at various locations. In her historical account of the commemorations, the historian Annet Mooij (b. 1961) asked the rhetorical question whether 'in the quarrelsome ambiance of the remembrance there was anybody left who sympathised with the Jews?'.[11] Indeed it seemed as if the origin of the victims did not matter, neither to the left-wing, anti-fascist movement nor to the city council. What mattered was either class solidarity or Amsterdam citizenship. Moreover, emphasising resistance and heroism – though in agreement with longstanding commemorative traditions[12] – was to the detriment of Jews who were primarily remembered as passive victims. In this sense, there was at least agreement as to whom were *not* to be remembered.

In the late 1960s there was an urge to link the strike to contemporary issues such as the Vietnam War, the German rearmament and the conflict in the Middle East. Piet Nak (1906-1996) was one of the communist organisers of the 1941 strike. After the war he had remained politically active, mostly in defiance of the 'Politburo' of the CPN.[13] Nak set up a Vietnam Committee and was co-founder of the Dutch Palestine Committee. The Yad Vashem Memorial Centre awarded him with the honorary title of 'Righteous among the Nations' as co-organiser of the strike. After the Six-Day War and after having participated in a tour through the Arab world during which he managed to meet all Arab leaders ('Only President Nasser was not available'), Nak returned his medal.[14] Nak was ridiculed because of his humble origins and presumed ignorance of world politics. When a critic reproached him for being judgmental while being unable to pinpoint Hebron on the map, Nak replied, with rhetorical skill, that his presumed ignorance about the location of Mauthausen had not prevented him from opposing oppression in 1941. Here, arguably, lies the key to Nak's commitment, which specifically

11   Annet Mooij, *De strijd om de Februaristaking* (Amsterdam: Balans, 2006).
12   For the myth of the fallen soldier *see* George L. Mosse, *Fallen Soldiers. Reshaping the Memory of the Two World Wars* (New York, Oxford: Oxford University Press, 1990).
13   Piet Nak also figures in chapter 7.
14   Interview Bertus Hendriks by Remco Ensel, 15 November 2011; Max Arian, 'Profiel Piet Nak. Verzetsman en dwarsligger', *De Groene Amsterdammer*, 13 May 2000. *See* chapter 7.

focused on the role of the bystander in his warning that 'the bystanders of the past remain passive again'.

Addressing the position of citizens as bystanders resembled the manner in which the protest generation was concerned about the alleged passivity of their parents. The 'Persecution and Destruction' (*vervolging en verdelging*) of the Jews, the subtitle of Jacques Presser's imposing 1965 history of *Ondergang* [the demise] of Dutch Jewry, had become part of public consciousness and collective memory in the late 1960s.[15] Dutch students reproached the war generation for its passivity then and now. When Loe de Jong, the national historian of the Second World War, was invited to defend his pro-American stance in a teach-in, he was booed for siding with the 'imperialists', but also for having pardoned Claus Von Amsberg, the future husband of Princess Beatrix, when it became known that he had been a member of the Hitler Youth.[16]

In 2000, a street in Amsterdam was named after Piet Nak.

Migrants join the commemoration

In the late 1970s, the Moroccan Workers Committee (KMAN) joined the tumultuous commemoration. The KMAN was founded by migrants with a lot of experience in contentious action in Morocco and France.[17] It appropriated the leftist signature of the commemoration as can be seen from their 1980 pamphlet.

> THE MOROCCAN WORKERS ALSO COMMEMORATE THE ANNIVERSARY OF THE FEBRUARY STRIKE. Today we pay homage to the Dutch men and women who went on strike in 1941 against the fascist deportation of Jewish citizens. We Moroccans live and work in Amsterdam and are prepared to participate in a memorial service which unites the Dutch and the foreigners in the fight against fascism. In the years that we were required to work here, far away from our family and our country, The Docker became our symbol for unity and resistance against racism and discrimination in the Netherlands, a living hope in our common struggle

15   English translation: Jacques Presser, *Ashes in the Wind. The Destruction of Dutch Jewry* (Detroit: Wayne State University Press, 1988). *See* part I.

16   Remko van der Maar, *Welterusten mijnheer de president. Nederland en de Vietnamoorlog 1965-1973.* (PhD thesis, Universiteit Utrecht, 2007), 82.

17   *See* chapter 7.

for a just society. To us Moroccan People, The Docker also represents our
hope in the struggle for freedom in Morocco.

Judging from the pamphlet, the KMAN gave its own twist to the leftist
culture of remembrance, expressing a combative attitude, while referring
to the victims of racism and exclusion. The Moroccan migrants identify
with the strikers as rebellious bystanders as well as with the Jews as targets
of racism and social exclusion.

The pamphlet was full of current issues and addressed all 'guest workers'
that felt oppressed by the capitalist system 'forced as we are to work here,
far away from our family'. The strike inspired them to fight oppression in
Morocco. The pamphlet evokes an image of the migrant worker as an exile
seeking a safe escape from a repressive regime only to be confronted with
the capitalist economic system and ethnic identity politics of Western
Europe. The pamphlet included an invitation to commemorate the 'popular [student] uprising' of 1965 in Casablanca. 'One of the best historical
examples of how people have joined forces to fight against discrimination
has been the February Strike, which the Amsterdam population organised
in 1941 as a protest against the deportation of their Jewish fellow citizens.
At that time people were played off against each other too.' The Moroccan
migrants thus remembered the February Strike in anti-racist and postcolonial terms.

The KMAN deployed Nazi antisemitism in its battle for citizenship in the
Netherlands. Chairman Abdu Menehbi's comparison between the Jews in
the 1930s and the migrant labourers of the 1970s and 1980s struck a sensitive
cord. It was a weak comparison if applied to the German Jews because it
lacked, for instance, any form of racist legislation. Instead, migrants' rights
were expanded in the 1980s.

Over the years, the KMAN continued to participate in collective actions
against expressions of antisemitism in the Netherlands. It joined the above-
mentioned gathering to commemorate the antisemitic attack in Antwerp,
after having agreed to leave 'Palestine shawls' at home – in exchange the
CIDI kept Israeli flags out of sight.

The only reported incident during the commemoration that may count
as a disturbance occurred in 1988 when a protester suddenly lifted a banner
stating 'Zionism = racism'. The police removed the man from the square.
According to the newspaper *Het Parool*, parliamentarian Jan Schaefer (1940-
1994) commented that this could not possibly be reckoned as a serious
protest: 'Equating Zionism with fascism and racism. That's unacceptable!'.
He clearly seemed to have failed to take notice of the fact that the equation

had been a regular feature of protest ever since it was included in the United Nations resolution of 1975.

The February Strike is a typical example of how a war commemoration offers a possibility – also to leftist first-generation migrants – to communicate either leftist or universal messages about resistance, solidarity and citizenship without explicating the Holocaust or even the war. The overall anti-fascist and anti-racist message connects the commemoration to other modes of remembering. In contrast, the Jewish commemorative culture was marginalised.

Postwar Dutch racism: from slavery to 'Black Pete'

The death of the fifteen-year-old Kerwin (Duinmeijer) on 20 August 1983 was a key moment in defining postwar Dutch racism. The synchronised articulation of remembering different forms of racist violence, in particular the Holocaust and slavery, in the past, with present-day forms of racism, was an important strategy in that process.

After an exchange of words at a night out, a sixteen-year-old boy stabbed Kerwin. A taxi driver dragged the heavily bleeding victim out of his cab and the ambulance arrived too late. The shock over Kerwin's death was huge and the murder received the epithet of 'the first racist murder after the Second World War'. The country had failed to live up to the maxim of 'Never Again'. The epithet had to do with the alleged perpetrator's motive. It was established that the suspect was dressed as a skinhead, had a tattoo saying '100% white' and, by some accounts, had made racist remarks and gestures ('dirty Turk' – to the man behind the counter of a diner –, a 'Nazi salute' and 'dirty negro') just before his attack. At the time, there seemed to be a public understanding that Kerwin was killed because of the colour of his skin, but the judge decided that there was no conclusive evidence for a racist motive. This reinforced the feeling that not only everyday racism but also institutionalised racism in the judicial system was still alive in the Netherlands. The estrangement got underlined when it became clear that Kerwin had grown up in a white foster family. Kerwin's mother, who was from the Dutch Antilles, argued that the foster family should be held accountable for letting Kerwin sneak out of his room. Because of this, Kerwin's surname became a sensitive issue. The municipality where he was born named a street after him, but then decided to rename the street in accordance with his original surname (i.e. Kerwin Lucas street).

In 1983 an organisation was set up to commemorate Kerwin and to tackle present-day racism. A statue in Kerwin's memory was erected in the Vondelpark.[18] Up to this day, the Friends of Kerwin foundation organises an annual commemoration (*'so we never forget where intolerance and racism can lead'*). The epithet of 'first racist murder after the war' was one way to conjure up the terror of the Holocaust. The foundation also introduced a red triangle as symbol for its activities because,

> in the Second World War (1939-1945) the Nazis in Germany incarcerated many people in concentration camps. Everyone knows that there were many Jews in the camps, but many other groups were also captured and put to death. These people all had to wear a badge on their clothes. For the Jews, this was a yellow Star of David. For others it was a triangle in one of five colours: red – political prisoners and Communists; pink – homosexuals; purple – Jehovah's Witnesses; black – Roma and Sinti ('Gypsies') and 'anti-social'; green – criminals.[19]

The organisation followed suit with various anti-fascist organisations in Europe by utilising the red triangle as symbol for their struggle. Ironically, the suspect, Nico Bodemeijer, pleaded insanity in court because of the war trauma of his father, a merchant at the Waterlooplein flea market, who had lost his family in the war. Afterwards, doubts were being raised about the Jewish origins of the suspect. A 2008 documentary, four years before the death of the convict, failed to clarify this issue.[20]

Another trope was to relate the incident to the persistence of a rarely acknowledged yet deeply ingrained racism in Dutch society. The English poem 'Kerwin', written by Maurice Di, one year after the incident, set the tone: *'No one really believes there is a thing called racism / it's always something else'*. The poem associates Kerwin's death with the transatlantic slave trade:

---

18 Most Dutch people will remember the incident because of a very popular song *Zwart Wit* ('Black White' by the Frank Boeijen Groep): 'Don't think white, don't think black, don't think black and white, but think in the colours of your heart.'

19 Website Friends of Kerwin foundation: www.kerwin.nl.

20 *Profiel Nico Bodemeijer* (direction: Kees Vlaanderen, 2008); *Kerwin, teken van de tijd* (direction: Froukje Bos, 1985); the feature film *Skin* tells the story from the perspective of the perpetrator (direction: Hanro Smitsman, 2008). In 1986 the anglicist and writer Frans Kellendonk (1951-1990) was (wrongly) accused of antisemitism when his highly acclaimed novel *Mystiek lichaam: een geschiedenis* (Amsterdam: Meulenhoff, 1986) appeared. Accordingly Kellendonk conceived the idea of writing his next novel about the case of Kerwin (which his premature death prevented from finishing).

Age-old Dutch racism … the jingle of the guilder is the rattle of the chains /
The chains they used to bind the blacks.

But it also refers to the Second World War:

Racism – fascism – Adolf Hitlerism or just plain Amsterdam snobbism.

The topic at the Kerwin memorial was broadened to include the commemoration of the abolishment of slavery as well as a campaign against
the character of black-faced *Zwarte Piet* [Black Pete] of the children's feast
Sinterklaas. This latter campaign was relaunched in 2013 in a highly publicised project by Quinsy Gario entitled *'Zwarte Piet is Racisme'* followed by
an intensive nation-wide debate in which opponents occasionally referred
to the war and the 'Black Holocaust'. The question of Black Pete continues
to stir the emotions in the Netherlands, with the Holocaust remaining a
fixed point of reference. One rapper tried to convey his aversion against
Black Pete in the following words: 'Imagine all opponents dressing up in
Hitler outfits and beginning to give out "Jewish Cookies" [a regular brand
in the Netherlands, RE] on May 4th.' Or: 'It is no wonder that so many of
you supported the Nazis during the war,' as one well-known boxer stated.
Another argument is precisely that because of the weight of the Shoah, the
Dutch are not capable of imagining any other racist suffering, not in the
least one for which they bear the responsibility: 'May 4th is by no means a
commemoration of the historical fact of genocide. It is the commemoration
of an ideological construction that upholds the greatness and supremacy
of the white Dutch establishment.'[21]

In 1985, two years after the murder of Kerwin, the city hall sponsored
a large conference that was organised by, among others, KMAN chairman
Menehbi. For two days, representatives from migrant organisations, anti-
racist groups and officials in the field of education, sports, police and media
discussed issues of institutional and everyday racism. In the periphery of
this *Prinsenhof conferentie* an interesting incident took place. According to a
newspaper report, 'a Moroccan man' complained that 'his children were being
taught about the Second World War and Nazism. He believed that Zionism is
fascism, because Zionism is killing our children.' His linking the Holocaust

---

21   Rapper Daryll Ossenga in *De Telegraaf,* 24 October 2013; Regilio Tuur in *Algemeen Handels-*
blad, 11 November 2014; Abulkasim Al Jaberi and Bryan van Hulst Miranda, 'Why the Dutch
never learned from the Holocaust', www.doorbraak.eu/dutch-never-learned-nazi-holocaust/.
For Black Pete *see also* the Epilogue.

to the Middle East conflict was a preview of the aforementioned protest at the commemoration of the February Strike and the numerous incidents after 2000. A representative of a Jewish organisation retorted that if this man indeed believed Zionism equalled racism he had better leave the conference. Which he did. It is rather ironic that Menehbi, whose views were similar to those of the protester, was awarded with a prestigious medal for his achievements in the field of anti-racism at the 2012 reunion of the *Prinsenhof conferentie*. At that reunion the social democratic mayor of Amsterdam, Eberhard van der Laan, came up with an explanation for the slow acknowledgment of the harmful effects of mass migration and multicultural politics in Amsterdam. It was all because of the Holocaust and the city's intense feelings of guilt and shame about the deportation of its Jewish citizens. Therefore, the city had been terrified to encourage a new wave of stigmatisation of a population group. The shameful memory of the Holocaust blocked the city's readiness to tackle the challenges of multiculturalism. As well as antisemitism. Again the Holocaust was framed as a barrier for gaining an accurate world view or for developing healthy social relationships.

Kristallnacht

In 1992 the new anti-racist organisation *Nederland Bekent Kleur* [literally: The Netherlands Shows its Colours] took the initiative for a public commemoration of the November 1938 Pogrom better known as the *Kristallnacht*. The initiative was triggered by the arson of a house in Solingen, Germany, which left five members of a Turkish family dead. In an atmosphere of great anxiety, the Jewish social democratic mayor Ed van Thijn warned in his speech that Nazi terror had also started in a democracy. So the first commemoration was set up as a 'protest rally against the rise of fascism'. Again chaired by Abdu Menehbi, the commemorations continued to focus on contemporary issues of racism or xenophobia. In Germany, the commemorations were accompanied by upheaval and controversy, but in the Netherlands there were no incidents. That is, until the year 2000 when the Second Intifada triggered a wave of protests in the Netherlands in which the commemoration of the Kristallnacht got tangled up.

The street protests of October 2000 were the first public display of a changed atmosphere. There were some incidents with protesters who had referred to Hitler and the Holocaust and there was an overall riotous mood.[22] It was decided to extend the organising committee with representatives

22 *See* chapter 14.

of CIDI, the city council and the Dutch Auschwitz Committee. It was also decided to change location, from the small area in front of the Kristallnacht memorial to the J.D. Meijer Square. Finally, all participating associations agreed on a code of conduct including a self-imposed ban on mentioning the Middle East conflict.

Menehbi, who no longer chaired the organising committee, had been asked to say a few reconciliatory words to the young participants of the October protests because, as he explained in an interview, 'you cannot go around discriminating other people [e.g. make antisemitic remarks at the protest rallies] because you are a victim of racism yourself.' But, as he continued,

> on the other hand there was this serious clash in Palestine. There was a war going on .... You do need to speak out against repression. Taking a stance is going to solve a big problem because that's where the commotion of these Moroccan kids is all about. They watch television every day and what they do is the consequence of what they see on the telly. They need to understand that not all Jews concur with the Israeli government .... I offer them a way out.[23]

When Menehbi started his speech he did not stop at calming things down. By presenting his views on the conflict, mainly referring to Israel's failure to comply with UN resolutions, one part of the audience got annoyed. In the end, the chairman of the Auschwitz Committee urged Menehbi to abort his speech.

It looked as if Menehbi had ignored the code of conduct, but afterwards he claimed to have distributed his speech days in advance. 'Everyone knew about it. Nobody had complained.' One of the organisers at the time recollected the incident: 'I can still remember what he literally said, to be exact, that Israel has to comply with Resolutions 242 and, er well, the famous UN resolutions .... It was all very friendly though, someone got up on the stage and whispered something in his ear.' Menehbi is still indignant years after the event: 'They say I politicised the event, I talked about politics. Should we not talk about politics? That's weird. We need to talk about the Kristallnacht in Berlin. No? You talk about a political event. It's nonsense to deem one thing as politics, and not the other.' The UN resolutions had been on the agenda for years and Menehbi's remarks should not have surprised anyone. But all were confronted with a new situation. Firstly, he made

23   Interview Abdu Menehbi by Ensel, 8 April 2011.

his comments on the occasion of a commemoration of the Kristallnacht where antisemitism is a central issue, whereas the February Strike is mainly remembered as a key event in the history of heroic resistance. Secondly, the Second Intifada protests had created a new and tense atmosphere. No longer was the stage occupied by secular, left- and right-wing opponents who were always at each other's throats. A new generation had knocked on the door with a new repertory of contentious action.

In the following years, everything about the Kristallnacht commemoration remained agitated. The organisation received a lot of criticism as if it had suddenly dawned upon opponents that there happened to be an annual Kristallnacht commemoration with a recognisable leftist anti-racist tenor. The representative of the antisemitism monitor *Meldpunt Discriminatie Internet* (MDI) blamed the organisation for making the commemoration *Judenrein*[24]. This harsh criticism was meant to point out how *all* forms of contemporary racism could be a topic at the commemorations apart from, apparently, 'new antisemitism'. The same applies to International Day for the Elimination of Racial Discrimination on 21 March, which is organised by the same people.

The commemoration was condemned as a 'falsified Kristallnacht commemoration ... that abuses the Shoah for phony leftist teachings'. The liberal politician Frits Bolkestein (b. 1933) voiced a similar opinion in a talk show.

> I held a speech to commemorate the umpteenth 'birthday' of the Kristallnacht ... and I have spoken there. There were other people. Jews have spoken there. Mayor Job Cohen has also spoken there. And to my utter surprise no one supported me when I talked about the fact that antisemitic incidents were mainly perpetrated by Muslims, not even the Jews who spoke there. That is submissive behaviour.[25]

The topos of submissive behaviour was derived from the work of the Egyptian-British writer Bat Ye'or. In a number of publications she had introduced the concept of 'dhimmitude': non-Muslims who are submissive towards Muslims as if we are still, or again, living in the Islamic Caliphate.[26] The average naive or left-wing citizen, for example the one participating in

24 Ronald Eissens, 'Graag een Judenreine Kristallnachtherdenking?', 3 November 2003, Magenta.nl
25 Frits Bolkestein in the TV talkhow *Pauw en Witteman*, 9 december 2010.
26 Bat Ye'or claims to be the inventor of the francophone concept 'dhimmitude', but in his study of the Islamophobic world of Anders Breivik (who on 22 June 2012 killed 77 youths on the island of Utoya), Bangstad argues that the term was introduced in Lebanon by Bashir Gemayel

the anti-racism movement, was ignorant of the larger Islamic danger that was lurking behind the incidents, the terror and the presence of Islamic migrant communities in Western Europe.

Eventually, a second Kristallnacht commemoration was set up, with a more explicit Jewish signature and situated in the synagogue on J.D. Meijer Square. In 2011, Mirjam Ohringer (1924-2016) talked about her experiences in 1938 at the 'old' memorial. A group of protesters in the audience, decked in Israeli flags, distributed a flyer in which Ohringer was disqualified as speaker because of her critical comments on Israel, thus denying a survivor to talk about her memories.

Referencing the Holocaust has become part of public discourse in postwar Dutch society. It is thus not uncommon to connect contemporary politics with the past by referring to the Holocaust. At the Kerwin Memorial present-day racism was criticised alluding to Dutch involvement in the slave trade and to Nazi antisemitism. Similarly, at several war commemorations the Middle East conflict was addressed. In almost all cases, these references were accompanied by debate and conflict in the run-up to the ceremony or in the aftermath.

It is unrealistic to expect everybody involved in a commemoration to agree on who or what to commemorate, but usually these disagreements remain hidden at the actual ceremony. It is up to the organising committees to reach some kind of compromise to avoid improvised interventions as happened at the Kristallnacht Memorial when a speaker had to be dragged off the stage. Still, outsiders may seize a public ceremony to give their own interpretation of past events. This happened at the commemoration of the February Strike in 1988 when as mentioned above a young man appeared with a banner denouncing Israel as a racist state. It is plausible the protester respected and accepted the commemoration as such, but wished to profit from its symbolic power in a 'multidirectional sense'. In retrospect, however, this incident appears to fit in with the events after 2000 when in several instances local war commemorations were disturbed.

Breaking the silence

We are now better equipped to understand the disturbances of 2003. It was not the first time commemorations got linked to current issues and the insertion of the Middle East conflict into a war commemoration was also

in 1982. Breivik called himself a 'first-generation dhimmi'. Sindre Bangstad, *Anders Breivik and the Rise of Islamophobia* (London: Zed Books, 2014), 73. *See also* Epilogue.

not something entirely new. The participation of Moroccan migrants goes back to their initial years in the Netherlands when they already coupled the remembrance of the war to current issues. We also saw an early complaint about the prominent place of the Shoah in Dutch society, to which 'the Jews' should not be entitled because of their behaviour in the Middle East conflict. Finally, over time there have been recurring attempts to connect the remembrance of the Shoah with slavery and colonialism. We shall now turn to the annual 4 May Commemoration.

The 4 May ceremony is reserved to commemorate the victims of the Second World War and is directly followed by Liberation Day on 5 May. The ceremonies weren't set from the start in 1945, but were assembled out of several distinct practices. At present, 4 May consists of hundreds of memorial services throughout the country, with some more prominent than others due to their location or to the attendance of politicians, members of the Royal Family and other dignitaries. The National Commemoration takes place on Dam Square, Amsterdam. The service there mainly consists of a number of speeches, two minutes of silence, the hoisting of the Dutch flag at half-mast while the national anthem is played and, finally, the laying of wreaths. The second most important is the televised ceremony at the war cemetery in the dunes near The Hague which consists of a walk, the ringing of a bell, two minutes of silence and the laying of wreaths.

The two-minute silence at eight o'clock in the evening has become a general feature of all commemorations. Usually, this is preceded by one or two speeches and followed by the laying of wreaths. Respecting this silence is ingrained in the postwar generation as a sign of respect and inner civilisation. This meant that, occasionally, those breaking the silence were lectured about their uncivilised behaviour or that cars were violently stopped when the driver ignored the silence. These examples also serve to show that breaking the silence is nothing new. However, breaking the silence by shouting antisemitic slogans was.[27]

In 2003, the events in the Amsterdam neighbourhood De Baarsjes received most publicity. A multicultural commemoration service had been organised with part of the commemoration held in a local mosque. Among other things, the attendants were shown a film about the contribution of Moroccan soldiers during the Second World War. Subsequently, wreaths

---

27   In 2010 there was a lot of commotion on Dam Square when a man, 'dressed like an "orthodox Jew"', who subsequently became known as 'The Dam Screamer', suddenly started screaming. Probably because of fears of a terrorist attack – someone else started shouting 'a bomb, a bomb!', causing great panic and a number of injured.

were laid at the monument. 'The horn blew, silence fell.' Then, a group of youngsters, aged between ten and fifteen, started chanting *Joden die moeten we doden'* [Let us kill the Jews]. That year, there were similar incidents at six other neighbourhood-oriented commemorations in Amsterdam. There is no evidence that these incidents were coordinated, but they are also not entirely coincidental.

Let us take a closer look at one of these commemorations. The borough of East Amsterdam organises two local commemorations, one in the 'Indische Buurt' and one in the 'Transvaalbuurt'. Both neighbourhoods were built in the early twentieth century when it was customary to express the supposedly everlasting bond with the 'overseas territories' and the South African Boers by naming streets after them. Due to an influx of migrants from Surinam, Morocco and Turkey the neighbourhoods became 'multicultural', so the visible reminders of the colonial past started to pinch. In 1977, for instance, Pretorius Square was renamed Steve Biko Square. The city council, however, turned down a proposal to rename *all* the streets, accepting the argument that this would further the forgetting of the deported and murdered Jewish families that had lived in the Transvaalbuurt or were forced to move there.[28] The council thus preferred the memory of the Jewish community over the everyday annoyance and embarrassment about the Afrikaner connection. With respect to the Jewish community of the Indische Buurt in 2014 a plaque was revealed at the entrance of the neighbourhood grocery store to mark the location of the pre-war synagogue.

The war monument on Ceram Square consists of a low wall with a plaque. The rest of the square is a grassy field that serves as a playground. The war commemoration has been following a fixed order since the 1950s: a silent march, one or two speeches, a choir, the 'Last Post', silence and coffee. In 2003, a lot of things happened at the same time and not all breaches of the conventional ceremonial order can be accounted for. There was, for example, a local Moroccan migrant organisation distributing flyers to raise awareness about the Palestinian cause; unknown protesters wrote slogans on the pavement, one of which called on 'white Jews' to leave the neighbourhood and move to the new town of Almere. Finally, there was a group of youngsters that harassed one of the invited guests. Ironically, the harassment can be construed as a failed attempt to give the ceremony a multicultural makeover.

28   Daniel Metz, 'Transvaalbuurt, tussen Boerenoorlog en anti-apartheid', *Ons Amsterdam*, 4 April 2012.

Pastor Nederstigt has been involved in the organisation of the ceremony for over fifteen years. In an interview, he explains how the 2003 incidents were in line with previous disturbances. 'In the first years when I was responsible for the ceremony everything went well, but at the turn of the century we were confronted with the first incidents.' It was because of these incidents that the organising committee came up with a plan:

As an experiment [in 2003] we invited a popular Moroccan singer to perform. But the man, who obviously had a big ego, just kept on singing. I asked him to stop, because of the two-minute silence at eight o'clock sharp, but he didn't. The music itself was not bad though. Meanwhile, there appeared to be some strife between his fans and those of another singer .... All in all, that year's commemoration was very disorderly and undignified.[29]

The pastor could not recall the name of the 'Moroccan singer', but it was hip-hop artist Raymzter who had become famous with the rap song 'Kut-Marokkanen' [bloody Moroccans]. The song was about the negative stigma of Moroccan-Dutch adolescents and was intended as a response to a slip of the tongue by an Amsterdam alderman in 2002 who had used the word 'Kut-Marokkanen' to refer to the troublesome adolescents in the suburbs. In the thematisation of xenophobia and Islamophobia, the song acted as a kind of anthem of the Mocros, the Moroccan-Dutch second generation. Incidentally, the pastor didn't remember the eggs that were thrown at the rapper.[30]

When we go back one year we can understand the 'experiment' with the hip-hop artist as an answer to the call for a less 'monocultural' commemoration in a period of post-9/11 agitation and amidst the protests of the Second Intifada. Or, as one resident optimistically envisioned her ideal multicultural commemoration: 'A Dutch brass band and a Moroccan rapper side by side.' In the year prior to the disturbances, a debate unleashed about the nature of Remembrance Day. There seemed to be an overall urge in Amsterdam to add a 'multicultural' ingredient to the ceremony. While in the neighbourhood of De Baarsjes the organising committee had decided to screen a film about the involvement of Moroccan soldiers in the Second World War, the organisers in the borough of East Amsterdam invited the hip-hop artist to address the post-9/11 social climate. In the neighbourhood

29 Interview Leo Nederstigt by Ensel, 2011.
30 See chapter 14 on egging and on the curse of 'Kut-Marokkanen.'

a rather highbrow debate ensued about religion in the public sphere, the lack of historical knowledge among 'Moroccans', Islamophobia and the conflict in the Middle East.

Two incidents affected the outcome of this debate. First there was the alderman's slip of the tongue about *Kut-Marokkanen*, as discussed in chapter 14. Second, on 13 April 2002 an anti-Israel protest march got out of hand with people waving flags with swastikas, and others climbing on the National Monument shouting 'Hamas Hamas, all Jews to the gas'. How was the local Remembrance Day organisation to react to these 'signs of the times'?

Two days before the anti-Israel protest, the district committee held a meeting. 'A delicious Moroccan meal' was followed by a discussion. It was particularly stressed that the suffering in the world wasn't over. 'It is embarrassing that no space is created for the Palestinian issue at official commemorations. After all, we should not look at groups or nations; the Jew of the Kristallnacht is the same as the Palestinian now.'[31]

A special role in the neighbourhood discussions was reserved for Ron Haleber, a scholar of Islam and a local resident. Haleber had been present at the first debates in the Anne Frank House in the 1960s. He argued with a lot of clamour that 'we had to recognise that the Moroccan-Dutch have little time for the Second World War. That's not their war.' And 'when these same Moroccans organise a memorial for the February Strike, the Dutch do not show up'. Then Haleber made a remarkable turn by referring to the way the Dutch government had dealt with 'the tragedy in Srebrenica: *Wir haben es nicht gewusst*', using the expression, which, according to Dutch folklore, people in postwar Germany used to exclaim to whitewash their role as accomplice to the genocide of the Jews.

And what about connecting the war memory to present-day issues? This wasn't a solution either because, as Haleber maintained, 'the special relationship' between the Netherlands and Israel would turn 'any detailed account' of the conflict into an accusation of antisemitism. The Dutch trade off their bad conscience about the war with unremitting support to Israel. Moroccans are supposed to commemorate something which, in their view, is related to what they perceive as an open wound, i.e. the founding of the state of Israel. If we don't succeed in finding a common ground for remembrance, Remembrance Day will persist as a ritual for 'a small white minority'. And

31   The debates were posted on a local website, for instance Simon Haagsma, www.zee-burgnieuws.nl, 12 April 2002. Information was also acquired through conversations with those concerned at the annual commemorations.

if this was not provocative enough, Haleber also suggested include the recitation of the Fatiha, the first Sura of the Quran, in the commemoration.

Clearly, this rant went beyond what most community members could accept. The tenor of his critique however fitted in with the search for a multicultural commemoration. This involved 'looking for the symbols of the other'. It was even a 'right of stigmatised Moroccan youths to share their individual commemoration with others'. The initiative to invite a rapper to the commemoration must have been conceived in this opinionated climate. Thus, as a local journalist afterwards defended the decision, 'If you want to preclude the exclusion of people, what nicer gesture than inviting them to your party? Of course, it was also a big gamble .... But if you don't try, you will never win.' Singing 'Bloody Moroccans' at a commemoration which had been running according to the same fixed pattern since the 1950s and was never meant to be 'a party', may be called a bold move indeed. Even Pastor Nederstigt had his doubts, but

> the then chair of the committee was very much in favour of the experiment and I supported her. Two weeks before 4 May she got ill. Next, some disturbing reports came through. But then I thought, that woman is ill, so I'm just going to stand right behind her, because it is not fair to cancel the performance in her absence. So, even though I had my doubts, I kept them to myself.[32]

As said, the disturbances of 2003 followed on incidents in previous years: throwing stones – once even a beer can –, vandalising flowers, cursing and making offensive remarks. Pastor Nederstigt remembers one incident in particular: 'I dare to speak about it now, but at the time I felt humiliated, standing there, doing something for the community and getting small stones thrown at you because obviously you represent a hostile organisation to them.' The pastor opposed the idea their behaviour should be qualified as misschief. 'You know, for some reason, you could feel the hate and sense that their parents or siblings had told them that the commemoration was in favour of the Jews and against the Arabs or the Palestinians.'

32 Interview Leo Nederstigt by Ensel, 2011.

'White Jews go to Almere!'

As said, the seven incidents weren't planned, but they weren't incidental either. They were part of the history of the boroughs of East Amsterdam and West Amsterdam where ethnic relations were strained and where 'Jews' had become a figure of speech for powerful 'natives'.[33] All the major incidents took place in neighbourhoods with a history of skirmishes, including New West, the scene of the only real 'race riot' in 1998. This, incidentally, explains why the neighbourhood police were prepared for riots and disturbances in 2003.[34] But the neighbourhood's history is even more complex, as the slogan 'white Jews' suggests.

East Amsterdam had already witnessed a white exodus to new towns like Almere. In the 1970s, the composition of the neighbourhood population began to change. It became ethnically diverse and 'lower class'. In statistical terms, the neighbourhood became classified as a 'lower-class immigrant area' with 30% Moroccans and Turks and a small pocket of long-established white residents. It's remarkable how this change already involved confrontations between these established residents and 'foreigners' on 4 May. When asked on behalf of a newspaper article, a thirty-year-old secretary indicated in 1989 that 'it's not so bad in the neighbourhood, but sometimes you become aware of the tension. For example, with the Remembrance of the Dead on Ceram Square. You think, how nice those immigrants and natives happily standing together. Well, actually, there were a few brats, dark boys, who were just walking through the flowers and stuff and some white people took offense. I understand their anger and I agree with them. But they immediately referred to them as dark kids. Then I think, no, they're just rascals.'[35]

After the white exodus and the influx of lower-class migrants, at the turn of the century the Indische Buurt got into a process of gentrification. Thus after 2000 – and much later than elsewhere – middle-class households moved into the neighbourhood causing a change in shops, restaurants and cafés: 'Everywhere you come across a *Jan Willem* or an *Anne-Fleur* [i.e. people with posh names]. The neighbourhood is changing in front of your eyes. All those people who used to live in East. They all moved to North [Amsterdam] as well as [the new towns of] Purmerend and Almere. This Amsterdam has become

---

33   Hans Moll and Hella Rottenberg, 'Joden maken de dienst uit in Nederland. Het antisemitische wereldbeeld van Marokkaanse jongeren', *NRC Handelsblad*, 14 June 2003.

34   Frank Bovenkerk, 'Rassenrellen of criminaliteit?', *Migrantenstudies* 4 (1999), 255-270.

35   Quoted in Gerard Andriessen and Arnold Reijndorp, *Eigenlijk een geniale wijk. Dagelijks leven in de Indische Buurt* (Amsterdam: Het Spinhuis, 1990).

a Manhattan. For yuppies.' Perhaps the slogan 'white Jews' was an answer to this development. The return of the white Jews who had once fled the area and were now slowly returning, albeit with a different income and education. Or maybe the slogan should be read as an encouragement to the last remaining 'old whites' to move out and leave the neighbourhood to the 'migrants'?

Dealing with the disturbances

The chair of the borough where the wreath football made world news, wanted to avoid another incident the next year. The politician Ahmed Marcouch (who became the next district mayor and subsequently Member of Parliament) was asked to lend a hand:

> In 2004, I was asked by the district mayor if I wanted to help since the entire international press was present in De Baarsjes to see whether things would go wrong again. The district mayor was terrified that it would happen again. And so he asked for help. I said: 'By all means.' He continued: 'But what are we going to do?' I answered: 'What we will do is to make sure that these young people learn the meaning of the remembrance. We are going to train them.' I took these guys to the youth centre. I began by working on the idea of 'remembering'. What is it and which symbols does it involve? Flag at half-mast, the trumpet, the light that goes on at eight o'clock sharp. How long are two minutes of silence? What kind of posture is suitable? What are you supposed to think of during the silence? We stood upright, chest forward, quietly breathing. You show respect by the way you stride towards the memorial. What's a memorial? Is there anything buried underneath or is it just a symbol? Is it only about the Jews? Is it a problem if it only involves Jews? What have you got against the Jews? Phew, that was quite some training.[36]

Marcouch's intervention led to a tranquil remembrance without incidents. The discontent of the regular attendants centred on the new role for the same youngsters that had been responsible for the disturbances. There already was a meeting in the mosque and a film about the Moroccan soldiers and on top of that the ringleaders of the year before were granted a role in the ceremonies. They were allowed to read out the names of the deceased

---

36 Interview Ahmed Marcouch by Ensel, 21 March 2011. Report of the 2003 events in: Wilma Kieskamp, 'Antisemitisme Marokkaanse jongens komt van buiten', *Trouw*, 19 May 2003. Disturbances weren't unique for Amsterdam. In 2003, the city of Leiden also had two incidents involving youths messing about with wreaths. For Marcouch *see also* chapters 14, 15 and 16.

Moroccan soldiers buried in the southwestern province of Zeeland. In the East District the district council first assumed control over the neighbourhood commemoration and gradually restored the local authority.

Between 2012 and 2014 the commemorations on Ceram Square proceeded without major problems, although noisy and interfering small children remained an issue. The ceremony once again consisted of speeches, a choir, the 'Last Post', silence and coffee. The 'multicultural' aspect consisted of messages of peace read out in different languages.

Remembrance envy

In his hefty study on the history of the 4 May commemorations in the Netherlands, the anthropologist Rob van Ginkel left the 2003 disturbances undocumented. He did, however, very thoroughly chart the historical dynamics of the Remembrance of the Dead ceremonies: the numerical increase in monuments and the emergence of ever more specific mnemonic communities that claim a place in the memorial landscape. This process cannot take place without some competition. According to Van Ginkel, the driving force behind this process is the existence of 'remembrance hierarchy' with 'victim rivalry' and 'remembrance envy' as potent emotions. The ensuing skirmishes were signs of the democratisation of the collective memory and, therefore, by far preferable to an interventionist government deciding how we all should remember.[37] In a way this viewpoint corresponds to Rothberg's approach: an act of remembering evokes other memories and for this reason one should avoid an overwrought response to the divergent ways in which people deploy the past or relate their own present-day concerns to past events. Yet Rothberg admitted, in an additional essay on the analogy between Gaza and the Warsaw ghetto, how 'multidirectional' remembering sometimes goes astray[38]. In this chapter, we have tried to find a balance between looking at the varied ways in which historical events are commemorated and remembered, and the ways in which people deny Jews to remember their past and commemorate their dead.

In 2012, a genuine remembrance war broke out when the poem selected by the National Committee for 4 and 5 May talked about the death of a young man, the young poet's great-uncle, who was enlisted in the Waffen-ss.

37   Rob van Ginkel, 'Herdenkingscultuur en herinneringspolitiek.' Speech at the book presentation of Jet Bussemaker, *Dochter van een kampkind*, Amsterdam, 20 April 2011.
38   Michael Rothberg, 'From Gaza to Warsaw: Mapping multidirectional memory', *Criticism* 53, 4 (Fall 2011), 523-548.

Several organisations protested against the initiative to have this poem recited at the ceremony on Dam Square. Although criticism came from various sides, 'Jewish organisations' were accused of monopolising the commemoration, or as the reproach in rhyme went: *'Dodenherdenking is geen Jodenherdenking'* ('Remembrance of the Dead is not Remembrance of the Jews'). But it never had been. Until 2016, when a radical change in the commemorative ceremony was implemented, no official wreath for the Jewish victims was laid at the National Monument on Dam Square.[39] For decades there was an unwritten rule dictating that no separate victim groups may be distinguished, just as had been the case in the early years after the war. Nevertheless, according to comments in the media, 'Jews' were hypersensitive, presumptuous, whining and manipulatively cherishing their victimhood and telling others how to think and act. Similar commotion erupted when, in that same year, a small memorial committee took the initiative to walk past the graves of ten German soldiers on 4 May.

Using phrases such as 'the dynamics' or 'the democratisation' of remembering may euphemistically conceal an array of rowdy commemorative practices. In the Netherlands, the remembering of the Holocaust became part of the identity politics of (former) migrants. They could hark back to already existing ways of thinking: resentment about the alleged hegemony of the Holocaust in public memory, combined with victim envy. Again, we find ideas about how the Jewish community tries to monopolise the commemoration, continuing to profit from its victimhood by keeping everyone in a moral headlock.

All of these issues also arise at a local level where they mingle with urban social problems. In East Amsterdam, Moroccan first-generation migrants have partaken in the Dutch commemorative culture and continue to do so. In De Baarsjes, the Moroccan soldiers in Zeeland were necessary in order to establish empathy and identification, in East Amsterdam an attempt was made with a rapper with Moroccan roots. It seemed difficult for some second-generation youngsters to conceive the memorial as a moment to reflect on the deceased from the neighbourhood, including the deported and murdered Jews and to conceive the commemoration of the Holocaust as a responsibility for all Dutch citizens.

39 Personal communication, Jacques Grishaver, chairman of the *Dutch Auschwitz Comité*, 2014. Ewoud Sanders, 'Maak van de Dodenherdenking geen Jodenherdenking', NRC *Handelsblad*, 7 May 2012. *See also* Epilogue.

18   Epilogue

Instrumentalising and Blaming 'the Jew', 2011-2016

Evelien Gans

'The war' and the Shoah: they remain subjects of endless discussion – reflected in the 'story' about them –, historiography, academic and public debate. The notion mooted in 2010 that it might be time to 'pension off' the war (*'De oorlog met pensioen?'*) turned out to be premature, or a rhetorical question.[1] Memory and commemoration are in perpetual flux. The same turbulence applies to the position of Jews and Judaism, including all the variant forms of antisemitism. And last but not least, the cauldron of views and actions relating to the establishment, the functioning and the continued existence of the state of Israel is constantly being stirred and boiling over. And this is only to look at the way all these issues surface, develop and become enmeshed in the Netherlands. Still, the rest of the world is never far away. This book has also dwelt at length on two main ethnic minorities in the Netherlands: Dutch people of Moroccan and Turkish descent. The international dimension is further enhanced by the multi-faceted involvement of many Jewish and non-Jewish people with Israel, and by the role of the internet.

At the heart of this book is the proposition that the Shoah and Israel have come to function as the two most important new – i.e. postwar – points of fixation for expressions of antisemitism. Both, in their very different ways, continue to work against the Jews. At the same time, they provided the signposts for twentieth-century Jewish history and identity. This curious mirror image is not in any sense, of course, exclusive to the Netherlands. Nonetheless, the Dutch – so often mythologised as a tolerant, broadminded people – occupy a central position here, viewed from a multicultural perspective. The following pages will suggest certain connections between themes listed in earlier chapters and a number of new elements and recent developments.

---

1   In 2010, a symposium was organised, entitled 'De oorlog met pensioen?' ('Time to pension off the war?') with the historians Hans Blom, Jolande Withuis and Chris Klep, Leiden, 11 May 2010; Ismee Tames, 'De oorlog als entertainment', *Trouw*, 16 October 2010. *See also* Maarten Asscher, 'De doorwerking van de Shoah in de Lage Landen. Nederland: Drie vragen die niet weggaan', in *Ons Erfdeel* 4 (November 2015), 42-50: 44.

The *leitmotif* is the tension that exists between universalism and particularism. The British sociologist Robert Fine (b. 1945) has said that today's crisis-ridden universalism may make Jews more frequent targets of aggression. Universalism has always had two faces, he writes:

> Its emancipatory face has been manifest in movements for legal recognition of Jews as equal citizens and for social recognition of Jews as equal human beings. Its repressive face has been manifest in depictions of 'the Jews' as a particularistic people incapable of embracing or actively hostile to the values of universal humanity.[2]

Amid this tension, we have seen the emergence of 'selective philosemitism' and 'anti-antisemitic enthusiasm', for instance in Geert Wilders' support for a ban on the ritual slaughter of animals. Wilders is also active on the world stage, and the proposed ban stirred up international controversy. This battle too involved a clash between real or imagined universal versus particularist values. To what extent can universalism manifest itself as a *diktat*: thou shalt not practise ritual slaughter?[3] Finally, the bloody attacks by Islamist extremists in Europe, on the satirical magazine *Charlie Hebdo* and the kosher supermarket in Paris in January 2015, and on Jewish targets in Toulouse, Brussels, Paris and Copenhagen, have continued unrelentingly. The threat of more attacks has remained present, in the Netherlands as well, and indeed Paris was the scene of further acts of terrorism on 13 November 2015 – and Brussels in March 2016. This Epilogue reviews the public debate that took place in the Netherlands following the attacks in Paris in January 2015. Do the jihadists see Jews as the primary representatives of an abominated, allegedly Western, universalism? The Dutch debate revolved largely around a conflict between those who claimed undiluted freedom of expression as a 'universal' right and those who wished to question this approach on principle. In the meantime, hate speech directed against Jews and Muslims – in other words, antisemitism and Islamophobia – were consigned to the margins of the debate.

'The Jew' with all his 'attributes' is a supremely versatile figure. He can be transplanted, gas chamber and all, into other undesirable individuals and minority groups, such as today's refugees from Syria and elsewhere.

---

2   Robert Fine, 'Two faces of Universalism: Jewish Emancipation and the Jewish Question', *Jewish Journal of Sociology* 56, 1/2 (2014), 29-47: 30.
3   Email from Remco Ensel to Evelien Gans, 6 December 2015.

Selective philosemitism as an instrument of Islamophobia: oddly close to antisemitism[4]

When the Amsterdam Chief Rabbi Aron Schuster (1907-1994) spoke at the official festivities held to mark ten years of the Netherlands' liberation from Nazi occupation, he denounced the postwar treatment of the Jews in the Netherlands in strong terms. In the presence of Queen Juliana, Prince Bernhard and a throng of prominent politicians and ecclesiastical authorities, he declared: 'an antisemitic ideology has left its mark on the Netherlands, even in circles where it would once have been unthinkable'.[5] He and his predecessor Justus Tal (1881-1954) closely monitored antisemitic tendencies and utterances among shopkeepers, among former resistance workers, and among public officials. They followed the debates on kosher slaughter, opening hours in the retail trade, as well as antisemitic utter-ances in the press, in the street and elsewhere. The government did not practise any form of systematic political antisemitism. However, the wheels of restorative justice moved laboriously,[6] and indifference combined with gross negligence produced reactions that at times amounted to antisem-itism. In Amsterdam's population register, the cards of Jewish people were still being marked with a letter 'J' in 1946, until the *Nederlands-Israëlitisch Kerkgenootschap* (the umbrella organisation for Jewish communities in the Netherlands; NIK) protested against it. Some Jews were still receiving

4   For the phenomenon of philosemitism, *see* chapter 6; Jonathan and Karp and Adam Sutcliffe (eds.), *Philosemitism in History* (Cambridge: Cambridge University Press, 2011). *See also* Frank Stern, *The Whitewashing of the Yellow Badge: Antisemitism and Philosemitism in Postwar Germany* (Studies in Antisemitism Series) (Oxford: Pergamon Press, 1992).

5   *Algemeen Handelsblad*, 6 May 1955, quoted in Joel Fishman, 'Een keerpunt in de naoorlogse geschiedenis van de Nederlandse joden: De toespraak van opperrabbijn Schuster in de Nieuwe Kerk (1955).' In: Hetty Berg and Bart Wallet (eds.), *Wie niet weg is, is gezien. Joods Nederland na 1945* (Zwolle: Waanders, 2011), 119-129: 122. *See also* A.E. Cohen, 'Tien jaar na de bevrijding van nationaal-socialisme en jodenvervolging in Nederland (1955).' In: J.C.H. Blom et al. (eds.), *A.E. Cohen als geschiedschrijver van zijn tijd* (Amsterdam: Boom, 2005), 317-328: 321-322.

6   The most recent example is the restitution of money unlawfully collected for leasehold on property, in cases in which the Jewish owners had been dispossessed and had either been deported or had gone into hiding: *see* Hinke Piersma and Jeroen Kemperman, *Openstaande rekeningen. De gemeente Amsterdam en de gevolgen van roof en echtsherstel* (Amsterdam: Boom, 2015). Another very recent publication discusses the struggle to obtain payment of Jewish insurance benefits that have remained unpaid: Regina Grüter, *Strijd om gerechtigheid: Joodse verzekeringstegoeden en de Tweede Wereldoorlog* (Amsterdam: Boom, 2015).

tax forms marked with a letter 'J' as late as 1951.[7] In any case, Schuster's comment about antisemitism 'even in circles where it would once have been unthinkable' was a reference to the government, for instance in connection with its capricious attitude to kosher slaughter.[8]

There have been recurrent requests to the government, as the successor to the government in exile and its representatives in the occupied Netherlands, to apologise for its failure to protect the Jewish community, both during and after the war. The Netherlands has a track record of preferring not to apologise for anything at all.[9] The person who has persisted longest and hardest in trying to wrest apologies from the Dutch government has been the Dutch-Israeli chemist and publicist Manfred Gerstenfeld. As a young journalist, he took part in a debate about antisemitism in the Netherlands in 1962 for the *Nieuw Israëlietisch Weekblad* (*NIW*), along with several older, prominent Dutch Jews.[10] Gerstenfeld is attached to the Jerusalem Centre for Public Affairs, a think tank that concerns itself with 'Israel's security needs and international standing', and is a prolific author, largely in English. He is what the Jewish-American scholar and rabbi Arthur Hertzberg (1921-2006) has called a 'professional anti-antisemite'.[11] Gerstenfeld has doggedly pursued the goal of getting the government to apologise – most recently in 2015 – though without success.[12] His controversial book, published in Dutch,

7   Chaya Brasz, 'Na de Tweede Wereldoorlog: Van Kerkgenootschap naar culturele minderheid.' In: J.C.H. Blom, R.G. Fuks-Mansfeld and I. Schöffer (eds.), *Geschiedenis van de Joden in Nederland* (Balans: Amsterdam, 1995), 351-403: 356.

8   Fishman, 'Een keerpunt in de naoorlogse geschiedenis van de Nederlandse joden', 125-126. Schuster may also have been referring to the passive attitude adopted by the Royal House of Orange in relation to the Jews. In contrast to their actions before the war, neither Queen Wilhelmina nor her daughter Juliana, who came to the throne in 1948, had visited any synagogues or other Jewish institutions at this point. In this respect, Schuster's intervention made a difference. The first major events were the reception of the Conference of European rabbis at Soestdijk Palace in 1957 and a royal visit to the Portuguese Synagogue in 1958. For more criticism and bitter recollections of the Royal House on the part of Dutch Jews, on matters such as the mildness with which pardons were granted to German war criminals who had played a key role in the persecution of the Jews, *see, ibid.* and Bart Wallet, 'Van vergeten Joden en een spirituele koningin', *NIW*, 26 June 2015.

9   *See, e.g.*, the laborious efforts to procure an apology for the Dutch army's violent suppression of the Indonesian independence movement in 1947-1949, and for the Dutch slave trade.

10   *See* chapter 5.

11   Arthur Hertzberg, 'Is Anti-Semitism Dying out?', *The New York Review of Books*, 24 June 1993. For an extensive survey of English-language publications by Manfred Gerstenfeld, *see* https://en.wikipedia.org/wiki/Manfred_Gerstenfeld.

12   Abraham Cooper and Manfred Gerstenfeld, 'Tijd dat Nederland excuses aanbiedt voor lot van Joden', *NRC Handelsblad*, 31 July 2015. The article was originally published in *The Wall Street Journal*, but adapted by Gerstenfeld (Cooper is vice-dean of the Simon Wiesenthal Center, Los

Het Verval: Joden in een stuurloos Nederland [The Decay: Jews in a Rudderless Netherlands] (2010) contains a long and interesting list of subtle and less subtle instances of antisemitism as experienced by his respondents – a far from random group that he had indeed selected himself, and some of whom he interviewed anonymously. He made the remarkable assertion that while living Jews are not indispensable to Dutch society, society cannot do without Jews in their symbolic role.[13]

In his book and in interviews, however, he frequently goes off into a tirade, shorn of rational argument, against the 'Left' and 'the Muslim'. He calls Muslims the new Evil who will light the fuse of a new Holocaust. He paints a vivid picture of the square that will be named one day after Mohammed B. (the murderer of Theo van Gogh), where the so-called *Protocols of the Elders of Zion* and *Mein Kampf* will be on sale. He has attacked Job Cohen on two counts: as leader of the PvdA, the social democratic party that Gerstenfeld describes as the Dutch standard-bearer of 'Eurabia', and for Cohen's willingness to speak to Hamas, whom he calls 'Muslim propagandists of the mass murder of the Jews'. Gerstenfeld also describes Job Cohen as 'a Jew without any Jewish substance'. Indeed, he blames Cohen for the rise in antisemitism in Amsterdam in the twenty-first century, since Cohen (when still mayor) felt thoroughly at home in the city's mosques, but did not visit a synagogue for years. He was one of those whose attitude would lead to a new Shoah – this time carried out by Muslims.[14]

Angeles). Gerstenfeld's proposal was largely rejected – by historians, politicians, journalists, writers and a more general public – as too late, too simple, or gratuitous. The general sentiment was that it was more valuable to carry on remembering and studying the history of the persecution of the Jews. Moreover, some suggested that such apologies might be seen (however wrongly) as hypocritical, in the light of Israel's possible crimes against the Palestinians: Andreas Kouwenhoven, 'Afgedwongen excuses WO II "weinig waard"', *NRC Handelsblad*, 31 July 2015; 'Reinout Labberton, 'Te laat en overigens ook niet gewenst', *NRC Handelsblad*, 4 August 2015; several letters to the editor, *ibid.* The prominent Dutch Jewish author Arnon Grunberg wrote that while the behaviour of the Dutch government had left a great deal to be desired, what mattered most in the present era was to admit more refugees: Arnon Grunberg, 'Menselijkheid', *de Volkskrant*, 3 August 2015.

13   Manfred Gerstenfeld, *Het Verval. Joden in een stuurloos Nederland* (Amsterdam: Van Praag, 2010), *passim*: 26, 112.

14   *Ibid.*, 28, 36-37, 67-69, 72-73. Els van Tiggele, 'De polderdelta in verval. Boek van Manfred Gerstenfeld', *NIW*, 10 December 2010; Evelien Gans, 'Verbaal misdrijf, reactie op het artikel van rabbijn Evers "Job Cohens onmogelijke vergelijking"', *NIW*, 24 December 2010; Evelien Gans, 'De strijd tegen antisemitisme is verworden tot ideologie tegen moslims', *NRC Handelsblad*, 8 January 2011; Manfred Gerstenfeld, 'Laffe Jood, Joodse Zelfhaat. Dat zijn niet mijn woorden', *NRC Handelsblad*, 22 January 2011. In 2010 Job Cohen resigned as mayor to accept the leadership of the PvdA. *See also* chapters 12 and 14.

In many of the above points, Gerstenfeld (b. 1937) and PVV leader Geert
Wilders (b. 1963) are in profound agreement: they are anti-Islam and anti-
Muslim; anti-Left, fiercely pro-Israel. Both borrow the term 'Eurabia' from
the far-right Jewish American Bat Ye'or, whose book *Eurabia* (2005) conjures
up a nightmare image of an Islamised Europe. It was Wilders, whether or
not inspired by Gerstenfeld, who called on the Dutch government, in 2012,
to apologise for its 'spineless attitude' during the Second World War.[15] To
no avail.[16] Wilders is first and foremost an anti-Islam and anti-Muslim
populist. It is a position that has brought him huge electoral gains and
numerous invitations from kindred spirits abroad. At the same time it
makes it essential for him to have a permanent bodyguard.[17] At first sight
he appears to be a philosemite. His party, the PVV (which has no members,
only a leader and parliamentarians) was only founded in 2006. He has never
been a right-wing extremist – at least, not in a traditional sense – and does
not share the ballast of antisemitic ideas. Wilders presents himself as a
bosom friend of Israel and takes a stand against antisemitism. Looked at
more closely, however, his philosemitism turns out to be instrumental – it
has a not-so-hidden agenda. It is certainly true that Wilders developed great
sympathy for Israel as a young man. During his political life, however, he
has allied himself solely with the right-wing and far-right elements in Israel;
to Wilders, Israel represents above all a military and nationalist bastion
against Islam. He takes no interest whatsoever in achieving reconciliation
with the Palestinians or with the Arab countries. He supports the old 'Jordan
option': Judea and Samaria for Israel and Jordan for the Palestinians.[18]

15   David Haakman, 'PVV wil excuses voor "slappe houding" regering in WOII', *NRC Handelsblad*, 4 January 2012; Hans Klis, 'Oud-politici willen excuus Nederland voor jodenvervolging',
ibid. For Bat Ye'or *see also* chapter 17.
16   'Rutte: geen excuses voor negeren Jodenvervolging', *NRC Handelsblad*, 13 January 2012.
17   *See, e.g.*, his recent visit to Dallas (Texas, USA) to attend a contest for the best cartoons of the
prophet Muhammed: Bob Price, 'EXCLUSIVE: Geert Wilders to Keynote Muhammad Art Exhibit
and Contest in Texas', 15 February 2015: www.breitbart.com/texas/2015/02/15/geert-wilders-to-
keynote-muhammad-art-exhibit-and-contest-in-texas/ (consulted 24 November 2015). There
was a bomb attack by two – probably Islamist – terrorists, who were shot and killed; it was not
clear if Wilder and Pamela Geller were the targets: Victor Morton, 'Two killed in gunfight outside
Muhammad cartoon contest', *The Washington Times*, 3 May 2015; 'Wat deed Wilders in de VS?',
de Volkskrant, 4 May 2015. Wilders also visited the United Kingdom, Germany, Australia and
Israel, where he was both sponsored, welcomed and openly abused. After his appeal for 'fewer
Moroccans' (*see* note 28) some of his political friends and sponsors thought he had gone too
far: *see* Emilie van Outeren, 'Buitenlandtrips voor Wilders steeds lastiger', *de Volkskrant*, 6 May
2015.
18   Wilders visited Israel several times as a young man. Later he made friends with the
former Minister of Foreign Affairs (and present Defence Minister) Avigdor Lieberman and

Wilders can get on fine with Jews provided they share his ideas. But when confronted with left-wing or progressive Jews such as Job Cohen, the 'lefty crowd',[19] he expresses his disgust, referring to them – borrowing another term from his mentor, Bat Ye'or – as *dhimmis*. This term has been taken completely out of its original, ancient historical context. In the Islamic world, Jews and Christians were seen as *dhimmis*, second-class citizens who nonetheless had more privileges than other minorities because both groups were 'People of the Book'. Today, the term's sense has been twisted and vulgarised to mean one who bows to, or is in league with, Islam.[20] Wilders' approach, then, is best described as 'selective philosemitism', as a counterpart to historian Peter Gay's concept of 'selective antisemitism'.[21] Wilders' fight against antisemitism, too, is largely selective. He and his parliamentarians practise anti-antisemitism mainly as an instrument in their campaigns against Muslims and Islam. As we have seen in this book, there is undoubtedly a large – not infrequently extreme – measure of anti-semitism to be found in Muslim circles. The relevant point here, however, is the fact that the PVV's protests chiefly target *Muslim* antisemitism.[22] We

Arjeh Eldad – both far-right Israeli politicians who want 'the Arabs' out of Israel: Evelien Gans, 'Anti-Antisemitic Enthusiasm and Selective Philosemitism: Wilders, the PVV and the Jews': wwww.jmberlin.de/main/DE/05-Publikationen/07-online-publikationen.php, and Evelien Gans, 'Anti-Antisemitischer Enthusiasmus & selektiver Philosemitismus: Geert Wilders, die PVV und die Juden', *Jahrbuch für Antisemitismusforschung* 23 (2014), 95-104.

19   The Dutch term is *'linkse kerk'* ('left-wing Church'), an allusion to the now long-dissolved compartmentalisation of Dutch society, primarily along religious lines.

20   Gans, 'On gas chambers, Jewish Nazis and noses', 78. Dik van Arkel, 'Genealogisch verband van antisemitische vooroordelen', in Dik van Arkel, R. Munk (ed.) et al., *Wat is antisemitisme? Een benadering vanuit vier disciplines* (Kampen: Kok, 1991), 54; Allan Harris Cutler and Helen Elmquist Cutler, *The Jew as Ally of the Muslim: Medieval Roots of Antisemitism* (Notre Dame: University of Notre Dame Press, 1986); Gans, 'Anti-Antisemitic Enthusiasm and Selective Philosemitism', 3; Ralph Pluim, 'Hoe nemen Nederlanders het Jodendom van Job Cohen en van andere Joodse politici waar?' (unpublished paper, Amsterdam 2010), 90-91. I thank Ralph Pluim. For other, known and controversial, anti-Islam activists and political friends of Wilders, including Pamela Geller and Robert Spencer, *see* Guus Valk, 'Geert Wilders' marginale vrienden', *NRC Handelsblad*, 5 May 2015. *See also* chapter 15.

21   Peter Gay used the concept of 'selective antisemitism' in the context of early twentieth-century attitudes among Berlin Jews and non-Jews, in which Jewish immigrants from Eastern Europe were seen as primitive and hence inferior. It is a classic example of a supposed dichotomy between 'good' and 'bad' Jews: Peter Gay, *Freud, Jews and other Germans: Masters and Victims in Modernist Culture* (New York: Oxford University Press, 1978), 152; Evelien Gans, *De kleine verschillen. Een historische studie naar joodse sociaal-democraten en socialistisch-zionisten in Nederland* (Amsterdam: Vassallucci, 1999), 208-210.

22   Fleur Agema, a prominent PVV MP, claimed in 2009 that antisemitism and homophobia were not 'Dutch customs', but attitudes largely imported from Morocco. This is obviously far from the truth: *see, e.g.*, Gans, 'Hamas, Hamas, All Jews to the gas', 96. This remark was made by Agema

may label such an approach 'anti-antisemitic enthusiasm' – being a form of anti-antisemitism that has a suspiciously eager ring to it, because it has a hidden meaning, a double, political agenda – in this case, Islam bashing. The PVV likes to emphasise that Islam teaches that it is Allah's wish to kill the Jews, and that Islam is 'essentially antisemitic', with the Quran stating that Jews are apes, swine and the Devil's servants. This is an extremely crude interpretation in which anti-Islam activists and Islamists form grotesque allies.[23]

Wilders' condemnation of the antisemitic utterances in 2014 of Jean-Marie Le Pen, the father of Marine Le Pen, the current leader of the Front National (FN), was half-hearted.[24] He cooperates closely with Le Pen Junior in the European Parliament. Like the FN, other parties too within this paradoxically Nationalist International, which is anti-Europe, anti-Islam and anti-immigration, have an antisemitic ideological past that the party leadership is trying to shake off. This is no easy task, given that these views are always lurking just around the corner.[25] Wilders adopted a similarly non-chalant attitude to *Voorpost*, a far-right Dutch group that is both antisemitic

on 15 April 2009: website PVV www.pvv.nl/index.php?option=com_content&task=view&id=1906; an audio recording of her entire speech was posted on YouTube: www.youtube.com/watch?v=CDSvXoFrDd8 (both were consulted in June 2009, but they are no longer available).

23   In this case it was PVV MP Joram van Klaveren: Emergency debate on the rapid rise of antisemitism in the Netherlands. Tweede Kamer [House of Representatives], 24 June 2010, Tweede Kamer 91, 91-7576; 'Verslag Algemeen Overleg Vaste Commissie voor Binnenlandse Zaken', 2 February 2011, Tweede Kamer, 2010-2011, 30 950, no. 22, 11-12. For a critical analysis of this kind of interpretation of Islam, *see, e.g.*, Mark Cohen, who writes that Christianity was bound to Judaism willy-nilly, while Islamic law 'lacked a specific focus on Jews': Mark Cohen, *Under Crescent and Cross: The Jews in the Middle Ages* (Princeton NJ: Princeton University Press, 1995), 54. The term 'anti-antisemitic enthusiasm' is inspired by Abram de Swaan's use of the term 'anti-Israel enthusiasm' in his article 'Anti-Israëlische enthousiasmes en de tragedie van het blind proces', *De Gids* 168 (2005), 349-367; *see also* chapter 14.

24   In June 2014, Jean-Marie Le Pen, the founder of the FN, notorious for his repeated assertion that the gas chambers were a mere detail in the history of the Second World War, made the following comment with regard to French artists who spoke out against the FN, with particular reference to the Jewish singer Patrick Bruel: 'On fera une fournée la prochaine fois' (We'll stick them/him in the oven next time'). Marine Le Pen blamed her father mainly for his failure to foresee that these words might be subjected to 'a malicious interpretation'. Wilders said that Le Pen's words were 'disgusting – *if actually uttered and intended in this sense*' (italics added): 'Jean-Marie Le Pen splijt Front National na antisemitische uithaal', and 'Uitspraak Jean-Marie Le Pen is meer dan "een politieke fout"', *NRC Handelsblad*, 10 June 2014.

25   Maurice Swirc, 'Geert Wilders, geen vriend van de Joden', *NIW*, 25 September 2013. Other allies include the Austrian FPÖ, the Italian Liga Nord, the Belgian Vlaams Belang, and certain members of the Polish Congress of the New Right (KNP) and the British UK Independence Party (UKIP): *NRC Handelsblad*, 16 June 2015. Austrian FPÖ leader Strache posted an antisemitic caricature of a Jewish banker on his Facebook page, but after their meeting in Vienna Wilders

Illustration 26 **Photo of a demonstration against the politics of Geert Wilders, 22 March 2014**

Remco Ensel, 22 March 2014

'The Holocaust a detail in History.' A man protests against Geert Wilders' rapprochement with Le Front National (FN) at the annual International Day against Racism, 2014. Jean-Marie Le Pen, the father of the present FN leader Marine Le Pen, had repeatedly called the Holocaust a detail in history.

and Islamophobic, which waved the Prince's Flag at a PVV demonstration. This orange-white-and-blue historical flag has its roots with the Orangists who fought in the Eighty Years' War (1568-1648). But in the 1930s it became tainted, when the Dutch National Socialists (NSB) adopted it as their flag.[26] On the day following the demonstration, Wilders was compelled to dissociate himself and his supporters from extremism and antisemitism in the Dutch Parliament. Yet even as he did so, four PVV members of parliament

tweeted that he had met a 'very impressive man': The PVV had more in common with the FPÖ 'than with the rest of Dutch Parliament': Swirc, 'Geert Wilders geen vriend van de Joden'.
26   André Horlings, 'Prinsenvlag niet van NSB-smetten vrij': http://historiek.net/prinsenvlag-nsb-smettenvrij/37267/ (consulted 13 November 2015).

sat demonstratively wearing pins in the shape of the Prince's Flag. It is evidently hard for Wilders and for Martin Bosma (b. 1964), who frames the PVV's ideology, to unequivocally cut all ties with the far right.[27]

We have already seen that parties once clearly ranked among the far right have been modifying their political accents. It is no longer easy to make political capital out of antisemitism. Moreover, the commemoration of the Holocaust may serve, in the words of Tony Judt, as 'the contemporary European entry ticket'.[28] And as Israel moves ever further to the right, its instrumentalisation as a partner in the struggle against Islam is all the more convenient. After a long string of incidents culminating in her father's profession of sympathy for the Vichy regime, Marine Le Pen first suspended him and subsequently expelled him from the party. By then he had become too great a liability, threatening her nationalist-populist course and her

27   De Volkskrant, 23 September 2013; Evelien Gans, 'Door PVV'ers gedragen vlag symboliseert politiek van uitsluiting', de Volkskrant, 8 October 2013, with a rectification in de Volkskrant, 9 October 2013; NRC Handelsblad, 10 October 2013. For Martin Bosma the Israeli flag symbolises explicitly 'liberated territory': Robert van Heuven, Interview Martin Bosma (PVV): 'Kunstenaars beschadigen wat niet-links is', 4 August 2011. wwww.robbertvanheuven.nl/?tag=ivo-van-hove (consulted 26 February 2014). Martin Bosma sees the 'Prince's Flag' as a bastion against the so-called Islamisation of the Netherlands and Europe. He warns that if 'the Left' gets its way, the Netherlands will be forced – like Israel – to give up 'land for peace', abandoning territory 'in order to appease Islam': Martin Bosma, De Schijn-elite van de valsemunters [The bogus elite of the counterfeiters], Drees, extreem rechts, de sixties, nuttige idioten, Groep Wilders en ik (Amsterdam: Bert Bakker, 2010), 274. In 2015 Bosma published Minderheid in eigen land: Hoe progressieve strijd ontaardt in genocide en ANC-apartheid (IJmuiden : Bibliotheca Africana Formicae, 2015) [A minority in one's own country: How progressive struggle degenerates into genocide and ANC apartheid]. This is essentially a book that defines white supremacy in opposition to black (ANC) terror. It is interesting that Amsterdam's former (Jewish) mayor Ed van Thijn, as a figurehead of the anti-racist movement in the Netherlands, features on the cover of the book. For a critical review, see Bas Kromhout, 'Recensie: Martin Bosma doet de waarheid over Zuid-Afrika geweld aan: Bij het boek Minderheid in eigen land', ThePostOnline, 4 June 2015. http://politiek.tpo.nl/2015/06/04/recensie-martin-bosma-doet-de-waarheid-over-zuid-afrika-geweld-aan/; Tom-Jan Meeus, 'Bosma, zijn boek, en zijn soms vernederende leven in de PVV', NRC Handelsblad, 30/31 May 2015 (both consulted 13 November 2015).
28   Tony Judt, Postwar: A History of Europe since 1945 (New York: Penguin, 2005), 803. Inevitably this invokes the parallel observation, by Heinrich Heine, that conversion to Christianity was the Jews' entry ticket into European civilisation. See also David Wertheim, 'Wilders, Le Pen kapen de Joodse zaak', NRC Handelsblad, 13 November 2013; The Dutch historian David Wertheim organised an international conference on 'The Jew as Legitimation' in Amsterdam, in August 2013; David Werheim (ed.), The Jews as Legitimation. Jewish-Non-Jewish Relationships beyond Antisemitism and Philosemitism (under review); David Wertheim, 'Geert Wilders and the Nationalist Populist Turn toward the Jews in Europe', ibid.

hugely-expanded support base: in other words, he stood in the way of the FN's path to power.[29]

It should be noted that the PVV was among the political parties that expressed outrage in Parliament at the antisemitic slogans shouted by football crowds in 2011. However, although the PVV cooperated with other MPs to draft a memorandum that sought to make football 'fun for everyone' again, the PVV's next comment on the issue omitted all mention of the word 'antisemitic'. Instead, the party called for Ajax supporters to be told immediately to stop calling themselves 'the Jews', their traditional affectionate nickname.[30] This reaction to native Dutch football hooligans was worlds apart from Wilders' earlier reaction to football hooligans of Moroccan descent in 2007. When these youngsters had been found guilty of repeated misconduct, Wilders not only demanded a long prison sentence, but added that the offenders should first be forced to clean a few football stadiums with their own toothbrushes.[31] Cleaning a floor or street with a small brush is a traditional humiliating punishment meted out at schools and in the army. This particular form of humiliation has its own icon: a photograph of Austrian Jews cleaning a street in Vienna in 1938, with Nazis and Austrian bystanders looking on.[32]

Concluding, what Wilders does, practising his selective philosemitism is instrumentalising a so-called 'universalistic Jewry', and using the stereotype of 'the Jew' to help bolster and justify his anti-Islam policies.[33]

29   Peter Vermaas, '"Vadermoord" stort het Front National in crisis', *NRC Handelsblad*, 9 April 2015; idem, 'Geschorste Le Pen père voelt zich verraden', *ibid.*, 5 & 6 May 2015.
30   Questions asked by MPs, with the government's replies, Tweede Kamer, 2010-2011, *Aanhangsel*, 2522, 17 May 2011. *See also* chapter 11.
31   *NRC Handelsblad*, 23 May 2007.
32   Evelien Gans, 'Weg met vernedering. Extreem-rechts keert zich niet per se tegen joden', *de Volkskrant* Opinie online, 17 December 2009: www.volkskrant.nl/search/?query=Weg+met +vernedering.+Extreem-rechts+keert+zich+niet+per+se+tegen+joden. For the photos, *see, e.g.,* Geert Mak, 'Zo werd verzet uitgevonden... Toespraak bij de herdenking van de Februaristaking', 25 February 2010: wwww.geertmak.nl/nl/Land/Essays%20en%20lezingen/461.html (consulted 28 January 2016); and Huib Riethof, 'De tien walgelijkste Wilders-ismes: 4. De tandenborstels', Krapuul.nl, 26 February 2011: www.krapuul.nl/overig/blog/27762/de-10-walgelijkste-wilderis-mes-4-de-tandenborstels/ (consulted 17 November 2015); Ernst Hirsch Ballin, 'Je moet eerst de ander zien te begrijpen', *Vrij Nederland*, 10 May 2008.
33   Wertheim, 'Wilders, Le Pen kapen de Joodse zaak.' Gans, 'Anti-Antisemitic Enthusiasm and Selective Philosemitism', 2.

The ritual slaughter of animals: the primitive, cruel, bloodthirsty Jew – and Muslim

The bill to ban the ritual slaughter of animals that was introduced into Parliament in June 2011 must have driven a wedge between Wilders and Gerstenfeld.[34] Public opposition to the ritual (i.e. unstunned) slaughter of animals is not a new phenomenon. The Dutch Animal Protection Society protested about it even before the Second World War, occasionally in terms that resonate with anti-Jewish propaganda, such as in the title of the pamphlet *Tegen Dieren martelen* [Against the torture of animals].[35] In Germany, the abolition of ritual slaughter was one of the first measures introduced by the Nazis, and they quickly did the same in the occupied Netherlands. This is not to say that to protest or take action against unstunned slaughter is necessarily antisemitic. It depends on the wording and context whether the opposition to kosher slaughter takes on a subtle or explicit anti-Jewish dimension. We shall not deal here with the highly complex issue of whether unstunned slaughter – provided it is carried out according to the rules, in other words with the use of a single razor-sharp cut through the carotid artery – causes more or less pain to an animal than industrial slaughter carried out under electronic anaesthesia or gas. The debate constantly gravitated towards this bone of contention, on which the experts remain divided. The question to be examined here is why the bill submitted in 2011 acquired so much support. We shall also seek to identify where the reactions to Jewish protests, in particular, overstepped the mark.[36]

Immediately after the liberation of the Netherlands from occupation, the reintroduction of *shechita*, the kosher, unstunned slaughter of animals, was a bone of contention. Here, as in the legislation on compulsory closing hours,[37] the government (this time the health ministry in consultation with the Animal Protection Agency) was inclined to maintain the ban

34 Manfred Gerstenfeld, 'Open brief aan Tweede Kamer over ritueel slachten', *Dagelijkse standaard*, 14 June 2011; www.dagelijksestandaard.nl/2011/06/open-brief-aan-tweede-kamer-over-ritueel-slachten and idem, 'Argumenten tegen ritueel slachten kloppen niet', *de Volkskrant*, 14 June 2011: www.volkskrant.nl/opinie/argumenten-tegen-religieus-slachten-kloppen-niet~a2447178/ (consulted 8 September 2011 and 29 January 2016).

35 F.F.W. Kattenbusch, 'Tegen Dierenmartelen. Wat gij niet wilt dat u geschiedt …. Open brief aan den Heer Joodschen Medewerker van "Het Vaderland"' (Gorinchem: J. Noorduyn en Zoon N.V., 1934).

36 The Muslim community also protested, of course (halal slaughter displays many similarities to *shechita*, such as its non-anaesthetised nature), as did Christian parties for whom religious freedom is a key priority.

37 See chapter 5.

on *shechita*. After persistent protests from the Jewish community, most notably Chief Rabbi Tal, a compromise was reached in 1949: *shechita* was to be permitted, but had to be done henceforth in public slaughterhouses designated by the Minister, of which there were to be just thirteen. Although in principle the conflict involved balancing freedom of religion against animal protection, under both constitutional and criminal law, it was the power of numbers that decided the issue. It was much the same as with the delayed legislation to permit shops to open on Sundays: the reduced number of Jews produced less power, in the well-known snowball effect. Few were left who ate kosher meat, whether for religious reasons or from habit, and if they happened to live too far from one of the thirteen slaughterhouses, they were out of luck. The same applied to Jewish butchers who had survived the war. Thus in this way, the Shoah worked against the Jews again.

The arguments employed by certain civil servants were at least as crude, if not cruder. During the occupation, the Chief Rabbi had acquiesced with prior anaesthesia – for health reasons; meat was a source of protein. 'In such a life-or-death emergency, we are entitled to say "yes".'[38] After the war, this was used against the Jews. In 1949, the health ministry wrote 'what was kosher then will have to be kosher now ... exaggerated orthodoxy prompts the Jews to desire more than is necessary.'[39] Similar arguments resurfaced in the 1980s, when ritual slaughter was being debated again, as it had indeed been debated in the intervening years.[40] The chief inspectorate of the Animal Protection Society in Hilversum published a study on ritual slaughter that once again urged the introduction of a ban. One of the arguments put forward in the study was that Jews were permitted to eat non-kosher meat in an emergency. Well, such an emergency would now be created: after all, Jews had not been able to adhere to their laws in the camps either. In a discussion with State Secretary Ad Ploeg and his officials, in 1984, similar words were used.[41]

38 Justus Tal, 'Rapport inzake het rituele slachten vanwege het Opperrabbinaat voor Nederland', 1 September 1949, 13.
39 Letter from Quadvlieg, 4 May 1949, Nationaal Archief [National Archives], Archief Volksgezondheid (1902) 1918-1950 (1976) (2.15.37), inv. no. 829.
40 In 1975, for example, the export of ritually slaughtered meat was banned, which provoked vehement protests from Jewish organisations: *see, e.g.,* 'Renate Katz, 'Centrale Commissie oefent kritiek op landbouw uit', *NIW*, 31 January 1975; 'Protest tegen verbod koosjer slachten', *NRC Handelsblad*, 8 January 1975, 'Verbod op ritueel slachten voor export veroorzaakt onrust', *NRC Handelsblad*, 13 January 1975.
41 The chief inspector concerned was D. van Oers: *see* Lody van de Kamp, 'Oude koeien uit de sloot', column (unpublished) sent to the author, email, 6 March 2011, and idem, *Dagboek van een verdoofd rabbijn: Persoonlijke notities bij een politieke aardverschuiving* (Zoetermeer:

Following the gradual influx of Islamic immigrants, since the 1960s, *dhabiyah*, or halal slaughter, which shares many, though not all, characteristics of *shechita*, was also approved in 1977 – if only to prevent the illegal slaughter of animals in private.[42] This was grist to the mill of Hans Janmaat (1934-2002), chairman and parliamentary leader of the far-right Centrum Party, who referred to 'medieval torture', and a fellow party member spoke of an 'animal holocaust'.[43] Far-right and right-wing populist parties took a firm and immovable stand against unstunned slaughter. The historian Bart Wallet (b. 1977) shows how the supporters and opponents of ritual slaughter switched sides in the postwar period. The Christian parties were initially opposed to it, on the principle that the Netherlands was a country in which Christian standards were to be applied. For left-wing and liberal parties such as PvdA, D66, and PPR, on the other hand, ritual slaughter was a laudable litmus test of the multicultural society – for the centre-right party VVD it was a proof of the principle of equality.

These positions started to shift when, following the attacks of 11 September 2001 and Pim Fortuyn's arrival on the political scene, Islam and the multicultural society attracted increasingly harsh criticism. And as secular standards became more and more dominant, and religious values started to be suppressed, people changed sides. In 2011, the progressive Party for Animals, which had been founded – like the PVV – in 2006, tabled a motion to prohibit non-anaesthetised slaughter, and gained support from progressive parties such as the Socialist Party (SP), Green Left and D66.[44] The social democrats (PvdA), as so often, dithered on the fence for a while, but in the end the PvdA voted in favour of the ban, which Parliament passed by a large majority on 28 June 2011.[45] The passage of this bill – and the events leading

---

Boekencentrum, 2012), 82-83. In the 1980s, Rabbi Van de Kamp was often a member of the Jewish delegations that consulted with the Ministry of Agriculture and Fisheries. *See also* Bas Kromhout, 'Kritiek op ritueel slachten soms antisemitisch. Dierenbeschermers wilden in 1945 Duits verbod handhaven', Interview with Evelien Gans, *Historisch Nieuwsblad*, 3, 2011.

42 *Shechita* is 'stricter' than *dhabiyah* in some areas, for instance in relation to training, the use of the knife, and the removal of the blood. This means that Muslims are always permitted to eat kosher meat, while the reverse does not necessarily apply.

43 Bart Wallet, 'Hoe voor- en tegenstanders van de rituele slacht van rol wisselen', *Trouw*, 14 May 2011; Max van Weezel, 'We hebben er weer een godsdienstoorlog bij', *Vrij Nederland*, 20 April 2011. *See also* 'Immigratie is sociaal-culturele vivisectie op het Nederlandse volk. Vraaggesprek Alfred Vierling voor Nationalistische Agenda / Vooraan!', *NRC Handelsblad*, 2 June 1984. Janmaat asked questions in parliament about this issue in 1985. For the Centrum Party, *see also* chapter 4.

44 *Ibid.*

45 Ron Meerhof, 'VVD in senaat tegen verbod rituele slacht', *de Volkskrant*, 19 October 2011.

up to it – caused considerable international controversy. One academic journal carried an article in which it was observed that 'liberal secularism is on its way to becoming the new group-think'.[46] Jewish organisations, in particular, protested vehemently. The Simon Wiesenthal Center (SWC) in Los Angeles, for instance, sent a letter to party leaders who had supported the ban seeking to persuade them otherwise. In addition, the bill was one of the main subjects of discussion at a meeting of European rabbis in Warsaw.[47] The British Chief Rabbi Jonathan Sacks (b. 1948) defended Jewish ritual slaughter in a public hearing of the Dutch Parliament. Here and there, these vigorous Jewish interventions led to accusations, or blunt observations, that the omnipresent 'Jewish lobby' was at work again.[48] Predictably, the vilest reactions came from the neo-Nazi Stormfront.[49]

Animal rights and religious freedom went into battle and animal rights came out on top: that is one of the many interpretations. The subject was in danger of becoming oversimplified, since the conflict was framed in terms of an opposition between animal lovers and animal tormenters. Viewed from a different perspective, the issue revolved around the rights of the majority as against those of a minority. Once again, it was numbers that mattered. Opponents of the ban labelled it political tokenism and opportunism. After all, the ban affected the slaughter of a relatively small number of animals, as opposed to industrial livestock production, which

46 Markha Valenta, 'The Future of Islamophobia: the Liberal, the Jew, the Animal', 8 June 2011: wwww.berfrois.com/2011/06/liberal-secularism-new-group-think/. *See also* Argemira Florez, Jesse Hettema, Alma Ibrahimovic, 'Reading Between the Lines: How the Debate on Ritual Slaughter Exposed Dutch Racism': wwww.humanityinaction.org/knowledgebase/540-reading-between-the-lines-how-the-debate-on-ritual-slaughter-exposed-dutch-racism (both consulted 23 November 2015).

47 'Joden lobbyen voor rituele slacht', *NRC Handelsblad*, 16 February 2011; *Trouw*, 31 October 2011. Manfred Gerstenfeld names many more Jewish organisations, including the World (and European) Jewish Congress, the Assembly of Italian Rabbis, Jewish community organisations in France, Great Britain, Austria etc.: Manfred Gerstenfeld, 'Ending the Anne Frank myth', 16 May 2011, posted on the blog of Kehilat Elz Hayim, 27 June 2011: http://etzhayimministry.webs.com/apps/blog/show/7527481-ending-the-anne-frank-myth (consulted 23 November 2015).

48 *See, e.g.*, Janny Groen, 'Samen in het geweer tegen aanval op halalvlees, "we zijn in shock"', *de Volkskrant*, 13 September 2011; reply to the Open Letter of Manfred Gerstenfeld to the Lower House about ritual slaughter: http://opinie.volkskrant.nl/artikel/show/id/8705/Argumenten_tegen_religieus_slachten_kloppen_niet (consulted 16 September 2011). *See also* note 62.

49 The following reply appeared in response to the letters sent by the SWC: 'And that's why I hate Jews. F*cking whiney bastards, ugh! ugh!' and 'I thought that sh*tty Jew Simon Wiesenthal died years ago. Some stuff you just can't get rid of', www.stormfront.org/forum/t780528/ (consulted 25 November 2015).

is supported by an influential agriculture lobby: as if there were no abuses in industrial livestock production. It looked as though the political parties had said farewell to the principle of the multicultural society, and were bidding against each other, as the legal scholar Wouter Veraart (b. 1971) wrote, to 'single out everything that diverged from the norm in a cultural, and especially a religious, sense, to make it suspect, and then to neutralise it by banning it by law'.[50] The historian Jaap Cohen (b. 1980) coined the phrase 'animal populism'.[51] In Belgium, a similar objection was raised, in 2015, against the proposal of a bill by the Flemish-Belgian Minister of, among others, Animal Welfare, Ben Weyts, in favour of a total ban on ritual slaughter.[52] A Dutch supporter of the ban, however, pointed out the archaic nature of non-anaesthetised slaughter, and suggested, not entirely without reason, that some Jews were lending force to their arguments with manipulative references to the Holocaust.[53] He himself advocated removing religious freedom from the Constitution, and proposed *en passant* another ban, on the circumcision of boys, as an expression of 'obscurantism'.[54] He was not the only commentator to suggest a link between ritual slaughter and circumcision. In consequence, a fierce debate erupted (one that has not yet been decided either way) between the supporters and opponents of a ban on circumcision.[55] Both debates are taking place all over the Western

50   Wouter Veraart opposed the ban in 'Een regen van verboden lost niets op', *NRC Handelsblad*, 9/10 April 2011.

51   Jaap Cohen, 'De slachtstrijd is weer opgelaaid', *NRC Next* 28 June 2011. A spokesperson for the Muslims and Government Contact Organisation (CMO) acknowledged, it should be said, that 'a lot still goes wrong in our slaughterhouses': 'Joodse en Islamitische organisaties gekrenkt door slachtvoorstel', *NRC Handelsblad*, 16 June 2011.

52   Rik Torfs, 'Mens(enrecht) versus dier(enrecht)', *De Standaard*, 13 August 2015. Rik Torfs is the rector of the Katholieke Universiteit Leuven. There were reactions too on the part of both Jews and Muslims, *see, e.g.,* Marjan Justaert, '"De laatste die onze rituele slachtingen verbood, was Adolf Hitler". Interview with Michael Freilich (Joods Aktueel)', *ibid.*, 11 August 2015; Dyab Abou Jahjah (the former chairman of AEL, now of Movement X, *see* chapters 12 and 14) attacked Freilich on his 'Holocaust argument' and on the fact that he (like Gerstenfeld) stated that a Jewish ritual slaughter (*shochet*) has a much more thorough education than his Muslim brothers. Jahjah denied that non-anaesthetised slaughter was by definition not halal, denouncing, however, both the opportunist policy of Weyts and warning the Belgian Muslims to focus on more relevant issues like the struggle against Islamophobia: 'Met verdoofd slachten is niks mis, met islamofobie wel', *ibid.,* 13 August 2015.

53   The literary theorist and committed 'freethinker' August Hans den Boef, in 'Er kómt helemaal geen verbod op rituele slacht', *ibid.* Several of the protests, though not all, referred to the Holocaust. Some were phrased in a manipulative way, in terms of context and phrasing.

54   Den Boef, 'Er kómt helemaal geen verbod op rituele slacht'.

55   *See, e.g.,* two Dutch intellectuals of (partly) Jewish descent who took opposing positions: the sociologist and publicist Herman Vuijsje (against circumcision), 'Besnijden, het weigeren van

world.[56] We are put in mind of Robert Fine's words on efforts to depict 'the Jews' as 'a particularistic people incapable of embracing the values of universal humanity'.[57]

The right-wing daily newspaper *De Telegraaf* (the paper with the largest circulation in the country) has called the Bible 'a book that is dripping with blood; the cruelly-slaughtered lambs virtually spill from its pages'.[58] A similar picture is sketched by the leader of the Party for Animals, Marianne Thieme, who writes that the Amsterdam rabbi Raphael Evers advocates 'the bloody ritual of cutting a creature's throat'.[59]

The conflict has been fought out in social media as well as in the mainstream press.[60] A cartoon published by the popular, deliberately 'politically incorrect' and right-wing populist weblog *GeenStijl* depicting two stereotypical Orthodox Jews, with the caption 'But is it all right if we carry on slaughtering Palestinians without stunning them?' provoked a flurry of divergent reactions. The cartoon thus forges a direct link between a traditional religious method of slaughtering animals and the politics of Israel. In view of the profile of *GeenStijl*, most commentators advocated freedom of expression (cartoons and captions like this must be allowed), while others contributed anti-Islam and anti-Muslim views, such as that there had certainly been more Jews slaughtered without stunning by Arabs than the other way round in the past 1400 years, and that Muslims were

---

vaccinatie: dat gebeurt niet om het geloof', *NRC Handelsblad*, 8/9 September 2012 and a critical response by Emeritus Professor of Sociology Abram de Swaan, 'Klagen besneden joden dan?', *ibid.*, 15/16 September 2012. We shall not go into the pros and cons of circumcision here.

56 *See, e.g.*, RD.nl, 'Interreligieuze actie Duitse Joden en moslims voor besnijdenis', 10 September 2012; Frank Furedi, 'The bigotry of the anti-circumcision zealots', *Sp!ked Online*, 2 July 2012: www.spiked-online.com/newsite/article/12595#.VlQ9m3ldGmw (consulted 24 November 2015). Matthea Westerduin, Yolande Jansen, Karin Neutel, 'Jongensbesnijdenis tussen religie, recht en geschiedenis,' in *Filosofie & Praktijk*, Vol. 35, Nr. 3, 35-55.

57 Fine, 'Two faces of Universalism', 29-30.

58 Orig. 'een boek dat druipt van het bloed; de wreed geslachte lammetjes vallen zowat van de pagina's af'; quoted in Bas Kromhout, 'Kritiek op ritueel slachten soms antisemitisch'.

59 Marianne Thieme, 'Onverdoofd slachten niet te rijmen met joodse voorschriften', RD.nl (*Reformatorisch Dagblad*), 10 December 2010: wwww.refdag.nl/opinie/ onverdoofd_slachten_niet_te_rijmen_met_joodse_voorschriften_1_523118

60 Some examples in the mainstream press are given above. A vast number of articles have been published by authors on both sides of the debate; the author has preserved them in her personal archive. A few may be mentioned here, however: an article by the internationally respected agriculture and food expert, Professor Louise Fresco: 'Bloed en rituelen', *NRC Handelsblad*, 13 April 2011; *see also* Louise Fresco, *Hamburgers in het paradijs: voedsel in tijden van schaarste en overvloed* (Amsterdam: Bert Bakker 2012) 142-144. Translated into English as *Hamburgers in Paradise: The stories behind the food we eat* (Princeton/New Jersey: Princeton University Press, 2015).

Illustration 27   Cartoon on ritual slaughter by D.C. Lama

D.C. Lama / geenstijl.nl, 6 June 2011

'But is it all right if we carry on slaughtering Palestinians without stunning them?'

'creepy, totalitarian, autistic gnus'.[61] A few writers drew attention to Gaza, where 'thousands of homes were destroyed in the Israeli anti-rocket invasion two and a half years ago and have not been rebuilt'. There were also other types of criticism: ultra-Orthodox, in some cases defined even more precisely than that: Haredi Jews were exempt from military service, so the caption made no sense. A few comments included jokes along the lines of 'the noses are too small'. The word 'antisemitism' was mentioned only once, and then to refute any such implication. And only one respondent

---

61   For all these replies, *see* wwww.geenstijl.nl/mt/archieven/2011/07/een_jodencartoon_kan_ dat_wel_z.html (consulted 22 November 2015). The same was said about Palestinians: they slaughtered Jews and not the other way around. The cartoon was drawn by D.C. Lama, who produced many of the cartoons on Theo van Gogh's website, 'De gezonde roker' (The healthy smoker): www.theovangogh.nl/lama/5jaar_lama.htm. I thank Katie Digan.

pointed out that the true venom of the caption was in the word 'slaughter': it is true that Palestinians were being killed, but 'there is no Palestinian holocaust going on'.[62]

When Manfred Gerstenfeld wrote an open letter to the Dutch Parliament objecting to the ban on unstunned slaughter,[63] his letter provoked hundreds of reactions on both sides, from cautious to crass,[64] some of them antisemitic and/or Islamophobic. The present section focuses on the latter categories. A return of the topos of 'the Jew' and 'the Muslim' as child murderers cropped up in the proposition that arguments in favour of ritual slaughter do not differ in principle from those in favour of the ritual slaughter of children. To allow one implied allowing the other too. The replies revived the old blood libel – whereas kosher and halal slaughter are designed precisely to prevent contact with blood. Another response: would a Jew facing certain death be given morphine first, or would his throat merely be cut without anaesthesia? The ritual slaughter of animals was compared to stoning, wife-beating, slavery, the massacre of infidels, and human sacrifices. Some accusations singled out Jews, some singled out Muslims, and often no clear distinction was drawn.[65]

In practice, Jews and Muslims alike were targeted in this polemic. Revisiting the rhetoric of medieval Christianity,[66] both groups were frequently depicted as 'the primitive enemy':

> Judaism is just as primitive an ideology as Islam. Both subject children and animals to ill-treatment for their personal pleasure. This is perverse and archaic, and should be punished. There should be an END to this special position enjoyed by religious fanatics.[67]

62   The killing of Palestinians was explicitly played down: 'as people, unfortunately, lose their lives in every conflict': see wwww.geenstijl.nl/mt/archieven/2011/07/een_jodencartoon_kan_dat_wel_z.html (consulted 22 November 2015).

63   Point 1 of Gerstenfeld's letter referred to 'the great difference between kosher and halal slaughter' (to the benefit of the former). He went on to confine himself exclusively to kosher slaughter, for which many respondents later took him to task. Reactions on: Gerstenfeld, 'Argumenten tegen religieus slachten kloppen niet': http://opinie.volkskrant.nl/artikel/show/id/8705/Argumenten_tegen_religieus_slachten_kloppen_niet (consulted 16 September 2011).

64   For instance, a well-argued exposition of the differences in eating culture was followed by the assertion that non-Dutch people must in any case keep to 'our rules'. This provoked a string of protests: *ibid*.

65   *Ibid.*

66   Cutler and Cutler, *The Jew as Ally of the Muslim*; see note 20.

67   'Voor mij een reden' in response to Bart-Jan Spruyt, 'Geert Wilders en de Joden', 24 August 2012 (consulted 4 November 2013). The anonymous author also fiercely denounces circumcision; Gans, 'Anti-Antisemitic Enthusiasm and Selective Philosemitsm', 8.

With arguments of this kind, observes the writer, journalist and blogger Daphne Meijer (b.1961), Christians and 'secularised post-Christians', i.e. the majority, use such arguments to triumph over Jews and Muslims, after which they can carry on eating their blood sausage on a bed of boiled lobster.[68] The British philosopher Brian Klug has noted that in the UK, the far-right National Front, fanatical hunters, and vegetarians all agree that religious slaughter by both Jews and Muslims amounts to 'sheer bloody murder'.[69]

Because of this, and in spite of numerous tensions and conflicts between the two groups, their representatives came together for mutual support. An initial meeting resulted in both official and unofficial consultations.[70] All the arguments, pressure and protests led the Senate to vote against the proposed ban; it was replaced by a voluntary agreement providing, among other things, for stricter controls by veterinarians in the slaughterhouses concerned; the animals must lose consciousness within forty seconds.[71] In October 2015, the official supervisory body again urged the introduction of a ban, on account of too many infringements of the regulations.[72] Some Jews have also advocated changes to *shechita* while keeping the basic principles intact.[73]

In the Senate too, the PVV voted in favour of the ban. It seems clear that Geert Wilders and his parliamentarians, with their consistent anti-Islam position, were primarily concerned to curb what they see as the 'Islamisation'

68 Daphne Meijer, 'Onbedwelmd slachten VI: ik spreek de tegenstander toe', 28 February 2011: http://daphnemeijer.com/blog/onbedwelmd-slachten-vi-ik-spreek-de-tegenstanders-toe/ (consulted 25 November 2015).
69 Brian Klug, 'Ritual Murmur in Britain: Flying the Flag for Animals.' In Brian Klug, *Being Jewish and Doing Justice: Bringing Argument to Life* (Middlesex and Portland: Vallentine Mitchell 2011), 241-254: 249.
70 'Open brief van JMNA [Jewish Moroccan Network Amsterdam] aan Job Cohen inz. ritueel slachten', NIK, 24 April 2011/20 Jamada |1432/20 Nissan 5771: www.w.nik.nl/2011/04/open-brief-joods-marokkaans-netwerk-aan-job-cohen-inz-ritueel-slachten/ (consulted 24 November 2015); 'Joden en moslims verenigd in platform', Joop.nl, 13 September 2011; Groen, 'Samen in het geweer tegen aanval op halalvlees'; Danielle Pinedo, 'Samen tegen het slachtverbod', *NRC Handelsblad*, 18 June 2011; 'Joodse en islamitische organisaties gekrenkt door slachtvoorstel'.
71 'Senaat steunt slachtverbod niet', *NRC Handelsblad*, 13 June 2012; Kemal Rijken, 'Opluchting na afwijzing verbod rituele slacht', NIW, 16 December 2012.
72 In October 2015, the admissibility of ritual slaughter was challenged once again: Joram Bolle and Bastiaan Nachtegaal, 'Advies warenautoriteit: verbied onverdoofd slachten. Volgens de NVWA zorgt de rituele slacht voor veel pijn en stress bij de dieren', *NRC Handelsblad*, 30 October 2015.The article suggests that Jewish organisations are for the first time considering making changes to the rules; *see also* Daphne Meijer, 'Terug naar het onverdoofd ritueel slachten': http://daphnemeijer.com/blog/onverdoofd-ritueel-slachten/ (consulted 23 November 2015).
73 Joop Jacobs, 'Sjechita 6', NIW, 27 May 2011.

of the Netherlands, and the Jews, in this case, were collateral damage.[74] For
their grassroots supporters, however, this was not necessarily the case. In
the party's social media, one found Jews and Muslims being presented as
equally objectionable in their particularism – in short, as 'backward' and
as aliens. On the PVV 'Forum for realists', one finds people writing that
Jews are as 'backward' as Muslims, that both 'come from the same bit of the
desert', and 'Jews were always bleating about having a country of their own,
why they don't simply go there?'[75] Most striking of all is the systematic and
public reference by the prominent PVV Member of Parliament Dion Graus,
responsible for animal well-being, to 'ritual torture'. In an interview he
added that Jews indulged in these practices under the 'pretext of freedom of
religion'.[76] This actually amounts to two antisemitic allegations in a single
sentence. Graus was never rebuked for these remarks by his party's leader.

Lodewijk Asscher (b. 1974), Deputy Prime Minister and Social Affairs
Minister, comes from a Jewish background. He has received a great deal of
antisemitic hate mail. Some messages address him as a 'Zionist dog', while
others call him 'the Jew', a 'stranger' who opposes the portrayal of 'Black
Pete' as part of the Dutch celebrations of the feast of St Nicholas. (Black Pete
has attracted international controversy as fostering a discriminatory, if not
racist, stereotype.)[77] His stand against Black Pete has led some to attack him
as an opponent of Dutch 'folk culture'. In addition, by putting two capital
'S'es in his (Jewish) name, they achieve a reversal of victim and perpetrator.
Other offensive messages accuse Asscher of collaborating with Islam and
of 'suckholing Muslims'; note the pornographic touch. The stereotypes
that are used in relation to Asscher imply the Janus face of 'the Jew', who is

74   See, e.g., Mostafa Mouftafi 'Over dubbele moraal gesproken', in response to Ludo Hellebrek-
ers, 'Onbedwelmd slachten', Joop.nl, 1 March 2011; Jager Verzamelaar, 'Het gaat ze niet om het
lot van de dieren', ibid., 28 February 2011 (both consulted 17 March 2011).

75   'Forum voor realisten' (consulted 12 July 2011). The forum was removed after a time. See
http://kafka.antenna.nl/?p=4548 and wwww.alertmagazine.nl/?p=1328. The same goes for
the acceptance of gays and lesbians, which is lower among PVV voters than among any other
non-religious party – roughly the same, ironically enough, as those among poorly-educated
Dutch people of Moroccan heritage: Jan Willem Duyvendak, 'Ook PVV'ers houden niet van
homoseksuelen', De Groene Amsterdammer, 10 March 2016.

76   See, e.g., Trouw, 30 October 2012; Gans, 'Door PVV'ers gedragen vlag symboliseert politiek van
uitsluiting'; Gans, 'Anti-antisemitic Enthusiasm and Selective Philosemitism', 8; Hans Knoop,
'Hoeveel gekker kan het worden', NIW, 19 October 2012.

77   For the debate on Black Pete see, e.g., Rebecca P. Brienen, 'Types and Stereotypes: Zwarte
Piet and his Early Modern Sources', and Joy L. Smith, 'The Dutch Carnivalesque: Blackface, Play
and Zwarte Piet.' In: Philomena Essed and Isabele Hoving (eds.), Dutch Racism (Amsterdam/
New York: Rodopi, 2014), 179-200 and 219-238.

accused of being both a racist and an anti-racist at the same time.[78] Asscher took an unusual step for someone in his position: he put several of the anti-Jewish tweets on his Facebook page together with his own ironic but sharp comments, which were later published in the mainstream media.[79] Although some of this abuse came from anti-Zionist and anti-racist 'authors', most originated from PVV circles. Former mayor Job Cohen also received antisemitic letters, first as a mayor and later on, as leader of the PvdA, but never published them.[80]

'The Jew': navigating between antisemitism, jihadism and Islamophobia

The Paris attacks on the offices of the French satirical weekly *Charlie Hebdo* on 7 January 2015, and two days later on a kosher supermarket, sent shock waves surging through the Netherlands, as indeed around the world – especially in the West, and particularly in Europe, where attacks of this kind are rarer than elsewhere. People were stunned that such an event could have happened in Paris, the city of the Enlightenment, which romantics dubbed the City of Light. But Paris is also a city with a highly polarised society, a split world with suburban slums or *banlieues* populated mainly by French nationals of Algerian and Moroccan parentage and other ethnic minorities with poor prospects for advancement, districts in which Islam – interpreted and practised in diverse ways – is the dominant religion. Among the frustrations and resentments that ferment in the *banlieues*, hatred of Israel, combined with antisemitism, plays an important part. Israel, here, serves to represent 'the Jew'. The attackers were the two brothers Cherif and Saïd Kouachi, of French-Algerian descent, who operated in the name of Al-Qaida; they murdered eleven people at the weekly's offices, eight of them journalists, before going out into the street, where they killed the policeman

78   Evelien Gans, "'[Lodewijk] Asscher, de twee SS in zijn naam geeft zijn ware aard aan ...."' Hedendaags antisemitisme.' Paper presented at the reunion of the Werkgroep Andere Tijden, Amsterdam, 12 March 2016 (unpublished).

79   Lodewijk Asscher, 'Beste reageerders, een bericht van Lodewijk', *NRC Handelsblad*, 10 February 2016.

80   Interview with Job Cohen, *Joodse omroep* [Jewish Radio Broadcast], 29 November 2009; *see also* Ralph Pluim, 'Hoe nemen Nederlanders het Jodendom van Job Cohen en dat van andere joodse politici in Nederland waar?' (unpublished paper, 2010). One hate mail (28 February 2011) read: '... Hitler's turning in his grave, he forgot to gas the Cohen family!' In the personal archive of Evelien Gans. I thank Job Cohen.

Ahmed Marabet, another French Muslim. An acquaintance of the brothers, Amedy Coulibaly, of French-Malian parentage, first murdered a French policewoman, then took hostages among the personnel and customers of a Jewish supermarket, where he murdered four people. Amedy Coulibaly invoked the group calling itself Islamic State. There are indications that Coulibaly was primarily planning to attack one or more Jewish schools.[81]

Earlier events had heralded this antisemitic violence. In 2006, a young Jewish Moroccan man, Ilan Halimi, was kidnapped and tortured for three weeks until he died from his injuries. The perpetrators, a gang calling themselves *Les Barbares* led by a man whose parents came from Côte d'Ivoire, had demanded a ransom. Knowing that their victim was Jewish, the group assumed that he must be wealthy. A large protest demonstration was held in response to Halimi's death, and the police was accused of having been too slow to acknowledge the antisemitic dimension of the case. In May 2015, just a few months after the January attacks, Halimi's memorial plaque was vandalised. In 2012, in Toulouse, another Islamist terrorist murdered several French soldiers, a rabbi and three pupils at a Jewish school.[82] The far right also committed a series of hate crimes: hundreds of Jewish graves were destroyed in February 2015, and the controversial statue *Dirty Corner* at the Palace of Versailles, made by the Indian-British artist Anish Kapoor, whose mother was a Jewish Iraqi, was daubed with antisemitic graffiti several times later that year.[83]

But this section is not about the highly complex and – as is clear – toxic social and ethnic relations in the French capital, nor about that country as such. It seeks to provide a brief overview and an initial analysis of the Dutch reactions to the attacks in Paris in January 2015, and to those in Copenhagen a month later. The latter capital witnessed an attack on 14 February on a café that was hosting a debate on 'Art, Blasphemy and Freedom of Expression', with the Swedish cartoonist Lars Viks as the main guest speaker. The latter remained unhurt, but the Danish filmmaker Finn Nörgard was

---

81   'Maps of Jewish schools found in terrorist's car', *Jewish Press*, 11 January 2015 www.jewishpress. com/uncategorized/maps-of-paris-jewish-schools-found-in-terrorists-car/2015/01/11/; 'Amédy Coulibaly. Il aurait tenté de viser une école juive de Montrougé', *Ouest France*, 4 November 2015, www.ouest-france.fr/societe/faits-divers/amedy-coulibaly-il-aurait-tente-de-viser-une-ecole-juive-de-montrouge-3816256 (both consulted 13 July 2016).

82   David Haakman, 'Vier doden bij schietpartij op school in Toulouse – Sarkozy: nationale tragedie', *NRC Handelsblad,* 19 March 2012.

83   'Schennis 200 joodse graven', *NRC Handelsblad*, 16 February 2015; Titia Ketelaar, 'Fantastisch: ik hang naast Rembrandt', *NRC Handelsblad*, 26 November 2015. Kapoor's work of art, intended to confront the power of Versailles as a 'queen', was nicknamed 'the queen's vagina'.

killed. This was followed soon afterwards by an attack on the city's main synagogue, at which the Jewish guard was murdered. The perpetrator was of Palestinian-Danish origin. The aim here is not to analyse the motives of the jihadists who committed their attacks in the name of Al-Qaida or IS. We shall not examine the role played by Islam, for instance, in a religious and/or political sense. That it played a role is clear, but expert opinion is divided on the extent of that involvement.[84] Experts also disagree on the subject of the West's responsibility for such attacks, either because of its military interventions in the Middle and Far East or because of its *failure* to intervene in Syria.[85] The focus here is on violence against Jews and verbal assaults on 'the Jew', and the role played by both in the debate on these attacks in the Netherlands.

The attacks evidently singled out two targets: freedom of expression, which – particularly in relation to images of the prophet Mohammed – was seen as blasphemy, and Jewry. While the issue of unstunned slaughter brought Jews and Muslims together, the attacks in the name of Allah drove them apart again. And while the majority of the Dutch population tended to lump 'the Muslims' together, including those who did not comment on the attacks, the Jews seemed initially to have been 'forgotten'.

Charlie Hebdo's publication of cartoons featuring the prophet Mohammed as an actor in a pornographic video at the end of 2012 – a form of pornographic Islamophobia? – elicited a sharp reaction from Sheikh Al-Azhar, the highest authority in Sunni Islam; he accused the West of deliberately provoking a confrontation. Al-Azhar also referred to the existence of a 'Zionist plot'. In January 2015, the sheikh condemned the attack.[86] The myth of a Jewish conspiracy is a product of Western society – as evidenced for

---

84   That Islam played a role of some kind is clear, but precisely what role is difficult to define: *see* Thijs Kleinpaste, 'Wrekers van de scherts: De stroman van rechts', *De Groene Amsterdammer*, 26 November 2015. As mentioned in chapter 1, Mark Cohen adopts a very cautious position. Neither the Dutch Arabists Jan Jaap de Ruiter and Halim El Madkouri nor the historian Remco Ensel are 'alarmists', but they do identify certain anti-Jewish elements in Islam and/or the Quran: Ted de Hoog, 'Antisemitisme als Arabische traditie: Een gesprek met Arabist Jan Jaap de Ruiter over het islamitische antisemitisme', *NIW*, 20 March 2015; Halim El Madkouri, 'IS is in niets strijdig met de islam', *de Volkskrant*, 1 December 2015; Ensel, *Haatspraak*, 151-152.

85   Markha Valenta, 'Charlie Hebdo, één week later', in Menno Grootveld, *Het woord. Charlie Hebdo* (Amsterdam: Editie Leesmagazijn, 2015), 85-96. Valenta refers to 'two universalist, radical barbarisms that are both willing to go to extremes in order to attain victory: an Americanist-led war on terror and a revolutionary global Islamicism', in the original English version: 'Charlie Hebdo, one week later', *Open Democracy*, 16 January 2015. Valenta is a researcher at Radboud University Nijmegen in the Netherlands.

86   Gert van Langendonck, 'Reageert Midden-Oosten anders dan het Westen?', *NRC Handelsblad*, 9 January 2012. For pornographic antisemitism and Islamophobia, *see* chapter 12.

instance by the so-called *Protocols of the Elders of Zion*.[87] And this was neither the first nor the last time that 'Zionism' was described as the key power seeking to discredit Islam. The Netherlands is no exception, as was made clear in earlier chapters by Ensel and Stremmelaar.[88]

In August 2014, a respected civil servant working for the Ministry of Security and Justice, Yasmina Haifi (whose mother is Dutch and father Moroccan) tweeted: 'ISIS has nothing to do with Islam. It's a deliberate plan by Zionists out to discredit Islam'.[89] Her tweet caused a minor commotion, and Haifi was suspended. But a Facebook group set up to support her – by Turkish- and Moroccan-Dutch initiators – attracted six thousand 'likes' within a few days. The group's spokesman claimed that Haifi could well be right, given that it was in the interests of Zionists, defined as those who supported Israel, to sow dissent among Muslims. He also condemned what he called 'class-based justice'. VVD politicians who had posted racist tweets, such as a member of parliament who had tweeted on the danger of a 'Muslim takeover' and suggested that it might be a good idea 'to put a fence around them', was let off with a reprimand. The Dutch Moroccan Alliance (SMN) lodged a formal protest about this particular tweet.[90] The charge of double standards had been made by Dutch Muslims before, and repeated by the Arab European League (AEL); it is discussed elsewhere in this book.[91] The support group won its case in a legal sense: the Advisory Committee on the Fundamental Rights and Functioning of Public Servants, chaired by Job Cohen, concluded that Haifi's utterance was improper, but that it was also improper for her to be dismissed.[92] This incident too provides an interesting mirror image. While Job Cohen had been accused by the Right of 'cosying up' to Muslims,[93] the old myth of a Jewish plot was still well and alive among Muslims. And the ultimate irony was that it should be Cohen, of all people, who decided in Haifi's favour.

After the Paris attacks of January 2015, too, the protests against the myth of a Zionist or Jewish plot – and other questionable or antisemitic utterances

---

87 For the so-called *Protocols of the Elders of Zion*, see also chapter 15.

88 *See* chapters 10 and 15.

89 Arjen Schreuder, 'Zo gek is dat niet, om te denken aan zionistische betrokkenheid bij IS'. Interview with Ismail Selvi, *NRC Handelsblad*, 25 August 2014.

90 *Ibid.*, 'SMN vraagt Rutte VVD-Statenlid tot de orde te roepen', *Republiek Allochtonie*, 18 August 2014: www.republiekallochtonie.nl/smn-vraagt-rutte-vvd-statenlid-tot-de-orde-te-roepen (consulted 30 November 2015).

91 *See* chapters 6, 14 and 15

92 Merijn Rengers and Andreas Kouwenhoven, 'Domme tweet, maar ontslag? Nee', *NRC Handelsblad*, 12 March 2015.

93 *See* chapter 12.

about Jews – collided several times with the charge of double standards: the claim that insults directed against Jews were considered a more serious matter than those against Muslims. The bone of contention remained the notion of unbounded freedom of speech, which was questioned by some and staunchly upheld by others. It is interesting to ponder the extent to which Islamophobia and antisemitism function as communicating vessels. Islamophobia and the feeling among Muslims that double standards are applied may tend to provoke more antisemitism, which leads to more Islamophobia – a spiralling movement that is not exclusive to Muslims. See also the theory of the French historian and sociologist Emmanuel Todd (b. 1951), who shortly after the January attacks in Paris stated – as quoted in *The Guardian* – 'that the rise in Islamophobia is in turn stoking antisemitism in run-down suburbs, and that antisemitism is growing in the middle class'.[94]

Dutch Muslims were divided. The evidence suggests that they – like French Muslims – certainly did not in general applaud the attacks. Any such profession of support, it should be added, would scarcely have been publicly acceptable, and would possibly have constituted a criminal offence. Some bodies explicitly condemned the attacks, such as the Muslims and Government Contact Organisation (CMO).[95] The anthropologist Martijn de Koning (b. 1978) estimates that roughly eight percent of Dutch Muslims are open to the influence of Salafism – of which Saudi Arabian Wahhabism is a powerful exponent – and that some of this minority sympathised with the attack on *Charlie Hebdo*.[96] But just as in France, one Tunisian-French man blamed the attack on *Charlie Hebdo* itself – the magazine should have stopped publishing its cartoons featuring the prophet Mohammed, he argued the Dutch Deputy Prime Minister Lodewijk Asscher found himself confronted, at VMBO schools,[97] by pupils who defined the attacks – following

94 Angelique Chrisafis, 'Emmanuel Todd: the French thinker who won't toe the Charlie Hebdo line', *The Guardian*, 28 August 2015. Todd published the controversial *Qui est Charlie: Sociologie d'une crise religieuse* (Paris: Seuil 2015), translated as: *Who is Charlie?: Xenophobia and the new middle class* (Cambridge: Polity 2015). *See* for a both critical and appreciative comment on Todd: Duyvendak, 'Ook PVV'ers houden niet van homoseksuelen'.

95 Andreas Kouwenhoven, 'Charlie Hebdo: een legitiem doelwit?', *NRC Handelsblad*, 9 January 2015; *see also* Fouad Laroui, 'Hooligans v/d intolerantie' and Youssef Azghari, 'Ook moslims aangeslagen', *NRC Handelsblad*, 8 January 2015. This was before the attack on the kosher supermarket.

96 Kouwenhoven, 'Charlie Hebdo: een legitiem doelwit?'.

97 Children in the Netherlands attend different schools after the age of twelve, based on tests and reports of academic ability. Roughly half, the 'lower' half of the ability range, which includes a relatively high proportion of children from ethnic minorities, attend schools for preparatory secondary vocational education (VMBO).

in Haifi's footsteps – as a 'hundred percent Zionist plot'. In the same period, an Amsterdam Muslim asserted that the IS leader Abu Bakr al-Baghdadi was Jewish, and reports circulated on the internet that *Charlie Hebdo* was controlled by Zionists who were trying to unleash a war against Muslims.[98] It should be added that those who felt that *Charlie Hebdo* had gone much too far with its provocative cartoons included many non-Muslims.[99]

The attention paid to the attack on the kosher supermarket attracted remarkably little attention in the mainstream media. In the first place, this was undoubtedly because it happened two days after the attack on *Charlie Hebdo*. The horror at the latter appears to have eclipsed that provoked by the antisemitic murder of the customers of a Jewish shop. The initial media coverage of the supermarket attack was meagre.[100] The debate in the Netherlands was heavily dominated by the issue of freedom of expression, linked to the disputed *Charlie Hebdo* cartoons. On the one side were passionate supporters of the unbounded freedom of expression – regardless of whether they were Jews, Muslims, Christians, atheists or others. On the other were those who argued that freedom of expression has certain limits, not only in a legal and constitutional sense (where it clashes with religious freedom and hate speech, for instance), but also in a moral sense. The first group identified with the new international slogan 'We are all Charlie', while others explained why they were *not* Charlie. While this confrontation was hardly a Dutch affair, the memory of Theo van Gogh played a role in this country's debate that was specific to the Netherlands.[101]

Immediately after the murder of Van Gogh, the writer and poet Remco Campert had observed that someone who had written, 'What's that caramel smell? Today they are burning Jews with diabetes', should not enter history as a hero of freedom of speech. As mentioned in chapter 12, however, that was precisely what would happen, although some more critical voices were raised as time went by.[102] But in November 2014, ten years after the assassination, when jihadi attacks in Europe had become a reality, Theo

98 Bas Heijne, 'Kleine mensen', *NRC Handelsblad*, 17/18 January 2015.

99 *See, e.g.*, Martijn de Koning, 'Denk even na voor je islamofobe cartoons verspreidt.' In: Grootveld (ed.), *Het woord*, 105-113, orig. in *de Volkskrant*, 17 January 2015; *see also* note 106.

100 'Ook veiligheid van Joden staat nu in Frankrijk op het spel', *ibid.*, 12 January 2015.

101 For Theo van Gogh, *see* chapters 1, 12 and 15.

102 This happened in 2009, five years after Van Gogh's death, *see, e.g.*, the many-sided artist Jeroen Henneman (b. 1942) in: Coen Verbraak, "'Hij kon een monster zijn". Profiel Theo van Gogh', *Vrij Nederland*, 24 October 2009; Coen Verbraak, *Profiel*, documentary about Theo van Gogh, broadcast on Dutch television by KRO broadcasting company, 25 October 2009: http:// tvblik.nl/profiel-1/theo-van-gogh.

**Illustration 28   Photo of a protest against the assault on Charlie-Hebdo, 8 January
2015**

Herman Wouters / Hollandse Hoogte

Je Suis Charlie, Je Suis Theo Van Gogh. People gather in front of the French
Embassy in Amsterdam to protest against the attack on Charlie Hebdo.

van Gogh was largely celebrated and honoured on a national scale. The
NPO TV news was only one of many media to describe Van Gogh reverently
as a 'champion of freedom of speech'. To the cultural historian Eva Rovers (b. 1978), Van Gogh's work epitomised the use of irony, and included
'sardonic exaggeration', 'carnivalesque social criticism', and the unmasking
of 'moral crusaders'.[103] Rovers adds that Van Gogh did not understand
that what he intended as irony could not be interpreted as such within
the cultural context of many Muslims. With such assertions, Rovers fell
into the trap of the supposed 'clash between two civilisations'. As if it was

103 Eva Rovers, 'De scherpe rand van ironie. Hoe de dorpsgek een duivelse spotter werd', *De
Groene Amsterdammer*, 23 October 2010. *See also* Evelien Gans, 'Theo van Gogh (1957-2004):
Copulerende gele sterren, geitenneukers en held van de vrije meningsuiting.' Paper presented
at the symposium 'Joden en moslims in een veranderende samenleving' [Jews and Muslims in
a changing society], Amsterdam, 31 March 2015. A publication of the papers presented at this
symposium is in preparation.

only Muslims who did not construe Van Gogh's utterances as ironic. Irony can serve as a protective shield behind which a writer hides and seeks to conceal (or thinks that he is concealing) his real intentions.[104]

Rovers never uses the words 'Islamophobe' or 'anti-Islam'. She does occasionally mention antisemitism, if only to deny its presence. Leon de Winter, though not a Muslim, was evidently someone else who was outside the 'shared Dutch cultural context' and therefore failed to understand Van Gogh's 'irony'.[105] De Winter has long since ceased to be viewed with sympathy, especially in leftist Jewish and non-Jewish circles, largely because of his 'Israel my country right or wrong' attitude.[106] But to assert, as Rovers claims, that Theo van Gogh's use of metaphors such as yellow stars copulating in a gas chamber, in his 1984 pamphlet against De Winter, was his way of standing up for the Jews, is to turn the world upside down. This is reversing the roles of victim and offender. More informally: it's the crudest *chutzpah*. Rovers was not alone in this respect. She derived her vision in part from Theo's boyhood friend Roeland Hazendonk, who wrote the stage monologue *Van Gogh Speaks* (2014):

> He was not antisemitic. What mattered to him was integrity. If you read his article carefully [you'll see that] he seeks to protect the Jewish people from the abuse of their identity by Leon de Winter.[107]

Hazendonk also said (unlike Rovers) that Van Gogh expressed himself in 'scandalous' terms. The cabaret artist and columnist Micha Wertheim (b. 1972) followed the two authors to their logical conclusion: 'What we miss most today is someone who can protect the Jews from De Winter'.[108] There now – *that* is what you call irony.

Two months after the commemoration of his assassination, after the attacks in Paris, Theo van Gogh still epitomised an absolute form of freedom of expression and was seen as someone who had not only testified to an

---

104 *See, e.g.*, Joost de Vries, 'Het einde van de apenrots: Waar blijven de nieuwe Grote Drie?', *De Groene Amsterdammer*, 6 August 2015.

105 Rovers, 'De scherpe rand van de ironie'.

106 For instance, at a gathering held to express solidarity with Israel, Leon de Winter made the tasteless 'joke' (he himself called it sarcasm): 'Perhaps it might be an idea to sneak a contraceptive into the drinking water in Gaza': Pim van den Dool, 'Anticonceptie oplossing voor situatie Gaza? Leon de Winter pareert kritiek', *NRC Handelsblad*, 24 November 2012. *See also* chapter 12.

107 *NRC Handelsblad*, 27 October 2014. Hazendonk's monologue and interviews did not in fact treat Van Gogh with veneration.

108 Micha Wertheim, 'Theo', *Het Parool*, 9 November 2014.

encroaching Islamisation but had also foretold the rise of Islamist terror in Europe. The focus here, of course, was on the attacks on *Charlie Hebdo*, described as a revenge murder and as such comparable to the killing of Van Gogh.[109] It was not about the attack on the kosher supermarket. On the other hand, Van Gogh has become a symbol – within and outside the Netherlands – of the attitude that claims the right to be offensive.[110] Take the view expressed by Van Gogh's close friend, the columnist and writer Theodor Holman (b. 1953), who maintains that vulgar, harsh and relentless cursing is 'an obligation' as part of cultural renewal.[111]

The legal scholar Egbert Dommering (b. 1943), commenting on some of Wilders' statements (such as equating the Quran to *Mein Kampf*), wrote that freedom of expression was too often detached from the substance of the debate. He saw language pollution and hate speech, pioneered by Theo van Gogh, as major negative elements of the polarised Dutch debate on integration.[112]

The American sociologist Ron Eyerman states in *The Assassination of Theo van Gogh* (2008) that Van Gogh was above all part of an international Western discourse that focuses on the 'clash between two civilisations'. In addition, however, Van Gogh – like his kindred spirits Pim Fortuyn and Hirsi Ali – translated this discourse into the idiom of the Second World War, which is deeply embedded in the Dutch collective memory, for instance by referring to radical Islam as fascist and to the Muslims as a fifth column.[113] The American social scientist Benjamin Barber (b. 1939) had described the assassinations of Fortuyn and Van Gogh, as far back as the end of December 2004, as violent and horrifying answers to people who used words in violent ways. The right of freedom of speech must certainly be protected, but immigrants had the right to be protected from hate speech.[114]

109 Folkert Jansma, 'Als het fatsoen opspeelt is niemand meer Charlie', *NRC Handelsblad*, 10/11 January 2015.

110 *See, e.g.*, Ian Buruma, 'Stel van Gogh en Charlie niet gelijk aan democratie', *NRC Handelsblad*, 17/18 January 2015; Willem Schinkel, 'Woorden zijn maar woorden', in Grootveld (ed.), *Het woord*, 49-60, orig. in *De Groene Amsterdammer*, 21 January 2015; De Koning, 'Denk even na voor je islamofobe cartoons verspreidt'.

111 Yoeri Albrecht, '"Schelden is plicht". Interview with Theodor Holman', *Vrij Nederland*, 25 September 2004.

112 Egbert Dommering, 'De vrijheid van wat? De ondergrens van de vrije meningsuiting', *Vrij Nederland*, 24 October 2009.

113 Ron Eyerman, *The Assassination of Theo van Gogh: From Social Drama to Cultural Trauma* (Durham and London: Duke University Press, 2008), 137. Eyerman scarcely pays any attention to Van Gogh's first target: the Jews. He refers only casually to mayor Job Cohen who 'often [bore] the brunt of Theo van Gogh's anti-Semitic statements': *ibid.*, 53; *see also ibid.*, 47.

114 Marc Leijendekker, 'De stellingen van Benjamin Barber: 1. Wie bang is, tast de democratie aan', *NRC Handelsblad*, 18/19 December 2014.

Finally, it is characteristic that in the age of what Europe has labelled the 'refugee crisis', people in Dutch refugee camps are aware of what happened to Van Gogh, and say that they take into account the fear that it aroused. In a packed and poorly-equipped camp, a Syrian refugee who had been living in the Netherlands for two months observed in an interview that 'even before Paris' – and in this case he was referring to the attacks of November 2015 – refugees had already been seen as 'fortune hunters, or worse, as terrorists', but that since then the 'negative vibes' had only increased. 'Theo van Gogh as a symbol' is the title of the interview: the inference is that he symbolises fear of Muslims.[115]

This entire book consists of a constant attempt to navigate between two or more extremes and to strike a nuanced balance. Some Jewish organisations and individuals are extremely worried about the antisemitism that they fear Muslim refugees may bring with them, but other voices within the Jewish community disagree, and active attempts are being made to set up a dialogue. In the same way, groups have endeavoured, time and again, to organise a dialogue between Jews and Dutch Moroccans.[116]

Both after the assassination of Van Gogh and after the attacks in Paris in January and November 2015, Dutch Muslims were called on to distance themselves from their terrorist fellow religionists. Some did so with great conviction, passionately and of their own accord, others did so in more lukewarm terms or not at all. Some French people, not all of them Muslims, considered the November attacks incomparably worse than those of January. For this time, 'innocent people' had been killed – in other words, neither cartoonists who drew pictures of Mohammed nor Jews.[117] It should be recalled that France's colonial history has created a generation that does not love France: 'I am not a patriot. There is no equality in this country.'[118]

---

115   Toine Heijmans, 'Theo van Gogh als symbool: De hypergevoeligheid van Hollandse Publieke Opinie', *de Volkskrant*, 25 November 2015.

116   *See, e.g.*, Hanne Obbink, 'Syriërs in buurt met veel Joden? Niet verstandig', *Trouw*, 12 October 2015; NOS Journaal (Dutch public news broadcast), 13 October 2015: www.youtube.com/watch?v=OUfwJt39F3U; Daphne Meijer, 'Vluchtelingenopvang in Amstelveen?', 13 October 2015: http://daphnemeijer.com/blog/vluchtelingenopvang-amstelveen/; Max van Weezel and Ron van de Wieken, 'Mensen in doodsnood help je. Zeker als Jood', *de Volkskrant*, 17 October 2015; Sander van Walsum, 'Joden met muziek naar Syriërs', *ibid.*, 28 October 2015; Ensel, *Haatspraak*, 295*ff*. *See also* chapter 16. 'Chantal Suissa', Dialoog met espresso', *NIW*, 15 May 2015. For Germany, *see*, *e.g.*, Michael Brenner, 'Bringen Flüchtlinge Antisemitismus nach Deutschland?', *Süddeutsche Zeitung*, 20 September 2015.

117   Gert van Langendonck and Peter Vermaas, 'Grote anti-terreuractie in Parijs', *NRC Handelsblad*, 18 November 2015.

118   Peer Vermaas, 'Deze oorlog draait om angst', *ibid.*

What is more, the Bataclan theatre, where by far the majority of deaths took place, was once Jewish-owned, and is still partly so; it used to host Jewish events. Furthermore, an annual reunion of a group of Israeli border police is held there. In 2007 and 2008 the Bataclan theatre was threatened by Muslim extremists for this reason.[119] Is this a coincidence? Or are the Jews, in this instance, 'collateral gain'?[120]

In the Netherlands, many Muslims spoke out openly against the attacks in November. However, no Muslim platform, whether official or informal, did so openly and systematically against jihadism and at the same time against discrimination of women, Jews and LGBT people. And there is also friction. Those who feel no kinship whatsoever with these jihadists are nonetheless held to account for the terrorists' actions. This is reflected in an increase in Islamophobia, and sometimes in violent actions against individual Muslims.[121] Mosques have fallen victim to diverse kinds of vandalisation for years, including acts of arson and the depositing of a pig's head.[122] The same – putting down a pig's head – has happened in a quarter of The Hague and at a centre for asylum seekers (of whom most are Muslims).[123] Indeed, such aggressive rituals are becoming more and more common; activists who are anti-Muslim and oppose the admission of asylum seekers have also started wearing pig's head caps. Mosques receive threatening letters decorated with swastikas calling their congregation 'pigs'.[124]

119 Véronique Mortaigne and Nathalie Guitbert, 'Le Bataclan: un haut lieu de culture ciblé de longue date par les islamistes', *Le Monde*, 15 November 2015; *The New York Times* chooses the wording: 'There is some speculation....': www.nytimes.com/live/paris-attacks-live-updates/paris-theater-had-been-owned-by-a-jewish-family/; http://fr.timesofisrael.com/les-anciens-proprietaires-juif-avaient-recemment-vendu-le-bataclan/ (all consulted 18 November 2015). For Dutch papers, *see, e.g.*, Ariejan Korteweg and Fokke Obbema, 'Ze stappen uit en schieten tot niemand meer beweegt', and Robert van Gijssel, 'The Dictators speelden in Parijs, na de terreur', *de Volkskrant*, 16 and 23 November 2015; 'Theater Bataclan is in Joodse handen', *Reformatorisch Dagblad*, 14 November 2015.
120 I thank Frank Diamand.
121 Sheila Kamerman and Andreas Kouwenhoven, 'Moslims nemen nooit genoeg afstand', *NRC Handelsblad*, 21/22 November 2015.
122 Andreas Kouwenhoven, 'Moskeeën weren zich tegen geweld', *ibid.*, 6 January 2015.
123 Ed., 'Racisme en intimidatie in Haagse volkswijk', AD.nl, 17 April 2014: www.ad.nl/ad/nl/1012/Nederland/article/detail/3637163/2014/04/17/Racisme-en-intimidatie-in-Haagse-volkswijk.dhtml; Stijn Tielemans, 'Verbazing over "zieke, laffe daad" met varkenskop', *ibid.*, 25 January 2016: wwww.ad.nl/ad/nl/34072/Groene-Hart/article/detail/4232509/2016/01/26/Verbazing-over-zieke-laffe-daad-met-varkenskop.dhtml.
124 *See* e.g. Julia Broos, 'As-Soennah schroeft beveiliging op na dreigbrief', *Algemeen Dagblad*, 26 February 2016; Janny Groen, 'Moskeeën veel vaker doelwit van agressie dan vermeld', *de Volkskrant*, 11 March 2016; Christiaan Pauwe, 'Amsterdamse moskee meldt haat niet bij de politie', *Het Parool*, 11 March 2016; Kim Bos, 'Extreem-rechts heeft het tij mee', *NRC Handelsblad*,

The latter immediately recalls both the anti-Jewish medieval image of the *Judensau* and the abusive, antisemitic song that vilified the Jewish Foreign Minister, who would indeed be murdered in 1922: *'Knallt ab den Walther Rathenau / Die gottverdammte Judensau'*.[125] That is an interesting parallel: Jews and Muslims alike are insulted by identifying them with the animal that they regard as 'unclean', while at the same time being branded as 'filthy'.[126]

In November 2015, a Dutch Muslim sighed, 'However hard you try, it's never good enough.'[127] Jews have plenty of experience of the mechanisms of collective liability: if one or more Jews misbehave, it stains the image of the group as a whole. Nowadays, some call on Jews to distance themselves openly from Israel or its policies.[128] Moroccan, Turkish, Jewish, Surinamese and Antillean Dutch people, and many others, cultivate – or are assumed to have cultivated – a hyphenated identity, says Remco Ensel. The Surinamese-Dutch journalist Harriet Duurvoort uses the phrase 'jigsaw-puzzle people'.[129] Like Jews, Muslims and other minorities experience a double bind situation: you think that you belong, you have adapted, but at the end of the day, you're always that 'Other'.[130] Some go on the counter-offensive: what are all those dead in Paris compared to all the dead in the Middle East? We also find recalcitrant, anti-Zionist and sometimes pro-jihadist and/or antisemitic reactions. At some secondary schools, pupils disrupted the official one-minute silence for the victims in Paris by shouting out 'Allahu Akbar!' or 'Free Palestine!'.[131]

It is a murky trio: jihadist terror, Islamophobia and antisemitism. The Dutch government recently commissioned a study of attitudes among young Muslims to Jews and Zionists. The findings revealed that the students did not feel particularly hostile to Jews, but they felt considerable aggression

17 March 2016. It may be noted that depositing dead animals in public spaces was already a familiar manifestation of protest in the seventeenth century: Kim Bos and Freek Schravesande, 'Varkenskop: een aloud dreigement', *NRC Handelsblad*, 27/28 February 2016.

125 'Gun down Walther Rathenau / that Goddamned Jew-sow'.

126 Bos and Schravesande, 'Varkenskop'.

127 Kamerman and Kouwenhoven, 'Moslims nemen nooit genoeg afstand'.

128 *See, e.g.*, Daan Rosenberg Polak, 'Joden zouden afstand moeten nemen van beleid regering-Netanyahu' [Jews should distance themselves from the policies of the Netanyahu government], *NRC Handelsblad*, 14/15 March 2015. The Dutch Jewish organisation *Een Ander Joods Geluid* [A Different Jewish Voice] does so.

129 *See* chapters 1, 14, 15. Harriet Duurvoort, 'Moord op multicultureel Parijs', *de Volkskrant*, 23 November 2015.

130 *See* chapter 1; Gans, *De kleine verschillen*, 207.

131 Kamerman and Kouwenhoven, 'Moslims nemen nooit genoeg afstand'.

vis-à-vis Zionists, a term they defined as Jews and Israelis who support the occupation of the West Bank and Gaza and the idea of a Greater Israel. Their view of Zionists, however, frequently incorporated old and new anti-Jewish stereotypes: they saw Zionists as people who control the media, as child killers, as immoral people involved in a conspiracy to gain world power and, last but not least, as perpetrators (equivalent to Nazis), whose aim is the genocide of the Palestinian people.[132]

The investigative journalist Margalith Kleijwegt (b. 1951) wrote a report, commissioned by the Education Minister, on the tensions that exist between pupils with different ethnic backgrounds, and on how teachers deal with them. The findings of this important piece of research (2016) demonstrate a clear rift between pupils of native descent and their classmates of Moroccan or Turkish descent. Kleijwegt discovered a striking contrast. While many Muslim pupils hold to the view that the Western World, the United States and Israel or 'the Zionists' are behind IS and behind the attacks on *Charlie Hebdo*, their non-Muslim counterparts, several of them sympathisers of Wilders and his PVV, think that the three-year old Syrian refugee boy Aylan, who drowned during his crossing to Europe and was found on the Turkish coast, triggering a gulf of emotions worldwide, was constructed by the media in order to arouse compassion. Two opposite conspiracy theories. A most alarming phenomenon: neither 'truth' nor facts seem to count any more. The report also deals with themes such as the danger of (Islamist) radicalisation, religion (Islam) as a source of consolation, antisemitism, xenophobia and the frustrating lack of social integration and of socio-economic perspectives.[133] Teachers are often in despair; some leave their Magen David at home. The report also states that the recruitment of fighters for the conflict in Syria takes place almost openly.[134]

In the summer of 2014, relations between Israel and Hamas escalated once again into convulsions of violence: three Israeli teenagers were abducted and murdered, Hamas fired rockets, and Israel invaded and bombed Gaza. Both Israel and Hamas committed war crimes, according to Amnesty

132 Ron van Wonderen and Willem Wagenaar, with contributions by Annemarike Stremmelaar, 'Nader onderzoek beelden van islamitische jongeren over zionisten en Joden' (Anne Frank House/Verwey-Jonker Institute), Utrecht, 13 October 2015.

133 Margalith Kleijwegt, 'Twee werelden, twee werkelijkheden. "Dat klopt niet juf, het staat niet in de koran"', *De Groene Amsterdammer*, 28 January 2016. This article is a shortened version of the report of the same name.

134 Bas Blokker, 'Juf, we kunnen de vormen van uw lichaam zien', *NRC Handelsblad*, 2 February 2016.

International.[135] At numerous anti-Israel or 'pro-Gaza' demonstrations in
The Hague, which included IS sympathisers, several demonstrators chanted
not only 'Death to Israel' but also 'Death to the Jews'.[136] The mayor of The
Hague was much criticised for his initial statement that 'no red lines had
been crossed'.[137]

The tendency to conflate stereotypical Jews and Zionists, and complaints
of double standards, reach well beyond the Dutch Muslim community.
The Austrian historians Helga Embacher (b. 1959) and Jan Rybak (b. 1987)
argue that antisemitism in Muslim circles must be taken seriously, and
its motives explored in depth. They also point out, however, much like
Todd, that a one-sided focus on 'Muslim antisemitism' may serve to suppress debate about antisemitism in 'the majority society'.[138] A turbulent
public debate erupted in relation to the Second World War Memorial Day
in the Netherlands in 2012. Each year, the main ceremony, at Dam Square
in Amsterdam, includes a poem written and recited by a school pupil. In
2012, the National Committee for the Commemoration selected a poem that
a boy had written about his great-uncle, an ss soldier who was killed on the
German Eastern Front. This man too, the poem suggests, was a victim – of
history, of his own wrong choices. The decision provoked a tirade of protest,
resulting in the poem's replacement. Still, some expressed the opposite point
of view. The highly-respected daily newspaper NRC Handelsblad carried
a front-page article entitled: 'Don't turn the Commemoration of the Dead

---

135 See, e.g., Amnesty International, 'Israeli forces displayed "callous indifference" in deadly
attacks on family homes in Gaza', 5 November 2014: www.amnesty.org/en/countries/middle-
east-and-north-africa/israel-and-occupied-palestinian-territories/report-israel-and-occupied-
palestinian-territories/; Amnesty International, 'Gaza "Black Friday": Cutting-edge investigation
points to Israeli war crimes in Rafah', 29 July 2015: www.amnesty.org/en/latest/news/2015/07/
gaza-cutting-edge-investigation-rafah/ (both consulted 10 December 2015); idem, 'Unlawful and
Deadly: Rocket and mortar attacks by Palestinian armed groups during the 2014 Gaza/Israel
Conflict' (London: Amnesty International, 2015).
136 NOS Journaal (Dutch public news broadcast), 25 July 2014: http://nos.nl/video/679266-
demonstranten-scanderen-dood-aan-de-joden.html (consulted 3 December 2015); 'Anti-Joodse
betoging van Haagse moslims', NRC Handelsblad, 25 July 2014.
137 Shari Deira, 'Kamerleden willen meer weten over anti-Joods protest Den Haag', Elsevier,
25 July 2014; Sander van der Werff, 'Duizenden eisen vertrek van burgemeester van Aartsen', AD.nl, 28 July 2014: www.ad.nl/ad/nl/1040/Den-Haag/article/detail/3703147/2014/07/28/
Duizenden-eisen-vertrek-burgemeester-Van-Aartsen.dhtml (consulted 3 December 2015).
138 Helga Embacher and Jan Rybak, 'Anti-Semitism in Muslim communities and Islamophobia
in the context of the Gaza War 2014: Austria and Germany', Open Democracy. free thinking for
the world, 1 October 2015: www.opendemocracy.net/mirrorracisms/helga-embacher-jan-rybak/
anti-semitism-in-muslim-communities-islamophobia-gaza-war (consulted 23 December 2015).
The authors also refer to Wilders.

into the Commemoration of the Jews'.[139] And one of many reactions in the social media read: 'They [the Jews] are just like spoilt children .... "WE must always be the centre of attention" .... I get so tired of it. And then, if you want some amusement, have a look at what is happening in Israel.'[140] It should be mentioned, though, that the debate led to the political decision that Memorial Day in the Netherlands would always focus on victims (including – in a much-criticised section – those killed during later Dutch military campaigns), not on possible former perpetrators, German or otherwise.[141]

To commemorate everything is to commemorate nothing, asserted the writer, legal scholar and bookseller Maarten Asscher (b. 1957).[142] Even so, the National Committee's decision constituted a break with a trend towards levelling,[143] which was marked by a certain blurring (whether or not intentional) of the dividing lines between victims, perpetrators, accomplices and bystanders – including in public memorial ceremonies. We see the same counter-reaction in the most recent Dutch historiography of the Second World War. It appears to show a more thoughtful attitude to the concepts of 'heroes' and 'bystanders', and a shift towards a more nuanced approach to the history of the Dutch resistance, including the Jewish resistance.[144]

139 Ewoud Sanders, 'Maak van Dodenherdenking geen Jodenherdenking', *NRC Handelsblad*, 7 May 2012; *see also* chapter 17.

140 www.welingelichtekringen.nl/21129-dodenherdenking-moet-geen-jodenherdenking-worden.html, 7 May 2012 (consulted 20 June 2012). On a very different level, the Dutch political scientist Cas Mudde states that many 'professional critics' practise self-censorship, and are more cautious in relation to Jews and Israel than in relation to other groups and states, for fear of being condemned: Cas Mudde, 'Nee, we zijn niet allemaal Charlie (en dat is een probleem).' In: Grootveld (ed.), *Het woord*, 35-40: 37-38; for the English version: www.opendemocracy.net/can-europe-make-it/cas-mudde/no-we-are-not-all-charlie-and-that%e2%80%99s-problem (consulted 30 March 2015).

141 *See, e.g.*, Hilbert Meijer, 'Comité 4 en 5 mei: herdenk geen Duitsers', *Nederlands dagblad*, 26 April 2014; Max van Weezel, 'Om wie draait het op de Dam', *Auschwitzbulletin* 59, 3 (September 2015), 11. Martine Kamsma, 'Het kan: 4 mei zonder heisa', *NRC Handelsblad*, 4 May 2015, including an interview with the historian Ilse Raaijmakers, who wrote a PhD on what she calls the 'commemoration arena'. Ilse Raaijmakers, *De stilte en de storm. 4 en 5 mei sinds 1945* ['The silence and the storm'] (2014); Jan Kuitenbrouwer, 'Rekbaar alibi', *NRC Handelsblad*, 9/10 May 2015.

142 Asscher, 'De doorwerking van de Shoah in de Lage Landen', 43, 45.

143 *See* chapters 1 and 13.

144 NIOD director Marjan Schwegman launched a debate on the concept of the 'hero' in the Van der Lubbe lecture: 'Waar zijn de Nederlandse verzetshelden?' ('Where are the Dutch war heroes?'; 2008); Frits Abrahams, 'Feilbare held', *NRC Handelsblad*, 4 May 2015. The NIOD promotes studies of multiple aspects of resistance, including the phenomenon of Jews who went into hiding during the Second World War, from new angles. *See also* Ahmed Aboutaleb, *Tussen droom en daad* (essay written for national history month, October 2015), Amsterdam: CPNB 2015. On the concept of a 'bystander', *see, e.g.*, Ensel and Gans, 'We know something of their fate: Bart van

After the attack on the synagogue in Copenhagen, the antisemitic message of the jihadists appears to have attracted more attention in the Netherlands. It appears as if only now, with the cumulative force of Brussels and Toulouse, the antisemitic message has broken through the frame of freedom of expression and the Islam debate. There is also a little more attention for the vulnerability of Jews facing an ever-increasing threat, while their institutions have already been guarded for years. *NRC Handelsblad* wrote plainly of the growing antisemitism in Europe, including among those of Dutch parentage.[145] On 6 April 2015, a small group of fans of the football club FC Utrecht sang the following macabre lyrics during a match against the Amsterdam team Ajax:

'Mijn vader zat bij de commando's	[My father was in the commandos,
Mijn moeder zat bij de SS	My mother was in the SS
Samen verbrandden ze joden	Together they've burned the Jews
Want joden die branden het best[146]	'Cos Jews they burn the best]

As we have seen, the association between 'Jews' (even imaginary Jews) and the gas chamber is indestructible. Other FC Utrecht fans described the offenders as 'nasty Nazi singers'. Even so, the national football federation fined the club as a whole €10,000. Furthermore, it ruled that no FC Utrecht fans at all were to be admitted to the next match against Ajax. In the end,

der Boom's history of the Holocaust in the Netherlands', and chapter 13. In 2015 an international conference was organised by the Germany Institute in Amsterdam (DIA): 'Probing the Limits of Categorisation: The "Bystander" in Holocaust History', Amsterdam, 24-26 September 2015. A selection of the papers presented at this conference will be published. For Jewish resistance, *see* chapters 3 and 13.

145 Mark Beunderman and Derk Walters, 'Europese Joden worden bedreigd maar emigreren nog niet massaal', *NRC Handelsblad*, 17 February 2015. *See also* 'Joden moeten zich in heel Europa kunnen thuis voelen, *NRC Handelsblad.*, 16 February 2015; 'Frankrijk zonder Joden is Frankrijk niet meer', an excerpt from the speech by the French Prime Minister Manuel Valls, in *de Volkskrant*, 17 February 2015; 'Alle Europeanen zijn Joden, alle Joden Europeaan', *ibid.*; Harriet Duurvoort, 'Antisemitisme gaat ons allemaal aan', *de Volkskrant*, 2 June 2015.

146 A video recording exists, for instance on the website of Amsterdam's local TV channel AT5, 6 April 2015 : http://www.at5.nl/artikelen/141886/minutenlang_antisemitische_spreekkoren_utrecht_fans and on YouTube: Sander Schomaker., 'FC Utrecht in de maag met antisemitische spreekkoren', *Metro*, 6 April 2015: http://www.metronieuws.nl/sport/2015/04/fc-utrecht-in-de-maag-met-antisemitische-spreekkoren. *See also* Evelien Gans, '...Cause Jews burn the best. Football antisemitism: The different historical manifestations of an ever-existing phenomenon in the Netherlands', paper presented at the International Conference *Tackling anti-Semitism in Professional Football* (organised by the Anne Frank House), Amsterdam Arena, 11-12 June 2015 (unpublished).

this latter ruling was overturned for the 2,000 people who had purchased season tickets.[147]

When the decision was announced, the mayor of Utrecht decided that the whole thing was too confusing, and posed a threat to public order. He therefore decided, to the astonishment of many, to turn the decision around: Ajax fans would have to stay at home, besides which they were banned from holding a protest demonstration.[148] *NRC Handelsblad* wrote that this was a case of racism – oddly enough it did not refer to antisemitism – in which 'the victims were being punished and the perpetrators would have better seats in a different part of the stadium'.[149] The contested 'song' took root. It was shouted again by PSV supporters, after their club had beaten Ajax, in May 2016. A PSV spokesman expressed his horror at the incident; the Centre for Information and Documentation on Israel (CIDI) filed a complaint with the police.[150] In March 2016, some Feyenoord supporters were taken to court for chanting 'Hamas, Hamas, all Jews to the gas' at an Ajax match. As noted above, antisemitism among Dutch football 'fans' does not go unnoticed abroad.[151] Racist abuse abounds: both against the Ajax player of Curaçao descent Riechedly Bazoer (by ADO) and against the former Ajax but now Feyenoord goalkeeper Kenneth Vermeer of Surinamese descent, regarded as a traitor by Ajax fans. One man made a black puppet representing a hanging Vermeer – thus referring, consciously or not, to lynching practices; he was banned from admission to the stadium.[152]

In December 2015, the Moroccan-Dutch rapper Ismo (Ismail Houllich) was acquitted of separate charges brought against him by the CIDI and

147 John Kroon, 'De nazi-zangers en hun triomf in Utrecht', *NRC Handelsblad*, 15 December 2015.
148 Freke Remmers, 'Utrecht verbiedt demonstratie Ajax-fans', *Algemeen Dagblad*, 9 December 2015.
149 Kroon, 'De nazi-zangers en hun triomf in Utrecht'.
150 For the 'song', *see* www.dumpert.nl/mediabase/6768311/cb0be623/antisemitisme_in_de_mac.html It is not certain if PSV can take measures itself, because the supporters in question were outside the stadium and moreover perhaps not owners of season tickets: 'CIDI doet aangifte tegen 'SS-lied', CIDI, 11 May 2016: www.cidi.nl/cidi-doet-aangifte-tegen-ss-lied/ (both consulted 13 July 2016).
151 'Feyenoordfans voor rechter om roepen antisemitische leuzen', *Het Parool*, 15 March 2016; Peter McVitie, '"If you don't jump you're a Jew" – Does Dutch football have an anti-Semitism problem?', *Goal*, 7 December 2015: www.goal.com/en-us/news/1956/europe/2015/12/07/18075042/if-you-dont-jump-youre-a-jew-does-dutch-football-have-an. The club Feyenoord has a 'good behaviour' and anti-racism programme: Feyenoord Fancoach: www.feyenoord.nl/samenleving/projecten/projecten-overzicht/Feyenoord%20Fancoachcoach (both consulted 18 March 2016).
152 Wilfried de Jong, 'Opblaaspop', *NRC Handelsblad*, 8 February 2016; Bart Hinke, 'Vermakelijk, maar vieze smaak blijft', *ibid.*

the gay rights organisation COC. Ismo's rap video *Eenmans* includes lyrics such as 'I don't shake hands with queers' and 'I hate those fucking Jews more than the Nazis'.[153] Ismo said in court that he had meant 'Zionists', not Jews. The court allowed the right to freedom of expression to prevail; furthermore, exaggerating is part of the rap genre. CIDI and COC called on the Public Prosecution Service to appeal the judgment, and they were successful.[154]

Many Dutch Jews think that the issue of antisemitism receives too little substantial attention.[155] The same applies to French Jews.[156] Whether this (real or imagined) relatively meagre attention stems from what was called in the introductory essay the three-piece suit of the stereotypical Jew, who first lays claim to ultimate victimhood, then benefits from this victimhood, but is 'actually' a victimiser – in Israel –, is hard to prove. Characteristically, however, during the prestigious weekly Dutch television programme *Buitenhof* [Outer Court, named after a government building in The Hague], prime minister Mark Rutte was extensively interviewed on 11 January, the day before he would join the international protest demonstration in Paris after the November 2015 attacks, the whole conversation centred on Charlie Hebdo and not one question was asked about the attack on the kosher supermarket.[157] Also hard to demonstrate is the proposition that *Charlie Hebdo* itself represents 'the Jew' – not so much because of its relatively large number of Jewish editors, but more as a symbol of modernity, the Western world, decadence, free speech and godlessness. The weekly has been called a symbol of a universalism that is both hated and envied. As for the Arab-French police officer who was murdered: in the Netherlands, during confrontations with football fans (who are largely native Dutch), police officers are often called 'Jews'. That is, they are seen as part, or

153 Wouter van Dijke, 'Rapper Ismo vrijgesproken van belediging. Bredaër rapte over "flikkers" en het haten van Joden', *NRC Handelsblad*, 8 December 2015; The #Eenmans clip was seen over 4.7 million times. Look and listen for yourself: www.youtube.com/watch?v=frTkFOPZfiE.

154 Esther Voet, 'Haatexpressie', *NIW*, 11 December 2015; COC, 'Vrijspraak Ismo: CIDI en COC roepen OM op in beroep te gaan', 9 December 2015: www.coc.nl/algemeen/vrijspraak-ismo-cidi-en-coc-roepen-om-op-in-beroep-te-gaan (consulted 23 December 2015); 'Hoger Beroep tegen "beledigende" rapper Ismo', *Brabants Dagblad*, 16 December 2015. As of the present moment – July 2016 – the appeal has not yet been heard.

155 Hans Vuijsje, 'Overheid, bescherm Joden blijvend', *de Volkskrant*, 20 February 2015. Vuijsje is the director of the Jewish Welfare Agency (JMW), where many sections of the Jewish community make their voices heard.

156 Peter Giesen, 'In regen van eieren naar de synagoge', *de Volkskrant*, 16 February 2015.

157 Theo van Praag, 'Hoe is het mogelijk dat Paul Witteman de Joodse slachtoffers in Parijs negeerde?', *Jonet*, 21 February 2016. I thank Theo van Praag.

instruments, of the establishment.[158] You don't need to be Jewish to be
called a Jew.

   After the attack in Copenhagen, Israeli Prime Minister Benjamin Netanyahu urged the Jews in Europe to move to Israel. The suggestion prompted
a largely negative response; nor was it embraced by all Israelis. Those in
positions of authority in Europe did not want to lose 'their' Jews, not so many
Jews were interested in making *aliyah*, and public opinion largely dismissed
the intervention.[159] After the November attacks, the French-Italian Jewish
historian Diana Pinto (b. 1949) warned of the possibility of an alarmist
reaction. She referred to comparisons with the 1930s as 'an "affront" and an
"insult" to the memory of those who suffered and died in the Holocaust'.
From Portugal to Russia, there is no government-led antisemitism: Jewish
people are given protection in abundance. Pinto rejects the 'lachrymose
conception of Jewish history', to use a phrase coined by the Jewish historian
Salo Baron.[160] Rightly so. Over the ages, Jews have enjoyed relative prosperity
and safety – and since 1945 they have experienced little physical violence in
the Western world. Nonetheless, the antisemitic attacks of recent years are
an ominous sign. Furthermore, antisemitism in the form of verbal aggression has simply continued with the passage of time. It is too often forgotten,
writes the Dutch sociologist Willem Schinkel (b. 1976), that words may be
deeds, and there is a fundamental lack of understanding for views (religious
or otherwise) that do experience words as deeds.[161]

158 *See* chapter 11.
159 *See, e.g., NRC Handelsblad*, 16 February 2016; Derk Walters and Mark Beunderman, 'Europese
Joden worden bedreigd maar emigreren nog niet massaal', *NRC Handelsblad*, 17 February 2015;
'Denen verontwaardigd over oproep Netanyahu', *de Volkskrant*, 16 February 2015. Thijs Niemantsverdriet, 'Asscher: oproep Netanyahu aan Joden is kwalijk opportunisme', *NRC Handelsblad*,
7 March 2015. Claude Lanzmann, director of the famous documentary *Shoah* (1985), stated that if
the Jews would leave France, this would imply a posthumous victory of Hitler: Ariejan Korteweg,
'"Mij kun je over Shoah niet kwetsen". Interview Claude Lanzmann (90)', *de Volkskrant*, 24 May
2016.
160 Amanda Borschel-Dan, 'Europe's Jews not sitting on bags ready to leave'. An interview
with Professor Diana Pinto, *The Times of Israel*, 10 November 2015: www.timesofisrael.com/
europes-jews-not-sitting-on-packed-bags-ready-to-leave-says-prof/ (consulted 3 December
2015). Salo Baron, *A Social and Religious History of the Jews* (Philadelphia: Jewish Publication
Society of America 1937), 2:32, quoted in Karp and Sutcliffe, *Philosemitism in History*, 4. *See also*
chapter 6.
161 Schinkel, 'Woorden zijn maar woorden', 51, 53. Schinkel focused on the attack on Charlie
Hebdo, and was highly critical concerning the notion of 'absolute' freedom of speech. He supports
his argument by invoking the British linguistic philosopher John Austin (1911-1960), not Judith
Butler: *see* chapters 1 and 14.

The same Diana Pinto who considers it nonsense that the European Jews should pack their bags and leave Europe, wrote in her book *Israel has moved* (2013) that the Jewish state is not part of its own neighbourhood, the Middle East, but 'thinks of itself as living in its own cyberspace at the very heart of a globalised world.' Israel 'lives inside its own utopia, in the literal sense of non-place'. Because of the uprooted history of the Jews, Zionism has not succeeded in interacting with neighbours or other states, and 'sees itself as always acted on rather than acting'. Such a state, 'living in its own utopia', where the Palestinians are invisible, is based on hubris and cannot, at the end of the day, be viable.[162]

As was noted in earlier chapters, the Dutch affection for Israel has gradually cooled.[163] That is partly a result of the Dutch finally putting behind them their longstanding sense of guilt as a result of the murder of the Jews in the Netherlands, as well of slumbering or open antisemitism, but it is certainly also related to Israel's politics. One need only read the critical, nuanced views of the left-wing quality Israeli newspaper *Haaretz* and the Dutch quality press to see how Israel's repressive apparatus has steadily grown, not only in relation to Palestinians and refugees, but also in relation to NGOs regarded as 'hostile', people considered second-rate citizens (such as Ethiopian Jews), troublemakers and dissidents – including a great many artists. One can say there is an area of tension between Israel as a point of fixation for postwar antisemitism and as a target of legitimate criticism.[164] In reaction to the new bloody tactic of Palestinians, mostly

---

162 Linda Grant, '*Israel has moved*, by Diana Pinto', review, *The Independent*, 28 February 2013.

163 For the concept 'Israëlgevoel' ('Israel feeling'), *see* Gans, *De kleine verschillen*, e.g. 894.

164 *See, e.g.*, Amira Hass, 'Relative of Arson Attack Victims: I Saw Two Masked Men Standing by as They Burned', *Haaretz*, 31 July 2015; Amira Hass, 'Ten Bullets, and She Never Got Near the Israeli Soldiers, *Haaretz*, 4 October 2015; Gideon Levy, 'Mohammed Allaan's Blood Is on Our Hands', *Haaretz*, 17 August 2015; etc. Critical so-called 'Leftist' Israelis like Gideon Levy (who actually requires protection) are often seen as traitors: Derk Walters, 'Landverraders, dat zijn linkse mensen volgens veel Israëliërs', *NRC Handelsblad*, 22 December 2015; idem, 'Jonge Ethiopische Joden staan op', *ibid.*, 5 May 2015. On Israeli football, *see* idem, 'Een Jood mag meer dan wij Arabieren', *ibid.*, 11 May 2015; Jan Franke, 'Het racismespook', *NIW*, 8 May 2015; Jan van der Putten, 'De status-quo is over de houdbaarheidsdatum', *De Groene Amsterdammer*, 12 March 2015; Daan Kloek, 'Migranten Israël protesteren bij ambassades', *Jonet.nl*, 7 January 2014: https://jonet.nl/migranten-israel-protesteren-bij-ambassades/ (consulted 10 December 2015). But then, don't forget, there is the following statement by Ayatollah Ali Khamenei (Iran) who said: 'Israël bestaat over 25 jaar niet meer' ('Israel will no longer exist in 25 years'), *de Volkskrant*, 11 September 2015; Evelien Gans, 'Het spanningsveld tussen Israël als aanhechtingspunt voor naoorlogs antisemitisme en doelwit voor legitieme kritiek', paper presented at CIDI meeting 'Hoe besmettelijk is de "Engelse ziekte"? De dunne lijn tussen antizionisme en antisemitisme', 9 June 2016 (unpublished).

youngsters, to stab and murder Israeli citizens in the public domain, the Israeli repression has increased. While more Palestinians than Israelis have been killed in the process, Netanyahu supports the proposal to expand the rule of 'collective punishment'. It has been common policy to demolish the houses of relatives of Palestinian attackers or terrorists. Under the new proposal, these family members would be deported. According to the Geneva Convention of 1949, collective punishment is a war crime.[165] Israel is pre-eminently a country of opposites. It has a relative, though substantial, right to freedom of expression. And let us not forget that Israel twice chose the famous transgender Dana to represent the country at the European Song Festival. This would be inconceivable in many countries, not only in Israel's neighbours.[166] Israel itself is living proof of the tension between universalism and particularism.

The twinning cooperation agreement that was planned between Amsterdam, Tel Aviv and Ramallah was voted down at the last moment by the left-wing parties in the Amsterdam city council. A compromise was eventually struck in the form of a cooperative arrangement.[167] The calls to boycott companies and products that are linked to the occupied territories continue to proliferate, in the Netherlands and elsewhere. There are also calls for a cultural boycott. But just as non-Jews complain of the supposed double standards that are applied to Jews and their 'sensitivities', critics of the boycott movement claim the same in relation to Israel. Why boycott Israel and not China, which occupies Tibet, or Morocco, which occupies the

165 'Israel's Government Reaches a New Moral Low', *Haaretz*, 6 March 2016; 'Netanyahu wil familie aanslagpleger deporteren', *NRC Handelsblad*, 3 March 2016. For the advancing Israeli annexation of the Westbank, *see* Oscar Garschagen, 'Geen uitweg meer uit de Jordaanvallei', *NRC Handelsblad*, 21 April 2006; Sam de Voogt, 'Israël bevestigt annexatie op de Jordaanoever', *ibid.*, 21 January 2016, and for inequal distribution of water between Israeli and Palestinians, *see e.g.* Amira Hass, 'Israel Incapable of Telling Truth About Water It Steals From Palestinians', *Haaretz*, 14 July 2016.

166 For example, the Israeli state still censors all kind of journalistic and cultural manifestations, both by Jewish Israelis and by Palestinians. *See, e.g.*, the Palestinian documentary *The Wanted 18* by Amer Shomali and Paul Cowan: Derk Walters, 'Israel vreest Palestijnse koeienfilm', *NRC Handelsblad*, 3 December 2015. At the same time, highly critical films such as *The Gatekeeepers* (Dror Moreh; 2012) and *Censured Voices* (Mor Loushy; 2015) are made and screened – though not without having to overcome certain obstacles – and have won several awards. For the Israeli transgender celebrity Dana, *see, e.g.*, http://newsfeed.time.com/2011/03/09/israel-chooses-transsexual-dana-international-for-eurovision-2011/ (consulted 4 December 2015).

167 *See, e.g.*, Remco Ensel, 'Israël zorgt voor heftige emoties, daarom is stedenband belangrijk', *Het Parool*, 27 Juni 2015; 'Definitief geen stedenband met Tel Aviv en Ramallah', *ibid.*, 15 October 2015; 'Gemeenteraad akkoord met samenwerking Ramallah en Tel Aviv', *ibid.*, 6 November 2015.

Western Sahara, or Turkey, which occupies northern Cyprus?[168] And why choose to isolate dissident Israeli artists?[169]

The world-famous Israeli writer Amos Oz (b. 1939), who has been a leading peace activist since 1967, writing devastating criticism of his country, is the son of Jewish parents who emigrated to Palestine before the Second World War because of the antisemitism in Russia. During a lecture he gave in Amsterdam in 2015, which happened to be on the day after the November attacks in Paris, Oz remarked with some cynicism that the slogan in the 1930s had been: 'Jews out! Go to Palestine!'. Now the slogan is: 'Jews get out of Palestine!'[170] While the Dutch historian Chris van der Heijden has referred to Israel as an 'irreversible error',[171] Oz says the exact opposite. The establishment of Israel, he claims, was the fulfilment, however inherently imperfect, of a dream, for millions of Jews who are now better off than their ancestors. Oz speaks of disillusionment, of lies and shadows. Israel could have been much better, but 'I would not say that Israel was a mistake'.[172]

Finally, antisemitism renews itself again and again, as does the myth of the Jewish plot. After the accusations that 'Zionism' controls IS and planned the attacks in Paris, rumours have started circulating in a number of countries, including Germany, Hungary and the Czech Republic, that Israel or 'the Jews' are the driving force behind the flow of refugees. The rumour is backed up by a story about Israel's determination to take revenge on Europe for the Shoah.[173]

168 Ton Nijhuis, 'EU-actie Israël is hypocriet', de Volkskrant, 13 November 2015.
169 Loes Gompes, 'Culturele boycot Israël verzwakt oppositie', de Volkskrant, 2 May 2015. For supporters and opponents of a cultural boycott in the UK, see NIW, 30 October 2015, 8-9.
170 Amos Oz, keynote lecture at the 2015 Nexus conference, Waiting for the Barbarians, Amsterdam, 14 November 2015.
171 See chapter 13.
172 Amos Oz in Buitenhof (a prestigious debate programme on Dutch television), 15 November 2015.
173 Peter Kreko, Director of the Political Capital Institute, untitled paper presented at the IHRA conference, The Holocaust in Public Discourse: Use and Abuse, Budapest (Hungary), 6 November 2015. For Hungary, see also Istvan Pogany, 'George Soros and the Refugee Crisis: Conspiracy Theories in Hungary', paper presented at the international conference 'Antisemitism in Europe. Cross-Front Antisemitism, Conspiracy Theories, Calls for Boycotts, Islamism, the Extreme Right and the Left' (IIBSA), Berlin, 12-13 December 2015; for the Czech Republic: Zbyněk Tarant, 'Organised Import: Conspiracy theory in responses to the 2015 refugee wave in the Czech Republic', ibid.; Zbyněk Tarant, 'Friends or Foes? Attitudes of the Czech Anti-Semitic Scene to Islam and Muslims' (Journal for the Study of Antisemitism (JSA); forthcoming). For Germany, see, e.g., http://tapferimnirgendwo.com/2015/09/19/albrecht-schroters-judenhassende-bruder (consulted 24 November 2015). I thank Kim Stoller.

**Illustration 29   Photo of a demonstration against the entry of refugees in Europe,
12 March 2016**

Maarten Brante/ ANP, 12 March 2016

During the recent refugee crisis, symbols of neo-Nazism, classic and football antisemitism assumed new meanings. Protesting against the Dutch refugee policy with a banner that says 'Defend Europe', two demonstrators of the *Nederlandse Volks-Unie* embody an eclectic combination of symbols: on their jackets they wear the logo of Rock Against Communism as well as a prohibitory sign for the antisemitic icon of the 'nose'. The protester on the left wears a Nazi iron cross as eardrop and furthermore has the football anthem YNWA (You Never Walk Alone) tattooed on his knuckles. According to a ruling of January 12, 2017 the combination of symbols constitutes an offense (group defamation) under article 137c of the Dutch Criminal Law.

Furthermore, 'the Jew' turns out to be transferable. The antisemitic jargon is so deeply internalised that it is applied on social media to the masses of Syrian, Afghan, Eritrean and other refugees moving through Europe. The 'migrant crisis' is swelling the ranks of the far right. Splinter groups such as *Voorpost* [Outpost], *Pro Patria, Dutch Self Defense Army* (DSDA) and *Identitair Verzet* ('Identity resistance', whose leader Paul Peters has a previous conviction for vandalising Jewish graves) exploit Islamophobic sentiments that are felt across a far broader spectrum of public opinion. They recently started taking part in demonstrations of the German-born anti-Islam and anti-refugee movement Pegida, which originated in Germany but now has an active Dutch branch too. On the 4th of May 2016, World War II Memorial Day, *Identitair Verzet* laid a wreath with a ribbon which bore the words 'Nooit meer broederoorlog' [Nie wieder Bruderkrieg; No more fratricidal war]: a well-known international neo-Nazi slogan.[174]

The neo-Nazi Constant Kusters of the Dutch ultranationalist *Nederlandse Volks-Unie* (NVU) has also joined in.[175] On 12 March 2016, Kusters and other NVU members demonstrated in Amsterdam against 'leftist violence', 'leftist fascism' and the 'asylum invasion in Europe'. Their slogans and outfit amalgamate xenophobia, Islamophobia, anti-communism and the age-old antisemitic icon of 'the nose', which has now migrated from the world of football to neo-Nazism. The Dutch Counter-Terrorism Service maintains that the organised Dutch far right is as yet incapable of mobilising large groups nationwide. However, the political scientist Sarah de Lange (b. 1981) points out that the far right's increased visibility may lead to its growth, and to a certain habituation, with a minimal response from society. A Rotterdam trainee metro driver was fired after he had posted a tweet calling for refugees to be sent to the gas chambers.[176]

A statement made by a Dutch social democrat who favoured providing more assistance to refugees was followed by a stream of vicious reactions on Facebook: 'It's about time that a second Hitler came along, to deal with them [refugees] the same way as the Jewish people were dealt with. No pity … just deal with them'; 'totally agree, gas them'; 'dirty fucking cunts, into the ovens with them'; 'the gas chambers are still there'. Then came the direct link to antisemitism itself: 'Yeah, what can I say … Hitler was

174 'Identitair Verzet organiseert nazistische provocatie op Dodenherdenking', Anti-fascistische ondezoeksgroep Kafka, 11 May 2016: http://kafka.nl/identitair-verzet-organiseert-nazistische-provocatie-op-dodenherdenking/ On Sunday 10 July 2015, a tiny group RVF Landstorm, connected with the English neo-Nazi Racial Volunteer Force marched with a 'Freedom for Palestine' banner of the Anti-Zionist Front (AZF), which has a swastika on its website; Guy Muller, 'Extreem-rechts marcheert "For Palestine"', CIDI, 13 July 2016: www.cidi.nl/extreem-rechts-marcheert-for-palestine/ (both consulted 14 July 2016).
175 Freek Schravesande, 'Extreem-rechts heeft het zwaar', *NRC Handelsblad*, 13 February 2015; 'Je struikelt bijna over de nieuwe Hitlers', *Algemeen Dagblad*, 27 November 2015. For Voorpost, see above; *see also* chapter 4.
176 The Post online, 'Rotterdamse metrobestuurder baan kwijt na vluchtelingen-naar-de-gaskamer-tweet', 31 August 2015: http://nieuws.tpo.nl/2015/08/31/rotterdamse-metrobestuurder-baan-kwijt-na-vluchtelingen-naar-de-gaskamer-tweet/ (consulted 3 December 2015). The dismissal led to several protests online.

right, really, exterminating people like that', and 'Yes, it's true, Hitler was not a sweetie-pie, but he warned us all about this'. These statements were published on the Facebook page of the supporters of the PVV.[177] The page has 25,000 followers.[178]

Antisemitism is a multifunctional projection screen, and since 1945 it has acquired two additional, crucial, points of fixation: the Shoah and Israel. 'The Jew' can be used for a variety of purposes – by anyone.

177 A friend of Willem Minderhout drew his attention to these statements. Minderhout, a historian and active member of the PvdA in the Provincial Executive, published them on his own Facebook account as a warning: 'Perhaps the PVV can start a "Complaints Website for Twitter Nazis"'. The PVV started websites of this kind for people to leave their complaints against Muslims and Poles. I thank Willem Minderhout and Onk Maas.
178 http://debestesocialmedia.nl/pvv-aanhangers-willen-asielzoekers-vergassen-verzuipen-en-verbranden/ (consulted 5 December 2015).

References

Archival sources

Anne Frank House
– archives and documentation
– documentation Karen Polak

Beeld en Geluid, Hilversum
– audiovisual material

Centrum voor documentatie en informatie Israël (CIDI)
– documentation archive
– antisemitism reports (2000-2015)

Internationaal Institute for Social History (IISH)
– archive Komitee Marokkaanse Arbeiders Nederland (KMAN)
– archive Algemene Studenten Vereniging Amsterdam (ASVA)
– archive Paspoort
– archive HITB

National Library Morocco
– Moroccan periodicals

Noord-Hollands Archief, Haarlem
– archive Gerechtshof Amsterdam

NIOD
– corresponded archive, Loe de Jong
– news clippings

Stadsarchief [City Archive], Amsterdam
– minutes of the City Council, Amsterdam

Personal Archive, Evelien Gans

Personal Archive, Ronald van den Boogaard

Piranha trial Documentation, Roel Meijer

Audiovisual sources

Andere Tijden (TV documentary) (18 november 2013).
Berg, Rudolf van den (dir.), *Bastille* (drama, 91 min., 1984).
Bos, Froukje (dir.), *Kerwin, teken van de tijd* (documentary, 1985).

Bromet, Frans, and Willemijn Francissen (dir.), *Ajax! Joden! Amsterdam!* (documentary, 60 min., 2013).

Campen, Catherine van (dir.), *Painful Painting* (documentary, 53 min., 2011).

Chomsky, Marvin J. and Gerald Green (dir.), *Holocaust* (TV series, 475 min., 1978).

Derakhshi, Ali (dir.) *Zahra's Blue Eyes* (TV drama series, 2004).

Diamand, Frank (dir.), *When Memory Comes. A Film about Saul Friedländer* (documentary, 65 min., 2012).

Earp, Jeremy, and Sud Jhally (dir.), *Reel Bad Arabs. How Hollywood vilifies a people* (documentary, 50 min., 2005).

Eickelboom, Jan, and Monique Wijnants (dir.), *De strijd van Ayaan Hirsi Ali* (TV report NOVA, 20 November, 2004).

Gibson, Mel (dir.), *The Passion of the Christ* (drama, 127 min., 2004).

Gogh, Theo (dir.), *Cool* (drama, 89 min., 2004).

—, *Luger* (drama, 85 min., 1982).

—, *Najib en Julia* (TV drama series, 2001).

—, and Ayaan Hirsi Ali (script), *Submission*. Part I (2004).

Jong, L. de, and NIOD (script), *De Bezetting* (documentary TV series, 21 episodes, 1960-1965).

'Joods op zondag', Joodse Omroep, 3 March 2013.

Keller, Hans, Henk Hofland and Hans Verhagen (eds.), *Vastberaden, maar soepel en met mate* (documentary, 1974).

Libsker, Ari (dir.), *Stalags: Holocaust and Pornography in Israel* (documentary, 63 min., 2007).

Loushy, Mor (dir.), *Censured Voices* (documentary, min. 84., 1015).

Mohammed, Jan (dir.). *International Guerrillas* (drama, 167 min., 1990).

Moreh, Dror (dir.), *The Gatekeepers* (documentary, 96 min., 2012).

Oz, Amos, Interview in *Buitenhof.* NPR television, 15 November 2015.

Resnais, Alain (dir.), *Nuit et Brouillard* (documentary, 32 min., 1955).

Shomali, Amer and Paul Cowan (dir.), *The Wanted 18* (animated documentary, 75 min., 2014).

Smitsman, Hanro (dir.), *Skin* (drama, 85 min., 2008).

Surányi, András, Sándor Simó and Edit Kőszegi (dir.), *Midön a vér* (documentary, 85 min., 1994).

Verhoeven, Paul (dir.), *Portret van Anton Adriaan Mussert* (documentary, 50 min., 1968).

Vlaanderen, Kees (dir.), *Profiel Nico Bodemeijer* (documentary, 25 min., 2008).

Wachowski Brothers, The (dir.), *The Matrix* (drama, 136 min., 1999).

Weerdt, Janneke de (dir.), *NTR Onbevoegd gezag: Kennis is macht* (documentary, 25 min, 2013).

Wilders, Geert (script) and 'Scarlet Pimpernel' (script, dir.), *Fitna* (documentary, 16 min., 2008).

Bibliography

Aalders, Gerard, *Berooid. De beroofde joden en het Nederlands restitutiebeleid sinds 1945* (Amsterdam: Boom, 2001).

Aalders, 'Dachau-spel' *Aantreden. Orgaan van de Nederlandse Vereniging van Ex-politieke gevangenen uit de Bezettingstijd,* 17, 11 (November 1962), 401-402.

Abidin Kılıç, Zeynel, 'Yazıklarolsun, yazıklarolsun', *Doğuş,* May 2002.

—, 'Utanıyorum', *Doğuş,* November 2000.

—, 'İnanç ve umudunuzu tüketmeyin!', *Doğuş,* December 2000.

Abou Dyab, Jahjah, *Tussen twee werelden. De roots van een vrijheidsstrijd* (Antwerp, Amsterdam: Meulenhoff, Manteau, 2003).

—, 'Met verdoofd slachten is niks mis, met islamofobie wel', *De Standaard,* 13 August 2015.

Aboutaleb, Ahmed, *Tussen droom en daad* (Amsterdam: CPNB, 2015).

Abrahamian, Ervand, *Khomeinism: Essays on the Islamic Republic* (Berkeley: University of California Press, 1993).

Abrahams, Frits, 'Terug', *NRC Handelsblad*, 11 November 2004.

—, 'Feilbare held', *NRC Handelsblad*, 4 May 2015.

Abram, Ido, 'Wat wisten Joodse en niet-Joodse Nederlanders tijdens "de" oorlog? Volgens historicus Bart van der Boom niet genoeg om adequaat te kunnen handelen.' *Kol Mokum*, September 2012.

Abrams, Nathan, 'Nathan Abrams on Jews in the American porn industry', *Jewish Quarterly* 196 (2004), 27-30.

Abzug, Robert, *Inside the Vicious Heart. Americans and the Liberation of Nazi Concentration camps* (Oxford: Oxford University Press, 1985).

Achcar, Gilbert, *Arabs and the Holocaust. The Arab-Israeli War of Narratives* (New York: Metropolitan Books, 2010).

Adamson, Kay, 'Issues of Culture and Identity in Contemporary France: The Problem of Reconciling a Colonial Past with a Present Reality', *Sociology* 40, 4 (2006), 627-643.

Adorno, Theodor W., 'Zur Bekämpfung des Antisemitismus heute.' In: Rolf Tiedeman (ed.), *Theodor W. Adorno. Kritik. Kleine Schriften zur Gesellschaft* (Frankfurt am Main: Suhrkamp Verlag, 1971), 105-133.

Aerts, Koen, 'A Belgian view of (the debate on) "Dat nooit meer" – "Never Again"', *BMGN* 128, 2 (2013), 81-89.

Akgündüz, Ahmet, 'Een analytische studie naar de arbeidsmigratie van Turkije naar West-Europa, in het bijzonder naar Duitsland en Nederland (1960-1974)', *Sociologische Gids* xl 50 (1993), 352-385.

Alberts Jaco et al., 'De wereld van Mohammed B.', *NRC Handelsblad*, 9 July 2005.

Albrecht, Yoeri, 'Schelden is plicht', *Vrij Nederland*, 25 September 2004.

—, and Thijs Broer, 'Ik hou niet van verlossers. Theo van Gogh 1957-2004', *Vrij Nederland*, 6 November 2004.

Alexander, Jeffrey C., *Remembering the Holocaust. A Debate* (Oxford: Oxford University Press, 2009).

Alkema, Klaas and Ger van der Drift, 'Mist tussen de dijken. De stemming in de weekbladpers en de opvang van oorlogsslachtoffers.' In: Conny Kristel (ed.), *Polderschouw. Terugkeer en opvang na de Tweede Wereldoorlog. Regionale verschillen* (Amsterdam: Bert Bakker, 2002), 263-292.

Allen, Jim, *Perdition* (London: Al Saqi, 1987).

Alphen, Ernst van, 'Pijnlijke schilderijen', *De Witte Raaf*, Edition 125, January-February 2007: www.dewitteraaf.be/artikel/detail/nl/3153.

Altglas, Véronique, 'Anti-Semitism in France: Past and Present', *European Societies* 14, 2 (2012), 259-274.

Amberg, Freico-Jan, and Maarten Post, *Van preek tot porno. De ontwikkeling van het Nijmeegs Universiteitsblad, 1951-1968* (Nijmegen, Uitgeverij Valkhof Pers, 2001).

Amerongen, Martin van, 'De vrienden van Israël krijgen koude voeten', *Vrij Nederland*, 10 November 1973.

—, 'Kuifje in Zwitserland of Beter een halfjood dan een lege dop.' In: Martin van Amerongen, *De muichelmoordenaar. Artikelen en polemieken* (Amsterdam: De Arbeiderspers, 1978), 266-290.

—, 'Een schijngestalte uit een ver (en fout) verleden.' In: Henk Rouwenhorst (ed.), *Koersbeweging. De zes Zeemanlezingen uit 1997* (Nijmegen: Nijmegen University Press, 1997), 84-95.

Amrani, Issandr El, 'In the Beginning There was Souffles. Reconsidering Morocco's most radical literary quarterly', *Bidoun* 13 ('Glory'): online magazine (www.bidoun.org).

Andel, C.P. van, *Jodenhaat en jodenangst. Over meer dan twintig eeuwen antisemitisme* (Amersfoort: De Horstink, 1984).
Anderson, Benedict, *Imagined Communities. Reflections on the Origin and Spread of Nationalism* (London, New York: Verso, 1991).
Anderson Toussaint, Paul, 'Ik haat Joden. Klaar', *Elsevier,* 7 June 2014.
Andriessen, Gerard, and Arnold Reijndorp, *Eigenlijk een geniale wijk. Dagelijks leven in de Indische Buurt* (Amsterdam: Het Spinhuis, 1990).
Anten, Hans, 'Bordewijk en de joden', *Nederlandse letterkunde* 7 (2002), 61-86.
Anne Frank Stichting/ Panteia, *Antisemitisme in het voorgezet onderwijs. Eindrapport,* ed. Eva Wolf, Jurriaan Berger and Lennart de Ruig (Projectnr. C10000, Zoetermeer, 8 July 2013).
Anne Frank Stichting/Verwey-Jonker Instituut, *Nader onderzoek beelden van islamitische jongeren over zionisten en Joden,* ed. Ron van Wonderen and Willem Wagenaar (Utrecht, 13 October 2015).
Anti-Fascistische Actie Nederland and Onderzoeksgroep Turks extreem-rechts, *'Ik sterf voor jou, Turkije'. Turks extreem-rechts in Nederland'* (Utrecht: Alert! & Onderzoeksgroep Turks extreem-rechts, 2009).
Antisemitisme in Nederland. WVC Literatuurrapport nr. 20, ed. M.T. Josephus Jitta-Geertsema and J.H. Sanders (The Hague: Ministerie van Welzijn, Volksgezondheid en Cultuur, 1983).
Appignanesi, Lisa, and Sara Maitland (eds.), *Het internationale Rushdie dossier* (Amsterdam: Van Gennep, 1989).
Arendt, Hannah, *Eichmann in Jerusalem. A Report on the Banality of Evil* (New York: Viking Press, 1963).
Arian, Max, 'Profiel Piet Nak. Verzetsman en dwarsligger', *De Groene Amsterdammer,* 13 May 2000.
Arib, Khadija, *Couscous op zondag. Een familiegeschiedenis* (Amsterdam: Balans, 2009).
Arkel, Dik van, *The Drawing of the Mark of Cain, A Socio-historical Analysis of the Growth of Anti-Jewish Stereotypes* (Amsterdam: Amsterdam University Press, 2009).
—, 'Genealogisch verband van antisemitische vooroordelen.' In: D. van Arkel, R. Munk et al. (eds.), *Wat is antisemitisme? Een benadering vanuit vier disciplines* (Kampen: Kok, 1991), 48-74.
Asad, Talal, *Genealogies of Religion. Discipline and Reasons of Power in Christianity and Islam* (Baltimore: Johns Hopkins University Press, 1993).
Aschheim, Steven E., 'Caftan and Cravat. The Ostjude as a Cultural Symbol in the Development of German anti-Semitism.' In: Semour Dreschen et al. (eds.), *Political Symbolism in Modern Europe* (New Brunschwick: Transaction, 1992), 81-99.
Asscher, Lodewijk, 'Beste reageerders, een bericht van Lodewijk', *NRC Handelsblad,* 10 February 2016.
Asscher, Maarten, 'De doorwerking van de Shoah in de Lage Landen. Nederland: Drie vragen die niet weggaan', *Ons Erfdeel* 4 (November 2015), 42-50.
Atacan, Fulya, *Kutsal Göc. Radikal Islamcı bir Grubun Anatomisi* (Ankara: Bağlam, 1993).
Austin, John L., *How to do things with words. The William James Lectures delivered at Harvard University in 1955* (Oxford: Clarendon Press, 2004).
Avci, Gamze, 'Religion, transnationalism and Turks in Europe', *Turkish Studies* 6, 2 (2005), 201-213.
Azghari, Youssef, 'Ook moslims aangeslagen', *NRC Handelsblad,* 8 January 2015.

Baer, Alejandro and Paula López, 'The Blind Spots of Secularization. A Qualitative Approach to the Study of Antisemitism in Spain', *European Societies* 14, 2 (2012), 203-221.
Baer, Marc D., *The Dönme: Jewish Converts, Muslim Revolutionaries, and Secular Turks* (Stanford, CA: Stanford University Press, 2010).

—, 'An Enemy Old and New: The Dönme, Anti-Semitism, and Conspiracy Theories in the Ottoman Empire and Turkish Republic', *Jewish Quarterly Review* 103, 4 (2013), 523-555.

Baggerman, Arianne and Rudolf Dekker, 'Egodocument als bron', *De Groene Amsterdammer*, 24 January 2013.

Bahara, Hassan, 'Een antisemitische ananas. De ongemakkelijke populariteit van Dieudonné', *De Groene Amsterdammer*, 16 January 2014.

Baile, David, 'The Discipline of Sexualwissenschaft Emerges in Germany, Creating Divergent Notions of the Sexuality of European Jewry.' In: S. Gilman and J. Zipes (eds.), *Yale Companion to Jewish Writing and Thought in German Culture 1096-1996* (New Haven: Yale University Press, 1997), 273-279.

Bakker, Niels, 'Webfilm: Painful Painting', *De Filmkrant,* 2 February 2012.

Bal, Margreet, 'Laveren tussen het orthodoxe en het liberale Jodendom', *Trouw*, 24 april 1999.

Bali, Rifat, 'The Image of the Jew in the rhetoric of political islam in Turkey', *Cahiers d'Etudes sur la Méditerranée Orientale et le monde Turco-Iranien* 28 (1999), 2-10.

—, *Musa'nın evlatları, Cumhuriyet'in yurttaşları* (Istanbul: İletişim, 2001).

—, *Cumhuriyet Yıllarında Türkiye Yahudileri: Devlet'in Örnek Yurttaşları*, 1950-2003 (Istanbul: Kitabevi, 2009).

Balk-Smit Duyzentkunst, Frida, 'De macht van het woord', *De Gids* 143 (1972), 152-158.

Bangstad, Sindre, *Anders Breivik and the Rise of Islamophobia* (London: Zed Books, 2014).

Barend, Frits, *Ajax' roemruchte Europacup* (Amsterdam: Born, 1971).

—, *Ajax' 2^e roemruchte Europacup* (Amsterdam: Born, 1972).

—, and Henk van Dorp, *2 x 45 minuten: interviews met Johan Cruijff … et al.* (Baarn: Thomas Rap, 1978).

—, and Manon Colson (eds.), *De Nederlandse sportliteratuur in 80 en enige verhalen* (Amsterdam: Prometheus, 2013).

Barnouw, David, *Rost van Tonningen. Fout tot het bittere eind* (Amsterdam: Walburg Pers, 1994).

—, 'Review of Chris van der Heijden, *Kinderen van foute ouders. Hun verhaal* (Amsterdam: Atlas Contact, 2014)', 11, *BMGN* 130, 1 (2015), review 14.

Baron, Salo, *Social and Religious History of the Jews* (Philadelphia: Jewish Publication Society of America, 1937).

—, 'Newer emphases in Jewish history.' In: Salo Baron, *History and Jewish Historians: Essays and Addresses* (Philadelphia: Jewish Publication Society of America, 1964), 90-108.

Bar-On, Tamir, 'El Tri: 'A pagan religion for all', *The Washington Post*, 4 June 2014.

—, *The World Through Soccer. The Cultural Impact of a Global Sport* (Lanham, MD: Rowman & Littlefield, 2014).

Bastiaanse, J.F.L., *De Jodenzending en de eerste decennia van de Hervormde Raad voor Kerk en Israël 1925-1965: een generatie in dienst van de Joods-Christelijke toenadering* (Zoetermeer: Boekencentrum, 1995).

Baudelaire, Charles, *Petits poèmes en prose. Le Spleen de Paris* (Paris: Flammarion, 1969).

Bauer, Yehuda, 'Beyond the Fourth Wave: Contemporary anti-Semitism and Radical Islam', *Judaism* 55, 127 (2006), 55-62.

Bayraktar, Hatice, 'Türkische Karikaturen über Juden (1933-1945)', *Jahrbuch für Antisemitismusforschung* 13 (2004), 85-108.

Beaman, Jean, 'Identity, marginalization, and Parisian banlieues.' In: Mark Clapson and Ray Hutchison (eds.), *Suburbanization in Global Society* (Bingley: Emerald, 2010), 153-175.

Begemann, F.A., 'Transgenerationele traumatisering: klachten bij kinderen van oorlogsgetroffenen.' In: F.A. Begemann, *Arbeidsongeschiktheid en traumatische (oorlogs)ervaringen* (Utrecht: Icodo, 1993), 49-66.

Beller, Steven, '"Pride and Prejudice" or "Sense and Sensibility"?' In: Daniel Chirot and Anthony Reid (eds.), *Essential Outsiders. Chinese and Jews in the Modern Transformation of Southeast Asia and Central Europe* (Seattle and London: University of Washington Press, 1997), 99-124.

Bemmel, M.A. van, '"We are Superjews, Ajax is the name." A study of identity of Ajax supporters' (MA thesis, Universiteit van Amsterdam, 20 August 2012).

Ben Barka, Bachir (ed.), *Mehdi Ben Barka en héritage. De la tricontinentale à l'altermondialisme* (Paris, Casablanca: Éditions Seyllepse, Tarik Éd., 2007).

Ben Barka, Mehdi, *Option révolutionnaire au Maroc. Suivi de Écrits politiques, 1960-1965* (Paris: Maspéro, 1966).

Bennani-Chraïbi, Mounia, *Soumis et rebelles: les jeunes au Maroc* (Paris: CNRS, 1994).

Benz, Wolfgang, 'Zwischen Antisemitismus und Philosemitismus: Juden in Deutschland nach 1945.' In: Katja Behrens (ed.), *Ich bin geblieben – warum? Juden in Deutschland – heute* (Gerlingen: Psychosozial-Verlag, 2002), 7-33.

Bendelac, Alegria, *Mosaïque. Une enfance juive à Tanger (1930-1945)* (Casablanca: Wallada, 1992).

Benschop, Albert, *Kroniek van een aangekondigde politieke moord. Jihad in Nederland* (Utrecht: Forum, 2005).

Bensoussan, Georges, *Antisemitism in French Schools. Turmoil of a Republic* (s.n.: Hebrew University of Jerusalem, Vidal Sassoon International Center for the Study of Antisemitism, 2004).

Benzakour, Mohammed, *Abou Jahjah. Nieuwlichter of oplichter? De demonisering van een politiek rebel* (Amsterdam, Anwerp: L.J. Veen, 2004).

Berg, Alexis and Dominique Vidal, 'De Gaulle's lonely predictions', *Le Monde diplomatique* (June 2007).

—, 'Même de Gaulle était isolé...', *Le Monde diplomatique* (June 2007).

Berger, Joel, 'Zweites Bild; "In der Synagoge."' In: Julius H. Schoeps and Joachim Schlör (eds.), *Antisemitismus. Vorurteile und Mythen* (München, Zürich: Piper, 1995), 67-73.

Berger, Mark T., 'After the Third World? History, Destiny and the Fate of Third Worldism', *Third World Quarterly* 25, 1 (2004), 9-39.

Berger, Maurits, 'Meer dan antisemitisme: een botsing van trauma's', *NRC Handelsblad*, 5 August 2014.

Bergmann, Martin S., and Milton E. Jucovy (eds.), *Generations of the Holocaust* (New York: Columbia University Press, 1990, with new pref. and postscripts; orig. 1982 Basic Books).

Bergmann, Werner, '"Störenfriede der Erinnerung." Zum Schuldabwehr-Antisemitismus in Deutschland.' In: Klaus-Michael Bogdal, Klaus Holz and Matthias N. Lorenz (eds.), *Literarischer Antisemitismus nach Auschwitz* (Stuttgart, Weimar: J.B. Metzler, 2007), 13-35.

—, 'Anti-Semitic Attitudes in Europe: A Comparative Perspective, *Journal of Social Issues* 64, 2 (2008), 343-362.

—, 'Sekundärer Antisemitismus.' In: Wolfgang Benz et al. (eds.), *Handbuch des Antisemitismus. Judenfeindschaft in Geschichte und Gegenwart. Bd. 3: Begriffe, Theorien, Ideologien. Im Auftrag des Zentrums für Antisemitismusforschung* (Berlin, New York: De Gruyter, K.G. Saur Verlag, 2010), 300-302.

—, and Rainer Erb, *Antisemitismus in der Bundesrepublik Deutschland. Ergebnisse der empirischen Forschung von 1946-1989* (Opladen: Verlag Leske und Budrichs, 1991).

Berkhoff, Karel C., *Motherland in Danger. Soviet Propaganda During World War II* (Cambridge MA, London: Harvard University Press, 2012).

Beunderman, Mark, and Derk Walters, 'Europese Joden worden bedreigd maar emigreren nog niet massaal', *NRC Handelsblad*, 17 February 2015.

Bilge Criss, Nur, 'A short history of anti-Americanism and terrorism: The Turkish case', *The Journal of American History* 89, 2 (2002), 472-484.

Bijl, Maarten, *Nooit meer Auschwitz! Het Nederlands Auschwitz Comité, 1956-1996* (Bussum: Thoth, 1997).

Bleich, Anet, 'Gruwelsprookjes uit naam der solidariteit', *De Groene Amsterdammer*, 13 July 1988.

Blokker, Bas, '"Wij hebben de zaak onder controle." Uzeyir Kabaktepe, voorman van Milli Gorus, stelt Nederland gerust', *NRC Handelsblad*, 5 September 1998.

—, 'Juf, we kunnen de vormen van uw lichaam zien', *NRC Handelsblad*, 2 February 2016.

Blom, J.C.H., *In de ban van goed en fout? Wetenschappelijke geschiedschrijving over de bezettingstijd in Nederland* (Bergen: Octavo, 1983).

—, 'De vervolging van de joden in internationaal vergelijkend perspectief', *De Gids* 150, 6/7 (June/July 1987), 494-507.

—, 'De vervolging van de joden in internationaal vergelijkend perspectief.' In: J.C.H. Blom, *Crisis, bezetting en herstel. Tien studies over Nederland 1930-1950* (The Hague: Nijgh & Van Ditmar Universitair, 1989), 134-150.

—, 'The persecution of the Jews in the Netherlands from a comparative international perspective.' In: Jozeph Michman (ed.), *Dutch Jewish History II* (Assen, Maastricht: Van Gorcum, 1989), 273-28.

—, 'The persecution of the Jews in the Netherlands in a comparative Western European perspective', *European History Quarterly* 19 (1989), 333-351.

—, 'Grijs verleden?', *BMGN* CXVI, iv (2001), 483-489.

—, 'Een kwart eeuw later. Nog altijd in de ban van goed en fout.' In: J.C.H. Blom, *In de ban van goed en fout? Geschiedschrijving over de bezettingstijd in Nederland* (Amsterdam: Boom, 2007), 55-179.

—, and J.J. Cahen, 'Joodse Nederlanders, Nederlandse joden en joden in Nederland.' In: J.C.H. Blom, R.G. Fuks-Manfeld and I. Schöffer (eds.), *Geschiedenis van de Joden in Nederland* (Amsterdam: Balans, 1995), 245-310.

—, R.G. Fuks-Manfeld and I. Schöffer (eds.), *Geschiedenis van de Joden in Nederland* (Amsterdam: Balans, 1995).

—, R.G. Fuks-Manfeld and I. Schöffer (eds.), *The History of the Jews in the Netherlands* (Portland Oregon: Littman Library of Jewish Civilisation, 2002).

Boerstra, Padu, 'Woorden zijn soms ook daden', *Filosofie magazine* 3 (2007), 16-17, 19-20.

Bock, Harald, 'Burhan Karkutli, 1932-2003', Das Pälestina Portal, www.arendt-art.de/deutsch/palestina/Stimmen_Palaestina/burhan_karkutli.htm.

Bok, Réne de, 'Nieuw PLO-kantoor in Den Haag', *Elsevier Magazine*, 13 November 1982, 17-21.

Bolle, Joram, and Bastiaan Nachtegaal, 'Advies warenautoriteit: verbied onverdoofd slachten. Volgens de NVWA zorgt de rituele slacht voor veel pijn en stress bij de dieren', *NRC Handelsblad*, 30 October 2015.

Bolwerk, Paul, 'Jeugdwerker ligt eruit in wijk', *De Gelderlander*, 12 March 2013.

—, 'Ophef over uitzending is afleidingsmanoeuvre', *De Gelderlander*, 15 March 2013.

Boom, Bart van der, 'Review J.J. Huizinga, 'Friesland en de Tweede Wereldoorlog', *de Volkskrant*, 3 January 1997.

—, *'We leven nog.' De stemming in bezet Nederland* (Amsterdam: Boom, 2003).

—, 'Den Haag: de Waalsdorpervlakte. Verzet en repressie in de Tweede Wereldoorlog.' In: Wim van den Doel (ed.), *Plaatsen van herinnering. Nederland in de twintigste eeuw* (Amsterdam: Prometheus, 2005), 122-133.

—, *Wij weten niets van hun lot. Gewone Nederlanders en de Holocaust* (Amsterdam: Boom, 2012).

—, 'Ordinary Dutchmen and the Holocaust: A Summary of Findings.' In: Peter Romijn et al. (eds.), *The Persecution of the Jews in the Netherlands 1940-1945. New Perspectives* (Amsterdam: Vossiuspers/ UvA, 2012), 29-52.

Boroujerdi, Mehrzad, *Iranian Intellectuals and the West. The Tormented Triumph of Nativism* (Syracuse, NY: Syracuse University Press, 1996).

Borschel-Dan, Amanda, 'Europe's Jews not sitting on bags ready to leave'. Interview with Professor Diana Pinto, *The Times of Israel*, 10 November 2015.

Bos, Kim, 'Extreem-rechts heeft het tij mee', *NRC Handelsblad*, 17 March 2016.

—, and Freek Schravesande, 'Varkenskop: een aloud dreigement', *NRC Handelsblad*, 27/28 February 2016.

Bosma, Martin, *De schijn-elite van de valsemunters: Drees, extreem rechts, de sixties, nuttige idioten, Groep Wilders en ik* (Amsterdam: Bert Bakker, 2010).

—, *Minderheid in eigen land: Hoe progressieve strijd ontaardt in genocide en ANC-apartheid* (IJmuiden: Bibliotheca Africana Formicae 2015).

Botje, Harm Ede & Jaco Alberts, 'Abou Jahjah, tien jaar later', *Vrij Nederland*, 8 August 2014.

Bossenbroek, Martin, *De Meelstreep. Terugkeer en opvang na de Tweede Wereldoorlog* (Amsterdam: Bert Bakker, 2001).

Boterman, Frits, *Duitse daders. De Jodenvervolging en de Nazificatie van Nederland (1940-1945)* (Amsterdam: Arbeiderspers, 2015).

Bouadi, Omar et al. (eds.), *De vele gezichten van Marokkaans Nederland* (Amsterdam: Mets & Schilt, 2001).

Boum, Aomar, *Memories of Absence. How Muslims Remember Jews in Morocco* (Stanford: Stanford University Press, 2013).

Bouw, Carolien, Jaap van Donselaar and Carien Nelissen, *De Nederlandse Volks-Unie: portret van een racistische splinterpartij* (Amsterdam: Wereldvenster, 1981).

Bovenkerk, Frank, 'Rassenrellen of criminaliteit?', *Migrantenstudies* 4: 255-270.

Boyarin, Daniel, Daniel Itzkovitz, and Ann Pellegrini (eds.), *Queer Theory and the Jewish Question* (New York: Columbia University Press, 2003).

Boym, Svetlana, 'Conspiracy Theories and Literary Ethics: Umberto Eco, Danilo Kiš and the Protocols of Zion', *Comparative Literature* 51, 2 (1999), 97-122.

Braam, Stella, and Mehmet Ülger, *Grijze Wolven: een zoektocht naar Turks extreem-rechts* (Amsterdam: Nijgh & Van Ditmar, 1997).

Braber, Ben, *Zelfs als wij zullen verliezen. Joden in verzet en illegaliteit, 1940-1945* (Amsterdam: Balans, 1990).

Brands, Maarten, 'Beslagen buitenspiegels. Over de grenzen van zelfreflectie.' In: Conny Kristel (ed.), *Met alle geweld. Botsingen en tegenstellingen in burgerlijk Nederland* (Amsterdam: Balans, 2003), 34-47.

Brants, Kees, and Willem Hogendoorn, *Van vreemde smetten vrij. Opkomst van de Centrumpartij* (Bussum: De Haan, 1983).

Brasz, Chaya, 'Na de Tweede Wereldoorlog: van kerkgenootschap naar culturele minderheid.' In: J.C.H. Blom, R.G. Fuks-Mansfeld and I. Schöffer (eds.), *Geschiedenis van de Joden in Nederland* (Amsterdam: Balans, 1995), 351-403.

—, 'Onontbeerlijk maar eigengereid. De zionistische inmenging in de naoorlogse joodse gemeenschap.' In: Conny Kristel (ed.), *Binnenskamers. Terugkeer en opvang na de Tweede Wereldoorlog. Besluitvorming* (Amsterdam: Bert Bakker, 2002), 235-260.

—, 'Na de Tweede Wereldoorlog: van kerkgenootschap naar culturele minderheid.' In: J.C.H. Blom, Rena Fuks-Mansfeld et al. (eds.), *Geschiedenis van de joden in Nederland* (Amsterdam: Balans, 1995), 351-352.

Braum, Christina von, 'Blut und Butschande. Zur Bedeutung des Blutes in der antisemitischen Denkwelt.' In: Julius Schoeps and Joachim Schlör (eds.), *Antisemitismus. Vorurteile und Mythen* (München: Piper, 1995), 80-95.

Bregstein, Philo, 'De Nederlandse paradox.' In: Philo Bregstein, *Het kromme kan toch niet recht zijn: Essays en interviews* (Baarn: de Prom, 1996), 45-72.

—, and Salvador Bloemgarten, *Herinnering aan Joods Amsterdam* (Amsterdam: De Bezige Bij, 1978).

Brenner, Emmanuel, *The Lost Territories of the Republic* (s.l.: American Jewish Committee, 2006; first French ed. 2002).

Brienen, P., 'Types and Stereotypes: Zwarte Piet and his Early Modern Sources.' In: Philomena Essed and Isabele Hoving (eds.), *Dutch Racism* (Amsterdam/New York: Rodopi, 2014), 179-179-200.

Broder, Henryk, *Der Ewige Antisemit. Über Sinn und Funktion eines beständigen Gefühls* (Frankfurt am Main: Fischer, 1986).

Bromet, Joop, 'Kritiek op Israël: ja/nee?', *NIW* (16 January 1967).

Broos, Julia, 'As-Soennah schroeft beveiliging op na dreigbrief', *Algemeen Dagblad*, 26 February 2016.

Broszat, Martin et al., *Bayern in der NS-Zeit. Herrschaft und Gesellschaft im Konflikt* (München: Oldenbourg, 1979).

—, and Saul Friedländer, 'A controversy about the historicization of National Socialism', *New German Critique* 44, 1 (April 1988), 85-126.

—, and Saul Friedländer, 'Um die "Historisierung des Nationalsozialismus": ein Briefwechsel', *Vierteljahrshefte für Zeitgeschichte* 36, 2 (1988), 339-372.

Browning, Christopher, *Ordinary Men: Reserve Police Battalion 101 and the Final Solution in Poland* (New York: Harper Collins, 1992).

Bruckner, Pascal, 'Racisme tegen blanke bestaat heus, Dieudonné', *NRC Handelsblad*. 11/12 January 2014.

Buber, Martin, *Chassidische Legenden*, ed. J. Martinet, in cooperation with F.R.A. Henkels and drawings by H.N. Werkman (Haarlem: Grafische Bedrijven, 1967).

Bunzl, Matti, *Symptoms of Modernity: Jews and Queers in Late-twentieth-century Vienna* (Berkeley, Los Angeles: University of California Press, 2004).

—, *Anti-Semitism and Islamophobia: Hatreds Old and New in Europe* (Chicago: Chicago University Press, 2007).

Burgat, François, *L'Islamisme au Maghreb* (Paris: Payot et Rivages, 1995).

Buruma, Ian, *Murder in Amsterdam. The Death of Theo van Gogh and the Limits of Tolerance* (New York: Penguin Press, 2006).

—, *Dood van een gezonde roker* (Amsterdam/Antwerp: Atlas/Contact 2006).

—, 'Stel van Gogh en Charlie niet gelijk aan democratie', *NRC Handelsblad*, 17/18 January 2015.

—, and Avishai Margalit, *Occidentalism. The West in the eyes of its enemies* (New York: Penguin Press, 2004).

Butler, Judith, *Excitable Speech: a Politics of the Performative* (New York: Routledge, 1997).

—, *Opgefokte taal: een politiek van de performatief* (Amsterdam: Parrèsia, 2007).

Butz, Arthur, *The Hoax of the Twentieth Century* (Torrance, CA.: Institute for Historical Review, 1976).

Byford, Jovan, *Conspiracy Theories. A Critical Introduction* (Houndmills: Palgrave MacMillan, 2011).

Caldwell, Christopher, 'Faith and Death', *New York Times*, 10 September 2006.

Campert, Remco, 'Gemengde gevoelens', *de Volkskrant*, 3 November 2004.

Canneyt, Hilde van, 'Interview met Ronald Ophuis', Gesprekken met hedendaagse kunstenaars, Amsterdam, 12 May 2011: http://hildevancanneyt.blogspot.nl/2011/07/v-behaviorurldefault-vmlo.html.

Cassuto, Carine, 'Op zoek naar de Superjood', *NIW*, 16 August 2013.

Cesarani, David, 'Anti-Zionism in Britain, 1922-2002: Continuities and Discontinuities.' In: Jeffrey Herf (ed.), *Anti-Semitism and Anti-Zionism in historical perspective. Convergence and divergence* (London, New York: Routledge 2007), 114-158.

—, *Eichmann. His Life and Crimes* (London: Heinemann, 2004).

Chazan, Robert, *Medieval Stereotypes and Modern Antisemitism* (Berkeley: University of California Press, 1997).

Cherribi, Oussama, *Imams d'Amsterdam. À travers l'exemple des imams de la diaspora Marocaine* (Phd Thesis, Universiteit van Amsterdam, 2000).

Chorus, Jutta, and Ahmet Olgun, 'Op de thee bij de jongens van de Hofstadgroep', *NRC Handelsblad*, 10-11 September 2011.

Chrisafis, Angelique, 'Emmanuel Todd: the French thinker who won't toe the Charlie Hebdo line', *The Guardian*, 28 August 2015.

Cleveland, William L., *A History of the Modern Middle East* (Boulder, CO: Westview Press, 2001).

Clifford, Rebecca, *Commemorating the Holocaust. The Dilemmas of Remembrance in France and Italy* (Oxford: Oxford University Press, 2013).

Cohen, A.E., 'Tien jaar na de bevrijding van nationaal-socialisme en jodenvervolging in Nederland' (1955), 'Verslag van bespreking, 8 October 1956.' In: J.C.H. Blom et al. (eds.), *A.E. Cohen als geschiedschrijver van zijn tijd* (Amsterdam: Boom, 2005), 317-328.

Cohen, Elie, *Beelden uit de nacht. Kampherinneringen* (Baarn: de Prom, 1992).

Cohen, Ies B., 'Slechts anti-Israëlische joden in forum. Asva wil tijdens congres "Lacunes gaan opheffen"', *NIW*, 15 May 1970.

Cohen, Jaap, 'De slachtstrijd is weer opgelaaid', *NRC Next*, 28 June 2011.

—, 'Hoe cruciaal is onwetendheid?', *NRC Next*, 3 April 2013.

—, 'Provoceren: over de top kwetsend of heel erg lomp', *NRC Next*, 5 February 2014.

Cohen, Mark R., *Under Crescent and Cross: The Jews in the Middle Ages* (Princeton, NJ: Princeton University Press 1995).

—, 'The "Convivencia" of Jews and Muslims in the High Middle Ages.' In: Moshe Maoz (ed.), *The Meeting of Civilizations. Muslims, Christians and Jewish* (Brighton, Portland: Sussex Academic Press, 2009), 54-65.

Cohn, Norman, *Warrant for Genocide. The Myth of the Jewish World-conspiracy and the Protocols of the Elders of Zion* (New York: Harper & Row, 1967).

Cohn, Werner, 'From Victim to Shylock and Oppressor: The New Image of the Jew in the Trotskyist Movement', *Journal of Communist Studies* 7, 1 (1991), 46-68.

Connelly, John, 'From enemy to brother.' Lecture at the international conference 'The Jew as legitimation', Menasseh ben Israel Institute, Amsterdam, 29 August 2013.

—, *From Enemy to Brother. The Revolution in Catholic Teaching on the Jews, 1933-1965* (Cambridge, MA: Harvard University Press, 2012).

Coolen, Anton, *Bevrijd vaderland* (Rotterdam: Nijgh & Van Ditmar, 1945).

Cooper, Abraham, and Manfred Gerstenfeld, 'Tijd dat Nederland excuses aanbiedt voor lot van Joden', *NRC Handelsblad*, 31 July 2015.

Cornelisse, Louis, 'Volkert houdt iets achter', *Trouw*, 30 June 2003.

Cornelissen, Igor, *Paul de Groot. Staatsvijand nr. 1* (Amsterdam: Nijgh & Van Ditmar, 1996).

Cottaar, Annemarie, Nadia Bouras and Fatiha Laouikili, *Marokkanen in Nederland. De pioniers vertellen* (Amsterdam: Meulenhoff, 2009).

Croes, Marnix, and Peter Tammes, *'Gif laten wij niet voortbestaan.' Een onderzoek naar de over-levingskansen van Joden in de Nederlandse gemeenten 1940-1945* (Amsterdam: Aksant, 2004).

Cutler, Allan Harris, and Helen Elmquist Cutler, *The Jew as Ally of the Muslim: Medieval Roots of Antisemitism* (Notre Dame: University of Notre Dame Press, 1986).

Damsma, J.M., *Nazis in the Netherlands: a social history of National Socialist collaborators, 1940-1945* (PhD thesis, Universiteit van Amsterdam, 2013).

Dangermond, Karin, 'Het heft in eigen handen: Joodse zelfmoorden in Nederland tijdens de Tweede Wereldoorlog', *Misjpoge* 25, 1 (2012), 4-12.

Daoud, Hassan, 'Een moord zonder echo', *De Groene Amsterdammer*, 14 January 2005.

Daoud, Zakya, *Les années Lamalif. 1958-1988. Trente ans de journalisme au Maroc* (Casablanca: Tarik, 2007).

Debus, Esther, *Die islamisch-rechtlichen Auskünfte der Millî Gazete im Rahmen des 'Fetwa-Wesen' der Türkischen Republik* (Berlin: Klaus Schwarz, 1984).

Deelen, René, *Voor altijd verbonden. Een onderzoek naar de invloed van de Holocaustherinnering op de Nederlandse geopolitieke relatie met Israël* (MA thesis, History Politics and Parliament, Radboud Universiteit, 2015).

Deira, Shari, 'Kamerleden willen meer weten over anti-Joods protest Den Haag', *Elsevier*, 25 July 2014.

De Kessel, M., 'Tango met de Dood. Over Mohammed Bouyeri's *Open Brief aan Hirsi Ali*.' Lecture at the symposium *'It takes two to tango: Religie in de publieke ruimte'*, Erasmus University Rotterdam, Faculty of Philosophy, 21 September 2005.

Dercksen, Jan Gerrit (Bennebroek), 'Betoging', *Trouw*, 3 April 1992.

Deutscher, Isaac, 'On the Israeli-Arab War', *New Left Review* I (1967).

Devji, Faisal, 'Looking back at Salman Rushdie's The Satanic Verses.' In: Barbara Daly Metcalf (ed.), *Making Muslim space in North America and Europe* (Berkeley, Los Angeles: University of California Press, 2002), 167-185.

Dommering, Egbert, 'De vrijheid van wat? De ondergrens van de vrije meningsuiting', *Vrij Nederland*, 24 October 2009.

Donselaar, Jaap van, *Fout na de oorlog. Fascistische en racistische organisaties in Nederland, 1950-1990* (Amsterdam: Bert Bakker, 1991).

—, *De staat paraat? De bestrijding van extreem-rechts in West-Europa* (Amsterdam: Babylon De Geus, 1995).

Dool, Pim van den, 'Anticonceptie oplossing voor situatie Gaza? Leon de Winter pareert kritiek', *NRC Handelsblad*, 24 November 2012.

Douwes, Jolan, 'RAP. Hollandse rap deukt, scheurt en beukt', *Trouw*, 27 April 1995.

Drayer, Elma, 'Het taboe op jodenhaat is verdwenen', *Trouw*, 28 februari 2013.

Dreyfuss, Havi, 'Changing Perspectives on Polish-Jewish Relations during the Holocaust. Search and Research. Lectures and Papers' (Jerusalem, Yad Vashem / The International Institute for Holocaust Research / Center for Research on the Holocaust in Poland, 2012.

Driessen, Camiel, 'Eieren gooien is de nieuwste kinderrage', *Dagblad De Pers*, 16 November 2009.

Dros, Lodewijk, 'AIVD wist van coup Milli Görüs', *Trouw*, 6 June 2007.

Duivenvoorden, Eric van, *Een voet tussen de deur: geschiedenis van de kraakbeweging (1964-1999)* (Amsterdam: De Arbeiderspers, 2000).

—, *Rebelse jeugd. Hoe nozems en provo's Nederland veranderden* (Amsterdam: Nieuw Amsterdam, 2015).

Dunk, Hermann von der, 'Conservatism in the Netherlands', *Journal of Contemporary History* 13, 4 (1978), 741-763.

Duyvendak, Jan Willem, 'Ook PVV'ers houden niet van homoseksuelen', *De Groene Amsterdammer*, 10 March 2016.

Duurvoort, Harriet, 'Antisemitisme gaat ons allemaal aan', *de Volkskrant*, 2 June 2015

—, 'Moord op multicultureel Parijs', *de Volkskrant*, 23 November 2015.

Dwyer, Kevin, *Moroccan Dialogues. Anthropology in Question* (Baltimore: The Johns Hopkins University Press, 1982).

Edgren, Henrik (ed.), *Looking at the Onlookers and Bystanders. Interdisciplinary Approaches to the Causes and Consequences of Passivity* (Stockholm: The Living History Forum, 2012).

Éditorial, 'La guerre, La paix et le reste, *Lamalif* (June-July 1967), 16-19.

Efron, John, 'When is a Yid not a Jew? The strange case of Supporter Identity at Tottenham Hotspur.' In: Michael Brenner and Gideon Reuveni (eds.), *Emancipation through Muscles. Jews and Sports in Europe* (Lincoln: University of Nebraska Press, 2006), 242-244.

Ehrlich, Howard J., 'The Swastika Epidemic of 1959-1960: Anti-Semitism and Community Characteristics', *Social Problems* 9, 3 (1962), 264-272.

Einhorn, Daniel Benjamin, 'Superjoden? Een onderzoek naar de herkomst en implicaties van het joodse zelfbeeld bij sommige Ajax-supporters 1900-2011' (MA thesis, Vrije Universiteit Amsterdam, August 2011).

Eisenmenger, Johan Andreas, *Entdecktes Judenthum: oder Gründlicher und wahrhaffter Bericht, welchergestalt die verstockte Juden die hochheilige Drey-Einigkeit... lästern... In zweyen Theilen verfasset* (Königsberg in Preussen, s.n., 1711).

El Madkouri, Halim, 'IS is in niets strijdig met de islam', *de Volkskrant*, 1 December 2015.

Elkerbout, Jaël, 'Fear and Hatred of "the Other": Comparing Stereotypes of Anti-Semitism and Islamophobia' (MA thesis Conflict Resolution and Governance, Universiteit van Amsterdam).

Embacher, Helga, 'Neuer Antisemitismus in Europa – ein historischer Vergleich.' In: Moshe Zuckermann (ed.), *Antisemitismus – Antizionismus – Israelkritik. Tel Aviver Jahrbuch für deutsche Geschichte* XXXIII (Göttingen: Wallstein Verlag, 2005), 50-69.

—, and Jan Rybak, 'Anti-Semitism in Muslim communities and Islamophobia in the context of the Gaza War 2014: Austria and Germany', *Open Democracy. free thinking for the world*, 1 October 2015: https://www.opendemocracy.net.

—, and Margit Reiter (eds.), *Europa und der 11. September 2001* (Wien, Köln, Weimar: Böhlau Verlag, 2011).

—, and Margit Reiter, 'Israel-Kritik und (neuer) Antisemitismus seit der Zweiten Intifada in Deutschland und Grofbritannien im Vergleich.' In: Monika Schwarz-Friesel, Evyatar Friesel and Jehuda Reinharz (eds.), *Aktueller Antisemitismus- ein Phänomen der Mitte* (New York: De Gruyter, 2010), 187-212.

Ende, Hanna van den, *'Vergeet niet dat je arts bent'. Joodse artsen in Nederland 1940-1945* (Amsterdam: Boom, 2015).

Ensel, Remco, *Saints and Servants in Southern Morocco* (Leiden, Köln: Brill, 1999).

—, *Haatspraak. Antisemitisme – een 21e-eeuwse geschiedenis* (Amsterdam: Amsterdam University Press, 2014).

—, 'Singing about the death of Muhammad al-Durrah and the emotional mobilization for protest', *International Journal of Media and Cultural Politics*, 10: 1 (2014), 21-38.

—, 'Als het antisemitisme is, moet je het ook zo noemen', *NRC Handelsblad*, 13 August 2014.

—, 'Pennestrijd. Public historians Geyl en Toynbee debatteren in de schaduw van de Holocaust (1948-1961)', *Ex Tempore* 34, 2 (2015), 145-157.

—, 'Slag of stoot: Over het strijdtoneel van het historisch debat', *Ex Tempore* 34 (2015), 86-94.

—, 'Israël zorgt voor heftige emoties, daarom is stedenband belangrijk', *Het Parool*, 27 Juni 2015.

—, 'Postcolonial memories. Frantz Fanon in/on Europe.' In: Marjet Derks, Martijn Eickhoff, Remco Ensel and Floris Meens (eds.), *What's Left Behind. The Lieux de Mémoire on Europe Beyond Europe* (Nijmegen: Vantilt, 2015), 199-206, 237-239 (notes).

—, and Annemarike Stremmelaar, 'Speech Acts. Observing Antisemitism and Holocaust Education in the Netherlands.' In: Günther Jikeli and Joëlle Allouche-Benayoun (eds.), *Perceptions of the Holocaust in Europe and Muslim Communities. Sources, Comparisons and Educational Challenges* (Dordrecht: Springer, 2013), 153-171.

—, and Evelien Gans, 'De inzet van joden als "'controlegroep". Bart van der Boom en de Holocaust', *Tijdschrift voor Geschiedenis* 126, 3 (2013), 388-396.

—, and Evelien Gans, 'The Bystander as a non-Jew.' Paper presented at the international conference *Probing the Limits of Categorization: The 'Bystander' in Holocaust History*, 24-26 September 2015, Amsterdam, 25 September.

—, and Evelien Gans, 'We know something of their fate. Bart van der Boom's history of the Holocaust in the Netherlands': https://independent.academia.edu/Remco Ensel and https://independent.academia.edu/EvelienGans.

Ephimenco, Sylvain, 'Straatterrorist', *Trouw*, 12 November 2010.

Erkel, Arjan, *Samir* (Amsterdam: Balans, 2007).

Etty, Elsbeth, 'De erfzonde van de linkse kerk', *NRC Handelsblad*, 1 November 2011.

Eyerman, Ron, *The Assassination of Theo van Gogh: From Social Drama to Cultural Trauma* (Durham and London: Duke University Press, 2008).

Eyl, H.R., 'De oliebronnen van Verhagen', *Propria Cures*, 10 May 1958.

Exter, Jak den, *Diyanet: een reis door de keuken van de officiële Turkse islam* (Beverwijk: Centrum Buitenlanders Peregrinus, 1990).

Fallaux, Emile, 'Een groot filmer zou hij worden', *NRC Handelsblad*, 5 November 2004.

Farner, Steve, *Whiteness. An introduction* (London, New York: Routledge, 2007).

Fassbinder, R.W., *Het vuil, de stad en de dood*. Vertaling en nawoord door Gerrit Bussink (The Hague: BZZTôH, 1986).

Fein, Helen, *Accounting for Genocide: National Responses and Jewish Victimization During the Holocaust* (repr. 1984; Chicago/London: University of Chicago Press, 1979).

—, 'Dimensions of Antisemitism: Attitudes, Collective Accusations, and Actions.' In: Helen Fein (ed.), *The Persisting Question: Sociological Perspectives and Social Contexts of Modern Antisemitism* (Berlin: Walter de Gruyter, 1987), 67-85.

—, 'The Impact of antisemitism on the enactment and success of "the Final Solution of the Jewish Question".' In: Helen Fein, *The Persisting Question: Sociological Perspectives and Social Contexts of Modern Antisemitism* (Berlin: Walter de Gruyter), 283-284.

Feinberg, Anat,'Ein missglückter Versuch: Klaus Pohls Jud Süss-Drama.' In: Hans-Peter Bayderdörfer and Jens Malte Fischer, in cooperation with Frank Halbach (eds.), *Judenrollen. Darstellungsformen im europäischen Theater von der Restauration bis zur Zwischenkriegszeit* (Tübingen: Max Niemeyer Verlag, 2008), 189-198.

Fine, Robert, 'Fighting with Phantoms: A Contribution to the Debate on Antisemitism in Europe', *Patterns of Prejudice* 43, 5 (2009), 459-479.

—, 'Two Faces of Universalism: Jewish Emancipation and the Jewish Question', *Jewish Journal of Sociology* 56, 1/2 (2014), 29-47: 30.

—, and Glynn Cousin, 'A Common Cause. Reconnecting the Study of Racism and anti-Semitism', *European Societies* 14, 2 (2012), 166-185.

Fischer, Lars, 'Anti-"Philosemitism" and Anti-Antisemitism in Imperial Germany.' In: Jonathan Karp and Adam Sutcliffe (eds.), *Philosemitism in History* (New York: Cambridge University Press, 2011), 170-189.

Fischer, Torben, and Matthias N. Lorenz (eds.), *Lexikon der 'Vergangenheitsbewältigung' in Deutschland: Debatten- und Diskursgeschichte des National-sozialismus nach 1945* (Bielefeld: Transkript, 2007).

Fishman, Joel, 'Een keerpunt in de naoorlogse geschiedenis van de Nederlandse joden: De toespraak van opperrabbijn Schuster in de Nieuwe Kerk (1955).' In: Hetty Berg and Bart Wallet (eds.), *Wie niet weg is, is gezien. Joods Nederland na 1945* (Zwolle: Waanders, 2010), 119-129.

Fisk, Robert, 'The forgotten massacre', *The Independent*, 15 September 2002.

Fitzgerald, Sean, 'The Anti-Modern Rhetoric of Le Mouvement Poujade', *The Review of Politics* 32, 2 (1970), 167-190.

F.N., 'Emoties laaiden op tijdens forum over de Arabische vluchtelingen', *NIW*, 15 February 1963.

Foer, Franklin, *How Soccer Explains the World. An Unlikely Theory of Globalization* (New York: Harper Perennial, 2004).

Fogteloo, Margreet, 'Grijsdenken. Het zwart-witdenken over de Tweede Wereldoorlog heeft afgedaan', *De Groene Amsterdammer*, 6 May 2005.

—, and Eduard van Holst Pellekaan, 'August Allebépleinvrees. Marokkanen in West, vijf jaar na de explosie', *De Groene Amsterdammer*, 20 December 2003.

Forster, Arnold and Benjamin R. Epstein, *The New Anti-Semitism* (New York: Mc-Graw-Hill, 1974).

Fortuin, Arjen, 'Een ander moreel oordeel propageren. De Oogst van het Decennium: "Grijs verleden" (2001) van Chris van der Heijden', *NRC Handelsblad*, 12 July 2010.

—, 'Wat haalt de filosemiet nu weer in zijn hoofd? ', *NRC Handelsblad*, 15 January 2016.

Fortuyn, Pim, *Tegen de islamisering van onze cultuur: Nederlandse identiteit als fundament* (Utrecht: A.W. Bruna, 1997).

Frank, Anne, *The Diary of Anne Frank: The revised critical edition* (New York: Doubleday, 2003).

Franke, Jan, 'Het racismespook', *NIW*, 8 May 2015.

Fransen, Ad, 'Theo van Gogh: "Wat is er mis met geitenneuker"', *HP/De Tijd*, 28 October 2009.

Fresco, Louise, 'Bloed en rituelen', *NRC Handelsblad*, 13 April 2011.

—, *Hamburgers in het paradijs: voedsel in tijden van schaarste en overvloed* (Amsterdam: Bert Bakker 2012).

—, *Hamburgers in Paradise: The Stories Behind the Food We Eat* (Princeton/New Jersey: Princeton University Press 2015).

Freud, Sigmund, *Civilization and Its Discontents* (London: Penguin, 2002); first Austrian ed.: Sigmund Freud, *Das Unbehagen in der Kultur* (Wien: Internationaler psychoanalytischer Verlag, 1930).

Friedländer, Saul, *Nazi-Duitsland en de joden I: De jaren van vervolging 1933-1939* (Utrecht: Het Spectrum, 1998).

—, *Nazi-Duitsland en de joden II: De jaren van vernietiging* (Amsterdam: Nieuw Amsterdam, 2007).

—, *Nazi Germany and the Jews. Volume I: The years of persecution, 1933-1939* (New York: Harper Collins, 2007).

—, *The Years of Extermination. Nazi Germany and the Jews, 1939-1945* (New York: Harper & Collins, 2007).

Friedman, Carl, 'Heksenjacht', *Trouw*, 30 June 2001.

Friedmann, Elise, *Monitor antisemitische incidenten in Nederland: 2008. Met een verslag van de Gaza periode (27 December 2008-23 January 2009)* (The Hague: CIDI, 2009).

Frosh, Stephen, 'Freud, Psychoanalysis and Anti-Semitism', *Psychoanalytic Review,* 91, 3 (2004): 309-333.

Fuks-Mansfeld, Rena, 'Verlichting en Emancipatie omstreeks 1750-1814.' In: J.C.H. Blom, R.G. Fuks-Manfeld and I. Schöffer (eds.), *Geschiedenis van de Joden in Nederland* (Amsterdam: Balans, 1995), 177-203.

Fulbrook, Mary, *A Small Town near Auschwitz. Ordinary Nazis and the Holocaust* (Oxford: Oxford University Press, 2012).

Furedi, Frank, 'The bigotry of the anti-circumcision zealots', *Sp!ked Online,* 2 July 2012.

Fürtig, Henner, 'Die Bedeutung der iranischen Revolution von 1979 als Ausgangspunkt für eine antijüdisch orientierte Islamisierung' *Jahrbuch für Antisemitismusforschung* 12 (Berlin: Metropol, 2003), 73-98.

Galan, Menno de, *De trots van de wereld. Michels, Cruijff en het Gouden Ajax van 1964-1974* (Amsterdam: De Arbeiderspers, 2006).

Galen Last, Dick van, 'Wetenschapsbeoefening en revisionisme.' In: Jaap van Donselaar, Teresien de Silva and W. Sorgdrager (eds.), *Weerzinwekkende wetenschap. Holocaustontkenning en andere uitingen van historisch revisionisme* (Amsterdam: Anne Frank Stichting, 1998), 16-33.

Gans, Evelien, 'Are Zionist socialists bad socialists? A 1929 Amsterdam left-wing polemic about Zionism.' In: Jozeph Michman (ed.), *Dutch Jewish History,* Vol. III (Assen, Maastricht: Van Gorcum, 1993), 321-338.

—, *Gojse nijd & joods narcisme. Over de verhouding tussen joden en niet-joden in Nederland* (Amsterdam: Arena, 1994).

—, 'Sam de Wolff (1878-1960): een typisch geval van én-én.' In: Francine Püttmann et al. (eds.), *Markante Nederlandse Zionisten* (Amsterdam: De Bataafsche Leeuw, 1996), 50-63.

—, 'Formalisme, lafheid en nalatigheid', *De Groene Amsterdammer,* 29 October 1997.

—, *De kleine verschillen die het leven uitmaken: een historische studie naar joodse sociaal-democraten en socialistisch-zionisten in Nederland* (Amsterdam: Vassallucci, 1999).

—, 'De politiek van het joods gevoel.' In: Marita Mathijsen (ed.), *Hartstocht in contrapunt* (Amsterdam: De Bezige Bij, 2002), 193-209.

—, '"Vandaag hebben ze niets, maar morgen bezitten ze weer een tientje." Antisemitische stereotypen in bevrijd Nederland.' In: Conny Kristel (ed.), *Polderschouw. Terugkeer en opvang na de Tweede Wereldoorlog. Regionale verschillen* (Amsterdam: Bert Bakker, 2002), 313-353.

—, 'Gojse broodnijd: de strijd tussen joden en niet-joden rond de naoorlogse Winkelsluitingswet 1945-1951.' In: Conny Kristel (ed.), *Met alle geweld. Botsingen en tegenstellingen in burgerlijk Nederland* (Amsterdam: Balans, 2003), 195-213.

—, 'De Joodse almacht. Hedendaags antisemitisme', *Vrij Nederland,* 29 November 2003.

—, *De weg terug. Het kantelend zelfbeeld van de joodse historicus Jaap Meijer (1912-1993)* (Amsterdam: Vossiuspers, Amsterdam University Press, 2003).

—, 'Volgend jaar in Jeruzalem', *Vrij Nederland,* 5 April 2003.

—, 'De almachtige jood. Hedendaags antisemitisme', *Vrij Nederland,* 29 November 2003.

—, 'The Netherlands in the Twentieth Century.' In: Richard Levy (ed.), *Antisemitism. A Historical Encyclopedia of Prejudice and Persecution* (Santa Barbara/Denver/Oxford: ABC-CLIO, 2005), Vol. 2, 498-500.

—, 'The omnipotent Jew. Antisemitism today', www.niod.nl/nl/hedendaags-antisemitisme (first published in *Vrij Nederland,* 29-11-2003; transl. by Wendie Shaffer).

—, '"The Jews" as products of globalisation', *Engage Journal* 2, May 2006.

—, 'Antisemitisme: evolutionair en multi-functioneel.' Paper presented at the *Anne Frank Stichting,* Amsterdam, 3 October 2007.

—, *Jaap en Ischa Meijer. Een joodse geschiedenis 1912-1956* (Amsterdam: Bert Bakker, 2008).

—, 'Next Year in Paramaribo: Galut and Diaspora as Scene-changes in the Jewish life of Jakob Meijer.' In: Yosef Kaplan (ed.), *The Dutch Intersection: The Jews and the Netherlands in Modern History* (Leiden / Boston: Brill, 2008), 369-387.

—, 'Weg met vernedering. Extreem-rechts keert zich niet per se tegen joden', *de Volkskrant* Opinie online, 17 December 2009.

—, 'Over gaskamers, Joodse nazi's en neuzen.' In: Peter Rodrigues and Jaap van Donselaar (eds.), *Monitor Racisme & Extremisme. Negende Rapportage* (Amsterdam: Anne Frank Stichting, Amsterdam University Press, 2010), 129-152.

—, 'On gas chambers, Jewish Nazis and noses.' In: Peter Rodrigues and Jaap van Donselaar (eds.), *Racism and Extremism Monitor. Ninth Report* (Amsterdam: Anne Frank Stichting, Universiteit Leiden, 2010), 74-87.

—, '"The Jew" as a multifunctional projection screen.' Introduction at the international symposium *The Dynamics of Contemporary Antisemitism in a Globalizing Context*, Amsterdam, 12 May 2010.

—, 'Iedereen een beetje slachtoffer, iedereen een beetje dader. De Nederlandse *Historikerstreit* over de grijze oorlog', *De Groene Amsterdammer*, 28 January 2010.

—, '"Verbaal misdrijf", Reactie op het artikel van rabbijn Evers "Job Cohens onmogelijke vergelijking"', *NIW*, 24 December 2010.

—, 'De strijd tegen het antisemitisme is verworden tot ideologie tegen moslims', *NRC Handelsblad*, 8 January 2011.

—, 'It is antisemitic – no, it isn't. The public debate on antisemitism and the Holocaust in the Netherlands.' Paper presented at the IIBSA symposium 'Perceptions of the Holocaust and Contemporary Antisemitism', Berlin, 31 May 2011.

—, 'Eigentlich waren doch alle ein bisschen Täter *und* Opfer... Nivellierungstendenzen und sekundärer Antisemitismus im Geschichtsbild des niederländischen Historikers Chris van der Heijden.' In: Nicole Colin, Matthias Lorenz and Joachim Umlauf (eds.), *Täter und Tabu. Grenzen der Toleranz in deutschen und niederländischen Geschichtsdebatten* (Essen: Klartext, 2011), 33-47.

—, 'Het waarom van de weerstand in academisch-intellectuele kring tegen het uitdelen van het stempel "antisemitisme."' Paper, NIOD researchers lunch, NIOD, 5 September 2011.

—, 'The Feuchtwanger-effect. Jud Süss as a testing ground for philosemitic and antisemitic stereotypes.' Paper presented at the symposium 'The many guises of Jud Süss', Menasseh ben Israel Institute, Amsterdam, 10 & 11 May 2012.

—, '"Hamas, Hamas, all Jews to the gas". The history and significance of an antisemitic slogan in the Netherlands, 1945-2010.' In: Günther Jikeli and Joëlle Allouche Benayoun (eds.), *Perceptions of the Holocaust in Europe and Muslim Communities. Sources, Comparisons and Educational Challenges* (Dordrecht: Springer, 2013), 85-103.

—, '"They have forgotten to gas you." Post-1945 Antisemitism in the Netherlands.', In: Philomena Essed and Isabele Hoving (eds.), *Dutch Racism* (Amsterdam/New York: Rodopi, 2014), 71-100.

—, 'Ischa Meijer, De soldaat van Oranje en de Fassbinderaffaire.' In: Hetty Berg and Bart Wallet (eds.), *Wie niet weg is, is gezien. Joods Nederland na 1945* (Zwolle: Waanders, 2010), 164-165.

—, 'Anti-antisemitischer Enthusiasmus & selektiver Philosemitismus: Geert Wilders, die PVV und die Juden', *Jahrbuch für Antisemitismusforschung* 23 (2014), 95-104.

—, '... Cause Jews burn the best. Football antisemitism: The different historical manifestations of an ever-existing phenomenon in the Netherlands.' Paper presented at the International Conference *Tackling anti-Semitism in Professional Football* (organised by the Anne Frank Stichting), Amsterdam Arena, 11-12 June 2015.

—, 'Theo van Gogh (1957-2004): Copulerende gele sterren, geitenneukers en held van de vrije meningsuiting.' Paper presented at the symposium 'Joden en moslims in een veranderende samenleving', Amsterdam, 31 March 2015.

—, 'Anti-Antisemitic Enthusiasm and Selective Philosemitism: Wilders, the PVV', Website Jüdisches Museum Berlin, www.jmberlin.de/main/DE/05-Publikationen/07-online-publikationen.php.

—, 'Anti-antisemitischer Enthusiasmus und selektiver Philosemitismus: Geert Wilders, die PVV und die Juden.' In: Stefanie Schüler-Springorum (ed.), Juliane Wetzel (Geschäftsführende Redakteurin), *Jahrbuch für Antisemitismusforschung* für das Zentrum für Antisemitismusforschung der Technischen Universität Berlin (Berlin: Metropol, 2014), 93-104.

—, '"[Lodewijk] Asscher, de twee SS in zijn naam geeft zijn ware aard aan...". Hedendaags antisemitisme.' Paper presented at the reunion of the Werkgroep Andere Tijden, Amsterdam, 12 March 2016.

—, 'Het spanningsveld tussen Israël als aanhechtingspunt voor naoorlogs antisemitisme en doelwit voor legitieme kritiek', paper presented at CIDI-meeting 'Hoe besmettelijk is de 'Engelse ziekte'? De dunne lijn tussen antizionisme en antisemitisme,' 9 June 2016.

—, 'Disparaging responsibility. The stereotype of the Passive Jew as a legitimizing factor in Dutch remembrance of the Shoah.' In David Wertheim (ed.), *The Jew as Legitimation. Jewish-Non-Jewish Relationships beyond Antisemitism and Philosemitism* (under review).

—, *Antisemitisme? Het beeld van 'de Jood' in Naoorlogs Nederland* (typoscript).

—, and Remo Ensel, 'Wij weten iets van hun lot. Nivellering in de geschiedschrijving', *De Groene Amsterdammer*, 13 December 2012, 32-35.

Garbarini, Alexandra, *Numbered Days. Diaries and the Holocaust* (Ann Arbor: Yale University Press 2006).

Gay, Peter, *Freud, Jews and other Germans: Masters and Victims in Modernist Culture* (New York: Oxford University Press, 1978).

Garschagen, Oscar, 'Geen uitweg meer uit de Jordaanvallei', *NRC Handelsblad*, 21 April 2006.

Gazzah, Miriam, *Rhythms and Rhymes of life. Music and Identification Processes of Moroccan-Dutch Youth* (Amsterdam: Amsterdam University Press, 2008).

Gebert, Malte, and Carmen Matussek, '"Selbst wenn sie under Land verlassen würden..." Die Adaptation der Protokolle der Weisen von Zion in der arabischen Welt', *Jahrbuch für Antisemitismusforschung* 18 (2009), 67-87.

Gelder, Frederik van, 'Commemoration, a philosophical view.' *The Ashworth Program for Social Theory*, University of Melbourne, 2007: www.amsterdam-adorno.net/fvg2013_crescas_ENG.pdf.

Gender-Killer, A.G. (ed.), *Antisemitismus und Geschlecht. Von 'effiminierten Juden, maskulinierten Judinnen' und andere Geschlechterbildern* (Münster: Unrast, 2005).

Genoud, François (ed.), *Hitlers politisches Testament. Die Bormann Diktate vom Februar und April 1945. Mit einem Essay von Hugh R. Trevor-Roper und einem Nachwort von André François-Poncet* (Hamburg: Albrecht Knaus, 1981).

Gentile, Emilio, 'A provisional dwelling. The origin and development of the concept of fascism in Mosse's historiography.' In: Stanley G. Payne, David J. Sorkin and John S. Tortoise (eds.), *What History Tells. George L. Mosse and the Culture of Modern Europe* (Madison: The University of Wisconsin Press, 2004), 41-109.

Gerrits, André, *The Myth of Jewish Communism: A Historical Interpretation* (New York: Peter Lang, 2009).

Gerstenfeld, Manfred, *Het Verval. Joden in een stuurloos Nederland* (Amsterdam: Van Praag, 2010).

—, 'Laffe Jood, Joodse Zelfhaat. Dat zijn niet mijn woorden', *NRC Handelsblad*, 22 January 2011.

—, 'Open brief aan Tweede Kamer over ritueel slachten', *Dagelijkse standaard*, 14 June 2011.

—, 'Onderzoek naar Jodenhaat in Nederland hard nodig', *Reformatorisch Dagblad*, 14 March 2013.

—, 'Dutch press tries to hide anti-Semitic incident', *Jerusalem Post*, 17 March 2013.

Geyl, Pieter, *Napoleon for and against* (New Haven: Yale University Press, 1949; first Dutch ed. 1946).

—, *Die Diskussion ohne Ende. Auseinandersetzungen mit Historikern* (Darmstadt: Gertner, 1958).

Ghiles-Meilhac, Samuel, 'Les Juifs de France et la guerre des Six Jours: solidarité avec Israël et affirmation d'une identité politique collective', *Matériaux pour l'histoire de notre temps* 4, 96 (2009), 12-15.

Giesen, Peter, 'In regen van eieren naar de synagoge', *de Volkskrant*, 16 February 2015.

Gijssel, Robert van, 'The Dictators speelden in Parijs, na de terreur', *de Volkskrant*, 16 November 2015.

Gilliat-Ray, Sophie, *Muslims in Britain. An Introduction* (Cambridge: Cambridge University Press, 2010).

Gilman, Sander, *Jewish Self-Hatred. Anti-Semitism and the Hidden Language of the Jews* (Baltimore, Maryland: The Johns Hopkins University Press, 1986).

—, *The Jew's Body* (New York, London: Routledge, 1991).

Ginkel, Rob van, *Rondom de stilte. Herdenkingscultuur in Nederland* (Amsterdam: Bert Bakker, 2011),

Ginniken, Jaap van, 'Palestina of Israël', *Nijmeegs Universiteitsblad* 27, 9 June 1967.

—, 'Palestijns Dagboek II', *Nijmeegs Universiteitsblad* 28, 16 June 1967.

—, 'Naar aanleiding van...', *Nijmeegs Universiteitsblad* 29, 23 June 1967.

Givet, Jacques, *La Gauche contre Israël? Essai sur le néo-antisémitisme* (Paris: Jean-Jacques Pauvert, 1968).

Glenn, Susan, 'In the Blood? Consent, Descent, and the Ironies of Jewish Identity', *Jewish Social Studies* 8, 2/3 (2002), 139-152.

Gogh, Theo van, 'Een Messias Zonder Kruis (Enige kanttekeningen bij Leon de Winter)', *Moviola* 1 (1984).

—, 'Snif, Snif. Ruikt het hier naar antisemitisme?', *Moviola* 2 (1985).

—, 'Rubriek: Wassenaarse brieven over onderwijs, kunst en wetenschap. A correspondence between Boudewijn Büch and Theo van Gogh', *Folia*, 10 and 17 September 1993.

—, 'Een columnist die voor Sonja Barend zwicht.' In: Theo van Gogh, *Er gebeurt nooit iets* (Amsterdam, Antwerp: Veen 1993), 30-33.

—, 'Vooruitgang', *Haagse Post/De Tijd*, 24 March 1994.

—, 'Lang leve de racist!', *HP/DeTijd*, 24 March 1995.

—, 'Eigen schuld dikke bult', *HP/DeTijd*, 20 October 1995.

—, 'Leve de islam', *HP/De Tijd*, December 1995.

—, *Allah weet het beter* (Amsterdam: Xtra, 2003).

—, 'De boel bij elkaar houden', *Metro*, 13 March 2004.

—, 'Zelfportret', *HP/De Tijd*, 4 June 2004.

—, 'Lof der besnijdenis', *Metro*, 8 October 2004.

—, 'Onze burgemeester', Van Gogh, *Metro*, 22 October 2004.

Gompes, Loes, *Fatsoenlijk land. Porgel en Porulan in het verzet* (Amsterdam: Rozenberg Publishers, 2013).

Goossensen, Jan, 'Op het randje', *Hervormd Nederland*, 9 May 1998.

Gouda, Frances, 'Divided Memories of World War II in the Netherlands and the Dutch East Indies: Sukarno and Anne Frank as Icons of Dutch Historical Imagination.' In: Daniel Chirot,

Gi-Wook Shin and Daniel Sneider (eds.), *Confronting Memories of World War II: European and Asian Legacies* (Seattle: The University of Washington Press, 2014), 105-134.

Graaf, Bram de, *Voetbalvrouwen. De glorietijd van het Nederlandse voetbal 1970-1978* (Amsterdam: Ambo, 2008).

Graaf, B.A. de, 'Religion bites: Religieuze orthodoxie op de nationale veiligheidsagenda.' *Tijdschrift voor Religie, Recht en Beleid* 2 (2012), 62-80.

Grant, Linda, '*Israel has moved*, by Diana Pinto', review, *The Independent*, 28 February 2013.

Grevers, Heleen, *Van landverraders tot goede vaderlanders: de opsluiting van collaborateurs in Nederland en België, 1944-1950* (Amsterdam: Balans, 2013).

Griffioen, Pim, and Ron Zeller, *Jodenvervolging, in Nederland, Frankrijk en België. Overeenkomsten, verschillen, oorzaken* (Amsterdam: Boom, 2011).

—, 'Comparing the Persecution of the Jews in the Netherlands, France and Belgium, 1940-1945: Similarities, Differences, Causes.' In: Peter Romijn et al. (eds.), *The Persecution of the Jews in the Netherlands, 1940-1945: new perspectives* (Amsterdam: Vossiuspers, 2012), 55-91.

Groen, Janny, 'Intifada-taferelen in Amsterdams stadsbeeld', *de Volkskrant*, December 12, 2001.

—, 'Samen in het geweer tegen aanval op halalvlees, "we zijn in shock"', *de Volkskrant*, 13 September 2011.

—, 'Weinig steun bedreigde onderzoeker', *de Volkskrant*, 11 March 2013.

—, '"Verketterd omdat ik de vinger op de zere plek heb gelegd"', *de Volkskrant*, 26 April 2013.

—, 'Moskeeën veel vaker van doelwit van agressie dan vermeld', *de Volkskrant*, 11 March 2016.

Gross, Jan T., Fear: *Anti-Semitism in Poland after Auschwitz: An Essay in Historical Interpretation* (Princeton: Princeton University Press, 2003).

Grosz, Ronald, 'Der Talmud im Feuer der Jahrhunderte.' In: Jüdisches Museum der Stadt Wien (ed.), *Die Macht der Bilder. Antisemitische Vorurteilen und Mythen* (Wien: Picus, 1995), 111-116.

Grunberg, Arnon, 'Vreedzame broeders', *Het Parool*, 6 November 2004.

—, 'Menselijkheid', *de Volkskrant*, 3 August 2015.

Grünfeld, Fred, *Nederland en het Nabije Oosten. De Nederlandse rol in de internationale politiek ten aanzien van het Arabisch-Israëlisch conflict 1973-1982* (Deventer: Kluwer, 1991).

Grüter, Regina, *Strijd om gerechtigheid: Joodse verzekeringstegoeden en de Tweede Wereldoorlog* (Amsterdam: Boom, 2015).

Guttman, Anna, '"People set apart": representations of Jewishness in the fiction of Salman Rushdie', *Ariel* 42, 3 (2011), 103-121.

Haakman, David, 'Van der Laan wil af van Jodenleus bij Ajax', *NRC Handelsblad*, 13 May 2011

—, 'PVV wil excuses voor "slappe houding" regering in WOII', *NRC Handelsblad*, 4 January 2012.

—, 'Vier doden bij schietpartij op school in Toulouse – Sarkozy: nationale tragedie', *NRC Handelsblad*, 19 March 2012.

Haan, Ido de, *Na de ondergang. De herinnering aan de jodenvervolging in Nederland, 1945-1995* (The Hague: Sdu, 1999).

—, 'The paradoxes of Dutch history. Historiography of the Holocaust in the Netherlands.' In: David Bankier and Dan Michman (eds.), *Holocaust Historiography in Context: Emergence, Challenges, Polemics and Achievements* (Jerusalem: Yad Vashem, Berghahn Books, 2008), 355-376.

Halsema, Femke, *Pluche. Politieke memoires* (Amsterdam: Ambo/Anthos, 2016).

Hanloser, Gerhard, 'Bundesrepublikanischer Linksradikalismus und Israel – Antifaschismus und Revolutionismus als Tragödie und als Farce.' In: Moshe Zuckermann (ed.), *Antisemitismus, Antizionismus, Israelkritik. Tel Aviver Jahrbuch für deutsche Geschichte XXXIII* (2005), 181-213.

Hart, Jan 't, '"Rooie advocaat" schudde gevestigde orde wakker', *de Volkskrant*, 7 June 1997.

Hartmans, Rob, 'Who's afraid of grey, black and white', *De Groene Amsterdammer*, 7 April 2001.

Hass, Amira, 'Relative of Arson Attack Victims: I Saw Two Masked Men Standing by as They Burned', *Haaretz*, 31 July 2015.

—,'Israel Incapable of Telling Truth About Water It Steals From Palestinians', *Haaretz*,14 July 2016.

—, 'Ten Bullets, and She Never Got Near the Israeli Soldiers, *Haaretz*, 4 October 2015.

Haveman, Ben, 'Anti-joodse bomdreiging "werk van een gek"', *de Volkskrant*, 25 October 1985.

Havenaar, Ronald, 'Een grenzeloze passie voor grijs', *Vrij Nederland*, 5 November 2011.

Heijden, Chris van der, *Grijs verleden. Nederland en de Tweede Wereldoorlog* (Amsterdam, Antwerp: Contact, 2001).

—, 'Fout en foutjes', *Vrij Nederland*, 3 March 2001.

—, 'Van zwart, wit en grijs. Oorlog en mensbeeld.' In: Louis Paul Boon et al., *Hij was een zwarte. Over oorlog en collaboratie* (Amsterdam: Meulenhoff, 2003), 69-83.

—, 'De oorlog is voorgoed voorbij', *Vrij Nederland*, 26 April 2003.

—,*Joodse NSB'ers: De vergeten geschiedenis van Villa Bouchina in Doetinchem* (Utrecht: Begijnekade 18 Uitgevers, 2006).

—, 'Vertel het hele verhaal van de oorlog en betrek de NSB erbij', *NRC Handelsblad*, 9/10 December 2006.

—, *Israël. Een onherstelbare vergissing* (Amsterdam/Antwerp: Contact 2008).

—, 'Moordenaars onder ons', *De Groene Amsterdammer*, 27 November 2009.

—, 'Die NSB – eine ganz normale politische Partei? Ein Plädoyer für historische Korrektheit jenseits der Political Correctness.' In: Nicole Colin, Matthias N. Lorenz and Joachim Umlauf (eds.), *Täter und Tabu: Grenzen der Toleranz in deutschen und niederländischen Geschichtsdebatten* (Essen: Klartext, 2011), 25-31.

—, *Dat nooit meer: de nasleep van de Tweede Wereldoorlog in Nederland* (Amsterdam, Antwerp: Contact, 2011).

—, 'Het laatste appèl. Het verhaal van een foto', *De Groene Amsterdammer*, 27 April 2011.

—, 'Het einde van de historische correctheid', *Vrij Nederland*, 6 December 2012.

—, 'Onnozele geiten. Auschwitz door de lens van de SS', *De Groene Amsterdammer*, 20 February 2013.

—, 'Waarheidsversneller', *De Groene Amsterdammer*, 9 October 2013.

—, 'Waar is hun menselijkheid?', *De Groene Amsterdammer*, 8 April 2015.

—, 'En behoed ons voor het kwade. De Tweede Wereldoorlog – De oorlog als sociaal houvast', *De Groene Amsterdammer*, 15 April 2015.

—, and Leon De Winter, *Handleiding ter bestrijding van extreem-rechts* (Amsterdam: De Bezige Bij, 1994).

Heijmans, Toine, 'Theo van Gogh als symbool: De hypergevoeligheid van Hollandse Publieke Opinie', *de Volkskrant*, 25 November 2015.

Heijne, Bas, 'Kleine mensen', *NRC Handelsblad*, 17/18 January 2015.

Henry, Patrick, 'Introduction. Jewish Resistance Against the Nazis', in Patrick Henry (ed.),*Jewish Resistance Against the Nazis* (Washington, D.C.: The Catholic University of American Press, 2014), XIII-XXXVIII.

Hettema, Douwe, 'Nederlandse verzetshelden en joodse onderduikers. De Duitse bezetting in de romanliteratuur.' In: Conny Kristel (ed.), *Polderschouw. Terugkeer en opvang na de Tweede Wereldoorlog: regionale verschillen* (Amsterdam: B. Bakker, 2002), 355-377.

Herzberg, Abel J., *Kroniek der Jodenvervolging, 1940-1945* (Amsterdam: Meulenhoff, 1978; reprint of *Onderdrukking en verzet. Nederland in oorlogstijd*, 1950).

Hertzberg, Arthur, 'Is Anti-Semitism Dying out?', *The New York Review of Books*, 24 June 1993.

Herzog, Yaacov, *A people that dwells alone. Speeches and writings of Yaacov Herzog* (London: Weidenfeld and Nicolson, 1975).

Heuves, Willem and Ad Boerwinkel (eds.), *Een wijze van kijken: psychoanalyse en schaamte. Liber Amicorum voor Louis Tas* (Amsterdam: Het Spinhuis, 1996).

Hijmans, Maarten Jan, 'Nogmaals: de Socialistische Zionisten', *Joodse Wachter*, February 1977.

—, 'De geheime hulp aan Israël', *NIW*, 28 March 1997.

Hilberg, Raul, *The Destruction of the European Jews* (Chicago: Quadrangle Books, 1961).

—, *Perpetrators, Victims, Bystanders. The Jewish Catastrophe 1933-1945* (New York: Aaron Asher Books, 1992).

Hillesum, Ettty, *Het werk. 1941-1943*. 6th rev. ed. (Amsterdam: Balans, 2012).

Hirsch, Marianne, *The Generation of Postmemory: Writing and Visual Culture After the Holocaust* (Columbia University Press, 2012).

Hirsch Ballin, Ernst, 'Je moet eerst de ander zien te begrijpen', *Vrij Nederland*, 10 May 2008.

Hitchens, Christopher, 'Assassins of the mind', *Vanity Fair*, February 2009.

Hödl, Klaus, 'Masculinity.' In: Richard S. Levy (ed.), *Antisemitism: A Historical Encyclopedia of Prejudice and Persecution* (Santa Barbara, CA: ABC-CLIO, 2005), Vol. 1: 447-448.

Hoek, J. S., Politieke geschiedenis van Nederland. Oorlog en herstel (Leiden: A.W. Sijthoff, 1970).

Hoekstra, E.H., and M.H. Ipenburg, *Wegwijs in religieus en levensbeschouwelijk Nederland: handboek religies, kerken, stromingen en organisaties* (Kampen: Kok, 2000).

Hoffman, Michael A., and Alan R. Critchley, *The Truth about the Talmud, Judaism's Holiest Book* (Coeur d'Alene, Idaho: Independent History and Research, 1998).

Holz, Klaus, *Die Gegenwart des Antisemitismus. Islamistische, demokratische und antizionistische Judenfeindschaft* (Hamburg: Hamburger Edition, 2005).

—, and Michael Kiefer, 'Islamistischer Antisemitismus Phänomen und Forschungsstand.' In: Wolfram Stender, Guido Follert and Mihri Özdogan (eds.), *Konstellationen des Antisemitismus* (Wiesbaden: VS Verlag für Sozialwissenschaften, 2010), 109-137.

Hondius, Dienke, 'De holocaust als hype. Goldhagen onderscheidt maar twee groepen Duitsers: daders en slachtoffers. Daartussenin zit niets', *De Groene Amsterdammer*, 23 April 1997.

—, *Terugkeer. Antisemitisme in Nederland rond de bevrijding*. With a story by Marga Minco (The Hague: Sdu, 1998; first ed. 1990).

—, *Gemengde huwelijken, gemengde gevoelens. Hoe Nederland omgaat met etnisch en religieus verschil* (The Hague: Sdu Uitgevers, 2001; rev. ed. of 1999).

—, *Return: Holocaust Survivors and Dutch Anti-Semitism* (Westport, CO.: Praeger, 2003).

—, *Oorlogslessen. Onderwijs over de oorlog sinds 1945* (Amsterdam: Bert Bakker, 2010).

—, 'Modderige mierenhoop. Chris van der Heijden: dat nooit meer', *De Groene Amsterdammer*, 2 November 2011.

Hoog, Ted de, 'Antisemitisme als Arabische traditie: Een gesprek met Arabist Jan Jaap de Ruiter over het islamitische antisemitisme', *NIW*, 20 March 2015.

Hoogstraten, Diederik van, 'Verplaatste Intifada', *Elsevier*, 28 October 2000.

Horlings, André, 'Prinsenvlag niet van NSB-smetten vrij': http://historiek.net/prinsenvlag-nsb-smettenvrij/37267/, 29 September 2013.

Horst, Pieter van der, *Joden in de Grieks-Romeinse wereld. Vijftien miniaturen* (Zoetermeer: Meinema, 2003).

Houwink ten Cate, J.T.M., 'Het jongere deel. Demografische en sociale kenmerken van het jodendom in Nederland tijdens de vervolging.' In: *Oorlogsdocumentatie 1940-1945. Jaarboek van het Rijksinstituut voor Oorlogsdocumentatie* (Amsterdam: Walburgpers, 1989), 9-66.

Huf, Philip, *Niemand in de stad* (Amsterdam: De Bezige Bij, 2012).

Hulsman, Bernard, 'Getto's op het web. Op internet heeft elke groep zijn eigen waarheid', *NRC Handelsblad*, 8/9 January 2005.

—, 'Khomeiny en de geitenneukers', *NRC Handelsblad*, 8/9 January 2005.

—, 'Doe het niet, zou je willen schreeuwen', *NRC Handelsblad*, 12 July 2013.

Hyman, Paula, *Gender and Assimilation in Modern Jewish History. The Roles and Representation of Women* (Seattle, London: University of Washington Press, 1995).

Iddekinge, P.R.A. van, and A.H. Paape, *Ze zijn er nog. Een documentatie over fascistische, nazistische en andere rechtsradicale denkbeelden en activiteiten na 1945* (Amsterdam: De Bezige Bij, 1970).

Imhof, R., and R. Banse, 'Ongoing Victim Suffering Increases Prejudice: the Case of Secondary Antisemitism', *Psychological Science* 20 (2009), 1443-1447.

IOT, 'Quickscan antisemitisme in de Turkse gemeenschap in Nederland.' 2013.

Israeli Commission of Inquiry, 'Final Report of the Israeli Commission of Inquiry into the Events at the Refugee Camps in Beirut', *Journal of Palestine Studies* 12, 3 (1983), 89-116.

Jacobs, Jane, *The Death and Life of Great American Cities* (New York: Random House, 1961).

Jacobs, Joop, 'Sjechita 6', *NIW*, 27 May 2011.

Jacobson, Howard, *The Finkler Question* (New York: Bloomsbury, 2010).

Jansma, Folkert, 'Als het fatsoen opspeelt is niemand meer Charlie', *NRC Handelsblad*, 10/11 January 2015.

Jansen, Corjo, and Derk Venema, *De Hoge Raad en de Tweede Wereldoorlog. Recht en rechtsbeoefening in de jaren 1930-1959* (Amsterdam: Boom, 2012).

Jansen, Ludger, 'Alles Schlußstrich – oder was? Eine philosophische Auseinandersetzung mit Martin Walsers Friedenspreisrede',*Theologie und Philosophie* 80 (2005), 412-422.

Janssen, Esther H., *Faith in public debate. An Inquiry into the relationship between freedom of expression and hate speech pertaining to religion and race in France, the Netherlands and European and international law* (PhD thesis, Universiteit van Amsterdam, 9 September 2014).

Jikeli, Günther, 'Anti-Semitism in youth language: the pejorative use of the terms for "Jew" in German and French today', *Conflict & Communication online* 9, 1 (2010), 1-13.

Jong, J.D. de, *Kapot moeilijk: Een etnografisch onderzoek naar opvallend delinquent groepsgedrag van 'Marokkaanse' jongens* (Amsterdam: Aksant, 2007).

—, 'Straatracisme is niet typisch Marokkaans', *de Volkskrant*, 15 May 2012.

Jong, Loe de, *Het Koninkrijk der Nederlanden in de Tweede Wereldoorlog* (The Hague: Martinus Nijhoff, 1969-1976).

Jong, Steven de, 'Mohammed Jabri: 'Allochtonen kunnen niet tegen kritiek'', *Politiek-digitaal*, 18 December 2005.

Jong, Wilfried de, 'Opblaaspop', *NRC Handelsblad,* 8 February 2016.

Joris, Lieve, 'Onze jongens in Libanon. "Die stomme joden hebben in het jaar 3000 nog oorlog"', *Haagse Post*, 23 June 1979.

J.S. (Jacob Soetendorp), 'Eerbied voor onze monumenten', *NIW,* 22 June 1945.

Judaken, Jonathan, 'So, What's New? Rethinking the "New" Anti-Semitism' in a Global Age', *Patterns of Prejudice*, 42, 5/5 (2008), 531-560.

Judt, Tony, *Postwar. A History of Europe since 1945* (New York: Penguin, 2005).

Justaert, Marjan, '"De laatste die onze rituele slachtingen verbood, was Adolf Hitler". Interview with Michael Freilich (Joods Aktueel)', *De Standaard*, 11 August 2015.

Kaddouri, Yehya, *Lach met de duivel. Autobiografie van een 'rotte-appel'-Marokkaan* (Amsterdam: Van Gennep, 2011).

Kalman, Aaron, '"Hitler should have killed all Jews", teens in Holland say', *The Times of Israel*, 7 March 2013.

Kamerman, Sheila, and Andreas Kouwenhoven, 'Moslims nemen nooit genoeg afstand', *de Volkskrant*, 21/22 November 2015.

Kamp, Justus van de, and Jacob van der Wijk, *Koosjer Nederlands. Joodse woorden in de Nederlandse taal* (Amsterdam, Antwerp: Contact, 2006).

Kamp, Lody van de, *Dagboek van een verdoofd rabbijn: Persoonlijke notities bij een politieke aardverschuiving* (Zoetermeer: Boekencentrum, 2012).

Kamsma, Martine, 'Het kan: 4 mei zonder heisa', *NRC Handelsblad*, 4 May 2015.

Kansteiner, Wulf, 'What is the opposite of genocide? Philosemitic television in Germany, 1963-1995. Adam Sutcliffe and Jonathan Karp (eds.), *Philosemitism in History* (New York: Cambridge University Press, 2011), 289-313.

Karacaer, Haci, 'Keulen locuta, causa finita', *NRC Handelsblad*, 19 May 2006.

Kattenbusch, F.F.W., 'Tegen Dierenmartelen. Wat gij niet wilt dat u geschiedt... Open brief aan den Heer Joodschen Medewerker van "Het Vaderland"' (Gorinchem: J. Noorduyn en Zoon N.V., 1934).

Katz, Renate, 'Centrale Commissie oefent kritiek op landbouw uit', *NIW*, 31 January 1975.

—, 'Aantal gemeenten geeft toch ariërverklaring af', *NIW*, 23 September 1977.

Ka-tzetnik 135633 (Yehiel De-Nur), *House of Dolls* (New York, Simon and Schuster, 1955; orig. ed. *Beit habubot*, 1953).

Keilson, Hans, *Sequential traumatization in children: a clinical and statistical follow-up study on the fate of the Jewish war orphans in the Netherlands* (Jerusalem: The Magnes Press / The Hebrew University, 1992).

Keizer, B., 'Ingezonden', *NIW*, 29 March 1968.

Keizer, Madelon de, *Het Parool 1940-1945. Verzetsblad in Oorlogstijd* (Amsterdam: Otto Cramwinckel, 1991).

—, 'Inleiding.' In: Madelon de Keizer (ed.), *Een dure verplichting en een kostelijk voorrecht. Dr. L. de Jong en zijn Geschiedwerk* (The Hague: Sdu Uitgeverij, 1995), 7-20: 12.

Kellendonk, Frans, *Mystiek Lichaam: een geschiedenis* (Amsterdam: Meulenhoff, 1986).

—, *De Brieven. Samengesteld, ingeleid en geannoteerd door Oek de Jong en Jaap Goedgebuure* (Amsterdam, Antwerp: Em. Querido's Uitgeverij BV, 2015).

Kepel, Gilles, 'Radical Islamism in Europe.' Interview with Irshad Manji, Steven Emerson, and Gilles Kepel, *Aspen Alert*, Aspen Institute, Washington, D.C., Dec. 2004.

Kershaw, Ian, *Hitler 1936-1945. Nemesis* (London: Allen Lane, 2000).

Kershner, Isabel, 'Israel's unexpected spinoff from a Holocaust trial', *The New York Times*, 6 September 2007.

Ketelaar, Titia, 'Fantastisch: ik hang naast Rembrandt', *NRC Handelsblad*, 26 November 2015.

Kieft, Ewoud, *Oorlogsmythen. Willem Frederik Hermans en de Tweede Wereldoorlog* (Amsterdam: De Bezige Bij, 2012).

—, 'Fouten na de oorlog', *NRC Handelsblad*, 31 October 2011.

—, 'Dat nooit meer', *NRC Handelsblad*, 4 November 2011.

Kleerekoper, Salomon, *Het antisemitisme en zijn randverschijnselen* (Deventer: Van Loghum Slaterus, 1970).

Kleinpaste, Thijs, 'Wrekers van de scherts: De stroman van rechts', *De Groene Amsterdammer*, 26 November 2015.

Kleijwegt, Margalith, 'De buurt van Mohammed B.' *Vrij Nederland*, 13 November 2004.

—, 'Super-Turk wil de politiek in', *Vrij Nederland,* 18 March 2006.

—, 'Twee werelden, twee werkelijkheden. "Dat klopt niet juf, het staat niet in de koran"', *De Groene Amsterdammer,* 28 January 2016.

Klinken, G.J. van, *Opvattingen in de gereformeerde kerken in Nederland over het Jodendom, 1896-1970* (Kampen: Kok, 1996).

Klinken, J. van, and J. Visscher, 'Omstreden moslims. Turks-orthodoxe islamaanhangers in Nederland schuwen antisemitisme niet', *Reformatorisch Dagblad,* 25 July 1998.

Klis, Hans, 'Oud-politici willen excuus Nederland voor jodenvervolging', *NRC Handelsblad,* 4 January 2012.

Kloek, Daan, 'Migranten Israël protesteren bij ambassades', *Jonet.nl,* 7 January 2014.

Klug, Brian, 'Ritual Murmur in Britain: Flying the Flag for Animals.' In Brian Klug, *Being Jewish and Doing Justice: Bringing Argument to Life* (Middlesex and Portland: Vallentine Mitchell 2011), 241-254.

Kluveld, Amanda, '60 jaar Israël is tijd voor een kus', *de Volkskrant,* 14 May 2008.

Knoop, Hans, 'Over citaten en stenen', *NIW,* 29 June 1979.

—, 'Hoeveel gekker kan het worden', *NIW,* 19 October 2012.

Koelewijn, Jannetje, '"Ik ben niet begonnen." Vrije meningsuiting volgens Theo van Gogh', *NRC Handelsblad,* 6/7 November 2004.

Kohlbauer-Fritz, Gabrielle, '"La belle juive" und die "schöne Schickse".' In Sander L. Gilman, Robert Jütte, Gabrielle Kohlbauer-Fritz (eds.), *'Der Schejne Jid'. Das Bild des 'jüdischen Körpers' in Mythos und Ritual* (Wien: Picus Verlag, 1998), 109-121.

Koning, Martijn de, 'Denk even na voor je islamofobe cartoons verspreidt.' In: Menno Grootveld (ed.), *Het woord. Charlie Hebdo* (Amsterdam: Editie Leesmagazijn 2015), 105-113 (orig. in *de Volkskrant,* 17 January 2015).

Kopuit, Mau, 'Anti-boycot comité gelijk met parlementair onderzoek gestart', *NIW,* 2 June 1978.

—, 'Bnee Beriet neemt bestrijding van het antisemitisme serieus', *NIW,* 25 July 1980.

—, and Tamarah Benima, 'Libanese gebeurtenissen klieven joodse gemeenschap', *NIW,* 1 October 1982.

Kopuit, Robert J., 'Uitgever Johan Polak: Voor mij is het niet nodig Israël van de kaart te vegen', *NIW,* 31 July 1970.

Kossmann, E.H., *De Lage Landen 1780/1980. Deel II 1914-1980* (Amsterdam, Brussels: Elsevier, 1986).

Kosto, A. 'Het voornemen van Van Thijn', *Elsevier Magazine,* 13 August 1986.

Kouwenhoven, Andreas, 'Hij stortte graag zijn gal over je uit', *NRC Handelsblad,* 30 November 2014.

—, 'Moskeeën weren zich tegen geweld', *NRC Handelsblad,* 6 January 2015.

—, 'Charlie Hebdo: een legitiem doelwit?', *NRC Handelsblad,* 9 January 2015.

—, 'Afgedwongen excuses WO II "weinig waard"', *NRC Handelsblad,* 31 July 2015.

Kozlowski, Maciej, *Naród Wybrany. Cracovia Pany. Z wielokulturowej historii poskiego sportu* (Warszawa-Krakow: Nigdy Wiecej, 2015).

Kristel, Conny, *Geschiedschrijving als opdracht. Abel Herzberg, Jacques Presser en Loe de Jong over de jodenvervolging* (Amsterdam: Meulenhoff, 1998).

—, 'Leiderschap na de ondergang. De strijd om de macht in joods naoorlogs Nederland.' In: Conny Kristel (ed.), *Binnenskamers. Terugkeer en opvang na de Tweede Wereldoorlog. Besluitvorming* (Amsterdam: Bert Bakker, 2002), 209-234.

— (ed.), *Met alle geweld: botsingen en tegenstellingen in burgerlijk Nederland* (Amsterdam: Balans, 2003).

—, 'J.C.H. Blom of het midden van de cirkel.' In: Conny Kristel (ed.), *Met alle geweld: botsingen en tegenstellingen in burgerlijk Nederland* (Amsterdam: Balans, 2003), 275-292.

—, 'Survivors as historians: Abel Herzberg, Jacques Presser and Loe de Jong on the Nazi Persecution of the Jews in the Netherlands.' In: David Bankier and Dan Michman (eds.), *Holocaust Historiography in Context. Emergence, Challenges, Polemics and Achievements* (Jerusalem: Yad Vashem, Berghahn Books, 2008), 207-226.

Krogt, J. van der, and Magenta, *Rechtsextremisme op het internet* (2009): www.magenta.nl

Kromer, Frank, 'Overheid aan zet', *NIW*, 15 March 2013.

Kromhout, Bas, 'Kritiek op ritueel slachten is soms antisemitisch. Dierenbeschermers wilden in 1945 Duits verbod handhaven.' Interview with Evelien Gans, *Historisch Nieuwsblad* (April 2011).

—, *De voorman. Henk Feldmeijer en de Nederlandse SS* (Amsterdam: Atlas Contact, 2012).

—, 'Nederlanders hebben het nicht gewusst', *Historisch Nieuwsblad*, 24 April 2012.

—, '"We hebben het nicht gewusst". Bart van der Boom over *Nederlanders* en de Holocaust', *Historisch Nieuwsblad*, May 2012.

—, 'Recensie: Martin Bosma doet de waarheid over Zuid-Afrika geweld aan: Bij het boek Minderheid in eigen land', 'ThePostOnline. Voorbij het eigen gelijk', 4 June 2015, http://politiek. tpo.nl/2015/06/04/recensie-martin-bosma-doet-de-waarheid-over-zuid-afrika-geweld-aan/.

—, 'Het ware gezicht van de NSB', *Historisch Nieuwsblad*, 24 November 2015.

—, *Fout! Wat Hollandse nazi-kranten schreven over Nederland, Joden en het verzet* (Amsterdam: Veen Media, 2016).

Kroon, John, 'De nazi-zangers en hun triomf in Utrecht', *NRC Handelsblad*, 15 December 2015.

Kuiper, Arie, 'Inleiding.' In: Abel J. Herzberg, *Zonder Israël is elke jood een ongedekte cheque. Essays*. Selected and introduced by Arie Kuiper (Amsterdam: Querido, 1992), 9-19.

—, *Een wijze ging voorbij: het leven van Abel J. Herzberg* (Amsterdam: Querido, 1997).

Kuitenbrouwer, Jan, 'De 150 hatelijkheden van Theo van Gogh', *NRC Handelsblad*, 30 October 2014.

—, 'Rekbaar alibi', *NRC Handelsblad*, 9/10 May 2015.

Kuper, Simon, 'Ajax, de joden, Nederland', *Hard Gras. Voetbaltijdschrift voor lezers* 22 (March 2000).

—, *Ajax, the Dutch, the War. Football in Europe during the Second World War* (London: Orion, 2003).

Kuyper, Abraham, *Liberalisten en Joden* (Amsterdam: Kruyt, 1878).

LaCapra, Dominick, *Representing the Holocaust. History, Theory, Trauma* (Ithaca: Cornell University Press, 1994), 63-66.

Lagrou, Pieter, 'Victims of Genocide and National Memory', *Past & Present* 154 (February 1997), 181-222.

Landau, Jacob M., *Radical politics in modern Turkey* (Leiden: Brill, 1974).

—, 'Muslim Turkish Attitudes towards Jews, Zionism and Israel', *Die Welt des Islams* 28, 1/4 (1988), 291-300.

Landman, Nico, *Van mat tot minaret: de institutionalisering van de islam in Nederland* (Amsterdam: VU uitgeverij, 1992).

Lang, Berel, 'Why didn't they resist more?' In: Patrick Henry (ed.), *Jewish Resistance Against the Nazis* (Washington, D.C.: The Catholic University of American Press, 2014), 27-39.

Lange, Freddy, 'Is Israël een land van Pausen, d.w.z. onfeilbaar?', *NIW*, 9 January 1970.

Lange, Yasha, 'Joden bezorgd over reeks incidenten', *NRC Handelsblad*, 17 October 2000.

Langendonck, Gert van, 'Reageert Midden-Oosten anders dan het Westen?', *NRC Handelsblad*, 9 January 2012.

Langeveld, Herman, 'Beeld van de NSB behoeft geen bijstelling', *NRC Handelsblad*, 12 December 2006

Lans, Jos van der, and Herman Vuijsje, *Het Anne Frank Huis, Een biografie* (Amsterdam: Boom, 2010).

Laroui, Fouad, 'Hooligans van de intolerantie', *NRC Handelsblad*, 8 January 2015.

Laskier, Michael M., 'Aspects of the Activities of the Alliance Israelite Universelle in the Jewish Communities of the Middle East and North Africa: 1860-1918', *Modern Judaism* 3, 2 (1983), 147-171.

Laskier, Michael M., and Eliezer Bashan, 'Morocco.' In: Reeva Spector Simon, Michael Menachem Laskier and Sara Reguer (eds.), *The Jews of the Middle East and North Africa in Modern Times* (New York: Columbia University Press, 2003), 471-504.

Lassner, Phyllis, and Lara Trubowitz (eds.), *Antisemitism and Philosemitism in the Twentieth and Twenty-first Centuries* (Newark: University of Delaware Press, 2008).

Lebovic, Nitzan, 'An Absence With Traces: The Reception of Nuit et Brouillard in Israel.' In: Ewout van der Knaap (ed.), *Uncovering the Holocaust: The International Reception of Night and Fog* (London: Wallflower Press, 2006), 86-105.

Lechner, Frank J., *The Netherlands. Globalization and National Identity* (New York. London: Routledge, 2008).

Leibovici, Solange, 'Het pornografisch antisemitisme', *De Groene Amsterdammer*, 17 May 1995.

Leijendekker, Marc, 'De stellingen van Benjamin Barber: 1. Wie bang is, tast de democratie aan', *NRC Handelsblad*, 18/19 December 2014.

Leijser, Ron, 'Derde Weg, christelijk antimilitarisme en pacifistisch-socialisme.' In: Joost Divendal et al. (eds.), *Nederland, links en de Koude Oorlog: breuken en bruggen* (Amsterdam: De Populier, 1982), 99-116.

Leiken, Robert S., *Europe's Angry Muslims: The Revolt of the Second Generation* (Oxford: Oxford University Press, 2012).

Léon, Abraham, *La Conception matérialiste de la question Juive* (Paris: EDI, 1968).

—, *The Jewish Question. A Marxist Interpretation* (New York: Pathfinder, 1970).

Leurs, Koen, *Digital Passages. Moroccan-Dutch youths performing diaspora, gender and cultural identities across digital space* (PhD thesis, Universiteit Utrecht, 2012).

Levisson, R.A., 'Knipoog naar de actualiteit', *NIW,* 10 January 1992.

Levy, Gideon, 'Mohammed Allaan's Blood Is on Our Hands', *Haaretz*, 17 August 2015.

Lewis, Bernard, *Semites and Anti-Semites: An Inquiry into Conflict and Prejudice* (London: Weidenfeld and Nicolson, 1986).

—, 'The New Anti-Semitism', *The New York Review of Books*, April 1986.

—, 'Muslim Anti-Semitism', *Middle East Quarterly* 5, 2 (June 1998), 43-49.

Leydesdorff, Selma et al. (eds.), *Israël een blanco cheque?* (Amsterdam: Amphora Books, Van Gennep, 1983).

Liagre Böhl, Herman de, and Guus Meershoek, *De Bevrijding van Amsterdam: een strijd om macht en moraal* (Zwolle: Waanders, 1989).

Liebman, Herman de, 'Antisémitisme et antisionisme – l'impossible amalgame', *Mai* 10 (1970).

Liempt, Ad van, and Jan H. Kompagnie, *Jodenjacht. De onthutsende rol van de Nederlandse politie in de Tweede Wereldoorlog* (Amsterdam: Balans2011).

Lindeman, Yehudi, and Hans de Vries, '"Therefore Be Courageous, Too." Jewish Resistance and Rescue in the Netherlands.' In: Patrick Henry (ed.), *Jewish Resistance against the Nazis* (Washington, D.C.: The Catholic University of American Press, 2014), 185-219.

Lindholm Schulz, Helena, and Juliane Hammer, *The Palestinian Diaspora. Formation of Identities and Politics of Homeland* (London, New York: Routledge, 2003).

Lindo, Flip, *Heilige wijsheid in Amsterdam: Ayasofia, stadsdeel De Baarsjes en de strijd om het Riva-terrein* (Amsterdam: Het Spinhuis, 1999).

—, *Activiteiten en doelstellingen van Nederlandse organisaties gelieerd aan Millî Görüş*. Report (FMG: Institute for Migration & Ethnic Studies, 2008).

Lipstadt, Deborah E., *Denying the Holocaust: The Growing Assault on Truth and Memory* (New York, Toronto: Free Press, Maxwell Macmillan, 2005).

Litvak, Meit, 'The Islamic Republic of Iran and the Holocaust: Anti-Semitism and Anti-Zionism.' In: Jeffrey Herf (ed.), *Anti-Semitism and anti-Zionism in Historical Perspective: Convergence and Divergence* (Abingdon: Routledge, 2013), 250-267.

Logtenberg, Hugo, and Marcel Wiegman, *Job Cohen: burgemeester van Nederland* (Amsterdam: Nieuw Amsterdam, 2010).

Longerich, Peter, *Hitlers Stellvertreter: Führung der Partei und Kontrolle des Staatsapparates durch den Stab Hess und die Parteikanzlei Bormann: Eine Publikation des Instituts für Zeitgeschichte* (München: K.G. Saur, 1992).

Lowe, Keith, *Savage Continent. Europe in the Aftermath of World War II* (London: Viking, 2012).

Lucardie, Paul, *Nederland stromenland: een geschiedenis van de politieke stromingen* (Assen: Van Gorcum 2002).

Maar, Remko van der, *Welterusten mijnheer de president. Nederland en de Vietnamoorlog 1965-1973*. (PhD thesis, Universiteit Utrecht, 2007).

Maas, Jurgen, and Annemarike Stremmelaar, 'Ik heb een missie.' Interview met Haci Karacaer.' In: Maurits van den Boogert and Jan Jonker Roelants (eds.), *De Nederlands-Turkse betrekkingen. Portretten van een vierhonderdjarige geschiedenis* (Hilversum: Verloren, 2012), 106-111.

Majiti, Rachid, and Ahmed Dadou, 'Weg met mea-culpa-media-Marokkanen', *NRC Handelsblad*, 11 November 2004.

Malik, Kenan, *From Fatwa to Jihad. The Rushdie Affair and its Legacy* (London: Atlantic, 2009).

Malik, Zaiba, *We are a Muslim, Please* (London: Windmill Press, 2011).

Manske, Ariane, 'Das ist doch nicht normal, oder doch? Kontext und Funktion der U.S.-amerikanischen PC-Diskussion der 90er Jahre und warum Barack Obama PC ist.' Paper presented at the Internationale Tagung: 'Political Correctness. Aufforderung zur Toleranz oder Selbstzensur? Geschichte und Aktualität eines kulturellen Phänomens', Amsterdam, 11.12.-12.12.2008.

—, *Political Correctness und Normalität. Die amerikanische PC-Kontroverse im kulturgeschichtlichen Kontext* (Heidelberg: Synchron Wissenschaftsverlag der Autoren, 2002).

Marcotti, Gabriele, 'Star of David, For Entertainment Only', *The Wall Street Journal*, 11 November 2012.

Marrus, Michael, 'Acts that speak for themselves', *The New York Times*, 20 September 1993.

Marsman, Hendrik, 'Brief over de joodsche kwestie; antwoord aan Dr. G.D. Knoche', *Het Kouter* 1 (1936), 289-302.

McVitie, Peter, '"If you don't jump you're a Jew" – Does Dutch football have an anti-Semitism problem?', *Goal*, 7 December 2015: www.goal.com/en-us/news/1956/europe/2015/12/07/18075042/ if-you-dont-jump-youre-a-jew-does-dutch-football-have-an.

Meerhof, Ron, 'VVD in senaat tegen verbod rituele slacht', *de Volkskrant*, 19 October 2011.

Meershoek, Guus, *Dienaren van het gezag. De Amsterdamse politie tijdens de bezetting* (Amsterdam: Van Gennep, 1999).

—, 'Een aangekondigde massamoord. Wat wisten Nederlanders van de jodenvervolging?', *De Groene Amsterdammer*, 31 January 2013.

Meeus, Tom-Jan, 'Bosma, zijn boek, en zijn soms vernederende leven in de PVV', *NRC Handels-blad*, 30/31 May 2015.

Meihuizen, Joggli, *Sans égards. Prof. mr. A. Pitlo en zijn conflicten met joodse juristen* (Boom: Amsterdam 2007).

Meijer, Hilbert, 'Comité 4 en 5 mei: herdenk geen Duitsers', *Nederlands dagblad*, 26 April 2014.

Meijer, Ischa, 'Het zionisme is geen acceptabele ideologie', *Vrij Nederland*, 2 December 1967.

—, 'Uitgever Johan Polak', *De Nieuwe Linie*, 25 February 1967.

—, 'Allemaal symptomen', *Haagse Post*, 14 July 1979.

Meijer, Maaike, *M. Vasalis. Een biografie* (Amsterdam: G.A. van Oorschot, 2011).

Meijer, Sietse, 'Theo moest and zou. The Making of Luger', *VPRO gids*, 17-23 September 2005.

Meijer, Roel, 'Inhoud van de religieuze en ideologische documenten aangetroffen in het beslag van verdachten in het Piranha-onderzoek. Deskundigenrapportage opgesteld voor de Arrondissementsrechtbank Rotterdam' (2007).

Melching, Willem, *Hitler. Opkomst en ondergang van een Duits politicus* (Amsterdam: Bert Bakker, 2013).

Melkman, J., 'Jodin in Israël', *NIW*, 16 February 1968.

Melsen, P.M.W., *Antisemitisme langs de lijn* (Thesis for the Police Academy in Apeldoorn, 1985).

Memmi, Albert, *Portrait d'un Juif* (Paris: Gallimard, 1962-1966).

—, *Portret van een Jood. De impasse* (Amsterdam: De Bezige Bij, 1964).

Menting, Marcel, *Verslonden door de revolutie. Het politieke leven van Sal Santen (1915-1998)* (MA thesis in political history, Radboud Universiteit, 2007).

Messel, Saul van, *Zeer zeker en zeker zeer. Joodse gedichten*. Haagse Cahiers 10 (Rijswijk Z.H.: De Oude Degel, 1967).

Metcalf, Barbara Daly, 'Introduction: Sacred Words, Sanctioned Practices, New Communities.' In: Barbara Daly Metcalf (ed.), *Making Muslim Space in North America and Europe* (Berkeley, Los Angeles: University of California Press, 2002), 1-27.

Metz, Tracy, '"Ik heb altijd geleerd weerbaar te zijn." Ronny Naftaniel, jood van beroep en van overtuiging', *NRC Handelsblad*, 11 March 2000.

Michman, Dan, 'Rewriting the Jewish History of the Holocaust.' Center for Jewish Studies, University of Florida, Gainesville, 17-19 March, 2012 (keynote lecture on 'The Jewish Dimension of the Holocaust in Dire Straits? Current Challenges of Interpretation and Scope').

—, 'Waren die Juden Nordafrikas im Visier der Planungen zur Endlösung? Die "Schoah" und die Zahl 700.000 in Eichmanns Tabelle am 20. Januar 1942.' In: Norbert Kampe and Peter Klein (eds.), *Die Wannsee-Konferenz am 20. Januar 1942. Dokumente, Forschungsstand, Kontroversen* (Köln/Weimar/Wien: Böhlau, 2013), 379-397.

Michman, Jozeph, Hartog Beem and Dan Michman, *Pinkas. Geschiedenis van de joodse gemeenschap in Nederland* (Ede/Antwerp: Kluwer, 1985).

Middleton-Kaplan, Richard, 'The Myth of Jewish Passivity.' In: Patrick Henry (ed.), *Jewish Resistance Against the Nazis* (Washington, D.C.: The Catholic University of American Press, 2014), 3-26.

Mierlo, L.P. van (Helmond), 'Leuzen', *NRC Handelsblad*, 4 April 1992.

Minerbi, 'Sergio I., 'The Passion by Mel Gibson: Enthusiastic Response in the Catholic World, Restrained Criticism by the Jews', *Jewish Political Studies Review* 17: 1-2 (Spring 2005): www.jcpa.org/phas/phas-minerbi-s05.htm.

Mitscherlich, Alexander and Margaretha, *Die Unfähigkeit zu trauern. Grundlagen kollektiven Verhaltens* (München: Piper, 1967).

Mok, G. Philip, 'Palestina Komité verspreidt gif', *Elseviers Magazine*, 29 April 1978.

—, '"Groeiende anti-semitisme beu". Joodse knokploeg opgericht', *Elseviers Magazine*, 7 July 1979.

Moll, Hans, and Hella Rottenberg, 'Joden maken de dienst uit in Nederland. Het antisemitische wereldbeeld van Marokkaanse jongeren', *NRC Handelsblad*, 14 June 2003.

Mooij, Annet, 'Nak, Pieter Frederik Willem (1906-1996)', in: *Biografisch Woordenboek van Nederland*. (www.historici.nl/Onderzoek/Projecten/BWN/lemmata/bwn6/nak).

—, *De strijd om de Februaristaking* (Amsterdam: Balans, 2006).

Moore, Bob, *Victims and Survivors: the Nazi Persecution of the Jews in the Netherlands, 1940-1945* (London: Arnold, 1997).

—, 'The war that won't go away', *BMGN* 128, 2 (2013), 73-80.

Moorman, Mark, 'Theo van Gogh was een lastpost met een heftig filminstinct', *Het Parool*, 1 November 2014.

Morina, Christina, 'The "Bystander" in Recent Dutch historiography', *German History* 32, 1 (2014), 101-111.

Mortaigne, Véronique and Nathalie Guitbert, 'Le Bataclan: un haut lieu de culture ciblé de longue date par les islamistes', *Le Monde*, 15 November 2015.

Morton, Victor, 'Two killed in gunfight outside Muhammad cartoon contest', *The Washington Times*, 3 May 2015.

Mosse, George, *Nationalism and Sexuality: Respectability and Abnormal Sexuality in Modern Europe* (New York: Howard Fertig, 1985).

—, *Fallen Soldiers. Reshaping the Memory of the Two World Wars* (New York, Oxford: Oxford University Press, 1990).

—, *The Image of Man: The Creation of Modern Masculinity* (New York and Oxford: Oxford University Press, 1996).

Mügge, Liza, *Beyond Dutch Borders: Transnational Politics among Colonial Migrants, Guest Workers and the Second Generation* (Amsterdam: Amsterdam University Press, 2010).

Müller, Sven Oliver, *Deutsche Soldaten und ihre Feinde. Nationalismus an Front und Heimatfront im Zweiten Weltkrieg* (Frankfurt am Main: S. Fischer, 2007).

Munson, Jr., Henri, *Religion and Power in Morocco* (New Haven: Yale University Press, 1993).

Naftaniel, Ronny, *De Arabische boykot en Nederland: een zwartboek met feiten en documenten over de houding van het bedrijfsleven en overheid onder Arabische druk* (The Hague: CIDI, 1978).

—, *Nieuwe feiten over de Arabische Boycot en Nederland: elf originele dokumenten en achttien kranteartikelen die de invloed van de Arabische boycot op het Nederlandse bedrijfsleven aantonen* (The Hague: CIDI, 1979).

Neitzel, Sönke, and Harald Welzer, *Soldaten. Protokolle vom Kämpfen, Töten und Sterben* (Frankfurt am Main: S. Fischer, 2011).

Nell, Liza M., 'The shadow of homeland politics: Understanding the evolution of the Turkish radical Left in the Netherlands', *Revue européenne des migrations internationales* 24, 2 (2008), 121-145.

Nesser, Peter, *The Slaying of the Dutch filmmaker. religiously motivated violence or Islamist terrorism in the name of global Jihad? FFI report*. Norwegian Defence Research Establishment, 2005.

Niedermüller, Peter, 'Zwei und zwanzigstes Bild; "Der Kommunist."' In: Julius Schoeps and Joachim Schlör (eds.), *Antisemitismus. Vorurteile und Mythen* (München: Piper, 1995), 273-278.

Niemantsverdriet, Thijs, 'Asscher: oproep Netanyahu aan Joden is kwalijk opportunisme', *NRC Handelsblad*, 7 March 2015.

Nijhuis, Ton, 'EU-actie Israël is hypocriet', *de Volkskrant*, 13 November 2015.

Nolte, Ernst, 'Die Vergangenheit die nicht vergehen will. Eine Rede, die geschrieben, aber nicht gehalten werden konnte', *Frankfurter Allgemeine Zeitung*, 6 June 1986.

Noorloos, Marloes van, *Hate Speech Revisited. A Comparative and Historical Perspective on Hate Speech Law in the Netherlands and England & Wales* (Cambridge: Intersentia, 2011).

Norel, K., *Tusken Dea en Libben* (Bolsward: Osinga, 1946).

Obbink, Hanne, 'Syriërs in buurt met veel Joden? Niet verstandig', *Trouw*, 12 October 2015.

Olgun, Ahmet, and Guido de Vries, 'Koerdisch-Turks conflict smeult ook in Arnhem', *NRC Handelsblad*, 31 October 2007.

Olson, Robert W., 'Al-Fatah in Turkey: its influence on the March 12 coup', *Middle Eastern Studies* 9, 2 (1973), 197-205.

Oltmans, Willem, 'Anti-Joods?', *Elsevier Magazine*, 21 July 1979.

—, *Memoires 1979-B* (Breda: Papieren Tijger, 2011).

Ornstein, Leonard, 'De FC Bunnikzijde. "Overal waar we komen, maken we er een zooitje van"', *Vrij Nederland*, 9 January 1982, 2-22.

Oudheusden, J. van, et al. (eds.), *Brabantse biografieën. Levensbeschrijvingen van bekende en onbekende Noordbrabanders*. Vol. 2 (Amsterdam, Meppel: Uitgeverij Boom & Stichting Brabantse Regionale Geschiedbeoefening, 1994).

Outeren, Emilie van, 'Buitenlandtrips voor Wilders steeds lastiger', *de Volkskrant*, 6 May 2015.

Oyevaar, Wytske, 'Antisemitisme in voetbalstadions. Een onderzoek naar de racistische spreek-koren en liederen van voetbalhooligans.' Paper, UvA course Contemporary Antisemitism. Lecturer: Evelien Gans, 9 August 2010.

Paans, Arjan, 'Nederlandse joden en moslims zeggen salaam en shalom', *Algemeen Dagblad*, 28 October 2000.

Palmen, Connie, 'Moord. In memoriam Theo van Gogh 1957-2004', *Vrij Nederland*, 20 November 2004.

Pam, Max, 'Ik haat Joden', *Het Parool*, 2 March 2013.

—, 'De geschiedenis van het woord "geitenneuker"', *The Max Pam Globe*, 28 January 2016: www.maxpam.nl/2014/11/geschiedenis-van-het-woord-geitenneuker/

Pas, Niek, *Aan de wieg van het nieuwe Nederland. Nederland en de Algerijnse Oorlog, 1954-1962* (Amsterdam: Wereldbibliotheek, 2008).

Pasterkamp, R., 'Verbazing over beledigen joden', *Reformatorisch Dagblad*, 21 March 1995.

Paulson, Gunnar, *Secret City: The Hidden Jews of Warsaw, 1940-1945* (New Haven, CT: Yale University Press 2002).

Pauwe, Christiaan, 'Amsterdamse moskee meldt haat niet bij de politie', *Het Parool*, 11 March 2016.

Peace, Timothy, 'Un antisémitisme nouveau? The debate about a "new antisemitism" in France', *Patterns of Prejudice* 43, 2 (2009), 103-121.

Peeters, Frans, *Gezworen vrienden. Het geheime bondgenootschap tussen Nederland en Israël* (Amsterdam, Antwerp: L.J. Veen, 1997).

Peters, Ruud, *De ideologische en religieuze ontwikkeling van Mohammed B. Deskundigenrapport in de strafzaak tegen Mohammed B. in opdracht van het openbaar ministerie opgesteld voor de Arrondissementsrechtbank Amsterdam* (May 2005).

—, *Overzicht teksten geschreven of vertaald door Mohammed B. Bijlage bij het deskundigenrapport 'De ideologische en religieuze ontwikkeling van Mohammed B.'* (May 2005).

Peijster, E., 'Paul van Tienen, en...', *Mededelingen van Actie 'De Vrije Richting'* – Den Haag (Extra Edition).

Perry, Marvin, and Frederick Schweitzer, *Antisemitism. Myth and Hate from Antiquity to the Present* (New York: Palgrave Macmillan, 2002).

Pieloor, R.A., B. van de Meer and M. Bakker, *F-side is niet makkelijk! Over vriendschap, geweld, humor, Amsterdam en Ajax* (Utrecht: Het Spectrum, 2002).

Piersma, Hinke, *Bevochten recht. Politieke besluitvorming rond de wetten voor oorlogsslachtoffers* (Amsterdam: Boom 2010).

—, *De drie van Breda. Duitse oorlogsmisdadigers in Nederlandse gevangenschap, 1945-1989* (Amsterdam: Balans, 2005).

—, and Jeroen Kemperman, *Openstaande rekeningen: de gemeente Amsterdam en de gevolgen van roof en rechtsherstel, 1940-1950* (Amsterdam: Boom, 2015).

Pinedo, Danielle, 'Samen tegen het slachtverbod', *NRC Handelsblad*, 18 June 2011.

—, and Sheila Kamerman, 'De minister is niet meer verrast als jongeren Hitler prijzen', *NRC Handelsblad*, 15 March 2013.

Pinner, Frank A., 'Student trade-unionism in France, Belgium and Holland: anticipatory socialization and role seeking', *Sociology of Education* 37, 3 (1964), 177-199.

Pinto, Diana, *Israel has moved* (Cambridge, MA: Harvard University Press, 2013).

Piper, Ernst, 'Achtes Bild: 'Die jüdische Weltverschwörung.' In: Julius H. Schoeps and Joachim Schlör (eds.), *Antisemitismus. Vorurteile und Mythen* (München, Zürich: Bechtermünz Verlag, 1995), 127-135.

Ploeg, Harry van der, 'Krikke roept op tot les tegen antisemitisme', *De Gelderlander*, 12 March 2013.

Pluim, Ralph, 'Hoe nemen Nederlanders het Jodendom van Job Cohen en van andere Joodse politici waar?' (typoscript), Amsterdam 2010.

—, '1981: een keerpunt in het antisemitisme in Nederland?', (typoscript), June 2011.

Podolska, Johanna, Staszek Goldstein and Andrew Tomlinson, 'Something fishy in the town of Lodz. The word "Jew" is an insult for soccer fans, but is it anti-Semitic?', *Fanatismo. One-off magazine on today's fanaticism*, May 2011 (initiated by Castrum Peregrini, Amsterdam), 40-43.

Pogany, Istvan, 'George Soros and the Refugee Crisis: Conspiracy Theories in Hungary.' Paper presented at the international conference 'Antisemitism in Europe. Cross-Front Antisemitism, Conspiracy Theories, Calls for Boycotts, Islamism, the Extreme Right and the Left' (IIBSA), Berlin, 12-13 December 2015.

Polak, Henri, *Het 'wetenschappelijk' antisemitisme. Weerlegging en betoog* (Amsterdam: Blitz, 1933).

Pollmann, Tessel, *Mussert & Co. De NSB-Leider en zijn vertrouwelingen* (Amsterdam: Boom, 2012).

Poorthuis, Marcel, and Theo Salemink, *Een donkere spiegel. Nederlandse katholieken over joden. Tussen antisemitisme en erkenning, 1870-2005* (Nijmegen: Valkhof Pers, 2006).

Postone, Moishe, 'History and Helplessness: Mass Mobilization and Contemporary Forms of Anticapitalism', *Public Culture* 18, 1 [special issue on *Anticapitalism, Xenophobia, Imperialism*], 93-110: 99.

Poulton, Emma, and Oliver Durell, 'Uses and meanings of "Yid" in English football fandom: A case study of Tottenham Hotspur Football Club', *International Review for the Sociology of Sport*' (2014), 1-20.

Praag, Carlo van, *Marokkanen in Nederland: een profiel* (The Hague: NIDI, 2006).

Praag, Marga van, and Ad van Liempt, *Jaap & Max. Het verhaal van de broers Van Praag* (Amsterdam: Nijgh & Van Ditmar 2011).

Praag, Theo van, 'Hoe is het mogelijk dat Paul Witteman de Joodse slachtoffers in Parijs negeerde?, '*Jonet*, 21 February 2016.

Presser, J., 'Het verzet van joden in Nederland 1940-1945.' In: J. Presser, *Schrijfsels en Schrifturen* (Amsterdam: Moussault, 1961).

—, *Ondergang. De vervolging en verdelging van het Nederlandse jodendom* (Staatsuitgeverij: The Hague, 1965).

—, *Ashes in the Wind. The Destruction of Dutch Jewry* (Detroit: Wayne State University Press, 1988).

Protocoles des Sages de Sion. La vérité sur Israël, ses plans, ses visées, révélée par un document israélite (Beyrouth, Presses Islamiques, 1967); transl. Roger Lambelin (1912), introd. Faëz Ajjaz.

Putten, Jan van der, 'De status-quo is over de houdbaarheidsdatum', *De Groene Amsterdammer*, 12 March 2015.

Quispel, Chris, 'Introduction.' In: Dik van Arkel, *The Drawing of the Mark of Cain, A Socio-historical Analysis of the Growth of Anti-Jewish Stereotypes* (Amsterdam: Amsterdam University Press, 2009), 11-19.

—, *Anti-Joodse beeldvorming en Jodenhaat. De geschiedenis van het antisemitisme in West-Europa* (Hilversum: Verloren, 2016).

Raaijmakers, Ilse, *De stilte en de storm. 4 en 5 mei sinds 1945* (PhD thesis, Universiteit Maastricht, 2014).

Rabbae, M., *Naast de Amicales ook de Ummon. De mantelorganisaties van de Marokkaanse autoriteiten in Nederland* (Utrecht: NCB, 1993).

Rahnema, Ali, *An Islamic Utopian. A Political Biography of Ali Shari'ati* (London: I.B. Tauris, 1998).

Ramadan, Tariq, 'Il faudra que la France comprenne que Mohamed Merah était un enfant de la France, non de l'Algérie', *Le Monde des religions.fr.*, 28 March 2012.

Rassinier, Paul, *Le Mensonge d'Ulysse: regard sur la littérature concentrationnaire* (Bourg-en-Bresse: Editions Bressanes, 1950).

Reiner, A.S., and H.J. Kisch, 'Verhagen de pekel in?', *Propria Cures*, 10 May 1958.

Reijzer, Hans, 'De Swaans dans rond het Joodse sentimentalisme.' In: Annet Mooij et al. (eds.), *Grenzeloos nieuwsgierig. Opstellen voor en over Abram de Swaan* (Amsterdam: Bert Bakker, 2007), 251-260.

Reitlinger, Gerhard, *The Final Solution* (London: Sphere Books, 1953).

Remmers, Freke, 'Utrecht verbiedt demonstratie Ajax-fans', *Algemeen Dagblad*, 9 December 2015.

Renders, Hans, 'Eigenlijk was bijna iedereen fout', *Het Parool*, 2 November 2011.

Rensmann, Lars, *Demokratie und Judenbild. Antisemitismus in der politischen Kultur der Bundesrepublik Deutschland* (Wiesbaden: Verlag für Sozialwissenschaften, 2004).

—, and Julius H. Schoeps (eds.), *Feindbild Judentum. Antisemitismus in Europa* (Berlin: Verlag für Berlin-Brandenburg, 2008).

Rich, Frank, '2004: The Year of "The Passion"', *The New York Times*, 19 December 2004.

Ridder van Rappard, L.J.R., *Hoe was het ook weer. Burgemeester voor, tijdens en direct na de bezetting van het Koninkrijk der Nederlanden in de Tweede Wereldoorlog* (Meppel: Boom, 1979).

Riessen, H. van, and Rogier van Aerde (eds.), *Het grote Gebod; Gedenkboek van het verzet van LO en LKP* (Kampen: Kok, 1989; first ed. 1951).

Riethof, Huib, 'De tien walgelijkste Wilders-ismes: 4. De tandenborstels, *Krapuul.nl,* 26 February 2011.

Righart, Hans, *De eindeloze jaren zestig. Geschiedenis van een generatieconflict* (Amsterdam, Antwerp: De Arbeiderspers, 1995).

Rijken, Kemal, 'Welles-nietes tussen BAN en ADO', *NIW*, 5 August 2011.

—, 'Opluchting na afwijzing verbod rituele slacht', *NIW*, 16 December 2012.

Rodinson, Maxime, 'Israel, fait colonial?', *Les Temps Modernes* (*Le conflit Israélo-Arabe*) 253 bis (1967), 17-88.

—, *Israel. A Colonial-Settler state?* (New York: Monad Press, 1973).

Roegholt, Richter, *Amsterdam in de 20ᵉ eeuw – deel II (1945-1970)* (Utrecht, Antwerp: Het Spectrum, 1979).

Rogalla von Bieberstein, Johannes, 'Judeo-Bolshevism.' In: Richard S. Levy (ed.), *Antisemitism. A Historical Encyclopedia of Prejudice and Persecution*. Vol. 1 (Santa Barbara: ABC-CLIO, 2005), 389-391.

Rogier, Jan, *De geschiedschrijver des Rijks en andere socialisten. Politieke Portretten I* (Nijmegen: SUN, 1979).

Rohling, August, *Der Talmudjude: zur beherzigung für Juden und Christen aller Stände* (Münster: Adolph Russel, 1877).

Rollinde, Marguerite, *Le mouvement Marocain des droits de l'Homme: entre consensus national et engagement citoyen* (Paris: Karthala, 2003).

Romijn, Peter, *Burgemeesters in oorlogstijd. Besturen onder Duitse bezetting* (Amsterdam: Balans, 2006).

—, 'Ambitions and Dilemmas of Local Authorities in the German Occupied Netherlands, 1940-1945.' In: Bruno De Wever, Herman van Goethem and Nico Wouters (eds.), *Local Government in Occupied Europe (1939-1945)* (Gent: Academia Press, 2006), 33-66.

—, 'Er is volop aandacht voor de NSB', *NRC Handelsblad*, 12 December 2006.

Rooij, Piet de, '"De reuk des doods." De fakkel van het antipapisme in Nederland 1848-1865.' In: Conny Kristel (ed.), *Met alle geweld. Botsingen en tegenstellingen in burgerlijk Nederland*. (Amsterdam: Balans, 2003), 60-77.

Roos, Robert, 'Ophuis tart de goede smaak', *Trouw*, 5 September 2000.

Rosenberg Polak, Daan, 'Joden zouden afstand moeten nemen van beleid regering-Netanyahu', *NRC Handelsblad*, 14/15 March 2015.

Rost van Tonningen-Heubel, F.S., *Op zoek naar mijn huwelijksring* (Erembodegem: De Krijger, 1993).

Rothberg, Michael, *Multidirectional Memory. Remembering the Holocaust in the Age of Decolonization* (Stanford: Stanford University Press, 2009).

—, 'From Gaza to Warsaw: Mapping multidirectional memory', *Criticism* 53, 4 (Fall 2011), 523-548.

Rovers, Eva, 'De scherpe rand van ironie. Hoe de dorpsgek een duivelse spotter werd', *De Groene Amsterdammer*, 23 October 2010.

Roy, Olivier, *The Failure of Political Islam* (London: IB Tauris, 1994).

Rozett, R., 'Jewish Resistance.' In: D. Stone (ed.), *The Historiography of the Holocaust* (Basingstoke: Palgrave Macmillan, 2004), 341-363.

Rubinstein, Renate, 'Actie', *Vrij Nederland*, 22 June 1963.

—, 'Deugd, ondeugd, deugd', *Opinie, veertiendaags orgaan van de Partij van de Arbeid*, 19 March 1965.

—, *Jood in Arabië, Goi in Israël* (Amsterdam: Meulenhoff, 1967).

—, 'Antwoord aan dr. Melkman', *NIW*, 22 March 1968.

Ruiter, Robin de, *De Protocollen van de wijzen van Sion ontsluierd* (Enschede: Mayra publications, 2007).

Rushdie, Salman, *Midnight's Children* (New York: Knopf, 1981).

—, *Shame* (New York: Knopf, 1983).

—, *The Satanic Verses* (New York: Viking Penguin, 1989).

—, *Joseph Anton. A Memoir* (New York: Random House, 2012).

Rutven, Malisse, *A Satanic Affair: Salman Rushdie and the Wrath of Islam* (London: Hogarth Press, 1991).

Ryan, William, *Blaming the Victim* (New York: Pantheon Book, 1971).

Sack, John, *An Eye for An Eye: The Untold Story of Jewish Revenge Against Germans in 1945* (New York: Basic Books, 1993).

Sanders, Charles, 'Er is nog volop antisemitisme', *De Telegraaf,* 9 January 1999.

Sanders, Ewoud, *Allemaal woorden* (Amsterdam, Rotterdam: Prometheus/NRC, 2005).

—, 'Maak van Dodenherdenking geen Jodenherdenking', *NRC Handelsblad,* 7 May 2012.

—, and Rob Tempelaars, *Krijg de vinkentering! IOOI Nederlandse en Vlaamse verwensingen* (Amsterdam: Contact, 1998).

Sanos, Sandrine, *The Aesthetics of Hate. Far-Right intellectuals, Antisemitism, and Gender in 1930s France* (Stanford: Stanford University Press, 2012).

Sartre, Jean-Paul, *Réflexions sur la question juive* (Paris: Gallimard, 1946).

—, *Anti-Semite and Jew* (s.l.: Schocken, 1948).

Sas, Niek van, 'Het beroerd Nederland. Revolutionair geweld en bezinning omstreeks 1800.' In: Conny Kristel (ed.), *Met alle geweld. Botsingen en tegenstellingen in burgerlijk Nederland.* (Amsterdam: Balans, 2003), 48-59.

Sayari, Sabri, 'The terrorist movement in Turkey: Social composition and generational changes', *Conflict Quarterly* (1987), 21-32.

Schäfer, Peter, *Judeophobia. Attitudes towards the Jews in the Ancient World* (Cambridge, MA: Harvard University Press, 1997).

Scheepmaker, Nico, 'Antisemitisch voetballen', *Vrij Nederland,* 23 January 1965.

Scheffel-Baars, Gondel, 'Transgenerationele traumatisering: problemen bij de naoorlogse generatie', *Bulletin Stichting Werkgroep Herkenning* 23, 3 (2008), 19-23.

Scheffer, Paul 'Het multiculturele drama', *NRC Handelsblad,* 29 January 2000.

—, *Immigrant Nations* (Cambridge: Polity Press, 2011).

—, 'De lange schaduw van de bezetting', *de Volkskrant,* 29 October 2011.

Schmidt, Maurits, 'De Schaduw van de Islam', *Het Parool,* 18 February 1995.

Seufert, Günter, 'Die Millî Görüş Bewegung (AMGT/IGMG): Zwischen Integration und Isolation.' In: Günter Seufert and Jacques Waardenburg (eds.), *Turkish Islam and Europe: Europe and Christianity as reflected in Turkish Muslim discourse and Turkish Muslim life in the diaspora* (Istanbul, Stuttgart: Steiner, 1999), 295-322.

Schie, A.J. van, 'Restitution of economic rights after 1945.' In: Jozeph Michman and Tirtsah Levie (eds.), *Dutch Jewish History. Proceedings of the Symposium on the History of the Jews in the Netherlands* (Jerusalem, Tel Aviv: Tel Aviv University, Hebrew University of Jerusalem, 1984), 401-420.

—, 'A Disgrace? Postwar Restitution of Looted Jewish Property in the Netherlands.' In: Chaya Brasz and Yosef Kaplan (eds.), *Dutch Jews as perceived by themselves and by others. Proceedings of the Eighth International Symposium on the History of the Jews in the Netherlands* (Leiden: Brill, 2001), 393-404.

Schiffauer, Werner, 'Verfassungsschutz und islamische Gemeinden.' In: Uwe E. Kemmesies (ed.), Terrorismus und Extremismus – der Zukunft auf der Spur: Beiträge zur Entwicklungsdynamik von Terrorismus und Extremismus – Möglichkeiten und Grenzen einer prognostischen Empirie (München: Luchterhand, 2006), 237-254.

—, *Nach dem Islamismus. Eine Ethnographie der Islamischen Gemeinschaft Milli Görüs* (Berlin: Suhrkamp, 2010).

Schimel, Lawrence (ed.), *Kosher Meat* (Santa Fe, NM: Sherman Asher, 2000).

Schinkel, Willem, 'Woorden zijn maar woorden.' In Menno Grootveld (ed.), *Het woord. Charlie Hebdo* (Amsterdam: Editie Leesmagazijn, 2015), 49-60.

Schlör, Joachim, 'Der Urbantyp.' In: Julius Schoeps and Joachim Schlör (eds.), *Antisemitismus. Vorurteile und Mythen* (München: Piper, 1995), 229-240.

Schmitz, Ben, *Van Goede Doelen en Loterijen. Een biografie van de stichting Algemene Loterij Nederland* (Nijmegen: Valkhof Pers, 2009).

Schnabel, Paul, 'De multiculturele illusie', *de Volkskrant*, 17 februari 2000.

Schoenmaker, Ben and Herman Roozenbeek (eds.), *Vredesmacht in Libanon. De Nederlandse deelname aan UNIFIL 1979-1985* (Amsterdam: Boom, 2004), 175-176

Schomaker, Sander, 'FC Utrecht in de maag met antisemitische spreekkoren', *Metro*, 6 April 2015.

Schot, Laura, 'Zeggen wat je denkt', *NIW*, 26 November 2004.

Schravesande, Freek, 'Extreem-rechts heeft het zwaar', *NRC Handelsblad*, 13 February 2015.

Schreuder, Arjen, 'Zo gek is dat niet, om te denken aan zionistische betrokkenheid bij IS'. Interview with Ismail Selvi, *NRC Handelsblad*, 25 August 2014.

Schubert, Florian, *Rechtsextreme Fans beim Bundesligafußball: Ihre Strategien und die Maßnahmen der Vereine – Eine Fallstudie am Beispiel des HSV* (Saarbrücken: VDM-Verlag Dr. Müller, 2009).

—, 'Antisemitismus in Fußball-Fankulturen.' In: Martin Endemann et al. (eds.), *Zurück am Tatort Stadion: Diskriminierung und Antidiskriminierung in Fußball-Fankulturen* (Münster: Die Werkstatt, 2015).

Schul, Yaacov, and Henri Zukier, 'Why do stereotypes stick?' In: Robert Wistrich (ed.), *Demonizing the Other. Antisemitism, Racism, and Xenophobia* (London and New York: Routledge, 2003), 31-43.

Schumacher, Erik, 'Blond antisemitisme', *Hard/hoofd. Online tijdschrift voor kunst en journalistiek*, 11 April 2011.

Schumacher, Peter, 'Ministerie van WVC terughoudend met verspreiding van rapport antisemitisme', *NRC Handelsblad,* 12 May 1985.

Schuyt, C.J.M., and Ed Taverne, *1950. Welvaart in zwart-wit* (The Hague: Sdu Uitgevers, 2000).

Semang, Fabian van, 'Wij weten niets van hun lot. Een nieuwe benadering van de Jodenuitroeiing in Nederland', *Sporen van herinnering, Pedagogie en Geschiedenisoverdracht* 2, 6 (2012), 2-4.

Serfaty, Abraham, 'Le judaïsme marocain et le sionisme', *Souffles* 4, 16-17 (1969), 24-37.

—, and Mikhaël Elbaz, *L'Insoumis. Juifs, Marocains et rebelles* (Paris: Ed. Desclée de Brouwer, 2001).

Sharobeem, Heba M., 'The Hyphenated Identity and the Question of Belonging. A Study of Samia Serageldin's *The Cairo House*', *Studies in the Humanities* 30, 1 & 2 (2003), 60-84.

Shindler, Colin, *A History of Modern Israel* (Cambridge: Cambridge University Press, 2008).

Shlaim, Avi, 'Israel and the Arab Coalition in 1948.' In: Eugene Rogan and Avi Shlaim (eds.), *The War for Palestine: Rewriting the United States and the Israeli-Palestinian Conflict History of 1948* (Cambridge: Cambridge University Press, 2001), 79-103.

Sijes, Ben, 'Enkele opmerkingen over de positie van de Joden in de Tweede Wereldoorlog in Nederland', *Jaarboek van de Maatschappij der Nederlandsche Letterkunde te Leiden*, 1973-1974 (Leiden, 1975), 14-38.

Silberstein, Laurence, *Postzionism Debates. Knowledge and Power in Israeli Culture* (London: Routledge, 1999).

Simmel, Ernst (ed.), *Anti-Semitism. A Social Disease* (New York: International University Press, 1946).

—, 'Einleitung.' In: Ernst Simmel (ed.), *Antisemitismus* (Frankfurt am Main: Fischer Taschenbuch Verlag, 1993), 12-19.

Sivan, Emmanuel, 'Eavesdropping on radical Islam', *Middle East Quarterly* (March 1995), 13-24.

Slaa, Robin te, and Edwin Klijn, *De NSB. Ontstaan en opkomst van de Nationaal-Socialistische Beweging, 1931-1935* (Amsterdam: Boom, 2009).

Sligter, Anja, 'Joods centrum vermoedt kwade opzet achter octopussymbool tijdens moslim-demonstratie', *de Volkskrant*, 4 April 1995.

Sluyser, M., *Voordat ik het vergeet* (Amsterdam: Het Parool, 1957).

Slooter, Luuk, 'Wijkidentiteiten in voorstedelijk Frankrijk: Gevangen tussen misère en trots', *Migrantenstudies* 27, 1 (2011), 43-57.

Slotemaker de Bruine, M.C., *Het Joodse vraagstuk* (Nijkerk: Callenbach, 1946).

Smid, Ally, 'Ik weet nu dat Jodenhaat verkeerd is', *Trouw*, 13 September 2009.

Smits, Boudewijn, *Loe de Jong 1914-2005. Historicus met een missie* (Amsterdam: Boom, 2014).

Smeulers, Alette, 'In opdracht van de staat: gezagsgetrouwe criminelen en internationale misdrijven.' Inaugural speech, Tilburg University, 27 April 2012.

Smit, Susan, 'De bal bleef rollen. Ajax binnen voetballend Amsterdam tijdens de Tweede Wereldoorlog' (MA Thesis, Nieuwe en Theoretische Geschiedenis, Universiteit van Amsterdam, 1997).

Smith, Joy L., 'The Dutch Carnivalesque: Blackface, Play and Zwarte Piet.' In: Philomena Essed and Isabele Hoving (eds.), *Dutch Racism* (Amsterdam/New York: Rodopi, 2014), 219-238.

Snel, Jan Dirk, 'Nederland en de band met Israël. Sympathie voor een jonge staat', *Historisch Nieuwsblad* 5 (2008).

Soetendorp, R.B., *Het Nederlandse beleid ten aanzien van het Arabisch-Israëlisch conflict 1947-1977* (Meppel: Krips Repro, 1982).

—, *Pragmatisch of principieel. Het Nederlandse beleid ten aanzien van het Arabisch-Israëlisch conflict* (Leiden: Martinus Nijhoff, 1983).

—, 'The Netherlands and Israel: from a special to a normal relationship', *Internationale Spectator* 43 (November 1989), 697-700.

Sontrop, T., H. Brandt Corstius, H.U. Jesserun d'Oliveira and H. Leupen, 'Tegen een overslaande stem', *Propria Cures*, 24 May 1958.

Spaanstra-Polak, B.H., 'Werkman, Hendrik Nicolaas (1882-1945).' In: *Biografisch Woordenboek van Nederland*: http://resources.huygens.knaw.nl/bwn1880-2000/lemmata/bwn2/werkman.

Spaaij, Ramón, *Understanding Football Hooliganism. A Comparison of Six Western European Football Clubs* (Amsterdam: Amsterdam University Press, 2006).

Spee, Ine, and Maartje Reitsma, *Puberaal, lastig of radicaliserend? Grensoverschrijdend gedrag van jongeren in het onderwijs* ('s-Hertogenbosch: KPC groep, 2010).

Speet, B.M.J., 'De Middeleeuwen.' In: J.C.H. Blom, R.G. Fuks-Manfeld and I. Schöffer (eds.), *Geschiedenis van de Joden in Nederland* (Amsterdam: Balans, 1995), 19-49.

Stangneth, Bettina, *Eichmann Before Jerusalem: The Unexamined Life of a Mass Murderer* (New York: Alfred A. Knopf, 2014).

Stauber, Roni, 'Auschwitz lie.' In: Richard S. Levy (ed.), *Antisemitism. A Historical Encyclopedia of Prejudice and Persecution*. Vol. 1 (Santa Barbara: ABC-CLIO 2005), 45.

—, 'Holocaust Denial, Negationism, and Revisionism.' In: Richard S. Levy (ed.), *Antisemitism. A Historical Encyclopedia of Prejudice and Persecution*. Vol. 1 (Santa Barbara: ABC-CLIO, 2005), 319-322.

Steen, Paul van der, 'De Derde Weg', *Historisch Nieuwsblad* 9 (2009).

Steenhuis, Paul, 'Aïsja: de verboden sterke vrouw', *NRC Handelsblad*, 1 December 2000.

Stein, Richard, 'Nabeschouwing: Nederlands antisemitisme en de strijd tegen ideeën.' In: *Veertig jaar na '45. Visies op het hedendaagse antisemitisme*. Introduced by Prof Dr L. de Jong (Amsterdam: Meulenhoff Informatief, 1985), 278-329.

Stein, Yoram, 'De rabbijn verhaalt vandaag van het feest van de vrede', *Trouw*, 14 oktober 2000.

—, 'Als moslim hier gelukkig leven', *Trouw*, 28 September 2001.

—, 'Gezellig praten over jodenhaat en moslimangst', *Trouw*, 7 December 2001.

—, 'De titanenklus van Karacaer', *Trouw*, 24 January 2002.

Steiner, George, 'Woorden van de nacht.' In George Steiner, *Verval van het woord* (Amsterdam: Athenaeum-Polak en Van Gennep 1990).

Steinz, Pieter, *Waanzin in de literatuur* (Amsterdam: CPNB, 2015).

Stern, Frank, *The Whitewashing of the Yellow Badge: Antisemitism and Philosemitism in Postwar Germany* (Studies in Antisemitism Series) (Oxford: Pergamon Press, 1992).

Stokkom, Bas van, *Mondig tegen elke prijs. Het vrije woord als fetisj* (The Hague: Boom Juridische Uitgevers, 2008).

—, Henny Sackers and Jean-Pierre Wils, *Godslastering, discriminerende uitingen wegens godsdienst en haatuitingen. Een inventariserende studie* (Ministerie van Justitie, 2006).

Stölting, Erhard, 'Sechzehntes Bild; "Der Verräter."' In: Julius Schoeps and Joachim Schlör (eds.), *Antisemitismus. Vorurteile und Mythen* (München: Piper, 1995), 218-228.

Stone, Dan, *Histories of the Holocaust* (Oxford: Oxford University Press, 2011).

Stroeken, Harry, *Nieuw psycho-analytisch woordenboek – begrippen, termen, personen* (Amsterdam: Boom, 2000).

Stremmelaar, Annemarike, 'Sharing stories. A history of multicultural war remembrance in the Netherlands. In: Philipp Gassert, Alan E. Steinweis and Jacob Eder (eds.), *Holocaust Memory in a Globalizing World* (Göttingen: Wallstein, 2015) (under review).

Stutje, Jan Willem, *Ferdinand Domela Nieuwenhuis. Een romantisch revolutionair* (Amsterdam: Atlas/Contact, 2012).

Sunier, Thijl, *Islam in beweging. Turkse jongeren en islamitische organisaties* (Amsterdam: Het Spinhuis, 1996).

— et al., *Diyanet. The Turkish Directorate for Religious Affairs in a changing environment* (VU University, Utrecht University, 2011).

Sutcliffe, Adam, and Jonathan Karp, 'Introduction. A brief history of philosemitism.' In: Adam Sutcliffe and Jonathan Karp (eds.), *Philosemitism in History* (New York: Cambridge University Press, 2011), 1-26.

Swaan, Abram de, 'Het joods sentimentalisme betrapt', *NIW* (*Niweau*), 27 November 1964.

—, 'De linkse oppositie. De stijl op zoek naar een situatie', *De Gids* 131(1968), 28-39.

—, 'Les enthousiasmes anti-israéliens: la tragédie d'un processus aveugle', *Raisons politiques* 4, 16 (2004), 105-124.

—, 'Anti-Israëlische enthousiasmes en de tragedie van het blind proces', *De Gids* 168 (2005), 349-367.

—, 'Klagen besneden joden dan?', *NRC Handelsblad*, 15/16 September 2012.

—, *Compartimenten van vernietiging. Over genocidale regimes en hun daders* (Amsterdam: Prometheus/Bert Bakker 2014).

—, 'Achter deze discussie gaat een schuldvraag schuil', *NRC Handelsblad*, 1 February 2014.

—, 'Klaag niet alle Nederlanders aan om de Holocaust en pleit ze ook niet allemaal vrij', *NRC Handelsblad*, 14/15 June 2014.

—, 'Nooit meer Auschwitz lezing', Amsterdam, 21 January 2015 (Amsterdam: Nederlands Auschwitz Comité, 2015).

Swijtink, André, *In de pas. Sport en lichamelijke opvoeding in Nederland tijdens de Tweede Wereldoorlog* (Haarlem: De Vrieseborch, 1992).

Swirc, Maurice, 'Geert Wilders, geen vriend van de Joden', *NIW*, 25 September 2013.

Tames, Ismee, *Besmette jeugd. Kinderen van NSB'ers na de oorlog* (Amsterdam: Balans, 2009).

—, *Doorn in het vlees. Foute Nederlanders in de jaren vijftig en zestig* (Amsterdam: Balans, 2013).

—, 'De oorlog als entertainment', *Trouw*, 16 October 2010.

Tarant, Zbynêk, 'Friends or Foes? Attitudes of the Czech Anti-Semitic Scene to Islam and Mus-
    lims.' Paper presented at the international conference 'Antisemitism in Europe. Cross-Front
    Antisemitism, Conspiracy Theories, Calls for Boycotts, Islamism, the Extreme Right and the
    Left' (IIBSA), Berlin, 12-13 December 2015.
Tegel, Susan, *Jew Süss. Life, Legend, Fiction, Film* (London: Continuum, 2011).
Teunissen, Jos, 'Psycholoog Jaap Sanders: Leeft het antisemitisme op? Ik geloof er niets van',
    Het Vrije Volk, 8 June 1984.
Tezcan, Levent, 'Inszenierungen kollektiver Identität. Artikulationen des politischen Islam-
    beobachtet auf den Massenversammlungen der türkisch-islamistischen Gruppe Milli Görüs',
    Soziale Welt 53, 3 (2002), 303-324.
Theeboom, Piebe, '150 jaar Corps in Amsterdam: een geschiedenis van het ASC/AVSV.' In: J.W.
    Ebbinge et al. (eds.), *Wij Amsterdamsche Studiosi. 150 jaar ASC/AVSV* (Amsterdam: ASC/
    AVSV, 2002), 12-206.
Thieme, Marianne, 'Onverdoofd slachten niet te rijmen met joodse voorschriften', *RD.nl,*
    10 December 2010.
Thijn, Ed van, and Ies Vuijsje: Anne Burgers, 'Ed van Thijn: "Boek Van der Boom misleidend"',
    Historisch Nieuwsblad, 7 May 2012.
Tielemans, Stijn, 'Verbazing over "zieke, laffe daad" met varkenskop', AD.nl., 25 January 2016.
Tierolf, Bas, and Lisanne Drost (eds.), *Poldis rapportage Antisemitisme 2012* (Utrecht: Verwey-
    Jonker Instituut, 2012).
Tiggele, Els van, 'De polderdelta in verval. Boek van Manfred Gerstenfeld', *NIW,* 10 December 2010.
Tinnemans, Will, *Een gouden armband: Een geschiedenis van Mediterrane immigranten in
    Nederland (1945-1994)* (Utrecht: Nederlands Centrum Buitenlanders, 1994).
Tjepkema, Almar and Jaap Walvis, *'Ondergedoken.' Het ondergrondse leven tijdens de Tweede
    Wereldoorlog* (Weesp: De Haan, 1985).
Todd, Emmanuel, *Qui est Charlie? Sociologie d'une crise religieuse* (Paris: Seuil 2015
—, *Who is Charlie?: Xenophobia and the new middle class* (Cambridge, MA: Polity 2015).
Todorov, Tzvetan, *Les morales de l'histoire* (Paris: B. Grasset, 1991).
Top, Bart, 'Evelien Gans: De grens van assimilatie verlegt zich keer op keer.' In: Bart Top, *Religie
    en verdraagzaamheid. 10 gesprekken over tolerantie in een extreme tijd* (Kampen: Ten Gave,
    2005), 47-60.
Torfs, Rik, 'Mens(enrecht) versus dier(enrecht), *De Standaard,* 13 August 2015.
Toynbee, Arnold J., 'Jewish Rights in Palestine', *The Jewish Historical Quarterly* 52, 1 (1961), 1-11.
—, *The Study of History* (Oxford: Oxford University Press, 1935-1961).
Trabulsi, Fawwaz, 'The Palestine problem: Zionism and Imperialism in the Middle East', *New
    Left Review* I, 57 (1969).
Trevisan Semi, Emanuela, 'Double trauma and manifold narratives: Jews' and Muslims' rep-
    resentation of the departure of Moroccan Jews in the 1950s and 1960s', *Journal of Modern
    Jewish Studies* 9, 1 (2010), 107-125
Trigt, Marjolein van, 'Afgebrand door Van Gogh', *Babel. Maandblad van de faculteit der
    Geesteswetenschappen* 13, 3 (November 2004), 4-5.
Truijens, Aleid, 'Hugo Brandt Corstius 1945-2014', *NRC Handelsblad,* 1 March 2014.
Türesay, Özgür, 'Antisionisme et antisémitisme dans la presse ottomane d'Istanbul à l'époque
    jeune turque (1909-1912) ', *Turcica* 41 (2009), 147-178.
Trotsky, Leon, 'On the Jewish Problem', a 1945 collection of writings, Leon Trotsky Internet
    Archive, www.marxists.org.

Ülger, Mehmet, 'Soldaten van Milli Gorus tegen scheiding kerk en staat', *Trouw*, 22 January 2002.

Ultee, Wouter, and Henk Flap, 'De Nederlandse paradox: waarom overleefden zoveel Nederlandse joden de Tweede Wereldoorlog niet?' In: Harry Ganzeboom and Siegwart Lindenberg (eds.), *Verklarende sociologie. Opstellen voor Reinhard Wippler* (Amsterdam: Thela Thesis, 1996), 185-196.

—, and Ruud Luijks, 'De schaduw van een hand. Joods-gojse huwelijken en joodse zelfdodingen in Nederland 1936-1943', in: H. Flap and W. Arts (eds.), *De organisatie van de bezetting* (Amsterdam: Amsterdam University Press, 1997), 55-76.

Valenta, Markha, 'Charlie Hebdo, één week later.' In: Menno Grootveld, *Het woord. Charlie Hebdo* (Amsterdam: Editie Leesmagazijn 2015), 85-96.

Valk, Guus, 'Geert Wilders' marginale vrienden', *NRC Handelsblad*, 5 May 2015.

Valk, Ineke van der, *Van migratie naar burgerschap. Twintig jaar Komitee Marokkaanse Arbeiders in Nederland* (Amsterdam: IPP, 1996).

Veen, Gerrit Jan van der, *De Vrije Kunstenaar*, 15 March 1944.

Velde, Koert van der, and Yoram Stein, 'Allemaal typisch Turkse retoriek', *Trouw*, 2 January 2002.

Vegterlo, Anne, 'Hitlergroet is geen discriminatie', *NRC Handelsblad*, 26 August 2015.

Ven, Colet van der, 'Ik vond Cohen genoeg', *NIW*, 19 September 1998.

Veraart, Wouter, 'Een regen van verboden lost niets op', *NRC Handelsblad*, 9/10 April 2011.

—, and Laurens Winkel (eds.), *The Post-war Restitution of Property Rights in Europe: Comparative Perspectives* (Amsterdam: Scientia Verlags, 2011).

Verbraak, Coen, '"Het wordt tijd om terug te slaan"', *Vrij Nederland*, 27 November 2004.

Verhagen, A.R.H.B., 'Israël de zee in?', *Propria Cures*, 3 May 1958.

—, 'Terreur', *Propria Cures*, 17 May 1958.

Verhey, Elma, *Om het joodse kind* (Amsterdam: Nijgh & Van Ditmar, 1991).

Verkijk, D., *Die slappe Nederlanders of viel het toch wel mee in 1940-1945?* (Soesterberg: Aspekt, 2001).

Vermaas, Peter, '"Vadermoord" stort het Front National in crisis', *NRC Handelsblad*, 9 April 2015.

—, 'Geschorste Le Pen père voelt zich verraden', *NRC Handelsblad*, 5 & 6 May 2015.

Vinen, Richard C., 'The End of an Ideology? Right-Wing Antisemitism in France, 1944-1970', *The Historical Journal* 37, 2 (1994), 365-388.

Vodka, Amir, *The Human Chameleon. Hybrid Jews in Cinema* (PhD thesis, Universiteit van Amsterdam 5 July 2016).

Voerman, G., 'Een geval van politieke schizofrenie. Het gespleten gedachtengoed van DS'70', *Jaarboek 1990 Documentatiecentrum Nederlandse Politieke Partijen* (Groningen 1991), 92-114.

Voet, Esther, 'Haatexpressie', *NIW*, 11 December 2015.

Volkov, Shulamit, *Antisemitismus als kultureller Code. Zehn Essays* (München: Beck, 2000).

Von Braun, Christina, 'Der sinnliche und der übersinnliche Jude.' In Sander L. Gilman, Robert Jütte, Gabrielle Kohlbauer-Fritz (eds.), *'Der Schejne Jid'. Das Bild des 'jüdischen Körpers'in Mythos und Ritual* (Wien: Picus Verlag, 1998) 97-108.

Voogt, Sam de, 'Israël bevestigt annexatie op de Jordaanoever, *NRC Handelsblad*, 21 January 2016.

Voren, Robert van, *Undigested Past: The Holocaust in Lithuania* (Amsterdam: Rodopi, 2013).

Vos, Evert de, '"Verliest den moed toch niet." Joodse voetbalclubs in Amsterdam 1908-1948' (MAthesis, Social History, Universiteit Leiden, October 2000).

Vree, Frank van, *In de schaduw van Auschwitz. Herinneringen, beelden, geschiedenis* (Groningen: Historische uitgeverij, 1995).

—, 'De dynamiek van de herinnering. Nederland in een internationale context.' In: Frank van Vree and Rob Laarse (eds.), *De dynamiek van de herinnering. Nederland en de Tweede Wereldoorlog in een internationale context* (Amsterdam: Bert Bakker, 2009), 17-40.

—, 'Iedere dag en elk uur. De jodenvervolging en de dynamiek van de herinnering in Nederland.' In: Hetty Berg and Bart Wallet (eds.), *Wie niet weg is, is gezien. Joods Nederland na 1945* (Zwolle: Waanders, 2010), 57-72.

—, Hetty Berg and David Duindam (eds.), *De Hollandsche Schouwburg. Theater, deportatieplaats, plek van herinnering* (Amsterdam: Amsterdam University Press, 2013).

Vries, Anne de, 'Het opgejaagde volk.' In: K. Norel et al., *Den vijand wederstaan: Historische schetsen van de Landelijke Organisatie voor hulp aan onderduikers, landelijke knokploegen en centrale inlichtingendienst* (Wageningen: Zomer & Keuning, 1946), 22-28.

Vries, Joost de, 'Het einde van de apenrots: Waar blijven de nieuwe Grote Drie?', *De Groene Amsterdammer*, 6 August 2015.

Vuijsje, Hans, 'Overheid, bescherm Joden blijvend', *de Volkskrant*, 20 February 2015.

Vuijsje, Herman, 'Besnijden, het weigeren van vaccinatie: dat gebeurt niet om het geloof', *NRC Handelsblad*, 8/9 September 2012.

Wacquant, Loïc, 'Territorial stigmatization in the age of advanced marginality', *Thesis Eleven* 91 (November 2007), 66-77

Wagenaar, Aad, 'Nederland 2003: De nieuwe Jodenhaat', *Panorama*, 24 September 2003.

Wal, Jessica ter, *Moslim in Nederland. De publieke discussie over de islam in Nederland: een analyse van artikelen in de Volkskrant 1998-2002*. SCP-werkdocument (The Hague: SCP, 2004), 78-86.

Wallet, Bart, 'Hoe voor- en tegenstanders van de rituele slacht van rol wisselden', *Trouw*, 14 May 2011.

—, 'Rituele slacht en godsdienstvrijheid in een seculiere samenleving', *Religie & Samenleving* 7, 2 (September 2012), 166-183.

—, '"Een levend gedenkteken." Israël, joods Nederland en de herinnering aan de Shoa.' In: Frank van Vree, Hetty Berg and David Duindam (eds.), *De Hollandsche Schouwburg. Theater, deportatieplaats, plek van herinnering* (Amsterdam: Amsterdam University Press, 2013), 190-199.

—, 'Van vergeten Joden en een spirituele koningin', *NIW*, 26 June 2015.

Walters, Derk, 'Jonge Ethiopische Joden staan op', *NRC Handelsblad*, 5 May 2015.

—, 'Een Jood mag meer dan wij Arabieren', *NRC Handelsblad*, 11 May 2015.

—, 'Israël vreest Palestijnse koeienfilm', *NRC Handelsblad*, 3 December 2015.

—, 'Landverraders, dat zijn linkse mensen volgens veel Israëliërs', *NRC Handelsblad*, 22 December 2015.

—, and Mark Beunderman, 'Europese Joden worden bedreigd maar emigreren nog niet massaal', *NRC Handelsblad*, 17 February 2015.

Wasserstein, Bernard, *Vanishing Diaspora. The Jews in Europe since 1945* (Cambridge, MA: Harvard University Press, 1996).

—, *Het einde van een diaspora. Joden in Europa sinds 1945* (Baarn: Ambo, 1996).

Waterman, Peter, 'Saint Theo', *Risq. Review of International Social Questions*, 9 November 2004.

Webman, Esther, 'The challenge of Assessing Arab/Islamic Anti-Semitism', *Middle Eastern Studies*, 46, 5 (September 2010), 677-697.

Weezel, Max van, '2/11. Theo van Gogh 1957-2004', *Vrij Nederland*, 6 November 2004.

—, 'We hebben er weer een godsdienstoorlog bij', *Vrij Nederland*, 20 April 2011.

—, 'Om wie draait het op de Dam', *Auschwitzbulletin* 59, 3 (September 2015).

—, and Margalith Kleijwegt, 'Terug naar Amsterdam-West', *Vrij Nederland*, 29 October 2005.

Weller, Paul, *A Mirror of Our Times. The Rushdie Affair and the Future of Multiculturalism* (London: Continuum, 2009).

Werbner, Pnina, 'Stamping the Earth with the Name of Allah: Zikr and the Sacralizing of Space among British Muslims.' In: Barbara Daly Metcalf (ed.), *Making Muslim Space in North America and Europe* (Berkeley, Los Angeles: University of California Press, 2002), 167-185.

Werff, Sander van der, 'Duizenden eisen vertrek van burgemeester Van Aartsen', *AD.nl*, 28 July 2014.

Werkman, Evert, 'Het woord JOOD in onze woordenboeken', *Het Parool*, 13 February 1965.

Wertheim, David, 'Hypotheek op een ongedekte cheque. De betekenis van Israël voor de Nederlandse-joodse schrijvers Abel Herzberg, Leon de Winter en Arnon Grunberg.' In: Hetty Berg and Bart Wallet (eds.), *Wie niet weg is, is gezien. Joods Nederland na 1945* (Zwolle: Waanders, 2010), 135-147.

—, 'Wilders, Le Pen kapen de Joodse zaak', *NRC Handelsblad*, 13 November 2013.

Wertheim, Micha, 'Theo', *Het Parool*, 9 November 2014.

Westerduin, Matthea ,Yolande Jansen & Karin Neutel, 'Jongensbesnijdenis tussen religie, recht en geschiedenis,' *Filosofie & Praktijk* 35, 3 (2014), 35-55.

Wetboek van Strafrecht [Criminal Code], 19th ed. [up to 1968], ed. by C. Fasseur. (Zwolle: Tjeenk Willink, 1969).

Wetzel, Juliane, 'Die Täter-Opfer-Umkehr', *Der Freitag*, 22 April 2012.

—, 'Antisemitism and Holocaust remembrance.' In: Günther Jikeli and Joëlle Allouche-Benayoun (eds.), *Perceptions of the Holocaust in Europe and Muslim Communities. Sources, Comparisons and Educational Challenges* (Dordrecht: Springer, 2013), 19-28.

Wieken, Ron van der, *Jodenhaat. Het verhaal van een uiterst explosief en destructief element in de westerse cultuur* (Amsterdam: Mastix Press, 2014).

Wielek, H., *De oorlog die Hitler won* (Amsterdam: Amsterdamse Boek- en Courantmij. N.V., 1947).

Wielen, J.E. van de, 'Wel protest', *NIW*, 21 October 1966.

Wielenga, Friso, 'Tale after Tale after Tale. The lost chance of a great project', *BMGN* 128, 2 (2013), 90-99.

Wind, E. de, 'Transgenerationele overdracht.' In: *Kinderen van de oorlog: opstellen naar aanleiding van een lezingencyclus, georganiseerd in de periode januari-april 1986 door de RIAGG's Centrum/Oud-West Amsterdam en Zuid/Nieuw-West Amsterdam, in samenwerking met de Stichting ICODO te Utrecht* (1987), 9-2.

Wijfjes, Huub, *Journalistiek in Nederland 1850-2000. Beroep, cultuur en organisatie* (Amsterdam: Boom, 2004).

Wijmenga, Rianne, 'De passie van de toeschouwer. Receptieonderzoek naar de reacties van het publiek op Mel Gibsons *The Passion of the Christ*' (MA thesis, Universiteit van Amsterdam, 29 April 2011).

Wijnen, Harry van, 'Wat niet hoort wat niet deert', *NRC Handelsblad*, 30 June 1998.

Winter, Leon de, *La Place de la Bastille* (Amsterdam: De Bezige Bij, 1981).

—, *De ruimte van Sokolov* (Amsterdam: De Bezige Bij, 1992).

—, *VSV* (Amsterdam: De Bezige Bij, 2012).

Wistrich, Robert, 'Anti-Zionism as an expression of Anti-Semitism in recent years.' Lecture delivered to the study circle on World Jewry in the home of the President of Israel, 10 December 1984.

—, 'Left-wing anti-Zionism in Western Societies.' In: Robert Wistrich (ed.), *Anti-Zionism and Antisemitism in the Contemporary World* (Basingstoke: Macmillan, 1990), 46-52.

—, *A Lethal Obsession. Anti-Semitism from Antiquity to the Global Jihad* (New York: Random House, 2010).

Withuis, Jolande, *Erkenning. Van oorlogstrauma naar klaagcultuur* (Amsterdam: De Bezige Bij, 2005).

—, and Annet Mooij (eds.), *The Politics of War Trauma. The Aftermath of World War II in Eleven European Countries* (Amsterdam: Aksant, 2010).

Witte, Rob, *'Al eeuwenlang een gastvrij volk': Racistisch geweld en overheidsreacties in Nederland (1950-2009)* (Amsterdam: Aksant, 2010).

Wolf, Eva, Jurriaan Berger and Lennart de Ruig, 'Antisemitisme in het voorgezet onderwijs', *Panteia. Research to Progress* (Projectnr. C10000, Zoetermeer, 8 July 2013).

Wolff, Sam, de, *Geschiedenis van de Joden in Nederland. Laatste Bedrijf* (Amsterdam: Arbeiders-pers, 1946).

Wolf, Udo, *Beispiel Al-Quds-Tag. Islamistische Netzwerke und Ideologien unter Migrantinnen und Migranten in Deutschland und Möglichkeiten zivilgesellschaftlicher Intervention Erstellt im Auftrag der Beauftragten der Bundesregierung für Migration, Flüchtlinge und Integration* (Berlin, 2004): (www.ufuq.de/pdf/WolterQuds.pdf).

Wolitz, Seth L., 'Imagining the Jew in France: From 1945 to the Present', *Yale French Studies* 85 (1994), 119-134.

Wreede, Jaap de, '"Bin Laden is mijn held van deze tijd." Publicist Willem Oltmans kan het dwarsliggen niet laten', *Reformatorisch Dagblad*, 24 May 2003.

Ye'or, Bat, *Eurabia. The Euro-Arab Axis* (Madison, NJ: Fairleigh Dickinson University Press, 2005).

Yesilgöz, Dilan, 'Alle vormen van discriminatie kennen één gemeenschappelijke deler', *Republiek Allochtonië*, 5 March 2013.

Young, Robert, *Postcolonialism. An Introduction* (Oxford, UK, Malden, MA: Blackwell Publishers, 2001).

Yükleyen, Ahmet and Gökçe Yurdakul, 'Islamic activism and immigrant integration: Turkish organizations in Germany', *Immigrants & Minorities* 29, 01 (2011), 64-85.

Zahraoui, Yassine, 'Hoe racistisch is een Marokkaan', *NRC Next*, 14 October 2006.

Zeitlin, Solomon, 'Jewish Rights in Eretz Israel (Palestine)', *The Jewish Historical Quarterly* 52, 1 (1961), 12-34.

Zondergeld, Gjalt, 'Continuïteit en discontinuïteit in de moderne Nederlandse geschiedenis. De these van J.C.H. Blom nader bezien', *Kleio, tijdschrift van de Vereniging van Geschiedenisler-aren in Nederland* 25, 8 (1984), 1-6.

Zonneveld, Loek, 'Het citatenkerkhof. Kroniek van R.W. Fassbinders "Het vuil, de stad en de dood", 1975-2002': www.loekzonneveld.nl/2004/fassb01.htm.

—, 'Fassbinder, het geniale monster. Bij wijze van Inleiding.' In: Rainer Werner Fassbinder, *Het vuil, de stad en de dood / Rainer Werner Fassbinder* (Transl. by Gerrit Bussink) (Utrecht: Signature, 2002), 7-16.

Zukier, Henri, 'The Transformation of Hatred: Antisemitism as a Struggle for Group Identity.' In: Robert Wistrich (ed.), *Demonizing the Other. Antisemitism, Racism, and Xenophobia* (London and New York: Routledge, 2003), 118-130.

Zwaap, René, 'De opstand der incorrecten', *De Groene Amsterdammer*, 17 January 1996.

Zwagerman, Joost, 'De eeuw van zijn vader', *de Volkskrant*, 11 April 2001.

Index

Personal Names

Subject Index

For Product Safety Concerns and Information please contact our EU
representative GPSR@taylorandfrancis.com
Taylor & Francis Verlag GmbH, Kaufingerstraße 24, 80331 München, Germany

www.ingramcontent.com/pod-product-compliance
Lightning Source LLC
Chambersburg PA
CBHW070614270326
41926CB00011B/1691